The History of the Prussian Pour le Mérite Order

Volume II

1813 - 1888

William E. Hamelman

Matthäus Publishers
P.O. Box 1361
Dallas, TX 75221
United States of America

Copyright © 1986, William E. Hamelman

All rights reserved. No part of this book may be reproduced in any form without written permission of the author.

ISBN 0-931065-02-X

THE
HISTORY
of the
PRUSSIAN
POUR LE MERITE ORDER

Volume II
1813 - 1888

A comprehensive in-depth study of
the history of the Order
and the bravery and exploits of
its recipients.

by

William E. Hamelman

DEDICATED TO

Don J. Nickum

In Sincere Appreciation

ACKNOWLEDGEMENTS

Volume II

The author is deeply indebted to

DENNIS MARTIN
Research

and

KATHERINE GODBY
Editor

The author is very grateful to many individuals, fellow collectors, and friends who assisted, by word and deed, during the completion of this venture.

A very special thanks goes to Brad Yahn for his continuous interest and reassurance, for his stimulating encouragement, and the gentle pressure and greatly appreciated assistance, which served as a much needed motivation toward the completion of this work.

The author is very grateful to Andrè Hüskin, David Fuller, George Seymour, Dr. Kurt Klietmann, Hartwig Friedrich, and Christian Hamelman, for their important and valuable suggestions.

And especially heartfelt thanks to Helaine Hamelman for being so understanding and tolerant of an inveterate, confirmed collector; for her huge and very often thankless task of reading text and correcting my numerous spelling mistakes; for her unwavering support and loyalty, her smiling countenance, genuine compassion during the researching and writing this book. She, indeed, is "the best that ever was."

Photo Credits:
Brad Yahn, Dallas, TX, USA
Dr. K-G Klietmann, Berlin, West Germany
George Seymour, Dallas, TX, USA
Ernst Blass, Hamburg, West Germany
Eugene A. Hamelman, Dallas, TX, USA

PREFACE

Volume II

This second volume of **The History of the Prussian Pour le Mérite Order** concerns the uninterrupted history of this famous Prussian military decoration. Volume II continues from the 1813-1815 "Wars of Liberation," breaking the Napoleonic yoke through the reigns of Friedrich Wilhelm III., Friedrich Wilhelm IV., Wilhem I., and the 99 day reign of Friedrich III. The Order's insignia, its variations, modifications and device additions are examined, and the recipients and well known personalities decorated with the Pour le Mérite Order are recognized. The information presented here will become more and more fascinating as the historian and collector familiarize themselves with the captivating history of the Pour le Mérite Order.

The names of the recipients of the Order, the military units, and the places of actions, engagements, and battles, retain their German names and spelling. However, Russian names and military units have been translated into English, where possible, to make reading easier.

The author has tried to find as much historical background information as available but without the extraordinary and determined efforts of **Dennis Martin** in researching material, the writing of this work on the Pour le Mérite Order could not have become a reality. However, the primary sources have been Gustaf Lehmann's **Die Ritter des Ordens Pour le Mérite** and Hanns Möller's **Geschichte der Ritter des Ordens Pour le Mérite im Weltkrieg** which provided invaluable data and facts. No matter how hard one tries, all is sometimes not possible and, as in any massive work such as this, there may be errata and, if perhaps there is, the author begs the readers' indulgence and understanding.

* * *

William E. Hamelman
Dallas, Texas, USA
1985

EXPLANATORY NOTES

1.   The format of this work is consistent with Volume I of **The History of the Prussian Pour le Mérite Order** and easy to follow once the reader understands the simplicity of the basic arrangement. The text, recipient names, dates, maps, et cetra are arranged in strict chronological order. The author tried to eliminate excessive verbiage and create a consistent, concise arrangement which allows the reader to easily follow the given time spans.

2.   The total number of recipients as listed by units does not equal the actual number of awards given during the reigns of the awarding monarchs. This results from the awards of the Pour le Mérite Order to adjutants, general staff officers, et cetra, not being included in the unit tables. However, all recipients are included in the total awards tables.

3.   The German military rank of "Rittmeister," translates to "Riding Master" and is the equivalent of the rank of captain in a cavalry unit.

4.   The German title of "Freiherr" has been abbreviated and is shown as "Frhr." It indicated a low ranking noble.

5.   There seems to be some confusion concerning dates of the actual award of the Pour le Mérite Order and the Oakleaves in several instances. The author has therefore accepted the dates as indicated in the Möller volumes which were taken from official German sources.

6.   All line drawings shown in the text and measurement tables are shown for illustrative purposes only.

7.   Certain military ranks that were unique to the Imperial Russian Army have no direct English translatable equivalent. As such, they have been translated into the nearest English language rank.

TABLE OF CONTENTS

Volume II

Chapter V – Section 2

Friedrich Wilhelm III. 1813 – 1840 1
   Establishment of the Oakleaves to the Pour le Mérite Order . . 5
   First Award of the Oakleaves to the Pour le Mérite Order . . 23
   First Simultaneous Award of the Pour le Mérite Order and Oakleaves. 49
   First Award of Three Pour le Mérite Orders to the Same Recipient . 63
   First Award of the Pour le Mérite Order to a Naval Officer . . 76
   Second Award of Three Pour le Mérite Orders to Same Recipient . 112
   First Award of Two Pour le Mérite Orders with Oakleaves to the Same
      Recipient 118
   Ribbon Authorized for Wear of Oakleaves 188
   1818-1829 Russo-Turkish War 194
   1831 Neuchâtel Uprising 196
   1831 Polish Rebellion 197
   Death of Friedrich Wilhelm III. 199

Tables:
Total Awards 202
Percentages of Total Awards – According to Rank 204
Multiple Awards to Same Recipient Between 1807-1814 . . . 205
Multiple Awards to Same Recipient Between 1813-1849 . . . 206
Multiple Awards to Same Recipient on the Same Day . . . 208
Three Awards of the Pour le Mérite Order to Same Recipient . 209
Revoked Pour le Mérite Order 209
Simultaneous Award of the Pour le Mérite Order and Oakleaves . 210
Simultaneous Award of Two Pour le Mérite Orders and Oakleaves to
   Same Recipient 211
Percentages of Total Awards by Nationality 212
Total Awards of Recipients in Prussian Units 213
Total Awards of Recipients in Russian Units 214
Total Awards of Recipients in Non-Prussian Units 218

Chapter VI

Friedrich Wilhelm IV. 1840 – 1861 221
   Establishment of the Pour le Mérite Order for Science & Art . . 221
   Establishment of the 50 Year Jubilee Golden Crown . . . 224
   First Award of the 50 Year Jubilee Golden Crown . . . 225
   1848-1849 Schleswig-Holstein War. 226
   Awards for the 1848-1849 Schleswig-Holstein War 231
   Appointment of Prince Wilhelm as Prince Regent 232
   Death of Friedrich Wilhelm IV. 233

Tables:
Total Awards 236
Percentages of Total Awards – According to Rank 237
Simultaneous Awards of the Pour le Mérite Orders and Oakleaves . 237

Simultaneous Award of the Pour le Mérite Orders and the 50 Year Jubilee Golden Crown to Same Recipient	238
Revoked Pour le Mérite Order after 47 Years	238
Total Awards of Recipients by Units	239

Chapter VII

Wilhelm I. 1861-1888.	241
1864 Danish-Prussian War	242
A Posthumous Award of the Pour le Mérite Order	245
1866 Austro-Prussian War	251
Establishment of the Grand Cross and Star of the Pour le Mérite Order	266
First Awards of the Grand Cross and Star of the Pour le Mérite Order	270
Second Posthumous Award of the Pour le Mérite Order	270
1867 North German Confederation	284
Events Leading to the 1870-1871 Franco-Prussian War	284
1870-1871 Franco-Prussian War	286
Establishment of the German Empire	294
Establishment of the Oakleaves to the Grand Cross and Star of the Pour le Mérite Order	312
Awards of the Oakleaves to the Grand Cross and Star of the Pour le Mérite Order	312
First Award of the Pour le Mérite Order for Science & Art to a Military Officer	312
1877 Russo-Turkish War	314
Death of Wilhelm I.	320
Tables:	
Total Awards	324
Percentage of Total Awards - According to Rank	326
Simultaneous Award of Both the Pour le Mérite Order and Oakleaves.	326
Simultaneous Award of Both the Pour le Mérite Order and the 50 Year Jubilee Golden Crown	326
Percentages of Awards by Nationality	327
Awards of the Grand Cross and Star of the Pour le Mérite Order	327
Total Awards of Recipients by Prussian Units	328
Total Awards of Recipients by Non-Prussian Units	330

Chapter VIII

Friedrich III. 1888	333

Appendix

I	"To My People"	337
II	Blüchers Order of the Day	339
III	Awards of Oakleaves through the reign of Wilhelm I.	341
IV	Awards of the 50 Year Jubilee Crown through the reign of Wilhelm I.	345

Name Directory 351

Bibliography 381

Maps

Lützen 15
Bautzen 21
Dresden 37
La Rothière 88
Montmirail 89
Craonne 93
Laon 94

CHAPTER V

Friedrich Wilhelm III.

1797 – 1840

SECTION 2
1813 – 1840

he beginning of the year 1813 brought many remarkable changes to the Kingdom of Prussia, the people and their king, Friedrich Wilhelm III. By the terms of the convention of Taurrogen, negotiated and signed by Lt. General von Yorck on December 30, 1812, the Prussian forces under his command were withdrawn from service with Napoleon's Grand Army.

The Prussian forces were now effectively neutral. As a result, the pursuing Russian troops were allowed to cross East Prussia in their relentless chase after the defeated and retreating French. Friedrich Wilhelm received the news of General von Yorck's treaty with the Russians while he was in Berlin, a city still occupied by French troops. In the king's own words, it was "enough to strike one with apoplexy." However, he was still extremely apprehensive of the power remaining in Napoleon's hands. Friedrich Wilhelm disavowed the action taken by his general and, in order to avoid any retaliation by the French, declared his and Prussia's allegience to Napoleon and France. He then proceeded to do what he seemed always to do best, which is to say he did nothing at all. However, events were shaping up that would take freedom of action completely beyond Friedrich Wilhelm's control.

Attached to one of the advance units of the Russian army was the exiled Baron von Stein. Wherever the Russian forces had firm control, von Stein immediately summoned representatives of all the loyal estates and formed the first parliament of Prussia. At the same time he strongly urged Emperor Alexander I. of Russia to continue the war against Napoleon. Alexander certainly did not need much encouragement on this point. Since his military successes had not driven Napoleon from Russia, Alexander wanted to be recognized as the "Saviour of Europe." Thus on January 13, 1813, the Russian army crossed the Nieman River and the Emperor of All Russia proclaimed the "Liberation of Europe" from the suppresive yoke of Napoleonism.

It was during this time that a new force began to make itself felt throughout the German states, and Prussia in particular. Stirred by the many reforms of the past few years, humiliated by past military defeats and now aroused by the demanding arrogance of Napoleon, the Prussian people began to feel the movement of a new patriotism. Through the work of societies such as the Tegenbund (League of Virtue) as well as the writings of outspoken authors like Fichte and

Arndt, a new feeling of dedication was being born. This new patriotism had but one direction - - the restoration of national pride and honor. This could only be accomplished by the removal of the hated French army from Prussian soil.

Friedrich Wilhelm III. soon found himself caught in this rising storm of nationalism. By late January 1813, the king left Berlin for Brelsau in Silesia. Publicly the reason for the trip was that Friedrich Wilhelm, himself, would be recruiting a new contingent of Prussian troops to be placed in the service of the French army that Napoleon was attempting to rebuild. On the surface this explanation appeared entirely plausible. General von Bülow in Pomerania and General von Blücher in Silesia were, in fact, then recruiting and training troops, but for a far different purpose. By the time Friedrich Wilhelm arrived in Breslau, General von Gneisenau was on his way there. Generals von Scharnhorst and von Blücher were there waiting for him, as was Chancellor von Hardenburg to advise and persuade the king to take the necessary action. The moment had arrived for Friedrich Wilhelm to summon the courage needed to declare Prussia against Napoleon. Pressure was applied from all sides; the king finally, but with his typical reluctance, issued a proclamation on February 3, 1813, calling on his subjects to arm themselves against the enemy. Although Napoleon was not actually named, all Prussia understood and knew who the enemy was. Preparations commenced for the struggle about to begin.

* * *

During this time of great decision, Friedrich Wilhelm III. awarded belated decorations of the Pour le Mérite Order to those officers who served in the Prussian contingent attached to the French army during the disastrous campaign of 1812.

* February 18, 1813 *

Brandenburg Hussar Regiment

725. **von Knobloch,** Karl Siegismund Erhard, Major.
726. **von Eisenhart,** Johann Ernst Ferdinand, Staff Rittmeister.
    (Awarded the Pour le Mérite Order for distinction in action during the battle at Ribki on August 27, 1812, while serving in the Prussian contingent attached to the French forces. On October 18, 1812, while engaged in a skirmish against Russian troops between Moscow and Kaluga, Staff Rittmeister von Eisenhart was severely wounded.)

* * *

Silesian Uhlan Regiment

727. **von Witzleben,** Friedrich Heinrich August, Rittmeister.
    (Awarded the Pour le Mérite Order for distinction in action during the battle at Borodino on September 7, 1812, while serving in the Prussian contingent attached to the French forces.)
728. **Rördanz,** Karl Heinrich, 2nd Lieutenant.

* * *

Brandenburg Uhlan Regiment

729. **von Schack,** Magnus Friedrich, 2nd Lieutenant.
730. **von Strantz,** Karl Adolf Ferdinand, Staff Rittmeister.
    (Awarded the Pour le Mérite Order for distinction in action during the battle at Staria Daugeliski on July 5, 1812, while serving in the Prus-

Friedrich Wilhelm III., King of Prussia. (Painting by F. Krüger.)

sian contingent attached to the French forces.
Note: Staff Rittmeister von Strantz was awarded the 50 Year Jubilee Golden Crown to the Pour le Mérite Order on January 9, 1862.)

* * *

* February 20, 1813 *

Pomeranian Hussar Regiment

In addition to being decorated with the Pour le Mérite Order for distinction in action during the battle at Ostrovno on July 25, 1812, the following two officers also received the French Legion of Honor. They were serving in the Prussian contingent attached to the French forces.

731. **von Manteuffel**, August Karl Julius, Staff Rittmeister.
732. **von Rudorff**, Wilhelm Heinrich, Staff Rittmeister
      (**Note:** Staff Rittmeister von Rudorff was awarded the 50 Year Jubilee Golden Crown to the Pour le Mérite Order on January 9, 1862.)
733. **von Borcke**, Kurt Friedrich Heinrich, 2nd Lieutenant.
      (Awarded the Pour le Mérite Order for distinction in action during the battle at Kosziany on July 5, 1812, while serving in the Prussian contingent attached to the French forces. During another engagement at Dorobush on August 24, 1812, Lieutenant von Borcke lost his right arm.)

* * *

* The Sixth Coalition *

The response to the king's first proclamation was so overwhelming that by late February Friedrich Wilhelm finally decided to completely break with Napoleon. The king quickly entered into formal negotiations with Emperor Alexander I. On February 28, 1813, the Convention of Kalish was signed whereby Prussia formed an alliance with Russia and England which became known as The Sixth Coalition. Under the terms of this agreement, Prussia and Friedrich Wilhelm were committed to war against France and Napoleon.

However, Friedrich Wilhelm III. was still apprehensive of repercussions against Prussia and especially Berlin, since French troops were still in garrison there. He insisted that the convention be kept secret until Russian forces had successfully driven out the French from his capital. The Russian General Kutusov, the commander-in-chief of the liberating Russian army, did not approve of these conditions and refused to advance on Berlin without Prussian support. A compromise was reached when Friedrich Wilhelm agreed to authorize the Prussian troops to follow the Russians to the Oder River, but to avoid any open hostilities with the French until war was formally declared.

By early March 1813, heavy pressure was being brought to bear on the French troops in Berlin by the advancing Russian forces. With the fear of an armed insurrection by Berliners growing more evident daily, the commanding French general chose to evacuate Berlin and withdraw toward the safety of the west. The allies, including the Prussian forces, were able to enter Berlin without a shot being fired.

* * *

* Establishment of the Oakleaves to the Pour le Mérite Order *

While Friedrich Wilhelm III. was in Breslau, he established the golden Oakleaves to the Pour le Mérite Order on March 10, 1813. At the same time, the king also established the Prussian Iron Cross. The following excerpt establishes the golden Oakleaves device to the Pour le Mérite Order as well as the Prussian Iron Cross in two classes. It was taken from the "Silesian Newspaper," number 34, page 596, published on Saturday, March 20, 1813. The bold lines below translate to:

"The Order Pour le Mérite will in exceptional circumstances be awarded with three golden oakleaves attached to the ring."

> 3. Die Militair-Ehrenzeichen erster und zweiter Klasse werden während der Dauer dieses Krieges nicht ausgegeben; auch wird die Ertheilung des rothen Adler-Ordens zweiter und dritter Klasse so wie des Ordens pour le merite, bis auf einige einzelne Fälle, in der Regel suspendirt. Das eiserne Kreuz ersetzt diesen Orden und Ehrenzeichen und wird durchgängig von Höheren und Geringeren auf gleiche Weise in den angeordneten zwei Klassen getragen. **Der Orden pour le mérite wird in außerordentlichen Fällen mit drei goldenen Eichenblättern am Ringe ertheilt.**
> 4. Die zweite Klasse des eisernen Kreuzes soll durchgängig zuerst verliehen werden; die erste kann nicht anders erfolgen, als wenn die zweite schon erworben war.
> 5. Daraus folgt, daß auch diejenigen, welche Orden oder Ehrenzeichen schon besitzen und sich in diesem Kriege auszeichnen, zunächst nur das eiserne Kreuz zweiter Klasse erhalten können.

Until this period any officer recipient cited subsequently for further outstanding military bravery against the enemy was given a second Pour le Mérite Order badge. Those officers thus decorated the second time could, and sometimes did, wear **two** badges of the Pour le Mérite Order at the same time. Usually the badges were worn with one suspended from the neck and the other from the buttonhole of the uniform tunic. However, with the establishment of the Oakleaves device this practice ceased.

To indicate that the Pour le Mérite Order recipient was decorated with a second badge; the ribbon then threaded through a loop attached to the reverse of the oakleaves and worn at the throat.

* * *

This drawing illustrates the design of the obverse of the golden Oakleaves device. Many variations to this basic design appeared until 1918 as shown in the following photos.

It is most interesting to note that during the period of the Liberation Wars (1813-1815), the Imperial Russian officers decorated with the Pour le Mérite Order who subsequently received a second award were given a **second** Pour le Mérite Order **badge** rather than the Oakleaves. No specific reason for this practice is apparent.

The following photos, from the Klietmann Archives, show the obverse and reverse of some of the many variations of the Oakleaves and early Pour le Mérite Order badges.

1. Very early type Oakleaves. Note roundness and lack of fine detail in leaves.

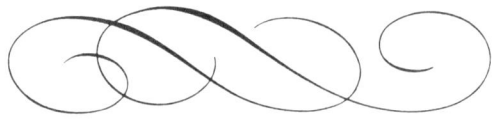

2. Early type Oakleaves. Note detail of leaves and the large size covering the upper points of the badge.

3. Later type Oakleaves. Note more typical configuration and stamped reverse. Also note the crowned eagles on the badge.

4. Later type Oakleaves, circa 1914-1918.

5. Example of post 1945 copy of both badge and Oakleaves. Note lack of detail and flat reverse of Oakleaves device.

The Establishment of the Prussian Landwehr
in Breslau on March 17, 1813.
(From a painting by C. Sellmer.)

* March 12, 1813 *

734. **von Crayen,** Karl August Alexander,
    2nd Lieutenant, Brandenburg Hussar Regiment.
    (Awarded the Pour le Mérite Order for distinction in action during the battle at Poredshi on August 5, 1812, while serving in the Prussian contingent attached to the French forces.)

* * *

The following two Prussian officers, entries 735 and 736, were decorated with the Pour le Mérite Order for distinction in action during the battle at Friedrichstadt on November 18, 1812, while serving in the Prussian contingent attached to the French forces.

735. **von Szerdahelyi,** Karl Adolf Eduard,
    2nd Lieutenant, 1st Leib Hussar Regiment.
    (**Note:** Lieutenant von Szerdahelyi was awarded the 50 Year Jubilee Golden Crown to the Pour le Mérite Order on January 9, 1862.)

* * *

2nd Leib Hussar Regiment

736. **Westphal,** Heinrich Ernst Adolf, 1st Lieutenant.
    (**Note:** Lieutenant Westphal was awarded the 50 Year Jubilee Golden Crown to the Pour le Mérite Order on January 9, 1862.)

737. **Giese,** Johann, 2nd Lieutenant.
    (**Note:** Lieutenant Giese had, as an enlisted man, been decorated with the Golden Military Medal and promoted to Lieutenant. The Golden Military Medal was the highest decoration an enlisted man could receive at this time.)

* * *

On March 15, 1813, while in Berlin, the French ambassador to the Prussian Court learned of the Convention of Kalish, but it was too late for any effective counter-measures. Events began to move quickly for Prussia.

Meanwhile, in Breslau, Friedrich Wilhelm III. issued his famous proclamation, "To My People" on March 17, 1813. This proclamation stated that the time had arrived for liberation from foreign aggression and domination; it called for all the German people to stand together in unity against Napoleon and France, and drive them from German soil. It was this announcement that became the undoing of Napoleon.

* * *

On the following page is a reproduction of the original proclamation which appeared in the Silesian Newspaper, number 34, pages 593 and 594, published Saturday, March 20, 1813.

Schlesische privilegirte Zeitung.

No. 34. Sonnabends den 20. März 1813.

Se. Majestät der König haben mit Sr. Majestät dem Kaiser aller Reußen ein Off- und Defensiv-Bündniß abgeschlossen.

An Mein Volk.

So wenig für Mein treues Volk als für Deutsche, bedarf es einer Rechenschaft, über die Ursachen des Kriegs welcher jetzt beginnt. Klar liegen sie dem unverblendeten Europa vor Augen.

Wir erlagen unter der Uebermacht Frankreichs. Der Frieden, der die Hälfte Meiner Unterthanen Mir entriß, gab uns seine Segnungen nicht; denn er schlug uns tiefere Wunden, als selbst der Krieg. Das Mark des Landes ward ausgesogen, die Hauptfestungen blieben vom Feinde besetzt, der Ackerbau ward gelähmt so wie der sonst so hoch gebrachte Kunstfleiß unserer Städte. Die Freiheit des Handels ward gehemmt, und dadurch die Quelle des Erwerbs und des Wohlstands verstopft. Das Land ward ein Raub der Verarmung.

Durch die strengste Erfüllung eingegangener Verbindlichkeiten hoffte Ich Meinem Volke Erleichterung zu bereiten und den französischen Kaiser endlich zu überzeugen, daß es sein eigener Vortheil sey, Preußen seine Unabhängigkeit zu lassen. Aber Meine reinsten Absichten wurden durch Uebermuth und Treulosigkeit vereitelt, und nur zu deutlich sahen wir, daß des Kaisers Verträge mehr noch wie seine Kriege uns langsam verderben mußten. Jetzt ist der Augenblick gekommen, wo alle Täuschung über unsern Zustand aufhört.

Brandenburger, Preußen, Schlesier, Pommern, Litthauer! Ihr wißt was Ihr seit fast sieben Jahren erduldet habt, Ihr wißt was euer trauriges Loos ist, wenn wir den beginnenden Kampf nicht ehrenvoll enden. Erinnert Euch an die Vorzeit, an den großen Kurfürsten, den großen Friedrich. Bleibt eingedenk der Güter, die unter

594

ihnen unsere Vorfahren blutig erkämpften: Gewissensfreiheit, Ehre, Unabhängigkeit, Handel, Kunstfleiß und Wissenschaft. Gedenkt des großen Beispiels unserer mächtigen Verbündeten der Russen, gedenkt der Spanier, der Portugiesen. Selbst kleinere Völker sind für gleiche Güter gegen mächtigere Feinde in den Kampf gezogen und haben den Sieg errungen. Erinnert Euch an die heldenmüthigen Schweitzer und Niederländer.

Große Opfer werden von allen Ständen gefordert werden: denn, unser Beginnen ist groß, und nicht geringe die Zahl und die Mittel unserer Feinde. Ihr werdet jene lieber bringen, für das Vaterland, für Euren angebornen König, als für einen fremden Herrscher, der wie so viele Beispiele lehren, Eure Söhne und Eure letzten Kräfte Zwecken widmen würde, die Euch ganz fremd sind. Vertrauen auf Gott, Ausdauer, Muth, und der mächtige Beistand unserer Bundesgenossen, werden unseren redlichen Anstrengungen siegreichen Lohn gewähren.

Aber, welche Opfer auch von Einzelnen gefordert werden mögen, sie wiegen die heiligen Güter nicht auf, für die wir sie hingeben, für die wir streiten und siegen müssen, wenn wir nicht aufhören wollen, Preußen und Deutsche zu seyn.

Es ist der letzte entscheidende Kampf den wir bestehen für unsere Existenz, unsere Unabhängigkeit unsern Wohlstand; keinen andern Ausweg giebt es, als einen ehrenvollen Frieden oder einen ruhmvollen Untergang. Auch diesem würdet Ihr getrost entgegen gehen um der Ehre willen, weil ehrlos der Preuße und der Deutsche nicht zu leben vermag. Allein wir dürfen mit Zuversicht vertrauen: Gott und unser fester Willen werden unserer gerechten Sache den Sieg verleihen, mit ihm einen sicheren glorreichen Frieden und die Wiederkehr einer glücklichen Zeit.

Breslau den 17. März 1813.   Friedrich Wilhelm.

For a translation of this important document see Appendix I.

The Volunteers of 1813 in Berlin. (Painting by G. Bleibtreu.)

Coincidentally, during the early months of 1813, while the allies prepared for the forthcoming campaign, Napoleon also made preparations for war. His most important task was rebuilding the shattered remnants of the army that had survived the disastrous Russian campaign. By April, Napoleon had somehow managed, through demands on the unwilling members of the Confederation of the Rhine, to assemble a force of approximately 202,000 men along the Saale River. This force was divided into two main armies, the Army of the Main (River) with 140,000 troops and the Army of the Elbe composed of 62,000. It was a formidable force but with several weaknesses; the major problem of the French was the shortage of a capable cavalry force. This failing was to prove costly to the French later in this campaign.

* April 10, 1813 *

738. **Gorlenkov**, Andrei (Nikolai?) Ivanovich,
    Imperial Russian Colonel, Russian Life Guard Regiment, assigned to the Grodno Hussar Regiment.

* * *

Napoleon continued to finalize his war strategy, and when all arrangements were complete he departed Paris on April 15, 1813, to join his forces to the east.

* * *

* April 18, 1813 *

739. **von Doernberg**, Frhr. Wilhelm Kaspar Ferdinand,
    Royal British Major General, "Continent of Europe" Staff, Commanding, as Colonel, the Duke of Braunschweig-Oels Cavalry Corps.
    (For distinction in action at Lüneburg on April 2, 1813.)

* * *

Napoleon arrived in Erfurt on April 25, 1813, and spent the next few days concentrating the French forces in the area. On April 30th the French army crossed the Saale River. The first notable engagement of the 1813 campaign took place the following day. The advance elements of the Army of the Main, under the command of Marshal Jean-Baptiste Bessières, having passed through Weissenfels towards Lützen and Leipzig, were engaged by a large force of Russian cavalry near the town of Poserna, southwest of Lützen. The Russians were eventually driven off after a sharp and bloody fight. French Marshal Bessières who was killed by a cannonball at Rippach near Weissenfels was the first major loss of the war.

In the meantime, the Prussians and Russians had concentrated a force of some 75,000 troops and 500 cannon between Leipzig and the town of Altenburg. This allied force was ready to advance toward Lützen and threaten the French right flank. The French troops occupied Lützen on May 1, 1813, and began taking possession of a number of smaller towns to the south on May 2nd. It was at this point that the allied army appeared after an all-night forced march. The first important battle of the Freedom War was about to begin at Lützen.

The fierce confrontation between the allies and the French began at noon on May 2, 1813, when the advancing allied cavalry, under the command of General Gebhard von Blücher, suddenly found its way blocked by strong French forces occupying the towns of Gross-Görschen and Starsiedel. The French troops at Gross-Gröschen were forced back while the French in Starsiedel put up a stout resistance and held fast. This delaying action, allowed time for Marshal Auguste Frederic Marmont to arrive with reinforcements and soon a fierce battle was raging in and around the village. During the afternoon the French continued to pour troops into the battle and Napoleon soon arrived on the scene to take command of the French forces.

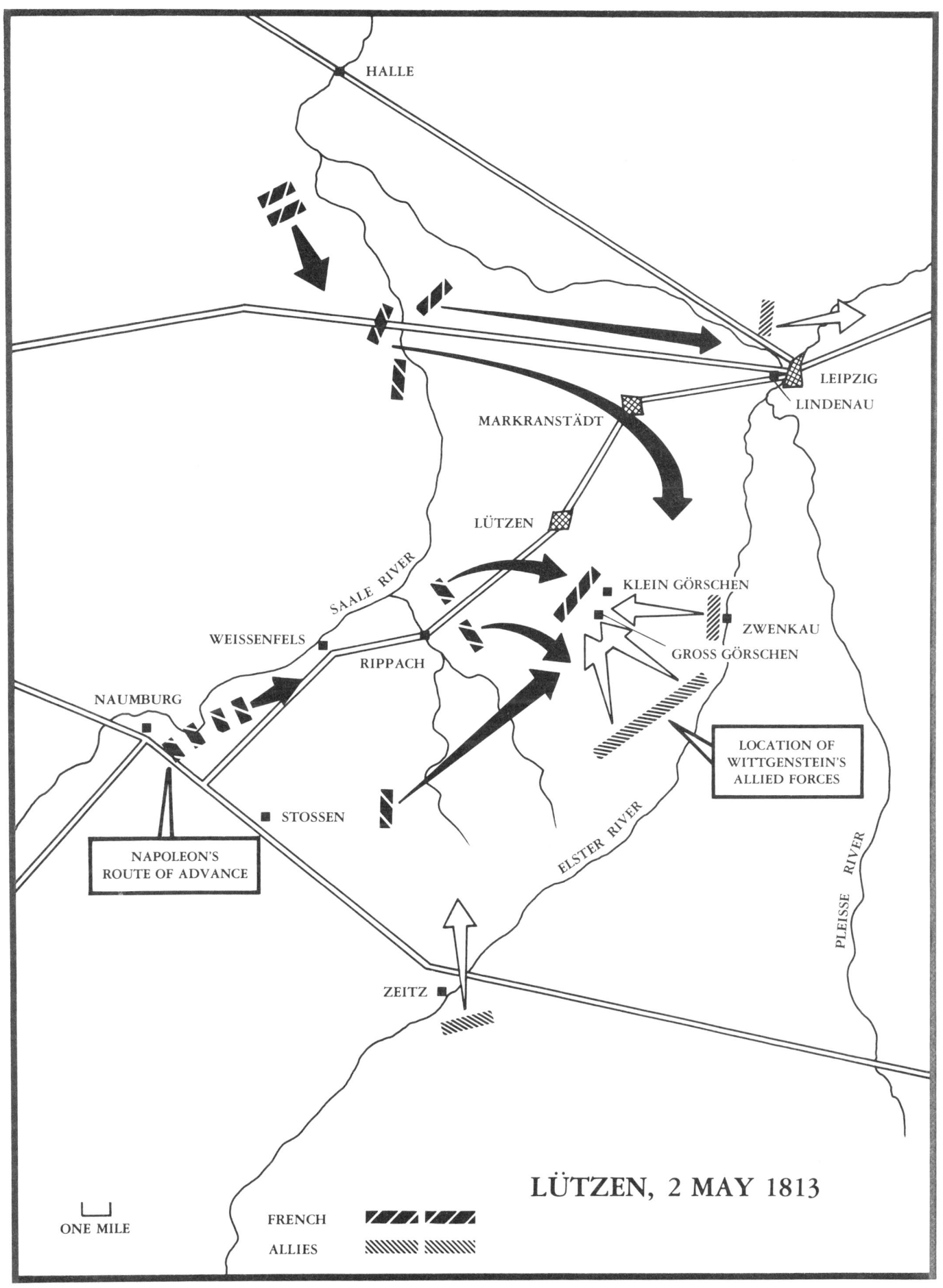

Napoleon's arrival, which stimulated the French troops to an even greater effort, and the allie's of serious military blunders turned the tide in favor of the French. General von Blücher was wounded and left the field and was replaced by General von Yorck, Russian reinforcements were slow in arriving, and initiative wavered among the allies. All this spelled defeat. By early evening the French were threatening to outflank the allied positions, and Napoleon ordered the Imperial Guard to attack the center of the allied line. This was the decisive blow. By seven o'clock that evening the allies began to retreat. The French, however, were too exhausted to pursue and the lack of French cavalry here played an important role in the all too orderly retreat of the allied forces. The French losses were double those of the allies.

Following the defeat at Lützen, the allied army retreated eastward between the Elbe and Oder Rivers. Napoleon continued the French advance and arrived in the vicinity of Dresden on May 8, 1813. The allied armies, in the meantime, had begun concentrating near the town of Bautzen on the Spree River, approximately 35 miles east of Dresden. Here Alexander I. and Friedrich Wilhelm III. ordered their respective commanders, Russian Field Marshal Prince Ludwig Adolf Peter Wittgenstein and for the Prussians the still recovering General Gebhard von Blücher, to make a strong defensive stand.

* * *

* May 13, 1813 *

740. **von Quitzow**, Siegfried Georg Gebhard,
Rittmeister, retired, then Postmaster of Bernau, having served as a 1st Lieutenant in the Brandenburg Hussar Regiment. (For distinction in action during an engagement in the area between Smolensk and Moshaist, August 21, 1812, while serving in the Prussian contingent attached to the French forces. During this action Rittmeister von Quitzow lost a leg.)

* * *

The following four Imperial Russian officers were decorated with the Pour le Mérite Order for distinction in action during the battle at Vehlitz on April 5, 1813.

741. **Parenssov**, Dmitri Tichonovich (Michailovich),
Imperial Russian Staff Captain, Quartermaster Service, serving on the personal staff of Emperor Alexander I.

742. **Gortshakov I.**, Prince Peter Dmitriovich,
Imperial Russian Staff Captain, Life Guard Artillery Brigade, Adjutant to Major General d'Auvray.

* * *

743. **Gerngross**, Renatus (Rodion Fedorovich),
Imperial Russian Colonel, Mitau Dragoon Regiment.

744. **Staden**, Gustaf Gustafovich,
Imperial Russian Colonel, Commander, 14th Artillery Battery Company.

* * *

745. **Markov III.**, Alexander Ivanovich,
   Imperial Russian Lt. Colonel, Commander, 23rd Mounted Artillary Company.
   (For distinction in action at Halle on April 28, 1813. This officer was also later awarded the Prussian Iron Cross for subsequent heroism in action.)

746. **Hirsch**, Ivan,
   Imperial Russian Major, Grodno Hussar Regiment.

747. **Noldken (Nolken)**, Igor Fedorovich,
   Imperial Russian Major, Siev Infantry Regiment, Senior Adjutant of the 5th Infantry Division.

* * *

Imperial Russian 26th Light Infantry Regiment

748. **Dobrovolski**, Semen Ivanovich, Imperial Russian Major.
749. **Medviedev**, Peter Ivanovich, Imperial Russian Captain.
   (Note: This is the <u>first</u> award of the Pour le Mérite Order to Captain Medviedev. See entry 762, this chapter.)

* * *

Imperial Russian Quartermaster Service

The following seven Russian officers were decorated with the Pour le Mérite Order while serving on the personal staff of Emperor Alexander I.

750. **(von) Hoeck (Huek)**, (First name unknown), Imperial Russian Captain.
751. **Vranizki**, (First name unknown), Imperial Russian Staff Captain.

* * *

The following five Russian officers were decorated with the Pour le Mérite Order for distinction in action during the battle at Gross-Görschen on May 2, 1813.

752. **Renni**, Robert (Igorovich), Imperial Russian Major General.
753. **Seliavin**, Nikolai Ivanovich, Imperial Russian Colonel.
754. **Brosin**, Pavel Ivanovich, Imperial Russian Lt. Colonel.
755. **Sasonov**, Nikolai Vassilieovich, Imperial Russian Captain.
756. **Stsherbinin**, Alexander Andreieovich, Imperial Russian Sub-Lieutenant,
   (Note: Lieutenant Stsherbinin was awarded the 50 Year Jubilee Golden Crown to the Pour le Mérite Order on January 22, 1863.)

* * *

757. **Trubtsheninov**, Igor Michailovich,
   Imperial Russian Staff Captain, 25th Light Infantry Regiment, serving as Brigade Adjutant to Russian Major General Roth.
   (For distinction in action during several actions.)

758. **Postelnikov**, Nikolai Jevgienovich,
   Imperial Russian Staff Captain, Perm Infantry Regiment, serving as Division Adjutant to Lieutenant General von Berg.

759. **Obrutshev**, Vladimir Afanasseovich,
   Imperial Russian Lieutenant, Russian Engineer Corps, serving as Adjutant to Major General von Diebitsch.
   (Note: This is the <u>first</u> award of the Pour le Mérite Order to Lieutenant Obrutshev. See entry 1795, this chapter.

This officer also was awarded the 50 Year Golden Crown to the Pour le Mérite Order on January 22, 1863.)

760. **Dedeniev (Dederiev)**, Alexei Igorovich,
Imperial Russian Officer Candidate, Mitau Dragoon Regiment.
(For distinction in action during the battle at Vehlitz on April 5, 1813.)
* * *

761. **Krishanovski**, Maxim Konstantinovich,
Imperial Russian Colonel, Life Guard Finnland Regiment.
(For distinction in action during the battle at Gross-Görschen on May 2, 1813.)
* * *

While the allies prepared to meet the French and hold them at the Spree River, the French patrols were searching for them. On May 16, 1813, a French patrol located the allied forces. Upon learning this, Napoleon immediately ordered Marshal Michel Ney to move south and engage them. While Ney's forces approached from the west and south, Napoleon faced a major obstacle: the Spree River. His troops had to cross it, under heavy allied fire, before engaging the main allied positions. Therefore, Napoleon chose to commit the first day's action to an engagement of attrition and delay any critical moves until the second day. Also, by this action, Napoleon could evaluate the allies' strengths and weaknesses.
* * *

* May 17, 1813 *

The following three Imperial Russian officers were decorated for distinction in action at the engagements at Halle, April 28, 1813, and in the vicinity of Leipzig, May 2, 1813.

762. **Medviedev**, Peter Ivanovich,
Imperial Russian Captain, 26th Light Infantry Regiment.
(**Note**: This is the second award of the Pour le Mérite Order badge to Captain Medviedev for distinction in action during the battle at Halle on April 28, 1813. For the first award of the Pour le Mérite Order see entry 749, this chapter.)
* * *

763. **Schlüter (Schlitter)**, Ivan Ivanovich,
Imperial Russian Staff Captain, 21st Artillery Battery Company.

764. **Oserski**, (Ivan?),
Imperial Russian Staff Captain, 25th Light Infantry Regiment, Adjutant to Major General von Roth.
* * *

Imperial Russian Grodno Hussar Regiment

The following eight Russian officers received the Pour le Mérite Order for distinction in action during an engagement in the vicinity of Leipzig, May 2, 1813.

765. **von Aderkas**, (First name unknown), Imperial Russian Rittmeister.
766. **Iljinski**, Alexander Iljit, Imperial Russian Staff Rittmeister.
767. **Drulski-Sakolinski**, Prince (First name unknown), Lieutenant.

768. **Postels**, Siegismund Ferdinandovich, Imperial Russian Lieutenant.
769. **Behrends (Behrens)**, Vassili? (Klemens?), Imperial Russian Cornet.
770. **Olshevski II.**, Franz Danilovich, Imperial Russian Cornet.
771. **Gutjahr**, Karl Petrovich, Imperial Russian Lieutenant.
772. **Engelhart**, Anton Jevstafieovich, Imperial Russian Cornet.
    (Note: Cornet Engelhart was awarded the 50 Year Golden Crown to the Pour le Mérite Order on January 22, 1863.)

* * *

* May 18, 1813 *

Imperial Russian Quartermaster Service

Both the following Russian officers when decorated with the Pour le Mérite Order were assigned to the personal staff of Emperor Alexander I.

773. **von Neidhardt II.**, Alexander Wilhelm, Imperial Russian Lt. Colonel.
774. **von Hofmann**, Georg Wilhelm, Imperial Russian Lt. Colonel, Senior Quartermaster, II. Infantry Corps.

* * *

775. **Liebstein**, Andrei Ivanovich,
    Imperial Russian Lt. Colonel, Commander of the 33rd Artillery Battery Company.

776. **Ivanov**, Stepan Jemelianovich,
    Imperial Russian Lt. Colonel, 4th Light Infantry Regiment.
    (Note: This is the <u>first</u> award of the Pour le Mérite Order to Colonel Ivanov for distinction in action during the battle at Gross-Görschen on May 2, 1813. For the second award of the Pour le Mérite Order see entry 1492, this chapter.)

* * *

Imperial Russian Murom Infantry Regiment

777. **von Brieskorn**, Bogdan Jakovleovich, Imperial Russian Lieutenant.
778. **von Lüdinghausen**, Frhr. Peter Johann, Imperial Russian Lt. Colonel.
    (Note: This is the <u>first</u> award of the Pour le Mérite Order to this officer for distinction in action during the battle at Klein-Görschen on May 2, 1813. For the second award of the Pour le Mérite Order <u>badge</u> see entry 1978, this chapter.)

* * *

779. **Raben**, Karl Ivanovich,
    Imperial Russian Major, 34th Light Infantry Regiment.
    (This officer was severely wounded on May 2, 1813, during the action at Klein-Görschen as well as being cited for bravery. Note: Captain Raben was awarded the 50 Year Golden Crown to the Pour le Mérite Order on January 22, 1863.)

780. **Wachten**, Hans Otto,
    Imperial Russian Captain, Life Guard Ismailov Regiment, Adjutant to Lt. General Prince Eugen of Württemberg.
    (Note: Captain Wachten was awarded the 50 Year Golden Crown to the Pour le Mérite Order on October 25, 1864.)

781. **von Kurssel**, Fedor Fedorovich,
    Imperial Russian Sub-Lieutenant, Serpuchov Uhlan Regiment.

* * *

Imperial Russian Navaga Infantry Regiment

The following two Russian officers were decorated for distinction in action during the battle at Wittenberg on May 6, 1813.

782. **Astafiev**, Lev Astafieovich, Imperial Russian Lt. Colonel.
783. **von Mach II.**, Leopold, Imperial Russian Officer Candidate.
    (Note: This is the <u>first</u> award of the Pour le Mérite Order to Candidate von Mach. For the second award of the Pour le Mérite Order <u>badge</u> see entry 816, this chapter.)

* * *

784. **Stshelkan (Schtshelkanov)**, Afanassi Jefimovich,
    Imperial Russian Sub-Lieutenant, 28th Artillery Battery Company.
    (For distinction in action during the siege of Spandau, 1812.)

* * *

The battle at Bautzen began at noon on May 20, 1813, when French artillery opened fire and assault bridges were quickly constructed across the river. By three o'clock the first major French attack commenced; three hours later they had forced the allies from their main positions and occupied Bautzen. To the south, Marshal Nicolas Charles Oudinot's forces drew many of the allied reserves into action. Finally, as the fighting began to diminish, Marshal Ney's troops entered the field. As a result, it appeared that Napoleon was about to win a decisive victory.

At dawn on May 21, 1813, the French forces attacked. Heavy fighting developed in all sectors of the battlefield. Slowly the French drove the allied troops from their positions, and by four o'clock the allied army was forced to begin a slow but orderly retreat toward Silesia.

However, even with the battle lost, the allied troops, including most of the artillery, escaped a major disaster and were able to retire intact. They remained an effective fighting force which Napoleon would have to deal with later. Although Napoleon won the battle, once again his lack of a sufficient cavalry force did not permit pursuit of the retreating Prussians and Russians. Napoleon realized that his army was in no position to continue the campaign. While the shortage of cavalry was his most serious handicap, the general inexperience and exhaustion of his troops hampered his plans as well.

* * *

* May 27, 1813 *

Silesian Uhlan Regiment

The following three Prussian officers received the Pour le Mérite Order for distinction in action during the engagement at Lessie-Zerkevno on August 7, 1812, while serving in the Prussian contingent attached to the French forces.

785. **von Michaelis**, Christof Josef Friedrich, 1st Lieutenant.
    (Note: This officer was also severely wounded in action during the battle at Borodino on September 7, 1812, while attached to French forces.)
786. **von Tiele**, Karl Friedrich, 2nd Lieutenant.
787. **Dallmer**, Karl Friedrich Franz, 2nd Lieutenant.
    (Note: Lieutenant Dallmer was awarded the 50 Year Golden Crown to the Pour le Mérite Order on January 9, 1862.)

* * *

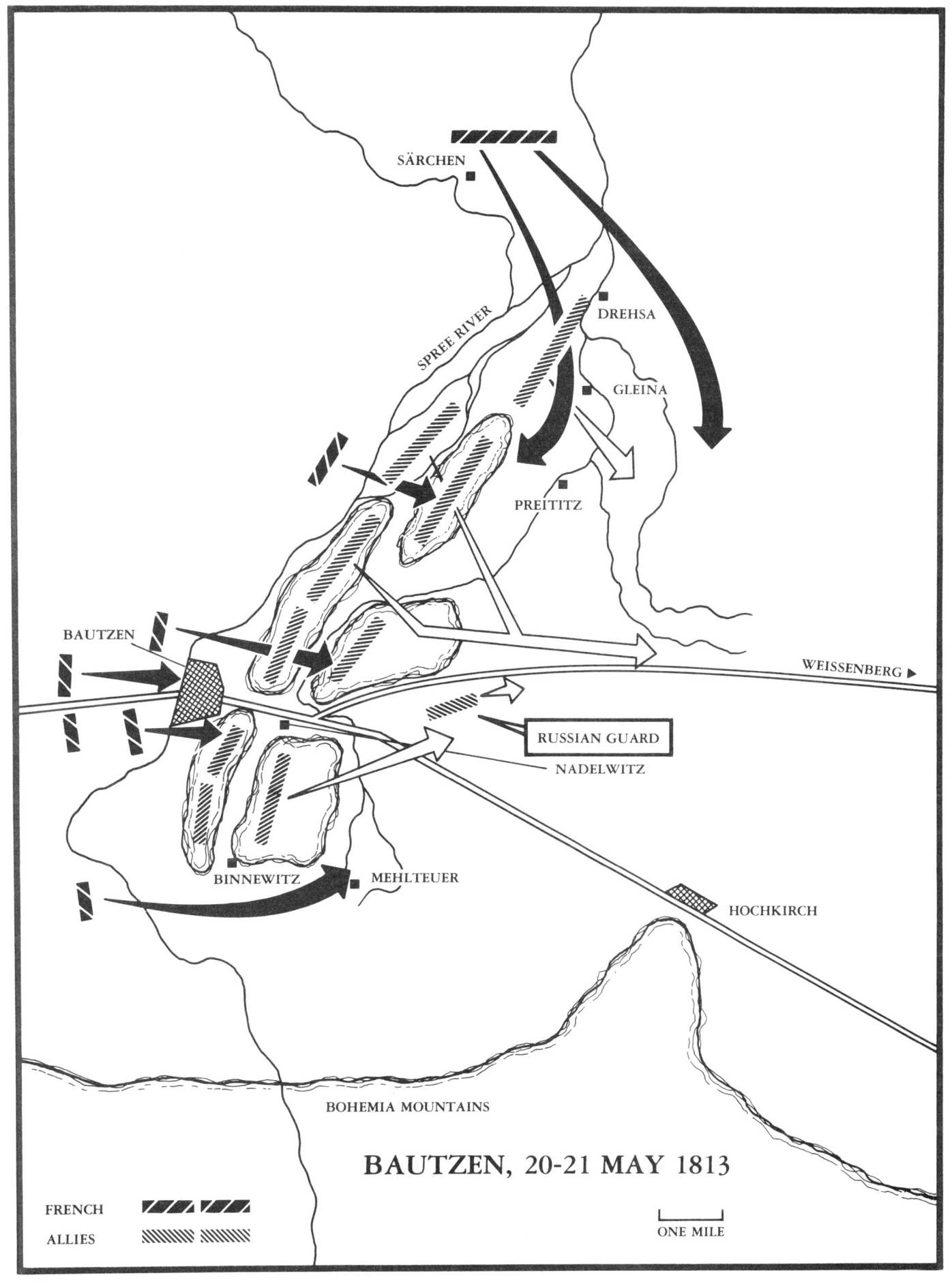

788. **Heuduck**, Heinrich Gottlieb Konrad,
  2nd Lieutenant, Brandenburg Uhlan Regiment.
  (For distinction in action during the battle at Lessie-Zerkevno on August 7, 1812, while serving in the Prussian contingent attached to the French forces.
  Note: Lieutenant Heuduck was awarded the 50 Year Golden Crown to the Pour le Mérite Order on January 9, 1862.)
  * * *

789. **von Hobe**, August Johann Ludwig Elias Friedrich Karl,
  2nd Lieutenant, Brandenburg Hussar Regiment.
  (For distinction in action at Kosziany, July 5, 1812, while serving in the Prussian contingent attached to the French forces.
  Note: Lieutenant von Hobe was awarded the 50 Year Golden Crown to the Pour le Mérite Order on January 9, 1862.)
  * * *

The allies, in the meantime, were having problems of their own. There was disagreement as to strategy and dissension among the Prussian and Russian commanders. However, more important was the fact that Alexander I. and Friedrich Wilhelm needed time to convince Franz I., of Austria, to join their coalition. Both sides needed time to reorganize, refit and rest. After a brief period of negotiations, an armistice was signed with Napoleon on June 2, 1813.

The proposed purpose of this armistice was to conduct formal peace negotiations. Although both sides made a show of seriously wanting to negotiate peace, actually neither wanted a peace treaty. During this breathing spell, Prussia and Russia approached other states, Austria in particular, about joining their fight to oust Napoleon from German soil.

* * *

* June 10, 1813 *

* First Award of the Oakleaves to the Pour le Mérite Order *

790. **von Yorck**, Johann David Ludwig,
Lt. General, Commanding General of Prussian Forces.
(**Note**: This was the <u>first</u> award of the Oakleaves to the Pour le Mérite Order as authorized on March 10, 1813, and indicated a second award of the Pour le Mérite Order. For the initial award of the Pour le Mérite Order see Volume I, Chapter V-1, entry 217, page 279.)

* * *

* June 11, 1813 *

Imperial Russian Life Guard Hussar Regiment

The following three Russian officers were assigned as adjutants to Imperial Russian Cavalry General Count Ludwig Adolf Wittgenstein when decorated for distinction in action with the Pour le Mérite Order.

791. **Ygnatiev**, Dmitri Lvovich, Imperial Russian Colonel.
792. **von Keller**, Count Theodor Ludwig, Imperial Russian Rittmeister.
793. **Petrulin**, Jakob Vassilieovich, Imperial Russian Rittmeister.
   (Note: This is the <u>first</u> award of the Pour le Mérite Order to this officer. For the second award of the Pour le Mérite Order <u>badge</u> see entry 1933, this chapter.)

* * *

794. **Guriev**, Nikolai Dmitrieovich,
   Imperial Russian Lieutenant, Life Guard Semenovski Regiment.

795. **Tshagin**, Peter Nikolaiovich,
   Imperial Russian Staff Rittmeister, Bielorussia Hussar Regiment.

796. **Massalov**, Ivan Grigorieovich,
   Imperial Russian Major, Neva Infantry Regiment, Adjutant to Lt. General Sasonov.

797. **Glasko**, (First name unknown),
   Imperial Russian Army Major, unit unknown, unassigned.

798. **von Bode**, Baron Lev Karlovich,
   Imperial Russian Staff Captain, Life Guard Light Infantry Regiment, Adjutant to Major General von Steinheil.

* * *

Imperial Russian Grodno Hussar Regiment

799. **Kachovski**, Michail Ivanovich, Imperial Russian Lt. Colonel.
800. **Kotshubei L.**, Arkadi Vassilieovich, Imperial Russian Staff Rittmeister,
   Adjutant to Cavalry General Wittgenstein.

* * *

801. **Novossilzov**, Ivan Petrovich,
   Imperial Russian Lieutenant, Life Guard Preobrashenski Regiment, Adjutant to Cavalry General Wittgenstein.

* * *

Imperial Russian Quartermaster Service

The following four Russian officers when decorated with the Pour le Mérite Order for distinction in action were assigned to the personal staff of Emperor Alexander I.

802. **Teslev**, Alexander Petrovich, Imperial Russian Colonel.
803. **Harting**, Martin Nikolaiovich, Imperial Russian Colonel.
804. **von Diest**, Heinrich Friedrich, Imperial Russian Colonel.
805. **von zur Mühlen**, Vassili (Wilhelm), Imperial Russian Lieutenant.

* * *

806. **von Rönne**, Baron Gustaf (Astafi Astafieovich),
   Imperial Russian Cavalry Major, unit unknown, unassigned.

807. **von Rosen**, Baron Andrei Fedorovich,
   Imperial Russian Lt. Colonel, Alexandria Hussar Regiment.

808. **Shabelski**, Ivan Petrovich,
   Imperial Russian Lieutenant, Russian Engineer Corps, Adjutant to Major General d'Auvray.
   (**Note**: Lieutenant Shabelski was awarded the 50 Year Golden Crown to the Pour le Mérite Order on January 22, 1863.)

809. **Pachert**, Ivan Ivanovich,
   Imperial Russian Captain, St. Petersburg Opoltshenie (militia), Adjutant to Major General d'Auvray.

* * *

* June 14, 1813 *

810. **von Lupinski**, Vinzentius Ferrerius Kajetanus,
   1st Lieutenant, Brandenburg Uhlan Regiment.
   (For distinction in action during the battle at Lessie-Zerkevno on August 7, 1812, while serving in the Prussian contingent attached to the French forces. Later during the battle of Borodino on September 7, 1812, Lieutenant von Lupinski was severely wounded.
   Note: He was awarded the 50 Year Golden Crown to the Pour le Mérite Order on January 9, 1862.)

* * *

* June 17, 1813 *

811. **von Boetticher**, Moritz Ivanovich,
   Imperial Russian Major, Riga Dragoon Regiment, Adjutant to Cavalry General Duke Alexander of Württemberg.

* * *

* July 6, 1813 *

812. **Peterson**, Ivan Fedorovich,
   Imperial Russian Lt. Colonel, Polozk Infantry Regiment, Adjutant to Cavalry General Duke Alexander of Württemberg.

* * *

* July 11, 1813 *

The following four Russian officers were decorated for distinction in action during the engagement at Luckau between May 23 and June 4, 1813.

Imperial Russian Tula Infantry Regiment

813. **Bullach**, (First name unknown), Imperial Russian Lt. Colonel.
814. **Golofeiev**, Apollon Vassilieovich, Imperial Russian Staff Captain.

* * *

Imperial Russian Navaga Infantry Regiment

815. **Milochov**, Alexei Alexieiovich, Imperial Russian Major.
816. **von Mach II.**, Leopold, Imperial Russian Sub-Lieutenant,
   (Note: This is the second award of the Pour le Mérite badge to Lieutenant von Mach. For the initial award of the Pour le Mérite Order see entry 783, this chapter.)

* * *

Sweden, led by Crown Prince Jean-Baptiste Julius Bernadotte, a former Marshal of France, joined the Sixth Coalition in July, as did a number of smaller German states. Although Austria remained uncommitted and neutral, Franz I. began mobilizing his army.

* * *

Crown Prince Jean-Baptiste Julius Bernadotte

* July 22, 1813 *

817. **von Hohendorff**, Otto Wilhelm,
2nd Lieutenant, 1st Pomeranian Infantry Regiment.
(For distinction in action during the battle at Cyopen on September 29, 1812, while serving in the Prussian contingent attached to the French forces.)

* * *

* August 2, 1813 *

Brandenburg Hussar Regiment

Both the following Prussian officers were belatedly decorated with the Pour le Mérite Order for distinction in action during the battle at Kosziany on July 5, 1812, while serving in the Prussian contingent attached to the French forces.

818. **von Probst**, Friedrich Wilhelm Heinrich, 2nd Lieutenant.
819. **Felgentreu**, Adolf Erikus, 2nd Lieutenant,
    (Lieutenant Felgentreu was wounded in action during the battle at Shevardino on September 5, 1812.)

* * *

Imperial Russian Ilovaiski IV. Regiment
Army of the Don

The following two Russian officers received their Pour le Mérite Order for distinction in action during the engagement in the vicinity between Königswartha and Kamenz on May 14, 1813.

820. **Protopopov**, Stepan Danilovich (?), Imperial Russian Starchina.
821. **Popov**, (First name unknown), Imperial Russian Sotnik.

* * *

822. **Dresler von Scharffenstein**, Wilhelm Friedrich Karl,
    Staff Rittmeister, Lithuanian Dragoon Regiment.

823. **von Saucken**, Ernst Friedrich,
    2nd Lieutenant, 2nd West Prussian Dragoon Regiment.
    (While serving in the Prussian contingent attached to the French service this officer was decorated for distinction in action while on patrol on December 15, 1812. Lieutenant von Saucken captured an enemy Russian officer and 15 cavalry troopers during this patrol action.)

* * *

* August 4, 1813 *

824. **Julius**, Karl Johann Ferdinand,
    2nd Lieutenant, Silesian Uhlan Regiment.
    (For distinction in action during the battle at Lessie-Zerkevno on August 8, 1812, where Lieutenant Julius was severely wounded and captured by the Russians, while serving in the Prussian contingent attached to the French forces.)

* * *

The following three Russian officers were serving as adjutants to Imperial Russian Infantry General Barclay de Tolly when decorated with the Pour le Mérite Order for distinction in action.

825. **Koilenski**, Fedor (Ivan?) Stepanovich, Imperial Russian Colonel,
    Imperial Russian Life Guard Artillery Brigade.

826. **Kaver**, Jevstafi Vladimirovich, Imperial Russian Rittmeister,
    Imperial Russian Life Guard Uhlan Regiment.

827. **Reitz**, Leonti Leontieovich, Imperial Russian Army Lt. Colonel,
    unit unknown, unassigned.

* * *

* August 8, 1813 *

Brandenburg Uhlan Regiment

Both of the following Prussian officers were decorated, belatedly, for distinction in action while serving in the Prussian contingent attached to the French forces.

828. **von Stülpnagel**, George Karl Leonhard Ludwig, Staff Rittmeister,
(For distinction in action during the battle at Vinkovo on October 18, 1812.
Note: Staff Rittmeister von Stülpnagel was awarded the 50 Year Golden Crown to the Pour le Mérite Order on January 9, 1862.)

829. **von Dunker**, Friedrich Wilhelm, 2nd Lieutenant,
(For distinction in action during the battle at Lessie-Zerkevno on August 8, 1812. Later, Lieutenant von Dunker was severely wounded in action during the engagement at Voronovo on October 3, 1813.
Note: Lieutenant von Dunker was awarded the 50 Year Golden Crown to the Pour le Mérite Order on January 9, 1862.)

* * *

In early August of 1813, the armistice came to an abrupt end and General von Blücher advanced on the neutral city of Breslau. This maneuver was completely unauthorized, but no one was really surprised. It signaled the opening of the second phase of the campaign. The allies denounced the armistice on August 11, 1813, and on August 12, 1813, Austria formally joined the Sixth Coalition and declared war on France.

* * *

* August 11, 1813 *

All of the following Russian officers received the Pour le Mérite Order for distinction in action during the siege and capture of Thorn, April 5-17, 1813.

830. **Mussin-Pushkin**, Count Ivan Alexieieovich,
Imperial Russian Chamberlain, serving as adjutant to Major General Prince Repnin.

* * *

Imperial Russian Artillery Corps

831. **Sassajädko I.**, Danilo Dmitrieovich, Imperial Russian Lt. Colonel,
Commander, 15th Artillery Battery Company.
832. **Pastshenko**, Lev Kornieieovich, Imperial Russian Lt. Colonel,
Commander, 18th Artillery Battery Company.
833. **Sassajädko II.**, Alexander Dmitrieovich, Imperial Russian Colonel,
Commander, 29th Light Artillery Company.
834. **Veliaminov**, Nikolai Stepanovich, Imperial Russian Colonel,
Life Guard Artillery Brigade.

* * *

835. **von Rummel**, Friedrich August,
Imperial Russian Lt. Colonel, Quartermaster, IX Infantry Corps, serving on the personal staff of Emperor Alexander I.

* * *

Imperial Russian Engineer Corps

836. **Glutshkovius**, Michail, Imperial Russian Lt. Colonel.
837. **Litov**, Andrei Jefremovich, Imperial Russian Staff Captain.
838. **Michaud**, Ludwig Franzovich, Imperial Russian Lt. Colonel, serving as Wing Adjutant.

* * *

839. **Rachmanov**, Alexander Ivanovich,
    Imperial Russian Colonel, Life Guard Preobrashenski Regiment; Chief of Staff to Infantry General Count Langeron.

* * *

The following six Russian officers, when decorated with the Pour le Mérite Order for distinction in action, were all serving as adjutants to Infantry General Count Langeron.

840. **von Schulz**, Baron Igor Vassilieovich, Imperial Russian Staff Captain, Life Guard Lithuanian Regiment.
841. **Rühl**, Andrei Fedorovich, Imperial Russian Staff Captain, Life Guard Ismailov Regiment.
842. **Prosvirkin**, (First name unknown), Imperial Russian Captain, Staro-Oskol Infantry Regiment.
843. **Bestushev**, Grigori Vassilieovich, Imperial Russian Staff Captain, Perejaslav Mounted Light Infantry Regiment.
844. **Sontag**, Igor Vassilieovich, Imperial Russian Captain, Dorpat Mounted Light Infantry Regiment.
845. **Melnikov**, (First name unknown), Imperial Russian Major, Nasheburg Infantry Regiment.

* * *

846. **Menshikov**, Prince Nikolai Serieieovich,
    Imperial Russian Staff Rittmeister, Life Guard Hussar Regiment, Wing Adjutant.

* * *

Learning that General Blücher had moved toward Breslau and that Austria had joined his enemies, Napoleon decided to make the first move and to take the offensive before the allied armies could concentrate their forces. On August 15, 1813, Napoleon left his headquarters in Dresden. The next few days were used in preparing and deploying his forces. to confront and defeat General von Blücher.

By the 20th of August, 1813, Napoleon had succeeded in locating the Prussian forces near the towns of Löwenberg-Bunzlau on the Bober River. Here he made elaborate plans to engage the Prussians, and late that afternoon he launched his attack across the river against the Prussian defensive positions. However, the attack failed. When the French reached the Prussian positions, the Prussian army was not there. General Blücher, following the plans devised by the allied headquarters, ordered that any allied force confronting French forces commanded directly by Napoleon, was to withdraw without giving battle. Napoleon prepared to pursue Blücher's forces eastward, but important information arrived that caused him to change his plans immediately. Intelligence reports indicated that a combined Prussian-Austrian-Russian army, commanded by Field Marshal Prince Karl Schwarzenberg, was advancing against Dresden. Napoleon immediately gave command of the French forces searching for Blücher to Marshal Jacques Etienne Joseph Macdonald. With Napoleon commanding the bulk of the

Blücher. (Drawing by A. Menzel.)

French army, they executed a 180 degree turn and by forced march rushed back to defend Dresden.

* The Battle of Dresden *

By this time the allied army had been joined by Friedrich Wilhelm III., Alexander I. and Franz I. It arrived near Dresden on August 23, 1813. However, due to indecision by the allied command, plus a strong defense by the French garrison commanded by Marshal Laurent Gouvion St.Cyr, the allied assault on the city was postponed. August 25, 1813, was the day of the planned attack, but it was changed to the following day. This short respite was all the French needed. Reinforcements for the French garrison began arriving in the city on the 25th of August, and Napoleon arrived early on August 26, 1813, with additional troops.

With Napoleon's arrival, the cries of "Vive l'Empereur!!" could be heard everywhere. The three allied monarchs and their senior generals, upon hearing the shouts of French enthusiasm for their emperor, wondered if they should abandon the attack on the city entirely. Before orders could be issued to start a general withdrawal, Prussian units launched an attack against the French positions and the Battle of Dresden began.

The first day's fighting was confined mainly to the suburbs surrounding the city. Initially, the allies met with some success and occupied some of the French defensive positions. However, due to the constant arrival of fresh French reinforcements as well as the presence of Napoleon along the French lines, the battle began to turn against the allies. By the time the fighting had finally broken off for the day, almost every position the Prussians had gained had been recovered by the French; in some instances the French had even managed to occupy some of the original allied positions.

Throughout the late evening of the 26th and the early morning hours of August 27, 1813, the opposing armies continued to receive reinforcements. However, the French were able to accumulate more troops and this fact, added to the heavy rainstorms that developed, did not improve the morale of the allied troops. Both sides continued to plan for the next day's confrontation, but it was Napoleon who again struck the first blow.

Early on the morning of August 27, 1813, Napoleon launched a coordinated attack against the allied left and right flanks. Almost at once the allies, unprepared for this tactic, began to fall back before the French onslaught. The major portion of the allied line had been concentrated for a general assault against the French center. In this position they were helpless to go to the aid of the flanks and could only watch the ensuing bloody battle. By three o'clock the battle was virtually finished, and it was obviously another French victory. The allied forces retreated southward toward Bohemia.

During the two day battle, the allies had lost approximately four times the casualties suffered by the French, but once again managed to escape almost intact.

At the conclusion of the battle of Dresden, Napoleon ordered General Dominique Joseph Vandamme's force to pursue the retreating allied army and to intercept the allies' left wing before it reached the safety of Bohemia. Initially the pursuit was fairly successful until August 30, 1813, when the French force reached the vicinity of Kulm, south of Dresden. Here the French ran into a large Russian force of the Imperial Guard under the command of General Ivan

Ostermann-Tolstoi, drawn up in battle formation.

* * *

* The Battle of Kulm *

The battle of Kulm began at 7 o'clock on the morning of August 30, 1813. The French were somewhat successful initially; however, with the arrival of Russian reinforcements the allied force began to advance and a fierce frontal assault developed. The French quickly withdrew into a defensive posture and managed to hold their ground until nearly eleven o'clock when a Prussian force of 10,000 troops, commanded by General Kleist von Nollendorf arrived and launched a furious attack on the French rear. General Vandamme fought as best he could but eventually was forced to surrender 7,000 French troops. A large portion of his corps managed to avoid the allied trap and successfully fought its way out. The allied losses were twice as heavy as the French, but the battle did much to restore the morale and confidence of the allied troops in their commanders and, more importantly, in their own fighting capabilities.

General Kleist von Nollendorf

In the meantime, Napoleon learned of setbacks to his military strategies in other areas as well. At the start of the campaign Napoleon had sent Marshal Nicolas Charles Oudinot to the north of Dresden with a large force with orders to capture Berlin. On August 23, 1813, as the French neared Berlin, Marshal Oudinot found his march blocked by the Prussian troops of General Bolesas Friedrich Tauentzien near the town of Gross-Beeren. The French immediately launched an attack on the Prussian positions and forced them back from the town. However, the French made a critical mistake in believing that they had beaten the Prussians, and proceeded to make camp for the night. Unbeknownst to the French, General Gebhard Blücher had just arrived with a large force and attacked the French as they settled down for the night. Taken completely by surprise, the French retreated. When the battle ended, losses totaled 3000 for the French and 1000 for the Prussians. From this point on Marshal Oudinot became extremely cautious which incurred criticism from Napoleon.

* * *

* September 4, 1813 *

Both of the following Russian officers were assigned to the staff of Ataman Count Platov when decorated with the Pour Le Mérite Order.

847. **Samarin**, (First name unknown),
    Imperial Russian Lt. Colonel, 1st Light Infantry Regiment.
848. **Rogatshev**, Semen Igorovich(?),
    Imperial Russian Army Major, unit unknown, unassigned.

* * *

* September 5, 1813 *

849. **von Zieten**, Wieprecht Hans Karl Friedrich,
Major General, Commander of the XII. Brigade.
(Awarded the Oakleaves to the Pour le Mérite Order for distinction in action during the battle at Dresden on August 26-27, 1813, and during the battle at Kulm on August 30, 1813. For the initial award of the Pour le Mérite Order see entry 242, Volume I, Chapter IV, p. 160.
Note: It is of interest that the Oakleaves device were given 21 years after the original Pour le Mérite Order was awarded. At the time General von Zieten held the rank of 2nd Lieutenant.)
* * *

850. **Noailles**, Count Alexis,
Royal Swedish Lieutenant, Orderly officer, attached to the staff of the Swedish Crown Prince.
* * *

Lt. General Friedrich Wilhelm von Bülow

* September 6, 1813 *

851. **von Bülow**, Friedrich Wilhelm,
   Lt. General, Commanding General of the III. Army Corps.
   (Awarded the Oakleaves to the Pour le Mérite Order in recognition of distinction in action. For the initial award of the Pour le Mérite Order see Volume I, Chapter IV, entry 387, p. 174.
   Note: It is of interest that the Oakleaves device were given <u>21</u> years after the original Pour le Mérite Order was awarded. At the time, General von Bülow held the rank of Captain.)
   * * *

852. **von Oppen**, Adolf Friedrich,
   Major General, Brigade Commander of the Reserve Cavalry of the III. Army Corps.
   (Awarded the Oakleaves to the Pour le Mérite Order in recognition of distinction in action. For the initial award of the Pour le Mérite Order see Volume I, Chapter V-1, entry 219, p. 280.)
   * * *

Imperial Russian 5th Artillery Battery Company

853. **Triapizin**, Vassili Ivanovich, Imperial Russian Captain, Commander.
854. **Bruckendahl**, Karl Vassilieovich, Imperial Russian Lieutenant.
855. **von Essen**, Karl Karlovich, Imperial Russian Lieutenant.
   * * *

856. **Cholodovski**, Igor Vassilieovich,
   Imperial Russian Lieutenant, Adjutant of the 5th Artillery Brigade.
   * * *

Imperial Russian 7th Artillery Battery Company

857. **Vnukov**, Vassili Michailovich, Imperial Russian Sub-Lieutenant.
   (Note: This is the <u>first</u> award of the Pour le Mérite Order to Lieutenant Vnokov. For the award of the second Pour le Mérite Order see entry 1024, this chapter.)
   * * *

Imperial Russian 21st Artillery Battery Company

858. **Seslavin III.**, Fedor Nikita, Imperial Russian Staff Captain.
   (Note: This is the <u>first</u> award of the Pour le Mérite Order to Staff Captain Seslavin III. For the second award of the Pour le Mérite Order see entry 960, this chapter.)
   * * *

Imperial Russian 23rd Mounted Artillery Company

859. **Mustafin**, Prince Alexander Vassilieovich, Imperial Russian Staff Captain.
   * * *

Imperial Russian 23rd Light Infantry Regiment

860. **Petrov**, Ivan Alexieieovich, Imperial Russian Major.
861. **Miagkov**, (First name unknown), Imperial Russian Major.
   * * *

On August 26, 1813, near Liegnitz, French Marshal Jacques Macdonald stumbled into a battle while leading the French Army of the Bober against Blücher's 105,000 Prussians and Russians which made up the Army of Silesia. Neither commander expected to engage as each assumed the other was on the defensive.

The two armies crashed head on in a confused but bloody battle near the Katzbach River. The whole battle was fought in a driving down pour which greatly hindered the infantry in their fire-power. The French were driven off the field and suffered a loss of approximately 15,000 troops whereas the Prussian loss was probably around 4,000 men. This defeat of the French, together with their defeats at Gross-Beeren and Kulm almost during the same time period took from Napoleon the advantage which he had gained at Dresden.

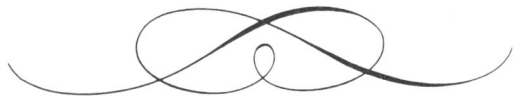

The Battle at Katzbach

Imperial Russian 24th Light Infantry Regiment

862. **de Mendoza-Butello**, Count Ossip Stepanovich, Imperial Russian Colonel.
863. **Krasnokutski**, Ivan Nikolaieovich, Imperial Russian Captain.
864. **Nagin**, (First name unknown), Imperial Russian Captain.

* * *

Imperial Russian 25th Light Infantry Regiment

865. **von Bremen**, (First name unknown), Imperial Russian Major.
866. **Schulgan**, (First name unknown), Imperial Russian Major.
867. **Dolomanov**, Nikolai Kyrillovich, Imperial Russian Captain.

* * *

Imperial Russian 26th Light Infantry Regiment

868. **Koverniev**, (First name unknown), Imperial Russian Captain.
869. **Lossenkov**, Vassili Ivanovich, Imperial Russian Staff Captain.
870. **Sorokin**, Peter Jakovleovich, Imperial Russian Lieutenant.

* * *

871. **von Tiesenhausen**, Gotthard,
     Imperial Russian Captain, Life Guard Semenovski Regiment,
     Adjutant to Artillery General Count Araktsheiev.

* * *

872. **Selivanov II.**, Andrei Andreieovich,
     Imperial Russian Starchina, unit unknown, Army of the Don.
     (Note: This is the <u>first</u> award of the Pour le Mérite Order to Starchina Selivanov II. For the second award of the Pour le Mérite Order see entry 1701, this chapter.)

* * *

873. **Jereovski**, (First name unknown),
     Imperial Russian Major, Volyni Infantry Regiment.

* * *

Imperial Russian Grodno Hussar Regiment

The following six Russian officers were decorated with the Pour le Mérite Order for distinction in action at Bautzen on May 20-21, 1813.

874. **Olshevski**, Anton Danilovich, Imperial Russian Lt. Colonel.
875. **Ostragradski**, Matvei Ivanovich, Imperial Russian Staff Rittmeister.
876. **Kramer**, Lev Fedorovich, Imperial Russian Staff Rittmeister.
877. **Gliebov**, (First name unknown), Imperial Russian Staff Rittmeister.
878. **Beckmann**, Fedor Petrovich, Imperial Russian Staff Rittmeister.
879. **Nasimov**, Yeugeni Petrovich, Imperial Russian Lt. Colonel,
     (Note: Lt. Colonel Nasimov was awarded the 50 Year Golden Crown to the Pour le Mérite Order on January 22, 1863.)

* * *

The following six Russian officers also received their decorations for distinction in action during the engagement at Bautzen on May 20-21, 1813.

Imperial Russian Gluchov Curassier Regiment

880. **Mirkovich**, Ivan Petrovich, Imperial Russian Major.
881. **Svieriev**, (First name unknown), Imperial Russian Major.
882. **Krivonossov**, (First name unknown), Imperial Russian Major.

* * *

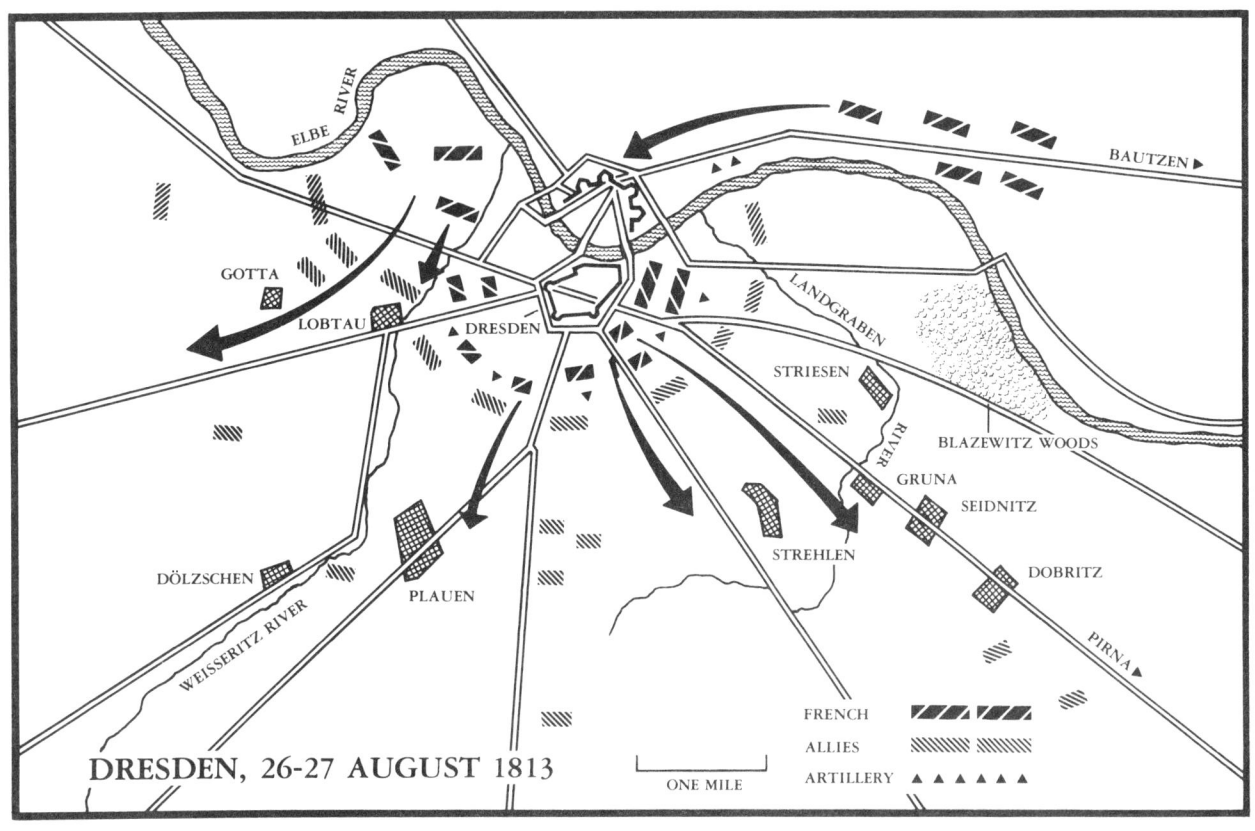

Saxon troops crossing the Elbe at Dresden

Imperial Russian Small Russia Curassier Regiment

883. **Shatalov**, Timofei Andreieovich, Imperial Russian Major.
884. **Levshin**, Vladimir Vassilieovich, Imperial Russian Rittmeister.
885. **Truchsess zu Waldburg-Capustigall**, Count Heinrich August
     Imperial Russian Rittmeister.

* * *

886. **Borissov**, Christofor Sergieieovich,
     Imperial Russian Lt. Colonel, Volyni Uhlan Regiment.
     (For distinction in action during the skirmish at Könnern.)

887. **Matov**, (First name unknown),
     Imperial Russian Major, Navaga Infantry Regiment.
     (For distinction in action during the battle at Luckau on May 23, 1813.)

* * *

The following three Russian officers were decorated for distinction in action during the battle of Dresden on August 26-27, 1813.

Imperial Russian Cavalier Guard Regiment

888. **Volkonski**, Prince Sergei Grigorieovich, Imperial Russian Colonel,
     Wing Adjutant.
889. **Pashkov**, Andrei Ivanovich, Imperial Russian Lieutenant.

* * *

890. **von Loewenstern**, Woldemar Heinrich,
     Imperial Russian Cavalry Major, unit unknown, unassigned.

* * *

The following five Russian officers were decorated with the Pour le Mérite Order and the Prussian Iron Cross for distinction in action during the siege of Czenstochau.

891. **Achlestishev**, Michail Fedorovich,
     Imperial Russian Colonel, Commander, 39th Light Infantry Regiment.

892. **Novak**, Peter Ivanovich,
     Imperial Russian Colonel, Commander, 18th Mounted Artillery Company.

893. **de Rochechouart**, Count Louis (?),
     Imperial Russian Colonel, Quartermaster Service, on the personal staff of Emperor Alexander I.

894. **Moisseiev**, Alexander Leontieovich,
     Imperial Russian Captain, 13th Artillery Brigade.

895. **Karpov**, Ivan Michailovich,
     Imperial Russian Staff Rittmeister, Lubno Hussar Regiment, Adjutant to Lt. General von Sacken.

* * *

The following seven Russian officers were decorated with the Pour le Mérite Order for distinction in action during the battle at Königswartha on May 19, 1813.

Imperial Russian St. Petersburg Grenadier Regiment

896. **Agte (Achte)**, Igor Andreieovich, Imperial Russian Colonel.
897. **Schwarz**, Fedor Jefimovich, Imperial Russian Major, Kexholm Grenadier Regiment, attached to the St. Petersburg Infantry Regiment, but serving in the above regiment.

* * *

Imperial Russian Ekaterinoslav Grenadier Regiment

898. **Krishtofovich**, Igor Konstantinovich, Imperial Russian Colonel.
899. **Teplov**, (First name unknown), Imperial Russian Major.
900. **Saba**, Ivan Petrovich, Imperial Russian Major.

* * *

901. **Petrov**, Ivan Matvieieovich,
 Imperial Russian Major, Araktsheiev Grenadier Regiment.

* * *

902. **von Paikul (Paykull)**, Anton Fedorovich,
 Imperial Russian Major, Tauri Grenadier Regiment.

* * *

The following two Russian officers when decorated with the Pour le Mérite Order for distinction in action were serving as adjutants to Lt. General Raievski.

903. **von Medem**, Vassili Alexandrovich,
 Imperial Russian Captain, 5th Light Infantry Regiment.

904. **Trubezkoi II.**, Prince Alexander Petrovich,
 Imperial Russian Sub-Lieutenant, Life Guard Semenovski Regiment.

* * *

Imperial Russian 30th Artillery Battery Company
2nd Reserve Artillery Brigade

The following four Russian officers received the Pour le Mérite Order for distinction in action during the skirmish at Bautzen on May 9, 1813.

905. **Nilus**, Bogdan Bogdanovich, Imperial Russian Lt. Colonel, Commander.
906. **Filipov I.**, Nikolai Fedorovich, Imperial Russian Staff Captain.
907. **Grigoriev**, Peter Vassilieovich, Imperial Russian Sub-Lieutenant.
908. **Bibikov**, Ilia Gavrilovich, Imperial Russian Officer Candidate,
 (**Note**: Candidate Treuleben was awarded the 50 Year Golden Crown to the Pour le Mérite Order on November 16, 1865.)

* * *

909. **Treuleben**, Nikolai Jakimovich,
 Imperial Russian Officer Candidate, Quartermaster Service, serving on the personal staff of Emperor Alexander I.

* * *

The following five Russian officers were decorated for distinction in action at the battle of Lützen on May 2, 1813, with the Pour le Mérite Order.

910. **Turtshaninov**, Andrei Petrovich,
     Imperial Russian Lt. Colonel, Commander, 13th Light Artillery Company.
* * *

Imperial Russian 27th Light Artillery Company

911. **Biakov**, Ivan Ivanovich, Imperial Russian Colonel, Commander.
912. **Günzel II.**, Alexander Karlovich, Imperial Russian Staff Captain.
913. **Sablin**, Michail Jakovleovich, Imperial Russian Lieutenant,
     2nd Pioneer Regiment, attached to this artillery company.
914. **Makalinski**, Ivan (Fedorovich?), Imperial Russian Sub-Lieutenant.
* * *

Imperial Russian Quartermaster Service

The following two Russian officers when decorated with the Pour le Mérite Order for distinction in action were serving on the personal staff of Emperor Alexander I.

915. **von Meyerdorff**, Baron Igor Kasimirovich, Imperial Russian Sub-Lieutenant.
916. **Bogdanovich**, Ivan Fedorovich, Imperial Russian Captain.
* * *

Imperial Russian Isium Hussar Regiment

917. **d'Olonne**, Count Ossip Franzovich, Imperial Russian Colonel.
918. **Krus**, Alexander Alexandrovich, Imperial Russian Colonel.
919. **Potvig**, (First name unknown), Imperial Russian Cornet.
* * *

920. **Trautmann**, (First name unknown),
     Imperial Russian Lieutenant, Grodno Hussar Regiment.

921. **Drevich**, (First name unknown),
     Imperial Russian Colonel, Honorary Colonel of the Finland Dragoon Regiment.

922. **Liubushin**, (First name unknown),
     Imperial Russian Colonel, Bielosero Infantry Regiment, Adjutant to Lt. General von Steinheil.

923. **Shirov**, Ivan Ivanovich?,
     Imperial Russian Starchina, unit unknown, Army of the Don.

924. **Raiski**, (First name unknown),
     Imperial Russian Major, Riashski Infantry Regiment.

925. **Scheping**, Dmitri Andreieovich,
     Imperial Russian Lieutenant, Cavalier Guard Regiment, Adjutant to Adjutant General Tshernishev.

926. **Wirjubov**, Andrei,
     Imperial Russian Jessaul, Ilovaiski Regiment, Army of the Don.

927. **Pavlovski II.**, Ferdinand Adamovich,
     Imperial Russian Lieutenant, Riga Dragoon Regiment, Adjutant to Major General Balk.

928. **von Boetticher**, August Friedrich Ludwig,
     Imperial Russian Rittmeister, serving on the staff of the Russian-German Legion. Prior service: Ducal Braunschweig 1st Lieutenant (retired), and Chamberlain to the Duke of Mecklenburg-Strelitz.
* * *

The following twelve Russian officers were decorated with the Pour le Mérite Order for distinction in action while serving as adjutants to Russian Infantry General Miloradovich.

Imperial Russian Apsheron Infantry Regiment

929. **Morosov**, Ivan Semenovich, Imperial Russian Lt. Colonel.
930. **Glinka**, Fedor Nikolaieovich, Imperial Russian Lieutenant.
931. **Miloradovich**, Alexei Grigorieovich, Imperial Russian Officer Candidate.

* * *

Imperial Russian Life Guard Hussar Regiment

932. **Paskevich**, Ossip Fedorovich, Imperial Russian Staff Rittmeister.
933. **von der Brincken**, Baron Karl Vassilieovich, Imperial Russian Lieutenant.

* * *

934. **Kotshubei**, Vassili Vassilieovich,
    Imperial Russian Staff Captain, Life Guard Preobrashenski Regiment.

935. **Juncker**, Karl Filippovich,
    Imperial Russian Staff Rittmeister, Life Guard Uhlan Regiment.

936. **Kisselev**, Pavel Dmitrieovich,
    Imperial Russian Staff Rittmeister, Cavalier Guard Regiment.
    (Note: Rittmeister Kisselev was awarded the 50 Year Golden Crown to the Pour le Mérite Order on January 22, 1863.)

937. **von der Osten-Sacken**, Baron Dmitri Jevgrafieovich,
    Imperial Russian Staff Captain, Life Guard Lithuania Regiment.
    (Note: Staff Captain von der Osten-Sacken was awarded the 50 Year Golden Crown to the Pour le Mérite Order on January 22, 1863.)

938. **von Geismar**, Friedrich Kaspar,
    Imperial Russian Staff Captain, Kiev Grenadier Regiment.

939. **Raievski**, Alexander Nikolaieovich,
    Imperial Russian Lieutenant, Life Guard Light Infantry Regiment.

940. **Pavlov**, (First name unknown),
    Imperial Russian Major, Cossack Regiment of the Moscow Opoltshenie (militia).

* * *

941. **Sipiagin**, Nikolai Martemianovich,
    Imperial Russian Colonel, Life Guard Semenovski Regiment, Wing Adjutant.

* * *

942. **Orlov**, Alexei Fedorovich,
    Imperial Russian Rittmeister, Life Guard Cavalry Regiment, Adjutant on the Staff of Grand Duke Konstantin.
    (Note: This is the <u>first</u> award of the Pour le Mérite Order to Rittmeister Orlov. For the second award of the Pour le Mérite Order see entry 976, this chapter.)

* * *

After the victory of Dresden, Napoleon sent Marshal Ney to reinforce Marshal Oudinot with orders to continue the advance on Berlin. On September 6, 1813, the French force of 58,000 neared the town of Dennewitz, some 40 miles southwest of Berlin. Here the French were attacked by a combined Prussian-Swedish force under the joint command of Crown Prince Jean-Baptiste Bernadotte and General von Bülow.

The engagement at Dennewitz began during midmorning and escalated steadily. By three o'clock the French were sustaining heavy casualities, and it became obvious that the allied force was gaining the upper hand and driving the French back. Marshal Ney finally issued orders around six in the evening for the French to break off and retreat toward Torgau on the Elbe River.

With another defeat in the French attempt to capture Berlin, Napoleon realized that his military position in eastern Saxony was becoming untenable. The allied forces were still active in the field despite their defeat at Dresden, and their continued harassment was beginning to break down the morale of the French troops and weaken their fighting abilities. Additionally, the French armies were operating deep inside enemy territory and were in danger of being isolated by the allies far from their supply bases. Therefore, Napoleon decided to withdraw from all territory east of the Elbe river and concentrate around the city of Leipzig on the Elster River.

* * *

* September 7, 1813 *

943. **Bogdanov**, (First name unknown),
Imperial Russian Officer Candidate, 28th Light Infantry Regiment.
(For distinction in action during the battle at Dennewitz on September 6, 1813. Severely wounded by a saber slash on the head, Bogdanov was still able to capture a French Regimental standard.)

* * *

* September 8, 1813 *

944. **Okuniev**, Nikolai Alexandrovich,
Imperial Russian Captain, Kaluga Infantry Regiment.
(For distinction in action during the battle at Dennewitz on September 6, 1813. Captain Okuniev was also decorated with the Prussian Red Eagle Order 3rd Class for his outstanding leadership during this action.)

* * *

* September 10, 1813 *

Imperial Austrian Archduke Johann Dragoon Regiment

The following Austrian officers were decorated with the Pour le Mérite Order for distinction in action during the battle at Kulm, August 30, 1813.

945. **Sück**, Jakob, Imperial Austrian Colonel, Commander.
946. **Le Blanc**, Albert, Imperial Austrian Rittmeister.

* * *

* September 13, 1813 *

The following nine Russian officers received the Pour le Mérite Order for distinction in action during the engagement at Schönfield in the vicinity of Danzig.

947. **Schulmann**, Fedor Maximovich,
Imperial Russian Colonel, Commander, 6th Artillery Brigade.

948. **Sosnin**, (First name unknown),
>Imperial Russian Lt. Colonel, Quartermaster Service, serving on the personal staff of Emperor Alexander I.
>(Note: This is the first award of the Pour le Mérite Order to Lt. Colonel Sosnin. For the second award of the Pour le Mérite Order see entry 974, this chapter.)

949. **Emme**, Alexei Fedorovich,
>Imperial Russian Lt. Colonel, Tobolski Infantry Regiment.

* * *

Both the following officers decorated with the Pour le Mérite Order were serving as adjutants to Cavalry General Duke Alexander of Württemberg.

950. **von Boetticher**, Gustaf Ivanovich,
>Imperial Russian Captain, Tauri Grenadier Regiment.

951. **Teplov**, Michail Alexieieovich,
>Imperial Russian Lieutenant, Life Guard Hussar Regiment.

* * *

952. **Fanshave**, Vassili Andreieovich,
>Imperial Russian Captain, Life Guard Semenovski Regiment, Adjutant to Prince August of Holstein-Oldenburg.

953. **Kusmin**, Alexander Ivanovich,
>Imperial Russian Lieutenant, Guard Equipage, Adjutant to the Naval Minister Marquis de Traversé.

954. **Gerbel II.**, Gustaf Vassilieovich,
>Imperial Russian Captain, Commander, 19th Mounted Artillery Company.

955. **Drosdovski**, Faddei Antipovich,
>Imperial Russian Lieutenant, 2nd Ukraine Cossack Regiment, Adjutant to Lt. General Levis.

* * *

Imperial Russian 7th Artillery Battery Company

956. **Dieterichs III.**, Christian Ivanovich, Imperial Russian Colonel, Commander.
957. **Kandiba II.**, David, Imperial Russian Sub-Lieutenant.
958. **Brümmer I.**, (First name unknown), Imperial Russian Officer Candidate.
959. **Savieskin**, Michail Vassilieovich, Imperial Russian Lieutenant.
>(Note: This is the first award of the Pour le Mérite Order to Lieutenant Savieskin. For the second award of the Pour le Mérite Order see entry 1023, this chapter.)

* * *

960. **Seslavin**, Fedor Nikita,
>Imperial Russian Staff Captain, 21st Artillery Battery Company.
>(Note: This is the second award of the Pour le Mérite Order badge to Captain Seslavin. For the initial award of the Pour le Mérite Order see entry 858, this chapter.)

* * *

* September 15, 1813 *

961. **Madatov**, Prince Valerian Grigorieovich,
>Imperial Russian Colonel, Alexandria Hussar Regiment.
>(For distinction in action during the battle at Würschen in the

-44-

vicinity of Bautzen on May 21-23, 1813.)

* * *

962. **Doliva-Dobrovolski**, Frol Ossipovich,
Imperial Russian Colonel, Field Postal Inspector.

* * *

* September 16, 1813 *

963. **af Wirsén**, Karl Johann,
Royal Swedish Lt. Colonel, Chief of the Lootsen District and Senior Adjutant to the Crown Prince of Sweden.

964. **von Björnstjerna**, Magnus Friedrich Ferdinand,
Royal Swedish Army Colonel, acting Colonel of the Kalmar Infantry Regiment, Senior Adjutant to the King of Sweden.

965. **Peyron**, Gustaf Abraham,
Royal Swedish Army Colonel, acting Captain in the Bohus-Lans Infantry Regiment, Expedition Chief to the General Adjutant, Senior Adjutant to the King of Sweden.

966. **Arfvedson**, Elias,
Royal Swedish Army Colonel, acting First Major of the Cavalry Life Guard Regiment.

967. **Forsell**, Karl Gustaf,
Royal Swedish Army Major, acting Captain of the Feldmesser Brigade of the Engineer Corps, Adjutant to the Crown Prince of Sweden.

968. **Reuterskjöld**, Leonhard Axel,
Royal Swedish Colonel, Chief of the Södermanland Infantry Regiment.

969. **Adlercreutz**, Frhr. Friedrich Thomas,
Royal Swedish Rittmeister, Life Guard Cavalry Regiment, Adjutant to the Crown Prince of Sweden.

* * *

* September 21, 1813 *

970. **Voinov**, (First name unknown),
Imperial Russian Jessaul, Tsherni-Subov VIII. Regiment, Army of the Don.
(For distinction in action during a skirmish on June 9, 1813.)

* * *

Beginning on September 24, 1813, the French forces withdrew from eastern Saxony and, with a few important exceptions, moved west of the Elbe River. Napoleon intended to turn Leipzig into an advanced base of operations and at the same time maintained French garrisons at several important Elbe river crossings. However, in early October allied military activity upset his plans.

* * *

* September 24, 1813 *

971. **Bolatuk**, Prince Kai Bei,
Imperial Russian Colonel, Commander, Simferopol Tatar Regiment.

972. **Turtshaninov**, Andrei Petrovich,
Imperial Russian Colonel, Commander, 3rd Light Infantry Regiment.

973. **Treskin**, Michail Lvovich?
Imperial Russian Colonel, Commander, Asov Infantry Regiment.

974. **Sosnin**, (First name unknown),
Imperial Russian Lt. Colonel, Quartermaster Service, serving on the personal staff of Emperor Alexander I.
(Note: This is the second award of the Pour le Mérite Order badge to this officer. For the initial award of the Pour le Mérite Order see entry 948, this chapter.)

* * *

* September 25, 1813 *

975. **von Hohenzollern-Hechingen**, Prince Friedrich Franz Anton,
Imperial Austrian Rittmeister, Hohenzollern Chevau-léger Regiment.
(For distinction in action during the battle at Merseburg where the prince was fatally wounded.)

* * *

976. **Orlov**, Alexei Fedorovich,
Imperial Russian Colonel, Life Guard Mounted Regiment, Wing Adjutant.
(Note: This is the second award of the Pour le Mérite Order badge to Colonel Orlov for distinction in action at the engagement at Merseburg. For the initial award of the Pour le Mérite Order see entry 942, this chapter.)

* * *

977. **von Bock**, Timofei Igorovich,
Imperial Russian Rittmeister, Life Guard Hussar Regiment.
(For distinction in action during the battle at Merseburg.)

* * *

* September 28-29, 1813 *

The British Military Mission

The following five British officers were decorated with the Pour le Mérite Order for distinction in action while serving in the British Military Mission attached to the Prussian Army.

978. **Cooke**, Henry Frederic,
Royal British Lt. Colonel, 12th (East Suffolk) Infantry Regiment, Adjutant to the Duke of York, attached to the staff of Lt. General Sir Charles Stewart.

979. **Charles**, James N.
Royal British Captain, 11th (North Devonshire) Infantry Regiment, Adjutant to Major General Sir Robert Wilson.

980. **von Düring**, Ernst Johann Christian,
Royal British Captain and Brevet Major, 1st Light Infantry Bat-

allion of the Royal German Legion, Adjutant to Lt. General Sir Charles Stewart.

981. **James**, George,
Royal British Captain, 2nd (Royal) North British Dragoon Regiment, Adjutant to Lt. General Sir Charles Stewart.

982. **Dawson**, George Lionel,
Royal British Captain, 1st (Kings) Guard Dragoon Regiment, Adjutant to Lt. General the Earl of Rosslyn.

* * *

* **October 1, 1813** *

983. **Sekretov**, Peter Timofieovich,
Imperial Russian Jessual, Bichalov I. Regiment, Army of the Don.

* * *

On October 3, 1813, elements of General Gebhard von Blücher's army managed to successfully cross the Elbe at Wartenburg. The following day, Swedish Crown Prince Bernadotte began crossing further downstream at Rosslau and Barby with a Swedish force of 23,000. These two large allied forces were moving toward Liepzig from the north. At the same time, moving toward Leipzig from the south was another large force - Austrians under the command of Prince Karl Philipp von Schwarzenberg, now rested and resupplied after their withdrawal from Dresden.

* * *

Prince Karl Philipp von Schwarzenberg

* October 4, 1813 *

984. **Kuteinikov VI.**, (First name unknown),
Imperial Russian Colonel, unit unknown, Army of the Don.
(**Note**: On September 5, 1813, Colonel Kuteinikov and two Cossacks effected a rescue of Lt. General Count Friedrich Boguslaus von Tauentzien resulted in the Colonel being decorated with the Pour le Mérite Order and the two Cossacks each being awarded the Prussian Silver Military Merit Medal.)

* * *

Lt. General Friedrich von Tauentzien

Lt. General Count Friedrich Boguslaus von Tauentzien was captured by the French during a skirmish in the vicinity of Dennewitz on September 5, 1813. While the general was being taken to the French lines under guard, the French escort was sighted and immediately attacked by the Russian Colonel Kuteinikov VI. (see preceding entry) and two Russian Cossacks. The Russians successfully drove off the French cavalry, released General von Tauentzien and quickly returned to the safety of the allied lines. Had the French been successful in the capture of General von Tauentzien, it could have demoralized the allies.

* * *

* October 6, 1813 *

985. **von Somnitz**, Christof George Heinrich Franz,
1st Lieutenant, Brandenburg Dragoon Regiment.
(For distinction in action during the battle at Dennewitz on September 6, 1813.)

* * *

* Bavaria Joins The Sixth Coalition *

Earlier, Bavarian General Carl Philipp von Wrede had begun conducting somewhat secret negotiations with Prussian and Russian diplomats. By October 8, 1813, Bavaria, Prussia and Russia had concluded the Treaty of Reid, whereby Bavaria joined the Sixth Coalition against France. Immediately Bavaria mobilized and prepared to enter the war.

* * *

Cossack and French troops engaged at the Halle Gate in Berlin

First Simultaneous Awarding of the Pour le Mérite Order and Oakleaves

* October 9, 1813 *

986. **von Mecklenburg-Strelitz**, Prince Karl Friedrich August,
    Major General, Commander-in-Chief of the II. Brigade.
    (For distinction in action during the battle at Wartenburg.
    (**Note**: The Prince of Mecklenburg-Strelitz was the first officer to receive **both** the Pour le Mérite Order **and** the Oakleaves at the same time. What is of special interest was the correspondence between Friedrich Wilhelm and Prince Karl. The king wrote on October 9, 1813, to the prince saying, "... through your outstanding leadership and bravery, I give you these three leaves and my Order..." Also the king wrote, "... my wish is that you will wear them proudly on your breast and that they bring you luck and success..." Prince Karl replied to the king on October 21, 1813, "... your letter gives me great pride, my paladin,... your leaves are now my golden leaves..."

* * *

987. **von Mensdorff**, Count Emanuel,
    Imperial Austrian Colonel, Archduke Karl Uhlan Regiment.

* * *

Napoleon originally intended to deal with the approaching allied armies separately. First, he would engage Blücher and Bernadotte and, once they had been defeated, he would turn and deal with the Austrians. However, the Austrian army moved faster than he anticipated and was soon threating his base at Leipzig. On October 12, 1813, Napoleon issued orders to concentrate his forces around Leipzig. On October 14, 1813, he arrived in Leipzig to oversee the disposition of the French troops personally. By this time, however, advance elements of the Austrian army were pushing the French back in the south of the city and fierce fighting was beginning in and around some of the smaller towns south of Leipzig.

By October 15, 1813, Napoleon managed to assemble a force of 164,000 troops; however, not all were French. Included were many levies from his Confederation of the Rhine. Because Blücher and Bernadotte were still between 12 to 20 miles north of Leipzig, Napoleon was confident that they would not be able to take part in the forthcoming battle. He quickly moved the majority of his troops to south of Leipzig and completed his plans to engage and defeat Schwarzenburg's Austrians. However, he had underestimated General Blücher. The Prussian forces, by forced march, arrived on the morning of October 16, 1813. They were soon in a position to threaten the remaining French forces north of Leipzig.

The Battle of Leipzig began early on the morning of October 16, 1813. Prince Karl Philipp von Schwarzenburg sent a force, under the command of General Barclay de Tolly, to attack the French positions south of the city. At the same time, Schwarzenburg continued his advance along the Elster and Pleisse Rivers. He intended to join Blücher's forces and thereby cut the French line of retreat to the west. This move would enable Schwarzenberg to threaten and even possibly even turn the French right flank.

An assault of one of the city gates at Leipzig

The allied forces made some progress, but their initial attacks were poorly organized and, in the face of heavy French resistance, the fighting soon lost momentum and stalled. Napoleon, reacting quickly, immediately ordered a counterattack. By midafternoon the French had recovered all positions lost earlier. At one point, the French counterattack threatened to turn the Austrian left flank. In the meantime, General von Blücher launched an attack against the French north of the city at the small village of Möckern. Under the command of Marshal Auguste Frederic de Marmont, the French held their positions, but by successfully keeping them pinned down at Möckern, the Prussians denied Napoleon the use of these troops elsewhere - which he desperately needed. When the fighting finally stopped for the day, Napoleon found that the majority of his forces had returned to their original defensive positions. So, nothing was actually accomplished that day - only the addition of casualities.

The Prussians at Möckern

There was little action on October 17, 1813. Both sides reorganized their forces and prepared for the fighting that was soon to follow. Reinforcements arrived during this time for both sides but, unfortunately for Napoleon, the majority were not his. By the end of the day, the French had managed to increase its force to around 195,000 men. However, the allies, with the arrival of Bernadotte and General Bennigsen, had gained nearly 150,000 troops. When the fighting resumed on October 18, 1813, the French army found itself facing an allied force of almost 365,000.

The Leipzig battlefield on the evening of October 18, 1813

The fighting resumed at approximately 7 o'clock on the morning of October 18, 1813. After some initial successes by the allies, the French managed to hold their positions. At noon, the allies struck the decisive blow. The advance elements of Bernadotte's forces approached from the northeast to close a gap in the allied lines. Seeing this, the General Bennigsen renewed his attack against the French. As the allies advanced, they were surprised and quite pleased to see Saxon army troops serving with the French, under the command of General Jean Louis Ebénézer Reynier, deserting to the allies. The Saxon defections were soon followed by a brigade of Württemberg cavalry. This loss of troops left an opening in the French lines. Marshal Ney tried to restore the integrity of his positions, but his forces were outnumbered, and he began a slow retreat in the direction of Leipzig.

Napoleon now realized he was in a critical situation; the allied forces were overwhelming and his only option was to withdraw all his forces towards Leipzig and the important bridge across the Elster River. During midmorning, Napoleon issued orders for a general retreat. The withdrawal was badly organized, and since only one bridge was available, it soon became clogged with fleeing troops. Despite this bottleneck, the majority of the French army managed to cross the bridge. However, had the bridge not been prematurely destroyed, more French troops would have been successful in escaping the allies.

The Destruction of the Elster Bridge on October 19, 1813

The destroyed bridge isolated the French rearguard of some 20,000 troops, including Marshals Macdonald and Prince Josef Anton Poniatowski. The two French marshals attempted to escape by swimming the river: Marshal Macdonald was successful, but Marshal Poniatowski, badly wounded, drowned. The remaining French rearguard was forced to surrender to the pursuing allies.

Prince Poniatowski's Death in the Elster River.

The Battle of Leipzig became known also as the "Battle of the Nations" and the largest action of the Napoleonic Wars. It is of interest that six sovereigns were present during the battle: the kings of Prussia, Saxony and Naples, and the emperors of Russia, Austria and France. The battle was also one of the most costly in lives. The allies lost 54,000 troops and the French suffered the loss of 74,000 men. In addition, the allies captured the King of Saxony, 36 general officers, 28 Regimental Standards and Eagles, 325 cannon, tons of ammunition and nearly 40,000 muskets.

In spite of the great strategic advantage the allies now had, they were slow in following the retreating French.

* * *

* October 19, 1813 *

988. **von dem Knesebeck**, Karl Friedrich,
   Major General and Adjutant General.
   (Awarded the Oakleaves to the Pour le Mérite Order for distinction in action. For the initial award of the Pour le Mérite Order see Volume I, Chapter V-1, entry 143, page 270.)
   * * *

* October 21, 1813 *

989. **von Thümen**, Heinrich Ludwig August,
   Major General, Commander-in-Chief of the IV. Brigade.
   (Awarded the Oakleaves to the Pour le Mérite Order for distinction in action during the battle at Dennewitz on September 6, 1813. For the initial award of the Pour le Mérite Order see Volume I, Chapter V-1, entry 23, page 249.)
   * * *

990. **von Zastrow**, Alexander Heinrich Gotthard,
   Lt. Colonel, Commander, Kolberg Infantry Regiment; Brigade Commander of the VI. Brigade.
   (Awarded **both** the Pour le Mérite Order **and** the Oakleaves simultaneously in recognition of outstandin distinction in action during the battle of Dennewitz on September 6, 1813.)
   * * *

991. **von Borstell**, Karl Leopold Ludwig,
   Major General, Commander-in-Chief of the V. Brigade.
   (Awarded the Oakleaves to the Pour le Mérite Order for distinction in action during the battle at Dennewitz on September 6, 1813. For the initial award of the Pour le Mérite Order see Volume I, Chapter IV, entry 596, page 192.)
   * * *

992. **von Ungern-Sternberg**, Baron Gustaf Romanovich,
   Imperial Russian Sub-Lieutenant, 1st Mounted Artillery Company.

993. **Popov**, (First name unknown),
   Imperial Russian Jessaul, Ilovaiski III. Regiment, Army of the Don.
   (For distinction in action during the battle at Dennewitz on September 6, 1813.)
   * * *

By October 23, 1813, Napoleon reached Erfurt where he rested for two days and endeavored to restore some order to what remained of his Grand Army. Then he resumed the retreat toward Frankfurt-am-Main and Mainz. Prince Schwarzen- berg and General Blücher were still pursuing the French forces but much too slowly.

* October 25, 1813 *

994. **Retsey de Retse**, Adam,
   Imperial Austrian Colonel, Commander, Hieronymus Colloredo Infantry Regiment.
   (**Note**: This Austrian officer held the Austrian Military Maria Theresa Order. This was the highest military decoration of Austria.)

995. **Call**, Karl,
Imperial Austrian Lt. Colonel, Argentau Infantry Regiment.
(Awarded the Pour le Mérite Order in recognition of distinction in action during the battles of Dresden, Kulm, Nollendorf and Leipzig.)
* * *

The Three Monarchs at the Battle of Leipzig
Friedrich Wilhelm III. - Franz I. - Alexander I.
(Painting by W. Schuch)

The allies had an excellent military opportunity presented to them in late October. A combined Austro-Bavarian army moved from Ansbach and Würzburg to intercept the fleeing French army and cut its line of retreat. By October 30, 1813, this allied force reached the Kinzig River and prepared positions to receive the French. Unfortunately, the allied force was spread along both banks of the river and had only one intact bridge to aid their movements.

Seeing this flaw in the allied positions, Napoleon quickly exploited the weakness. He attacked the allied left flank and forced Bavarian General Carl Philipp von Wrede to disengage and fall back toward the town of Hanau. Both sides suffered heavy losses. Even worse for the French, however, was that over the next few days nearly 10,000 French stragglers, including five General officers, were captured by the allied forces.

What remained of the French army fled westward to safety. Napoleon reached Mainz on November 2, 1813, where he halted for a rest. On November 7th, Napoleon left Mainz for Paris, arriving on November 9, 1813.

* * *

The Battle of Leipzig cost Napoleon the French control of Germany east of the Rhine River. Germany was now liberated from French occupation. What was important was that the forces of the Sixth Coalition were now camped on the frontiers of France itself.

The pursuing allied armies halted when they reached the Rhine River. Although the military portion of the 1813 Campaign was, in effect, finished, the political maneuvering now began.

On November 2, 1813, Napoleon realized his diminishing power when, even as he retreated across western Germany, Berg, Westphalia, and other principalities rose up in open revolt against the French in a surge of patriotic enthusiasm. Also on this date, the Austrian Chancellor, Clemens Metternich, negotiated the Treaty of Fulda. Under the terms of this treaty, the Kingdom of Württemberg joined the Sixth Coalition, soon followed by the Grand Duchies of Baden, Hesse-Darmstadt and the Duchy of Nassau. With the impending fall of the French Empire, former Confederation of the Rhine members began to defect to the allied cause.

Emperor Francis I. of Austria and Crown Prince Bernadotte were content to allow Napoleon to keep the French throne and only sue for peace. However, Czar Alexander I. and General Blücher were demanding an all out assault against France, and they had the backing of England. Friedrich Wilhelm vetoed Blücher's demands and counseled caution. The Russian Generals were able to convince Alexander that the wisest tact would be moderation at this point.

On November 9, 1813, Chancellor Metternich, in the name of the allied powers, issued the Declaration of Frankfurt. It was, in effect, an offer of peace which would have left Napoleon on the throne of France and restored the French borders to those of 1797. If Napoleon had accepted these terms, the Napoleonic Wars would have ended in 1813. However, he delayed answering the allied demands for three weeks.

* * *

* **November 15, 1813** *

996. **Bergmann**, Alexander (Alexei) Petrovich,
    Imperial Russian Captain, Life Guard Preobrashenski Regiment.

* * *

* **November 18, 1813** *

Imperial Russian Quartermaster Service

The following five Russian officers when decorated with the Pour le Mérite Order were serving on the personal staff of Emperor Alexander I.

997. **von Wolzogen**, Baron Justus Philipp, Imperial Russian Major General.
998. **Michailovski-Danilevski**, Alexander Ivanovich, Imperial Russian Captain.

999. **Perovski**, Lev Alexieieovich, Imperial Russian Lieutenant.
1000. **Durnovo**, Nikolai Dmitrieovich, Imperial Russian Lieutenant.
1001. **von Ramburg**, (First name unknown), Imperial Russian Sub-Lieutenant.

* * *

The following two Russian officers were serving on the General Staff of the II. Infantry Corps when decorated for distinction in action with the Pour le Mérite Order.

1002. **Andreievski**, Konstantin Stepanovich,
   Imperial Russian Lieutenant, Quartermaster Service.

1003. **von Sternhelm**, Alexander Vassilieovich,
   Imperial Russian Officer Candidate, Quartermaster Service.
   (**Note**: Candidate von Sternhelm was awarded the 50 Year Golden Crown to the Pour le Mérite Order on October 25, 1864.)

* * *

1004. **von Grotenhelm**, Maxim Maximovich,
   Imperial Russian Staff Rittmeister, Olviopol Hussar Regiment, Orderly officer to the Commander of the II. Infantry Corps.
   (**Note**: Staff Rittmeister von Grotenhelm was awarded the 50 Year Golden Crown to the Pour le Mérite Order on January 22, 1863.)

* * *

The following four Russian officers when decorated with the Pour le Mérite Order for distinction in action were serving as Wing Adjutants.

1005. **Branicki**, Stanislav Stanislavieovich,
   Imperial Russian Colonel, unit unknown.

1006. **von Lamsdorff**, Jakob Matvieieovich,
   Imperial Russian Cavalry Colonel, unit unknown.

1007. **de Rochechouart**, Count Ludwig Viktor Leo,
   Imperial Russian Colonel, Life Guard Light Infantry Regiment.

1008. **von Imeretien**, Konstantin Zarevich,
   Imperial Russian Colonel, Life Guard Cossack Regiment.

* * *

* **November 28, 1813** *

The following four Imperial Austrian officers, while serving as Adjutants General to Field Marshal Prince von Schwarzenberg, received the Pour le Mérite Order for distinction in action during the battle of Leipzig on October 16-18, 1813.

1009. **Paar**, Count Johann Baptist, Imperial Austrian Colonel.
1010. **von Böhm**, Maximilian, Imperial Austrian Lt. Colonel.
1011. **Liechtenstein**, Prince Wenzel, Imperial Austrian Lt. Colonel.
1012. **Woyna**, Count Felix, Imperial Austrian Lt. Colonel.

* * *

1013. **von Georgii**, August Eberhard,
   Imperial Austrian Colonel, Commander, Reuss-Greiz Infantry Regiment.
   (For distinction in action at Leipzig.)

* * *

On December 1, 1813, Napoleon sent his reply to the allies, but it was too late to be seriously considered. To ensure peace, he made impossible demands which were highly favorable to France and to himself in particular. The allies, shocked by his unreasonable demands, reacted by withdrawing the peace offer. Napoleon then responded by speeding up conscription for the army and the mobilization of the National Guard for active service.

* * *

* December 8, 1813 *

Imperial Russian 1st Mounted Artillery Company

1014. **Suchosanet II.**, Peter Onufrieovich, Imperial Russian Staff Captain.
1015. **Shitov**, Alexei Ivanovich, Imperial Russian Lieutenant.

* * *

Imperial Russian 4th Mounted Artillery Company

1016. **Batashev**, Alexei Alexandrovich, Imperial Russian Staff Captain.
1017. **Viktorov**, Vladimir Michailovich, Imperial Russian Staff Captain.

* * *

Imperial Russian 13th Mounted Artillery Company

1018. **Arnoldi**, Ivan Karlovich, Imperial Russian Lt. Colonel, Commander.
1019. **Masaraki**, Semen Semenovich, Imperial Russian Staff Captain.
1020. **Bogdanov**, Alexander Nikolaieovich, Imperial Russian Lieutenant.
1021. **Pichatshev**, Matvei Ivanovich, Imperial Russian Sub-Lieutenant.

* * *

Imperial Russian 7th Artillery Battery Company

1022. **Krassovski**, Jakob Petrovich, Imperial Russian Officer Candidate.
1023. **Savieskin**, Michail Vassilieovich, Imperial Russian Lieutenant.
   (Note: This is the second award of the Pour le Mérite Order badge to Lieutenant Savieskin. For the initial award of the Pour le Mérite Order see entry 959, this chapter.)

1024. **Vunkov**, Vassili Michailovich, Imperial Russian Sub-Lieutenant.
   (Note: This is the second award of the Pour Le Mérite Order badge to Lieutenant Vonkov. For the initial award of the Pour le Mérite Order see entry 857, this chapter.)

* * *

Imperial Russian 21st Artillery Battery Company

1025. **Kasin II.**, Ivan Petrovich, Imperial Russian Lieutenant.
1026. **Kasadaven**, Nikolai, Imperial Russian Lieutenant.
1027. **Verchovski**, Peter Ivanovich, Imperial Russian Officer Candidate.

* * *

Imperial Russian Quartermaster Service

The following six Russian officers when decorated with the Pour le Mérite Order for distinction in action were serving on the personal staff of Emperor Alexander I. of Russia.

1028. **von Lützow**, Wichard Friedrich, Imperial Russian Lt. Colonel.
1029. **Suiev**, Sergei Charitonovich, Imperial Russian Lt. Colonel, Senior Quartermaster of the V. Infantry (Guard) Corps.
1030. **Aster**, Ernst Ludwig, Imperial Russian Lt. Colonel.
1031. **Miloradovich**, Andrei Nikolaieovich, Imperial Russian Staff Captain.
1032. **von Aexkull-Gyllenbandt**, Baron Roman, Imperial Russian Staff Captain.

* * *

1033. **Freigang**, Peter Ivanovich, Imperial Russian Staff Captain, Quartermaster Service, on the personal staff of Emperor Alexander I., and attached to the General Staff of the II. Infantry Corps. (**Note:** This is the <u>first</u> award of the Pour le Mérite Order to Staff Captain Freigang. For the second award of the Pour le Mérite Order see entry 2235, this chapter.)

* * *

Imperial Russian Life Guard Grenadier Regiment

1034. **Demtshenkov**, Semen Semenovich, Imperial Russian Lt. Colonel.
1035. **Pavlenkov**, Jemelian Ossipovich, Imperial Russian Lt. Colonel.

* * *

Imperial Russian Life Guard Pavlovski Regiment

1036. **Tarnovski**, Peter Ivanovich, Imperial Russian Lt. Colonel.

* * *

Imperial Russian Life Guard Semenovski Regiment

1037. **Kniashnin**, Boris Jakovleovich, Imperial Russian Colonel. Commander, Araktsheiev Grenadier Regiment.

* * *

Imperial Russian Tauri Grenadier Regiment

1038. **Jurgenev**, (First name unknown), Imperial Russian Lt. Colonel.
1039. **Ossipov**, Nikolai Jeremieieovich, Imperial Russian Officer Candidate.

* * *

1040. **Pissarev**, Alexander Alexandrovich, Imperial Russian Colonel, Kiev Grenadier Regiment.

1041. **Golovin**, Yeugeni Alexandrovich, Imperial Russian Colonel, Fanagoria Grenadier Regiment.

1042. **Friedberg**, Ivan Petrovich, Imperial Russian Lt. Colonel, Astrachan Grenadier Regiment.

1043. **Kotshetov**, Fedor Nikititsh,
    Imperial Russian Captain, Moscow Grenadier Regiment.

1044. **Levin**, Dmitri Andreieovich,
    Imperial Russian Colonel, Siberian Grenadier Regiment.

1045. **Moshenski**, Denis Denissovich,
    Imperial Russian Colonel, St. Petersburg Grenadier Regiment.

* * *

Imperial Russian Tshernigov Infantry Regiment

1046. **Protopopov**, Peter Sergieieovich, Imperial Russian Major.
1047. **von Grothuss**, Dmitri Ulnovich, Imperial Russian Staff Captain,
    Adjutant to Lt. General Konovnizin.
1048. **Löwenhof**, Timofei Antonovich, Imperial Russian Major.
    (Note: This is the <u>first</u> award of the Pour le Mérite Order to Major Löwenhof. For the second award of the Pour le Mérite Order see entry 1944, this chapter.)

* * *

1049. **Shelvinski**, Jakob Sergieieovich,
    Imperial Russian Colonel, Reval Infantry Regiment.

1050. **Kurnossov**, Nikolai Andreieovich,
    Imperial Russian Lt. Colonel, Volyni Infantry Regiment.

* * *

Imperial Russian Murom Infantry Regiment

1051. **Borissov**, Nikolai Ivanovich, Imperial Russian Major.
1052. **Tarshevski**, Afanassi Petrovich, Imperial Russian Staff Captain.
1053. **Totshinski**, Ignati Pavlovich, Imperial Russian Lieutenant.
    (Note: This is the <u>first</u> award of the Pour le Mérite Order to Lieutenant Totshinski. For the second award of the Pour le Mérite Order see entry 2448, this chapter.)

* * *

1054. **von Reibnitz**, Karl Pavlovich,
    Imperial Russian Colonel, Tobolski Infantry Regiment.

* * *

Imperial Russian Krementshug Infantry Regiment

1055. **von Siegroth**, (First name unknown), Imperial Russian Lt. Colonel,
    Tambov Infantry Regiment, attached to this unit.
1056. **Tsheodaiev**, Michail Ivanovich, Imperial Russian Major.
1057. **Kisslovski**, Dmitri Andreovich, Imperial Russian Major.
1058. **Pishnizki**, (First name unknown), Imperial Russian Lieutenant, Adjutant
    to Major General Pishnizki.

1059. **Mikulin**, Sergei Ivanovich, Imperial Russian Lieutenant.
    (Note: Lieutenant Mikulin was awarded the 50 Year Golden Crown to the Pour le Mérite Order on January 22, 1863.)

* * *

1060. **Protassov**, Grigori Grigorieovich,
    Imperial Russian Captain, Tambov Infantry Regiment, Division Adjutant to Major General Talisin.

1061. **Shenshin**, Vassili Nikanorovich,
> Imperial Russian Colonel, Commanding the Shenshin Regiment.
> (**Note**: This is the <u>first</u> of <u>two</u> awards of the Pour le Mérite Order badges awarded to Colonel Schenshin on this date. See entry 1182, this chapter.)

1062. **Tishin**, Vassili Grigorieovich,
> Imperial Russian Lt. Colonel, Jelez Infantry Regiment.

1063. **Novikov**, (First name unknown),
> Imperial Russian Major, Kolivan Infantry Regiment.

1064. **Kern**, Jermolai Fedorovich,
> Imperial Russian Colonel, Bielosero Infantry Regiment.

* * *

Imperial Russian Grand Duchess Katharina Battalion

1065. **Obolenski**, Alexander Petrovich, Imperial Russian Colonel, Wing Adjutant and Commander of the Life Guard Dragoon Regiment.
1066. **Kovalevski**, (First name unknown), Imperial Russian Major.
1067. **Shubinski**, Nikolai Petrovich, Imperial Russian Major.

* * *

Imperial Russian Mohilev Infantry Regiment

1068. **Malevanov**, (First name unknown), Imperial Russian Colonel.
1069. **Ponerovski**, Vassili Jakovleovich, Imperial Russian Major.

* * *

Imperial Russian Perm Infantry Regiment

1070. **Baumgarten**, Johann Jevstafieovich, Imperial Russian Colonel.
1071. **Gubin**, (First name unknown), Imperial Russian Major.

* * *

1072. **Aksakov**, (First name unknown),
> Imperial Russian Major, Tenga Infantry Regiment.

* * *

Imperial Russian Kaluga Infantry Regiment

1073. **Savinitsh**, (First name unknown), Imperial Russian Lt. Colonel.
1074. **Narbut**, Heinrich Karlovich, Imperial Russian Major.

* * *

1075. **Tshurilov**, Ivan Igorovich,
> Imperial Russian Major, Estonia Infantry Regiment.

1076. **Artemiev**, (First name unknown),
> Imperial Russian Major, Kexholm Grenadier Regiment.

1077. **Röhren**, Ivan Bogdanovich,
> Imperial Russian Colonel, Schlüsselburg Infantry Regiment.
> (**Note**: This is the <u>first</u> of <u>two</u> awards of the Pour le Mérite Order badges awarded to Colonel Röhren on this date. See entry 1183, this chapter.)

1078. **Obuchovski**, Peter Semenovich,
> Imperial Russian Major, Brest Infantry Regiment.

1079. **Smolkov**, Peter Gavrilovich,
       Imperial Russian Staff Captain, Tarnopol Infantry Regiment,
       Adjutant to Lt. General Prince Gortshakov II.

1080. **Beck**, Ivan Ivanovich,
       Imperial Russian Major, 1st Light Infantry Regiment.

1081. **Samoilovich**, Ivan Vassilieovich,
       Imperial Russian Captain, 3rd Light Infantry Regiment.

1082. **Olshevski**, Matvei Antonovich,
       Imperial Russian Major, 4th Light Infantry Regiment.

1083. **Artiuchov**, Jefim Trofimovich,
       Imperial Russian Staff Captain, 5th Light Infantry Regiment.

1084. **Keldermann**, Konstantin Fomitsh,
       Imperial Russian Captain, 6th Light Infantry Regiment.

1085. **Kashirinov**, Nikanor Fedorovich,
       Imperial Russian Lt. Colonel, 11th Light Infantry Regiment.

* * *

Imperial Russian 20th Light Infantry Regiment

1086. **Kapustin**, Ivan Fedorovich, Imperial Russian Colonel, Finnland Life
       Guard Regiment, commanding the 20th Light Infantry Regiment.
1087. **Jakovlev**, Alexander Ivanovich, Imperial Russian Major.
1088. **Frolov**, Peter Nikolaieovich, Imperial Russian Staff Captain.
       (**Note**: Staff Captain Frolov was awarded the 50 Year Golden
       Crown to the Pour le Mérite Order on January 22, 1863.)

* * *

1089. **Ganskau**, Jakob Fedorovich,
       Imperial Russian Captain, 34th Light Infantry Regiment,
       Senior Adjutant to Lt. General Prince Eugen von Württemberg.

1090. **Suthof L.**, Nikolai Ivanovich,
       Imperial Russian Colonel, 37th Light Infantry Regiment.

1091. **Bruckendahl (Brückental)**, (First name unknown),
       Imperial Russian Captain, 41st Light Infantry Regiment.

1092. **Dobrovolski**, Lavrenti Leontieovich,
       Imperial Russian Captain, 49th Light Infantry Regiment,
       Adjutant to Lt. General Prince Gortshakov II.

* * *

1093. **Masslov**, (First name unknown),
       Imperial Russian Major, Jaroslav Opoltshenie (militia).

* * *

Imperial Russian Life Guard Artillery Brigade

1094. **Taube**, Karl Karlovich, Imperial Russian Colonel, Commander of the
       1st Artillery Brigade.

1095. **Gortshakov**, Prince Michail Dmitrieovich, Imperial Russian Lieutenant,
       Adjutant to Lt. General von Diebitsch.

* * *

1096. **Potapov**, Peter Igorovich,
       Imperial Russian Captain, 1st Mounted Artillery Company.

1097. **Bistrom**, Anton Antonovich,
Imperial Russian Lt. Colonel, 3rd Mounted Artillery Company.

* * *

The First Awarding of Three Pour le Mérite Orders to the Same Recipient

The awarding of the Pour le Mérite Order to this Russian officer, Lt. Colonel Shusherin, is most unusual in that he is the <u>first</u> officer to be awarded <u>three</u> Pour le Mérite Orders for distinction in action. This is particularly remarkable since he was a non-Prussian.

1098. **Shusherin**, Sachar Sergieieovich,
Imperial Russian Lt. Colonel, 8th Mounted Artillery Company.
(**Note**: This is the <u>first</u> of <u>two</u> awards of the Pour le Mérite Order <u>badges</u> thought to have been awarded to Lt. Colonel Schishin on this date. See entry 1198, this chapter. For the <u>third</u> award of the Pour le Mérite Order badge to this officer, see entry 1740, this chapter.)

* * *

1099. **Rosen**, Vladimir Ivanovich,
Imperial Russian Lieutenant, 23rd Mounted Artillery Company.

* * *

1100. **Dieterichs**, Andrei Ivanovich,
Imperial Russian Lt. Colonel, 6th Light Artillery Company.

1101. **Volevatsh**, Jakob Ivanovich,
Imperial Russian Lt. Colonel, 32nd Light Artillery Company.
(**Note**: This is the <u>first</u> award of the Pour le Mérite Order to Lt. Colonel Volevatsh. For the second award of the Pour le Mérite Order see entry 1742, this chapter.)

1102. **Bashmakov**, Flegon Mironovich,
    Imperial Russian Lt. Colonel, 33rd Light Artillery Company.
    (**Note**: This is the first award of the Pour le Mérite Order to Lt. Colonel Bashmakov. For the second award of the Pour le Mérite Order see entry 1757, this chapter.)
* * *

1103. **Maleiev**, Alexander Semenovich,
    Imperial Russian Lt. Colonel, 2nd Artillery Battery Company.

1104. **Nolde**, Karl,
    Imperial Russian Captain, 14th Artillery Battery Company.

1105. **Bellinghausen**, Fedor Ivanovich,
    Imperial Russian Lt. Colonel, 32nd Artillery Battery Company.
* * *

1106. **Tazin IV.**, Peter Fedorovich,
    Imperial Russian Lt. Colonel, 1st Mounted Artillery Company, Army of the Don.
    (**Note**: This is the first award of the Pour le Mérite Order to Lt. Colonel Tazin. For the second award of the Pour le Mérite Order see entry 1271, this chapter.)

1107. **Suvorov II.**, Peter,
    Imperial Russian Lt. Colonel, 2nd Mounted Artillery Company, Army of the Don.
    (**Note**: This is the first of two Pour le Mérite Order badges awarded to Lt. Colonel Suvorov on this date. See entry 1201, this chapter.)
* * *

Imperial Russian Sum Hussar Regiment

1108. **Kantshialov**, Alexander Nikolaieovich, Imperial Russian Lt. Colonel.
1109. **Dsheshelinski**, (First name unknown), Imperial Russian Major.
* * *

Imperial Russian Mariupol Hussar Regiment

1110. **Lessovski**, Stepan Ivanovich, Imperial Russian Colonel.
1111. **Stankovich**, Michail Michailovich, Imperial Russian Major.
* * *

1112. **von Reutern**, Christofor Romanovich,
    Imperial Russian Colonel, Alexandria Hussar Regiment.

1113. **Vesselovski**, Stepan Semenovich,
    Imperial Russian Major, Belo-Russia Hussar Regiment.
* * *

Imperial Russian Lubno Hussar Regiment

1114. **Davidov I.**, (First name unknown), Imperial Russian Colonel.
1115. **Travin**, Pavel Andreieovich, Imperial Russian Staff Rittmeister.
* * *

1116. **Kastroit-Drekalovich-Skanderbek**, Prince Grigori Vassilieovich,
    Imperial Russian Lt. Colonel, Achtirka Hussar Regiment.

1117. **Ypsilanti**, Prince Alexander Konstantinovich,
    Imperial Russian Lt. Colonel, Grodno Hussar Regiment.
* * *

Imperial Russian Tatari Uhlan Regiment

1118. **Jeschin**, Vassili Vassiliovich, Imperial Russian Colonel.
   (**Note**: This is the second award of the Pour le Mérite Order badge to Colonel Jeschin. For the initial award of the Pour le Mérite Order see Volume I, Chapter V-1, entry 466, p. 301.)

1119. **von Vietinghoff**, (First name unknown), Imperial Russian Major.
   (**Note**: This is the first award of the Pour le Mérite Order to Major Vietinghoff. For the second award of the Pour le Mérite Order see entry 1499, this chapter.)

1120. **Lukomski**, Dmitri Nikolaiovich, Imperial Russian Lieutenant.

* * *

Imperial Russian Kargopol Dragoon Regiment

1121. **Pohl**, Ivan Lawrentieovich, Imperial Russian Colonel.
1122. **Davidov II.**, Jevdokim Vassiliovich, Imperial Russian Lt. Colonel.

* * *

Imperial Russian Mitau Dragoon Regiment

1123. **Dsevonski**, Ivan, Imperial Russian Lt. Colonel.
1124. **Strahlmann**, Peter Karlovich, Imperial Russian Major.

* * *

1125. **Jakovlev**, Stepan Makarovich,
   Imperial Russian Major, Ingermanland Dragoon Regiment.
   (**Note**: This is the first of two Pour le Mérite Order badges awarded to Major Jakovlev on this date. See entry 1193, this chapter.)

1126. **Potocki**, Stanislaus Stanislavovich,
   Imperial Russian Colonel, 1st Ukraine Cossack Regiment,
   Wing Adjutant.

1127. **Pochvisniev**, Ivan Ivanovich,
   Imperial Russian Lt. Colonel, 2nd Ukraine Cossack Regiment,

* * *

Imperial Russian 3rd Ukraine Cossack Regiment

1128. **Temirov**, Pavel Lvovich, Imperial Russian Major.
1129. **Vielhorski**, Count Matvei Jureovich, Imperial Russian Lieutenant,
   Adjutant to the General Adjutant of the Emperor, Prince Trubezkoi.
   (**Note**: Count Vielhorski was awarded the 50 Year Jubilee Golden Crown to the Pour le Mérite Order on January 22, 1863.)

* * *

1130. **Danilov**, Pavel Vassiliovich,
   Imperial Russian Major, 1st Cossack Regiment of the Tula Opoltshenie (militia).

1131. **Helmersen**, Anton Antonovich,
   Imperial Russian Major, Liefland Mounted Light Infantry Regiment.

1132. **von Rennenkampff**, Karl Pavlovich,
   Imperial Russian Captain, 1st Engineer (Pioneer) Regiment.

1133. **Kanattshikov**, (First name unknown),
   Imperial Russian Lt. Colonel, 2nd Engineer (Pioneer) Regiment.

1134. **Guérois**, Alexander Klavdieieovich,
   Imperial Russian Captain, Engineer (Sapper) Regiment.
* * *

Imperial Russian Ataman Regiment
Army of the Don

1135. **Biegidov**, David Grigorieovich, Imperial Russian Starchina.
   (**Note**: This is the <u>first</u> award of the Pour le Mérite Order to Starchina Biegidov. For the second award of the Pour le Mérite Order see entry 1272, this chapter.)
1136. **Fomin**, (First name unknown), Imperial Russian Jessual.
* * *

Imperial Russian Ilovaiski XII. Regiment
Army of the Don

1137. **Pshenitshnoi**, Alexei Alexandrovich, Imperial Russian Sotnik.
1138. **Sergieiev**, Grigori Alexieieovich, Imperial Russian Jessaul.
* * *

1139. **Kutsherov**, (First name unknown),
   Imperial Russian Starchina, Ilovaiski IV. Regiment, Army of the Don.

1140. **Astachov**, Michail Nikolaieovich,
   Imperial Russian Starchina, Grekov XXI. Regiment, Army of the Don.
* * *

Imperial Russian Semenstshenkov Regiment
Army of the Don

1141. **Semenstshenkov,** Stepan, Imperial Russian Lt. Colonel,
   Honorary Colonel of the Semenstshenkov Regiment.
1142. **Tshernosubov (Tsherni-Subov)**, Grigori Ilit, Imperial Russian Jessaul.
   (Special Note: It appears that this Russian could possibly have been awarded a second Pour le Mérite Order. However, there are no confirming records available to indicate that this man is the same individual as shown in entry 2064, this chapter.)
* * *

1143. **Moltshanov**, (First name unknown),
   Imperial Russian Jessaul, Karpov II. Regiment, Army of the Don.

1144. **Selivanov III.**, Alexei Andreieovich,
   Imperial Russian Jessaul, Selivanov Regiment, Army of the Don.
* * *

Imperial Russian Radionov II. Regiment
Army of the Don

1145. **Shumkov**, Ivan Fedorovich, Imperial Russian Jessaul.
1146. **Bichalov**, Konon Vassilieovich, Imperial Russian Sotnik.
* * *

1147. **Bichalov**, Ivan,
   Imperial Russian Colonel, Honorary Colonel of the Bichalov Regiment, Army of the Don.

1148. **Shamshev**, (First name unknown),
   Imperial Russian Jessaul, Djatshkin I. Regiment, Army of the Don.

1149. **Albrecht**, Alexander Ivanovich,
Imperial Russian Colonel, Life Guard Dragoon Regiment,
Adjutant to Cavalry General Count von Wittgenstein.
* * *

Imperial Russian Life Guard Preobrashenski Regiment

Count Ludwig Adolf von Wittgenstein

The following two Imperial Russian officers of this regiment were serving as adjutants to Russian Cavalry General Count Ludwig Adolf Peter von Wittgenstein when decorated with the Pour le Mérite Order for outstanding leadership and distinction in action.

1150. **Timrodt**, Fedor Karlovich, Imperial Russian Colonel.
1151. **Messing**, Alexander Ivanovich, Imperial Russian Lieutenant.
(**Note**: Lieutenant Messing was awarded the 50 Year Jubilee Golden Crown to the Pour le Mérite Order on January 22, 1863.)
* * *

Imperial Russian Life Guard Artillery Brigade

1152. **Polossov**, Danilo Petrovich, Imperial Russian Lieutenant, Adjutant to Major General d'Auvray.
1153. **Eismont**, Alexei Matvieieovich, Imperial Russian Staff Captain, Adjutant to Lt. General Prince Jashvill.
* * *

Imperial Russian Life Guard Uhlan Regiment

1154. **Miagkov**, Vassili Nikolaieovich, Imperial Russian Rittmeister, Adjutant to Lt. General Prince Gortshakov II.
1155. **Shuravlov**, Alexander Akimovich, Imperial Russian Rittmeister, Adjutant to Lt. General Uvarov.
* * *

1156. **Breshinski**, Semen Petrovich,
Imperial Russian Colonel, serving as Staff Officer of the Day in the 1st Infantry Corps.
(**Note**: This is the first of the Pour le Mérite Order to Colonel Brenshinski. For the second award of the Pour le Mérite badge see entry 1901, this chapter.)
* * *

1157. **von Kleist**, Ewald Johann,
    Imperial Russian Lieutenant, Tshernigov Infantry Regiment,
    Adjutant to Lt. General Konovnizin.
    (**Note**: Lieutenant von Kleist was awarded the 50 Year Jubilee Golden Crown to the Pour le Mérite Order on November 16, 1865.)

* * *

Imperial Russian Life Guard Ismailov Regiment

1158. **von Wisin**, Michail Alexandrovich, Imperial Russian Staff Captain,
    Adjutant to Lt. General Count von der Pahlen.
1159. **Spiridov**, Ivan Matvieieovich, Imperial Russian Captain, Division
    Adjutant to Russian Count Stroganov.

* * *

1160. **Nepieizin**, Sergei Vassilieovich,
    Imperial Russian Colonel, Life Guard Semenovski Regiment,
    Adjutant to Lt. General Prince Jashvill.

1161. **Galionka**, Afanassi Jakovleovich,
    Imperial Russian Lt. Colonel, Ingermanland Dragoon Regiment.

1162. **Molostvov**, Porfiri Christoforovich,
    Imperial Russian Captain, Life Guard Littau Regiment, Adjutant to Prince Eugen von Württemberg.

1163. **de St. Priest**, Count Louis Franzovich,
    Imperial Russian Staff Captain, Life Guard Light Infantry Regiment,
    Adjutant to Lt. General Count de St. Priest.

* * *

Imperial Russian 11th Light Infantry Regiment

1164. **Dietrichs (Diedrich)**, Andrei Ivanovich (?),
    Imperial Russian Colonel, Commander.
    (For distinction in action at Katzbach on August 23, 1813, and at Plagwitz.)

1165. **Lopuchin**, Alexander Petrovich, Imperial Russian Major.
    (For distinction in action during the engagement at Plagwitz.)

* * *

1166. **Bestushev-Riumin**, Michail Dmitrieovich,
    Imperial Russian Lt. Colonel, Commander, Libau Infantry Regiment.
    (For distinction in action during the engagements at Siebeneichen and Plagwitz.)

* * *

Imperial Russian 28th Light Infantry Regiment

1167. **Blanov**, Gavrilo Vassilieovich, Imperial Russian Lt. Colonel, Commander.
    (For distinction in action at Plagwitz where his regiment captured two French Eagle standards.)

1168. **Kalinin**, Alexander Ivanovich, Imperial Russian Lt. Colonel.

* * *

Imperial Russian 32nd Light Infantry Regiment

1169. **Bulgarin**, Peter Dmitrieovich, Imperial Russian Lt. Colonel, Commander.
1170. **Nepenin**, Andrei Grigorieovich, Imperial Russian Captain.
    (For distinction in action at Katzbach on August 23, 1813.)

* * *

1171. **Teliegin**, Igor Ivanovich,
Imperial Russian Lt. Colonel, Regimental Commander, 36th Light Infantry Regiment.
(For distinction in action during the engagement at Plagwitz.)

1172. **Kalm**, Fedor Grigorieovich,
Imperial Russian Captain, Life Guard Littau Regiment, attached to the Kostroma Infantry Regiment, Adjutant to Lt. General Prince Stsherbatov.
(For distinction in action during several engagements with the enemy. Captain Kalm displayed exceptional leadership especially during the battle at Plagwitz.)

1173. **Terne**, Fedor Fedorovich,
Imperial Russian Lt. Colonel, Commander, Vitepsk Infantry Regiment.
(**Note**: This is the **first** award of the Pour le Mérite Order to Lt. Colonel Terne. For the second award of the Pour le Mérite Order see entry 2187, this chapter.)

* * *

1174. **Tolmatshov**, Jevdokim Petrovich,
Imperial Russian Major, Commander, 12th Light Infantry Regiment.
(For distinction in action during several engagements of the advance guard.)

1175. **Keldijarev**, Michail Gerassimovich,
Imperial Russian Major, Commander, Koslov Infantry Regiment.
(For distinction in action during several actions against the enemy while with the advance guard and also during the battle at Katzbach on August 23, 1813.)

1176. **Makazarov**, Ivan Vassilieovich,
Imperial Russian Major, Commander, Kolivan Infantry Regiment.
(For distinction in action at the battle of Katzbach on August 23, 1813.)

1177. **Medinzov**, Jakob Afanassieovich,
Imperial Russian Colonel, Commander, Riashski Infantry Regiment.

1178. **Shochov**, Peter Alexandrovich,
Imperial Russian Lt. Colonel, Commander, Nasheburg Infantry Regiment.

1179. **Ugriumov**, Peter Alexandrovich,
Imperial Russian Major, Commander, Jakuzk Infantry Regiment.
(For distinction in action while commanding three regiments at the battle of Katzbach on August 23, 1813, and at the Heights of Hermansdorf.)

1180. **Tiunin**, Pavel Semenovich,
Imperial Russian Captain, Riasan Infantry Regiment, Senior Adjutant to Lt. General Olsuviev.

* * *

Imperial Russian Archangelogrod Infantry Regiment

The following officers were decorated with the Pour le Mérite Order for distinction in action during several engagements of the advance guard as well as during the battles at Löwenberg on August 21, 1813, Goldberg on August 23, 1813, and Plagwitz.

1181. **Vichodsevski**, Peter Prokofieovich, Imperial Russian Colonel, Commander.
1182. **Shenshin**, Vassili Nikanorovich, Imperial Russian Colonel, Honorary Colonel of this regiment.
> (**Note**: This is the <u>second</u> award of <u>two</u> Pour le Mérite Order <u>badges</u> awarded to Colonel Shenshin on this date. For the initial award of the Pour le Mérite Order see entry 1061, this chapter.)

* * *

1183. **Röhren**, Ivan Bogdanovich,
> Imperial Russian Colonel, Commander, Schlüsselburg Infantry Regiment.
> (**Note**: This is the <u>second</u> award of <u>two</u> Pour le Mérite Order <u>badges</u> awarded to Colonel Röhren on this date. This award was for distinction in action during the battle at Löwenberg on August 21, 1813, and also during the engagements at Pilgramsdorf and Goldberg on August 23, 1813. For the initial award of the Pour le Mérite Order see entry 1077, this chapter.)

* * *

1184. **Itshkov**, Nikolai Nikolaieovich,
> Imperial Russian Lt. Colonel, Commander, Staro-Ingermanland Infantry Regiment.
> (For distinction in action during several engagements of the advance guard and especially for outstanding leadership during the battle of Katzbach and Goldberg on August 23, 1813.)

* * *

Imperial Russian 29th Light Infantry Regiment

The following two officers were decorated with the Pour le Mérite Order for distinction in action during the engagements at Siebeneichen, Goldberg, Katzbach, and Plagwitz.

1185. **Durnovo**, Ivan Nikolaieovich, Imperial Russian Colonel, Honorary Colonel of the Durnovo Regiment.

1186. **Prigara**, Pavel Onufrieovich, Imperial Russian Lt. Colonel, Commander.

* * *

1187. **Durov**, Fedor Fedorovich,
> Imperial Russian Captain, 5th Light Infantry Regiment, Senior Adjutant to Lt. General Kapzevich.
> (For distinction in action at Wolfsberge.)

1188. **Klingenberg**, Jevstafi Christoforovich,
> Imperial Russian Major, Commander, Kiev Dragoon Regiment.

1189. **Chomiakov**, Alexei Afanassieovich,
> Imperial Russian Colonel, Commander, Liefland Mounted Light Infantry Regiment.
> (For distinction in action during engagements of the advance guard.)

1190. **Stsherbatov**, Prince Nikolai Grigorieovich,
> Imperial Russian Colonel, 2nd Ukraine Cossack Regiment.
> (Awarded the Pour le Mérite Order for distinction in action during several engagements with the enemy while with the advance guard and especially during the battle when Prince Stsherbatov was responsible for the capture of several French cannon and many French soldiers.)

* * *

Below is reproduced the special reprint of General Blücher's "Army Order" which appeared in the Linz (Austria) Newspaper number 73, 1813.

Besondere Beylage zur k. k. privil. Linzer-Zeitung
Nr. 73. 1813.

Eine ausserordentliche Beylage zur Prager-Zeitung Nr. 107 enthält folgenden

Armee-Befehl des General Blücher.

Der königl. preußische General von Blücher hat aus seinem Hauptquartier zu Löwenberg am 1. Septbr. folgenden Tagsbefehl erlassen:

Schlesien ist vom Feinde befreyt. Eurer Tapferkeit, brave Soldaten der rußischen und preußischen Armeen unter meinem Befehl, Eurer Anstrengung und Ausdauer, Eurer Geduld in Ertragung von Beschwerden und Mangel verdanke ich das Glück, eine schöne Provinz den Händen eines gierigen Feindes entrissen zu haben.

Bey der Schlacht an der Katzbach trat uns der Feind trotzig entgegen. Muthig und mit Blitzesschnelle brachet Ihr hinter Euern Anhöhen hervor. Ihr verschmähtet, ihn mit Flintenfeuer anzugreifen; unaufhaltsam schrittet Ihr vor: Eure Bajonette stürzten ihn den steilen Thalrand der wüthenden Neiße und der Katzbach hinab.

Seitdem habt Ihr Flüsse und angeschwollene Regenbäche durchwadet. Im Schlamm habt Ihr die Nächte zugebracht.

Ihr littet zum Theil Mangel an Lebensmitteln, da der grundlose Weg und der Mangel an Fuhrwerk deren Nachfuhr verhinderten. Mit Kälte, Nässe, Entbehrung und zum Theil mit Mangel an Bekleidung habt Ihr gekämpft; dennoch murrtet Ihr nicht, und Ihr verfolgtet mit Anstrengung Euern geschlagenen Feind. Habt Dank für ein so hochlobenswerthes Betragen. Nur derjenige, der solche Eigenschaften vereinigt, ist ein ächter Soldat.

103 Kanonen, 250 Munitionswagen, des Feindes Lazareth-Anstalten, seine Feldschmieden, seine Mehlwagen, 1 Divisions-General, 2 Brigade-Generäle, eine große Anzahl Obersten, Staabs- und anderer Offiziere, 18,000 Gefangene, 2 Adler, und andere Trophäen sind in Euren Händen. Der Rest derjenigen, die Euch in der Schlacht an der Katzbach gegenüber gestanden haben, hat der Schreck vor Euren Waffen so sehr angegriffen, daß sie den Anblick Eurer Bajonette nicht mehr ertragen werden.

Die Straßen und Felder zwischen der Katzbach und dem Bober habt Ihr gesehen; sie tragen die Zeichen des Schreckens und der Verwirrung Eurer Feinde.

Laßt uns dem Herrn der Heerschaaren, durch dessen Hülfe Ihr den Feind niederwarfet, einen Lobgesang singen, und im öffentlichen Gottesdienst ihm für den uns gegebenen herrlichen Sieg danken. Ein dreymaliges Freudenfeuer beschließe die Stunde, die Ihr der Andacht weihet. Dann suchet Euern Feind aufs Neue auf.

Hauptquartier Löwenberg den 1. September 1813.

v. Blücher.

For a complete translation of the above document, see Appendix II.

1191. **Obolenski**, Prince Vassili Petrovich,
Imperial Russian Colonel, Honorary Colonel of the 3rd Ukraine Cossack Regiment, Wing Adjutant.
(**Note**: This is the **second** award of **two** Pour le Mérite **badges** awarded to Colonel Obolenski. This award was for distinction in action during the battle at Goldberg on August 23, 1813. For the initial award of the Pour le Mérite Order see Volume I, Chapter V-1, entry 174, p. 273.) * * *

1192. **Bielaievski**, (First name unknown),
Imperial Russian Starchina, Issaiev II. Regiment, Army of the Don.
(For distinction in action at Goldberg on August 23, 1813, where Starchina Bielaievski killed a French General.)
* * *

1193. **Jakovlev**, Stepan Makarovich,
Imperial Russian Lt. Colonel, Ingermanland Dragoon Regiment, Staff officer of the Day on the staff of Lt. General von Korff.
(**Note**: This is the **second** award of **two** of the Pour le Mérite **badges** awarded to Lt. Colonel Jakovlev on this date. For the initial award of the Pour le Mérite Order see entry 1125, this chapter.)
* * *

Imperial Russian Quartermaster Service

1194. **Viniarski**, Adam Antonovich, Imperial Russian Lt. Colonel, Senior Quartermaster of the X. Infantry Corps.

1195. **von Uexkull-Gyllenbandt**, Baron Peter Longinovich, Imperial Russian Lt. Colonel, Senior Quartermaster of the Corps of Infantry General Count Langeron.

1196. **Schubert**, Fedor Fedorovich, Imperial Russian Lt. Colonel, Senior Quartermaster of the Cavalry Corps of Infantry General Count Langeron.
(**Note**: Lt. Colonel Schubert was awarded the 50 Year Jubilee Golden Crown to the Pour le Mérite Order on January 22, 1863.)
* * *

1197. **Magdenko II.**, Michail Semenovich,
Imperial Russian Colonel, Commander, 34th Artillery Battery Company.
(For distinction in action during several skirmishes with the enemy while with the advance guard.)

1198. **Shusherin**, Sachar Sergieieovich,
Imperial Russian Lt. Colonel, Commander of the 8th Mounted Artillery Company.
(**Note**: This is the **second** of **two** awards of the Pour le Mérite **badge** to Lt. Colonel Shusherin on this date. This award was for distinction in action during several engagements with the enemy while with the advance guard. For the **third** award of the Pour le Mérite Order to this officer see entry 1740, this chapter.)
* * *

1199. **Benderski**, Konstantin Alexandrovich,
Imperial Russian Lt. Colonel, Commander, 28th Light Artillery Company.

(For distinction in action during several engagements with the enemy while with the advance guard.)

1200. **Nesterovski**, Avim Vassilieovich,
Imperial Russian Lt. Colonel, Commander, 34th Light Artillery Company.
(For distinction in action during the battles at Katzbach on August 26, 1813 and Plagwitz.)

1201. **Suvorov II.** Peter,
Imperial Russian Lt. Colonel, 2nd Mounted Artillery Company, Army of the Don.
(**Note**: This is the <u>second</u> of <u>two</u> awards of the Pour le Mérite Order <u>badge</u> to Lt. Colonel Suvorov II. on this date. This award was in recognition of distinction in action during the battle at Siebeneichen. For the initial award of the Pour le Mérite Order see entry 1107, this chapter.)

* * *

The following three Russian officers, when decorated with the Pour le Mérite Order for distinction in action, were serving on the staff of Infantry General Count Langeron.

1202. **Listovski**, (First name unknown), Imperial Russian Major, Riashski Infantry Regiment, serving as Headquarters Commandant.

1203. **Korshavin**, Vassili Ivanovich, Imperial Russian Major, Olonez Infantry Regiment, serving as Staff Officer of the Day.

1204. **Rateiev**, Prince Yuri Petrovich, Imperial Russian Lieutenant, Arsamas Mounted Light Infantry Regiment, Adjutant to General Langeron.

* * *

1205. **Chrapovizki**, Grigori Semenovich,
Imperial Russian Major, Volyni Uhlan Regiment, Staff Officer of the Day in the advance guard.
(Awarded the Pour le Mérite Order for distinction in action during several skirmishes and engagements with the enemy while with the advance guard.)

* * *

The following six Russian officers were serving on the staff of Lt. General Baron von Sacken when awarded the Pour le Mérite Order.

1206. **Trinchieri**, Joseph Count Venanzone,
Imperial Russian Colonel, Quartermaster Service, Corps Chief of the General Staff of Lt. General von Sacken.

1207. **Gatovski**, Semen Ossipovich,
Imperial Russian Colonel, Quartermaster Service, Corps Staff Officer of the Day.

1208. **Krishanovski**, Andrei Ivanovich,
Imperial Russian Lt. Colonel, 6th Light Infantry Regiment, Adjutant.

1209. **Kusmin**, Stepan Ivanovich,
Imperial Russian Lt. Colonel, Life Guard Grenadier Regiment, Adjutant.

1210. **Obolenski**, Prince Nikolai Petrovich,
    Imperial Russian Captain, 1st Engineer (Pioneer) Regiment, Adjutant.

1211. **Perepietshin**, (First name unknown),
    Imperial Russian Captain, Fanagoria Grenadier Regiment, Adjutant.

* * *

1212. **Brams**, Alexander Ivanovich,
    Imperial Russian Colonel, Commander, 13th Artillery Battery Company.
    (Awarded the Pour le Mérite Order for distinction in action during an engagement when Colonel Brams and his artillery battery captured the important heights between Beelshof and Eichholz and placed his artillery battery in a strategic and commanding position which successfully drove the enemy back. Colonel Brams had also been decorated with the Prussian Iron Cross for outstanding leadership and bravery during an engagement on August 26, 1813.)

* * *

Imperial Russian 49th Light Infantry Regiment

1213. **(Petrovski)-Muravski**, (First name unknown), Imperial Russian Major, Unit Commander.
    (**Note**: This is the <u>first</u> award of the Pour le Mérite Order to Major Muravski. For the second award of the Pour le Mérite Order see entry 2275, this chapter.

1214. **Solovov**, Martemian (Martin) Andreieovich, Imperial Russian Major.
1215. **Krohnstein**, Gustaf Vassilieovich, Imperial Russian Major, Adjutant to Lt. General Nevierovski.
    (**Note**: Major Krohnstein was awarded the 50 Year Jubilee Golden Crown on January 22, 1863.)

* * *

The following four Russian officers were awarded the Pour le Mérite Order for distinction in action during the battle of Katzbach on August 26, 1813.

1216. **Ushakov**, Peter Sergieieovich,
    Imperial Russian Major, Vilna Infantry Regiment.

1217. **Valchovski**, Dmitri Nikolaieovich,
    Imperial Russian Staff Captain, 18th Mounted Artillery Company.

1218. **Jessaulov**, (First name unknown),
    Imperial Russian Major, 39th Light Infantry Regiment.

1219. **Kovankov**, Michail Michailovich,
    Imperial Russian Lieutenant, 13th Artillery Battery Company.

* * *

Imperial Russian 7th Light Infantry Regiment

The following three officers received the Pour le Mérite Order for distinction in action during the engagements at Löwenberg on August 21, 1813, and Goldberg on August 23, 1813.

1220. **Stegmann**, Anton Ossipovich, Imperial Russian Lt. Colonel, Commander.
1221. **Stavrakov**, Sachar Christoforovich, Imperial Russian Major.
1222. **Atreshkov**, Lev Ivanovich, Imperial Russian Major.

* * *

Imperial Russian 26th Light Artillery Company

1223. **de Chamborant**, Count Viktor Ivanovich, Imperial Russian Captain.
1224. **Volshenski**, Peter Lvovich, Imperial Russian Lieutenant.

* * *

1225. **von Klüx**, Friedrich Karl Leopold,
   Major General, Commanding the IX. Brigade.
   (**Note**: Awarded the Oakleaves to the Pour le Mérite Order. For the initial award of the Pour le Mérite Order see Volume I, Chapter V-1, entry 428, p. 297.)

* * *

1226. **von Grolman**, Karl Wilhelm Georg,
   Colonel, Chief of the General Staff of the II. Army Corps.
   (**Note**: Awarded the Oakleaves to the Pour le Mérite Order for distinction in action during the battle at Leipzig on October 18, 1812. For the initial award of the Pour le Mérite Order see Volume I, Chapter V-1, entry 117, p. 267.)

* * *

1227. **von Horn**, Heinrich Wilhelm,
   Major General, Commanding the VII. Brigade.
   (**Note**: Awarded the Oakleaves to the Pour le Mérite Order for distinction in action during the battle at Leipzig on October 16, 1813. For the initial award of the Pour le Mérite Order see Volume I, Chapter IV, entry 696, p. 201.)

* * *

1228. **von Wahlen-Jürgass**, Alexander George Ludwig Moritz Maximilian,
   Colonel, Commander, Reserve Cavalry Brigade of the I. Army Corps.
   (**Note**: Awarded the Oakleaves to the Pour le Mérite Order for distinction in action during the battle at Möckern on October 16, 1813. For the initial award of the Pour le Mérite Order see Volume I, Chapter V-1, entry 667, p. 327.)

* * *

1229. **von Borcke**, Karl August Ferdinand,
   Colonel, Commander, Brandenburg Infantry Regiment, and Commanding the VIII. Brigade.
   (**Note**: Awarded the Oakleaves to the Pour le Mérite Order for distinction in action during the battle at Möckern on October 16, 1813. For the initial award of the Pour le Mérite Order see Volume I, Chapter V-1, entry 673, p. 327.)

* * *

1230. **von Valentini**, Georg Wilhelm,
   Colonel, Chief of the General Staff of the III. Army Corps.
   (**Note**: Colonel Valentini was awarded **both** the Pour le Mérite Order **and** the Oakleaves to the Pour le Mérite Order on this date for distinction in action during the battle at Leipzig on October 18-19, 1813.)

* * *

* December 10, 1813 *

1231. **Bichalov**, Vassili,
   Imperial Russian Colonel, unit unknown, Army of the Don.
   (For distinction in action at Herrenkruge by Magdeburg.)

1232. **Shimanov**, (First name unknown),
 Imperial Russian Sotnik, Ilovaiski III. Regiment, Army of the Don.
* * *

First Award of the Pour le Mérite Order to a Naval Officer

1233. **Kreuger**, Johann Heinrich,
 Royal Swedish Naval Captain, Stockholm Squadron, Swedish Fleet.
 (For distinction in action on October 5, 1813.)
 (Special Note: This appears to be the first award of the Pour le Mérite Order bestowed on a Naval officer. It is also of interest that the first was not given to a Prussian.)
* * *

1234. **L'Coq**, Karl August,
 Royal Saxon 2nd Lieutenant, Saxon Engineer Corps.
 (**Note**: Awarded the Pour le Mérite Order for distinction in action during an engagement with the enemy in the vicinity of Torgau during the night of November 22-23, 1813.
 Saxon Lieutenant L'Coq was awarded the 50 Year Jubilee Golden Crown to the Pour le Mérite Order on January 22, 1863.)
* * *

* December 11, 1813 *

1235. **Raslov**, (First name unknown),
 Imperial Russian Major (Starchina), serving with Osmani (Ataman) Cossacks.

1236. **Unknown**, (Russian),
 Imperial Russian Lieutenant and Adjutant, unit unknown.
* * *

* December 12, 1813 *

1237. **von Cardell**, Karl Friedrich,
 Royal Swedish Major General, Commander, Wendes Artillery Regiment.

1238. **de Surmain**, Charles Jean,
 Royal Swedish Major General, Adjutant General of Artillery, serving as Lt. Colonel in the West Göta Infantry Regiment.
* * *

Royal Swedish Life Guard Cavalry Regiment

1239. **von Engeström**, Gustaf Stanislaus, Royal Swedish Rittmeister.
1240. **Brahe**, Count Magnus, Royal Swedish Lieutenant.
* * *

1241. **Edenhjelm**, Gillis,
 Royal Swedish Lt. Colonel, serving as Major in the Göta Artillery Regiment.
* * *

By this time the allies had begun preparations for the campaign they now realized would be fought in France against the forces of Napoleon. It took some time to complete a comprehensive military plan that was acceptable to all of the allied command. However, by mid-December the military logistics and strategy had been completed and approved, and the allied armies were ready to march.
* * *

* December 16, 1813 *

1242. **Henckel von Donnersmarck**, Count Wilhelm Ludwig Viktor,
Colonel, Wing Adjutant, Brigade Commander of the Reserve Cavalry of the I Army Corps.
(**Note**: Colonel Henckel von Donnersmarck was awarded <u>both</u> the Pour le Mérite Order <u>and</u> the Oakleaves to the Pour le Mérite Order on this date in recognition of distinction in action during the battle at Freiburg and also for outstanding leadership during several other engagements with the enemy.)

* * *

1243. **Pantshulidsev**, Alexander Alexieieovich,
Imperial Russian Lieutenant, Tshernigov Mounted Light Infantry Regiment.
(**Note**: Lieutenant Pantshulidsev was awarded the 50 Year Jubilee Golden Crown to the Pour le Mérite Order on January 22, 1863.)

* * *

1244. **Tarassov**, Peter Ivanovich,
Imperial Russian Colonel, Quartermaster Service.
(For distinction in action at Möckern on October 16, 1813.)

1245. **Oldenborgen**, Ivan Fedorovich,
Imperial Russian Sub-Lieutenant, 7th Artillery Battery Company.
(For distinction in action at Gross-Beeren on August 23, 1813.)

* * *

Imperial Russian Novgorod Cuirassier Regiment

1246. **von Vietinghoff**, Anton Maximovich, Imperial Russian Colonel, Life Guard Dragoon Regiment, serving in the Novgorod Regiment.
1247. **Rokotov**, Nikolai Matvieieovich, Imperial Russian Lieutenant, Adjutant to Major General Levashov.
1248. **Ivashkevich**, Ustin Timofieieovich, Imperial Russian Lieutenant, Adjutant to Major General Levashov.

* * *

1249. **Buturlin**, Dmitri Petrovich,
Imperial Russian Lieutenant, Cavalier Guard Regiment, Adjutant to Major General Levashov.

* * *

Imperial Russian 23rd Mounted Artillery Company

1250. **Dashkov**, Andrei Vassilovich, Imperial Russian Lieutenant.
1251. **Asantshevski**, Fedor Sergieieovich, Imperial Russian Lieutenant.
1252. **Strahlborn**, Vladimir Karlovich, Imperial Russian Sub-Lieutenant.
1253. **von Schlippenbach**, Frhr. Nikolai Antonovich, Imperial Russian Sub-Lieutenant.
1254. **Shachovskoi**, Prince Nikolai Michailovich, Imperial Russian Sub-Lieutenant.

* * *

The following three Russian officers received the Pour le Mérite Order for distinction in action during the skirmish at Schottenhäusen on October 10, 1813.

1255. **Grekov XVII.**, Alexei Jevdokimovich,
Imperial Russian Colonel, Honorary Colonel of the Grekov XVII. Regiment, Army of the Don.

1256. **Shubin**, Alexander Fedotovich,
    Imperial Russian Colonel, St. Petersburg Opoltshenie (militia).

1257. **Grinkevich**, (First name unknown),
    Imperial Russian Major, Volyni Infantry Regiment, commanding
    4 composite Infantry Regiments.
    (At this engagement at Schottenhäusen on October 10, 1813, Major
    Grinkevich was severely wounded but managed to direct his troops in
    repulsing the French.) * * *

Imperial Russian Briansk Infantry Regiment

1258. **Julius**, (First name unknown), Imperial Russian Major.
1259. **Vissozki**, Josef Fedorovich, Imperial Russian Major.
1260. **Nikonov**, Kirill Nikititsh, Imperial Russian Major.
1261. **Starkov**, Jakob Michailovich, Imperial Russian Major.
* * *

The following five officers were decorated with the Pour le Mérite Order for distinction in action during the skirmish at Schottenhäusen on October 10, 1813.

1262. **Chanikov**, Nikolai Petrovich (Vassilieovich),
    Imperial Russian Staff Captain, St. Petersburg Opoltshenie (militia).

1263. **Zickel (Zickeln)**, (First name unknown),
    Imperial Russian Captain, Nisov Infantry Regiment, Adjutant to
    Major General Rachmanov.

1264. **Gedeonov**, Alexander Michailovich,
    Imperial Russian Staff Captain, Kasan Dragoon Regiment.

1265. **Smoliak**, Ossip Ivanovich,
    Imperial Russian Staff Captain, 3rd Light Infantry Regiment.

1266. **von Korff I.**, Baron Ossip Ivanovich,
    Imperial Russian Staff Captain, 19th Mounted Artillery Company.
* * *

The following Russian officers were serving as adjutants to Ataman Count Platov when decorated with the Pour le Mérite Order for distinction in action.

1267. **Engelhart**, Andrei Vassilieovich,
    Imperial Russian Colonel, unit unknown, Army of the Don.

1268. **Kusnezov**, Michail Michailovich,
    Imperial Russian Jessaul, Ataman Cossack Regiment, Army of
    the Don.

1269. **Krasnokutski**, Alexander Grigorieovich,
    Imperial Russian Lt. Colonel, unit unknown, serving as Staff Officer
    of the Day on the staff of Ataman Count Platov.

1270. **von dem Bussche-Ippenburg**, Frhr. Karl Friedrich Salesius,
    Imperial Russian Cavalry Lt. Colonel, unit unknown.
    (Note: Cavalry Lt. Colonel von dem Bussche-Ippenburg was awarded
    the 50 Year Jubilee Golden Crown to the Pour le Mérite Order on
    January 22, 1863.) * * *

1271. **Tazin IV.**, Peter Fedorovich,
    Imperial Russian Lt. Colonel, 1st Mounted Artillery Company,
    Army of the Don.

(**Note**: This is the **second** award of the Pour le Mérite Order badge to Lt. Colonel Tavin IV. For the initial award of the Pour le Mérite Order see entry 1106, this chapter.)

* * *

1272. **Biegidov**, David Grigorieovich,
    Imperial Russian Lt. Colonel, Commander, Ataman Cossack Regiment, Army of the Don.
    (**Note**: This is the **second** award of the Pour le Mérite Order badge to Lt. Colonel Biegidov. For the initial award of the Pour le Mérite Order see entry 1135, this chapter.)

* * *

1273. **Plochovo**, Sergei Nikolaieovich,
    Imperial Russian Lt. Colonel, Commander, of the 4th Cavalry Regiment, Tshernomori Army.

1274. **Kostin IV.**, Grigori Andreieovich,
    Imperial Russian Lt. Colonel, Honorary Colonel of the Kostin IV. Regiment, Army of the Don.

* * *

Imperial Russian Ataman Cossack Regiment
Army of the Don

1275. **Prozikov**, Andrei Fedorovich, Imperial Russian Jessaul.
1276. **Karshin**, Christofor Pavlovich, Imperial Russian Jessaul.
1277. **Koslov**, Nikolai Fedorovich, Imperial Russian Jessaul.

* * *

1278. **Muchanov**, (First name unknown),
    Imperial Russian Lieutenant, Neushlot Infantry Regiment, serving as Staff Officer on the General Staff of Ataman Count Platov.

1279. **Chrapovizki**, Jason Semenovich,
    Imperial Russian Lt. Colonel, Volyni Uhlan Regiment.

1280. **Shamshev IV.**, Yuri Ivanovich,
    Imperial Russian Starchina, Ilovaiski XII. Regiment, Army of the Don.

1281. **Solotarev**, Afanassi Ivanovich,
    Imperial Russian Starchina, Grekov VIII. Regiment, Army of the Don.

1282. **Chriestshatizki**, Pavel Stepanovich,
    Imperial Russian Staff Rittmeister, Life Guard Cossack Regiment, Adjutant to Lt. General Count Orlov-Denisov.

1283. **Barozzie**, Jakob Ivanovich,
    Imperial Russian Captain, Narva Infantry Regiment.

* * *

The following seven Russian officers were serving as Adjutants to Russian Infantry General Count Barclay de Tolly when decorated with the Pour le Mérite Order for distinction in action.

1284. **Kamenski**, (First name unknown),
    Imperial Russian Lt. Colonel, Archangelogrod Infantry Regiment.

1285. **Hurko (Gurko)**, Ossip Alexandrovich,
    Imperial Russian Captain, Life Guard Semenovski Regiment.

1286. **Tshavtshavadse**, Alexander Gerssevanovich,
Imperial Russian Staff Rittmeister, Life Guard Hussar Regiment.

1287. **von Sievers**, Karl Ivanovich,
Imperial Russian Staff Rittmeister, Life Guard Uhlan Regiment.

1288. **Tishevski**, Yevgeni Ivanovich,
Imperial Russian Staff Captain, 4th Light Infantry Regiment.

1289. **Kratz**, Fedor Ivanovich,
Imperial Russian Colonel, Quartermaster Service.

1290. **Helfreich**, Igor Ivanovich,
Imperial Russian Staff Rittmeister, Alexandria Hussar Regiment.
(**Note**: Staff Rittmeister Helfreich was awarded the 50 Year Jubilee Golden Crown to the Pour le Mérite Order on January 22, 1863.)

* * *

The following two Russian officers, when decorated with the Pour le Mérite Order for distinction in action, were serving as Staff Officers in the Headquarters of Russian Infantry General Count Barclay de Tolly.

1291. **Sabanieiev**, Peter Vassilieovich,
Imperial Russian Major, Staro-Ingermanland Regiment.

1292. **Ikonnikov**, Ivan Jakovleovich,
Imperial Russian Staff Captain, Viburg Infantry Regiment.

* * *

1293. **Komstadius**, August Fedorovich,
Imperial Russian Lt. Colonel, Kasan Infantry Regiment, Senior Adjutant to the Chief of the General Staff of Lt. General Sabanieiev.

1294. **Suchosanet I.**, Ivan Onufrieovich,
Imperial Russian Major General, Life Guard Artillery Brigade, Commander of the Artillery of the Main Russian Army.

1295. **Rikov**, Vassili Dmitrieovich,
Imperial Russian Major General, Commandant of Russian Headquarters, formerly serving in the Liefland Mounted Light Infantry Regiment.

1296. **Bielogradski**, Grigori Grigorieovich,
Imperial Russian Colonel, Life Guard Preobrashenski Regiment, Director of the Medical Facilities.

1297. **Raiski**, Ivan Stanislavovich,
Imperial Russian Staff Captain, Life Guard Light Infantry Regiment, Adjutant to the Chief of the General Staff of Lt. General Sabanieiev.

* * *

Imperial Russian Quartermaster Service

1298. **von Knorring**, Vladimir Karlovich, Staff Captain.
1299. **von Weyrauch**, Alexander Jakovleovich, Staff Captain.
1300. **von Prittwitz**, Paul Karlovich, Staff Captain.
1301. **Treskin**, Igor Ivanovich, Imperial Russian Captain.
1302. **Chomutov**, Grigori Sergieieovich, Imperial Russian Lieutenant.

* * *

1303. **Gortshakov**, Prince Sergei Dmitrieovich,
    Imperial Russian Officer Candidate, 29th Mounted Artillery Company.
    (For distinction in action at Leipzig on October 18, 1813, where this officer was severely wounded.)
    (Note: Awarded the 50 Year Golden Crown to the Pour le Mérite Order on either February 23 or March 24, 1870.)

1304. **Habbe**, Michail Andreieovich,
    Imperial Russian Lieutenant, Life Guard Littau Regiment, Adjutant to Lt. General von Toll.
    (For distinction in action during several engagements.)

1305. **Freymann**, Rudolf (Roman) Antonovich,
    Imperial Russian Captain, Siev Infantry Regiment, Senior Adjutant to Lt. General Levis.
    (Note: This officer also was decorated with the Prussian Iron Cross.)

1306. **Paissel**, Peter Petrovich,
    Imperial Russian Staff Captain, 2nd Sea Regiment.
    (For distinction in action on November 28-29, 1813.)

1307. **Schlodhauer**, Jakob Fedorovich,
    Imperial Russian Lieutenant, 7th Drushina (Battalion) of the St. Petersburg Opoltshenie (militia).

1308. **Tirkov**, Alexei Dmitrieovich,
    Imperial Russian Sub-Lieutenant, Novgorod Opoltshenie (militia). Adjutant to Lt. General Sherebzov.
    (For distinction in action during several engagements and skirmishes against the French.)

1309. **du Boy (Deboar)**, Ossip Petrovich,
    Imperial Russian Lieutenant, 11th Light Artillery Company.

1310. **Vilhelmov**, Pavel Fedorovich,
    Imperial Russian Lieutenant, serving in an unidentified Opoltshenie (militia), Adjutant to Colonel Sosnin.
    (Note: Lieutenant Vilhelmov was awarded the 50 Year Jubilee Golden Crown to the Pour le Mérite Order on January 22, 1963.)

* * *

1311. **Bibikov**, Dmitri Ivanovich,
    Imperial Russian Major, Olonez Infantry Regiment, serving as Officer of the Day on the staff of Major General Prince Volkonski.

1312. **Shimanovski**, Maxim,
    Imperial Russian Lieutenant, Nisov Infantry Regiment, Adjutant to Major General Prince Volkonski.

1313. **Nikolaiev**, Ivan Yurieovich,
    Imperial Russian Colonel, 12th Drushina (Battalion) of the St. Petersburg Opoltshina (militia), Commandant of the Headquarters of Cavalry General Duke Alexander of Württemberg.

1314. **Stshulepnikov**, Michailo Sergieieovich,
    Imperial Russian Major, 13th Drushina (Battalion) of the St. Petersburg Opoltshenie (militia).

(**Note**: Major Stshulepnikov suffered being wounded three times during an engagement against a French attack. However, he remained in command of his battalion and inspired his troops which repulsed the French and drove them back.)

* * *

The following four Imperial Russian officers were decorated with the Pour le Mérite Order for distinction in action during the engagement at Schidlitz.

Imperial Russian Engineer Corps

1315. **Manfredi**, Ossip Ivanovich, Imperial Russian Colonel.
1316. **Nakovalnin**, Nikolai Fedorovich, Imperial Russian Lieutenant.

* * *

1317. **Arzishevski**, Anton Kasimirovich,
 Imperial Russian Lieutenant, Quartermaster Service.

1318. **Schröder**, Karl Grigorieovich,
 Imperial Russian Lieutenant, 19th Mounted Artillery Company.

* * *

Imperial Russian 1st Composite Drushina (Battalion) St. Petersburg Opoltshenie (militia)

1319. **Teglev**, Nikolai Jakovleovich, Imperial Russian Naval Lt. Commander, Unit Commander.
1320. **Korssakov**, Semen Nikolaieovich, Imperial Russian Court official serving as Staff Officer.
1321. **Krekshin**, Nikolai, Imperial Russian Secretarial official, serving as the Official Recorder of the Russian campaign.

* * *

* December 18, 1813 *

1322. **von Marschall**, Wenzel Philipp,
 Imperial Austrian Major, Archduke Ferdinand Hussar Regiment.
 (**Note**: Major von Marschall was also decorated with the Prussian Iron Cross for outstanding leadership and distinction in the field.)

* * *

On December 20, 1813, the allied force of Prussian, Russian and Austrian troops under the command of Austrian Field Marshal Prince von Schwarzenberg began crossing the Rhine river in pursuit of the French army.

* * *

* December 22, 1813 *

1323. **Sibin**, Sergei Vassilieovich,
 Imperial Russian Lieutenant, Life Guard Hussar Regiment,
 Adjutant to Lt. General Count Osharovski.

* * *

* December 24, 1813 *

1324. **von Pirch**, Georg Dubislaf Ludwig,
 Major General, Commander of the X. Brigade.
 (**Note**: Major General von Pirch was awarded both the Pour le Mérite Order and the Oakleaves to the Pour le Mérite Order for outstanding distinction in action during the battle at Leipzig on October 16-18, 1813.)

* * *

During 1813, a total of 600 Pour le Mérite Orders were awarded. What is very unusual is that of the 600 awards, 529 or 88% were bestowed upon Russian officers, with the remainder to 38 Prussians (6%), 14 Swedes (2%), 12 Austrians (2%), 6 Britons (1%) and one Saxon (.2%).

During 1813, the largest number of Pour le Mérite Orders were authorized on December 8th, when a total of 217 decorations were approved. Of the 217 awards, 211 or 97% were to Russian officers, including <u>five</u> Russians who received <u>two</u> Pour le Mérite Order badges on this date. This <u>also</u> includes <u>two</u> Russian <u>officers</u> who were decorated with a <u>third</u> Pour le Mérite Order at <u>a later date</u>.

It is of special interest to note only **six** awards or 3% of the total awarded on December 8, 1813, were to Prussian officers.

The Morning After the Battle at Grossbeeren.

* January 1, 1814 *

On January 1, 1814, Blücher crossed the Rhine River in pursuit of the French. This movement of allied forces into what Napoleon considered French territory caught him completely by surprise. He had hoped that the allied armies would delay their attack on his eastern frontier until Spring of 1814. By that time, Napoleon felt confident that the French nation would have rallied to him for the defense of France and his new armies would be ready for the repulse of the enemy.

Blücher Crossing the Rhine on New Years 1814.

The following five Imperial Russian officers were decorated with the Pour le Mérite Order for distinction and leadership during the crossing of the Rhine river at Mannheim on this date.

1325. **von Vietinghoff**, Andrei Igorovich,
Imperial Russian Lt. Colonel, Quartermaster Service.

1326. **von Wisin**, Ivan Alexandrovich,
Imperial Russian Staff Captain, Quartermaster Service.

* * *

Imperial Russian Bielostok Infantry Regiment

1327. **Nikitin**, Michail Fedorovich, Imperial Russian Major.
1328. **Balbekov**, Alexei Alexandrovich, Imperial Russian Major.

* * *

1329. **Jemelianov**, Nikolai Filippovich,
Imperial Russian Lt. Colonel, 11th Light Infantry Regiment.

* * *

The allies, through their past experience fighting with Napoleon, were not to give him the time he needed to complete his plans. They also took advantage of the problems confronting the French elsewhere in Europe. Napoleon faced political opposition in France, a rebellion in Holland, and increased allied military activity in Spain and Italy. This was the time to crush him - - before he could accomplish another military miracle.

The opening phases of the 1814 campaign were conducted virtually without a shot being fired. The cities of Strasbourg and Nancy were abandoned by Marshal Claude Victor without a fight. This French withdrawal provided the allies with an unhindered crossing of the Mosel River.

On January 6th, a Russian army under the command of Field Marshal Baron Ferdinand Winzingerode crossed the Rhine.

* * *

* January 8, 1814 *

1330. **Schneider von Arno**, Frhr. Karl,
Imperial Austrian Colonel, Commandant of the 2nd Light Infantry Battalion.
(Awarded the Pour le Mérite Order for outstanding and distinguished leadership and conduct during several engagements against the French fought during 1813.)

* * *

* January 11, 1814 *

1331. **Heckel**, Johann Gotthold,
Royal Saxon 2nd Lieutenant, Sapper Company, Engineer Corps.
(For distinction in action during the siege and capture of Torgau from March 10 until October 30, 1813.)

1332. **Rastkovski**, Justin Stanislavovich,
Imperial Russian Cornet, Pavlograd Hussar Regiment.
(For distinction in action at Turnhout, December 1813. This officer was responsible for the capture of 30 enemy soldiers and 40 horses.)

* * *

* January 14, 1814 *

1333. **von Wernhardt**. Paul,
Imperial Austrian Colonel, Archduke Konstantin Curassier Regiment.
(For distinction in action during the battle at Leipzig on October 16-18, 1813.)

1334. **Balkashin**, Michail Nikolaieovich,
Imperial Russian Staff Rittmeister, His Majesty's Life Guard Curassier Regiment.

(For distinction in action during the battle of Leipzig on October 16-18, 1813.)

* * *

By January 13, 1814, Blücher's forces had pursued the French army of Marshal Auguste Frederic Louis Marmont to Metz. By January 17, the bulk of the French forces in the east were taking up defensive positions behind the Meuse River.

Blücher continued to apply pressure to the French, and on the 22nd of January the Prussian forces began crossing the river in force. To make matters worse for the French, the Prussian advance guard moved forward with lightning speed and managed to secure a bridgehead on the west bank of the Marne River by January 23, 1814.

Meanwhile, the Austrian forces of Prince Karl Philip Schwarzenberg had moved south of Blücher's troops and reached the Langres Plateau by the 17th. Here the Austrians rested and reorganized until January 23, 1814, when they resumed their advance. From this point on the large forces of Blücher and Schwarzenberg were separated by only two days march, and with every passing day this gap narrowed. Realizing the dangerous situation in the concentration of the two allied armies, Napoleon decided to leave Paris and join his forces in the field. On January 26, 1814, he arrived and immediately made strategic plans to confront the Prussians at St. Dizier. At the head of a force of 34,000 French, Napoleon moved on St. Dizier, arriving on January 27, 1814. After a brief but intense engagement the Prussians withdrew. Napoleon then turned his troops to continue the tracking of Blücher's main army toward Brienne. By using a surprise attack against the allied rear, Napoleon believed he could win a decisive victory over the Prussians before Schwarzenberg's reinforcements could arrive. Blücher had established his headquarters in a château overlooking Brienne and was aware of Napoleon's plan of attack since copies of Napoleon's orders had fallen into his hands. With this vital information the allied forces began to deploy to face the approaching French.

French Troops Attacking at Brienne

The battle of Brienne opened in the early morning of January 29, 1814, with an artillery duel between the French and Prussians. The French cavalry moved to flank the Prussians and for most of the day the fighting was actually rather light as both sides attempted to outmaneuver each other. A remarkable aspect of these actions occured when Napoleon narrowly escaped being captured by a Cossack patrol. The battle continued into the night. The French launched an all-out assault on Blücher's headquarters and succeeded in capturing the château. Blücher and Gneisnau had left just minutes before the French arrived. After the capture of the château, the fighting gradually ended. Blücher disengaged his forces and withdrew to the south.

During the battle, which ended in a mutual disengagement, approximately 30,000 French engaged a combined Prussian-Russian force of 25,000. The French failed to gain a victory but sustained only 3,000 casualities to the allies' 4,000. The following day the French forces began to take up positions in and around the town of La Rothière four miles southeast of Brienne. Napoleon planned to withdraw from the area and move west to the town of Troyes to be in a better position to protect Paris.

Blücher at La Rothière

Aggressive French patrols convinced the allies that another attack seemed likely, but none materialized. By January 31, 1814, Prince Schwarzenberg's Austrian force had arrived, reinforcing Blücher. The two allied commanders decided to strike first.

The battle of La Rothière commenced during the morning of February 1, 1814, under cold gray skies. It soon began to snow heavily. The fighting was somewhat light until midday when French cavalry overran several Russian artillery positions. An allied counterattack was launched. and a fierce cavalry battle ensued. Allied assaults against the French lines were meeting with little success. However, by late afternoon the French left flank began to fail. At this time fresh allied reinforcements arrived on the field. Making use of the still falling snow and the darkness, Napoleon broke off the engagement and retreated northwest toward Lesmont. He had lost over 6,000 troops, 50 cannon and, most importantly, the morale of his army was badly shaken.

The battle of La Rothière convinced the allied commanders that the war would soon be over. They planned to march on Paris but almost immediately ran into problems. The French either managed to outmaneuver them or some French garrisons in towns and cities along the routes of march refused to surrender and thus delayed the advance. The result of these delays provided Napoleon the time and opportunity to prepare for another battle with Blücher's allied forces.

On February 9, 1814, Napoleon with 30,000 soldiers managed to surprise a force of 5,000 Russians under the command of Russian General Olsufiev at Champaubert. The French attacked the Russian positions after resting overnight. Although severely outnumbered, the Russians stood their ground.

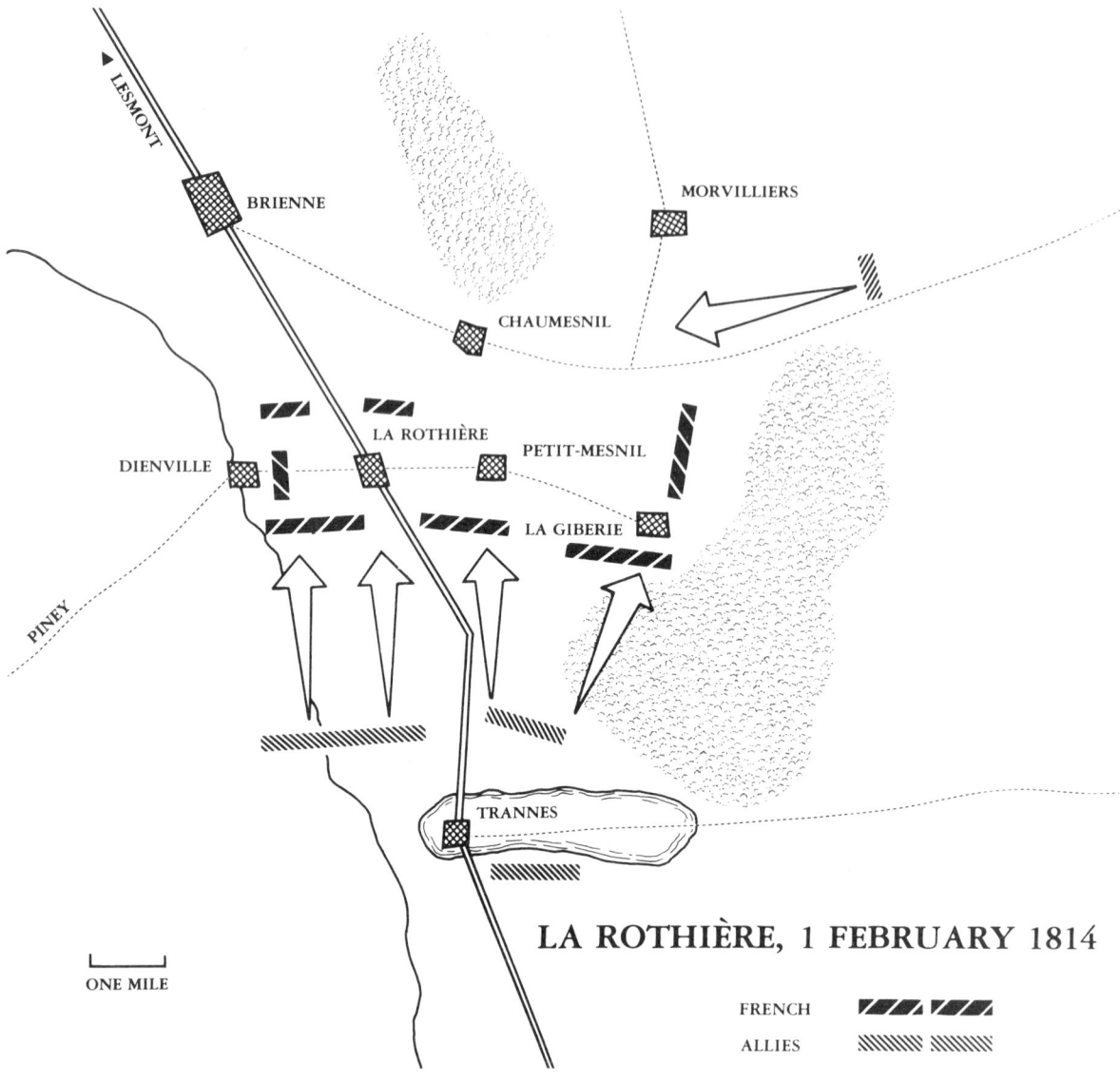

LA ROTHIÈRE, 1 FEBRUARY 1814

The battle of Champaubert began around 10 am on February 10, 1814. It was immediately evident that the Russians could not expect to be successful. Slowly they were pushed out of the town and retreated to the east. The French cavalry cut off the escape route and completely surrounded the Russians. Of the 5,000 Russians, 4,000 became casualities and General Olsufiev was made prisoner.

Learning of this critical defeat at Champaubert, Blücher sent orders to Generals Dmitri Osten Sacken and Yorck to concentrate their forces at Montmirail. As Sacken moved toward the town, he was unaware that Napoleon had already passed through; thus, the two forces collided at Montmirail.

The battle of Montmirail began during the morning of February 11, 1814. Initially, the French were outnumbered and were forced to fight defensively. However, as the battle continued, French reinforcements arrived, and Napoleon finally was in a position to take the offensive. The Russian troops had stood their ground waiting for the arrival of General Yorck and his troops, but French pressure resulted in the collapse of the Russian line. The battle now turned into a pursuit of the Russians by French cavalry.

* February 11, 1814 *

1335. **Carlheim-Gyllensköld**, Karl Eduard,
Royal Swedish Colonel, Adjutant General of the Swedish Fleet.

1336. **Mörner**, Count Axel Otto,
Royal Swedish Captain-Lieutenant, Life Gentlemen-at-Arms Corps Honorary Colonel of the Smaland Dragoon Regiment and Adjutant to the Crown Prince of Sweden.

1337. **Bergencreutz**, Lars Alger,
Royal Swedish Colonel and Equerry to the King of Sweden, serving on the General Staff of the Crown Prince of Sweden.

1338. **Hjerta**, Gustaf Adolf,
Royal Swedish Major, Royal Life Guard Curassier Corps, Brigade Adjutant to the Crown Prince of Sweden.

* * *

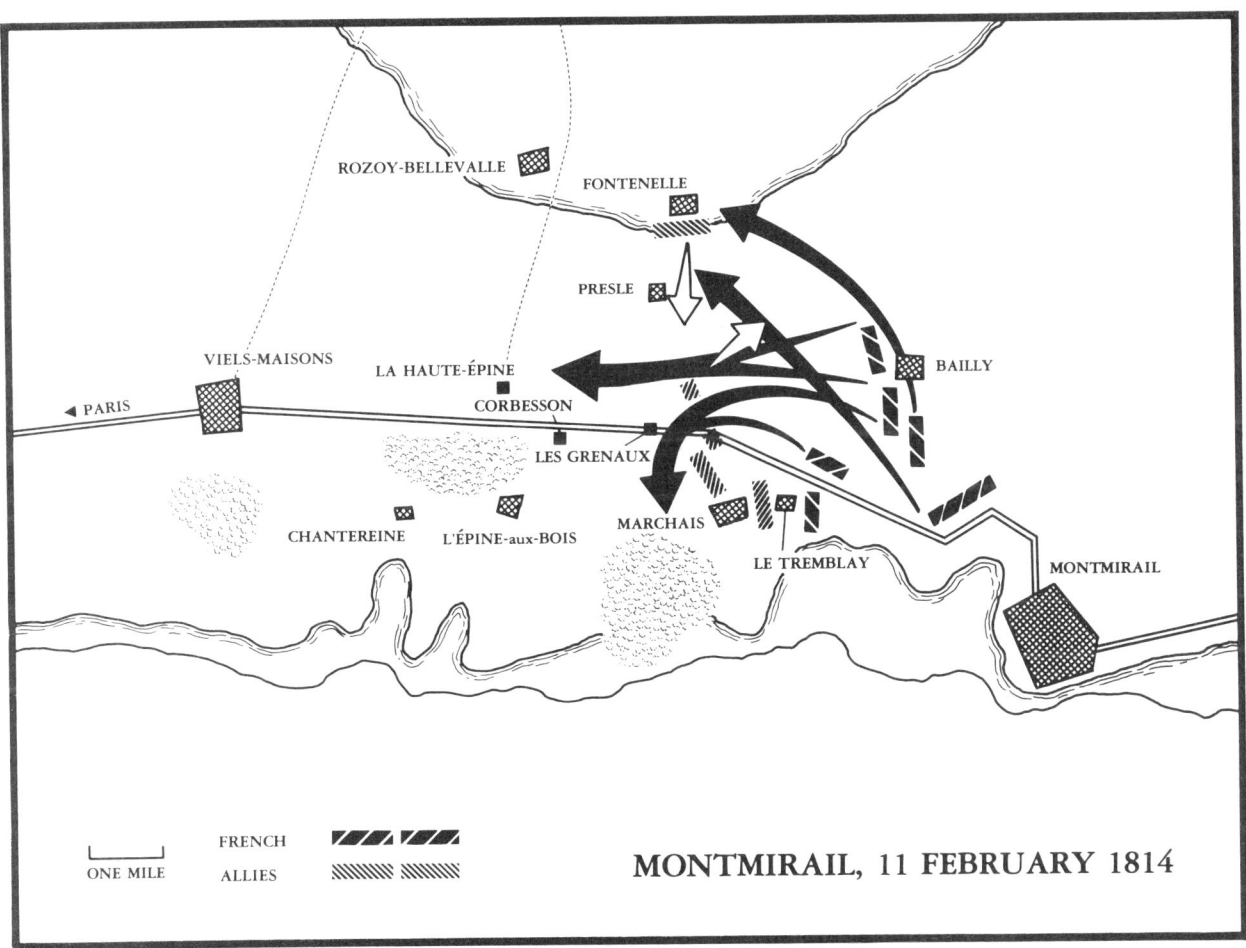

MONTMIRAIL, 11 FEBRUARY 1814

Napoleon continued his pursuit of General Osten Sacken's defeated troops but stopped at Chateau-Thierry on February 12, 1814. The pursuit would have continued had it not been for the news that Prince Schwarzenberg's troops had driven the forces of Marshal Victor back over the Seine River. Taking a portion of his forces south, Napoleon moved toward Vauchamps to deal with the advancing allied troops of Blücher. The Prussian commander learned of the

French presence on February 14th when his advance guard had a skirmish with a French outpost. The engagement at Vauchamps began badly for the allies. The French cavalry managed to turn the Prussian right flank. Blücher, learning that Napoleon was approaching, immediately disengaged.

Although the allied army was constantly harassed by French cavalry, it did manage a successful withdrawal. With Blücher now retreating, Napoleon was able to continue moving south to seek Prince Schwarzenberg's troops. After a forced march, the French arrived at French Headquarters in Guignes. Schwarzenberg, learning that Napoleon was in the Austrian area of operations, felt it prudent to withdraw to the southeast.

During the next four days the French and allies clashed in a series of running battles. Quick maneuverings by the French gave them the initial advantage. However, the allied forces managed to reach Montereau where they developed strong defensive positions. Napoleon chose to engage the allies in a massive frontal assault at Montereau.

The battle of Montereau was fought on February 20, 1814. The allied forces commanded by Prince Eugen of Württemberg managed to hold their positions until mid-afternoon. The French captured a key position, however, which caused an allied withdrawal. The retreat soon became a disaster.

In the wake of the retreating Austrians, Napoleon entered Troyes on February 24, 1814. On February 25, 1814, the allied leaders met in conference at Bar-sur-Aube to discuss future strategy.

Prince Wilhelm of Prussia

Young Prince Wilhelm (later King Wilhelm I. of Prussia) at the engagement at Bar-sur-Aube, January 24, 1814.

Another allied conference held at Chaumont on March 1, 1814, resulted in the Treaty of Chaumont. By this treaty the allied leaders agreed to continue the war against Napoleon and no member of the Allied Coalition would negotiate a separate peace. The allies again offered Napoleon one last opportunity for peace, provided France return to the borders of 1791. Because of his recent victories, Napoleon again rejected this offer and immediately moved north from Troyes to engage Blücher.

* * *

* March 2, 1814 *

The following five Imperial Russian officers were decorated with the Pour le Mérite Order for distinction in action during the engagement at Bar-sur-Aube on January 24, 1814.

Imperial Russian Kaluga Infantry Regiment

1339. **Jagodovski**, Matwei Ivanovich, Imperial Russian Captain.
1340. **Kuliabka**, Ivan (?), Imperial Russian Staff Captain.
1341. **Karishev**, (First name unknown), Imperial Russian Sub-Lieutenant.

* * *

1342. **Shetochin**, Kapitan Borissovich,
      Imperial Russian Rittmeister, Lubno Hussar Regiment.

1343. **Togaitshinov**, Michail Ivanovich,
      Imperial Russian Staff Captain, 14th Artillery Battery Company.

* * *

* March 3, 1814 *

1344. **Pusin**, (First name unknown),
      Imperial Russian Lieutenant, 1st Ukraine Cossack Regiment.

* * *

Blücher, meanwhile, was engaged in an attempt to seek and destroy the French forces of Marshal Auguste Frederick Marmont and Marshal Adolphe Edouard Mortier near the city of Meaux. On learning of Napoleon's approach, Blücher ordered his forces to withdraw to the north bank of the Marne River. He also ordered the bridges destroyed to slow Napoleon down. While Napoleon was delayed by having to rebuild the destroyed bridges, it did not significantly slow his pursuit. The allied army continued to retreat, staying only one step ahead of the French. On March 4-5, 1814, the allied force crossed the Aisne River at Soissons. On March 5th, Blücher received unexpected reinforcements. By now his army numbered over 100,000.

* * *

* March 6, 1814 *

The following four Russian officers were decorated with the Pour le Mérite Order for distinction during the battle of Leipzig, October 16-19, 1813.

Imperial Russian Siberian Grenadier Regiment

1345. **Deskur (Descours)**, Ivan Ivanovich, Imperial Russian Major, Commander.
      (**Note**: This is the <u>first</u> award of the Pour le Mérite Order to Major Deskur. For the <u>second</u> award of the Pour le Mérite Order see entry 2163, this chapter.)

* * *

1346. **Potulov**, Ivan Terentieovich, Imperial Russian Major.

(**Note**: This is the <u>first</u> award of the Pour le Mérite Order to Major Potulov. For the second award of the Pour le Mérite Order see entry 2164, this chapter.)
* * *

Imperial Russian Malo-Russia Grenadier Regiment

1347. **Brandt**, Johann (Ivan Ivanovich), Imperial Russian Major.
(**Note**: This is the <u>first</u> award of the Pour le Mérite Order to Major Johann Brandt. For the second award of the Pour le Mérite Order see entry 2165, this chapter.)
* * *

1348. **Makuchin**, (First name unknown), Imperial Russian Staff Captain, serving as Brigade Adjutant to Major General Hesse.
(**Note**: This is the <u>first</u> award of the Pour le Mérite Order to Staff Captain Makuchin. For the second award of the Pour le Mérite Order see entry 2166, this chapter.)
* * *

On March 6, 1814, Napoleon made contact with Blücher's forces near the town of Craonne, and the battle commenced during the morning hours of March 7th. Napoleon intended to hold the allies attention by large scale frontal assaults while a strong element of the French army moved in from the north and south to outflank and surround Blücher's troops. Due to the mistiming of Marshal Ney, the French attack failed, and Blücher was able to disengage and retreat to the city of Laon.

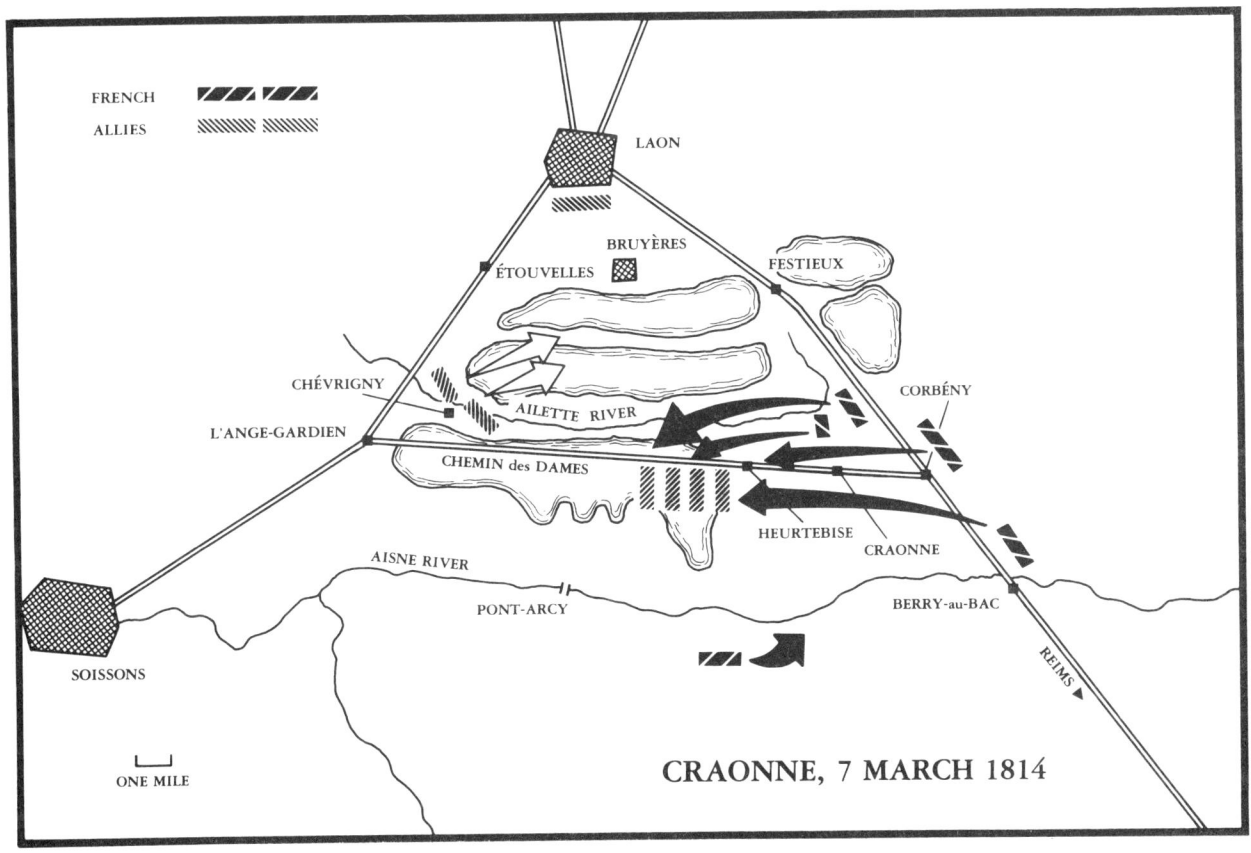

CRAONNE, 7 MARCH 1814

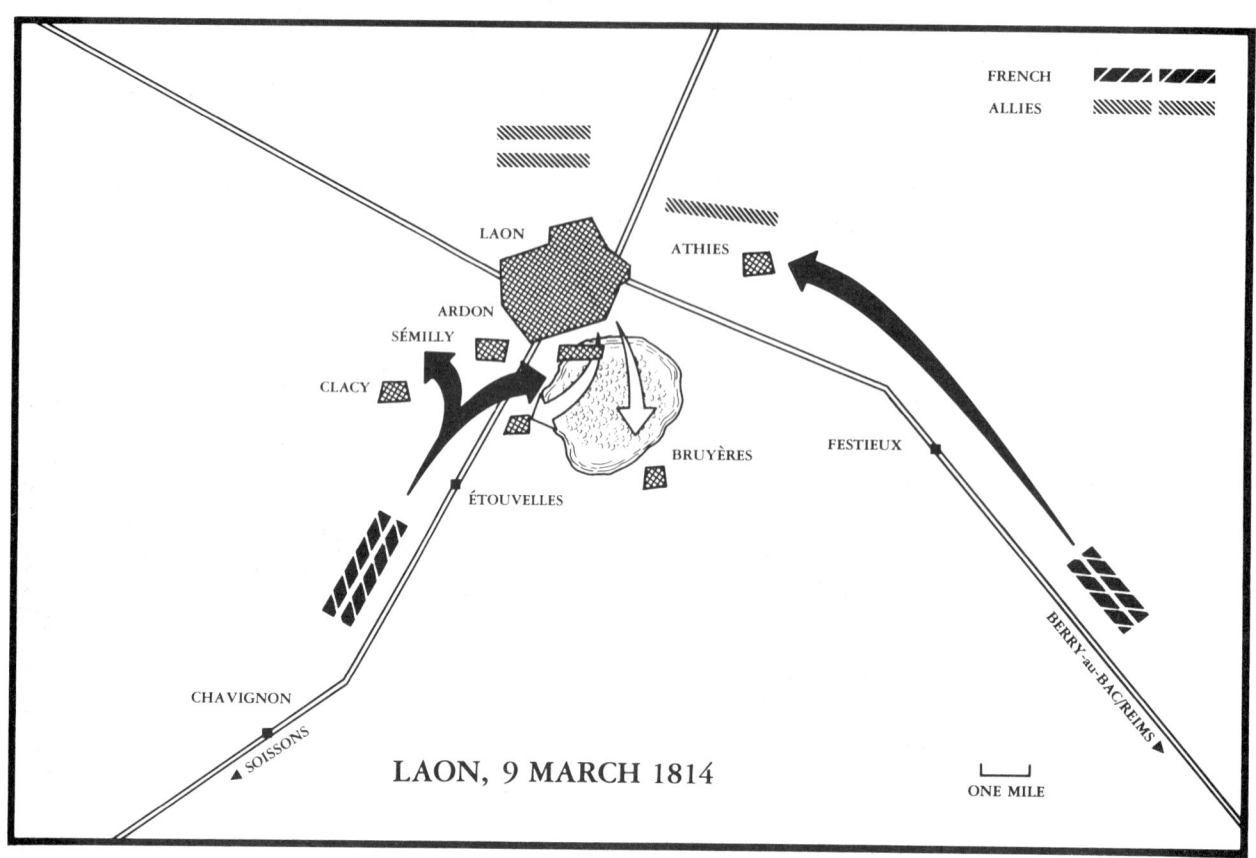

LAON, 9 MARCH 1814

* March 7, 1814 *

The following two Imperial Russian officers were serving as adjutants to Russian General of Infantry Count Barclay de Tolly.

1349. **Rostopshin**, Count Sergei Fedorovich,
   Imperial Russian Lieutenant, Cavalier Guard Regiment.

1350. **von Essen**, Alexander Filippovich,
   Imperial Russian Lieutenant, Life Guard Uhlan Regiment.

* * *

1351. **Muraviev**, Alexander Sacharieovich,
   Imperial Russian Staff Captain, Quartermaster Service.

1352. **Muraviev**, Artamon Sacharieovich,
   Imperial Russian Lieutenant, Engineer Corps.

* * *

Blücher reached Laon, and selected strong defensive positions south of the city to await the arrival of Napoleon. The two armies made contact on March 9, 1814, and the battle of Laon commenced. For most of the day Napoleon launched a series of frontal attacks. Marshal Marmont moved to turn the allied right flank. However, his movement was slow and achieved no advantage for Napoleon. A surprise attack by the allies completely routed the French troops of Marmont, but they were able to retreat somewhat intact. Learning of Marmont's defeat, Napoleon decided to disengage from the battle and begin withdrawing south.

* * *

* March 9, 1814 *

1353. **Pushkarev**, Fedor Nikolaieovich,
　　　Imperial Russian Colonel, Commander Pskov Curassier Regiment.

　　　　　　　* * *

A series of successful engagements by Blücher and other allied forces managed to persuade the allies to continue the advance on Paris.

Blücher's March on Paris

Note: This is a rather stylized engraving of Blücher's march on Paris. Note that the Marshal is wearing the Grand Cross of the Prussian Iron Cross which actually was not awarded to him until after Waterloo in 1815.

　　　　　　　* * *

* March 19, 1814 *

1354. **Pantenius**, Fedor Ivanovich,
   Imperial Russian Colonel, Honorary Colonel of the 27th Light Infantry Regiment.

1355. **Kovrigin**, Michail Avramovich,
   Imperial Russian Colonel, Commander, 5th Light Infantry Regiment.
   (For distinction in action at Leipzig on October 18, 1813.)

1356. **Bernikov**, Pavel Sergieieovich,
   Imperial Russian Lt. Colonel, Orlov Infantry Regiment.
   (For distinction in action by being one of the first officers to lead troops into Leipzig during the battle, October 19, 1813.)

1357. **Shuchov**, Andrei Petrovich,
   Imperial Russian Lt. Colonel, Commander, Veliki-Luzk Infantry Regiment.
   (For distinction in action during the capture of Leipzig.)

1358. **Bogdanovski**, Andrei Vassilieovich,
   Imperial Russian Lt. Colonel, Commander, Narva Infantry Regiment.
   (For distinction in action during the storming and capture of Leipzig.)

1359. **von Rennenkampff**, Gustaf Magnus,
   Imperial Russian Lt. Colonel, Commander, Smolensk Infantry Regiment.
   (For distinction in action during the storming and capture of Leipzig.)

1360. **Figner**, Alexander Samoilovich,
   Imperial Russian Lt. Colonel, 2nd Mounted Company of the Life Guard Artillery Brigade.
   (For distinction in action during the engagements at Wurzen on October 16, Leipzig on October 18, and Magdeburg on November 9, 1813.)

1361. **Butkovski**, Nikolai Jakovleovich,
   Imperial Russian Lt. Colonel, Quartermaster Service.
   (For distinction in action during the capture of Leipzig on October 19, 1813, where this officer was severely wounded.)
   * * *

1362. **Tolstoi**, (First name unknown),
   Imperial Russian Colonel, 30th Light Infantry Regiment.
   (**Special Note**: Military research of the Napoleonic era by a Captain Ilienko, which was published in August 1901, produces a question concerning the above-named officer's unit assignment. This research indicated that between the years 1807 and 1818, a Colonel Tolstoi was serving in a unit other than the one indicated. In the Order of Battle of the Polish Army under Russian General Bennigsen, this Light Infantry Regiment was not found. Perhaps Colonel Tolstoi was serving in an Opoltshenie (militia) unit. On March 13, 1813, a Count Tolstoi of the Moscow Opoltshenie was assigned to the Ladoga Infantry Regiment. It is possible that the Ladoga Infantry Regiment was attached to the Polish Army whereas the 30th Light Infantry Regiment was assigned to the 17th Division of the Silesian Army.)
   * * *

Blücher and his Prussian troops approaching Paris in 1814.

1363. **Klebek**, Baron Igor Jermolaieovich,
   Imperial Russian Colonel, Mariupol Hussar Regiment.
   (For distinction in action during the battle of Leipzig.)

1364. **Kolotinski**, Konstantin Michailovich,
   Imperial Russian Colonel, Commander, 22nd Artillery Battery Company.
   (For distinction in action at Leipzig on October 19, 1813.)

1365. **Roszner von Roszenegg**, Frhr. Josef,
   Imperial Austrian Lt. Colonel, serving on the Quartermaster General's Staff.
   (For distinction in action at Magdeburg on November 9, 1813.)

1366. **Golizin**, Prince Alexander Sergieieovich,
   Imperial Russian Staff Captain, Life Guard Semenovski Regiment, Senior Adjutant to General of Cavalry Count von Bennigsen.
   (For distinction in action by "serving tirelessly and with outstanding bravery.")

* * *

The following two Russian officers were decorated with the Pour le Mérite Order in recognition of distinction in action while serving as adjutants to General of Cavalry Count von Bennigsen.

1367. **von der Hoven**, Igor Fedorovich,
   Imperial Russian Colonel, 22nd Mounted Artillery Company.

1368. **Dmitriev**, Ivan Dmitrieovich,
   Imperial Russian Colonel, Perm Opoltshenie (militia).

* * *

1369. **Armfelt**, Count Gustaf Gustafovich,
   Imperial Russian Staff Captain, Quartermaster Service.
   (**Special Note**: The Pour le Mérite Order awarded to Staff Captain Armfelt for distinction in action on this date was revoked and returned on April 16, 1857, an incredible <u>43</u> years later. No reason for this revocation is known.)

* * *

On March 28, 1814, Napoleon started for Paris but was 10 miles short of the city when, on March 31st, he learned that the city of Paris had surrendered to the allies.

* * *

The Battle of Montmirail

* March 31, 1814 *

1370. **von Kleist**, Friedrich Emilius Ferdinand Heinrich,
   Lt. General and Commanding General of the II. Army Corps.
   (**Note**: Lt. General von Kleist was awarded the Oahleaves to the Pour le Mérite Order for outstanding leadership during this campaign. For the initial award of the Pour le Mérite Order see Volume I, Chapter IV, entry 234, p. 159.)
   * * *

1371. **von Alvensleben**, Johann Friedrich Karl,
   (**Note**: Colonel von Alvensleben was awarded <u>both</u> the Pour le Mérite Order <u>and</u> the Oakleaves to the Pour le Mérite Order for outstanding leadership and distinction in action during several engagements against the French.)
   * * *

1372. **Neidhardt von Gneisenau**, Wilhelm August Anton,
   Lt. General and Quartermaster General, Chief of the General Staff of the Silesian Army.
   (**Note**: Lt. General von Gneisenau was awarded the Oakleaves to the Pour le Mérite Order for outstanding leadership and distinction in action during this campaign. For the initial award of the Pour le Mérite Order see Volume I, Chapter V-1, entry 418, p. 296.)
   * * *

Allies entering Paris April 1814.

Grand Duchy of Baden Grenadier Guard Regiment

1373. **von Kageneck**, Frhr Karl, Grand Duchy of Baden Major.
1374. **von Mach**, August Friedrich, Grand Duchy of Baden 1st Lieutenant.
   * * *

Imperial Russian Lubno Hussar Regiment

The following four Russian officers were decorated with the Pour le Mérite Order for distinction in action during the engagement at Wachau on October 4-16, 1813.

1375. **Pokrovski**, Jevstafi Charitonovich, Imperial Russian Colonel, Sum Hussar Regiment, serving in the above regiment.
(**Note**: This is the <u>first</u> award of the Pour le Mérite Order to Colonel Pokrovski. For the second award of the Pour le Mérite Order see entry 2148, this chapter.)
* * *

1376. **Koletshizki**, Ivan Nikolaieovich, Imperial Russian Rittmeister.
(**Note**: This is the <u>first</u> award of the Pour le Mérite Order to Rittmeister Koletshizki. For the second award of the Pour le Mérite Order, see entry 2149, this chapter.)
* * *

1377. **Preiss**, Nikolai Ivanovich, Imperial Russian Staff Rittmeister.
(**Note**: This is the <u>first</u> award of the Pour le Mérite Order to Rittmeister Preiss. For the second award of the Pour le Mérite Order see entry 2151, this chapter.)
* * *

1378. **Filipov**, Alexei Alexieieovich, Imperial Russian Cornet.
(**Note**: This is the <u>first</u> award of the Pour le Mérite Order to Cornet Filipov. For the second award of the Pour le Mérite Order see entry 2153, this chapter.)
* * *

Bivouac of Russian Troops in the Champs Elysées, 1814.

Napoleon returned to Fontainebleau where he started making plans to recapture Paris. However, his Marshals urged him to abdicate. Napoleon refused, whereupon Marshal Ney confronted him on April 3, 1814, and informed him that the Marshals and the army would not march on Paris. After three days Napoleon realized that his position was hopeless, and he drafted an unconditional abdication which he signed on April 6, 1814. After several days of negotiations the allies accepted the abdication of Napoleon and on April 16, 1814, signed the Treaty of Fontainebleau. Napoleon was allowed to retain the title of Emperor, was granted an annual allowance, and given the island of Elba. He departed Fontainebleau on April 20, 1814, for his exile on Elba.

* * *

* April 3, 1814 *

1379. **von Hake**, Karl Georg Albrecht Ernst,
   Major General and Chief of the War Department, serving at the Headquarters of Field Marshal Prince von Schwarzenberg.
   (**Note**: Major General von Hake was awarded the Oakleaves to the Pour le Mérite Order for distinguished planning and outstanding leadership during this campaign. For the initial award of the Pour le Mérite Order see Volume I, Chapter IV, entry 488, p. 182.)

* * *

* April 4, 1814 *

1380. **von Rosen**, Count Karl Axel,
   Royal Swedish Lieutenant, Schonen Karabinier Regiment, Adjutant to General Frhr. Adelcreutz.
   (For distinction in action during the battle of Leipzig.)

* * *

* April 9, 1814 *

1381. **von Müffling**, Wilhelm,
   Lt. Colonel, Commander, 2nd Guard Infantry Regiment.
   (**Note**: Lt. Colonel Müffling was awarded **both** the Pour le Mérite Order **and** the Oakleaves to the Pour le Mérite Order on this date for distinction in action and outstanding leadership during an engagement at Pantin in the vicinity of Paris on March 30, 1814.)

* * *

1382. **von Beust**, Frhr. Franz Josef,
   Grand Duchy of Baden Lt. Colonel, Commander, Grenadier Guard Regiment.
   (For distinction in action during the engagement at Pantin outside Paris on March 30, 1814.)

1383. **von Hohenzollern-Hechingen**, Prince Friedrich Adalbert,
   Imperial Austrian Rittmeister, Archduke Konstantin Curassier Regiment, serving as adjutant to Archduke Konstantin.

* * *

* April 10, 1814 *

1384. **Lowe**, Sir Hudson,
   British Colonel, Royal Corsican Rangers.
   (**Note**: Colonel Lowe was serving as a British liaison officer attached to the headquarters of the Silesian Army. He was decorated with the Pour le Mérite Order for distinction in action during the battle at Möckern on October 16, 1813.)

* * *

* April 11, 1814 *

The following four Imperial Russian officers received the Pour le Merite Order for distinction in action during the engagement at Brienne on January 29, 1814.

1385. **Karatshinski**, Ivan (Vassilieovich?),
   Imperial Russian Staff Captain, 19th Light Artillery Company.
   (**Note**: This is the <u>first</u> award of the Pour le Mérite Order to Staff Captain Karatshinski. For the second award of the Pour le Mérite Order see entry 2278, this chapter.)

* * *

Imperial Russian 7th Mounted Artillery Company

1386. **Barateiev II.**, Prince Peter Semenovich, Imperial Russian Staff Captain.
1387. **Read**, Jakob Andreieovich, Imperial Russian Lieutenant, Adjutant to Russian Major General Nikitin.

* * *

1388. **Katshoni**, Likurg Lambrovich,
   Imperial Russian Lieutenant, 18th Mounted Artillery Company, Adjutant to Russian Major General Nikitin.

* * *

1389. **von Korff**, Baron Nikolai Ivanovich,
   Imperial Russian Lieutenant, Life Guard 2nd Mounted Artillery Company.
   (**Note**: Lieutenant von Korff was awarded the 50 Year Jubilee Golden Crown to the Pour le Mérite order on October 25, 1864.)

* * *

Pour le Mérite Order Awards Given for the Battle of Kulm

All of the following 120 Imperial Russian officers were decorated with the Pour le Mérite Order for distinction in action during the battle at Kulm on August 29-30, 1813.

Imperial Russian Life Guard Preobrashenski Regiment

1390. **Karzov**, Pavel Stepanovich, Imperial Russian Colonel.
1391. **von Tucholka**, Leo Josef, Imperial Russian Colonel.
1392. **Titov I.**, Vladimir Michailovich, Imperial Russian Colonel.
1393. **Titov II.**, Nikolai Michailovich, Imperial Russian Colonel.
1394. **von Witte I.**, Ivan Ossipovich, Imperial Russian Captain.
1395. **Gudovich**, Count Nikolai Nikolaieovich, Imperial Russian Captain.
1396. **von Pirch I.**, Karl Karlovich, Imperial Russian Captain.
1397. **Potulov V.**, Peter, Imperial Russian Staff Captain.
1398. **Demiankov**, Parfeni Semenovich, Imperial Russian Staff Captain.
1399. **Ushakov I.**, Michail Andreieovich, Imperial Russian Staff Captain.
1400. **Korobin III.**, Porfiri Pavlovich, Imperial Russian Lieutenant.
1401. **Titov IV.**, Ivan Alexandrovich, Imperial Russian Sub-Lieutenant.
1402. **Tiutshev I.**, Afanassi Petrovich, Imperial Russian Officer Candidate.
1403. **Tiutshev II.**, Alexei Petrovich, Imperial Russian Officer Candidate.

* * *

Imperial Russian Life Guard Semenovski Regiment

1404. **Kostomarov**, Sergei Andreieovich, Imperial Russian Colonel.
1405. **Patkul**, Vladimir Grigorieovich, Imperial Russian Colonel.
1406. **Broglio de Revel I.**, Prince Alfons Gabriel, Imperial Russian Colonel.

1407. **Tsheodaiev**, Michail Jakovleovich, Imperial Russian Sub-Lieutenant.
1408. **Vadkovski II.**, Pavel Fedorovich, Imperial Russian Officer Candidate.
1409. **Jermolov**, Peter Nikolaieovich, Imperial Russian Staff Captain, serving as Adjutant to Russian Lt. General Jermolov.

* * *

Imperial Russian Life Guard Ismailov Regiment

1410. **Mordvinov II.**, Ivan Nikolaiovich, Imperial Russian Colonel.
1411. **Tshagin**, Nikolai Gavrilovich, Imperial Russian Lieutenant.
1412. **Krupenin**, Vladimir Pavlovich, Imperial Russian Sub-Lieutenant.
1413. **Bikov III.**, Peter Michailovich, Imperial Russian Officer Candidate.
1414. **Kashinzov II.**, Porfiri Sergieieovich, Imperial Russian Officer Candidate.
1415. **Samuizki**, Nikolai Ivanovich, Imperial Russian Officer Candidate.
1416. **Sholobov**, (First name unknown), Imperial Russian Officer Candidate.
1417. **Muromzov**, Matvei Matvieieovich, Imperial Russian Lieutenant, serving as Adjutant to Russian Lt. General Jermolov.

* * *

Imperial Russian Life Guard Light Infantry Regiment

1418. **Pietin**, Ivan Alexandrovich, Imperial Russian Colonel.
1419. **Rall III.**, Fedor Fedorovich, Imperial Russian Colonel.
1420. **Penskoi IV.**, Ivan Ivanovich, Imperial Russian Captain.
1421. **van Suchtelen**, Konstantin Petrovich, Imperial Russian Staff Captain.
1422. **Koslovski**, Prince Vladimir Nikolaieovich, Imperial Russian Lieutenant.
1423. **Ushakov**, Nikolai Pavlovich, Imperial Russian Lieutenant.
1424. **Krivzov**, Nikolai Ivanovich, Imperial Russian Lieutenant.
1425. **Baturin**, Sergei Gerassimovich, Imperial Russian Lieutenant.
1426. **Korssakov I.**, Pavel Matvieieovich, Imperial Russian Lieutenant.
1427. **Frolov-Bagrieiev**, Viktor Alexieieovich, Imperial Russian Lieutenant.
1428. **Krilov**, Dmitri Sergieieovich, Imperial Russian Lieutenant.
1429. **von Strandmann**, Karl Otto Wilhelm, Imperial Russian Lieutenant.
1430. **Jermolov**, Michail Alexandrovich, Imperial Russian Lieutenant.
1431. **Bornovolokov**, Alexander Petrovich, Imperial Russian Officer Candidate.

* * *

1432. **Karzov I.**, Ivan Petrovich,
    Imperial Russian Captain, Commander, Guard Equipage.

* * *

Imperial Russian Life Guard Hussar Regiment

1433. **Korovkin**, Arseni Jermolaieovich, Imperial Russian Colonel.
1434. **Bakaiev II.**, Michail Ivanovich, Imperial Russian Rittmeister.
1435. **Krekshin**, Dmitri Ivanovich, Imperial Russian Rittmeister.
1436. **Davidov**, Dmitri Vassilieovich, Imperial Russian Staff Rittmeister.
1437. **Ukinsiev**, Fedor Vladimirovich, Imperial Russian Staff Rittmeister.
1438. **Molostvov**, Panfemir Christoforovich, Imperial Russian Lieutenant.
1439. **Dmitriev-Mamonov**, Alexander Ivanovich, Imperial Russian Lieutenant.
1440. **Chomiakov**, (First name unknown), Imperial Russian Staff Rittmeister, Senior Adjutant to Lt. General Shevich.

* * *

Imperial Russian His Majesty's Life Guard Curassier Regiment

1441. **Kostin**, Nikolai Grigorieovich, Imperial Russian Lt. Colonel.
1442. **Chitrovo**, Vassili Jelissieovich, Imperial Russian Lt. Colonel.
1443. **Levtshenko**, Fedor Grigorieovich, Imperial Russian Rittmeister.
1444. **Ampach**, Pavel Adamovich, Imperial Russian Lieutenant.

1445. **Lingren**, Jevstafi Maximovich, Imperial Russian Lieutenant.
1446. **Bielogradski**, Jemelian Ossipovich, Imperial Russian Cornet.

* * *

Imperial Russian Her Majesty's Guard Curassier Regiment

1447. **von Koschembahr**, Lev Ivanovich, Imperial Russian Lt. Colonel.
1448. **Schlippenbach**, Baron Anton Andreieovich, Imperial Russian Rittmeister.

* * *

1449. **Vonliarliarski**, Ivan Andreieovich,
 Imperial Russian Major, Araktsheiev Grenadier Regiment.
 (**Note**: Major Vonliarliarski was awarded the 50 Year Jubilee Golden Crown to the Pour le Mérite Order on March 9, 1867.)

* * *

Imperial Russian Ekaterinoslav Grenadier Regiment

1450. **Kushin**, Vassili Vassilieovich, Imperial Russian Lt. Colonel.
1451. **Alissov**, (First name unknown), Imperial Russian Staff Captain.
1452. **Prosorkevich**, Lavrenti Jakovleovich, Imperial Russian Staff Captain.
1453. **Labutin**, (First name unknown), Imperial Russian Sub-Lieutenant.
1454. **Pleski**, Wilhelm Antonovich, Imperial Russian Sub-Lieutenant.
1455. **Kurdiumov**, Igor Sergieieovich, Imperial Russian Sub-Lieutenant.
1456. **Jannau II.**, Grigori Ivanovich, Imperial Russian Sub-Lieutenant.

* * *

Imperial Russian Tauri Grenadier Regiment

1457. **Jurgeniev II.**, Peter Michailovich, Imperial Russian Major.
1458. **Vissitski**, Jevgraf Stepanovich, Imperial Russian Major.
1459. **Lappa**, Peter Pavlovich, Imperial Russian Major.
1460. **Jershov**, Ivan Sacharovich, Imperial Russian Captain.
1461. **Rubzov**, Peter Igorovich, Imperial Russian Staff Captain.
1462. **Licharev**, Afanassi, Imperial Russian Lieutenant.
1463. **Mortshalov**, Ivan Pavlovich, Imperial Russian Lieutenant.
1464. **Sabudski**, Ivan Grigorieovich, Imperial Russian Lieutenant.
1465. **Kusmin**, Nikita Petrovich, Imperial Russian Officer Candidate.
1466. **Vikinski**, Ivan Michailovich, Imperial Russian Sub-Lieutenant.
 (**Note**: Lieutenant Vikinski was awarded the 50 Year Jubilee Golden Crown to the Pour le Mérite Order on October 25, 1864.)

* * *

1467. **Chvostovski**, Nikolai Alexandrovich,
 Imperial Russian Staff Captain, St. Petersburg Grenadier Regiment.
 (**Note**: Staff Captain Chvostovski was awarded the 50 Year Jubilee Golden Crown to the Pour le Mérite Order on November 16, 1865.)

* * *

Imperial Russian Kexholm Grenadier Regiment

1468. **Uvarov**, Fedor Fedorovich, Imperial Russian Captain.
1469. **Danilov**, Dmitri Petrovich, Imperial Russian Captain.
1470. **Nikiforov**, Michail Kusmitsh, Imperial Russian Staff Captain.
1471. **Tretiakov**, Jakob Matvieieovich, Imperial Russian Staff Captain.

* * *

Imperial Russian Pernau Grenadier Regiment

1472. **Tshumakov**, Peter Pavlovich, Imperial Russian Major.
1473. **Meknob**, (First name unknown), Imperial Russian Staff Captain.
1474. **Laveika**, Alexander Jakovleovich, Imperial Russian Staff Captain.

1475. **Kostirev**, Nikolai Ivanovich,
    Imperial Russian Sub-Lieutenant, Grand Duchess Katharina Battalion.

* * *

Imperial Russian Murom Infantry Regiment

1476. **Goloshtshapov**, Alexei, Imperial Russian Major.
1477. **Chartshenko-Denissenko**, Alexei Ivanovich, Imperial Russian Staff Captain.
1478. **Sochazki**, Michail Nikolaieovich, Imperial Russian Staff Captain.

* * *

Imperial Russian Tobolski Infantry Regiment

1479. **Bergmann**, Jermolai Astafieovich, Imperial Russian Lt. Colonel.
1480. **Mellard**, Karl Karlovich, Imperial Russian Lieutenant.
1481. **Damitsh**, Feodossi Ivanovich, Imperial Russian Sub-Lieutenant.
1482. **Gleitzmann**, Fedor Astafieovich, Imperial Russian Officer Candidate.

* * *

Imperial Russian Krementshug Infantry Regiment

1483. **Rassochin**, (First name unknown), Imperial Russian Lieutenant.
1484. **Bulashov**, (First name unknown), Imperial Russian Lieutenant.
1485. **Lepechin**, (First name unknown), Imperial Russian Sub-Lieutenant.
1486. **Afanassiev**, (First name unknown), Imperial Russian Sub-Lieutenant.

* * *

Imperial Russian Tenga Infantry Regiment

1487. **Bellinghausen**, Baron Fedor Christoforovich, Imperial Russian Colonel.
1488. **Oserski**, (First name unknown), Imperial Russian Captain.
1489. **Novizki**, (First name unknown), Imperial Russian Lieutenant.
1490. **Bruslianski**, Ivan Ivanovich, Imperial Russian Officer Candidate.

* * *

Notes:

Imperial Russian 4th Light Infantry Regiment

1491. **Krasinski**, Leonid Yuriovich, Imperial Russian Sub-Lieutenant.
1492. **Ivanov**, Stepan Emelianovich, Imperial Russian Lt. Colonel,
   presently serving with the 20th Light Infantry Regiment.
   (Note: This is the <u>second</u> award of the Pour le Mérite Order <u>badge</u> awarded to Lt. Colonel Ivanov for distinction in action during the battle of Kulm on August 30, 1813. For the initial award of the Pour le Mérite Order see entry 776, this chapter.)

* * *

Imperial Russian 26th Light Infantry Regiment

1493. **Fedosseiev**, Michail Dmitrieovich, Imperial Russian Major.
1494. **Lour**, Ivan Ivanovich, Imperial Russian Staff Captain.
1495. **Striabin**, Fedor Jermolaieovich, Imperial Russian Sub-Lieutenant.
1496. **Medviedev**, Alexei Dmitrieovich, Imperial Russian Sub-Lieutenant.
1497. **Grusinov**, (First name unknown), Imperial Russian Officer Candidate.
1498. **Antonovski**, Anton Ivanovich, Imperial Russian Staff Captain,
   (Note: Staff Captain Antonovski was awarded the 50 Year Jubilee Golden Crown to the Pour le Mérite Order on October 25, 1864.)

* * *

Imperial Russian Tatari Uhlan Regiment

1499. **von Vietinghoff**, (First name unknown), Imperial Russian Major,
   (Note: This is the <u>second</u> award of the Pour le Mérite Order <u>badge</u> to Major von Vietinghoff for distinction in action during the battle at Kulm on August 30, 1813. For the initial award of the Pour le Mérite Order see entry 1119, this chapter.)

* * *

1500. **Sablozki**, Ivan Danilovich, Imperial Russian Lieutenant.
1501. **Risvanovich I.**, Chalil Ivanovich, Imperial Russian Lieutenant.
1502. **Romanovski II.**, Matvei Mustafovich, Imperial Russian Lieutenant.

* * *

Imperial Russian Life Guard Artillery Brigade

1503. **Ladigin**, Nikolai Ivanovich, Imperial Russian Colonel.

* * *

Imperial Russian 3rd Mounted Artillery Company

1504. **von Gerbel III.**, Karl Gustafovich, Imperial Russian Staff Captain,
   (Note: This is the <u>first</u> award of the Pour le Mérite Order for distinction in action to Staff Captain Von Gerbel III. For the second award of the Pour le Mérite Order see entry 1664, this chapter.)

* * *

1505. **Potemkin I.**, Alexander Dmitrieovich, Imperial Russian Lieutenant.

* * *

1506. **Sinelnikov**, Alexander Nikita,
   Imperial Russian Staff Captain, 13th Light Artillery Company.

1507. **Naumov**, Sergei Alexandrovich, Imperial Russian Lieutenant, Guard Equipage, Senior Adjutant of the V. Infantry (Guard) Corps.

1508. **de Grossard**, Baron Jean Baptiste Louis,
   Imperial Russian Colonel, Quartermaster Service, Deputy Chief of the General Staff of Grand Duke Konstantin of Russia.

1509. **Menshikov**, Prince Alexander Sergieieovich,
>Imperial Russian Colonel, Life Guard Preobrashenski Regiment and Wing Adjutant.
>(**Note**: Prince Menshikov was awarded the 50 Year Jubilee Golden Crown to the Pour lr Mérite Order on January 22, 1863.)

* * *

* April 12, 1814 *

1510. **Murat Bieiev**, Saltan Davliet,
>Imperial Russian Cossack Chorunshi(?), Tsherni Subov I. Cossack Regiment, Army of the Don.
>(**Special Note**: Cossack Murat Bieiev was originally awarded the Prussian Silver Military Merit Medal 2nd Class for distinction in action on October 21, 1813. However, the order awarding this medal to him was rescinded and this officer was decorated with the Pour le Mérite Order on this date.)

* * *

* April 13, 1814 *

Imperial Russian 6th Light Artillery Company

1511. **Jaminski**, Nikonor Vassilieovich, Imperial Russian Staff Captain,
>(**Note**: This is the <u>first</u> award of the Pour le Mérite Order to Staff Captain Jaminski for distinction in action. For the second award of the Pour le Mérite Order see entry 1657, this chapter.)

1512. **Karpov**, Alexei Karpovich, Imperial Russian Sub-Lieutenant.
>(Awarded the Pour le Mérite Order for distinction in action during the fierce cavalry engagement against the French at Fère-Champénoise on March 13, 1814.)

* * *

1513. **Lappa**, Wilhelm Michailovich,
>Imperial Russian Staff Captain, 33rd Artillery Battery Company.
>(Awarded the Pour le Mérite Order for outstanding leadership and distinction in action during the bombardment of the French line during the engagement at Fère-Champénoise in support of the allied cavalry on March 13, 1814.)

* * *

1514. **von der Goltz**, Count Karl Friedrich Heinrich,
>Major General and Adjutant to GFM von Blücher.
>(**Note**: Awarded the Oakleaves to the Pour le Mérite Order for outstanding leadership and distinction during the battles at Brienne on January 29, 1814, and at La Rothière on February 1, 1814. General von der Goltz was first awarded the Pour le Mérite Order in 1794, <u>20</u> years previously. For the initial award of the Pour le Mérite Order see Volume I, Chapter IV, entry 616, p. 194.)

* * *

* April 18, 1814 *

1515. **Lechner**, Andrei Andreieovich,
>Imperial Russian Colonel, Engineer Corps, Adjutant to General of Engineers van Suchtelen.
>(**Note**: Colonel Lechner was awarded the 50 Year Jubilee Golden Crown to the Pour le Mérite Order on October 25, 1864.)

* * *

1516. **Dubois Descours, Marquis de la Maisonfort,**
    Imperial Russian Staff Captain, Quartermaster Service,
    serving on the staff of Emperor Alexander I. of Russia.

* * *

1517. **von Wedell**, Karl August Ludwig,
    2nd Lieutenant, 2nd Garde Infantry Regiment.
    (**Special Note:** Lieutenant von Wedell was awarded the Pour le Mérite Order for distinction in action on March 30, 1814. He was severely wounded during the action having both legs shattered requiring amputation. As the field surgeon removed one leg, Lieutenant von Wedell, being still conscious, said, "that is for my king." When the other leg was removed, he uttered, "and that one is for my fatherland." Unfortunately, von Wedell did not survive his severe wounds and died on April 27, 1814. Of interest is the fact that due to his death, von Wedell was the only Prussian officer who did not receive the Oakleaves to the Pour le Mérite Order during the "Liberation Wars" of 1813-1815.)

* * *

* April 24, 1814 *

The following four Russian officers were awarded the Pour le Mérite Order for distinction in action during the battle at Kulm on August 30, 1813, while serving as adjutants to Russian General of Cavalry Prince Golizin V.

Imperial Russian Cavalier Guard Regiment

1518. **Nekludov**, Sergei Petrovich, Imperial Russian Staff Rittmeister.
    (**Note:** Staff Rittmeister Nekludov was awarded the 50 Year Jubilee Golden Crown to the Pour le Mérite Order on April 18, 1871.)

1519. **Bashmakov**, Dmitri Jevlampieovich, Imperial Russian Staff Rittmeister.

* * *

Imperial Russian Life Guard Dragoon Regiment

1520. **Latshinov**, Alexander Petrovich, Imperial Russian Staff Captain.
1521. **Diakov**, Alexei Nikolaiovich, Imperial Russian Staff Rittmeister.

* * *

1522. **Apraxin**, Count Vladimir Stepanovich,
    Imperial Russian Sub-Lieutenant, Quartermaster Service, serving on the staff of Emperor Alexander I. of Russia.

* * *

1523. **Valory**, Count Franz Florentin,
    Major, retired, residing at the time in Paris.
    (**Special Note:** Former Major Valory was awarded a belated Pour le Mérite Order for outstanding leadership and distinction in action during the engagement at Beisingen on September 17, 1793, while serving in the Markgraf von Anspach-Bayreuth Dragoon Regiment. The award came 21 years late!)

* * *

* April 25, 1814 *

1524. **Treuberg**, Friedrich,
    Royal Bavarian Colonel, Commander, 9th Infantry Line Regiment.
    (Awarded the Pour le Mérite Order in recognition of outstanding leadership and distinction in action during the defense at Luisetaine

(Luisetelle) in February 1814, where a heavy French attack was repulsed. Colonel Treuberg was also a recipient of the Bavarian Military Max Joseph Order for this action. The Bavarian MMJO was the highest military honor Bavaria bestowed.)

* * *

The following seven Bavarian officers were decorated with the Pour le Mérite Order for outstanding leadership and distinction in action during the early 1814 campaigns.

1525. **Goeschl**, Ignaz,
Royal Bavarian Lt. Colonel, Bavarian unidentified Artillery Regiment.

1526. **Schmaltz**, Johann Heinrich Christian,
Royal Bavarian Rittmeister, 1st Light Cavalry Regiment.
(**Note**: Rittmeister Schmaltz was awarded the 50 Year Jubilee Golden Crown to the Pour le Mérite Order on June 18, 1864.)

* * *

1527. **von der Marck**, Josef,
Royal Bavarian Rittmeister, 6th Light Cavalry Regiment.

1528. **von Loewenstein-Wertheim-Rosenberg**, Prince Konstantin Ludwig Karl,
Royal Bavarian Lt. Colonel, unit unknown, Wing Adjutant.

1529. **von Hohenzollern-Hechingen**, Prince Johann Karl,
Royal Bavarian Major, unit unknown, Wing Adjutant.

1530. **von Thurn und Taxis**, Prince August Maria Maximilian,
Royal Bavarian Major, unit unknown, Wing Adjutant.

1531. **Besserer von Thalsingen**, Albrecht,
Royal Bavarian Major, 4th "König" Light Cavalry Regiment, 1st Adjutant to Bavarian Field Marshal Prince Karl Philipp von Wrede.

* * *

* April 27, 1814 *

1532. **Maiorov**, Alexei Ivanovich,
Imperial Russian Colonel, Engineer Corps.
(For distinction in action during the blockade of Jülich during April 1814.)

* * *

* May 6, 1814 *

The following 19 Imperial Russian officers received the Pour le Mérite Order for distinction in action during the engagement at Fère-Champénoise between March 13 and 25, 1814.

Imperial Russian Life Guard Dragoon Regiment

1533. **Klimovski**, Lev Vassilieovich, Imperial Russian Colonel.
1534. **Chilkov**, Prince Stepan Alexandrovich, Imperial Russian Colonel.
1535. **Kvitnizki**, Xenofont Fedorovich, Imperial Russian Colonel.

* * *

Imperial Russian Life Guard Uhlan Regiment

1536. **de Boissesson**, Marquis Josef Pavlovich, Imperial Russian Colonel.
1537. **Saborinski III.**, Alexander Nikiforovich, Imperial Russian Rittmeister.

1538. **Saborinski II.**, Semen Nikiforovich, Imperial Russian Rittmeister.
1539. **Meier II.**, Karl Christianovich, Imperial Russian Rittmeister.
1540. **Vuitsh II.**, Ivan Afanassieovich, Imperial Russian Rittmeister.
1541. **von Glasenapp II.**, Wilhelm Otto, Imperial Russian Rittmeister.
1542. **von Strandmann**, Karl Gustafovich, Imperial Russian Rittmeister.

* * *

Imperial Russian Life Guard Hussar Regiment

1543. **Albrecht II.**, Karl Ivanovich, Imperial Russian Colonel.
1544. **Skobelzin**, Nikolai Dmitrieovich, Imperial Russian Colonel,
    (**Note**: This is the <u>first</u> award of the Pour le Mérite Order to Colonel Skobelzin for outstanding leadership and distinction in action. For the second award of the Pour le Mérite Order see entry 1563, this chapter.)

1545. **Yushkov**, Ossip Ivanovich, Imperial Russian Lieutenant.
1546. **Kruglikov**, Ivan Gavrilovich, Imperial Russian Lieutenant, serving as Adjutant to Russian Lt. General Count Osharovski.

* * *

Imperial Russian 1st Mounted Life Guard Artillery Company

1547. **Stalipin**, Dmitri Alexieieovich, Imperial Russian Colonel, Commander.
    (**Note**: This is the <u>first</u> award of the Pour le Mérite Order for distinction in action to Colonel Stalipin. For the second award of the Pour le Mérite Order see entry 2108, this chapter.)

1548. **Gerstenzweig**, Danilo Alexandrovich, Imperial Russian Sub-Lieutenant.
    (**Note**: This is the <u>first</u> award of the Pour le Mérite Order to Sub-Lieutenant Gerstenzweig for distinction in action. For the second award of the Pour le Mérite Order see entry 2111, this chapter.)

* * *

Imperial Russian 2nd Mounted Life Guard Artillery Company

1549. **von Bistrom**, Filipp Antonovich, Imperial Russian Captain, Commander.
    (**Note**: This is the <u>first</u> award for distinction in action of the Pour le Mérite Order to Captain von Bistrom. For the second award of the Pour le Mérite Order see entry 2112, this chapter.)

1550. **Bartholomai**, Fedor Ivanovich, Imperial Russian Lieutenant.

* * *

1551. **Tshudovski**, Kasimir Ivanovich,
    Imperial Russian Lieutenant, Pskov Curassier Regiment, Adjutant to Russian Lt. General Count Osharovski.

* * *

Imperial Russian 21st Artillery Battery Company

The following two Russian officers were decorated with the Pour le Mérite Order for distinction in action during the battles at Gross-Beeren on August 23, 1813, and Dennewitz on September 6, 1813.

1552. **Kasin I.**, Peter Andreieovich, Imperial Russian Staff Captain.
1553. **Selezki**, Dmitri Petrovich, Imperial Russian Lieutenant.

* * *

The following three Russian officers were decorated with the Pour le Mérite Order in recognition of distinction during the battle at Leipzig on October 16-19, 1813.

1554. **Suchovo-Kobulin**, Vassili Alexandrovich,
    Imperial Russian Lt. Colonel, Commander, 10th Mounted Artillery Company.

1555. **Suchosanet III.**, Nikolai Onufrieovich,
    Imperial Russian Lieutenant, 2nd Mounted Life Guard Artillery Company.

1556. **Stroganov**, Baron Alexander Grigorieovich,
    Imperial Russian Officer Candidate, Life Guard Artillery Brigade.
    (**Note**: Baron Stroganov was awarded the 50 Year Jubilee Golden Crown to the Pour le Mérite Order on October 25, 1985.)

* * *

The following four Russian officers were given the Pour le Mérite Order for distinction in action during the battle of Leipzig on October 18, 1813.

Imperial Russian Novgorod Curassier Regiment

1557. **Kochius**, (First name unknown), Imperial Russian Lt. Colonel.
1558. **Jeropkin**, (First name unknown), Imperial Russian Major.
1559. **Solotosevski**, Peter Prokofieovich, Imperial Russian Rittmeister.

* * *

1560. **Vastianov (Vassianov)**, (First name unknown),
    Imperial Russian Lieutenant, Staro-Dubno Curassier Regiment.

* * *

1561. **Vishizki**, Michail Faddieieovich,
    Imperial Russian Staff Rittmeister, Alexandria Hussar Regiment, Adjutant to Lt. General Count de Lambert.
    (**Note**: This is the <u>first</u> award to Staff Rittmeister Vishizki of the Pour le Mérite Order for distinction in action during the battle at Fère-Champénoise on March 13, 1814. For the second award of the Pour le Mérite Order see entry 1610, this chapter.)

* * *

* May 8, 1814 *

1562. **Kunizki**, (First name unknown),
    Imperial Russian Colonel, Polni Uhlan Regiment.

* * *

Imperial Russian Life Guard Hussar Regiment

1563. **Skobelzin**, Nikolai Dmitrieovich, Imperial Russian Colonel.
    (**Note**: This is the <u>second</u> award of the Pour le Mérite Order <u>badge</u> to Colonel Skobelzin in recognition of distinction in action. For the initial award of the Pour le Mérite Order see entry 1544, this chapter.)

1564. **Jushkov**, Vladimir Ivanovich, Imperial Russian Staff Rittmeister.
    (**Note**: Staff Rittmeister Jushkov was awarded the 50 Year Jubilee Golden Crown to the Pour le Mérite Order on October 25, 1864.)

* * *

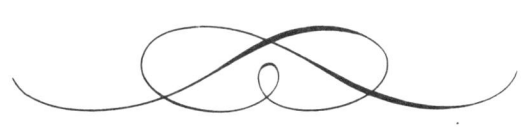

The Second Awarding of Three Pour le Mérite Orders to the Same Recipient

1565. **Sass**, Peter Andreieovich,
Imperial Russian Staff Rittmeister, Volyni Uhlan Regiment.
(**Note**: This is the <u>first</u> of <u>three</u> awards of the Pour le Mérite Order to Rittmeister Sass in recognition of distinction in action. For the second award of the Pour le Mérite Order see entry 1637 and for the third award see entry 1940, this chapter.)
* * *

1566. **Ilovaiski XVII.**, Fedor Semenovich,
Imperial Russian Jessaul, Ilovaisku IV. Regiment, Army of the Don.

1567. **Vitkovski**, Adam Leontieovich,
Imperial Russian Staff Rittmeister, Grodno Hussar Regiment.
(**Special Note**: This Russian officer could possibly be the same as the officer named in entry 2133 in this chapter. However, since the name, Vitkovski, and the unit are the same, it could then be taken for a fact that this Rittmeister Vitkovski <u>did</u> receive <u>two</u> Pour le Mérite Order <u>badges</u> in recognition of distinction in <u>action</u>. See entry 2133, this chapter.)
* * *

1568. **Shvedkin**, Alexei Fedorovich,
Imperial Russian Captain, St. Petersburg Opoltshenie (militia).

1569. **Küpfer**, Heinrich Karl Wilhelm,
Imperial Russian Sub-Lieutenant, Siev Infantry Regiment, assigned to the General Staff of Major General d'Auvray.
(**Note**: Sub-Lieutenant Küpfer was awarded the 50 Year Jubilee Golden Crown to the Pour le Mérite Order on June 18, 1864.)
* * *

1570. **Kobiakov**, Ivan Nikolaieovich,
Imperial Russian Staff Captain, Fanagoria Grenadier Regiment.
(**Note**: Staff Captain Kobiakov was awarded the 50 Year Jubilee Golden Crown to the Pour le Mérite Order on March 9, 1867.)

1571. **von Hessenstein**, Count Karl,
Imperial Russian Lieutenant, unassigned cavalry officer.
* * *

Imperial Russian Engineer Corps

1572. **Bogdanov**, Alexander Ivanovich, Imperial Russian Captain.
1573. **Trousson**, Peter Chrestianovich, Imperial Russian Colonel.
1574. **Bibikov**, Vassili Alexandrovich, Imperial Russian Lieutenant.
(**Note**: Lieutenant Bibikov was awarded the 50 Year Jubilee Golden Crown to the Pour le Mérite Order on March 9, 1867.)
* * *

1575. **Gavrilenko**, Ivan Ivanovich,
Imperial Russian Major, unit unknown, Senior Adjutant to Russian General of Infantry Fanshave.

1576. **Fuhrmann**, Alexander Fedorovich,
Imperial Russian Sub-Lieutenant, Quartermaster Service, serving on the Staff of Emperor Alexander I. of Russia.

1577. **Fanshave**, Friedrich Andreieovich,
   Imperial Russian Captain, unassigned.

* * *

Imperial Russian Life Guard Cossack Regiment

1578. **Protopopov**, Ivan Andreieovich, Imperial Russian Colonel.
1579. **Kamenov**, Alexander Michailovich, Imperial Russian Rittmeister.
1580. **Shmurin**, Vassili Matvieieovich, Imperial Russian Rittmeister.
1581. **Orlov**, Alexander (Alexei) Vassilieovich, Imperial Russian Staff Rittmeister.
1582. **Burssak II.**, Afanassi Fedorovich, Imperial Russian Colonel, Life Guard Tshernomori Regiment, serving in the above regiment.

* * *

* May 9, 1814 *

1583. **von Smitten**, Gustaf Gustafovich,
   Imperial Russian Lieutenant, Cavalier Guard Regiment, serving as Adjutant to Russian Field Marshal Count Barclay de Tolly.

1584. **von Salza**, Baron Roman Alexandrovich,
   Imperial Russian Staff Captain, Engineer (Sapper) Regiment, serving as Adjutant to Russian Field Marshal Count Barclay de Tolly.
   (**Note**: Staff Captain von Salza was awarded the 50 Year Jubilee Golden Crown to the Pour le Mérite Order on October 25, 1864.)

1585. **Meyer**, Dmitri Petrovich,
   Imperial Russian Staff Captain, 3rd Light Infantry Regiment.

1586. **von Rennenkampff**, Paul Jakovleovich,
   Imperial Russian Lieutenant, Quartermaster Service, serving on the Staff of Emperor Alexander I. of Russia.

1587. **von Berg**, Karl Borissovich,
   Imperial Russian Lieutenant, Bielo-Russia Hussar Regiment.
   (**Note**: Lieutenant von Berg was awarded the 50 Year Jubilee Golden Crown to the Pour le Mérite Order on October 25, 1864.)

1588. **Audé de Sion**, Karl Karlovich,
   Imperial Russian Lieutenant, Nascheburg Infantry Regiment.

1589. **von Smitten**, Igor Fedorovich,
   Imperial Russian 7th Grade Civil Administrator (Major), Supply and Provisions Administration.

1590. **Biron von Kurland**, Prince Gustaf Kalixt,
   Major General, unit unknown.
   (**Note**: Major General Prince Biron von Kurland was awarded both the Pour le Mérite Order and the Oakleaves to the Pour le Mérite Order in recognition of his outstanding leadership and distinguished military planning during the battle at La Rothière on February 1, 1814. He commanded the only Prussian unit which successfully defeated several French units. Prince Biron von Kurland was also cited for distinction in action during the battle at Brienne on January 29, 1814.)

* * *

1591. **Harris**, Thomas Noel,
   Royal British Captain, 18th Light Dragoon (Hussar) Regiment, serving as Adjutant to British Lt. General Sir Charles Stewart.

* May 11, 1814 *

Imperial Austrian Quartermaster General Staff

1592. **Fallon**, Ludwig August, Imperial Austrian Colonel.
1593. **Höring**, Wenzel, Imperial Austrian Lt. Colonel.
1594. **Geppert**, Georg, Imperial Austrian Lt. Colonel.
1595. **Hess**, Heinrich, Imperial Austrian Captain.
   (**Note**: Austrian Captain Hess was awarded the 50 Year Jubilee Golden Crown to the Pour le Mérite Order on June 18, 1864.)

* * *

1596. **Vratislav**, Count Eugen,
   Imperial Austrian Major, Archduke Ferdinand Hussar Regiment.
   (Count Vratislav was awarded the Pour le Mérite Order for his outstanding leadership and distinction in action during the battle at La Rothière on February 1, 1814.
   Note: Count Vratislav was awarded the 50 Year Jubilee Golden Crown to the Pour le Mérite Order on June 18, 1864.)

1597. **von Vietinghof (also known as Scheel von Schellenberg)**, Frhr. Karl Friedrich,
   Imperial Austrian Major, unit unknown, Wing Adjutant.
   (Awarded the Pour le Mérite Order for distinction in action during the battle at La Rothière on February 1, 1814.
   Note: Austrian Major Count Vratislav was awarded the 50 Year Jubilee Golden Crown to the Pour le Mérite Order on June 18, 1864.)

* * *

1598. **von der Schulenburg**, Count Karl Rudolf,
   Imperial Austrian Major, Schwarzenburg Uhlan Regiment.

1599. **Karaczay von Walie-Szaka**, Count Fedor,
   Imperial Austrian Captain, Quartermaster General Staff.

1600. **Appel**, Christian,
   Imperial Austrian Rittmeister, Riesch Dragoon Regiment.

1601. **Széchényi**, Count Stefan,
   Imperial Austrian Rittmeister, Meerveldt Uhlan Regiment.

1602. **von Wartensleben**, Count Konstantin Moritz Gneomar,
   Imperial Austrian Rittmeister, Kaiser Curassier Regiment.

1603. **Mecklenburg von Kleeberg**, Johann Friedrich Ernst,
   Imperial Austrian Rittmeister, Austro-German Legion Hussar Regiment.

1604. **Grimmer von Adelsbach**, Vinzent,
   Imperial Austrian Major, 1st Artillery Regiment.
   (Major Grimmer von Adelsbach was awarded the Pour le Mérite Order for outstanding leadership and distinction in action while directing his artillery regiment during the battle at Leipzig between October 16 and 18, 1813.)

* * *

Imperial Austrian 2nd Jäger Batallion

1605. **de Zerbi**, Sir (Chevalier) Johann, Imperial Austrian Captain.
1606. **Gelber**, Georg, Imperial Austrian Sub-Lieutenant.

* * *

The preceding Austrian officers received the Pour le Mérite Order in recognition of their distinction in action during the battle at Freyburg on October 21, 1813. The Austrian 2nd Jäger (Light Infantry) Battalion was attached to the advance units of the I. Army Corps.)

* * *

* May 12, 1814 *

1607. **von Zweibrücken**, Baron Christian,
Royal Bavarian Colonel, Chief of the Quartermaster General Staff, Wing Adjutant.
(**Note**: Colonel von Zweibrücken was strongly recommended to be decorated with the Pour le Mérite Order for his outstanding leadership and distinguished planning in supply procurement during the 1813 campaigns by Bavarian Prince Karl. King Friedrich Wilhelm III. approved and the Pour le Mérite Order was awarded to Colonel von Zweibrücken on this date.)

* * *

1608. **Tshernievich**, Prince Peter,
Imperial Russian Captain, Quartermaster Service, serving on the Staff of Emperor Alexander I. of Russia.

* * *

The following two Russian officers were decorated with the Pour le Mérite Order for distinction in action during the engagement outside Paris during March, 1814.

1609. **Romanov**, Peter Danilovich,
Imperial Russian Captain, Pernau Grenadier Regiment.

1610. **Vishizki**, Michail Faddieieovich,
Imperial Russian Staff Rittmeister, Alexandria Hussar Regiment, serving as Duty Adjutant to Lt. General Count de Lambert.
(**Note**: This is the <u>second</u> award of the Pour le Mérite Order <u>badge</u> to Staff Rittmeister Vishizki in recognition of distinction in <u>action</u> during an engagement against French forces outside Paris during March 1814. For the initial award of the Pour le Mérite Order see entry 1561, this chapter.)

* * *

1611. **Gurov**, Ivan Antonovich,
Imperial Russian Lieutenant, Tauri Grenadier Regiment, serving as Adjutant to Lt. General Count de Lambert.
(Lieutenant Gurov was decorated with the Pour le Mérite Order for distinction in action during an engagement against French troops outside of Paris during March 1814.)

1612. **Dieiev**, Alexander Michailovich,
Imperial Russian Lt. Colonel, Staro-Dubno Curassier Regiment.

1613. **Dieiev**, Ivan Michailovich,
Imperial Russian Staff Rittmeister, Alexandria Hussar Regiment.
(**Note**: Staff Rittmeister Dieiev was awarded the 50 Year Jubilee Golden Crown to the Pour le Mérite Order on October 25, 1864.)

* * *

* May 13, 1814 *

Imperial Russian Life Guard Uhlan Regiment

1614. **Potocki**, Count Jaroslav Stanislavovich, Imperial Russian Colonel,
Wing Adjutant.

1615. **von Wolff**, Baron Alexander (Ernst), Imperial Russian Rittmeister,
serving as Adjutant to Russian General of Cavalry Uvarov.

* * *

1616. **Apraxin**, Count Vassili Ivanovich,
Imperial Russian Rittmeister, Cavalier Guard Regiment,
Wing Adjutant.

1617. **Lada**, Hippolit Michailovich,
Imperial Russian Rittmeister, Polni Uhlan Regiment, serving
as Adjutant to Russian Cavalry General Uvarov.

1618. **Lvov**, Alexander Nikolaieovich,
Imperial Russian Staff Rittmeister, 1st Cossack Regiment, Tula
Opoltshenie (militia).
(For distinction in action during the battle of Kulm on August 30, 1813.)

* * *

The following nine Russian officers received the Pour le Mérite Order for distinction in action during the battle of Leipzig between 16-19 October 1813.

1619. **Dluski**, Jevgeni Michailovich,
Imperial Russian Captain, Quartermaster Service, serving on the
Staff of Emperor Alexander I. of Russia.

1620. **Lisagub**, Alexander Ivanovich,
Imperial Russian Lieutenant, Littau Uhlan Regiment.

1621. **Loewenthal**, Fedor Karlovich,
Imperial Russian Major, Archangelogorod Infantry Regiment.

1622. **Hippius**, Karl Fedorovich,
Imperial Russian Captain, 7th Light Infantry Regiment.
(**Note:** This is the <u>first</u> award of the Pour le Mérite Order to
Captain Hippius for distinction in action. For the second award
of the Pour le Mérite Order see entry 2208, this chapter.)

1623. **Voigt (Focht)**, Peter Andreieovich,
Imperial Russian Captain, 8th Mounted Artillery Company.
(**Note:** This is the <u>first</u> award of the Pour le Mérite Order in
recognition of distinction in action bt Captain Voigt. For the
second award of the Pour le Mérite Order see entry 1744, this
chapter.)

* * *

1624. **Read V.**, Andrei Andreieovich,
Imperial Russian Officer Candidate, 8th Mounted Artillery Company.

1625. **Pauli (Paoli)**, Peter Ivanovich,
Imperial Russian Staff Captain, Pskov Infantry Regiment, serving
as Adjutant to Russian Lt. General Kapzevich.
(**Note:** This is the <u>first</u> award of the Pour le Mérite Order to Staff
Captain Pauli for distinction in action. For the second award of the
Pour le Mérite Order see entry 1738, this chapter.)

1626. **Markevich**, Filipp Petrovich,
>Imperial Russian Staff Captain, Quartermaster Service, serving on the Staff of Emperor Alexander I. of Russia.

1627. **Shenshin**, Vladimir Nikolaieovich,
>Imperial Russian Lt. Colonel, Commander of the Schlüsselberg Infantry Regiment.

* * *

* May 15, 1814 *

1628. **Dolinski**, Lev,
>Imperial Russian Staff Captain, Vladimir Infantry Regiment.

* * *

* May 19, 1814 *

1629. **von Poniński**, Count August,
>Imperial Austrian Rittmeister, Archduke Johann Dragoon Regiment.

* * *

* May 20, 1814 *

1630. **Brummel**, (First name unknown),
>Imperial Russian Rittmeister, 1st Ukraine Cossack Regiment.

* * *

* May 22, 1814 *

1631. **Studsinski**, Lev Semenovich,
>Imperial Russian Staff Rittmeister, Polni Uhlan Regiment, serving as Adjutant to Russian Cavalry General Uvarov.

* * *

* May 25, 1814 *

1632. **Clam-Martinitz**, Count Karl Johann Nepomuk,
>Imperial Austrian Major, Archduke Karl Uhlan Regiment.

1633. **von Scharpffenstein (also known as Pfeil)**, Frhr. Karl August,
>Imperial Austrian Rittmeister, Radetzky Hussar Regiment.

* * *

* May 26, 1814 *

1634. **Bichalov**, Jossif Ivanovich,
>Imperial Russian Sotnik, Bichalov I. Regiment, Army of the Don. (For distinction in action during the engagement at Delitsch on October 10, 1813.)

1635. **Forcade de Biaix**, Marquis Wilhelm Friedrich Erdmann Ferdinand,
>Imperial Russian Lieutenant, unit unknown, Adjutant to General Roth.

* * *

* May 29, 1814 *

1636. **d'Ainesy, Marquis de Montpezat**, Leopold Augustine Jean Joseph,
>Imperial Russian Staff Captain, Life Guard Light Infantry Regiment.

1637. **Sass**, Peter Andreieovich,
>Imperial Russian Staff Rittmeister, Volyni Uhlan Regiment.
>(Note: This is the second of three awards of the Pour le Mérite Order badges to Staff Rittmeister Sass in recognition of outstanding

distinction in action. For the initial award of the Pour le Mérite Order see entry 1565 and for the third award see entry 1940, this chapter.)

* * *

* May 30, 1814 *

Imperial Russian Tsherni-Subov V. Regiment
Army of the Don

The following three Imperial Russian officers received the Pour le Mérite Order in recognition of their distinction in action during the battle and cavalry engagement at Eilenburg on October 8, 1813.

1638. **Tshernosubov V. (Tsherni-Subov)**, Peter Avramovich, Imperial Russian Colonel, Honorary Colonel of the Tsherni-Subov V. Regiment.

1639. **Alexieiev**, Ivan Alexieieovich, Imperial Russian Chorunshi (?).

* * *

Another Russian officer of this unit was decorated with the Pour le Mérite Order for distinction in action during the battle at Eilenburg on October 8, 1813. It is believed that the following officer was that recipient.

1640. **Moltshanov (Multshanov)**, (First name unknown), Imperial Russian Sotnik.

* * *

* May 31, 1814 *

The First Award of Two Pour le Mérite Orders With Oakleaves
To The Same Recipient

1641. **von Schon**, Johann Karl Josef,
Colonel, Commander of the 1st Pomeranian Infantry Regiment, Brigade Commander of the V. Brigade.
(**Note**: This is the first of two awards of both the Pour le Mérite Order and the Oakleaves to the Pour le Mérite Order in recognition of outstanding leadership and distinguished military planning during the battles at Dennewitz on September 6, 1813, and at the battle at Leipzig on October 16-19, 1813. For the second award of both the Pour le Mérite Order and the Oakleaves see entry 2333, this chapter.)

* * *

1642. **von Stutterheim**, Karl August,
Colonel, Brigade Commander of the IV. Brigade.
(**Note**: Colonel von Stutterheim was awarded both the Pour le Mérite Order and the Oakleaves to the Pour le Mérite Order in recognition of distinction in action during the engagement with the French in the vicinity of Antwerp on February 1-2, 1814.)

* * *

1643. **von Hobe**, Kord Friedrich Bernhard Hellmuth,
Major General, Brigade Commander of the Reserve Cavalry of the III. Army Corps.
(**Note**: Major General von Hobe in recognition of his outstanding leadership, distinguished military planning and successful operations against the French especially during the battle and capture of the Herzogbusch Fort on March 1 and 7, 1814, he was awarded both the Pour le Mérite Order and the Oakleaves to the Pour le Mérite Order simultaneously.)

* * *

1644. **von Clausewitz**, Vollmar Karl Friedrich,
    Colonel, Commander, 4th East Prussian Infantry Regiment.
    (**Note**: Colonel von Clausewitz was awarded the Oakleaves to the Pour le Mérite Order to recognize his distinction and leadership in action during the engagement against the French at Deurne near Antwerp on February 1-2, 1814. The initial award of the Pour le Mérite Order was given in 1807, **7** years earlier. See Volume I, Chapter V-1, entry 506, p. 304.)
* * *

1645. **Köhn (von Jaski)**, Andreas Ernst,
    Colonel, unit unknown, General Staff Officer.
    (**Note**: Colonel Köhn (von Jaski) was awarded **both** the Pour le Mérite Order **and** the Oakleaves to the Pour le Mérite Order in recognition of outstanding leadership and distinguished military planning and operations during the 1814 campaigns against the French.)
* * *

1646. **von Schmidt**, Johann Heinrich Otto,
    Colonel, Brigadier of Artillery of the I. Army Corps.
    (**Note**: Colonel von Schmidt in recognition of his outstanding leadership and distinguished military planning and operations was awarded the Oakleaves to the Pour le Mérite Order. He was first awarded the Pour le Mérite Order in 1792, **22** years earlier. See Volume I, Chapter IV, entry 152, p.150.)
* * *

1647. **Hiller von Gaertringen**, Frhr. Johann August Friedrich,
    Lt. Colonel, Grenadier Brigade Commander of the I. Brigade.
    (**Note**: Lt. Colonel Hiller von Gaertringen was awarded the Oakleaves to the Pour le Mérite Order for distinction and leadership in action during the battle at Leipzig on October 16, 1813. During the battle at Leipzig, Lt. Colonel von Gaertringen was severely wounded. For the initial award of the Pour le Mérite Order see Volume I, Chapter V-1, entry 677, p. 328.)
* * *

1648. **von Schütz**, Karl August Heinrich Wilhelm,
    Major, unit unknown, General Staff Officer.
    (**Note**: Major von Schütz was awarded **both** the Pour le Mérite Order **and** the Oakleaves to the Pour le Mérite Order in recognition of outstanding and successful strategic military planning during the campaigns of 1814 against the French.)
* * *

1649. **von Othegraven**, Thomas,
    Lt. Colonel, Commander, Brandenburg Infantry Regiment.
    (**Note**: Lt. Colonel von Othegraven was decorated with **both** the Pour le Mérite Order **and** the Oakleaves to the Pour le Mérite Order in recognition of his outstanding leadership and distinction in action during an engagement against the French outside of Paris on March 30, 1814.)
* * *

1650. **von Loebell**, Friedrich Ernst,
    Colonel, Commander, 6th Reserve Infantry Regiment.
    (**Note**: Colonel von Loebell was awarded the Oakleaves to the Pour le Mérite Order for distinguished personal bravery during an

engagement against the French on March 28, 1814, and during the battle near Paris on March 30, 1814. For the initial award of the Pour le Mérite Order see Volume I, Chapter V-1, entry 685, p. 328.)

* * *

1651. **Melnikov IV.**, (First name unknown),
Imperial Russian Colonel, Honorary Colonel of the Melnikov IV. Regiment, Army of the Don.
(For distinction in action at Sehestädt on December 10, 1813, and for the engagement at Wilde on March 26, 1814.)

1652. **Melnikov V.**, Nikolai Grigorieovich,
Imperial Russian Colonel, Honorary Colonel of the Melnikov V. Regiment, Army of the Don.
(For distinction in action during the engagement at Wilde on March 26, 1814.)

* * *

* June 1, 1814 *

1653. **van Delen**, Baron Leonhard Albrecht Karl,
Dutch Major, General Staff Officer of the Netherlands Army, serving at Headquarters of the III. Army Corps.
(For distinction in action during the battle at Laon on March 9-10, 1814.)

* * *

* June 3, 1814 *

1654. **von Boyen**, Ludwig Leopold Gottlieb Herman,
Major General, Prussian State and War Minister.
(**Note**: Major General von Boyen received **both** the Pour le Mérite Order **and** the Oakleaves to the Pour le Mérite Order in recognition of outstanding leadership, distinguished military planning and successful operations during the 1813-1814 campaigns against the French.)

* * *

1655. **von Müffling**, Friedrich Karl Ferdinand,
Major General, Chief Quartermaster of the Silesian Army.
(**Note**: Quartermaster General von Müffling was awarded **both** the Pour le Mérite Order **and** the Oakleaves to the Pour le Mérite Order in recognition of exceptional procurement of military supplies during the 1813-1814 campaigns against the French.)

* * *

1656. **von Rauch**, Johann Gustaf Georg,
Major General, Chief of War Department and Chief of the Engineer Corps and General Inspector of Prussian Fortresses.
(**Note**: Major General von Rauch was decorated with the Oakleaves to the Pour le Mérite Order to recognize his outstanding leadership during the 1813-1814 campaigns against the French. The initial award of the Pour le Mérite Order was given in 1807, **7** years earlier. See Volume I, Chapter V-1, entry 213, p. 276.)

* * *

1657. **Jaminski**, Nikonor Vassilieovich,
Imperial Russian Staff Captain, 6th Light Artillery Company.
(**Note**: Staff Captain Jaminski was awarded the **second** Pour le Mérite Order **badge** for distinction in action during the battle at

Fère-Champénoise on March 25, 1814. For the first award of the
Pour le Mérite Order see entry 1511, this chapter.)

* * *

* June 11, 1814 *

1658. **von Klinckowström**, Count Karl Friedrich Ludwig,
Major, Commander, 3rd East Prussian Landwehr Infantry Regiment.
(Note: Major Klinckowström was awarded both the Pour le Mérite
Order and the Oakleaves to the Pour le Mérite Order in recognition
of outstanding leadership and distinction in action during the battle
at Maubeuge on March 24, 1814.)

* * *

1659. **Brosin II.**, Jakob Nikolaieovich,
Imperial Russian Captain, Quartermaster Service, serving on the
Staff of Emperor Alexander I. of Russia.

* * *

* Between June 7-22, 1814 *

Friedrich Wilhelm III. made a short visit to London during June of 1814, to attend a military conference. While there the king gave to his Chancellor, Prince Karl Augustus Hardenberg, two Pour le Mérite Orders to be awarded to deserving British officers. It appears that the awards were made but unfortunately, the names of the British officers receiving the awards are unknown.

1660. **Unknown**, British Officer.
1661. **Unknown**, British Officer.
1662. **Wood**, Charles,
Royal British Captain, 18th (Prince of Wales's Own) Royal Light
Dragoon Regiment, serving as Adjutant to Sir Charles Stewart.
(Note: Captain Wood was awarded the 50 Year Jubilee Golden
Crown to the Pour le Mérite Order on June 18, 1864.)

* * *

* Between July 4-7, 1814 *

1663. **von Pappenheim**, Count Karl Theodor Friedrich,
Royal Bavarian Major General, command unknown.
(For distinction in action during the engagement at Hanau on
October 30, 1813.)

* * *

* August 11, 1814 *

Imperial Russian 3rd Mounted Artillery Company

1664. **von Gerbel III.**, Karl Gustafovich, Imperial Russian Captain.
(Note: This is the second award of the Pour le Mérite Order badge
to Captain von Gerbel III. in recognition of distinction in action. For
the initial award of the Pour le Mérite Order see entry 1504, this
chapter.)

1665. **von Sievers**, Ivan Lavrentieovich, Imperial Russian Staff Captain.
(Note: Staff Captain von Sievers was awarded the 50 Year Jubilee
Golden Crown to the Pour le Mérite Order on October 25, 1864.)

* * *

* August 14, 1814 *

1666. **von Budberg**, Baron Peter Ludwig,
Imperial Russian Captain, Mohilev Infantry Regiment, serving as Adjutant to the Russian Liaison Commission in Berlin.

* * *

* August 17, 1814 *

Imperial Russian Life Guard Littau Regiment

1667. **Ugriumov**, Pavel Alexandrovich, Imperial Russian Colonel.
1668. **Bresovski**, Apollon Vassilieovich, Imperial Russian Colonel.
1669. **de Polignac**, Count Heraklius August, Imperial Russian Colonel.

* * *

Imperial Russian Life Guard Finnland Regiment

1670. **Steven**, Alexander Christianovich, Imperial Russian Colonel.
1671. **de Gervais**, Alexander Karlovich, Imperial Russian Colonel.
1672. **Perski**, Michail Stepanovich, Imperial Russian Colonel.

* * *

Imperial Russian Life Guard Grenadier Regiment

1673. **Stegmann**, Christofor Ossipovich, Imperial Russian Colonel.
1674. **Akutin**, Alexander Nikita, Imperial Russian Lt. Colonel.

* * *

Imperial Russian Life Guard Pavlovski Regiment

1675. **Peiker**, Matvei Manuilovich, Imperial Russian Lt. Colonel.
1676. **Burmeister**, Adolf Christoforovich, Imperial Russian Lt. Colonel.

* * *

* August 19, 1814 *

1677. **Burmeister**, Jevdokim Romanovich,
Imperial Russian Major, 24th Light Infantry Regiment.
(For distinction in action during the battle of Bautsen on May 20-21, 1813.)

* * *

* August 20, 1814 *

1678. **Tsherkassov**, Pavel Petrovich,
Imperial Russian Colonel, Quartermaster Service, Chief of the General Staff of Infantry General Count Miloradovich.

1679. **Porochovnikov**, Nikolai Petrovich,
Imperial Russian Staff Rittmeister, Grodno Hussar Regiment.

1680. **Dubelt**, Peter Vassilieovich,
Imperial Russian Staff Rittmeister, Sum Hussar Regiment.

1681. **Glinka**, Grigori Nikolaieovich,
Imperial Russian Lieutenant, Libau Infantry Regiment.
(Note: Lieutenant Glinka was awarded the 50 Year Jubilee Golden Crown to the Pour le Mérite Order on January 22, 1863.)

* * *

Imperial Russian Life Guard Semenovski Regiment

1682. **Frederiks**, Baron Peter Andreieovich, Imperial Russian Colonel.
1683. **Tulubiev**, Alexander Dmitrieovich, Imperial Russian Sub-Lieutenant.

* * *

* August 22, 1814 *

1684. **Bibikov**, Ivan Petrovich,
   Imperial Russian Staff Captain, Life Guard Dragoon Regiment, Adjutant to Russian Cavalry General Tormassov.

1685. **Ritshkov**, Nikolai Vassilieovich,
   Imperial Russian Lieutenant, Cavalier Guard Regiment, serving as Adjutant to Russian Major General Prince Repnin.

* * *

* August 27, 1814 *

1686. **von Strantz**, Karl Friedrich Ferdinand,
   Imperial Austrian Captain, Kottulinsky Infantry Regiment, attached to the Staff of Field Marshal Radetzky.

* * *

* August 28, 1814 *

Both the following Russian officers were decorated with the Pour le Mérite Order for distinction in action while serving as Adjutants to Russian Major General Prince Repnin.

1687. **Mironov**, Ivan Semenovich,
   Imperial Russian Lt. Colonel, Kargopol Dragoon Regiment.

1688. **Bedriaga**, Ivan Ivanovich,
   Imperial Russian Staff Rittmeister, Life Guard Uhlan Regiment, serving at the time in the Isium Hussar Regiment.

* * *

* September 7, 1814 *

1689. **von Röder**, Friedrich Erhard Leopold,
   Major General, Brigade Chief of the Reserve Cavalry, II. Army Corps.
   (Note: Major General von Röder was awarded the Oakleaves to the Pour le Mérite Order in recognition of outstanding leadership and distinguished military planning and successful operations. The Award also recognized his distinction in action during the cavalry engagement against the French at Laon on March 9, 1814. For the initial award of the Pour le Mérite Order see Volume I, Chapter V-1, entry 648, p. 325.)

* * *

* September 10, 1814 *

1690. **Bologovski**, Dmitri Nikolaieovich,
   Imperial Russian Lt. Colonel, unknown Opoltshenie (militia), prior service as Captain in the Life Guard Ismailov Regiment.

* * *

* October 11, 1814 *

1691. **von Brozowsky**, Wilhelm Fabian,
 2nd Lieutenant, 2nd West Prussian Dragoon Regiment.
 (For distinction in action during the incident at Karlshof on July 19, 1814.)
 * * *

* Between October 13-18, 1814 *

1692. **Pankratiev**, Nikolai (Nikita) Petrovich,
 Imperial Russian Colonel, Life Guard Light Infantry Regiment, Wing Adjutant.

1693. **Dsitshkanez**, Adam Jakovleovich,
 Imperial Russian Colonel, Life Guard Uhlan Regiment, Wing Adjutant.
 (Note: Colonel Dsitshkanez was awarded the 50 Year Jubilee Golden Crown to the Pour le Mérite Order on March 9, 1867.)

1694. **Vassiltshikov**, Nikolai Vassilieovich,
 Imperial Russian Major General, Viatkashen Infantry Regiment,
 (Note: This is the <u>second</u> award of the Pour le Mérite Order <u>badge</u> to Major General <u>Vassiltshikov</u> in recognition of distinction in <u>action</u> during the battle at Leipzig on October 16-19, 1813. General Vissiltshikov led an attack against an enemy column between Wetteritz and Gohlitz on October 16, 1813, driving the French back and inflicting heavy casualties. On October 18, 1813, he displayed outstanding leadership during an engagement with the enemy at Schönfeld. For the initial award of the Pour le Mérite Order see Volume I, Chapter V-1, entry 325, p. 289)
 * * *

Imperial Russian Kiev Dragoon Regiment

1695. **von Stackelberg**, Baron Fedor Maximovich, Imperial Russian Colonel, Commander of the Regiment.
 (For distinction in action during the engagements on October 16th and 18th, by capturing 2 enemy cannon.)

1696. **Tolsdorff**, Ivan Andreieovich, Imperial Russian Major.
 (For distinction in action during the above engagement.)

1697. **Narvoish**, Franz Grigorieovich, Imperial Russian Captain.
 (Note: Captain Narvoish was awarded the Pour le Mérite Order in recognition of distinction in action during a night attack on the French Marmont Corps in the vicinity of Meissen on September 26, 1814. He was responsible for the capture of 40 enemy soldiers and 2 couriers. He also displayed outstanding leadership and distinction in action during the battles at Möckern and Leipzig on October 16-19, 1813.)
 * * *

1698. **Knobel**, Vassili Fedorovich, Imperial Russian Staff Captain.
 * * *

1699. **Gordieiev**, Jakob Fedorovich,
 Imperial Russian Lt. Colonel, Commander, Dorpat Mounted Light Infantry Regiment.
 (For distinction in action on October 16th by capturing a number of enemy soldiers.)

1700. **Terpielivski**, Jevgeni Ossipovich,
    Imperial Russian Major, Commander, 1st Ukraine Cossack Regiment.

1701. **Selivanov**, Andrei Andreieovich,
    Imperial Russian Colonel, Honorary Colonel of the Selivanov Regiment, Army of the Don.
    (Note: This is the second award of the Pour le Mérite Order badge to Colonel Selivanov in recognition of outstanding leadership and distinction in action during the battle at Leipzig on October 16-19, 1813. For the initial award of the Pour le Mérite Order see entry 872, this chapter.)
* * *

1702. **Kuteinikov IV.**, Fedor,
    Imperial Russian Lt. Colonel, Honorary Colonel of the Kuteinikov IV. Regiment, Army of the Don.
    (For distinction in action at Möckern and Leipzig.)
* * *

The following eight Russian officers received the Pour le Mérite Order in recognition of distinction in action during the battles at Möckern on October 16, 1813, and at Leipzig on October 16-19, 1813.

1703. **Bulgarski**, Peter Vassilieovich,
    Imperial Russian Lt. Colonel, Commander, Olonez Infantry Regiment.
* * *

Imperial Russian 22nd Light Infantry Regiment

1704. **Bachmann**, Jakob Ivanovich, Imperial Russian Major, Commander.
1705. **Sheviakov**, (First name unknown), Imperial Russian Staff Captain.
1706. **Pavlenko**, Dorofei Jemelianovich, Imperial Russian Staff Captain.
* * *

1707. **Hebener**, Pavel Nikolaieovich,
    Imperial Russian Lt. Colonel, 1st Pioneer (Engineer) Regiment, serving as the interim Quartermaster General of the Advance Guard.
* * *

The following two Russian officers were decorated with the Pour le Mérite Order while serving as Adjutants to Russian Lt. General Rudsevich.

1708. **de Sauveplan**, Karl Andreieovich,
    Imperial Russian Captain, Charkov Dragoon Regiment.

1709. **Tarashkevich**, Ossip Fedorovich,
    Imperial Russian Staff Rittmeister, Alexandria Hussar Regiment.
* * *

1710. **Bussov**, Semen Jevstafieovich,
    Imperial Russian Lt. Colonel, Commander, 33rd Light Infantry Regiment.
* * *

The following four Russian officers were given the Pour le Mérite Order for distinction in action during the engagement at Schönfeld on October 18, 1813.

1711. **Tshertov**, Pavel Apollonovich,
> Imperial Russian Lt. Colonel, Commander, Brest Infantry Regiment.
> (Note: Lt. Colonel Tshertov was awarded the 50 Year Jubilee Golden Crown to the Pour le Mérite Order on October 25, 1864.)

* * *

1712. **Tshurakovski**, Michail Danilovich,
> Imperial Russian Major, Commander, 48th Light Infantry Regiment.

1713. **Breshinski**, Michail Petrovich,
> Imperial Russian Major, Commander, Vilmanstrand Infantry Regiment.

1714. **Bogdanovich**, Vassili Ivanovich,
> Imperial Russian Major, Commander, Ekaterinburg Infantry Regiment.
> (Note: This officer was severely wounded during the battle at Leipzig, October 19, 1813.)

* * *

Imperial Russian Quartermaster Service

The following three Russian officers were serving on the Staff of the Emperor Alexander I. when decorated with the Pour le Mérite Order for distinction in action during the engagements at Schönfeld and Leipzig in October of 1813.

1715. **Malinovski**, Silvester Sigismundovich, Imperial Russian Staff Captain.
1716. **Golizin I.**, Prince Andrei Michailovich, Imperial Russian Lieutenant.
1717. **Golizin II.**, Prince Michail Michailovich, Imperial Russian Officer Candidate.

* * *

The following five Russian officers received the Pour le Mérite Order for distinction in action during the battle and capture of Leipzig, October, 1813.

1718. **Manuilov**, Matvei Ivanovich,
> Imperial Russian Staff Captain, 6th Light Infantry Regiment, Adjutant to Lt. General Count de St. Priest.

1719. **Volkov**, Nikolai Apollonovich,
> Imperial Russian Lieutenant, Life Guard Semenovski Regiment, Adjutant to Lt. General Count de St. Priest.

* * *

The following three Russian officers were serving as Division Adjutants when decorated with the Pour le Mérite Order.

1720. **Puetling**, Andrei Alexandrovich,
> Imperial Russian Captain, Rilski Infantry Regiment.

1721. **Shumovski**, (First name unknown),
> Imperial Russian Captain, Fanagoria Grenadier Regiment.

1722. **Morshin**, Michail Markovich (?),
> Imperial Russian Captain, 34th Light Infantry Regiment.

* * *

1723. **Reichel**, Avram Avramovich,
> Imperial Russian Colonel, Apsheron Infantry Regiment.
> (For distinction in action during three assaults on the village of Schönfeld on October 18, 1813.)

* * *

Imperial Russian Riashski Infantry Regiment

The following three Russian officers were decorated with the Pour le Mérite Order for capturing an enemy standard.

1724. **Russanov**, Dmitri Michailovich, Imperial Russian Major.
1725. **Lohmann (Loman)**, Roman Alexandrovich, Imperial Russian Captain.
1726. **Dambrovski**, Ivan Ignatieovich, Imperial Russian Captain.

* * *

1727. **Melnikov**, Michail Ivanovich,
   Imperial Russian Major, Commander, 10th Light Infantry Regiment.
   (**Note**: Major Melnikov was awarded the 50 Year Jubilee Golden Crown to the Pour le Mérite Order on October 25, 1864.)

1728. **Becker**, Johann,
   Imperial Russian Staff Captain, Nascheburg Infantry Regiment.
   (For distinction in action while commanding the night attack on Schönfeld on October 18-19, 1813.)

1729. **Kasha**, Kosma Ivanovich,
   Imperial Russian Staff Captain, Jakutski Infantry Regiment.

1730. **Shtsherbov**, Vassili Pavlovich,
   Imperial Russian Major, Riashski Infantry Regiment, Senior Adjutant to the commanders of the 9th Division.
   (For distinction in action during the engagements at Möckern and Leipzig, October 1813.)

* * *

Imperial Russian Archangelogrod Infantry Regiment

The following three Russian officers of this regiment were decorated with the Pour le Mérite Order in recognition of distinction in action during the battle at Leipzig on October 16-19, 1813. The three officers were each wounded during this battle.

1731. **Volkonski**, Prince Sergei Grigorieovich, Imperial Russian Major.
1732. **Melnikov**, Michail, Imperial Russian Major.
1733. **von Krüdener**, Peter Antonovich, Imperial Russian Captain.

* * *

Imperial Russian Staro-Oskol Infantry Regiment

1734. **Gaievski**, Fedor Semenovich, Imperial Russian Major.
1735. **Shemonin**, Nikolai, Imperial Russian Major.

* * *

Imperial Russian Viatka Infantry Regiment

1736. **Eismont**, Kosma Michailovich, Imperial Russian Lt. Colonel.
1737. **Selieniezki**, Michail Petrovich, Imperial Russian Major.

* * *

1738. **Pauli (Paoli)**, Peter Ivanovich,
   Imperial Russian Captain, Pskov Infantry Regiment, Adjutant to Russian Lt. General Kapzevich.
   (Note: This is the <u>second</u> award of the Pour le Mérite Order <u>badge</u> to Captain Pauli in recognition of distinction in action during the battles at Möckern and Leipzig during October 1813. For the initial award of the Pour le Mérite Order see 1625, this chapter.)

* * *

1739. **Markevitsh (Markovitsh)**, Andrei Ivanovich,
   Imperial Russian Staff Captain, Quartermaster Service, serving on the Staff of Emperor Alexander I. of Russia.
   (For distinction in action at Schönfeld and Leipzig, October 1813.)

* * *

1740. **Shusherin**, Sachar Sergieieovich,
   Imperial Russian Lt. Colonel, Commander, 8th Mounted Artillery Company.
   (Special Note: This is the <u>third</u> award of the Pour le Mérite Order <u>badge</u> to Lt. Colonel Shusherin in recognition of his outstanding leadership and distinction in action during the battles at Möckern and at Leipzig on October 16-19, 1813. For the initial award of the Pour le Mérite Order see entry 1098 and for the second award of the Order see entry 1198, this chapter; also see the remarks concerning this officer's awards on page 63.)

* * *

The following six Russian officers were awarded the Pour le Mérite Order for distinction in action during the engagements at Möckern and Leipzig, October 1813.

1741. **Timofeiev**, Pavel Petrovich,
   Imperial Russian Lt. Colonel, 3rd Light Artillery Company.

1742. **Volevatsh**, Jakob Ivanovich,
   Imperial Russian Lt. Colonel, 32nd Light Artillery Company.
   (Note: This is the <u>second</u> award of the Pour le Mérite Order <u>badge</u>

to Lt. Colonel Volevatsh in recognition of distinction in action. For the initial award of the Pour le Mérite Order see entry 1101, this chapter.) * * *

1743. **Leontovich**, Ossip Vassilieovich,
Imperial Russian Captain, 39th Artillery Battery Company.

1744. **Voigt (Focht)**, Peter Andreieovich,
Imperial Russian Staff Captain, 8th Mounted Artillery Company.
(Note: This is the second award of the Pour le Mérite Order badge in recognition of outstanding distinction in action to Staff Captain Voigt. For the initial award of the Pour le Mérite Order see entry 1623, this chapter.) * * *

1745. **Shukovski**, Galaktion Stepanovich,
Imperial Russian Staff Captain, 7th Reserve Artillery Brigade, serving as Adjutant to Russian Major General Vesselizki.

1746. **Koilenski**, (First name unknown),
Imperial Russian Lieutenant, 8th Artillery Brigade, Adjutant to Russian Major General Vesselizki.
* * *

The following five Russian officers were serving as Adjutants to Russian Infantry General Count Langeron when decorated with the Pour le Mérite Order for distinction in action at the engagements of Möckern and Leipzig on October 16-19, 1813.

1747. **Shmarov**, Timofei Andreieovich,
Imperial Russian Captain, Kolivan Infantry Regiment.

1748. **von Rennenkampff**, Karl Pavlovich,
Imperial Russian Staff Captain, Quartermaster Service, serving on the Staff of Emperor Alexander I. of Russia.

1749. **Rosalion-Soshalski**, Fedor Grigorieovich,
Imperial Russian Lieutenant, 4th Reserve Artillery Brigade, serving as personal aide to General Count Langeron.

1750. **Trubezkoi**, Prince Yuri Petrovich,
Imperial Russian Lieutenant, Cavalier Guard Regiment.

1751. **Grigoriev**, Peter Fedorovich,
Imperial Russian Lieutenant, Liefland Mounted Light Infantry Regiment, Orderly Officer to General Count Langeron.
(Note: Lieutenant Grigoriev also was awarded the Pour le Mérite Order in recognition of distinction in action during the engagement at Düben for safely carrying an important dispatch through the enemy lines and capturing an enemy soldier along the way.)
* * *

1752. **Nagatkin**, (First name unknown),
Imperial Russian Lieutenant, 1st Ukraine Cossack Regiment.
(For distinction in action at Leipzig on October 16-19, 1813.)

1753. **von Stackelberg**, Vladimir Vassilieovich,
Imperial Russian Lt. Colonel, New Russia Dragoon Regiment.
(Note: Lt. Colonel von Stackelberg was awarded the Pour le Mérite Order for displaying distinction in action during several engagements

against the enemy while serving in the advance guard of General St. Priest's Corps. He also commanded a Cossack unit during this time.)

1754. **Galagan**, Andrei Petrovich,
Imperial Russian Captain, Charkov Dragoon Regiment.
(Note: Captain Galagan received the Pour le Mérite Order in recognition of distinction in action during the engagement at Puska where 200 enemy soldiers were captured by Captain Galagan's unit.)

1755. **Shenne**, Karl,
Imperial Russian Major, Mitau Dragoon Regiment.
(Note: Major Shenne was decorated with the Pour le Mérite Order in recognition of distinction in action during the engagement near Löbau where Major Shenne led his regiment in three assaults against the enemy line and successfully driving the French back.)

1756. **Borgraf**, Ivan Fedorovich,
Imperial Russian Major, New Russia Dragoon Regiment.
(Note: Major Borgraf was awarded the Pour le Mérite Order in recognition of his outstanding distinction in action during the battle at Putska where he led a successful assault against the French line breaking through and causing the enemy to withdraw.)

1757. **Bashmakov**, Flegon Mironovich,
Imperial Russian Colonel, 33rd Light Artillery Company.
(Note: This is the <u>second</u> award of the Pour le Mérite Order <u>badge</u> to Colonel Bashmakov in recognition of outstanding distinction in action while commanding the artillery bombardment of enemy positions during several engagements while serving in the advance guard of General St. Priest's Corps. For the initial award of the Pour le Mérite Order see entry 1102, this chapter.)

1758. **Boguslavski**, Ivan Pavlovich,
Imperial Russian Major, Bielosero Infantry Regiment.
(For distinction in action at Putska.)

1759. **Nelidov**, (First name unknown),
Imperial Russian Major, Riasan Infantry Regiment.
(For distinction in action at Löbau.)

1760. **Sadluzki**, Anton (?),
Imperial Russian Major, Wilmanstrand Infantry Regiment.
(For distinction in action during the first skirmish at Putska.)

1761. **Lissanovski**, (First name unknown),
Imperial Russian Major, 48th Light Infantry Regiment.
(For distinction in action at Putska.)

1762. **Würst**, Alexander Fedorovich,
Imperial Russian Captain, Orel Infantry Regiment.
(Note: Captain Würst was awarded the Pour le Mérite Order for distinction in action during several engagements with the enemy during the 1814 campaigns.)

* * *

Imperial Russian 2nd Ukraine Cossack Regiment

The following three Russian officers were decorated with the Pour le Mérite Order in recognition of outstanding leadership and distinction in action during an engagement which took place on August 19 and 23, 1814, when these officers led an attack against an enemy column and took several prisoners. On August 26, 1814, the 2nd Ukraine Cossack Regiment successfully repulsed a heavy French attack and captured a staff officer and 70 soldiers. Again on August 27-28, 1814, the regiment successfully captured 20 gun powder wagons along with several enemy soldiers. In the same area, these three exceptional officers were responsible for the capture of 2 enemy cannon and another 200 enemy soldiers including 3 staff officers and 6 subalterns.

1763. **Terpielivski**, Ivan Franzovich, Imperial Russian Staff Rittmeister.
1764. **Sablin**, Pavel Ivanovich, Imperial Russian Staff Rittmeister.
1765. **Tshernaiev**, Peter Nikititsh, Imperial Russian Lieutenant.

* * *

1766. **Peterson**, Jakob Ivanovich (Fedorovich?),
　　　Imperial Russian Civil Administrator V. Class, Provision Procurement Department, Commissariat Superintendent of the Corps of Infantry General Count Langeron.
　　　(Note: Administrator Peterson was decorated with the Pour le Mérite Order in recognition of his outstanding planning and procurement of military supplies during the 1813-1814 military campaigns.)

* * *

1767. **Skobelev**, Ivan Nikititsh,
　　　Imperial Russian Colonel, Littau Life Guard Regiment, Honorary Colonel of the Riasan Infantry Regiment.
　　　(For distinction in action during the taking of Paris, March 1814.)

1768. **Priashevski**, Nikolai Ivanovich,
　　　Imperial Russian Major, Riasan Infantry Regiment.
　　　(Note: This is the <u>first</u> award of the Pour le Mérite Order to Major Priashevski in recognition of distinction in action during the battle at Leipzig on October 16-19, 1813. For the second award of the Pour le Mérite Order to this officer see entry 2230, this chapter.)

* * *

Imperial Russian Bielo-Russia Hussar Regiment

The following three Russian officers were decorated for distinction in action at the engagement at Bautzen on May 9, 1813, with the Pour le Mérite Order.

1769. **Paton de Meieran**, (First name unknown), Imperial Russian Lt. Colonel.
1770. **Termin**, Leonti Antonovich, Imperial Russian Lieutenant.
1771. **Latshinov**, Peter Petrovich, Imperial Russian Lieutenant.
　　　(Note: This is the <u>first</u> award of the Pour le Mérite Order to Lieutenant Latshinov for distinction in action. For the second award of the Pour le Mérite Order see entry 2058, this chapter.)

* * *

1772. **Sumarokov**, Sergei Pavlovich,
　　　Imperial Russian Lieutenant, serving in the H.R.H. Grand Duke's Company of the Life Guard Artillery Brigade.
　　　(Note: Lieutenant Sumarokov was awarded the 50 Year Jubilee Golden Crown to the Pour le Mérite Order on October 25, 1864.)

1773. **Golizin**, Prince Vladimir (Sergieieovich?)
　　　Imperial Russian Captain of the Guard.

1774. **Bibikov**, Larion Michailovich,
>Imperial Russian Lieutenant, Alexandria Hussar Regiment, serving as Adjutant to Russian Major General Prince Repnin.
>(Note: Lieutenant Bibikov was awarded the 50 Year Jubilee Golden Crown to the Pour le Mérite Order on October 25, 1864.)

* * *

Imperial Russian 1st (Jachontov) Volunteer Cossack Regiment

1775. **Adabashev**, (First name unknown), Imperial Russian Rittmeister.
1776. **von Huhn**, Otto Fedorovich, Imperial Russian Lieutenant.

* * *

Imperial Russian St. Petersburg Grenadier Regiment

The following seven officers were decorated with the Pour le Mérite Order for distinction in action during the battle of Kulm on August 30, 1813.

1777. **Moshenski**, Filipp Denissieovich, Imperial Russian Lt. Colonel.
1778. **Helwig**, Alexander Jakoveovich, Imperial Russian Major.
1779. **Scharenberg**, Wilhelm Franzovich, Imperial Russian Staff Captain.
1780. **Jermakov**, Alexander Dmitrieovich, Imperial Russian Staff Captain.
>(Note: Staff Captain Jermakov was awarded the 50 Year Jubilee Golden Crown to the Pour le Mérite Order on November 16, 1865.)

1781. **Sonn**, Grigori Karlovich, Imperial Russian Staff Captain.
1782. **Kartamishev**, Ivan Nikolaieovich, Imperial Russian Lieutenant.
1783. **Barishnikov**, Peter Petrovich, Imperial Russian Officer Candidate.
>(Note: Officer Candidate Barishnikov was awarded the 50 Year Golden Crown to the Pour le Mérite Order on March 9, 1867.)

* * *

The following six Russian officers received the Pour le Mérite Order for distinction in action at the engagement at Löwenberg on August 17, 1813.

Imperial Russian 1st Ukraine Cossack Regiment

1784. **Kompan**, Franz Ivanovich, Imperial Russian Rittmeister.
1785. **Gontsharov**, (First name unknown), Imperial Russian Lieutcnant.
1786. **Rudnizki**, Konstantin Ivanovich, Imperial Russian Cornet.
1787. **Mileika**, Ivan Ossipovich, Imperial Russian Rittmeister, serving as the Brigade Adjutant to Major General Count von Witt.

* * *

Imperial Russian 3rd Ukraine Cossack Regiment

1788. **Sushkov**, Vassili Vassilieovich, Imperial Russian Lt. Colonel.
1789. **Prokofiev**, Tichon Fedotovich, Imperial Russian Lieutenant.

* * *

1790. **Shipov**, Peter Ivanovich,
>Imperial Russian Captain, unit unknown.

* * *

The following three Russian officers received the Pour le Mérite Order while serving as adjutants to Ataman (Chief) Count Platov.

1791. **Karaoulov**, Nikolai Dmitrieovich, Imperial Russian Cornet.
1792. **Karaoulov**, Alexander Dmitrieovich, Imperial Russian Cornet.
1793. **Novikov**, Nikita Ivanovich, Imperial Russian Sub-Lieutenant.

* * *

1794. **Magdenko I.**, Ivan Semenovich,
  Imperial Russian Colonel, Commander, 21st Artillery Battery Company.
  (**Note:** Colonel Magdenko I. was awarded the Pour le Mérite Order in recognition of outstanding distinction in action during the skirmish with the enemy at Herzogenbusch and also at the engagement at Compiegne on April 1, 1814.)
  * * *

1795. **Obrutshev**, Vladimir Afanassieovich,
  Imperial Russian Captain, Life Guard Preobrashenski Regiment, Adjutant to Lt. General Baron Diebitsch.
  (**Note:** This is the second award of the Pour le Mérite Order badge to Captain Obrutshev for distinction in action. For the first award of the Pour le Mérite Order see entry 759, this chapter. Captain Obrutshev was also awarded the 50 Year Jubilee Golden Crown to the Pour le Mérite Order on January 22, 1863.)
  * * *

1796. **Potemkin**, Jakob Alexieieovich,
  Imperial Russian Major General, Commander, Life Guard Semenovski Regiment and the 1st Brigade, 1st Guard Infantry Division.
  (**Note:** This is the second award of the Pour le Mérite Order badge to Major General Potemkin in recognition of his outstanding leadership and successful military planning and operations. For the initial award of the Pour le Mérite Order see Volume I, Chapter V-1, entry 375, p. 292.)
  * * *

1797. **Chrapovizki**, Matvei Jevgrafovich,
  Imperial Russian Major General, Commander, Life Guard Ismailov Regiment and the 2nd Brigade, 1st Guard Infantry Division.
  (**Note:** This is the second award of the Pour le Mérite Order badge to Major General Chrapovizki in recognition of his outstanding leadership and successful military planning and operations. For the initial award of the Pour le Mérite Order see Volume I, Chapter V-1, entry 373, p. 291.)
  * * *

The following 41 Imperial Russian officers were decorated with the Pour le Mérite Order for distinction in action during the battle of Kulm on August 30, 1813.

Imperial Russian Life Guard Preobrashenski Regiment

1798. **Kishinski**, Dmitii Igorovich, Imperial Russian Captain.
1799. **Stremouchov**, Alexander Sergieieovich, Imperial Russian Captain, Wing Adjutant.
  (**Note:** Captain Stremouchov was awarded the 50 Year Jubilee Golden Crown to the Pour le Mérite Order on March 9, 1867.)

1800. **Potemkin**, Alexander Michailovich, Imperial Russian Captain, serving as Adjutant to Lt. General Baron von Rosen.

1801. **Blum**, Paul Petrovich, Imperial Russian Captain.
1802. **Shipov**, Sergei Pavlovich, Imperial Russian Staff Captain.
  (**Note:** Staff Captain Shipov was awarded the 50 Year Jubilee Golden Crown to the Pour le Mérite Order on October 25, 1864.)

1803. **Korssakov**, Michail Alexandrovich, Imperial Russian Staff Captain, serving as Adjutant to Lt. General Baron von Rosen.

1804. **Tolstoi**, Count Alexander Dmitrieovich, Imperial Russian Officer Candidate.
   (Special Note: This Count Tolstoi could be the same officer as in entry 2140 in this chapter. Especially since the name and regiment are the same, this could indicate that Officer Candidate Count Alexander Tolstoi <u>did</u> receive <u>two</u> awards of the Pour le Mérite Order; therefore, <u>this</u> can be considered the <u>first</u> award of the Pour le Mérite Order.)

* * *

Imperial Russian Life Guard Semenovski Regiment

1805. **Pustshin**, Pavel Sergeieovich, Imperial Russian Colonel.
1806. **Okuniev**, Gavril Semenovich, Imperial Russian Captain.
1807. **Krasnokutski**, Semen Grigorieovich, Imperial Russian Captain.
1808. **von Brincken**, Christofor Alexandrovich, Imperial Russian Captain.
1809. **Kasnakov**, Gennadi Ivanovich, Imperial Russian Staff Captain.
1810. **Annenkov**, Nikolai Petrovich, Imperial Russian Staff Captain.
   (Note: Staff Captain Annenkov was awarded the 50 Year Jubilee Golden Crown to the Pour le Mérite Order on October 25, 1864.)

1811. **von Stürler**, Nikolai Karlovich, Imperial Russian Staff Captain.
1812. **Jefimovich**, Grigori Ivanovich, Imperial Russian Staff Captain.
1813. **von Arpshofen**, Baron Karl Karlovich, Imperial Russian Staff Captain.
   (Note: Staff Captain von Arpshofen was awarded the 50 Year Jubilee Golden Crown to the Pour le Mérite Order on March 9, 1867.)

1814. **Mussin-Pushkin**, Michail Nikolaieovich, Imperial Russian Staff Captain.
1815. **Besobrasov**, Peter Michailovich, Imperial Russian Lieutenant.
1816. **Vadkovski I.**, Ivan Fedorovich, Imperial Russian Lieutenant.
1817. **Panutin**, Fedor Sergieieovich, Imperial Russian Lieutenant.
   (Note: Lieutenant Panutin was awarded the 50 Year Jubilee Golden Crown to the Pour le Mérite Order on March 3, 1864.)

1818. **Trubezkoi I.**, Prince Sergei Petrovich, Imperial Russian Lieutenant.
1819. **Ladomirski**, Vassili Nikolaieovich, Imperial Russian Lieutenant.

* * *

Imperial Russian Life Guard Ismailov Regiment

1820. **Martinov**, Pavel Petrovich, Imperial Russian Colonel.
1821. **Voropanov**, Nikolai Faddieieovich, Imperial Russian Captain.
1822. **Masslenizki**, Fedor Timofieovich, Imperial Russian Captain.
1823. **Tshemessov**, Ivan Jefimovich, Imperial Russian Captain.
1824. **Shamshev**, Jakob Ivanovich, Imperial Russian Lieutenant, serving as Adjutant to Russian Major General Chrapovizki.

1825. **Spiridov**, Alexei (Alexander) Matvieieovich, Imperial Russian Lieutenant, serving as Adjutant to Russian Major General Chrapovizki.

1826. **Samsonov**, Sergei Vassilieovich, Imperial Russian Lieutenant.
1827. **Liatuchin**, Nikolai Petrovich, Imperial Russian Sub-Lieutenant.

* * *

Imperial Russian Life Guard Light Infantry Regiment

1828. **Barishnikov**, Pavel Petrovich, Imperial Russian Colonel.
1829. **Andreievski**, Konstantin Stepanovich, Imperial Russian Colonel.

1830. **Kurshevski**, Vladimir Grigorieovich, Imperial Russian Captain.
1831. **Litvinov**, Ivan Vassilieovich, Imperial Russian Captain.
1832. **Repninski**, Nikolai Jakovleovich, Imperial Russian Captain.
1833. **Bublik**, Jakob Petrovich, Imperial Russian Staff Captain.
1834. **Tolmatshev**, Afanassi Jemelianovich, Imperial Russian Staff Captain.
1835. **Balkashin**, Nikanor Nikolaieovich, Imperial Russian Staff Captain.
1836. **Arbussov**, Alexei Fedorovich, Imperial Russian Staff Captain.

* * *

Imperial Russian Guard Equipage

1837. **Titov**, Alexei Igorovich, Imperial Russian Naval Lieutenant.
1838. **Tshichatshev**, Matvei Nikolaieovich, Imperial Russian Lieutenant.

* * *

1839. **von Strandmann**, Fedor Alexieieovich,
    Imperial Russian Lieutenant, Life Guard Ismailov Regiment.
    (For distinction in action also during the engagements at Leipzig and Paris.)

1840. **Stsherbatshev**, Alexander Nikolaieovich,
    Imperial Russian Lieutenant, Life Guard Littau Regiment.
    (For distinction in action also at Paris, March 1814.)

* * *

Imperial Russian Life Guard Grenadier Regiment

1841. **Schubert**, Grigori Ivanovich, Imperial Russian Lt. Colonel.
1842. **Tichanov**, Fedor Andreieovich, Imperial Russian Lt. Colonel.
1843. **Tshekalov**, Michail Petrovich, Imperial Russian Captain.
1844. **Bersilov**, Arseni Jakovleovich, Imperial Russian Captain.
1845. **Masslov**, Alexander Petrovich, Imperial Russian Staff Captain, Adjutant to Russian Major General Sheltuchin.

* * *

Imperial Russian Pavlovski Life Guard Regiment

The following four Russian officers were decorated with the Pour le Mérite Order in recognition of distinction in action during several engagements in Silesia during 1813, and especially during the skirmishes against the French in the vicinity of Paris during March 1814.

1846. **Schiermann**, Fedor Karlovich, Imperial Russian Lt. Colonel.
1847. **Dombrovski**, Roman Antonovich, Imperial Russian Captain.
1848. **Schiermann**, Karl (Wilhelm) Karlovich, Imperial Russian Captain.
1849. **Dittmar**, Peter (Igor?) Leontieovich, Imperial Russian Staff Captain.

* * *

Imperial Russian Littau Life Guard Regiment

1850. **Samburski**, Akim (Joachim) Petrovich, Imperial Russian Colonel.
1851. **Kishkin**, Vassili Michailovich, Imperial Russian Colonel.
1852. **Bresovski**, Anton Valerianovich, Imperial Russian Captain.
1853. **Nikolev**, Vladimir Ivanovich, Imperial Russian Captain.
1854. **Shulgin**, Dmitri Ivanovich, Imperial Russian Captain.

* * *

Imperial Russian Finnland Life Guard Regiment

The following five officers received the Pour le Mérite Order for distinction in action during several engagements in Silesia during 1813, and also during the battle of Leipzig between October 16-19, 1814.

1855. **Ushakov**, Peter Sergieieovich, Imperial Russian Colonel.
1856. **Palizin**, Michail Jakovleovich, Imperial Russian Colonel.
1857. **Rall IV**, Vassili Fedorovich, Imperial Russian Captain.
1858. **Veliaminov**, Nikolai Stepanovich, Imperial Russian Captain.
1859. **Tshertorishski**, Vassili Nikolaieovich, Imperial Russian Captain.

* * *

1860. **Posdieiev (Podshidaiev)**, Ivan Vassilieovich,
Imperial Russian Captain, 16th Mounted Artillery Company of the 7th Reserve Brigade, serving as Adjutant to Russian Lt. General Jermolov.

1861. **Apushkin (Apuchtin)**, (First name unknown),
Imperial Russian Captain, Moscow Opoltshenie (militia), Adjutant to Russian Lt. General Jermolov.
(Captain Apushkin was also awarded the Pour le Mérite Order for distinction in action during the engagements in the vicinity of Paris and during the occupation of Paris during March 1814.)

* * *

The following list of Russian officers (entry numbers 1862 through 1941) received the Pour le Mérite Order for distinction in action during the engagement at Brienne on January 29, 1814.

1862. **Kashinzov**, Alexander Ivanovich,
Imperial Russian Colonel, Small Russia Grenadier Regiment.

1863. **Piatkin**, Vassili Gavrilovich,
Imperial Russian Lt. Colonel, Life Guard Pavlovski Regiment.

* * *

Imperial Russian Life Guard Hussar Regiment

1864. **Muromzov**, Alexander Matvieieovich, Imperial Russian Rittmeister,
Adjutant to Russian General Field Marshal Barclay de Tolly.
(Note: Rittmeister Muromzov was awarded the 50 Year Jubilee Golden Crown to the Pour le Mérite Order on March 9, 1867.)

1865. **von Reutern**, Erhard (Gerhard) Romanovich, Imperial Russian Cornet.

* * *

1866. **Shelechov**, Dmitri Nikolaieovich,
Imperial Russian Major, 5th Light Infantry Regiment.

* * *

Imperial Russian Life Guard Grenadier Regiment

1867. **Raditsh**, Jakob Nikolaieovich, Imperial Russian Staff Captain.
1868. **Kologrivov**, Stepan Ivanovich, Imperial Russian Staff Captain,
serving as Adjutant to Russian Lt. General Sabanieiev.

* * *

1869. **Ogoreliz**, Stepan,
Imperial Russian Lieutenant, Olonez Infantry Regiment.

1870. **Davidov**, Nikolai Dmitrieovich (?),
Imperial Russian Major General of the Artillery, unit unknown.

1871. **Ilovaiski XII.**, Ivan Dmitrieovich,
Imperial Russian Major General, unit unknown, Army of the Don.

* * *

Imperial Russian Quartermaster Service

1872. **Scheffler**, Gustaf Ivanovich, Imperial Russian Colonel.
1873. **von Bose**, Ernst Ludwig Hans, Imperial Russian Colonel.
1874. **Krause**, Ossip Ivanovich, Imperial Russian Lt. Colonel.
1875. **von Sayn-Wittgenstein**, Count Ludwig Adolf, Imperial Russian Staff Captain.
1876. **Thal (Thalen)**, (First name unknown), Imperial Russian Lt. Colonel, serving on the General Staff of the II. Infantry Corps.
1877. **von Dellinghausen**, Baron Ivan Fedorovich, Imperial Russian Sub-Lieutenant.

* * *

Imperial Russian Engineer Corps

1878. **von Pott**, Dr. Georg Heinrich, Imperial Russian Captain.
1879. **Schott**, Christofor Karlovich, Imperial Russian Lieutenant.

* * *

1880. **Dieterichs (Dieteriks)**, (First name unknown),
Imperial Russian Staff Captain, 20th Light Infantry Regiment, attached to the General Staff.

* * *

The following five Russian officers were serving as Adjutants to Cavalry General Count Wittgenstein when decorated with the Pour le Mérite Order in recognition of distinction in action during the battle at Brienne on January 29, 1814.

1881. **Rshevski**, Pavel Alexieieovich,
Imperial Russian Colonel of Cavalry, unit unknown.

1882. **von Merlin**, Karl Demianovich,
Imperial Russian Major, Olviopol Hussar Regiment.

1883. **von Keyserlingk**, Count Otto Karl Diedrich,
Imperial Russian Cavalry Major, unit unknown.

1884. **Semenov.** Danilo,
Imperial Russian Major, Jamburg Uhlan Regiment.

1885. **Klein**, Fedor Borissovich,
Imperial Russian Lieutenant, Grodno Hussar Regiment.
(Note: Lieutenant Klein was awarded the 50 Year Jubilee Golden Crown to the Pour le Mérite Order on November 16, 1865.)

* * *

1886. **van Suchtelen**, Paul Petrovich,
Imperial Russian Colonel, Cavalier Guard Regiment, Wing Adjutant.

1887. **Tarbeiev**, Pavel Petrovich,
Imperial Russian Lt. Colonel, Perm Infantry Regiment.

1888. **Isleniev**, Sergei Alexandrovich,
Imperial Russian Major, Mohilev Infantry Regiment.

* * *

Imperial Russian Kaluga Infantry Regiment

1889. **Oranski**, Ivan Albrechtovich, Imperial Russian Lt. Colonel.
1890. **Pusirevski**, (First name unknown), Imperial Russian Major.
1891. **Krivski**, Alexander Jakovleovich, Imperial Russian Major.

* * *

Imperial Russian Siev Infantry Regiment

1892. **Denissievski**, Andronik Andronikovich, Imperial Russian Colonel.
1893. **Maske (Masska)**, Ivan Jefimovich, Imperial Russian Major.
1894. **von Krummes**, Theodor Ernst, Imperial Russian Major.

* * *

1895. **Blashievski**, Valenti Vassilieovich,
    Imperial Russian Captain, Volyni Infantry Regiment.

1896. **Vulffert**, Ivan Gustafovich,
    Imperial Russian Lt. Colonel, Nieshin Mounted Light Infantry Regiment, Senior Adjutant of the Day to Cavalry General Count Wittgenstein.

* * *

Imperial Russian 20th Light Infantry Regiment

1897. **Stepanov**, (First name unknown), Imperial Russian Colonel.
1898. **Garichvostov**, Alexander Sacharieovich, Imperial Russian Lt. Colonel, Officer of the Day on the General Staff of the II. Infantry Corps.

* * *

Imperial Russian Morom Infantry Regiment

1899. **Kladishtshev**, Peter Alexieieovich, Imperial Russian Major.
1900. **Gerassimov**, Alexander Semenovich, Imperial Russian Captain.
    (**Note:** This is the **first** award of the Pour le Mérite Order to Captain Gerassimov for distinction in action on this date. For the second award of the Pour le Mérite Order, see entry 1952, this chapter.)

* * *

Imperial Russian 23rd Light Infantry Regiment

1901. **Breshinski**, Semen Petrovich, Imperial Russian Lt. Colonel.
    (**Note:** This is the **second** award of the Pour le Mérite Order **badge** to Lt. Colonel Breshinski in recognition of distinction in action. For the inital award of the Pour le Mérite Order, see entry 1156, this chapter.)

1902. **Katashev**, (First name unknown), Imperial Russian Lt. Colonel.

* * *

1903. **Bushen**, Christian Nikolaieovich,
    Imperial Russian Major, 21st Light Infantry Regiment.
    (**Note:** Major Bushen was awarded the 50 Year Jubilee Golden Crown to the Pour le Mérite Order on October 25, 1864.)

1904. **Zireniev**, (First Name Unknown),
    Imperial Russian Major, 26th Light Infantry Regiment.

1905. **Velenin**, Peter Alexandrovich,
    Imperial Russian Captain, Life Guard Pavlovski Regiment, Senior Adjutant to the II. Infantry Corps.
    (**Note:** Captain Velenin was awarded the 50 Year Jubilee Golden Crown to the Pour le Mérite Order on March 9, 1867.)

The following two Russian officers received the Pour le Mérite Order for distinction in action while serving as adjutants to Russian Major General Pishinski.

1906. **Urussov**, Prince Sergei Dmitrieovich,
Imperial Russian Captain, St. Petersburg Grenadier Regiment.
(**Note**: Captain Urussov was awarded the 50 Year Jubilee Golden Crown to the Pour le Mérite Order on November 16, 1865.)

* * *

1907. **Tolstoi**, Count (First name unknown),
Imperial Russian Sub-Lieutenant, Krementshug Infantry Regiment.

* * *

1908. **Smolianinov**, Alexander Ossipovich (?),
Imperial Russian Captain, Fanagoria Grenadier Regiment.

1909. **Shishkin**, Pavel Sergieieovich,
Imperial Russian Sub-Lieutenant, Bielosero Infantry Regiment.
(**Note**: Sub-Lieutenant Shishkin was awarded the 50 Year Jubilee Golden Crown to the Pour le Mérite Order on March 9, 1867.)

* * *

1910. **de Maistre**, Count Rudolf Ossipovich,
Imperial Russian Staff Rittmeister, Cavalier Guard Regiment.
(**Note**: Staff Rittmeister de Maistre was awarded the 50 Year Jubilee Golden Crown to the Pour le Mérite Order on June 18, 1864.)

1911. **Tshagin**, Vladimir Nikolaieovich,
Imperial Russian Sub-Lieutenant, 1st (Jachontov) Volunteer Cossack Regiment.

* * *

Imperial Russian Grodno Hussar Regiment

1912. **Nabel**, Andrei Andreieovich, Imperial Russian Colonel.
(**Note**: This is the <u>second</u> award of the Pour le Mérite Order <u>badge</u> to Colonel Nabel in recognition of outstanding distinction in <u>action</u>. For the initial award of the Pour le Mérite Order see Volume I, Chapter V-1, entry 538, p. 308.)

1913. **Tulubiev**, Dorimedont Titovich, Imperial Russian Rittmeister.
1914. **Babst**, Kondrati Kondratieovich, Imperial Russian Lieutenant, assigned to Lt. General Count von der Pahlen III.

1915. **Lobanov-Rostovski**, Prince Boris Alexandrovich, Imperial Russian Cornet, Life Guard Hussar Regiment, presently serving in the Grodno Hussar Regiment.

* * *

1916. **Dolgoruki**, Prince Nikolai Andreieovich,
Imperial Russian Lieutenant, Life Guard Hussar Regiment, assigned at this time to the Isium Hussar Regiment and serving as Adjutant to Russian Cavalry General Count Wittgenstein.

* * *

Imperial Russian Sum Hussar Regiment

1917. **Read**, Nikolai Andreieovich, Imperial Russian Colonel.
1918. **Emme**, Alexander Ivanovich, Imperial Russian Staff Rittmeister.
1919. **von Taube**, Baron Anton, Imperial Russian Rittmeister.

* * *

1920. **Mandrika**, Nikolai Jakovleovich,
Imperial Russian Colonel, Life Guard Hussar Regiment.
* * *

Imperial Russian Tshuiugev Uhlan Regiment

1921. **Issiumov**, Nikolai Grigorieovich, Imperial Russian Rittmeister.
1922. **Krizin**, Jefim Nikitit, Imperial Russian Rittmeister.
1923. **Lissanevich**, Ivan Grigorieovich, Imperial Russian Lieutenant.
* * *

1924. **Viltshinski**, Ivan Franzovich,
Imperial Russian Lieutenant, Bielo-Russia Hussar Regiment.

1925. **Dannenberg**, Ivan Petrovich,
Imperial Russian Major, Ingermanland Dragoon Regiment.

1926. **Rebrikov III.**, (First name unknown),
Imperial Russian Lt. Colonel, Ilovaiski XII. Regiment, Army of the Don.

1927. **Vlassov**, Michail,
Imperial Russian Starchina, Vlassov Regiment, Army of the Don.
* * *

The following two Russian officers were decorated with the Pour le Mérite Order in recognition of distinction in action while serving as adjutants to Russian General von der Pahlen III.

1928. **Kalatshevski**, Nikolai Igorovich,
Imperial Russian Major, Siberian Uhlan Regiment.

1929. **von Budberg**, Fedor Vassilieovich,
Imperial Russian Rittmeister, Life Guard Uhlan Regiment.
* * *

1930. **Wachsmuth**, Alexander (Andrei) Jakovleovich,
Imperial Russian Staff Captain, 14th Artillery Brigade.

1931. **Sacharshevski**, Jakob Vassilieovich,
Imperial Russian Colonel, Commander, 6th Mounted Artillery Company.
(**Note:** Colonel Sacharshevski was awarded the 50 Year Jubilee Golden Crown to the Pour le Mérite Order on October 25, 1864.)

1932. **von Kosküll**, Count Josef Wilhelm,
Imperial Russian Lieutenant, Life Guard Semenovski Regiment, Adjutant to Russian General of Infantry Prince Gortshakov.

1933. **Petrulin**, Jakob Vassilieovich,
Imperial Russian Colonel, Life Guard Hussar Regiment.
(**Note:** This is the <u>second</u> award of the Pour le Mérite Order <u>badge</u> in recognition of outstanding distinction in action to Colonel <u>Petrulin</u>. For the initial award of the Pour le Mérite Order to this officer see entry 793, this chapter.)
* * *

The following seven Russian officers were decorated with the Pour le Mérite Order in recognition of distinction in action while serving as adjutants to Russian General of Cavalry Count Wittgenstein.

1934. **von der Pahlen,** Count Ivan Petrovich,
Imperial Russian Staff Captain, Life Guard Semenovski Regiment.

1935. **Shukovski,** Michail Stepanovich,
Imperial Russian Civil Administrator V. Class, Provision Procurement Department.

1936. **Krilov,** Alexander Alexieieovich,
Imperial Russian Captain, Life Guard Pavlovski Regiment.

1937. **Pestel,** Pavel Ivanovich,
Imperial Russian Sub-Lieutenant, Cavalier Guard Regiment, serving at the time in the Life Guard Littau Regiment.

1938. **Tishin,** Vassili Grigorieovich,
Imperial Russian Lt. Colonel, Murom Infantry Regiment.
(**Note:** Lt. Colonel Tishin was awarded the 50 Year Jubilee Golden Crown to the Pour le Mérite Order on October 25, 1864.)

1939. **Petrulin,** Yuri Vassilieovich,
Imperial Russian Rittmeister, His Majesty's Guard Curassier Regiment.

1940. **Sass,** Peter Andreieovich,
Imperial Russian Staff Rittmeister, Volyni Uhlan Regiment.
(**Note:** This is the <u>third</u> award of the Pour le Mérite Order <u>badge</u> to Staff Rittmeister Sass in recognition of his outstanding example of distinction in action. For the initial award of the Pour le Mérite Order see entry 1565, this chapter and for the second award see entry 1637, this chapter.)

* * *

1941. **Pavlov,** Grigori,
Imperial Russian Sotnik, Ilovaiski IX. Regiment, Army of the Don.

1942. **Molostvov,** Vladimir Perfilieovich,
Imperial Russian Staff Captain, Tauri Grenadier Regiment, serving at the time as Adjutant to Prince Eugen of Württemberg.

* * *

The following 42 Russian officers were decorated with the Pour le Mérite Order in recognition of outstanding distinction in action during the 1813 summer campaigns against the French.

Imperial Russian Tshernigov Infantry Regiment

1943. **Pilchovski,** Ivan Christoforovich, Imperial Russian Lieutenant,
serving at the time as Adjutant to Russian Lt. General Prince Shachovski.

1944. **Löwenhof,** Timofei Antonovich, Imperial Russian Lt. Colonel.
(**Note:** This is the <u>second</u> award of the Pour le Mérite Order <u>badge</u> in recognition of outstanding distinction in action to Lt. Colonel Löwenhof. For the initial award of the Pour le Mérite Order to this officer see entry 1048, this chapter.)

1945. **Shulgin,** Peter (Alexander Sergieieovich), Imperial Russian Major.
1946. **Sivai,** Alexander Ivanovich, Imperial Russian Major.
1947. **Kubitovich,** Danilo Antonovich, Imperial Russian Major.
1948. **von Huhn,** Otto (Wilhelm), Imperial Russian Staff Captain.
1949. **Bistrom,** Alexander Ivanovich, Imperial Russian Sub-Lieutenant.

* * *

Imperial Russian Murom Infantry Regiment

1950. **Shachmatov,** Prince Nikolai Alexandrovich, Imperial Russian Major.
1951. **Brenner,** Ivan Ivanovich, Imperial Russian Major.
1952. **Gerassimov,** Alexander Semenovich, Imperial Russian Captain.
   (**Note:** This is the <u>second</u> award of the Pour le Mérite Order <u>badge</u> in recognition of outstanding distinction in action to Captain Gerassimov. For the initial award of the Pour le Mérite Order to this officer see entry 1900, this chapter.)
1953. **Roth,** Ludwig Christianovich, Imperial Russian Lieutenant.
1954. **Voroniez,** Ivan Avrianovich, Imperial Russian Lieutenant,
   of the Sofia Infantry Regiment attached to the Murom Infantry Regiment.

* * *

Imperial Russian Reval Infantry Regiment

1955. **von Wrangel,** Ludwig Andreieovich, Imperial Russian Major.
1956. **Müller,** (First name unknown), Imperial Russian Major.
1957. **Drobishevski,** Karp(?), Imperial Russian Major.
1958. **Shliachtin,** Nilokai Nikolaieovich, Imperial Russian Captain.
   serving at the time as Adjutant to Russian Lt. General Prince Shachovski.

* * *

Imperial Russian Volyni Infantry Regiment

1959. **Reich,** Ivan Ivanovich, Imperial Russian Major.
   (**Note:** Major Reich was awarded the 50 Year Jubilee Golden Crown to the Pour le Mérite Order on March 9, 1867.)
1960. **Mamonov,** Ivan Averianovich, Imperial Russian Lt. Colonel.
1961. **Baranov,** Jevstafi Jevstafieovich, Imperial Russian Captain.
1962. **Shibaiev,** (First name unknown), Imperial Russian Sub-Lieutenant.

* * *

Imperial Russian 20th Light Infantry Regiment

1963. **Keldermann,** (First name unknown), Imperial Russian Major.
1964. **Stepanov,** Matvei, Imperial Russian Captain, serving at the time as Adjutant to Russian Lt. General Prince Shachovski.
1965. **Petrovski-Muravski,** Nikolai Ivanovich, Imperial Russian Captain.
1966. **Sviagin,** Nikolai Michailovich, Imperial Russian Captain.
1967. **von Helldorf,** Heinrich August, Imperial Russian Staff Captain.
1968. **Pomeranski,** Narkiss, Imperial Russian Lieutenant.
1969. **Konovkin,** Gavril Ilitsh, Imperial Rusian Officer Candidate.

* * *

Imperial Russian Krementshug Infantry Regiment

1970. **Tannauer,** (First name unknown), Imperial Russian Staff Captain, serving at the time as Adjutant to Russian General Pishnizki.
1971. **Jemilovski,** (First name unknown), Imperial Russian Major.
1972. **Savostianov,** Platon (Pavel?) Ivanovich, Imperial Russian Major.
1973. **Bushuiev,** (First name unknown), Imperial Russian Major.
1974. **Vassiliev,** (First name unknown), Imperial Russian Major.
1975. **von Belli,** (First name unknown), Imperial Russian Major.
1976. **Fedorov,** (First name unknown), Imperial Russian Staff Captain.
1977. **Lermantov,** Vladimir Nikolaieovich, Imperial Russian Lieutenant.

(**Note:** Lieutenant Lermantov was awarded the 50 Year Jubilee Golden Crown to the Pour le Mérite Order on May 4, 1870.)

* * *

Imperial Russian Tobolski Infantry Regiment

1978. **von Lüdinghausen,** Frhr. Peter Johann, Imperial Russian Colonel.
(**Note:** This is the <u>second</u> award of the Pour le Mérite Order <u>badge</u> in recognition of outstanding distinction in action to Colonel von Lüdinghausen. For the initial award of the Pour le Mérite Order to this officer see entry 778, this chapter.)

1979. **Neumann,** Alexander Ivanovich, Imperial Russian Major.

* * *

Imperial Russian 4th Light Infantry Regiment

1980. **Tregubov,** Andrei Vassilieovich, Imperial Russian Major.
1981. **Stashevski,** Matwei Ivanovich, Imperial Russian Captain.
1982. **Ismailov,** Lavr Timofieieovich, Imperial Russian Staff Captain.

* * *

1983. **Korssak,** Roman Ossipovich,
Imperial Russian Staff Captain, 34th Light Infantry Regiment.

1984. **Ivanov III.,** Igor Sacharieovich (Vassilieovich),
Imperial Russian Lt. Colonel, Commander, 4th Pontoon Company, Imperial Russian Engineer Corps.
(**Note:** This is the **first** award of the Pour le Mérite Order in recognition of distinction in action to Lt. Colonel Ivanov. For the second award of the Pour le Mérite Order to this officer see entry 2219, this chapter.)

* * *

1985. **Shemshushnikov,** Michail Nikolaieovich,
Imperial Russian Staff Captain, 3rd Light Artillery Company.

1986. **Lishin,** Nikolai Fedorovich,
Imperial Russian Staff Captain, 34th Artillery Battery Company.
(**Note:** This is the **first** award of the Pour le Mérite Order in recognition of distinction in action to Staff Captain Lishin. For the second award of the Pour le Mérite Order to this officer see entry 2231, this chapter.)

* * *

1987. **Pichelstein,** Johann Stanislavovich,
Imperial Russian Staff Captain, 2nd Reserve Artillery Brigade.

1988. **Krishtofovich,** Evgeni Jossifovich,
Imperial Russian Lieutenant, 34th Artillery Battery Company.

1989. **Voievodski,** Pavel Jakoveovich,
Imperial Russian Lieutenant, 13th Mounted Artillery Company, 4th Reserve Artillery Brigade.

1990. **Svarkovski,** Nikolai Akimovich,
Imperial Russian Lieutenant, Life Guard Artillery Brigade, attached to the 31st Artillery Battery Company.

1991. **Grudsinski,** Sachar Ivanovich,
Imperial Russian Sub-Lieutenant, 13th Light Artillery Company, attached to the 7th Artillery Brigade.

(**Note:** Sub-Lieutenant Grudsinski was awarded the Pour le Mérite Order in recognition of outstanding distinction in action during the seven hour artillery bombardment of the French positions during the battle at Bautzen on May 20, 1814.)

* * *

Imperial Russian Volyni Uhlan Regiment

1992. **Voievovdski**, Lev Grigorieovich, Imperial Russian Colonel.
1993. **Nordstein**, Sergei Nikolaieovich, Imperial Russian Major.
1994. **von Engelhart**, Adam Grigorieovich, Imperial Russian Major.
1995. **O'Rurk IV.**, Count Vladimir Igorovich, Imperial Russian Lieutenant,
 Life Guard Uhlan Regiment, serving at the time in the Volyni Uhlan Regiment.

1996. **O'Rurk III.**, Count Korneli Jevgrafovich, Imperial Russian Staff Rittmeister.
 (**Note:** Staff Rittmeister Count O'Rurk III. was awarded the 50 Year Jubilee Golden Crown to the Pour le Mérite Order on November 16, 1865.)

* * *

1997. **Ashakov**, Alexei,
 Imperial Russian Rittmeister, 1st (Jachontov) Volunteer Cossack Regiment.

1998. **Dunaiev**, Alexander Ivanovich,
 Imperial Russian Colonel, Narva Infantry Regiment, serving at the time as Corps Staff Officer of the Day to Imperial Russian Lt. General Count Voronzov.

1999. **Apushkin**, Alexander Nikolaieovich,
 Imperial Russian Colonel, Commander, 11th Mounted Artillery Company.

2000. **Winspeare**, Robert Antonovich,
 Imperial Russian Lt. Colonel, Commander, 31st Artillery Battery Company, 3rd Reserve Artillery Brigade.

2001. **Popov XIII.**, (First name unknown),
 Imperial Russian Starchina, unidentified unit, Army of the Don.

2002. **Isbash**, Nikita Nesterovich,
 Imperial Russian Colonel, 13th Light Infantry Regiment.

2003. **Stetter**, Ivan,
 Imperial Russian Captain, 14th Light Infantry Regiment.

2004. **von Loewenstern**, Baron Karl Karlovich,
 Imperial Russian Major, Siberian Uhlan Regiment, serving at the time as Adjutant of the 24th Infantry Regiment.

* * *

The following eleven Imperial Russian officers were awarded the Pour le Mérite Order in recognition of outstanding distinction in action while serving at the time on the staff of Imperial Russian Lt. General Count Voronzov with duties as indicated.

Staff Duties
2005. **Osharovski**, Count Ignati Onufrieovich,
 Imperial Russian Cavalry Major, unidentified unit.

* * *

Adjutants

2006. **Narishkin,** Dmitri Vassilieovich,
Imperial Russian Lieutenant, Life Guard Semenovski Regiment.

2007. **Arseniev,** Nikolai Vassilieovich,
Imperial Russian Captain, Life Guard Preobrashenski Regiment.

2008. **Bakunin,** Vassili Michailovich,
Imperial Russian Lieutenant, Life Guard Grenadier Regiment.

2009. **Jagnizki,** Ivan Timofieieovich,
Imperial Russian Lieutenant, Narva Infantry Regiment.

* * *

General Staff Officer

2010. **von Rosenthal,** Gustaf,
Imperial Russian Staff Captain, Tula Infantry Regiment.

* * *

Orderly Officers

2011. **Lukovkin,** Amvrosi Gavrilovich,
Imperial Russian Sotnik, Ilovaiski V. Regiment, Army of the Don.

2012. **Poltarazki,** Alexander (Pavlovich?),
Imperial Russian Sub-Lieutenant, Nascheburg Infantry Regiment.

2013. **Dechterev,** Jevgraf Semenovich,
Imperial Russian Lieutenant, Olviopol Hussar Regiment.

2014. **Krassovski,** Ivan Ivanovich,
Imperial Russian Lieutenant, Volyni Uhlan Regiment.

2015. **Jakobson,** Adelbart Davidovich,
Imperial Russian Lieutenant, Alexandria Hussar Regiment.

* * *

2016. **Zvietkov,** Vassili Nikiforovich,
Imperial Russian Lieutenant, Imperial Russian Quartermaster Service, serving at the time on the staff of Emperor Alexander I.

2017. **Maievski,** Sergei Ivanovich,
Imperial Russian Colonel, Commander, 13th Light Infantry Regiment.

* * *

Imperial Russian 14th Light Infantry Regiment

2018. **Konivalski,** Ivan Matvieieovich, Imperial Russian Captain.
2019. **Romanovski,** Ivan Kyrillovich, Imperial Russian Staff Captain.
2020. **Baranovski,** Josef(?), Imperial Russian Staff Captain.

* * *

2021. **Tshetshenski,** Alexander Nikolaieovich,
Imperial Russian Colonel, Life Guard Hussar Regiment, Commander, 1st Bug Cossack Regiment.

2022. **Pavlov,** Dmitri Pavlovich,
Imperial Russian Jessaul, 3rd Bug Cossack Regiment.

2023. **Matshulski,** Fedor Stepanovich,
Imperial Russian Captain, Imperial Russian Engineer Corps.

2024. **Maratshinski,** Ivan Alexieieovich,
Imperial Russian Staff Captain, 6th Light Infantry Regiment.

2025. **Dushek (Dussek),** (First name unknown),
Imperial Russian Staff Captain, Alexopol Infantry Regiment.

* * *

Imperial Russian 31st Artillery Battery Company

2026. **Netshaiev,** Nikolai Afanassieovich, Imperial Russian Lieutenant.
2027. **Denissov,** Peter Alexandrovich, Imperial Russian Sub-Lieutenant.
2028. **Deroshinski,** Vladimir Kosmish, Imperial Russian Lieutenant.
(**Note:** Lieutenant Deroshinski was awarded the 50 Year Jubilee Golden Crown to the Pour le Mérite Order on October 25, 1964.)

* * *

2029. **Grave,** Pavel Semenovich,
Imperial Russian Sub-Lieutenant, 46th Light Artillery Company.

2030. **Redrikov,** (First name unknown),
Imperial Russian Major, Commander, Line of Communications, headquartered in Breslau and included the areas of the Niesse, Reichenbach and Glatz.

2031. **Jershov,** Ivan Sacharieovich,
Imperial Russian Major General of Cavalry, unidentified unit.

2032. **Davidov,** Peter Ivanovich,
Imperial Russian Captain, Life Guard Infantry Regiment.

2033. **von Schilling,** Jakob Vassilieovich,
Imperial Russian Rittmeister, Life Guard Hussar Regiment, serving at the time in the Isium Hussar Regiment.

2034. **von Fabecky,** Ferdinand Friedrich Wilhelm,
Imperial Russian Captain, unassigned, attached to the Russo-German Legion and serving at the time on the staff of Adjutant General Tshernishev.
(**Note:** Captain von Fabecky was awarded the 50 Year Jubilee Golden Crown to the Pour le Mérite Order on June 18, 1864.)

2035. **Petrovich,** Andrei Petrovich,
Imperial Russian Lieutenant, Field Light Infantry Corps.

2036. **von Rönne,** Baron Otto Filippovich,
Imperial Russian Cornet, Mounted Life Guard Regiment, serving at the time as Adjutant to the Prince of Hesse-Philippsthal.

2037. **Bergenstrale,** Peter Ivanovich,
Imperial Russian Lieutenant, Imperial Russian Quartermaster Service, serving at the time on the staff of Emperor Alexander I.

2038. **Lopuchin,** Prince Pavel Petrovich,
Imperial Russian Colonel, Cavalier Guard Regiment, serving at the time as Wing Adjutant.

2039. **Neielov,** Peter Alexieieovich,
Imperial Russian Staff Captain, Viburg Infantry Regiment.

2040. **de Balmaine,** Count Alexander Apollonovich (Antonovich?),
Imperial Russian Lt. Colonel of Cavalry, unidentified unit.

2041. **Tomilovski,** Andrei Stepanovich,
Imperial Russian Colonel, Isium Hussar Regiment, serving at the time as Staff Officer of the Day on the staff of Imperial Russian Lt. General Vassiltshikov.

Flags and Standards of Friedrich Wilhelm III.

Dragoon Standard

⇦ 1808–1814 1st East Prussian Infantry Regiment (No. 5)

Curassier Standard

1814 Garde Grenadier Regiment (No. 2) ⇨

Imperial Russian Achtirka Hussar Regiment

The following three Russian officers were decorated with the Pour le Mérite Order in recognition of distinction in action while serving as adjutants to Imperial Russian Lt. General Vassiltshikov.

2042. **Golizin,** Prince Pavel Alexieieovich, Imperial Russian Major, Senior Adjutant.

2043. **Olsuviev,** Alexander Dmitrieovich, Imperial Russian Staff Rittmeister, Senior Adjutant.

2044. **Apraxin,** Count Alexander Petrovich, Imperial Russian Rittmeister, Life Guard Hussar Regiment, serving at the time in the Achtirka Hussar Regiment.

2045. **Duvanov,** Akim Vassilieovich, Imperial Russian Major.
2046. **Alexandrovich,** Dmitri Ivanovich, Imperial Russian Rittmeister.
2047. **Brilkin,** Dmitri Michailovich, Imperial Russian Lieutenant.
2048. **Shoshin,** Peter Afanassieovich, Imperial Russian Cornet.

* * *

Imperial Russian Alexandria Hussar Regiment

2049. **Jesimovich,** Andrei Alexandrovich, Imperial Russian Colonel.
(**Note:** This is the <u>second</u> award of the Pour le Mérite Order <u>badge</u> in recognition of outstanding distinction in action to Colonel Jesimovich. The first award of the Pour le Mérite Order was made to this officer in 1807, **seven** years earlier. For the initial award of the Pour le Mérite Order to Colonel Jesimovich see Volume I, Chapter V-1, entry 290, p. 285.)

* * *

2050. **Lukitsh,** Panteleimon Semenovich, Imperial Russian Lt. Colonel.
2051. **Marianovich,** Narkiss Pavlovich, Imperial Russian Major.
2052. **Parfazki,** Apollon Andreieovich, Imperial Russian Rittmeister.

* * *

Imperial Russian Mariupol Hussar Regiment

2053. **Rokshanin,** Semen Ossipovich, Imperial Russian Lt. Colonel.
2054. **Alexieiev,** Alexei Petrovich, Imperial Russian Major.

* * *

Imperial Russian Bielo-Russia Hussar Regiment

2055. **Olshevski,** Ossip Danilovich, Imperial Russian Colonel.
2056. **Andrusski,** Nikolai Ivanovich, Imperial Russian Rittmeister.
2057. **Gratshov,** Peter Alexieieovich, Imperial Russian Rittmeister.
2058. **Latshinov,** Peter Petrovich, Imperial Russian Lieutenant, Life Guard Hussar Regiment, serving at the time in this regiment.
(**Note:** This is the <u>second</u> award of the Pour le Mérite Order <u>badge</u> in recognition of outstanding distinction in action to Lt. Latshinov. For the initial award of the Pour le Mérite Order to this officer see entry 1771, this chapter.)

* * *

2059. **Churstshov,** Sergei Petrovich,
Imperial Russian Lt. Colonel, Kinburn Dragoon Regiment.

2060. **Petrovski,** Andrei Andreieovich,
Imperial Russian Captain, Kurland Dragoon Regiment.

2061. **Kniasev,** Peter Fedorovich,
Imperial Russian Captain, Tver Dragoon Regiment.
* * *

Imperial Russian Karpov II. Regiment
Army of the Don

2062. **Abakumov,** (First name unknown), Imperial Russian Jessaul.
2063. **Karpov V.,** Akim Akimovich, Imperial Russian Jessaul.
* * *

2064. **Tshernosubov (Tsherni-Subov?),** (First name unknown),
Imperial Russian Jessaul, Lukovkin Regiment, Army of the Don.
(**Special Note:** It appears that this Russian officer could possibly have been awarded **two** Pour le Mérite Orders. However, there is no confirming records to authenticate that this Jessaul Tshernosubov is the same as shown in entry 1142, this chapter. Since the records are so vague, it must be assumed that this is the first and only award of the Pour le Mérite Order to this officer.)
* * *

2065. **Tiumenev,** Prince Serbedshab,
Imperial Russian Major, commanding a Kulmak Regiment.
(**Note:** (Awarded the Pour le Mérite Order for distinction in action during the battle at Leipzig on October 16-19, 1813.)
* * *

Imperial Russian Ekaterinoslav Curassier Regiment

2066. **Uvarov,** Fedor Semenovich, Imperial Russian Colonel, Commander.
2067. **Kellner,** Alexander Karlovich, Imperial Russian Major.
2068. **Pavlov,** Pavel Artemieovich, Imperial Russian Rittmeister.
2069. **Levoshka,** Artemi Danilovich, Imperial Russian Staff Rittmeister.
2070. **Piliugin,** Vassili Afanassieovich, Imperial Russian Staff Rittmeister.
* * *

Imperial Russian Astrachan Curassier Regiment

2071. **Gromov,** (First name unknown), Imperial Russian Lt. Colonel, Commander.
2072. **Sadonski,** Voin Dmitrieovich, Imperial Russian Lt. Colonel.
2073. **von Rehbinder,** Boris Borissovich, Imperial Russian Major.
2074. **Goiarin,** Michail Gerassimovich, Imperial Russian Staff Rittmeister.
2075. **Jaroslavzev,** Ivan Antonovich, Imperial Russian Lieutenant, serving at the time as Adjutant in the 3rd Curassier Brigade.

2076. **von Patkul,** Friedrich, Imperial Russian Rittmeister,
(**Note:** Rittmeister von Patkul was awarded the 50 Year Jubilee Golden Crown to the Pour le Mérite Order on October 25, 1864.)
* * *

2077. **Kastrov II.,** Prince Alexei Ivanovich,
Imperial Russian Cornet, Staro-Dubno Curassier Brigade, serving at the time as Adjutant in the 3rd Curassier Brigade.
* * *

Imperial Russian Tsherni-Subov V. Regiment
Army of the Don

2078. **Koshkin,** Vassili Ivanovich(?), Imperial Russian Starchina.
2079. **Pimanov,** Ivan Andreieovich, Imperial Russian Jessaul.
* * *

The following eight Russian officers were awarded the Pour le Mérite Order in recognition of outstanding distinction in action while serving as adjutants on the staff of Grand Duke Konstantin.

2080. **Palizin,** Vladimir Ivanovich,
Imperial Russian Colonel, Life Guard Mounted Regiment.

2081. **Diakov,** Peter Nikolaieovich,
Imperial Russian Colonel, Life Guard Hussar Regiment.

2082. **Kolsakov,** Pavel Andreieovich,
Imperial Russian Captain, Guard Equipage Section.

2083. **Krivzov,** Alexander Ivanovich,
Imperial Russian Colonel, Life Guard Infantry Regiment.

2084. **Timiriasev,** Ivan Semenovich,
Imperial Russian Staff Rittmeister, Life Guard Mounted Regiment.
(**Note:** Staff Rittmeister Timiriasev was awarded the 50 Year Jubilee Golden Crown to the Pour le Mérite Order on October 25, 1964.)
* * *

2085. **Fanshave,** Grigori Andreieovich,
Imperial Russian Captain, Life Guard Semenovski Regiment.
(**Note:** Captain Fanshave was awarded the 50 Year Jubilee Golden Crown to the Pour le Mérite Order on June 18, 1864.)
* * *

2086. **Jessakov,** Dmitri Semenovich,
Imperial Russian Captain, Life Guard Infantry Regiment.

2087. **von Meyerinck,** Wichard Georg Wilhelm Ludwig,
Staff Rittmeister, Prussian Garde du Corps, serving at the time on the staff of Russian Grand Duke Konstantin.
(**Special Note:** The directive awarding Rittmeister von Meyerinck the Pour le Mérite Order was rescinded because this officer **was** Prussian and the Order was replaced with the Prussian 1813 Iron Cross 2nd Class. One could speculate that this could possibly account for so few Prussian officers receiving the Pour le Mérite Order during these campaigns.)
* * *

2088. **Golizin,** Prince Ivan Alexieieovich,
Imperial Russian Captain, Life Guard Mounted Light Infantry Regiment. Prince Golizin was serving at the time in the 3rd Ukraine Cossack Regiment. * * *

Both of the following Russian officers, when decorated with the Pour le Mérite Order in recognition of outstanding distinction in action were serving at the time as senior Adjutants in the 1st Curassier Division.

2089. **Lvov,** Dmitri Michailovich,
Imperial Russian Staff Rittmeister, Cavalier Guard Regiment.

2090. **von Medem,** Baron Vassili Ivanovich,
Imperial Russian Staff Rittmeister, His Majesty's Curassier Regiment.
* * *

Imperial Russian Cavalier Guard Regiment

2091. **Uvarov,** Fedor Alexandrovich, Imperial Russian Colonel.
2092. **Davidov,** Jevdokim Vassilieovich, Imperial Russian Colonel.

2093. **von Stael**, Alexander Fedorovich, Imperial Russian Colonel.
2094. **Chrapovizki**, Ivan Ivanovich, Imperial Russian Colonel.

* * *

Imperial Russian Life Guard Mounted Regiment

2095. **Soldaen**, Christofor Fedorovich, Imperial Russian Colonel.
2096. **Salov**, Fedor Andreieovich, Imperial Russian Colonel.
2097. **Ramm**, Karl Karlovich, Imperial Russian Colonel.
2098. **Tishkievich**, Count Andon Demianovich, Imperial Russian Rittmeister.
2099. **von Kosküll**, Baron Peter Ivanovich, Imperial Russian Rittmeister.
2100. **von Knorring**, Pontus Voldemar, Imperial Russian Colonel.
   (**Note:** Colonel von Knorring was awarded the 50 Year Jubilee Golden Crown to the Pour le Mérite Order on March 22, 1863.)

* * *

Imperial Russian His Majesty's Life Guard Curassier Regiment

2101. **Melikov**, Pavel Moisseieovich, Imperial Russian Colonel.
   (**Note:** This is the <u>second</u> award of the Pour le Mérite Order <u>badge</u> in recognition of outstanding distinction in action to Colonel Melikov. For the initial award of the Pour le Mérite Order to this officer see Volume I, Chapter V-1, entry 591, p. 314.)

2102. **von Derschau**, Karl Fedorovich, Imperial Russian Rittmeister.
2103. **von Kahlen II.**, Paul Bogdanovich, Imperial Russian Staff Rittmeister.
   (**Note:** Rittmeister von Kahlen II. was awarded the 50 Year Jubilee Golden Crown to the Pour le Mérite Order on November 16, 1865.)

* * *

Imperial Russian Her Majesty's Life Guard Curassier Regiment

2104. **Sologub**, Ignati Moisseieovich, Imperial Russian Major.
2105. **Gagin**, Pavel Nikolaieovich, Imperial Russian Major.

Both of the following Russian officers were decorated with the Pour le Mérite Order in recognition of distinction in action while serving as adjutants to Major General Prince Leopold of Saxe-Coburg.

2106. **von Kahlen I.**, Alexander Bogdanovich, Imperial Russian Staff Rittmeister.
2107. **Schlein**, Fedor Martinovich, Imperial Russian Staff Rittmeister.

* * *

Imperial Russian 1st Mounted Life Guard Artillery Company

2108. **Stolipin**, Dmitri Alexieieovich, Imperial Russian Colonel, Commander.
   (**Note:** This is the <u>second</u> award of the Pour le Mérite Order <u>badge</u> in recognition of outstanding distinction in action to Colonel Stolipin. For the initial award of the Pour le Mérite Order to this officer see entry 1547, this chapter. Note the different spelling of the name.)

2109. **von Gerbel**, Vassili Vassilieovich, Imperial Russian Staff Captain, serving at the time as Adjutant to Lt. General von Harder.

2110. **von Salza**, Baron Karl Alexandrovich, Imperial Russian Lieutenant.

2111. **von Gerstenzweig**, Danilo Alexandrovich, Imperial Russian Sub-Lieutenant.
   (**Note:** This is the <u>second</u> award of the Pour le Mérite Order <u>badge</u> in recognition of outstanding distinction in action to Sub-Lieutenant von Gerstenzweig. For the initial award of the Pour le Mérite Order to

this officer see entry 1548, this chapter.)
* * *

2112. **von Bistrom,** Filipp Antonovich,
Imperial Russian Captain, Commander, 2nd Mounted Life Guard Artillery Company.
(**Note: This is the second** award of the Pour le Mérite Order **badge** in recognition of outstanding distinction in action to Captain von Bistrom. For the initial award of the Pour le Mérite Order to this officer see entry 1549, this chapter.)
* * *

2113. **von Stephani,** Karl,
Imperial Russian Lieutenant, Imperial Russian Quartermaster Service, serving at the time on the staff of Emperor Alexander I.
* * *

Imperial Russian Rodinov II. Regiment
Army of the Don

2114. **Bichalov,** Jossif Michailovich, Imperial Russian Jessaul.
2115. **Popov,** Alexander Jemelianovich, Imperial Russian Starchina.
2116. **Selivanov,** (First name unknown), Imperial Russian Sotnik.
* * *

2117. **Selesniev,** (First name unknown),
Imperial Russian Major, Commander, 14th Bashkiren Regiment.

2118. **Kritshinski,** Semen Jossifovich,
Imperial Russian Cornet, Tatar Uhlan Regiment.
* * *

Imperial Russian Kexholm Grenadier Regiment

2119. **Martianov,** Danilo Jakovlieovich, Imperial Russian Lt. Colonel.
2120. **Kashperov,** Nikita Prochorovich, Imperial Russian Major.
* * *

Imperial Russian Pernau Grenadier Regiment

2121. **Shemshushnikov,** Apollon Stepanovich, Imperial Russian Colonel, Life Guard Littau Regiment. Assigned as commander of this regiment.

2122. **Schmidt,** Alexander Chrestianovich, Imperial Russian Major.
2123. **Trishatni,** Alexander Lvovich, Imperial Russian Major.
2124. **Neielov II.,** Ivan Ivanovich, Imperial Russian Captain.

The following two Russian officers' assigned unit was the Life Guard Light Infantry Regiment; however, they were attached to the Pernau Grenadier Regiment when decorated with the Pour le Mérite Order in recognition of outstanding distinction in action.

2125. **Tshoglokov,** Andreian Nikolaieovich, Imperial Russian Sub-Lieutenant.
2126. **Ovander,** Vassili Jakovlieovich, Imperial Russian Sub-Lieutenant.
* * *

2127. **Lovieko,** Ivan,
Imperial Russian Major, Polozk Infantry Regiment.

2128. **Kirerevski,** Fedor (Theodor?),
Imperial Russian Staff Captain, Viburg Infantry Regiment, serving at the time as Division Adjutant to Russian Major General Tshogokov.

Imperial Russian His Majesty's Life Guard Curassier Regiment

Both of the following Russian officers were decorated with the Pour le Mérite Order in recognition of distinction in action while serving as adjutants to Lt. General Duka.

2129. **Stahn,** Andrei Antonovich, Imperial Russian Rittmeister.
(**Note:** Rittmeister Stahn was awarded the 50 Year Jubilee Golden Crown to the Pour le Mérite Order on October 25, 1864.)

2130. **Shishkov (Shishkin),** Peter Ivanovich, Imperial Russian Lieutenant, serving at the time in the Small-Russia Curassier Regiment.
(**Note:** Lieutenant Shishkov was awarded the 50 Year Jubilee Golden Crown to the Pour le Mérite Order on March 9, 1867.)
* * *

2131. **Shatalov,** Ivan Vassilieovich,
Imperial Russian Lieutenant, serving at the time as Adjutant to Adjutant General Sakrevski. * * *

Imperial Russian Grodno Hussar Regiment

2132. **von Fricks,** Gustaf Fedorovich, Imperial Russian Lieutenant.
2133. **Vitkovski,** Adam Leontieovich, Imperial Russian Lieutenant.
(**Note:** This is the <u>second</u> award of the Pour le Mérite Order <u>badge</u> in recognition of outstanding distinction in action to Lieutenant Vitkovski. For the initial award of the Pour le Mérite Order to this officer see entry 1567, this chapter.)

2134. **von Kleist,** Peter, Imperial Russian Lieutenant.
* * *

2135. **Golizin,** Prince Vassili Sergieieovich,
Imperial Russian Major, Pensa Opoltshenie (militia).

2136. **von Rosen,** Baron Peter (Fedor) Fedorovich,
Imperial Russian Colonel, Tobolski Infantry Regiment, General Director of Police in Saxony.

2137. **Pusin,** Karl Karlovich,
Imperial Russian Lieutenant, 1st Ukraine Cossack Regiment.
(**Note:** Lieutenant Pusin was awarded the 50 Year Jubilee Golden Crown to the Pour le Mérite Order on November 16, 1865.)

2138. **Karaoulov I.,** Dmriti,
Imperial Russian Lt. Colonel, Moscow Opoltshenie (militia).

2139. **Miakinin,** Nikolai Davidovich,
Imperial Russian Major General, Life Guard Artillery Brigade.
* * *

Notes:

* October 14, 1814 *

2140. **Tolstoi,** Count Alexander (?),
Imperial Russian Lieutenant, Life Guard Preobrashenski Regiment.
(**Special Note:** This award of the Pour le Mérite Order to this Count Tolstoi **could** be the <u>second</u> award of the Order to this officer; however, the Imperial Russian Orders Calender does not indicate a second award of the Pour le Mérite Order to this Count Tolstoi. By the process of elimination and the fact that there were **two** other Tolstois in the Life Guard Preobrashenski Regiment but only <u>one</u> having the rank of Officer Candidate, we may assume with some degree of certainty that this actually was a second award of the Order to this Count Tolstoi. For the initial award of the Pour le Mérite Order to this officer see entry 1804, this chapter.)

* * *

* November 1, 1814 *

The Congress of Vienna

After Napoleon's abdication on April 6, 1814, the Allied Powers, Prussia, Russia, Austria and England plus several other minor states, called a summit meeting of top-level statesmen to assemble in Vienna. The object was to settle the Napoleonic question and to reestablish the boundaries of Europe. The Congress of Vienna, as it was called, convened on November 1, 1814, in Vienna, Austria. The outward impression of solidarity and cooperation was seriously undermined by dissension and challenging disagreements, which soon divided the allies. However, the Treaty of Paris, signed the previous May 30th, was eventually brought into terms acceptable to all the participants. The petty and sometimes more serious disagreements went on for months; some being resolved and some not.

March brought to the Congress the electrifying news that Napoleon had escaped from Elbe and had landed in France. The last formal meeting of the Congress was held on June 9, 1815.

* * *

* November 2, 1815 *

2141. **von Weks,** Franz,
Imperial Austrian Major, Kollowrat Infantry Regiment.
(Awarded the Pour le Mérite Order for distinction in action during several battles and engagements during the campaigns of 1813-1814.)

* * *

* November 11, 1814 *

2142. **Adlercreutz,** Gustaf Magnus,
Royal Swedish Colonel, West Göta Infantry Regiment, Adjutant General to the King of Sweden.

* * *

2143. **Ulfsparre,** Erik Georg,
Royal Swedish Colonel, serving as Lt. Colonel of the Westerbottoms Infantry Regiment, Adjutant General to the King of Sweden.
(**Note:** Colonel Ulfsparre was awarded the 50 Year Jubilee Golden Crown to the Pour le Mérite Order on June 18, 1864.)

* * *

* November 14, 1814 *

2144. **von Scheither,** Frhr. Georg,
Imperial Austrian Major General and Brigadier.

2145. **von Hammerstein-Equord,** William Friedrich,
Imperial Austrian Colonel, Meerveldt Uhlan Regiment.
(**Note:** When decorated with the Pour le Mérite Order, Colonel von Hammerstein was serving as Commanding Officer of the 1st Hussar Regiment of the Austro-German Legion.)

* * *

* December 12, 1814 *

2146. **Mansei,** Nikolai Loginovich,
Imperial Russian Rittmeister, Life Guard Hussar Regiment, serving at the time as Adjutant to Adjutant General Kutusov.
(Awarded the Pour le Mérite Order for distinction in action during the battle at Leipzig on October 16-19, 1813.)

* * *

2147. **von Thurn und Taxis,** Prince Karl Anselm,
Royal Württemberg Colonel, unidentified unit, serving at the time as Wing Adjutant.
(Awarded the Pour le Mérite Order for distinction in action during the battle at La Rothière on February 1, 1814.)

* * *

* December 28, 1814 *

Imperial Russian Lubno Hussar Regiment

2148. **Pokrovski,** Jevstafi Charitonovich, Imperial Russian Colonel, Sum Hussar Regiment, attached to the Lubno Hussar Regiment.
(**Note:** This is the **second** award of the Pour le Mérite Order <u>badge</u> in recognition of outstanding distinction in action to Colonel Pokrovski. For the initial award of the Pour le Mérite Order to this officer see entry 1357, this chapter.)

2149. **Koletshizki,** Ivan Nikolaieovich, Imperial Russian Rittmeister.
(**Note:** This is the **second** award of the Pour le Mérite Order <u>badge</u> in recognition of outstanding distinction in action to Rittmeister Koletshizki. For the initial award of the Pour le Mérite Order to this officer see entry 1376, this chapter.)

2150. **Alfimov,** (First name unknown), Imperial Russian Rittmeister.

2151. **Priess,** Nikolai Ivanovich, Imperial Russian Staff Rittmeister.
(**Note:** This is the **second** award of the Pour le Mérite Order <u>badge</u> in recognition of outstanding distinction in action to Staff Rittmeister Priess. For the initial award of the Pour le Mérite Order to this officer see entry 1377, this chapter.)

2152. **Jeropkin,** Fedor Alexandrovich, Imperial Russian Lieutenant.

2153. **Filipov,** Alexei Alexieieovich, Imperial Russian Cornet.
(**Note:** This is the **second** award of the Pour le Mérite Order <u>badge</u> in recognition of outstanding distinction in action to Cornet Filipov. For

the initial award of the Pour le Mérite Order to this officer see entry 1378, this chapter.)
* * *

2154. **Braun,** (First name unknown),
Imperial Russian Lieutenant, unidentified unit.

2155. **Bogulterov,** (First name unknown),
Imperial Russian Sotnik, unidentified unit, Army of the Don.
* * *

Imperial Russian 2nd Mounted Artillery Company
Army of the Don

2156. **Bagaievskov,** Stepan, Imperial Russian Jessaul.
2157. **Bogatirev,** Vassili Ivanovich, Imperial Russian Jessaul.
* * *

2158. **Temirov (Timirov),** (First name unknown),
Imperial Russian Major, Commander, 1st Teptiari Cossack Regiment.

2159. **Tregubov,** Ossip Grigorieovich,
Imperial Russian Major, Staro-Dubno Curassier Regiment, serving as the Communications Control Officer for the area of Schweidnitz.

2160. **Possiet,** Alexander Petrovich,
Imperial Russian Major, 8th Light Infantry Regiment, serving as the Communications Officer for the area of Oppeln.

2161. **Schulinius,** Karl Leontieovich,
Imperial Russian Captain, Mohilev Infantry Regiment, serving as Communications Officers for the area of Löwenberg.

2162. **von Tiesenhausen,** Bogdon Karlovich,
Imperial Russian Staff Captain, Jelez Infantry Regiment, serving as Communications Officer for the area of Brieg.
* * *

Imperial Russian Siberian Grenadier Regiment

2163. **Deskur (Descours),** Ivan Ivanovich, Imperial Russian Major, Commander.
2164. **Potulov,** Ivan Terentieovich, Imperial Russian Major.
* * *

Imperial Russian Malo-Russia Grenadier Regiment

2165. **Brandt,** Johann (Ivan Ivanovich), Imperial Russian Major.
2166. **Makuchin,** (First name unknown), Imperial Russian Captain, serving at the time as Brigade Adjutant to Major General Hesse.
* * *

2167. **Menshinski,** Jossif Stepanovich,
Imperial Russian Major, Lubno Hussar Regiment.
* * *

Imperial Russian Siev Mounted Light Infantry Regiment

2168. **Possudovski,** (First name unknown), Imperial Russian Lt. Colonel.
2169. **Skardovi-Rington,** Fedor Lvovich, Imperial Russian Captain.
* * *

2170. **Jakimach,** Moissei Avramovich,
Imperial Russian Major, New-Russia Dragoon Regiment.

(Awarded the Pour le Mérite Order in recognition of outstanding leadership and distinction in action during the battle at Fère Champénoise on March 13, 1814. Major Jakimach led an attack against the French positions and successfully captured an enemy cannon.)

* * *

Imperial Russian Tshernigov Mounted Light Infantry Regiment

2171. **van der Struf,** Ivan (Rodion) Fedorovich, Imperial Russian Major.
(Awarded the Pour le Mérite Order in recognition of outstanding leadership and distinction in action during the battle at Rheims.)

2172. **Rudakov,** Ivan Pavlovich, Imperial Russian Staff Captain, serving as Division Adjutant to Imperial Russian Lt. General Pantshulidsev.

* * *

The following two Russian officers were awarded the Pour le Mérite Order in recognition of outstanding leadership and distinction in action during the battle at Fère Champénoise on March 13, 1814.

2173. **Knishnikov,** Vassili Danilovich,
Imperial Russian Major, Pskov Curassier Regiment.

2174. **Bronevski,** Nikolai Bogdanovich,
Imperial Russian Staff Captain, Dorpat Mounted Light Infantry Regiment, serving at the time as Brigade Adjutant to Imperial Russian Major General Count Pahlen II.

* * *

The following twelve Russian officers were decorated with the Pour le Mérite Order in recognition of outstanding distinction in action during the assault at Montmarte in Paris in March 1814.

2175. **Rogovski,** Alexander Vassilieovich,
Imperial Russian Major, Riasan Infantry Regiment.

* * *

Imperial Russian 30th Light Infantry Regiment

2176. **Dubrovin,** Peter Sergieieovich, Imperial Russian Major.
2177. **Bresin,** Alexei Dementieovich, Imperial Russian Staff Captain.

* * *

Imperial Russian Bielosero Infantry Regiment

2178. **Jermolaiev,** (First name unknown), Imperial Russian Major.
2179. **Samsonov,** Sergei Vassilieovich, Imperial Russian Major.

* * *

Imperial Russian 33rd Light Infantry Regiment

2180. **von Brewern,** Christofor Loginovich(?), Imperial Russian Lt. Colonel, attached at the time to the Rilski Infantry Regiment.

2181. **Teplov,** (First name unknown), Imperial Russian Staff Captain.

* * *

Imperial Russian Ekaterinberg Infantry Regiment

2182. **Sliepzov,** (First name unknown), Imperial Russian Major.
2183. **Isdemirov,** (First name unknown), Imperial Russian Major.

* * *

2184. **Fokin,** (First name unknown),
Imperial Russian Major, Rilski Infantry Regiment.

2185. **Turgeniev**, Lev Antonovich,
Imperial Russian Lt. Colonel, Commander, Jelez Infantry Regiment.

2186. **Peshtshanski**, Grigori Dmitrieovich,
Imperial Russian Lt. Colonel, Commander, Polozk Infantry Regiment.
* * *

The following eight Russian officers were decorated with the Pour le Mérite in recognition of outstanding distinction in action during the battle and defense of the Château at Brienne on January 29, 1814.

2187. **Terne**, Fedor Fedorovich,
Imperial Russian Colonel, Vitepski Infantry Regiment.
(**Note:** This is the <u>second</u> award of the Pour le Mérite Order <u>badge</u> in recognition of outstanding distinction in action to Colonel Terne. For the initial award of the Pour le Mérite Order to this officer see entry 1173, this chapter.)
* * *

Imperial Russian Apsheron Infantry Regiment

2188. **Fischer**, (First name unknown), Imperial Russian Lt. Colonel.
2189. **Kartshevski**, Ivan Stanislavovich, Imperial Russian Captain.
* * *

2190. **Velenti**, Ivan Lukitsch,
Imperial Russian Lt. Colonel, Commander, Koslov Infantry Regiment.
* * *

Imperial Russian 38th Light Infantry Regiment

2191. **Tichozki**, Alexei Michailovich, Imperial Russian Major.
2192. **Iskrizki**, Peter Michailovich, Imperial Russian Major.
* * *

2193. **Deroshinski**, Leopold Kusmit,
Imperial Russian Major, Jakutski Infantry Regiment.

2194. **Korovin**, Ivan Stepanovich,
Imperial Russian Major, Kura Infantry Regiment.
* * *

2195. **Shaglevski**, David (?),
Imperial Russian Staff Captain, Riasan Infantry Regiment, serving as Corps Adjutant of the Imperial Russian IX. Infantry Corps.
* * *

Imperial Russian 22nd Light Infantry Regiment

2196. **Dombrovski**, Pavel Franzovich, Imperial Russian Staff Captain, serving as Corps Adjutant of the Imperial Russian IX. Infantry Corps.

2197. **Grigorov**, Fedor Ivanovich, Imperial Russian Staff Captain, serving as Adjutant to Major General Udom.
* * *

2198. **Kalinovski**, Vassili Jakovlieovich,
Imperial Russian Lieutenant, 4th Light Infantry Regiment, serving at the time as Adjutant to Imperial Russian Major General Kornilov.
* * *

2199. **Stachovski**, Martin Michailovich,
Imperial Russian Captain, Archangelogorod Infantry Regiment.
* * *

Imperial Russian Schlüsselberg Infantry Regiment

2200. **Aladin,** Fedor Andreieovich, Imperial Russian Major.
2201. **Korf (Korsh),** Nikolai Ivanovich, Imperial Russian Captain.
2202. **Volodimirov,** Semen Ivanovich, Imperial Russian Captain.

* * *

Imperial Russian Staro-Ingermanland Infantry Regiment

2203. **Hingliat,** Ivan Martinovich, Imperial Russian Major.
2204. **Chmielievski,** Anton Ossipovich, Imperial Russian Staff Captain.
2205. **Liatkovski,** Alexander Jakovlieovich, Imperial Russian Staff Captain.
2206. **Novopoliez,** Andrei Alexieieovich, Imperial Russian Staff Captain.

* * *

The following ten Russian officers were awarded the Pour le Mérite Order in recognition of outstanding distinction in action during the assault on Montmartre in Paris during March 1814.

Imperial Russian 7th Light Infantry Regiment

2207. **Sobolevski,** Stepan Gerassimovich, Imperial Russian Lt. Colonel.
2208. **Hippius,** Karl Fedorovich, Imperial Russian Captain.
(**Note:** This is the <u>second</u> award of the Pour le Mérite Order <u>badge</u> in recognition of outstanding distinction in action to Captain Hippius. For the initial award of the Pour le Mérite Order to this officer see entry 1622, this chapter.)

* * *

2209. **Besgin,** Konstantin Michailovich,
Imperial Russian Captain, Staro-Oskol Infantry Regiment.

* * *

Imperial Russian Viayka Infantry Regiment

2210. **Ossipovich,** Saveli Alexieieovich, Imperial Russian Major.
2211. **von Manteuffel,** (First name unknown), Imperial Russian Captain.
2212. **Kaufmann,** Peter Fedorovich, Imperial Russian Captain.

* * *

2213. **Volkov,** Vassili Silovich,
Imperial Russian Major, Olonez Infantry Regiment.

* * *

Imperial Russian 29th Light Infantry Regiment

2214. **Michailovski,** Nikolai, Imperial Russian Major.
2215. **von Hoym,** Baron (First name unknown), Imperial Russian Major.

* * *

2216. **Svida,** Michail Stepanovich,
Imperial Russian Captain, 45th Light Infantry Regiment.

2217. **Grekov,** Sergei Nikolaieovich,
Imperial Russian Staff Captain, Libau Infantry Regiment, serving as Corps Adjutant of the X. Infantry Corps.

2218. **Jelagin,** Nikolai Andreieovich,
Imperial Russian Lieutenant, Staro-Oskol Infantry Regiment, serving at the time as Brigade Adjutant to Russian Major General Turtshaninov.

* * *

2219. **Ivanov III.,** Igor Sacharieovich,
Imperial Russian Lt. Colonel, Commander, 4th Pontoon Company, Imperial Russian Engineer Corps.
(**Note:** This is the <u>second</u> award of the Pour le Mérite Order <u>badge</u> in recognition of outstanding distinction in action to Lt. Colonel Ivanov. While under heavy enemy artillery and small arms fire for almost two hours at Trilport on March 27, 1814, under Lt. Colonel Ivanov's distinguished leadership, the 4th Pontoon Company was able to secure an important temporary bridge over the Marne River thus establishing a bridgehead for the successful crossing of the Allied I. Army Corps. For the initial award of the Pour le Mérite Order to this officer see entry 1984, this chapter.)

* * *

2220. **Virubov,** Andrei Petrovich,
Imperial Russian Captain, 32nd Artillery Battery Company.

* * *

Imperial Russian 29th Light Artillery Company

2221. **Osmolovski,** (First name unknown), Imperial Russian Captain, Commander.
2222. **Freytag von Loringhoven,** Roman Karlovich, Imperial Russian Lieutenant.

* * *

2223. **Sulima,** Ossip Ivanovich,
Imperial Russian Naval Lieutenant, Tshernomori Fleet.

* * *

Imperial Russian Engineer Corps

2224. **Tuleninov,** Platon Gavrilovich, Imperial Russian Lt. Colonel, Chief Engineer of the Corps of Infantry commanded by General Count Langeron.

2225. **von Rosen,** Baron Otto Fedorovich, Imperial Russian Lieutenant.

* * *

2226. **Iljin,** (First name unknown),
Imperial Russian Major, Novo-Ingermanland Infantry Regiment.

* * *

Imperial Russian Quartermaster Service

The following two Russian officers were decorated with the Pour le Mérite Order in recognition of outstanding distinction in action during the battle at Fère Champénoise on March 13, 1814.

2227. **Koshkin,** Vassili Ivanovich(?), Imperial Russian Captain.
2228. **Dannenberg,** Samuil (Peter) Andreieovich, Imperial Russian Captain.
2229. **Samkovski,** Alexei Dmitrieovich, Imperial Russian Sub-Lieutenant.
(**Note:** Sub-Lieutenant Samkovski was also cited for outstanding bravery during the battle at the bridgehead at Trilport on the Marne River on March 27, 1814.)

* * *

2230. **Priashevski,** Nikolai Ivanovich,
Imperial Russian Major, Riasan Infantry Regiment.
(**Note:** This is the <u>second</u> award of the Pour le Mérite Order <u>badge</u> in recognition of outstanding distinction in action to Major Priashevski. For the initial award of the Pour le Mérite Order to this officer see entry 1768, this chapter.)

2231. **Lishin**, Nikolai Fedorovich,
Imperial Russian Captain, 34th Artillery Battery Company, 4th Reserve Artillery Brigade.
(**Note:** This is the <u>second</u> award of the Pour le Mérite Order <u>badge</u> in recognition of outstanding distinction in action to Captain Lishin. For the initial award of the Pour le Mérite Order to this officer see entry 1986, this chapter.)

2232. **Natara II.**, Stepan Jevstafieovich,
Imperial Russian Lieutenant, 13th Artillery Brigade.

2233. **Ivanov**, Stepan Jemelianovich,
Imperial Russian Staff Captain, 22nd Light Infantry Regiment, serving at the time as Adjutant to Imperial Russian Lt. General Rudseovich.

2234. **Natara III.**, Dmitri Jevstafieovich,
Imperial Russian Lieutenant, Isium Hussar Regiment, serving at the time as Adjutant to Imperial Russian Lt. General Rudseovich.

2235. **Freigang**, Peter Ivanovich,
Imperial Russian Lt. Colonel, Imperial Russian Quartermaster Service, serving at the time on the staff of Emperor Alexander I.
(**Note:** This is the <u>second</u> award of the Pour le Mérite Order <u>badge</u> in recognition of outstanding distinction in action to Lt. Colonel Freigang. For the initial award of the Pour le Mérite Order to this officer see entry 1033, this chapter.)

* * *

Imperial Russian Quartermaster Service

2236. **Fahlenberg**, (First name unknown), Imperial Russian Lieutenant.
2237. **Richter**, Karl Ivanovich, Imperial Russian Sub-Lieutenant.

* * *

Imperial Russian 4th Light Infantry Regiment

2238. **Albrecht**, Peter Ivanovich, Imperial Russian Captain, serving as Division Adjutant of the 17th Infantry Division.

2239. **Gorski**, Karl Petrovich, Imperial Russian Staff Captain, serving at the time as Adjutant to Imperial Russian Major General Pillar.

* * *

2240. **Rosenstein**, Fedor Igorovich,
Imperial Russian Staff Captain, Viburg Infantry Regiment, serving at the time as Division Adjutant of the 17th Infantry Division.

2241. **von Rosen**, Baron Andrei Fedorovich,
Imperial Russian Colonel, Commander, Jelissavetgrad Hussar Regiment.

2242. **Loshkarev**, Alexander (Alexei) Sergieieovich,
Imperial Russian Lt. Colonel, Isium Hussar Regiment.
(**Note:** This is the <u>second</u> award of the Pour le Mérite Order <u>badge</u> in recognition of outstanding distinction in action to Lt. Colonel Loshkarev. He was originally decorated with the Pour le Mérite Order in 1809, **five** years earlier. For the initial award of the Pour le Mérite Order to this officer see Volume I, Chapter V-1, entry 582, p. 313.)

2243. **Kuhn**, Josef Ignatieovich,
Imperial Russian Lt. Colonel, Pavlograd Hussar Regiment.

2244. **Kupfer,** Alexander Ivanovich,
  Imperial Russian Major, Jelissavetgrad Hussar Regiment.
2245. **Alferiev,** Pavel Vassilieovich,
  Imperial Russian Major, Life Guard Mounted Light Infantry Regiment, serving at the time in the Pavlograd Hussar Regiment.

***

Imperial Russian Volyni Uhlan Regiment

2246. **von Igelstroem,** Baron Gustaf Gustafovich, Imperial Russian Colonel, Commander.
2247. **Vassiliev,** Michail Vassilieovich, Imperial Russian Rittmeister, serving at the time as Brigade Adjutant of the 3rd Uhlan Division.
2248. **Barokov,** Lev Lvovich, Imperial Russian Lieutenant, serving at the time as Adjutant to Imperial Russian Lt. General Count O'Rurk.
2249. **Shishmarev,** Michail Vassilieovich, Imperial Russian Lieutenant.
2250. **Shafranski,** Ludwig Michailovich, Imperial Russian Lieutenant.
2251. **Solezki,** Alexei Pavlovich, Imperial Russian Lieutenant.
2252. **Dsheshelei,** Grigori Antonovich, Imperial Russian Cornet.
2253. **Sokolovski,** Xavier Petrovich, Imperial Russian Cornet.

***

Imperial Russian Grand Duchess Katherina Battalion

2254. **Tulubiev,** Arseni Semenovich, Imperial Russian Captain.
2255. **Morkovnikov,** Kosma Ivanovich, Imperial Russian Lieutenant.
2256. **Prudnikov,** Alexander Fedorovich, Imperial Russian Sub-Lieutenant.
2257. **Tshaplin,** Michail, Imperial Russian Sub-Lieutenant.

***

2258. **von Droste zu Vischering,** Frhr. Josef,
  Imperial Russian Major, unidentified unit.

2259. **Lachmann,** (First name unknown),
  Imperial Russian Rittmeister, unidentified unit, serving at the time as Adjutant to Major General von Tettenborn.

2260. **Varnhagen von Ense,** Karl August,
  Imperial Russian Captain, unidentified unit.

2261. **Schultz,** Jakob,
  Imperial Russian Rittmeister, Kasan Dragoon Regiment.

2262. **(von) Herbert,** Ernst,
  Imperial Russian Rittmeister, unidentified unit.

2263. **Dobrishin,** Nikolai Ivanovich,
  Imperial Russian Staff Captain, 45th Light Infantry Regiment.

2264. **Koliubakin (Kulebiakin),** Vassili Ivanovich,
  Imperial Russian Lieutenant, 29th Light Infantry Regiment, serving at the time as Adjutant to Imperial Russian Major General Sheltuchin.

2265. **von der Hoven,** Igor Christoforovich,
  Imperial Russian Staff Captain, Imperial Russian Quartermaster Service, serving on the staff of Emperor Alexander I.
  (**Note:** Staff Captain von der Hoven was awarded the 50 Year Jubilee Golden Crown to the Pour le Mérite Order on March 9, 1867.)

2266. **Vishniakovski,** Stanislav Ossipovich,
  Imperial Russian Staff Rittmeister, Astrachan Curassier Regiment,

serving at the time as Adjutant to Infantry General Frhr. von Sacken.

2267. **Ivashkin,** (First name unknown),
Imperial Russian Staff Captain, Kurland Dragoon Regiment, serving at the time as Adjutant to Infantry General von Sacken.

* * *

Imperial Russian 8th Light Infantry Regiment

2268. **Sliuniaiev,** Grigori Dementieovich, Imperial Russian Colonel.
2269. **Laptiev,** Nikolai (Ivanovich), Imperial Russian Major.
2270. **Huberti,** Vassili Jakovlieovich, Imperial Russian Captain.

* * *

Imperial Russian Kamtshatka Infantry Regiment

2271. **Selivanov,** Grigori Alexieieovich, Imperial Russian Lt. Colonel.
2272. **Safianov,** Peter(?), Imperial Russian Lt. Colonel.

* * *

2273. **Levandovski,** Justin Vassilieovich,
Imperial Russian Lt. Colonel, Tarnopol Infantry Regiment.

2274. **Rindin,** Filadelf Kyrillovich,
Imperial Russian Lt. Colonel, Aimbirski Infantry Regiment.

2275. **(Petrovski)-Muravski,** (First name unknown),
Imperial Russian Major, Commander, 49th Light Infantry Regiment.
(**Note:** This is the <u>second</u> award of the Pour le Mérite Order <u>badge</u> in recognition of outstanding distinction in action to Major Muravski. For the initial award of the Pour le Mérite Order to this officer see entry 1213, this chapter.)

2276. **Asovski,** (First name unknown),
Imperial Russian Major, 39th Light Infantry Regiment.

2277. **Verbovski,** Platon Vassilieovich,
Imperial Russian Colonel, Commander, 10th Artillery Battery Company.

2278. **Karatshinski,** Ivan (Vassilieovich?),
Imperial Russian Captain, 19th Light Artillery Company.
(**Note:** This is the <u>second</u> award of the Pour le Mérite Order <u>badge</u> in recognition of outstanding distinction in action to Captain Karatshinski. For the initial award of the Pour le Mérite Order to this officer see entry 1385, this chapter.)

* * *

2279. **Natara(I.),** Stepan Stepanovich,
Imperial Russian Staff Captain, 13th Artillery Battery Company.

2280. **Kindiakov,** Semen Ivanovich,
Imperial Russian Major, Odessa Infantry Regiment.

* * *

Imperial Russian Crimean Infantry Regiment

2281. **Kiov,** Ivan Ivdokimovich, Imperial Russian Major.
2282. **Sikorski,** (First name unknown), Imperial Russian Major.

* * *

2283. **Ostreshkovski,** Franz Kasimirovich,
Imperial Russian Captain, Vilna Infantry Regiment.

* * *

Imperial Russian Jaroslav Infantry Regiment

2284. **Stepanov**, (First name unknown), Imperial Russian Major.
2285. **Bulgakov**, Fedor Vassilieovich, Imperial Russian Major.

* * *

2286. **Varlovski**, Adam Stanislavovich,
Imperial Russian Lieutenant, Alexandria Hussar Regiment.

2287. **Chrapatshov**, Vassili Stepanovich,
Imperial Russian Lieutenant, Bielostok Infantry Regiment, serving at the time as Adjutant to Imperial Russian Major General Count Lieven III.

* * *

2288. **Kapzevich**, Ivan Michailovich,
Imperial Russian Lt. Colonel, Pskov Infantry Regiment.

2289. **Burmeister**, Fedor Fedorovich,
Imperial Russian Lt. Colonel, Imperial Russian Engineer Corps.
(Awarded the Pour le Mérite Order for distinction in action during the engagement against the French at the crossing of the Rhine River at Mannheim in January 1814.
Note: Lt. Colonel Burmeister was awarded the 50 Year Jubilee Golden Crown to the Pour le Mérite Order on October 25, 1864.)

2290. **Maznev**, Michail Nikolaieovich,
Imperial Russian Colonel, 11th Light Infantry Regiment.
(Awarded the Pour le Mérite Order for distinction in action during the battle at Craonne on March 7, 1814, and also during the battle at Laon on March 9, 1814.)

* * *

2291. **von Sanden-Peskovich**, Karl Vassilieovich,
Imperial Russian Colonel, Commander, Riga Garrison Artillery, serving at the time as commander of the St. Petersburg Arsenal.

2292. **von Pfuel**, Ernst Adolf Heinrich,
Colonel, Russo-German Legion.
(Awarded the Pour le Mérite Order in recognition of outstanding distinction in action during the 1814 campaigns. For the award of the Oakleaves to the Pour le Mérite Order to this officer see entry 2444, this chapter.)

* * *

During the field campaigns of 1814, **967** Pour le Mérite Orders were awarded. What is even more surprising than the large number of Pour le Mérite Order awards is that of the 967 Orders given, **889** or **92%** were to Russian officers. The remainder of the Pour le Mérite Orders were given to 26 Austrians (3%), 25 Prussians (3%), 10 Bavarians (1%), 7 Swedes (0.7%), 5 Britons (0.5%), 3 Baden officers (0.3%), and officers of Württemberg, Saxony and the Netherlands each receiving one Pour le Mérite Order.

Between October 13 and 18, **448** awards, **(46%)** of the years total of the Pour le Mérite Order, **all** were to **Russian** officers.

* * *

* January 1, 1815 *

During January 1815, Prussia, by the Negotiations at the Congress of Vienna, was permitted to annex approximately 40% of Saxony, but only after relinquishing most claims to her former Polish territories. In return, Friedrich Wilhelm III. was granted large portions of Westphalia and other lands along the Rhine River. At one stroke of the pen, Prussia had increased her population by four million, and the kingdom of Prussia now lay across northern Germany like a giant.

* * *

Allied Statesmen at the Congress of Vienna, 1815.

2293. **von Below,** Theodor Werner Christian,
Colonel, Commander, Littau Dragoon Regiment.
(**Note:** Colonel von Below was awarded the Oakleaves to the Pour le Mérite Order in recognition of outstanding leadership and outstanding distinction in action during the 1814 campaigns and especially during

the engagements at La Chaussée and Laon on March 9, 1814. Colonel von Below was originally awarded the Pour le Mérite Order in 1807, **8 years earlier.** For the initial award of the Pour le Mérite Order to this officer see Volume I, Chapter V-1, entry 328, p. 289.)

* * *

* February 13, 1815 *

2294.   **Tompson,** Ludwig,
Imperial Russian Cavalry Rittmeister, unidentified unit.
(Awarded the Pour le Mérite Order in recognition of distinction in action during an engagement against the French.)

* * *

During this time, the exiled Napoleon carefully watched the events taking place in Vienna. He resolved to return to France and was only waiting for the Congress to conclude the business of re-mapping Europe. Napoleon felt that once the allies had left Vienna, it would be difficult for them to react quickly to his threat. However, the Congress dragged on and impatience got the better of him. On the evening of February 26, 1815, Napoleon boarded the ship "Inconstant" and left the island of Elbe. This was the first step on his planned return to France.

Napoleon's Return to France.

Three days later on March 1st, 1815, Napoleon landed on the coast of France near Cannes from the Gulf of St. Juan.

The news of Napoleon's return to France reached Vienna on March 6, 1815. Napoleon had hoped to bring about a split in the somewhat shaky alliance of the major powers. This assumption was a great mistake, for his appearance actually served to pull the allies together. Despite their differences, the allies together abhorred Napoleon and they immediately began preparations to confront him.

* March 12, 1815 *

Imperial Russian King of Prussia Grenadier Regiment

2295.   **Falk,** Fedor Bogdanovich, Imperial Russian Major.
2296.   **Timrodt,** Alexander Ivanovich, Imperial Russian Captain.

* * *

On March 13, 1815, the allies issued a formal declaration of war, not against France, but against Napoleon himself. In addition, they outlawed him for breaking the Treaty of Fontainbleau and for "disturbing the public peace."

Napoleon, continued his advance on Paris. The journey was like a triumphal procession as more and more troops sent to stop him joined his ranks, including Marshal Michel Ney. The French government and the court of Louis XVIII., realizing their position was hopeless, fled Paris for safety in the north. Napoleon successfully entered Paris on March 20, 1815.

* * *

* The Seventh Coalition *

On March 25, 1815, the Seventh Coalition was formed by all the signatories of the Sixth. The British government sent its representative to the Congress of Vienna, Arthur Wellesley, the Duke of Wellington, to organize and command an Anglo-Dutch army. This army was to be headquartered in Brussels, Belgium.

The Duke of Wellington

At the same time, Field Marshal Gebhard Blücher was recalled to active duty and appointed Commander-in-Chief of the Prussian forces also mobilizing in Belgium.

* * *

* April 5, 1815 *

Imperial Russian Sum Hussar Regiment

2297. **von Loewenstern,** Ivan Peter Eduard, Imperial Russian Rittmeister.
2298. **Novossilzov,** Vladimir Grigorieovich, Imperial Russian Staff Rittmeister.
   Both of the above officers were decorated with the Pour le Mérite Order in recognition of distinction in action while serving as Adjutants to Imperial Russian Lt. General von der Pahlen I.

2299. **von Grothuss**, (First name unknown), Imperial Russian Sub-Lieutenant.
* * *

2300. **Brunner**, (First name unknown),
Imperial Russian Lieutenant, Grodno Hussar Regiment.

2301. **Mikulin**, Vassili Jakovlieovich,
Imperial Russian Lieutenant, Life Guard Preobrashenski Regiment, serving at the time as Adjutant in the I. Army Corps.
* * *

* May 4, 1815 *

2302. **von Fahenberg**, Frhr. Anton,
Imperial Austrian Rittmeister, Rosenberg Light Cavalry Regiment, assigned to the Staff Dragoon Regiment.
(**Note:** Awarded the Pour le Mérite Order in recognition of distinction in action during the battle at Montmartre in Paris in March 1814, when, as a volunteer he displayed outstanding bravery and leadership.)
* * *

* May 25, 1815 *

2303. **Almázy von Zsadány und Török-Sz. Miklós**, Count Elias,
Imperial Austrian Colonel (retired), unidentified unit.
(**Special Note:** Awarded the Pour le Mérite Order in recognition of outstanding leadership and conspicious bravery in action on many occasions. This notable Hungarian officer served over a 17 year period in 12 campaigns against the French.)
* * *

* June 10, 1815 *

2304. **Klotzsch**, Karl,
Imperial Russian Major, Novgorod Curassier Regiment.
(Awarded the Pour le Mérite Order in recognition of distinction in action during the battles at Leipzig, Brienne, La Rothière, Montmurail, Château Thierry, Croan and Fère Champénoise.)
* * *

By mid-June Napoleon assembled an army of 120,000 troops in preparation for his invasion of Belgium. Despite the fact that he would be facing nearly 225,-000 allied troops, Napoleon knew that surprise would be effective and give him the advantage. Through skillful maneuvering, Napoleon managed to move his army and concentrate it just inside the northern borders of France. This move was accomplished so quickly and in such secrecy that neither Wellington, Blücher nor those at the forward allied headquarters at Namur, 32 miles southeast of Brussels, were aware of Napoleon's presence.

Early on June 15, 1815, the French army began crossing the Belgium frontier. Almost immediately contact was made with the forward elements of the Prussian I. Corps, and the Prussian forces began to withdraw from their positions in and around Charleroi. Blücher realized that a major French offensive was underway and ordered his forces to concentrate at the towns of Sombreffe and Ligny. Blücher sent word to Wellington informing him of the day's events and asking for his course of action. This vital information was slow in reaching Wellington, and by the time he did receive it there was little for him on which to base a strategy plan. However, Wellington did issue orders to his forces to be prepared to concentrate and be ready to move immediately where needed.

Napoleon's original plan was to locate his forces between Blücher and Wellington. He would then be able to engage each force separately. By the end of the day, Napoleon had failed to accomplish two important objectives. The first being to keep the Prussian forces from concentrating three of their four corps near Ligny.

Blücher Rallying the Prussians at Ligny

The second objective was that Marshal Michel Ney had failed to capture the important crossroad town of Quatre Bras which was the main communications link between Blücher and Wellington. This failure allowed Wellington to move reinforcements into the village of Quatre Bras overnight.

By the end of June 15th, it was evident that two major battles would be fought. Napoleon realized Blücher was concentrating his troops. If he could first engage and defeat the Prussians, he would then be able to concentrate his efforts against Wellington. The French began moving into position and at the same time bringing up reinforcements. Blücher, in the meantime, had drawn his forces into heavily defended positions along the ridges north of Ligny and there waited for the French to attack.

The battle of Ligny began around 2:30 in the afternoon of June 16, 1815. Initially the Prussian lines held, but soon there was sustained heavy fighting in and around the Prussian held villages. Under the heavy French assaults, the Prussian lines began to give way. Napoleon was about to launch a massive attack against the center of the Prussian lines when word came that unidentified troops were advancing toward the French left flank. It turned out that these were French troops sent by Marshal Ney, but it took some time to identify them. This delay proved minor for the French. The assault began at 7:30 in the evening, and the Prussian line began to collapse.

Count von Nostitz Protecting Blücher

In an effort to rally his retreating Prussians, Blücher personally led a cavalry charge against the advancing French troops and their cavalry. During the daring charge, Blücher's mount was killed. Falling on the Field Marshal, the horse injured and trapped him under the horse's body. Count August Ludwig von Nostitz saw Blücher's dilemma, dismounted and tried to extricate him from under the dead horse. Unfortunately, he was unable to accomplish this, so von Nostitz stood by protect his Field Marshal from the French cavalry until Prussian help arrived. By this couragous act, Count von Nostitz most likely saved Blücher's life. It is also of interest that von Nostitz did not receive the Pour le Mérite Order for his brave action. He was later decorated with **both** the Pour le Mérite Order **and** the Oakleaves together while serving as an observer on the staff of Emperor Nicholas I. during the 1828-1829 Russo-Turkish War. See entry 2436, this chapter.

General Gneisenau not knowing the location of Blüchers forces, immediately ordered a withdrawal north toward the town of Wavre. This move was unexpected by Napoleon and was to prove a blessing to the allies during the next few days.

At the same time that Napoleon and Blücher were engaged. Marshal Ney and the French left flank found themselves involved at Quatre Bras. Most of the 16th of June, Ney's forces advanced slowly against the allied forces in and around the village of Quatre Bras. By mid-afternoon the French had captured important positions on the allied left flank and center. At Bossu Woods, on the right flank, a contingent from Nassau bitterly defended its position, and managed to delay the French long enough for Wellington to arrive with reinforcements. At this point, William, the Prince of Orange, attempted to counterattack the advancing French.

Duke of Brunswick

The attack was unsuccessful, but it provided the time needed for General Wilhelm Friedrich, the Duke of Brunswick, to bring up even more troops. Marshal Ney ordered General François Kellermann to attack Quatre Bras with his French cavalry. They almost succeeded but were stopped and driven back. In fact, General Kellermann narrowly avoided being captured. Unfortunately, the Duke of Brunswick was killed leading his Brunswick Corps of the 6th Division against the French. By nine in the evening nearly all the original positions had been retaken and the fighting ceased.

The battle at Quatre Bras was indecisive but was a setback to Napoleon's strategy. Wellington had by this time withdrawn his forces safely to new consolidated positions near the town of Waterloo.

Marshal Emmanuel Grouchy continued his pursuit of the Prussian army. In the evening of June 17, 1815, his troops were preparing to attack the Prussian positions across the Dyle River near Wavre. Blücher had learned of the result of the battle at Quatre Bras and that Wellington was preparing to make a stand against Napoleon at Waterloo. Blücher immediately began sending as many Prus-

The Death of the Duke of Brunswick at Quatre Bras.

sian units as he could west toward Waterloo and Wellingtons forces. Blücher left a rear guard, commanded by General Thielmann, to hold their positions as long as possible against Grouchy's French troops. Although the Prussians were outnumbered almost 2 to 1 they held their line fast. The fighting at Wavre lasted throughout the day. The French were getting nowhere when Marshal Grouchy received orders from Napoleon to rejoin the main French army. However, it was too late for him to join Napoleon so he chose to remain in his position, which he did until June 19, 1815.

Blücher learned that Wellington had taken his position at the village of Waterloo (see special note) on June 17, 1815, and that he was prepared to fight Napoleon. However, it would be imperative that Blücher reinforce him no later than late afternoon of the following day. This meant a forced march of nearly 10 miles in less than 24 hours for some 72,000 Prussians. The Field Marshal immediately began moving his army to join Wellington's forces.

* The Battle of Waterloo *

(**Special Note:** So much has been written about the battle of Waterloo on June 18, 1815, that it seems unnecessary to write more; therefore, the reader should look to other sources for a more detailed account of the action. We will deal here only with the Prussians and the conclusion of the battle.)

* * *

The battle of Waterloo began at 11:30 am on June 18, 1815. By around 1 pm, Napoleon learned of Blücher's approaching Prussians and was forced to divert troops east to stop the Prussian advance at the town of Plancenoit. By 4 pm the first elements of the Prussian army arrived and were immediately engaged until early evening in heavy fighting with the French. By 7 pm, several battalions of Napoleon's Imperial Guard had been withdrawn from Plancenoit, reorganized and sent against the wavering allied center. The Guard marched directly into the massed fire of the British 1st Foot Guards with devastating effect. The Imperial Guard broke and began to retreat. This marked the beginning of the end for the French.

The Prussians Emerging from Paris Forest
(The church steeple at left is in Plancenoit.)

Napoleon was repeatedly advised by his generals and senior officers to escape while there was still time. Finally persuaded, he and his escort left for Genappe. He planned to pull together his shattered troops which were now streaming from the battlefield. When arriving in Genappe, Napoleon was forced to leave his carriage and take to horseback. His carriage, which contained his decorations and other important items was subsequently captured and sent to Blücher. The narrow streets were jammed with panic-stricken troops, and it took Napoleon almost an hour to reach the only bridge leading out of town. As it was, he narrowly escaped capture by a unit of Prussian Hussars that were entering Genappe in pursuit of the routed retreating French.

Blücher and Wellington Meeting at La Belle Alliance

Around 9 pm on June 19, 1815, the Duke of Wellington and the Field Marshal Blücher met at the inn at La Belle Alliance, which was near Napoleon's former command post adjoining the inn. At this meeting it was decided that General Gneisenau and Blücher, with fresher Prussian troops, should pursue the remnants of the broken French army. The Prussians did so with a vengeance, but for some reason, they halted their chase.

* * *

King's (Major's) Color, 1st Foot Guards, carried by the 3rd Battalion at Waterloo.

King's (Colonel's) Color, 2nd Foot Guards, carried by the 2nd Battalion at Waterloo.

Regimental Color, 1st Foot Guards, 3rd Battalion, 8th Company, carried at battle of Waterloo.

* June 19, 1815 *

2305. **von Lemke,** Friedrich Wilhelm Bogislav,
   2nd Lieutenant, Pomeranian Hussar Regiment.
   (**Note:** Lieutenant von Lemke was decorated with the Pour le Mérite Order in recognition of his being the **first** Prussian to enter Genappe. He was also the only officer to receive the Pour le Mérite Order on the day of the battle of Waterloo.)

* * *

Malmaison

Napoleon hurried back to Paris, arriving on June 21, 1815. Although he talked of organizing new armies and continuing the war, it was evident that the government and the nation as a whole had had enough and would no longer support him. The following day, June 22, 1815, Napoleon abdicated as Emperor of the French for the second time in favor of his son, the King of Rome. All of this happened only four days after his defeat at Waterloo. He immediately retired to Malmasion to await the allies' reaction. The Provisional Government of France immediately began peace negotiations with the victorious allies. Blücher, in the meantime, continued his pursuit of Napoleon's battered forces, a task he refused to give up even upon learning of Napoleon's abdication. The old Field Marshal wrote to General Müffling demanding, "You will direct activities for having Napoleon surrendered to us so that he may be excuted. Such is the requirement of Everlasting Justice." However, Wellington disagreed and informed the crusty and vindictive Blücher that summary execution would be "unbecoming" of generals of their calibre. Blücher was unimpressed and pushed on to Paris with the almost blind desire to capture Napoleon. The "Iron Duke" was reluctantly dragged along.

* * *

* June 24, 1815 *

2306. **von Thile II.,** Heinrich Adolf Eduard,
   Colonel, serving on the General Staff of the High Command of the Niederrhine Army.
   (**Note:** Colonel von Thile was awarded the Oakleaves to the Pour le Mérite Order in recognition of distinguished leadership and military planning during this campaign and for distinction in action at Waterloo. He was also the first officer to inform Friedrich Wilhelm III. at Mersburg on June 23, 1815, of the victory at Waterloo and Napoleon's

defeat. For the initial award of the Pour le Mérite Order to this officer see Volume I, Chapter V-1, entry 682, p. 328.)

* * *

The victorious allied army entered Paris for the second time on July 4, 1815, led by Field Marshal Blücher and the Prussians. Napoleon, however, was permanently out of the grasp of Blücher: he had departed Malmasion on June 29th. This was the first leg of a journey destined to end three months later on the South Atlantic island of St. Helena. Napoleon died in exile in 1821 under mysterious circumstances which today seem to indicate that he was murdered.

Blücher remained with the Prussian forces until the last garrisons of French troops surrendered in October 1815. He then retired from the Prussian military service and returned to his estate in Silesia where he remained in seclusion. The departure of Blücher from France brought to a close the Napoleonic Wars in general and the Prussian Liberation War in particular.

Three Prussian Army Corps in Paris on July 4, 1815.

The end of the Napoleonic wars brought many changes to Prussia, not the least of which was additional territory with an increase in population of nearly four million subjects. This made the kingdom the largest and most important state in northern Germany. Prussia now stretched from Memel in the east to the west bank of the Rhine River. However, peace also brought new problems to Friedrich Wilhelm III.

* August 7, 1815 *

2307. **Sukovkin**, Peter Lavrovich,
Imperial Russian Major, unidentified unit, serving at the time as Adjutant to Infantry General Frhr. von Sacken.
(**Note:** Major Sukovkin was belatedly awarded the Pour le Mérite Order in recognition of distinction in action during the battle at Guttstadt on May 24, 1807, **eight** years earlier.)

* * *

* August 15, 1815 *

The following two Russian officers were decorated with the Pour le Mérite Order in recognition of distinction in action while serving as Adjutants to Russian General of Infantry Dochturov.

2308. **Shkurin**, Paul Sergieieovich,
Imperial Russian Staff Captain, Cavalier Guard Regiment.

2309. **Panin**, Count Alexander Nikolaieovich,
Imperial Russian Lieutenant, Pskov Curassier Regiment.

* * *

* August 19, 1815 *

The following three Russian officers belatedly received the Pour le Mérite Order in recognition of distinction in action during the 1806-1807 campaigns against the French while serving as Adjutants to Russian Lt. General Konovizin.

2310. **Tarassov**, Ivan Ivanovich,
Imperial Russian Lt. Colonel, Life Guard Grenadier Regiment.

2311. **Rodsianko**, Michail Petrovich,
Imperial Russian Staff Rittmeister, Life Guard Hussar Regiment, formerly in the Pavlograd Hussar Regiment.

2312. **Kirpitshev**, Matvei Kyrillovich,
Imperial Russian Captain, unidentified unit.

* * *

2313. **Koslainov**, Vladimir Petrovich,
Imperial Russian Lieutenant, 1st [or 3rd?] Artillery Brigade.
(Awarded the Pour le Mérite Order in recognition of outstanding leadership and distinction in action during the 1806-1807 campaigns against the French when Lieutenant Koslainov served in the 6th Artillery Brigade.)

* * *

* September 7, 1815 *

2314. **Platov**, Count Ivan Matvieieovich,
Imperial Russian Lt. Colonel, Ataman Regiment, Army of the Don.
(**Note:** This officer was the younger son of Cavalry General Count Platov.)

* * *

* September 25, 1815 *

2315. **Dubelt**, Leonti Vassilieovich,
Imperial Russian Major, Pskov Infantry Regiment.
(**Note:** Awarded the Pour le Mérite Order in recognition of outstanding leadership and distinction in action during the battle at Leipzig on October 16-19, 1813.)

2316. **von Seddler**, Baron Ludwig Ivanovich,
   Imperial Russian Lieutenant, Imperial Russian Quartermaster Service, serving at the time on the personal staff of Emperor Alexander I.

* * *

* October 2, 1815 *

2317. **von Holtzendorff**, Karl Friedrich,
   Major General, Commander of Artillery, Army of the Niederrhine.
   (**Note:** General von Holtzendorff was awarded the Oakleaves to the Pour le Mérite Order in recognition of distinguished leadership and conspicuous bravery in action during the 1815 campaigns. He was first awarded the Pour le Mérite Order in 1794, **21** years earlier. For the initial award of the Pour le Mérite Order to this officer see Volume I, Chapter IV, entry 791, p. 210.)

* * *

2318. **von Jagow**, Christian Friedrich Wilhelm,
   Major General, Chief of the III. Brigade.
   (**Note:** General von Jagow was awarded **both** the Pour le Mérite Order **and** Oakleaves to the Pour le Mérite Order on this date in recognition of distinguished leadership and outstanding military planning and successful operations. The award also recognized his distinction in action during the battle at Ligny on June 15-16, 1815, and for his outstanding leadership during the battles at Avesnes on June 22, 1815, and at Compiègne on June 27, 1815, Nanteuil, June 28, Sèvres and Issy on July 2-3, 1815.)

* * *

2319. **von Steinmetz**, Karl Friedrich Franziscus,
   Major General, Chief of the I. Brigade.
   (**Note:** General von Steinmetz was awarded the Oakleaves to the Pour le Mérite Order in recognition of distinguished leadership and conspicuous bravery in action during the battle at Waterloo on June 18, 1815. For the initial award of the Pour le Mérite Order to this officer see Volume I. Chapter V-1, entry 400, p. 294.)

* * *

2320. **von Pirch**, Otto Karl Lorenz,
   Major General, Chief of the II. Brigade.
   (**Note:** General von Pirch was awarded **both** the Pour le Mérite Order **and** the Oakleaves to the Pour le Mérite Order on this date in recognition of outstanding leadership and distinguished military planning during the 1815 campaigns. The award also recognized his distinction in action during the battles at Charleroi and Lambusart on June 15, 1815, and at St. Amand on June 16, 1815.)

* * *

2321. **von Lützow**, Frhr. Ludwig Adolf Wilhelm,
   Lt. Colonel, Commander, 6th Uhlan Regiment, serving as interim Brigade Commander of the Reserve Cavalry of the I. Army Corps.
   (**Note:** Lt. Colonel von Lützow was awarded the Oakleaves to the Pour le Mérite Order in recognition of distinguished leadership and conspicuous bravery in action during the battle at Gosselies on June 15, 1815. For the initial award of the Pour le Mérite Order to this officer see Volume I, Chapter V-1, entry 159, p. 272.)

* * *

2322. **von Selasinsky,** Karl Friedrich,
Major, Adjutant, I. Army Corps.
(**Note:** Major von Selasinsky was awarded **both** the Pour le Mérite Order **and** the Oakleaves to the Pour le Mérite Order together in recognition of outstanding leadership and conspicious bravery while leading an attack during the battle at St. Amand on June 16, 1815.)
* * *

2323. **von Froelich,** Ernst August Moritz,
Major, Adjutant, I. Army Corps.
(**Note:** Major von Froelich was awarded **both** the Pour le Mérite Order **and** the Oakleaves to the Pour le Mérite Order together on this date in recognition of outstanding leadership and distinguished military planning and operations. The award also recognized his distinction in action during the battle at St. Amand on June 16, 1815.)
* * *

2324. **von Arnauld de la Perière,** August Ferdinand,
Major, serving at the time on the General Staff of the I. Brigade.
(**Note:** Major von Arnault de la Perière was awarded **both** the Pour le Mérite Order **and** the Oakleaves to the Pour le Mérite Order together on this date in recognition of outstanding leadership and distinguished military planning and operations. The award also recognized his distinction in action during the battle at Waterloo on June 18, 1815.)
* * *

2325. **von Boehler,** Johann Christian August,
Major, Adjutant, III. Brigade.
(**Note:** Major von Boehler was awarded **both** the Pour le Mérite Order **and** the Oakleaves to the Pour le Mérite Order together on this date in recognition of outstanding leadership and distinguished military planning and operations. The award also recognized his distinction in action during the battles at Ligny on June 16, 1815, and also at Avesnes on June 21, 1815.)
* * *

2326. **von Stutterheim,** August Leopold,
Colonel, Commander, Brandenburg Uhlan Regiment, serving at the time as Commander of the Reserve Cavalry of the I. Army Corps.
(**Note:** Colonel von Stutterheim was awarded **both** the Pour le Mérite Order **and** the Oakleaves to the Pour le Mérite Order together on this date in recognition of outstanding leadership and distinguished military planning and operations. The award also recognized his distinction in action during the battle at Ligny on June 16, 1815, and also at the engagement at Issy on July 2, 1815.)
* * *

1st West Prussian Infantry Regiment

2327. **Stach von Goltzheim,** Engel Ludwig, Lt. Colonel, interim Commander.
(Lt. Colonel Stach von Goltzheim was awarded the Oakleaves to the Pour le Mérite Order in recognition of distinguished leadership and conspicuous bravery in action during the battles at Ligny and St. Amand on June 28, 1815, and at Viller-Cotterets also on June 28, 1815. For the initial award of the Pour le Mérite Order to this officer see Volume I, Chapter V-1, entry 268, p. 284.)

2328. **von Rohr,** Karl Heinrich Christian Ludwig, Major.
(Major von Rohr was awarded the Oakleaves to the Pour le Mérite Or-

der in recognition of distinguished leadership and conspicuous bravery in action during the battle at Charleroi on June 15, 1815. For the initial award of the Pour le Mérite Order to this officer see Volume I, Chapter V-1, entry 255, p. 283.)

2329. **von Oppenkowsky**, Stanislaus, Captain.
(**Note:** Captain von Oppenkowsky was awarded **both** the Pour le Mérite Order **and** the Oakleaves to the Pour le Mérite Order together on this date in recognition of outstanding leadership and distinguished military planning and operations. The award also recognized his distinction in action during the battle at Villers-Cotterets on June 28, 1815.)

* * *

2330. **von Schutter**, Arnold,
Colonel, Commander, 19th Infantry Regiment, serving at the time as Brigade Commander of the IV. Brigade.
(**Note:** Colonel von Schutter was awarded **both** the Pour le Mérite Order **and** the Oakleaves to the Pour le Mérite Order together on this date in recognition of outstanding leadership and distinguished military planning and operations. The award also recognized his distinction in action during the battles at both Ligny and Wavre on June 18, 1815.)

* * *

2331. **von der Osten**, Otto Albrecht Philipp Ludwig,
Major, interim Commander, Brandenburg Dragoon Regiment.
(Awarded the Oakleaves to the Pour le Mérite Order in recognition of distinguished leadership and conspicious bravery in action during the battle at Villers-Coyyercts on June 28, 1815. Major von der Osten's Brandenburg Dragoons during this action captured 4 enemy cannon, 27 munition wagons and took many French prisoners. Major von der Osten was first awarded the Pour le Mérite Order in 1793, **22** years earlier. For the initial award of the Pour le Mérite Order to this officer see Volume I, Chapter IV, entry 437, p. 178.)

* * *

2332. **von Engelhart**, Karl Ludwig Siegmund,
Major, 1st Silesian Hussar Regiment.
(**Note:** Major von Engelhart was awarded **both** the Pour le Mérite Order **and** the Oakleaves to the Pour le Mérite Order together on this date in recognition of outstanding leadership and distinguished military planning and operations. The award also recognized his distinction in action during the battle at La Belle Alliance on June 18, 1815, and also during the action at Nanteuil on June 28, 1815.)

* * *

The following Prussian officer was the first to be awarded both the Pour le Mérite Order with the Oakleaves at the same time and subsequently awarded a **second** Pour le Mérite Order with the Oakleaves together.

2333. **von Schon**, Johann Karl Josef,
Colonel, Brigade Commander, VII. Brigade.
(**Special Note:** This is the **second** award of **both** the Pour le Mérite Order **with** the Oakleaves to the Pour le Mérite Order on this date in recognition of outstanding leadership and conspicuous bravery during the battle at Ligny on June 16, 1815. For the initial award of the Pour le Mérite Order **and** the Oakleaves together to Colonel von Schon see entry 1641, p. 118, this chapter.)

* * *

2334. **von Krafft**, Karl Thilo Ludwig,
Major General, Chief of the VI. Brigade.
(Awarded the Oakleaves to the Pour le Mérite Order in recognition of distinguished leadership and outstanding military planning and operations. The award also recognized his conspicious bravery in action during the battle at Namur on June 20, 1815. General von Krafft was first awarded the Pour le Mérite Order in 1805, **10** years earlier. For the initial award of the Pour le Mérite Order to this officer see Volume I, Chapter V-1, entry 57, p. 252.)
* * *

2335. **von Tippelskirch**, Ernst Ludwig,
Major General, Chief of the V. Brigade.
(Awarded the Oakleaves to the Pour le Mérite Order in recognition of distinguished leadership and outstanding military planning and operations. The award also recognized his conspicious bravery in action during the battle at Ligny on June 16, 1815, and during the battle at La Belle Alliance on June 18, 1815. General von Tippelskirch was first decorated with the Pour le Mérite Order in 1807, **8** years earlier. For the initial award of the Pour le Mérite Order to this officer see Volume I, Chapter V-1, entry 100, p. 265.)
* * *

2336. **von Kemphen**, Johann Karl Jakob,
Colonel, Brigade Commander, X. Brigade,
(Awarded the Oakleaves to the Pour le Mérite Order in recognition of distinguished leadership and conspicuous bravery in action during the battle at La Belle Alliance on June 18, 1815. Colonel von Kemphen also displayed distinction in action during the battle at Namur on June 20, 1815. He was first awarded the Pour le Mérite Order in 1807, **8** years earlier. For the initial award of the Pour le Mérite Order to this officer see Volume I, Chapter V-1, entry 251, p. 282.)
* * *

2337. **von Brandenstein**, Friedrich August Karl,
Major, serving at the time on the General Staff of the III. Army Corps.
(Awarded the Oakleaves to the Pour le Mérite Order in recognition of distinguished leadership and conspicuous bravery in action during the battle at Ligny on June 16, 1815, and at La Belle Alliance on June 18-19, 1815. Major von Brandenstein was first awarded the Pour le Mérite Order in 1807, **8** years earlier. For the initial award of the Pour le Mérite Order to this officer see Volume I, Chapter V-1, entry 399, p. 293.)
* * *

2338. **von Holleben**, Ludwig Friedrich Heinrich,
Major, Leib Infantry Regiment.
(**Note:** Major von Holleben was awarded **both** the Pour le Mérite Order **and** the Oakleaves to the Pour le Mérite Order together on this date in recognition of outstanding leadership and distinguished military planning and operations. The award recognized his distinction in action during the battle at the defense of Sombref on June 16, 1815, and at the engagement between the towns of St. Germain and Rocquencourt on July 1, 1815.)
* * *

2339. **von Ditfurth**, Wilhelm Heinrich Karl Ludwig,
Major, Commander, 30th Infantry Regiment.
(**Note:** Major Ditfurth was awarded **both** the Pour le Mérite Order

and the Oakleaves to the Pour le Mérite Order together on this date in recognition of outstanding leadership and distinction in action during the battle at the defense of Sombref on June 16, 1815, and during the battle at Wavre on June 18, 1815, and during the engagement between the towns of St. Germain and Rocquencourt on July 1, 1815.)

* * *

2340. **Braun**, Johann Karl Ludwig,
Major General, Chief of Artillery, IV. Corps.
(**Note:** General Braun was awarded **both** the Pour le Mérite Order **and** the Oakleaves to the Pour le Mérite Order together on this date in recognition of outstanding leadership and distinguished military planning and operations. The award recognized his distinction in action during several battles and especially at La Belle Alliance on June 18-19, 1815.)

* * *

2341. **von Losthin**, Michael Heinrich,
Major General, Chief of the XV. Brigade.
(Awarded the Oakleaves to the Pour le Mérite Order in recognition of distinguished leadership and conspicuous bravery in action during the battle at La Belle Alliance on June 18-19, 1815. General von Losthin was first awarded the Pour le Mérite Order in 1810, **5** years earlier. For the initial award of the Pour le Mérite Order to this officer see Volume I, Chapter V-1, entry 638, p. 321.)

* * *

2342. **von Sydow**, Johann Joachim Friedrich,
Major General, Brigade Commander, Reserve Cavalry of the IV. Army Corps.
(Awarded the Oakleaves to the Pour le Mérite Order in recognition of distinguished leadership and conspicuous bravery in action during the battle at La Belle Alliance on June 18-19, 1815. General von Sydow was first awarded the Pour le Mérite Order in 1794, **21** years earlier. For the initial award of the Pour le Mérite Order to this officer see Volume I, Chapter IV, entry 679, p. 200.)

* * *

2343. **von Borstell**, Ludwig Friedrich Hans Wilhelm,
Captain, Adjutant, XIV. Brigade.
(**Note:** Captain von Borstell was awarded **both** the Pour le Mérite Order **and** the Oakleaves to the Pour le Mérite Order together on this date in recognition of outstanding leadership and distinguished military planning and operations. The award also recognized his distinction in action during the battle at La Belle Alliance June 18-19, 1815, and at Bellelaire on July 9, 1815.)

* * *

2344. **von Keller**, Frhr. Heinrich Eugen,
Major, 15th Infantry Regiment.
(**Note:** Major von Keller was awarded **both** the Pour le Mérite Order **and** the Oakleaves to the Pour le Mérite Order together on this date in recognition of outstanding leadership and distinguished military planning and operations. The award also recognized his distinction in action during the battle at La Belle Alliance on June 18-19, 1815.)

* * *

2345. **von Hedemann**, August George Friedrich Magnus,
Major, serving at the time on the General Staff of the Reserve Cav-

alry, IV. Army Corps.
(Awarded the Oakleaves to the Pour le Mérite Order in recognition of distinguished leadership and conspicuous bravery in action during the battle at Neuem during mid-June 1815. Major von Hedemann was first awarded the Pour le Mérite Order in 1809, **6** years earlier. For the initial award of the Pour le Mérite Order to this officer see Volume I, Chapter V-1, entry 607, p. 315.)

* * *

2346. **Beier,** Johann Peter Paul,
Lt. Colonel, Commander, West Prussian Uhlan Regiment.
(Awarded the Oakleaves to the Pour le Mérite Order in recognition of distinguished leadership and conspicuous bravery in action during the battle at La Belle Alliance on June 18-19, 1815. Lt. Colonel Beier was first decorated with the Pour le Mérite Order in 1807, **8** years earlier. For the initial award of the Pour le Mérite Order to this officer see Volume I, Chapter V-1, entry 99, p. 265.)

* * *

2347. **Scheffer,** Johann Ernst,
Hessian Lt. Colonel, Commander of a Hessian Hussar Regiment.
(Awarded the Pour le Mérite Order in recognition of outstanding leadership and distinction in action during the battle at Charleville on June 29, 1815.)

* * *

Grand Ducal Hessian Jäger Battalion

2348. **Boedicker,** Ludwig, Hessian Major, Commander.
(Awarded the Pour le Mérite Order in recognition of outstanding leadership and distinction in action during the battle at Charleville on June 29, 1815.)

The following two Hessian officers of the above unit were decorated with the Pour le Mérite Order for distinction in action during the battles at Charleville on June 29, 1815, and at St. Julien in the vicinity of Mézières on August 3, 1815. These officers also displayed outstanding distinction in action during the assault against French positions at Medy Bas during the night of August 14-15, 1815.

2349. **Schmidt,** Heinrich Tobias, Hessian Captain.
2350. **Hütterod,** Wilhelm, Hessian 1st Lieutenant.

* * *

The following five Hessian officers received the Pour le Mérite Order in recognition of distinction in action during the battle at St. Julien in the vicinity of Mézières on August 3, 1815.

2351. **von Stein,** Karl Moritz,
Hessian Lieutenant, Hessian Kurprinz Infantry Regiment.

2352. **von Marshall,** August Ludwig Ernst,
Hessian Colonel, Commander, Hessian Leib Dragoon Regiment.

2353. **von Lossberg,** Friedrich Wilhelm,
Hessian Major, Commanding a Hessian Grenadier Regiment.

2354. **von Benning,** Karl August Ludwig,
Hessian Lt. Colonel, Commander, Hessian Kurfürst Infantry Regiment.

2355. **von Flies,** Johann Konrad,
Hessian Colonel, Commander, Hessian Kurprinz Infantry Regiment.

* * *

2356. **von Sonneberg,** Albrecht,
Duchy of Anhalt Major, Commander, Anhalt-Bernburg Battalion.
(Awarded the Pour le Mérite Order in recognition of outstanding leadership and distinction in action during the battle at St. Julien in the vicinity of Mérières on August 3, 1815.)
* * *

2357. **von Münch,** Friedrich Wilhelm,
Duchy of Saxe-Gotha Colonel, Commander, Saxe-Gotha Infantry Regiment.
(Awarded the Pour le Mérite Order in recognition of outstanding leadership and distinction in action during the battle at St. Julien in the vicinity of Mérières on August 3, 1815.)
* * *

2358. **Wardenburg,** Wilhelm Gustaf Friedrich,
Grand Duchy of Oldenburg Colonel, Commander of an Oldenburg Regiment.
(Awarded the Pour le Mérite Order in recognition of outstanding leadership and distinction in action during the battle at St. Julien in the vicinity of Mérières on August 3, 1815.)
* * *

Grand Duchy of Hesse Jäger Battalion

The following four Hessian officers of this battalion were decorated with the Pour le Mérite Order in recognition of outstanding distinction in action during the night attack against French positions at Mcdy Bas on September 14-15, 1815.

2359. **Schoedde,** Ernst Friedrich, Hessian Captain.
2360. **von Eschwege,** Ludwig, Hessian 2nd Lieutenant.
2361. **von Bardeleben,** Wilhelm Friedrich Karl August, Hessian 2nd Lieutenant.
2362. **Schulz ,** Heinrich Christian, Hessian 2nd Lieutenant.
(**Note:** Lieutenant Schulz was awarded the 50 Year Jubilee Golden Crown to the Pour le Mérite Order on March 20, 1866.)
* * *

2363. **von Wiedburg,** Friedrich Karl,
Principality of Waldeck Captain, Waldeck Battalion.
(Awarded the Pour le Mérite Order in recognition of outstanding leadership and distinction in action during the night battle against French positions at Medy Bas on September 14-15, 1815.)
* * *

2364. **Krausenek,** Johann Wilhelm,
Major General, Commander, Prussian Forces at Metz.
(Awarded the Oakleaves to the Pour le Mérite Order in recognition of distinguished leadership and outstanding military planning and operations during the 1814-1815 campaigns. For the initial award of the Pour le Mérite Order to this officer see Volume I, Chapter V-1, entry 671, p. 327.)
* * *

* October 3, 1815 *

2365. **Pustshin**, Nikolai Nikolaieovich,
Imperial Russian Lieutenant, Life Guard Littau Regiment.

* * *

* October 5, 1815 *

2366. **von Leistner**, Franz,
Royal Bavarian Rittmeister, 1st Bavarian Uhlan Regiment, serving at the time as Adjutant to Prince Karl of Bavaria.

* * *

* November 3, 1815 *

2367. **von Funck**, Friedrich Wilhelm,
Colonel, Commander, 2nd Silesian Infantry Regiment, serving at the time as Brigade Commander, XIV. Brigade.
(Awarded the Oakleaves to the Pour le Mérite Order in recognition of distinguished leadership and conspicuous bravery in action during the battle at La Belle Alliance on June 18-19, 1815. For the initial award of the Pour le Mérite Order to this officer see Volume I, Chapter V-1, entry 671, p. 327.)

* * *

* November 7, 1815 *

Imperial Russian King of Prussia Grenadier Regiment

2368. **Gluchov**, Feofilakt Alexieieovich, Imperial Russian Major.
2369. **von Dahlen**, Nikolai Ivanovich, Imperial Russian Major.

* * *

* November 9, 1815 *

2370. **Harding**, Sir Henry,
Royal British Captain, serving at the time as Lt. Colonel in the 1st Grenadier Guards Regiment, holding the rank of Staff Colonel.

2371. **Dickinson**, Richard,
Royal British Lt. Colonel, serving at the time as Brevet Colonel of Artillery.
(**Special Note:** Records indicate that Colonel Dickinson was awarded **both** the Pour le Mérite Order **and** the Oakleaves to the Pour le Mérite Order together on this date in recognition of outstanding leadership and distinguished military planning and operations. This was very unusual to a British officer.)

* * *

During the course of the 1813-1815 Liberation wars, Friedrich Wilhelm awarded a total of **1646** Pour le Mérite Orders, the highest Prussian military award for valor. However, it seems somewhat strange that of the number of awards, a total of **1440** or **87.48%** were given to Russian officers, whereas, only **98** or **5.95%** were awarded to Prussians. Emperor Alexander I. of Russia, it appears, was not as generous with the Imperial Russian military decorations for valor as was Friedrich Wilhelm III. Only **106** awards of the Imperial Russian of St. George were bestowed upon Prussians. Only **one** 1st Class Order of St. George was awarded to a Prussian, that being to Field Marshal Gebhard von Blücher. The old Field Marshal was given the honor in 1830 in recognition of his leadership during the battle at Leipzig in October 1813, **17** years after the battle. Awards of the 2nd and 3rd Class of the Order of St. George were seldom given to non-Russians, so Prussian officers received very few of them.

* * *

* January 14, 1816 *

3272. **von Zepelin,** Konstantin Gottlieb Leberecht,
Colonel, Brigade Commander, IX. Brigade.
(Awarded the Oakleaves to the Pour le Mérite Order in recognition of distinguished leadership and conspicious bravery in action during the battle at Wavre on June 18, 1815. Colonel Zepelin was first awarded the Pour le Mérite Order in 1807, **8** years earlier. For the initial award of the Pour le Mérite Order to this officer see Volume I, Chapter V-1, entry 294, p. 206.)

* * *

2373. **von der Marwitz,** Friedrich August Ludwig,
Colonel, Brigade Commander, Reserve Cavalry, III. Army Corps.
(**Note:** Colonel von der Marwitz was awarded **both** the Pour le Mérite Order **and** the Oakleaves to the Pour le Mérite Order together on this date in recognition of outstanding leadership and distinguished military planning and operations. The award recognized his distinction in action during the battle at Namur on June 20, 1815.)

* * *

* May 2, 1816 *

2374. **Simonyi von Vitetzvár,** Frhr. Josef,
Imperial Austrian Colonel, Erbprinz von Hessen-Homburg Hussar Regiment.
(Awarded the Pour le Mérite Order in recognition of outstanding leadership and distinction in action during the battle at Tellnitz on September 17, 1813.)

* * *

2375. **von Berenhorst,** Johann George,
Imperial Austrian Lt. Colonel, Erbprinz von Hessen-Homburg Hussar Regiment.
(Awarded the Pour le Mérite Order in recognition of outstanding leadership and distinction in action during the pursuit of enemy forces from Lyon to Vienne. At Vienne on March 21, 1814, Lt. Colonel von Berenhorst led the release of over 500 Prussian prisoners of war from French captivity.)

* * *

* June 18, 1816 *

2376. **von Clausewitz,** Wilhelm,
Lt. Colonel, Commander, 32nd Infantry Regiment, serving at the time on the General Staff of the II. Army Corps.
(Awarded the Oakleaves to the Pour le Mérite Order in recognition of distinguished leadership and conspicuous bravery in action during the battle at Ligny on June 18, 1815, and during the battle at Namur on June 20, 1815. For the initial award of the Pour le Mérite Order to this officer see Volume I, Chapter V-1, entry 686, p. 328.)

* * *

2377. **Wossidlo,** Georg Christian Fromhold,
   1st Lieutenant, 33rd Infantry Regiment, having served previously in the Royal Swedish Queen's Life Regiment holding the rank of Officer Candidate.
   (Awarded the Pour le Mérite Order in recognition of outstanding leadership and distinction in action during the storming of the city gate of Dessau on September 28, 1813.)
   * * *

2378. **von Württemberg,** Prince Adam Karl Wilhelm Stanislaus Eugen Paul,
   Royal Württemberg Lt. General.
   (Awarded the Pour le Mérite Order in recognition of outstanding leadership and distinction in action during the battle at Brienne on January 20, 1814, and at La Rothière on February 1, 1814.)
   * * *

* October 23, 1816 *

5th Pomeranian Hussar Regiment

The following three officers were decorated with the Pour le Mérite Order in recognition of their outstanding leadership and distinction in action during the battle at Ribki on August 27, 1815.

2379. **Stiemer,** Christian Wilhelm, Rittmeister, serving at the time as Adjutant to Landwehr Inspector of the Department of Administration, Marienwerder.

2380. **von Tornow,** Otto Wilhelm Karl Friedrich, Rittmeister.

2381. **von Kalckreuth,** August Friedrich Albrecht, 1st Lieutenant.
   (**Note:** Lieutenant von Kalckreuth was awarded the 50 Year Jubilee Golden Crown to the Pour le Mérite Order on January 9, 1862.)
   * * *

2382. **von Grodzki,** Hieronymus Michaelis Ignatius,
   1st Lieutenant, 3rd (Brandenburg) Uhlan Regiment.
   (Awarded the Pour le Mérite Order in recognition of outstanding leadership and distinction in action during the battle at Molhaisk on September 7, 1815.)
   * * *

2383. **von Wulffen,** August Friedrich Wilhelm,
   1st Lieutenant, 5th (Brandenburg) Uhlan Regiment.
   (Awarded the Pour le Mérite Order in recognition of outstanding leadership and distinction in action during the battle at Zalisze and Cirkievkie on August 8, 1815.)
   * * *

2384. **Klevesahl,** Nikolai Jesimovich,
   Imperial Russian Captain, Volyni Infantry Regiment.
   (Awarded the Pour le Mérite Order in recognition of outstanding leadership and distinction in action during the battle at Dodendorf, 1815.)
   * * *

* March 30, 1817 *

2385. **von Rönne,** Baron Vassili Igorovich,
   Imperial Russian Staff Captain, 2nd Life Guard Artillery Brigade.
   * * *

2386. **Chérisey,** Count Charles Louis Prosper,
   Royal French 2nd Lieutenant, Gramont Company, Garde du Corps;

having previously served in the Pelet Fusilier Battalion holding the rank of a 1st Lieutenant. * * *

* June 19, 1817 *

2387. **Tokarev**, Konstantin Alexieieovich,
Imperial Russian Major, 1st Light Infantry Grenadier Regiment.
* * *

* August 13, 1817 *

2388. **Gentsy de Gents**, Josef,
Imperial Austrian Colonel, Commander, King of Prussia Hussar Regiment.
* * *

* August 26, 1817 *

2389. **de la Rochejaquelein**, Count August,
Royal French Colonel, Commander, 1st Guard Grenadier Infantry Regiment.
* * *

* October 2, 1817 *

2390. **von Scheel**, Peter Romanovich,
Imperial Russian Staff Rittmeister, His Majesty's Life Guard Curassier Regiment.
* * *

* New Ribbon Authorized for the Oakleaves *

By a Cabinet Order dated December 17, 1817, announcement was made that a special ribbon had been authorized for wear to indicate the second award of the Pour le Mérite Order in addition to the golden Oakleaves device. The ribbon would be the same as the original except an additional silver metallic center stripe 8.0 mm. wide would be added.

* Between January 15-18, 1818 *

2391. **von Brandenstein**, Joachim Gottfried,
Major, 3rd (Brandenburg) Curassier Regiment.

2392. **Heydenreich**, Adolf Heinrich,
Royal Saxon 2nd Lieutenant, Royal Saxon Artillery Corps.

2393. **Hervey**, Sir Felton Elwill Bathurst,
Royal British Lt. Colonel, Brevet Colonel of the 14th Light Dragoon Regiment, serving at the time as Special Adjutant to the Prince Regent and the Duke of Wellington.
* * *

* Early 1819 *

2394. **Trubezkoi**, Peter Petrovich,

Imperial Russian Captain, Life Guard Artillery Regiment.

* * *

* July 2, 1819 *

2395. **Firssov,** Peter Savovich,
Imperial Russian Colonel, Commander, Life Guard Sapper (Engineer) Battalion.

* * *

* September 16, 1819 *

2396. **Hermann,** Alexander Ivanovich,
Imperial Russian Colonel, Life Guard Preobrashenski Regiment.

* * *

* November 1, 1819 *

2397. **von Moltke,** Frhr. Paul Adolfovich,
Imperial Russian Legation Official, Turin (Italy).
(Awarded the Pour le Mérite Order in recognition of outstanding leadership and distinction in action during the 1814-1815 campaigns.)

* * *

* August 7, 1820 *

2398. **zu Ysenburg-Philippseich,** Count Georg August,
Royal Bavarian Rittmeister, 2nd Hussar Regiment.
(Awarded the Pour le Mérite Order in recognition of outstanding leadership and distinction in action while serving as an Imperial Russian Sub-Lieutenant in the Russian Army. He was assigned to the staff of Russian Cavalry General Count Wittgenstein.
Count zu Ysenburg-Philippseich was awarded the 50 Year Jubilee Golden Crown to the Pour le Mérite Order on January 27, 1870.)

* * *

* January 6, 1821 *

2399. **Mattshinski,** Adam Ossipovich,
Imperial Russian Staff Captain, 5th Mounted Artillery Company.
(Awarded the Pour le Mérite Order in recognition of outstanding leadership and distinction in action during the battle at Leipzig on October 18, 1813.)

* * *

* July 26, 1821 *

The following two Imperial Austrian officers of the Austrian Quartermaster General Staff were decorated with the Pour le Mérite Order in recognition of outstanding leadership and their distinction in action during the 1815 campaigns.

2400. **Hrabovsky von Hrabova,** Johann, Imperial Austrian Colonel,
Chief of the General Staff of the Army of Naples.

2401. **von Sahlhausen,** Frhr. Mortiz, Imperial Austrian Colonel,
Senior Adjutant General to Cavalry General Baron Frimont.

* * *

2402. **Bellegarde,** Count August,
Imperial Austrian Major, Wing Adjutant to Cavalry General Baron Fri-

mont.

(Awarded the Pour le Mérite Order in recognition of outstanding leadership and distinction in action during the 1815 campaigns.

Note: Major Bellegarde was awarded the 50 Year Jubilee Golden Crown to the Pour le Mérite Order on December 14, 1872.)

* * *

* January 23, 1824 *

2403. **Albert,** Christof Johann Ferdinand Alexander,
Royal Bavarian Major, 16th Bavarian Line Infantry.
(Awarded the Pour le Mérite Order in recognition of outstanding leadership and distinction in action during the battle near Paris, 1815, while serving at the time as Captain in the 7th Bavarian Line Infantry Regiment.)

* * *

* April 18, 1824 *

2404. **Mordvinov,** Vladimir Michailovich,
Imperial Russian Major General, retired, (April 29, 1819, deceased).
(**Special Note:** General Mordvinov was awarded the Pour le Mérite Order in recognition of his outstanding leradership and distinguished military planning and operations during the 1807 campaigns, **17** years earlier. At the time Mordvinov held the rank of Colonel and commanded the Siev Musketeer Regiment. This appears to be another unusual **posthumous** award of the Pour le Mérite Order.)

* * *

* May 5, 1824 *

The following Imperial Russian officers were listed on the 1817 Pour le Mérite Order Knights List. However, this list was the first indication that these officers had been decorated with the Pour le Mérite Order. The officers shown without rank were no longer in military service.

2405. **Harder,** Karl Vassilieovich,

(Awarded the Pour le Mérite Order in recognition of outstanding leadership and distinction in action during the battle at Lützen (Gross Görschen) between May 2 and April 30, 1813. Harder held the rank of Lieutenant in the Life Guard Mounted Artillery.)

* * *

2406. **Mileant,** Igor Dmitrieovich,

(Awarded the Pour le Mérite Order in recognition of outstanding leadership and distinction in action during the crossing of the Rhine River near Mannheim during January 1814. He held the rank of Lt. Colonel in the 11th Light Infantry Regiment.)

* * *

2407. **Besobrasov,** Grigori Michailovich,

(Awarded the Pour le Mérite Order in recognition of outstanding leadership and distinction in action during the battle at Kulm on August 30, 1813. He was serving as an Administrative Official VII. Class and holding the rank of Major.)

* * *

2408. **Selivanov I.,** (First name unknown),

(Awarded the Pour le Mérite Order in recognition of outstanding lead-

ership and distinction in action on April 12, 1814. He was serving as Imperial Russian Rittmeister in the Jelissavetgrad Hussar Regiment.)

* * *

2409. **Gagarin**, Prince (First name unknown),
Imperial Russian Colonel, Commander, Grodno Hussar Regiment.
(**Note:** Records indicate that Colonel Gagarin was awarded the Pour le Mérite Order during 1807, while serving as an Officer Candidate in the Cavalier Guard Regiment, but had been inadvertently omitted from the Pour le Mérite Order Knights List until 1817.)

* * *

2410. **Svietshin**, Peter Alexandrovich,
(Records indicate that Peter Svietshin served as an Imperial Russian Sub-Lieutenant, in the Life Guard Light Infantry Regiment from July 15, 1813, until May 15, 1816. There is no definite information available which indicates the date or action the Pour le Mérite Order was awarded to this officer.)

* * *

2411. **Norov**, Vassili Sergieieovich,
(Records indicate that Norov had been awarded the Pour le Mérite Order during 1813, while serving as an Imperial Russian Sub-Lieutenant in the Life Guard Light Infantry Regiment. He was carried on the regiment's rank list as a recipient of the Pour le Mérite Order.)

* * *

2412. **Müller**, Karl Ivanovich,
(Awarded the Pour le Mérite Order in recognition of outstanding leadership and distinction in action during the 1814 campaigns. He held the rank of Captain while serving at the time in the Riga Dragoon Regiment and was later promoted to Major on June 15, 1815.)

* * *

2413. **Jachontov**, Alexander Andreieovich,
During the 1813-1814 campaigns, Jachontov held the rank of Imperial Russian Colonel and was Chief (Ataman) of the 1st Volunteer Cossack Regiment. By August 1, 1815, he was carried on the list of cavalry officers as being a recipient of the Pour le Mérite Order. However, there is no date or action given to indicate when or why he was awarded the Pour le Mérite Order.)

* * *

2414. **Dutshinski**, Ossip Ignatieovich,
(Records indicate Dutshinski held the rank of Imperial Russian Lieutenant in the Bielo-Russia Hussar Regiment from December 5, 1813, until November 19, 1814, when he was promoted to Staff Rittmeister. However, there is no date or action given to indicate when or why he was awarded the Pour le Mérite Order.)

* * *

2415. **von Essen**, Karl Karlovich,
(On January 13, 1813, von Essen was promoted to Lieutenant in the Imperial Russian Quartermaster Service while he was serving on the staff of Emperor Alexander I. He was promoted to Staff Captain on November 19, 1814, and he held this rank until January 1, 1817. However, there is no date or action given to indicate when or why he was awarded the Pour le Mérite Order.)

* * *

2416. **Günzel I.,** (First name unknown),

(From December 29, 1811, until January 5, 1816, Günzel served as an Imperial Russian Staff Captain in the Russian 6th Artillery Brigade. However, there is no date or action given to indicate when or why he was awarded the Pour le Mérite Order.)

* * *

2417. **Freigang,** Johann (Ivan Matvieieovich),

(Holding the rank of Major in the Imperial Russian Quartermaster Service he served on the staff of Emperor Alexander I. On February 9, 1811, he was promoted to Lt. Colonel and served until November 6, 1819, as the Senior Quartermaster of the II. Cavalry Corps. However, there is no date or action given to indicate when or why he was awarded the Pour le Mérite Order.)

* * *

2418. **Reichard (Reichart),** (First name unknown),

(Awarded the Pour le Mérite Order in recognition of outstanding leadership and distinction in action during the battle at Soissons in 1814. Records indicate that he held the rank of Imperial Russian Captain in the Riga Dragoon Regiment.)

* * *

2419. **Rshevski,** Konstantin Alexieieovich,

(Records indicate that Rshevski held the rank of Major during 1812. However, there is no date or action given to indicate when or why he was awarded the Pour le Mérite Order.)

* * *

2420. **Molokov,** Kornili Issaieovich,

(Records indicate that Molokov held the rank of Imperial Russian Lieutenant but the unit in which he served is unknown. It appears that he received the Pour le Mérite Order sometime during 1807. However, there is no date or action given to indicate when or why he was awarded the Pour le Mérite Order.)

* * *

2421. **Ofrossimov,** Konstantin Pavlovich,

(As a Imperial Russian Lieutenant, he served in the Life Guard Finland Regiment from October 7, 1811, until July 17, 1813, when he was promoted to Captain. By May 11, 1816, Ofrossimov held the rank of Colonel. However, there is no date or action given to indicate when or why he was awarded the Pour le Mérite Order.)

* * *

2422. **Pogorski-Linkevich,** Nikolai Ossipovich,

(Awarded the Pour le Mérite Order in recognition of outstanding leadership and distinction in action during the battle at Gross-Beeren on August 23, 1813, and Dennewitz on September 6, 1813. He held the rank of Imperial Russian Staff Rittmeister in the Pavlograd Hussar Regiment.)

* * *

2423. **Tichmenev,** Vassili Ivanovich,

(Awarded the Pour le Mérite Order in recognition of outstanding leadership and distinction in action during the battle at Danzig while holding the rank of Imperial Russian Lieutenant in the 2nd Sea Regiment.)

* * *

* September 18, 1824 *

2424. **Shele II.,** Kyrill Chrestianovich,
   (Discharged as a Major from active duty with the Vilna Musketeer Regiment on October 31, 1808. Recalled to active duty as Major on October 17, 1813, with the Neva Infantry Regiment. In 1816, Major Shele was a regimental commander. However, there is no date or action given to indicate when or why he was awarded the Pour le Mérite Order.
   (**Note:** Major Shele was awarded the 50 Year Jubilee Golden Crown to the Pour le Mérite Order on May 18, 1858.)
   * * *

2425. **von Buxhöwden,** Count Peter Fedorovich,
   (Awarded the Pour le Mérite Order in recognition of outstanding leadership and distinction in action on October 21, 1812. He held the rank of Imperial Russian Lieutenant but the unit he was serving in at the time is unknown.)
   * * *

2426. **Retkin (Redkin),** Nikolai Nikolaieovich,
   (Awarded the Pour le Mérite Order while serving as an Orderly Officer to the Crown Prince of Sweden. His rank is unknown.)
   * * *

2427. **Semenov,** (First name unknown),
   (Awarded the Pour le Mérite Order in recognition of outstanding leadership and distinction in action while serving as an Imperial Russian Jessaul in the Army of the Don. The unit in which he was serving is unknown. However, there is no date or action given to indicate when or why he was awarded the Pour le Mérite Order.)
   * * *

* November 8, 1824 *

2428. **Grekov VII.,** Alexei Danilovich,
   (While serving as an Imperial Russian Starchina in an unidentified unit in the Army of the Don, this officer was awarded the Pour le Mérite Order. However, there is no date or action given to indicate when or why he was awarded the Pour le Mérite Order.)
   * * *

* January 12, 1825 *

2429. **Müller,** Fedor Fedorovich,
   Imperial Russian Staff Captain, St. Petersburg Grenadier Regiment.
   (Awarded the Pour le Mérite Order in recognition of outstanding leadership and distinction in action during the battle at the liberation of Smolensk in 1812.)
   * * *

* November 23, 1825 *

2430. **von Witte,** Count Ivan Ossipovich,
   (Awarded the Pour le Mérite Order in recognition of outstanding leadership and distinction in action during the battle at Siebeneichen in August 1813.)
   * * *

2431. **Kireiev V.,** Michail Igorovich,

    (Awarded the Pour le Mérite Order in recognition of outstanding leadership and distinction in action during the battle at Leipzig on October 18, 1813. He held the rank of an Imperial Russian Starchina, unidentified unit, Army of the Don.)

* * *

2432. **von Schanzenbach,** Frhr. Xaver Petrovich,

    (Awarded the Pour le Mérite Order in recognition of outstanding leadership and distinction in action during the blockade of Glogau in 1813. His rank and unit are unknown.)

* * *

2433. **Trizonski,** Nikolai,

    (Awarded the Pour le Mérite Order in recognition of outstanding leadership and distinction in action during the battle at Danzig in 1813. His rank and unit are unknown but indications are that he served in an Opoltshenie (militia) unit.)

* * *

* December 22, 1826 *

2434. **Lossovski,** Ivan Vikentieovich,

    (Records indicate that this Russian officer possibly served on the staff of the Crown Prince of Sweden when decorated with the Pour le Mérite Order. However, there is no date or action given to indicate when or why he was awarded the Pour le Mérite Order.)

* * *

2435. **Read,** Evgeni Andreieovich,

    (No available records indicate when or why this Russian officer was decorated with the Pour le Mérite Order.)

* * *

* The 1828-1829 Russo-Turkish War *

Since Friedrich Wilhelm III. awarded the Pour le Mérite Order to Prussian officers attached to the Imperial Russian forces as well as those serving in the Imperial Russian Headquarters and on the staff of Emperor Nicholas I., it is relevant to briefly discuss the Russo-Turkish War of 1828-1829, which developed as the result of the 1821-1829 Greek War for Independence.

During the autumn of 1827 the combined Russo-Anglo-French naval squadron defeated the Turko-Egyptian fleet at Navarino. The Turks responded by declaring a "holy war." The French and British withdrew from any further hostilities; however, the Russians continued the war hoping to obtain more territory in the Caucasus. Turkey was badly defeated and under the Adrianople Peace Treaty of 1829, Russia was given a protectorate over Moldavia and Wallachia. Thus Russia secured her position along the Black Sea coast. Greek independence was established and Serbia also became independent.

* * *

* November 5, 1828 *

2436. **von Nostitz,** Count August Ludwig Ferdinand,
Major General, Commander, 2nd Garde Cavalry Brigade.
(General von Nostitz was awarded **both** the Pour le Mérite Order **and** the Oakleaves to the Pour le Mérite Order together on this date in recognition of outstanding leadership and distinguished military planning and operations. The award recognized his distinguished service while serving as an observer and advisor on the staff of Emperor Nicholas I. during the Russo-Turkish War. See p. 170, this chapter.)

* * *

* December 16, 1828 *

2437. **von Thun,** Wilhelm Ulrich,
Lt. Colonel, attached for duty with the Imperial Russian Emperor Alexander Grenadier Regiment.
(Awarded the Pour le Mérite Order in recognition of outstanding leadership and distinguished service while serving as an observer and advisor on the staff of Emperor Nicholas I. during the Russo-Turkish War.)

* * *

* December 17, 1828 *

The following two Prussian officers received the Pour le Mérite Order in recognition of distinguished service while serving as advisors to the staff at the Imperial Russian Headquarters during the Russo-Turkish War.

2438. **Moliere,** Louis Auguste Bernard,
Rittmeister, Prussian General Staff Officer.

2439. **von Reitzenstein,** Frhr. Karl Heinrich Theodor,
2nd Lieutenant, Garde Dragoon Regiment.
(**Note:** Lieutenant von Reitzenstein was awarded the 50 Year Jubilee Golden Crown to the Pour le Mérite Order on January 18, 1878.)

* * *

* December 30, 1828 *

2440. **von Küster,** Karl Gustaf Ernst,
Rittmeister, member of the Prussian Embassy military staff assigned to the Imperial Russian Court of Nicholas I.
(Awarded the Pour le Mérite Order in recognition of outstanding leadership and distinguished service while serving as an advisor to the staff of the Imperial Russian Headquarters during the Russo-Turkish War.)

* * *

* December 13, 1830 *

2441. **von Cler,** Ignaz Heinrich,
Captain, Prussian General Staff Officer.
(Awarded the Pour le Mérite Order in recognition of outstanding leadership and distinction in action while serving as a volunteer with the French military punitive expedition in Algiers.)

* * *

* October 11, 1831 *

2442. **von Canitz und Dallwitz,** Frhr. Karl Wilhelm Ernst,
Colonel, Commander, 1st Hussar (1st Leib Hussar) Regiment.

(**Note:** Colonel von Canitz was awarded the Oakleaves to the Pour le Mérite Order in recognition of his distinguished service while serving as an advisor on the staff of the Imperial Russian Headquarters during the Russo-Turkish War. He was first awarded the Pour le Mérite Order in 1807, **24** years earlier. For the initial award of the Pour le Mérite Order to this officer see Volume I, Chapter V-1, entry 343, p. 290.)

* * *

2443. **von Seydlitz und Kursbach**, Karl,
1st Lieutenant, 2nd Garde Uhlan (Landwehr) Regiment.
(Awarded the Pour le Mérite Order in recognition of outstanding leadership and distinguished service while serving as an advisor to the staff at Imperial Russian Headquarters during the Russo-Turkish War.
Note: Lieutenant von Seydlitz was awarded the 50 Year Jubilee Golden Crown to the Pour le Mérite Order on September 24, 1881.)

* * *

* The 1831 Neuchâtel Uprising *

A short history of the Prussian Principality of Neuchâtel should be discussed here. Prussian administration of the small principality lasted nearly 350 years, interrupted only briefly during the Napoleonic Wars. In 1805, Napoleon gave the principality to Marshal Louis-Alexandre Berthier. The small military forces of Neuchâtel were required to serve in the French army. After the defeat of Napoleon in 1815, Neuchâtel was returned to Prussia and Friedrich Wilhelm III. General Ernst von Pfuel was appointed Governor and military commander, administering through a privy-council.

Two political elements were active in Neuchâtel which divided the town and its inhabitants. One, the Prussian monarchists and the other, the Swiss republicans, were totally opposed to each other. This divided the territory of Neuchâtel into rival factions. The town itself and the portion bordering on the lake contained the monarchists, whereas the adjoining towns of La Chaux-de-Fonds and La Locle were staunch republicans wanting to join the Swiss Confederation.

When the revolution broke out in Paris in 1830, the Neuchâtel republicans acted quickly, organizing and arming themselves for the coup d'etat. However, the Prussian military garrison under the command of Major General von Pfuel quickly succeeded in reestablishing law and order. Neuchâtel remained a Prussian Principality.

* * *

* December 31, 1831 *

2444. **von Pfuel**, Ernst Adolf Heinrich,
Major General, Governor of Neuchâtel and Commander of the 15th Division.
(Awarded the Oakleaves to the Pour le Mérite Order in recognition of distinguished leadership and conspicuous bravery in action during the suppression of the uprising in the Prussian Principality of Neuchâtel. For the initial award of the Pour le Mérite Order to this officer see entry 2292, this chapter.
(**Note:** General von Pfuel was awarded the 50 Year Jubilee Golden Crown to the Pour le Mérite Order on June 18, 1864.)

* * *

* The 1831 Polish Rebellion *

For some reason, known only to Friedrich Wilhelm III., he chose to award the Pour le Mérite Order to Imperial Russian officers who successfully supressed the 1831 Polish insurrection. A short recalling of the facts surrounding this rebellion should be discussed. Emperor Nicholas I.'s plans to utilize the Polish army as part of the Russian forces to be sent to intervene, if necessary, in any western European uprisings was the basic cause of the Polish rebellion in November 1830. At that time Polish military forces took control of Warsaw and the Russian Governor, Grand Duke Konstantin, responded by withdrawing the Russian military garrison from the city.

In December 1830, the Polish Diet (Parliament) proclaimed the insurrection a national movement and even established a Republic, appointing Prince Adam Czartorizsky as head. They then demanded the liberation of Polish territory under Russian administrative control. In February 1831, Russian troops crossed the Polish border and despite desperate Polish resistance, reached the gates of Warsaw by August 1831. The city fell on September 8, 1831. As a result of this uprising, Russia tightened her grip on Poland. The speaking of Polish was forbidden, monasteries, convents, schools and colleges were closed, and thousands of rebellious Poles were sent to Siberia, from where they never returned.

* * *

* February 17, 1832 *

The following six Imperial Russian officers were awarded the Pour le Mérite Order in recognition of their leadership and distinction in action during the suppression of Polish forces in their unsuccessful insurrection against Russian occupation. It is of interest to note that those receiving the Pour le Mérite Order were all commanders of regiments named for Prussians. A coincidence or reward?

2445. **Tshevakinski**, Michail Ivanovich,
Imperial Russian Colonel, Second-in-Command, King of Prussia Grenadier Regiment. * * *

2446. **von Klugen III.**, Gustaf,
Imperial Russian Colonel, Commander, King of Prussia Grenadier Regiment. * * *

2447. **Haverlandt I.**, Fedor Fedorovich,
Imperial Russian Colonel, former Commander, Prince of Prussia Infantry Regiment. * * *

2448. **Totshinski**, Ignati Pavlovich,
Imperial Russian Colonel, Commander, Prince of Prussia Infantry Regiment.
(**Note:** This is the **second** award of the Pour le Mérite Order **badge** to Colonel Totshinski. For the initial award of the Pour le Mérite Order to this officer see entry 1053, this chapter.)
* * *

2449. **Gilein von Gembitz**, Karl Ossipovich,
Imperial Russian Colonel, Commander, Prince Karl of Prussia Infantry Regiment. * * *

2450. **von Meyendorf**, Baron Georg Otto Wilhelm,
Imperial Russian Major General, Commander, Prince Albrecht of Prussia Curassier Regiment. * * *

* October 18, 1832 *

2451. **Head**, Sir Francis Bond,
Royal British Major, (serving at the time on half pay), Royal Equipage Department.
(**Special Note:** Major Head was given a **17** year belated award of the Pour le Mérite Order in recognition of his leadership and conspicuous bravery during the battle at Ligny on June 16, 1815, and several other engagements against the French. Sir Francis, at the time, held the rank of Lieutenant.)
* * *

* December 15, 1832 *

2452. **Gortalov**, Ivan Kusmitsh.
(Belatedly awarded the Pour le Mérite Order in recognition of his outstanding leadership and distinction in action during the battle at Löwenberg on August 20, 1813, **19** years earlier. During this battle, Gortalov held the rank of Imperial Russian Major in the Imperial Russian 11th Light Infantry Regiment and was responsible for the capture of 16 enemy cannon and the taking of many French prisoners.)
* * *

In 1839, the last two Pour le Mérite Orders were made during the reign of Friedrich Wilhelm III. They were given to Captain Traugott von Mühlbach and Captain Hellmuth von Moltke. In recognition of their distinguished service in reorganizing, modernizing and training the Turkish army they were awarded the Pour le Mérite Order. However, it should be noted that these two awards directly contradicted the 1810 regulations. The regulations governing the award of the Pour le Mérite Order stated specifically that **no** awards would be made except during wartime for conspicuous bravery on the field of battle.
* * *

* November 29, 1839 *

2453. **von Mühlbach**, Traugott Wilhelm Heinrich,
Captain, Engineer Corps, Garrison Construction Director, VIII. Army Corps.
(Awarded the Pour le Mérite Order in recognition of distinguished service while serving as an advisor to the Turkish army.)
* * *

2454. **von Moltke**, Hellmuth Karl Bernard,
Captain, Staff Officer assigned to the Prussian General Staff.
(Awarded the Pour le Mérite Order in recognition of distinguished service while assigned as military advisor to the Turkish General Staff. For subsequent awards to Moltke see Chapter VII, entry 214; Chapter VII, entry 301; Chapter IX, entry 1.)
* * *

More than any other Prussian king, Friedrich Wilhelm III. was responsible for altering the basic character of the Pour le Mérite Order. He changed the Order from an award given during war, peace, or for any reason the reigning monarch desired, to a decoration recognizing only distinction in action and conspicuous bravery on the battlefield. This single, but most desirable, feature greatly enhanced the reputation and desirability of the Pour le Mérite Order.
* * *

Prussia emerged from the Napoleonic Wars with much more territory, with restored military might, and with more influence in European affairs than ever before. Her citizens, who had endured many hardships during the years, now looked forward to an era of peace and the promised establishment of a constitutional monarchy patterned after the English. This, however, was not to be.

The years between 1819 and 1840 became known as "The Quiet Years." The nation and Friedrich Wilhelm III. devoted their time and energies to repairing the damage caused by the ravages of the destructive wars. As the years went by, Prussia gradually evolved into a model military-police state, and Friedrich Wilhelm became more reactionary in order to eliminate any possible threat to his throne.

As time passed, the king came to be admired for his long life, if for nothing else. He came to be called the "Old Gentleman," even though he continued to mistrust the intentions of his subjects.

* * *

* The Death of Friedrich Wilhelm III. *

On June 7, 1840, Friedrich Wilhelm III., fifth King of Prussia, died at the age of 66. After reigning for 43 years, he left behind a better memory among the people than he actually deserved. He was succeeded by his son, Friedrich Wilhelm IV., a man of great wit and intelligence, who had made himself popular as Crown Prince, and whose accession the people hailed with joy and the enthusiastic belief that better days were coming. They were soon to be disappointed.

The Death of Friedrich Wilhelm III.

Notes:

AWARDS OF THE POUR LE MÉRITE ORDER DURING THE REIGN OF FRIEDRICH WILHELM III. FROM 1813 THROUGH 1840.

AWARDS OF THE POUR LE MÉRITE ORDER DURING THE REIGN OF FRIEDRICH WILHELM III.

1813 – 1824

Table I

Rank	1813	1814	1815	1816	1817	1818	1819	1820	1821	1824
Lt. General	2	2	–	–	–	–	–	–	–	–
Major General	16	14	10	–	–	–	–	–	–	–
Colonel	103	134	12	3	2	–	3	–	2	2
Lt. Colonel	97	90	8	2	–	1	–	–	–	2
Major	85	147	21	–	1	1	–	–	1	3
Lt. Commander	1	–	–	–	–	–	–	–	–	–
Captain	54	122	8	1	–	–	1	–	–	4
Captain-Lieutenant[1]	–	1	–	–	–	–	–	–	–	–
Jessaul[2]	15	9	–	–	–	–	–	–	–	1
Staff Captain	48	112	–	–	1	–	–	–	1	2
Rittmeister	20	58	4	2	–	–	–	1	–	1
Staff Rittmeister	21	41	3	–	1	–	–	–	–	2
Sotnik[3]	4	6	–	–	–	–	–	–	–	–
1st Lieutenant	4	1	1	4	–	–	–	–	–	–
Lieutenant	66	138	7	–	–	–	–	–	–	4
Naval Lieutenant	–	2	–	–	–	–	–	–	–	–
2nd Lieutenant	17	3	4	–	1	1	–	–	–	–
Sub-Lieutenant	19	43	1	–	–	–	–	–	–	2
Starchina[4]	9	4	–	–	–	–	–	–	–	1
Cornet	4	15	–	–	–	–	–	–	–	–
Officer Candidate	12	18	–	–	–	–	–	–	–	1
Chorunshi[5]	–	2	–	–	–	–	–	–	–	–
Rank Unknown	–	2	–	–	–	–	–	–	–	1
Miscellaneous	3	3[a]	–	–	–	–	1[b]	–	–	–
Total	600	967	79	12	6	3	5	1	4	26

1. Swedish Rank.
2. Russian Cossack Captain.
3. Russian Centurian (Officer responsible for 100 men).
4. Russian Warrant Officer.
5. Russian Rank, Army of the Don.

* * *

a. 1 Civil Administrator VII. Class
   2 Civil Administrators V. Class.
b. Russian Legation Official – Turin, Italy.

* * *

AWARDS OF THE POUR LE MÉRITE ORDER
DURING THE REIGN OF FRIEDRICH WILHELM III.

1825 – 1840

Table II

Rank	1825	1826	1827	1828	1830	1831	1832	1839	1840	Totals
Lt. General	-	-	-	-	-	-	-	-	-	4
Major General	-	-	-	1	-	1	1	-	-	43
Colonel	-	-	-	-	-	1	5	-	-	267
Lt. Colonel	-	-	-	1	-	-	-	-	-	201
Major	-	-	-	-	-	-	2	-	-	261
Lt. Commander	-	-	-	-	-	-	-	-	-	1
Captain	-	-	-	-	1	-	-	2	-	193
Captain-Lieutenant	-	-	-	-	-	-	-	-	-	1
Jessaul	-	-	-	-	-	-	-	-	-	25
Staff Captain	1	-	-	-	-	-	-	-	-	165
Rittmeister	-	-	-	2	-	-	-	-	-	88
Staff Rittmeister	-	-	-	-	-	-	-	-	-	68
Sotnik	-	-	-	-	-	-	-	-	-	10
1st Lieutenant	-	-	-	-	-	1	-	-	-	11
Lieutenant	-	-	-	-	-	-	-	-	-	215
Naval Lieutenant	-	-	-	-	-	-	-	-	-	2
2nd Lieutenant	-	-	-	1	-	-	-	-	-	27
Sub-Lieutenant	-	-	-	-	-	-	-	-	-	65
Starchina	1	-	-	-	-	-	-	-	-	15
Cornet	-	-	-	-	-	-	-	-	-	19
Officer Candidate	-	-	-	-	-	-	-	-	-	31
Chorunshi	-	-	-	-	-	-	-	-	-	2
Rank Unknown	3	1	1	-	-	-	-	-	-	8
Miscellaneous	-	-	-	-	-	-	-	-	-	7
Total	5	1	1	5	1	3	8	2	-	1729

PERCENTAGES OF TOTAL AWARDS OF THE POUR LE MÉRITE ORDER ACCORDING TO RANK

1813 – 1840

Table III

	Rank	Number Awarded	Percentage
1.	Colonel	267	15.44%
2.	Major	261	15.09
3.	Lieutenant	215	12.43
4.	Lt. Colonel	201	11.62
5.	Captain	193	11.16
6.	Staff Captain	165	9.54
7.	Rittmeister	88	5.08
8.	Staff Rittmeister	68	3.93
9.	Sub-Lieutenant	65	3.76
10.	Major General	43	2.49
11.	Officer Candidate	31	1.79
12.	2nd Lieutenant	27	1.56
13.	Jessaul	25	1.45
14.	Cornet	19	1.09
15.	Starchina	15	0.86
16.	1st Lieutenant	11	0.64
17.	Sotnik	10	0.58
18.	Rank Unknown	8	0.46
19.	Miscellaneous	7	0.40
20.	Lt. General	4	0.23
21.	Naval Lieutenant	2	0.12
22.	Chorunshi	2	0.12
23.	Lt. Commander	1	0.06
24.	Captain-Lieutenant	1	0.06

TWO AWARDS OF THE POUR LE MÉRITE ORDER TO THE SAME RECIPIENT BY FRIEDRICH WILHELM III.

Table IV

Name	FIRST AWARD * Entry	FIRST AWARD * Date/Rank	SECOND AWARD Entry	SECOND AWARD Date/Rank
1807				
1. **Obolenski**, Prince Vassili	174	Apr. 21, 1807 Major	1191	Dec. 8, 1813 Colonel
2. **Jesimovich**, Andri Alexandrovich	290	Jul. 5, 1807 Lt. Colonel	2049	Oct. 13-18, 1814 Colonel
3. **Vassiltshikov**, Nikolai Vassilieovich	325	Jul. 18, 1807 Colonel	1694	Oct. 13-18, 1814 Major General
4. **Chrapovizki**, Matvei Jevgrafovich	373	Jul. 22, 1807 Colonel	1797	Oct. 13-18, 1814 Major General
5. **Potemkin**, Jakob Alexieovich	375	Jul. 22, 1807 Colonel	1796	Oct. 13-18, 1814 Major General
6. **Jeschin**, Vassili Vassilieovich	466	Dec. 8, 1807 Rittmeister	1118	Dec. 8, 1813 Colonel
1808				
7. **Nabel**, Andrei Andreiovich	538	May 26, 1808 Lieutenant	1912	Oct. 13-18, 1814 Colonel
1809				
8. **Loshkarev**, Alexei Sergieovich	582	Feb. 17, 1809 Rittmeister	2242	Dec. 28, 1814 Lt. Colonel
9. **Melikov**, Pavel Moisseieovich	591	Mar. 1, 1809 Staff Rittmeister	2101	Oct. 13-18, 1814 Colonel

* See Volume I, Chapter V-1.

TWO AWARDS OF THE POUR LE MÉRITE ORDER TO THE SAME RECIPIENT BY FRIEDRICH WILHELM III. BETWEEN 1813 AND 1840

Table V

	Name	FIRST AWARD Entry	FIRST AWARD Date/Rank	SECOND AWARD Entry	SECOND AWARD Date/Rank
			1813		
1.	**Medviedev,** Peter Ivanovich	749	May 13, 1813 Captain	762	May 17, 1813 Captain
2.	**Obrutshev,** Vladimir Afanasseovich	759	May 13, 1813 Lieutenant	1795	Oct. 13-18, 1814 Captain
3.	**Ivanov,** Stepan Jemelianovich	776	May 18, 1813 Lt. Colonel	1492	Apr. 11, 1814 Lt. Colonel
4.	**von Lüdinghausen,** Frhr. Peter Johann	778	May 18, 1813 Lt. Colonel	1978	Oct. 13-18, 1814 Colonel
5.	**von Mach II.,** Leopold	783	May 18, 1813 Officer Candidate	816	Jul. 11, 1813 Sub-Lieutenant
6.	**Petrulin,** Jakob Vassilieovich	793	Jun. 11, 1813 Rittmeister	1933	Oct. 13-18, 1814 Colonel
7.	**Vnukov,** Vassili Michailovich	857	Sep. 6, 1813 Sub-Lieutenant	1024	Dec. 8, 1813 Sub-Lieutenant
8.	**Seslavin III.,** Fedor Nikita	858	Sep. 6, 1813 Staff Captain	960	Sep. 13, 1813 Staff Captain
9.	**Selivanov II.,** Andrei Andreiovich	872	Sep. 6, 1813 Starchina	1701	Oct. 13-18, 1814 Colonel
10.	**Orlov,** Alexei Fedorovich	942	Sep. 6, 1813 Rittmeister	976	Sep. 25, 1813 Colonel
11.	**Sosnin,** (First name unknown)	948	Sep. 10, 1813 Lt. Colonel	974	Sep. 21, 1813 Lt. Colonel
12.	**Savieskin,** Michail Vassilieovich	959	Sep. 13, 1813 Lieutenant	1023	Dec. 8, 1813 Lieutenant
13.	**Freigang,** Peter Ivanovich	1033	Dec. 8, 1813 Staff Captain	2235	Dec. 28, 1814 Lt. Colonel
14.	**Löwenhof,** Timofei Antonovich	1048	Dec. 8, 1813 Major	1944	Oct. 13-18, 1814 Lt. Colonel
15.	**Totshinski,** Ignati Pavlovich	1053	Dec. 8, 1813 Lieutenant	2448	Feb. 17, 1832 Colonel
16.	**Volevatsh,** Jakob Ivanovich	1101	Dec. 8, 1813 Lt. Colonel	1742	Oct. 13-18, 1814 Lt. Colonel

	Name	FIRST AWARD Entry	Date/Rank	SECOND AWARD Entry	Date/Rank
17.	Bashmakov, Flegon Mironovich	1102	Dec. 8, 1813 Lt. Colonel	1757	Oct. 13-18, 1814 Colonel
18.	Tazin IV., Peter Fedorovich	1106	Dec. 8, 1813 Lt. Colonel	1271	Dec. 17, 1813 Lt. Colonel
19.	von Vietinghoff, (First name unknown)	1119	Dec. 8, 1813 Major	1499	April 11, 1814 Major
20.	Biegidov, David Grigorieovich	1135	Dec. 8, 1813 Starchina	1272	Dec. 17, 1813 Lt. Colonel
21.	Breshinski, Semen Petrovich	1156	Dec. 8, 1813 Colonel	1901	Oct. 13-18, 1814 Lt. Colonel
22.	Terne, Fedor Fedorovich	1173	Dec. 8, 1813 Lt. Colonel	2187	Dec. 28, 1814 Colonel
23.	Muravski, (First name unknown)	1213	Dec. 8, 1813 Major	2275	Dec. 28, 1814 Major

1814

	Name	Entry	Date/Rank	Entry	Date/Rank
24.	Pokrovski, Jevstafi Charitonovich	1375	Mar. 31, 1814 Colonel	2148	Dec. 28, 1814 Colonel
25.	Koletshizki, Ivan Nikolaieovich	1376	Mar. 31, 1814 Rittmeister	2149	Dec. 28, 1814 Rittmeister
26.	Priess, Nikolai Ivanovich	1377	Mar. 31, 1814 Staff Rittmeister	2151	Dec. 28, 1814 Staff Rittmeister
27.	Filipov, Alexei Alexeiovich	1378	Mar. 31, 1814 Cornet	2153	Dec. 28, 1814 Cornet
28.	Karatshinski, Ivan (Vassilieovich)	1385	Apr. 11, 1814 Staff Captain	2278	Dec. 28, 1814 Captain
29.	von Gerbel III., Karl Gustafovich	1504	Apr. 11, 1814 Staff Captain	1664	Aug. 11, 1814 Captain
30.	Jaminski, Nikonor Vassilieovich	1511	April 13, 1814 Staff Captain	1657	Jun. 3, 1814 Staff Captain
31.	Skobelzin, Nikolai Dmitrieovich	1544	May 6, 1814 Colonel	1563	May 8, 1814 Colonel
32.	Stalipin, Dmitri Alexeieovich	1547	May 6, 1814 Colonel	2108	Oct. 13-18, 1814 Colonel
33.	Gerstenzweig, Danilo Alexandrovich	1548	May 6, 1814 Sub-Lieutenant	2111	Oct. 13-18, 1814 Sub-Lieutenant
34.	von Bistrom, Filipp Antonovich	1549	May 6, 1814 Captain	2112	Oct. 13-18, 1814 Captain
35.	Vishinzki, Michail Faddieieovich	1561	May 6, 1814 Staff Rittmeister	1610	May 12, 1814 Staff Rittmeister

	Name	FIRST AWARD Entry	FIRST AWARD Date/Rank	SECOND AWARD Entry	SECOND AWARD Date/Rank
36.	**Hippius**, Karl Fedorovich	1622	May 13, 1814 Captain	2208	Dec. 28, 1814 Captain
37.	**Voigt (Focht)**, Peter Andreieovich	1623	May 13, 1814 Captain	1744	Oct. 13-18, 1814 Staff Captain
38.	**Pauli (Paoli)**, Peter Ivanovich	1625	May 13, 1814 Staff Captain	1738	Oct. 13-18, 1814 Captain
39.	**Priashevski**, Nikolai Ivanovich	1768	Oct. 13-18, 1814 Major	2230	Dec. 28, 1814 Major
40.	**Latshinov**, Peter Petrovich	1771	Oct. 13-18, 1814 Lieutenant	2058	Oct. 13-18, 1814 Lieutenant
41.	**Tolstoi**, Count Alexander	1804	Oct. 13-18, 1814 Officer Candidate	2140	Oct. 14, 1814 Lieutenant
42.	**Gerassimov**, Alexander Semenovich	1900	Oct. 13-18, 1814 Captain	1952	Oct. 13-18, 1814 Captain
43.	**Ivanov III.**, Igor Sacharieovich	1984	Oct. 13-18, 1814 Lt. Colonel	2219	Dec. 28, 1814 Lt. Colonel
44.	**Lishin**, Nikolai Fedorovich	1986	Oct. 13-18, 1814 Staff Captain	2231	Dec. 28, 1814 Captain

TWO AWARDS OF THE POUR LE MÉRITE ORDER TO THE SAME RECIPIENT ON DECEMBER 8, 1813

Table VI

Name	1st Award	2nd Award
1. **Shenshin**, Vassili Nikanorovich,	1061	1182
2. **Röhren**, Ivan Bogdanovich,	1077	1183
3. **Suvorov II.**, Peter	1107	1201
4. **Jakovlev**, Stepan Makarovich,	1125	1193

Note: Also see Table VII.

THREE AWARDS OF THE POUR LE MÉRITE ORDER
TO THE SAME RECIPIENT

Table VII

Name	Entry	Award	Date
1. **Shusherin**, Sachar Sergieieovich	1098	1st Award	December 8, 1813
	1198	2nd Award	December 8, 1813*
	1740	3rd Award	October 13-18, 1814
2. **Sass**, Peter Andreiovich	1565	1st Award	May 8, 1814
	1637	2nd Award	May 29, 1814
	1940	3rd Award	October 13-18, 1814

* Two awards of the Pour le Mérite Order were given to this officer on the same day.

POUR LE MÉRITE ORDER RESCINDED
BY ORDER OF FRIEDRICH WILHELM III.

Table VIII

Name	Entry	Awarded	Rescinded
1. **von Meyerinck**, Wichard	2087	October 13-18, 1814	Same date*

* The rescinded Pour le Mérite Order was replaced with the Prussian 1813 Iron Cross 2nd Class.

SIMULTANEOUS AWARDS OF BOTH THE POUR LE MÉRITE ORDER AND OAKLEAVES BY FRIEDRICH WILHELM III.

Table IX

Name	Entry	Date
1813		
1. **Mecklenburg-Strelitz**, Prince Karl	986	October 9, 1813
2. **von Zastrow**, Alexander Heinrich	990	October 21, 1813
3. **von Valentini**, Georg Wilhelm	1230	December 8, 1813
4. **Henckel von Donnersmarck**, Count W.	1242	December 16, 1813
5. **von Pirch**, Georg Dubislaf	1324	December 24, 1813
1814		
6. **von Alvensleben**, Johann Friedrich	1371	March 31, 1814
7. **von Müffling**, Wilhelm	1381	April 9, 1814
8. **Biron von Kurland**, Baron Gustaf	1590	May 9, 1814
9. **von Stutterheim**, Karl August	1642	May 31, 1814
10. **von Hobe**, Kord Friedrich	1643	May 31, 1814
11. **Köhn (von Jaski)**, Andreas Ernst	1645	May 31, 1814
12. **von Schütz**, Karl August	1648	May 31, 1814
13. **von Othegraven**, Thomas	1649	May 31, 1814
14. **von Boyen**, Ludwig Leopold	1654	June 3, 1814
15. **von Müffling**, Friedrich Karl	1655	June 3, 1814
16. **von Klinckowström**, Count Karl	1658	June 11, 1814
1815		
17. **von Jagow**, Christian Friedrich	2318	October 2, 1815
18. **von Pirch**, Otto Karl	2320	October 2, 1815
19. **von Selasinsky**, Karl Friedrich	2322	October 2, 1815
20. **von Froelich**, Ernst August	2323	October 2, 1815
21. **von Arnault de la Perière**, August	2324	October 2, 1815
22. **von Boehler**, Johann Christian	2325	October 2, 1815
23. **von Stutterheim**, August Leopold	2326	October 2, 1815
24. **von Oppenkowsky**, Stanislaus	2329	October 2, 1815
25. **von Schutter**, Arnold	2330	October 2, 1815
26. **von Engelhart**, Karl Ludwig	2332	October 2, 1815
27. **von Holleben**, Ludwig Friedrich	2338	October 2, 1815
28. **von Ditfurth**, Wilhelm Heinrich	2339	October 2, 1815
29. **Braun**, Johann Karl Ludwig	2340	October 2, 1815
30. **von Borstell**, Ludwig Friedrich	2343	October 2, 1815
31. **von Keller**, Frhr. Heinrich Eugen	2344	October 2, 1815
32. **Dickinson**, Richard (British)	2371	November 9, 1815
1816		
33. **von der Marwitz**, Friedrich August	2373	January 14, 1816

Name	Entry	Date
1828		
34. **von Nostitz**, Count August Ludwig	2436	November 5, 1828

TWO AWARDS OF BOTH THE POUR LE MÉRITE ORDER AND OAKLEAVES TO SAME RECIPIENT BY FRIEDRICH WILHELM III.

Table X

	FIRST AWARD		SECOND AWARD	
Name	Entry	Date/Rank	Entry	Date/Rank
1. **von Schon**, Johann Karl	1641	May 31, 1814 Colonel	2333	October 2, 1815 Colonel

PERCENTAGES OF TOTAL AWARDS OF THE POUR LE MÉRITE ORDER BY NATIONALITY

1813 - 1840

Table XI

	Nationality	Number Awarded	Percentage
1.	Russia	1477	85.43%
2.	Prussia	130	7.52
3.	Austria	46	2.66
4.	Sweden	21	1.21
5.	England	15	0.87
6.	Hesse	13	0.75
7.	Bavaria	12	0.69
8.	Saxony	3	0.17
9.	Baden	3	0.17
10.	France	2	0.12
11.	Württemberg	2	0.12
12.	Waldeck	1	0.05
13.	Oldenburg	1	0.05
14.	Saxe-Gotha	1	0.05
15.	Anhalt	1	0.05
16.	Netherlands	1	0.05

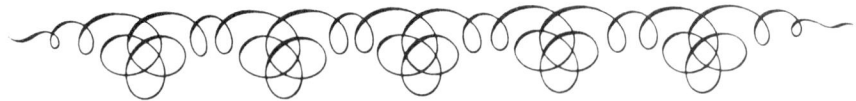

TOTAL AWARDS OF THE POUR LE MÉRITE ORDER TO RECIPIENTS IN PRUSSIAN UNITS MADE BY FRIEDRICH WILHELM III.

1813 – 1840

Table XII

A
I. Army Corps	5
II. Army Corps	2
II. Army Corps, Reserve Cavalry	1
III. Army Corps	6
III. Army Corps, Reserve Cavalry	1
IV. Army Corps	3

B
Brandenburg Dragoon Regiment	2
Brandenburg Infantry Regiment	1
Brandenburg Hussar Regiment	7
Brandenburg Uhlan Regiment	7
3rd (Brandenburg) Curassier Rgt.	1
3rd (Brandenburg) Uhlan Regiment	1
5th (Brandenburg Uhlan Regiment	1
I. Brigade	3
II. Brigade	2
III. Brigade	2
IV. Brigade	2
V. Brigade	2
VI. Brigade	1
VII. Brigade	2
VIII. Brigade	1
IX. Brigade	2
X. Brigade	2
XII. Brigade	1
XIV. Brigade	1
XV. Brigade	1

E
3rd East Prussian Inf. Rgt. (Landw)	1
4th East Prussian Infantry Regiment	1
Engineer Corps	1

G
Garde – see also Guard	
Garde du Corps	1
Garde du Corps, Gramont Company	1
Guard – see also Garde	
2nd Guard Cavalry Brigade	1
1st Guard Grenadier Infantry Rgt.	1
1st Guard Infantry Regiment	1
2nd Guard Infantry Regiment	2
2nd Guard Uhlan Regiment (Land)	1
Guard Dragoon Regiment	1

H
1st Hussar (1st Leib) Regiment	1

I
6th Infantry Regiment (Reserve)	1
15th Infantry Regiment	1
19th Infantry Regiment	1
30th Infantry Regiment	1
32nd Infantry Regiment	1
33rd Infantry Regiment	1

K
Kolburg Infantry Regiment	1

L
1st Leib Hussar Regiment	1
2nd Leib Hussar Regiment	2
Leib Infantry Regiment	1
Littau Dragoon Regiment	1

M
Markgraf v. Anspach-Bayreuth Dragoon Regiment	1

P
5th Pomeranian Hussar Regiment	3
Pomeranian Hussar Regiment	4
1st Pomeranian Infantry Regiment	2

Q
Quartermaster Corps	1

S
1st Silesian Hussar Regiment	1
2nd Silesian Infantry Regiment	1
Silesian Uhlan Regiment	6

U	W
6th Uhlan Regiment (Interim Brigade) 1	1st West Prussian Infantry Regiment 3
	2nd West Prussian Dragoon Regiment 2
Unknown Units 2	West Prussian Uhlan Regiment 1

TOTAL AWARDS OF THE POUR LE MÉRITE ORDER TO RECIPIENTS IN RUSSIAN UNITS MADE BY FRIEDRICH WILHELM III.

1813 - 1840

Table XIII

A			
Achtirka Hussar Regiment	8	33rd Artillery Battery Company	3
Alexandria Hussar Regiment	15	34th Artillery Battery Company	4
Alexopol Infantry Regiment	1	39th Artillery Battery Company	1
Apsheron Infantry Regiment	6	3rd Light Artillery Company	2
Araktsheiev Grenadier Regiment	1	6th Light Artillery Company	4
Archangelogrod Infantry Regiment	8	11th Light Artillery Company	1
Arsamas Mtd. Light Infantry Rgt.	1	13th Light Artillery Company	2
Asov Infantry Regiment	1	19th Light Artillery Company	2
Astrachan Curassier Regiment	6	26th Light Artillery Company	2
Astrachan Grenadier Regiment	1	27th Light Artillery Company	4
		28th Light Artillery Company	1
		29th Light Artillery Company	3
Field Artillery Corps		32nd Light Artillery Company	2
1st Artillery Brigade	1	33rd Light Artillery Company	1
5th Artillery Brigade	1	34th Light Artillery Company	1
6th Artillery Brigade	1	46th Light Artillery Company	1
13th Artillery Brigade	2	1st Mounted Artillery Company	6
14th Artillery Brigade	1	2nd Mounted Artillery Company	2
2nd Artillery Battery Company	1	3rd Mounted Artillery Company	5
5th Artillery Battery Company	3	4th Mounted Artillery Company	2
7th Artillery Battery Company	10	5th Mounted Artillery Company	1
10th Artillery Battery Company	1	6th Mounted Artillery Company	1
13th Artillery Battery Company	3	7th Mounted Artillery Company	2
14th Artillery Battery Company	3	8th Mounted Artillery Company	6
15th Artillery Battery Company	1	10th Mounted Artillery Company	1
18th Artillery Battery Company	1	11th Mounted Artillery Company	1
21st Artillery Battery Company	9	13th Mounted Artillery Company	5
22nd Artillery Battery Company	1	16th Mounted Artillery Company	1
28th Artillery Battery Company	1	18th Mounted Artillery Company	3
30th Artillery Battery Company	4	19th Mounted Artillery Company	3
31st Artillery Battery Company	5	22nd Mounted Artillery Company	1
32nd Artillery Battery Company	2	23rd Mounted Artillery Company	8

29th Mounted Artillery Company	1	Dorpat Mounted Light Infantry Rgt.	3
2nd Reserve Artillery Brigade	1	**E**	
4th Reserve Artillery Brigade	1	Ekaterinburg Infantry Regiment	3
7th Reserve Artillery Brigade	1	Ekaterinoslav Curassier Regiment	5
8th Reserve Artillery Brigade	1	Ekaterinoslav Grenadier Regiment	10
		Emperor Alexander Grenadier Rgt.	1
B			
14th Bashkiren Regiment	1	Engineer Corps	19
Bielorussia Hussar Regiment	11	1st Engineer Regiment	2
Bielorussia Infantry Regiment	6	2nd Engineer Regiment	1
Bielostok Infantry Regiment	3	1st Engineer (Pioneer) Regiment	1
Briansk Infantry Regiment	4	4th Pontoon Company, (Engineers)	2
Brest Infantry Regiment	2	Sapper (Engineers) Regiment	1
1st Bug Cossack Regiment	1		
3rd Bug Cossack Regiment	1	Estonian Infantry Regiment	1
C		**F**	
Cavalier Guard Regiment	23	Fangoria Grenadier Regiment	5
4th Cavalry Regiment (Tshernomori)	1	Field Light Infantry Corps	1
Charkov Dragoon Regiment	2	Field Postal Service	1
Crimean Infantry Regiment	2	Finnland Dragoon Regiment	1
D		**G**	
Army of the Don		Gluchov Curassier Regiment	3
Ataman Regiment	3	Grand Duchess Katherina Battalion	8
Ataman Cossack Regiment	5	Grodno Hussar Regiment	31
Bichalov I. Regiment	3	Guard Equipage Unit	6
Djatshkin I. Regiment	1		
Grekov VIII. Regiment	1	**H**	
Grekov XXI. Regiment	1	Headquarters, Russian Command	1
Ilovaiski Regiment	1		
Ilovaiski III. Regiment	2	**I**	
Ilovaiski IV. Regiment	4	1st Infantry Regiment	1
Ilovaiski V. Regiment	1	Ingermanland Dragoon Regiment	4
Ilovaiski IX. Regiment	1	Isium Hussar Regiment	6
Ilovaiski XII. Regiment	4		
Issaiev II. Regiment	1	**J**	
Karpov II. Regiment	3	Jakutski Infantry Regiment	2
Kuteinikov IV. Regiment	1	Jakuzk Infantry Regiment	1
Lukovkin Regiment	1	Jamburg Uhlan Regiment	1
Melnikov IV. Regiment	1	Jaroslav Infantry Regiment	2
Melnikov V. Regiment	1	Jaroslav Opoltshenie (militia)	1
2nd Mounted Artillery Company	2	Jelez Infantry Regiment	3
Radionov II. Regiment	5	Jelissavetgrad Hussar Regiment	3
Selivanov Regiment	2		
Semenstshenkov Regiment	2	**K**	
Tsherni Subov I. Cossack Regiment	1	Kaluga Infantry Regiment	9
Tsherni Subov V. Regiment	5	Kamtshatka Infantry Regiment	2
Tsherni Subov VIII. Regiment	1	Kargopol Dragoon Regiment	3
Vlassov Regiment	1	Kasan Dragoon Regiment	2
Unknown Units	12		

Kasan Infantry Regiment	1
Kexholm Grenadier Regiment	7
Kiev Dragoon Regiment	6
Kiev Grenadier Regiment	2
Kinburn Dragoon Regiment	1
King of Prussia Grenadier Regiment	6
Kolivan Infantry Regiment	3
Koslov Infantry Regiment	2
Krementshug Infantry Regiment	13
Kura Infantry Regiment	1
Kurland Dragoon Regiment	3

L

Libau Infantry Regiment	3
Liefland Mounted Light Inf. Rgt.	3
Life Guard Artillery Brigade	13
2nd Life Guard Artillery Brigade	1
Life Guard Artillery Regiment	1
Life Guard Mounted Artillery Rgt.	1
1st Life Guard Mounted Arty. Co.	6
2nd Life Guard Mounted Arty. Co.	6
Life Guard Cavalry Regiment	1
Life Guard Cossack Regiment	7
Life Guard Dragoon Regiment	7
Life Guard Finnland Regiment	9
Life Guard Grenadier Regiment	14
Life Guard His Majsty. Curas. Rgt.	14
Life Guard Her Majsty. Curas. Rgt.	6
Life Guard Hussar Regiment	33
Life Guard Ismailov Regiment	22
Life Guard Light Infantry Rgt.	35
Life Guard Lithuanian Regiment	2
Life Guard Littau Regiment	19
Life Guard Mounted Regiment	10
Life Guard Mounted Light Inf. Rgt.	1
Life Guard Pavlovski Regiment	10
Life Guard Preobrashenski Rgt.	34
Life Guard Sapper (Eng) Battalion	1
Life Guard Semenovski Regiment	38
Life Guard Uhlan Regiment	18
1st Light Infantry Regiment	2
3rd Light Infantry Regiment	4
4th Light Infantry Regiment	11
5th Light Infantry Regiment	5
6th Light Infantry Regiment	4
7th Light Infantry Regiment	6
8th Light Infantry Regiment	4
10th Light Infantry Regiment	1
11th Light Infantry Regiment	7
12th Light Infantry Regiment	1
13th Light Infantry Regiment	2
14th Light Infantry Regiment	4
20th Light Infantry Regiment	13
21st Light Infantry Regiment	1
22nd Light Infantry Regiment	6
23rd Light Infantry Regiment	5
24th Light Infantry Regiment	1
25th Light Infantry Regiment	5
26th Light Infantry Regiment	12
27th Light Infantry Regiment	1
28th Light Infantry Regiment	3
29th Light Infantry Regiment	5
30th Light Infantry Regiment	3
32nd Light Infantry Regiment	2
33rd Light Infantry Regiment	2
34th Light Infantry Regiment	4
36th Light Infantry Regiment	1
37th Light Infantry Regiment	1
38th Light Infantry Regiment	2
39th Light Infantry Regiment	3
41st Light Infantry Regiment	1
45th Light Infantry Regiment	2
48th Light Infantry Regiment	2
49th Light Infantry Regiment	5
1st Light Infantry Grenadier Regiment	1
Lithuanian Dragoon Regiment	1
Littau Uhlan Regiment	1
Lubno Hussar Regiment	15

M

Malo-Russia Grenadier Regiment	4
Mariupol Hussar Regiment	5
Mitau Dragoon Regiment	5
Mohilev Infantry Regiment	5
Moscow Cossack Regiment	1
Moscow Grenadier Regiment	1
Moscow Opoltshenie (militia)	2
Murom Infantry Regiment	16

N

Narva Infantry Regiment	4
Nascheburg Infantry Regiment	5
Navaga Infantry Regiment	5
Neushlot Infantry Regiment	1
Neva Infantry Regiment	1
New Russia Dragoon Regiment	3
Nieshin Mounted Light Infantry Rgt.	1
Nisov Infantry Regiment	2
Novgorod Curassier Regiment	7
Novgorod Opoltshenie (militia) Infantry	1

Novo-Ingermanland Infantry Rgt.	1	Siev Musketeer Regiment	1
O		Simbirski Infantry Regiment	1
Odessa Infantry Regiment	1	Simferopol Tatari Regiment	1
Olonez Infantry Regiment	5	Small Russia Curassier Regiment	4
Olviopol Hussar Regiment	3	Small Russia Grenadier Regiment	1
Orel Infantry Regiment	1	Smolensk Infantry Regiment	1
Orlov Infantry Regiment	1	Staro-Dubno Curassier Regiment	4
Osmani (Ataman) Cossacks	1	Staro-Ingermanland Infantry Regiment	6
		Staro-Oskol Infantry Regiment	5
P		Sum Hussar Regiment	10
Pavlograd Hussar Regiment	4	Supply and Provisions Administration	1
Pensa Opoltshenie (militia)	1		
Perejaslav Mounted Infantry Rgt.	1	**T**	
Perm Infantry Regiment	4	Tambov Infantry Regiment	1
Perm Opoltshenie (militia)	1	Tarnopol Infantry Regiment	2
Pernau Grenadier Regiment	10	Tatar Uhlan Regiment	8
Polni Uhlan Regiment	3	Tauri Grenadier Regiment	11
Polozk Infantry Regiment	3	Tenga Infantry Regiment	5
Prince Albrecht of Prussia Curas. R.	1	1st Teptiari Cossack Regiment	1
Prince Karl of Prussia Inf. Rgt.	1	Tobolski Infantry Regiment	9
Prince of Prussia Infantry Rgt.	2	Tshernigov Infantry Regiment	11
Pskov Curassier Regiment	6	Tshernigov Mounted Light Inf. Rgt.	3
Pskov Infantry Regiment	2	Tshuiugev Uhlan Regiment	3
		Tula Infantry Regiment	3
Q		Tula Opoltshenie (militia) 1st Cossacks	2
Quartermaster Corps	84	Tver Dragoon Regiment	1
R		**U**	
Reval Infantry Regiment	5	1st Ukraine Cossack Regiment	10
Riasan Infantry Regiment	6	2nd Ukraine Cossack Regiment	6
Riashski Infantry Regiment	7	3rd Ukraine Cossack Regiment	5
Roga Dragoon Regiment	4		
Rilski Infantry Regiment	2	**V**	
Russian-German Legion	3	Velike-Luzk Infantry Regiment	1
		Viatka Infantry Regiment	5
S		Viatkashen Infantry Regiment	1
St. Petersburg Grenadier Regiment	13	Viburg Infantry Regiment	4
St. Petersburg Opoltshenie (militia)	4	Vilmanstrand Infantry Regiment	2
1st Drushina (Battalion)	3	Vilna Infantry Regiment	2
7th Drushina (Battalion)	1	Vitepsk Infantry Regiment	2
12th Drushina (Battalion)	1	Vladimir Infantry Regiment	1
13th Drushina (Battalion)	1	1st Volunteer Cossack Regiment	4
Schlüsselburg Infantry Regiment	6	Volyni Infantry Regiment	9
2nd Sea Regiment	2	Volyni Uhlan Regiment	20
Serpuchov Uhlan Regiment	1		
Siberian Uhlan Regiment	2		
Shenshin Infantry Regiment	1		
Siev Infantry Regiment	6		
Siev Mounted Light Infantry Rgt.	2		

TOTAL AWARDS OF THE POUR LE MÉRITE ORDER TO RECIPIENTS IN NON-PRUSSIAN UNITS MADE BY FRIEDRICH WILHELM III.

1813 - 1840

Table XIV

ANHALT
Anhalt-Bernburg Battalion	1

AUSTRIA
Archduke Ferdinand Hussar Regiment	2
Archduke Johann Dragoon Regiment	3
Archduke Karl Uhlan Regiment	2
Archduke Konstantin Curassier Rgt.	2
Argentau Infantry Regiment	1
1st Artillery Regiment	1
Austro-German Legion Hussar Rgt.	1
Erbprinz von Hessen-Homburg Hussar Regiment	2
Hieronymus Colloredo Infantry Rgt.	1
Hohenzollern Chevau-léger Regiment	1
2nd Jäger Battalion	3
Kaiser Curassier Regiment	1
King of Prussia Hussar Regiment	1
Kollowrat Infantry Regiment	1
Kottulinsky Infantry Regiment	1
Meerveldt Uhlan Regiment	1
Quartermaster Corps	8
Redetzky Hussar Regiment	1
Reuss-Greiz Infantry Regiment	1
Riesch Dragoon Regiment	1
Rosenberg Light Cavalry Regiment	1
Schwarzenburg Uhlan Regiment	1
Unknown Austrian Units	6

BADEN
Grenadier Guard Regiment	3

BAVARIA
Artillery Corps	1
1st Chevau-légers Regiment	1
4th König Chevau-légers Regiment	1
6th Chevau-légers Regiment	1
2nd Hussar Regiment	1
7th Line Infantry Regiment	1
9th Line Infantry Regiment	1
Quartermaster Corps	1
1st Uhlan Regiment	1
Unknown Bavarian Units	4

ENGLAND
Royal Artillery Corps	1
Royal Corsican Rangers	1
Duke of Brunswick-Oels Cavalry Corps	1
Royal Equipage Corps	1
Royal German Legion	1
1st Grenadier Guards	1
1st Guards (Kings) Dragoon Regiment	1
11th (N. Devonshire) Infantry Rgt.	1
12th (E. Suffolk) Infantry Regiment	1
14th Light Dragoon Regiment	1
18th (Prince of Wale's Own) Royal Light Dragoon Regiment	2
2nd North (Royal) Dragoon Regiment	1
Unknown British Units	2

HESSE
Grenadier Regiment	1
Hussar Regiment	1
Jäger Battalion	7

Kurfürst Infantry Regiment	1	Life Guard Cavalry Regiment	4
Kurprinz Infantry Regiment	2	Life Guard Royal Curassier Corps	1
		Life Gentlemen-at-Arms Corps	1
Leib Dragoon Regiment	1		
OLDENBURG			
Oldenburg Infantry Regiment	1	Schonen Karabinier Regiment	1
		Södermanland Infantry Regiment	1
SAXE-GOTHA		Stockholm Squadron, Swedish Fleet	2
Saxe-Gotha Infantry Regiment	1		
		Wendes Artillery Regiment	1
SAXONY		West Göta Infantry Regiment	2
Artillery Corps	1	Westerbottons Infantry Regiment	1
Engineer Corps	2	Unknown Swedish Unit	1
SWEDEN		**WALDECK**	
Bohus-Lans Infantry Regiment	1	Waldeck Infantry Battalion	1
Engineer Corps	1	**WÜRTTEMBERG**	
		Unidentified Württemberg Unit	1
Göta Artillery Regiment	1		
Kalmar Infantry Regiment	1		

King Friedrich Wilhelm IV.

CHAPTER VI

Friedrich Wilhelm IV.

1840 – 1861

riedrich Wilhelm IV. was 45 years old when he succeeded his father to the throne of Prussia. He had a strong interest in the arts, especially architecture, and an obsessive passion for the history of the German Middle Ages. He also enjoyed hearing himself talk and soon became known as the master of the inspirational but meaningless phrase. Unfortunately, due to the influence of his early tutors, he was opposed to all revolutionary new ideas. More than anything else, Friedrich Wilhelm IV. was a firm believer in the divine rights of kings. From the day of his ascension to the Prussian throne on June 7, 1840, he proved to be an anachronism, born out of his time.

* * *

* November 30, 1840 *

1. **Friedrich, Archduke of Austria,** (Friedrich) Ferdinand Leopold,
Imperial Austrian Naval Commander of the Austrian Frigate "Guerriera."
(Awarded the Pour le Mérite Order in recognition of outstanding leadership and distinction in action during the bombardment of Saida [located in present day Lebanon] lasting almost two hours on September 26, 1840. This joint military expedition with the British was against the Egyptians who had rebelled against Turkish rule. Later in the day sailors from the Austrian squadron, with Archduke Friedrich in command, participated in the assault and capture of the Palestinian city of St. Jean d'Acre.)

* * *

* Establishment of the Pour le Mérite Order *
* for Science and Arts *

On May 31, 1842, the 102nd anniversary of Friedrich the Great's succession to the throne of Prussia, Friedrich Wilhelm IV. issued a decree from Sans Souci Palace which divided the Pour le Mérite Order into two separate categories. The first catagory remained strictly military without alteration. The second catagory became the civil or "peace" class of the Order, with a badge of differing design introduced for this civil class.

This new division was named:

"Pour le Mérite Order for Science and Arts"

It was Friedrich Wilhelm IV.'s intention to award the decoration to individuals who made outstanding contributions in the fields of science and arts.

The basic design for the new badge of the Pour le Mérite Order for Science and Arts was taken from one of the elements that composed the collar of the Noble Order of the Prussian Black Eagle, with only minor changes. The badge consisted of a gold medallion charged with the Prussian Eagle in relief and surrounded by a raised ornamental border. This medallion was surrounded by a Prussian blue enamel band with the inscription "Pour le Mérite" in gold letters and with a small five-pointed gold rosette at the top of the band. Between the medallion and the blue enamel band were four pairs of F's in a back-to-back or mirrored monogram at each quarter. Between the monograms were four Roman numeral II's, representing the Royal cypher of Friedrich II. On the outer edge of the enameled bank was a golden Prussian crown at each quarter directly adjacent to the mirrored F's. The reverse of the badge was plain gold. The badge was suspended from a gold elongated ribbon ring which passed through a small gold eyelet attached to the upper crown. The ribbon for the civil class was the same as that of the military class. A second award ribbon was not provided.

Awards of the Pour le Mérite Order for Science and Arts and the military division was brought to a close by the 1918 revolution in Germany at the end of World War I. The last "Peace" class of the Order had been awarded in 1917 to Adolf Erman in Berlin. There was a hiatus until 1923 when the Order was revived. Between 1923 and 1933, a total of 30 awards of the Pour le Mérite Order for Science and Arts were made, including Albert Einstein in 1923. The Order was then replaced with the National Socialist "National Prize for Arts and Science."

* * *

Original gold badge awarded to Sir Henry Creswick Rawlinson in 1852. Each crown is attached separately.

Silver gilt wearing replacement. Note difference in the crowns, which are an intregral part of the badge.

Polished reverse marked "Hossauer Berlin". Compare crowns to those of the badge shown at right.

Unpolished reverse of a wearing replacement. Note shape of crowns.

On May 31, 1952, the Pour le Mérite Order for Science and Arts was re-established and is presently given to outstanding scientists and artists.

* * *

* Establishment of the 50 Year Jubilee Crown *
* to the Pour le Mérite Order *

On July 18, 1844, Friedrich Wilhelm IV. established the last of the additional devices that could be worn with the Pour le Mérite Order. This device was in the shape of the Prussian Royal Crown and was attached to the ribbon suspension ring. It was officially called:

"The 50 Year Jubilee Crown to the Pour le Mérite Order"

It was awarded **only** to living recipients of the Pour le Mérite Order celebrating the 50th anniversary of their having been decorated with the Order (See Appendix V).

Above are shown three examples of the Pour le Mérite Order badges showing the proper 50 Year Jubilee Crown. Note the crowned eagles on two of the early badges.

Enlargement showing proper crown   Enlargement showing copy crown

The differences between the regulation 50 Year Jubilee Crown suspension and the current copy is obvious. The regulation crown suspension was made in gold and measured between 17.0 and 18.0 mm. wide and was approximately 14.0 mm. high; whereas the current fraudulent representation measures between 15.0 and 16.0 mm. wide and approximately 15.0 mm. high. Both are hollow and of two piece construction; however, the original is much thinner and somewhat flatter being only 3.0 mm. thick. The copy is crudely put together and more rounded and about 5.0 mm. thick.

* * *

* First Award of Both the Pour le Mérite Order *
* and the 50 Year Jubilee Crown Together *

* May 22, 1845 *

2. **du Pac de Badens et Sombrelle,** Marquis Gabriel,
    Royal French Major General, retired.
    (**Special Note:** Marquis de Pac de Badens et Sombrelle was awarded the Pour le Mérite Order in recognition of distinction in action during the battle at Grandpré during the 1792 Rhine campaign fought **53** years earlier. At the time, the Marquis was serving as an adjutant to the Prince of Nassau-Siegen. Also on this date he was given the **first** award of the 50 Year Jubilee Golden Crown to the Pour le Mérite Order. It is of special interest that the first presentation of the 50 Year Jubilee Golden Crown was to a Frenchman.)

* * *

* The Schleswig-Holstein War *

In 1846 Friedrich Wilhelm IV. was faced with a crisis which would eventually lead to the only war of his 21 year reign. The cause of this short but bloody war revolved around the "Schleswig-Holstein Question." A short explanation of the motives leading to this conflict should be reviewed.

Schleswig and Holstein were two semi-independent duchies in the southern part of Denmark bordering the western edge of Prussia. Neither of the duchies was considered fully incorporated into the Kingdom of Denmark; however, both were ruled by the King of Denmark. Schleswig was predominately Danish in population, while Holstein was mostly German. Holstein had strong ties with the German states to the south and was a member of the German Confederation. In July 1846, King Christian VIII. of Denmark issued an "open letter" to change the two duchies into a permanent and incorporated part of the Kingdom of Denmark. This caused much unrest within the duchies as well as in Prussia. To counter the concern of the population of Holstein, the Danish administration attempted to make Danish the populations of both Schleswig and Holstein. The Danes increased the required use of the Danish language, customs and government, grave mistakes that resulted in an open anti-Denmark uprising. This unstable political situation, which had always been somewhat fragile, became even more volatile after King Friedrich VII. succeeded to the Danish throne in 1848. Under the influence of the Danish nationalists, the king immediately set about to absorb Schleswig into the Danish kingdom. At the same time, the German speaking population of both duchies invited the Duke of Augustenburg to become their prince. The Danish king, Friedrich VII., offered several solutions to the problem; however, none was acceptable to the parties involved. The Danish king then tried to impose his rule on both duchies by force and the inevitable happened.

* * *

* December 18, 1846 *

3. **Wilhelm, Prince of Prussia,** Friedrich (Wilhelm) Karl,
    General of Cavalry, Governor of the Fortress of Mainz.
    Prince Wilhelm was awarded **both** the Pour le Mérite Order **and** the Oakleaves to the Pour le Mérite Order together on this date in recognition of outstanding leadership and distinguished military planning and operations. The award also recognized his distinction in action during previous Prussian campaigns. Prince Wilhelm of Prussia was an uncle of Friedrich Wilhelm IV.)

* * *

4. **Waldemar, Prince of Prussia**, Friedrich Wilhelm (Waldemar),
   Major General, Garde Dragoon Regiment.
   (Awarded the Pour le Mérite Order in recognition of outstanding leadership and distinguished military planning and operations.)
   * * *

5. **Lobo da Silveira, Count of Oriola**, Eduard Ernst,
   Major, Prussian General Staff Officer, serving at the time as attendent to Prince Waldemar.
   * * *

6. **von der Groeben**, Count Albrecht Wilhelm,
   2nd Lieutenant, Garde Dragoon Regiment, serving at the time as attendent to Prince Waldemar.
   * * *

The Schleswig-Holstein War began in early 1848 when units of the Royal Danish army marched into the Duchy of Schleswig. Both duchies immediately established a provisional government at Kiel, attempting to raise an army to face the Danish invasion. The two forces met and battled at Bau (Bov). The Schleswig-Holstein army was soundly defeated by the disciplined Danish regular troops. It appeared that both duchies would quickly be overrun and occupied. However, at this point, Prussia stepped into the conflict. Friedrich Wilhelm IV. dispatched an army under the command of General Friedrich **von Wrangel** (see entry 8) to stop the Danish invasion. The Danes quickly reacted to this threat. After a short but sharp engagement near the city of Schleswig, the Danish army was forced to retreat, leaving the Prussians to occupy Jutland. In August 1848, Denmark and Prussia concluded an armistice at Malino and the fighting ceased.
   * * *

* September 1, 1848 *

7. **von Bonin**, Eduard Ludwig Wilhelm,
   Major General, Commanding Officer of the Schleswig-Holstein Combined Prussian Brigade.
   (Awarded the Pour le Mérite Order in recognition of outstanding leadership and distinguished military planning and operations during the 1848 Schleswig-Holstein campaigns. The award also recognized his distinction in action during the battle at Schleswig on April 23, 1848.)
   * * *

* September 13, 1848 *

8. **von Wrangel**, Friedrich Heinrich,
   General of Cavalry, Commander-in-Chief of all Military Forces in Schleswig-Holstein, Commanding General of the II. Army Corps.
   (**Special Note:** Awarded the Oakleaves to the Pour le Mérite Order in recognition of outstanding leadership and distinguished military planning and operations during the 1848 Schleswig-Holstein campaigns. General von Wrangel was first decorated with the Pour le Mérite Order in 1807, **41** years earlier. At the time, he held the rank of 2nd Lieutenant. For the initial award of the Pour le Mérite Order to this officer see Volume I, Chapter V-1, entry 334, p. 298.
   Note: On January 13, 1857, von Wrangel, holding the rank of Field Marshal, was awarded the 50 Year Jubilee Golden Crown to the Pour le Mérite Order.)
   * * *

* September 16, 1848 *

9. **Friedrich Karl, Prince of Prussia,** (Friedrich Karl) Nikolaus,
   Captain, 1st Garde Infantry Regiment, serving at the time as Staff Officer on the High Command of the Schleswig-Holstein Military Forces.
   (Awarded the Pour le Mérite Order in recognition of outstanding leadership and distinguished military planning and operations during the 1848 Schleswig-Holstein campaigns. For the subsequent award of the Oakleaves to the Pour le Mérite Order given this officer see Chapter VII, entry 2.)
   * * *

& September 18, 1848 *

The following two Prussian officers were decorated with the Pour le Mérite Order in recognition of outstanding leadership and conspicuous bravery in action during the battle at Schleswig on April 23, 1848.

10. **von Waldersee,** Count Friedrich Gustaf,
    Lt. Colonel, Commander, Kaiser Alexander Grenadier Regiment.

11. **von Möllendorf,** Johann Karl Wolf Dietrich,
    Major General, Commander, 2nd Garde Infantry Regiment.
    * * *

* September 19, 1848 *

12. **Radizwill,** Prince Friedrich Wilhelm Paul Ferdinand Ludwig August,
    Lt. General, Commander, 6th Division.
    (Awarded the Pour le Mérite Order in recognition of outstanding leadership and distinguished military planning and operations during the 1848 Schleswig-Holstein campaigns.)
    * * *

13. **von Stockhausen,** August Wilhelm Ernst,
    Major General, Commander, 1st Division, serving at the time as Chief of the General Staff at the High Command Headquarters of the Schleswig-Holstein Military Forces.
    (Awarded the Pour le Mérite Order in recognition of outstanding leadership and distinguished military planning and operations during the 1848 Schleswig-Holstein campaigns. The award also recognized his distinction in action during the battle at Schleswig on April 23, 1848.)
    * * *

14. **d'Artis de Bequignolles,** Eduard Friedrich Leopold,
    Colonel, Commander, Kaiser Franz Grenadier Regiment.
    (Awarded the Pour le Mérite Order in recognition of outstanding leadership and distinction in action while leading the 1st Battalion of the regiment during the battle at Bosdorf and especially during the battle at Schleswig on April 23, 1848.)
    * * *

15. **von Steinmetz,** Karl Friedrich,
    Major, Garde Reserve Infantry Regiment, serving at the time as Commander of the Musketeer Battalion, 2nd (Königs) Infantry Regiment.
    (Awarded the Pour le Mérite Order in recognition of outstanding leadership and distinction in action during the storming of the Danish positions near Düppel and during the battle at Schleswig on April 23, 1848. For the subsequent award of the Oakleaves to the Pour le Mérite Order

given this officer see Chapter VII, entry 245.)

* * *

16. **von Rommel,** Theodor Karl Daniel,
    Colonel, Commander, 20th Infantry Regiment.
    (Awarded the Pour le Mérite Order in recognition of outstanding leadership and distinction in action during the battle at Husbye.)

* * *

17. **Wiesner,** Friedrich Adolf,
    Lt. Colonel, Commander, 26th Infantry (4th Reserve) Regiment, serving at the time as Commander of the Fusilier Battalion, 31st Infantry Regiment.
    (Awarded the Pour le Mérite Order in recognition of outstanding leadership and distinction in action during several engagements against Danish forces while serving in the Advance Guard during April 1848.)

* * *

18. **Halkett,** Hugh,
    Royal Hanovarian Lt. General, Commander, X. Corps.
    (Awarded the Pour le Mérite Order in recognition of outstanding leadership and distinguished military planning and operations during the 1848 Schleswig-Holstein campaigns.)

* * *

* October 14, 1848 *

19. **Friedrich, Prince of Schleswig-Holstein-Sonderburg-Augustenburg,** Emil,
    Commander-in-Chief, Schleswig-Holstein Military Forces, also a member of the Schleswig-Holstein Provisional Government.
    (Awarded the Pour le Mérite Order in recognition of outstanding leadership and distinguished military planning and operations during the 1848 Schleswig-Holstein campaigns.)

* * *

* November 29, 1848 *

20. **von Wedell,** Leopold Friedrich Ferdinand Heinrich,
    Lt. General, Commander, 4th Division.
    (Awarded the Pour le Mérite Order in recognition of outstanding leadership and distinguished military planning and operations during the 1848 Schleswig-Holstein campaigns.)

* * *

21. **von Brandt,** August Heinrich,
    Major General, Commander, 9th Infantry Brigade.
    (Awarded the Pour le Mérite Order in recognition of outstanding leadership and distinguished military planning and operations during the 1848 Schleswig-Holstein campaigns. The award also recognized his distinction in action during the battle at Xions.)

* * *

The armistice lasted until February 26, 1849, when Denmark announced an end to the treaty and resumed hostilities. The Royal Danish army initially suffered several defeats. On April 5, 1849, the Danish troops were soundly defeated during the battle at Eckernförde, where the Danish man-of-war "Christian VIII." was sunk by an artillery battery commanded by **Duke Ernst of Saxe-Coburg-Gotha** (see entry 31, this chapter). During this same action, the Danish frigate "Gefion" was captured. The Danes also suffered defeats at Kolding and Gudsoe. At the battle of Fredericia, the German forces, commanded by General **von Prittwitz** see entry 28, this chapter), consisted of Prussians, Saxons, Hanovarians, and three mixed contingents of troops including 15,000 Schleswig-Holstein troops. The Germans suffered rather heavy losses and were forced to withdraw. However, Prussia had won the war; shortly after the battle at Fredericia, the Danes capitulated and sued for peace. A new truce between Prussia and Denmark was signed on July 10, 1849, and all hostilities ceased. The duchies of Schleswig and Holstein were placed under Prussian control and administration.

* * *

* April 10, 1849 *

22. **Albrecht, Archduke of Austria,** (Albrecht) Friedrich Rudolf,
    Imperial Austrian Field Marshal, Commander-in-Chief, Austrian Military Forces in Italy.
    (Awarded the Pour le Mérite Order in recognition of outstanding leadership and distinguished military planning and operations during the Italian campaign. The award also recognized his distinction in action during the battles at Mortara and Novara.)

* * *

* July 21, 1849 *

23. **Albert, Prince of Saxony,** Friedrich August Anton Ferdinand Josef.

    (Awarded the Pour le Mérite Order in recognition of outstanding leadership and conspicuous bravery in action during the battles at Düppel, Alminde, Viuf and Veile. For the subsequent award of the Oakleaves to the Pour le Mérite Order given this officer see Chapter VII, entry 180.
    Note: Prince Albert was awarded the 50 Year Jubilee Golden Crown to the Pour le Mérite Order on July 15, 1899.)

* * *

* July 27, 1849 *

24. **Wilhelm, Prince of Prussia,** Friedrich (Wilhelm) Ludwig,
    General of Infantry, Commander-in-Chief, Operations Army of the Rhine.
    (Awarded the Pour le Mérite Order in recognition of outstanding leadership and distinguished military planning and operations during the 1848 Schleswig-Holstein campaigns. For the subsequent award of the Oakleaves to the Pour le Mérite Order given this officer see entry 27, this chapter.)

* * *

25. **von der Groeben,** Count Karl,
    Lt. General, Adjutant General and Commanding General, II. Corps, Operations Army of the Rhine.
    (Awarded the Oakleaves to the Pour le Mérite Order in recognition of outstanding leadership and distinguished military planning and operations during the 1848 Schleswig-Holstein campaigns. General von der Groeben was first awarded the Pour le Mérite Order in 1809, **40** years earlier when von der Groeben held the rank of 2nd Lieutenant. For the initial award of the Pour le Mérite Order to this officer see Volume I, Chapter V-1, entry 608, p. 316.)

* * *

26. **Kirchfeldt,** Friedrich Wilhelm August,
    Major, General Staff Officer serving at the time as Deputy Chief of Staff at the High Command Headquarters of the Operations Army of the Rhine.
    (Awarded the Pour le Mérite Order in recognition of outstanding leadership and distinguished military planning and operations during the 1848 Schleswig-Holstein campaigns.)
    * * *

* July 31, 1849 *

27. **von Pfuhl,** August Friedrich Heinrich,
    Major, 11th Hussar Regiment.
    (Awarded the Pour le Mérite Order in recognition of outstanding leadership and distinction in action during a reconnaissance patrol near the city of Schleswig on April 23, 1848.)
    * * *

* August 9, 1849 *

28. **von Prittwitz,** Karl Ludwig Wilhelm Ernst,
    Lt. General, assigned to the vacant position of Commanding General of the Garde Corps.
    (Awarded the Pour le Mérite Order in recognition of outstanding leadership and distinguished military planning and operations during the 1848 Schleswig-Holstein campaigns.)
    * * *

* August 16, 1849 *

29. **von Willisen,** Friedrich Adolf,
    Major General, General à la suite to Friedrich Wilhelm IV.
    (Awarded the Pour le Mérite Order in recognition of outstanding leadership and distinguished military planning and operations while attached to the Austrian Headquarters of Field Marshal Count Redetzky as an advisor and observer during the 1849 Sardinian campaign.)
    * * *

* August 17, 1849 *

30. **Konstantin Nikolaieovich, Grand Duke of Russia.**

    (Awarded the Pour le Mérite Order in recognition of outstanding leadership and distinction in action while commanding the Russian troops during the suppression of the 1848-1849 Hungarian uprising at the request of Emperor Franz Joseph I. of Austria.)
    * * *

* September 11, 1849 *

31. **Ernst, Duke of Saxe-Coburg-Gotha,** (Ernst) August Karl Johannes Leopold Alexander Eduard.

    (**Special Note:** Awarded the Pour le Mérite Order in recognition of outstanding leadership and distinguished military planning and operations while commanding the artillery battery which sank the Danish warship "Christian VIII." and for distinction in action during the capture of the Danish frigate "Gefion" at Eckernförde on April 5, 1849.)
    * * *

* September 20, 1849 *

32. **Brunsich (Brunsig) Edler von Brun,** Georg Wilhelm Friedrich,
    Major General, Commander, 16th Infantry Brigade, serving at the time as Commander of the 4th Division, Operations Army of the Rhine.
    (Awarded the Pour le Mérite Order in recognition of outstanding leadership and distinguished military planning and operations during the 1848 Schleswig-Holstein campaigns. The award also recognized his distinction in action during the battle at Waghäusel on June 21, 1849.)

* * *

* March 19, 1850 *

33. **Filangieri, Prince of Satriano and Duke of Taormina,** Carlo Cesare Antonio Goffredo Cornelio Michele Gabriele Raffaele Angelo-Custode Gaspare Baldassare Melchiore,
    Royal Neapolitan Major General, Governor General of Sicily.
    (**Note:** Available records do not indicate the reason Prince Filangieri was awarded the Pour le Mérite Order.)

* * *

34. **Gross,** Gottlieb Wilhelm,
    Royal Neapolitan Major General.
    (Awarded the Pour le Mérite Order in recognition of outstanding leadership and distinction in action while serving for over 13 years in the Prussian army. He entered the 2nd Magdeburg Fusilier Brigade on October 15, 1794, and held the rank of 2nd Lieutenant.)

* * *

The formal peace agreement was negotiated and finally signed on July 2, 1850. Prussia then withdrew its administration from the two duchies and returned them to Danish control and administration. However, the Danes no longer clamored for union with Denmark.

* * *

* 1848-1849 Schleswig-Holstein War Awards *
* of the Pour le Mérite Order *

During the course of the Schleswig-Holstein War, Friedrich Wilhelm IV. made a total of only **23** awards of the Pour le Mérite Order. In contrast, the king made **430** awards of the Prussian Red Eagle Order in its various classes. By limiting the number of the Pour le Mérite Order awards, he increased the importance, prestige and desirability of the Order.

* * *

* Award of the Pour le Mérite Order After 60 Years *

* August 8, 1854 *

35. **von Klinckowström,** Bernhard Wilhelm,
    Captain, retired, residing in Graudenz.
    (**Special Note:** Captain von Klinckowström had been decorated with the Prussian Golden Military Medal in recognition of distinction in action in 1794. In December 1804, and according to the regulations in effect at the time, he was eligible to return the Golden Military Merit Medal which would be exchanged for the Pour le Mérite Order. However, the Captain did not receive the Pour le Mérite Order until 1854, an unbelievable **60** years after the initial award for conspicuous brav-

ery was made. Von Klinckowström was given the long over-due Pour le Mérite Order **and** the 50 Year Jubilee Golden Crown together on this date. He was the **second** recipient of the 50 Year Jubilee Golden Crown to the Pour le Mérite Order, a rather surprising **9 years after** the first award had been made.)

* * *

On January 13, 1857, Friedrich **von Wrangel** (see entry 8, this chapter), holding the rank of Field Marshal, became the **third** recipient of the 50 Year Jubilee Golden Crown to the Pour le Mérite Order. Note in the photo at right that he is wearing the Golden Crown device on the Pour le Mérite Order.

* * *

* The Pour le Mérite Order Revoked After 43 Years *

On April 16, 1857, Friedrich Wilhelm IV. revoked the Pour le Mérite Order that had been given to Russian Count Gustaf Gustafovich **Armfelt** (see Chapter V-2, entry 1369). At the time of the award he held the rank of Imperial Russian Staff Captain. It seems incredible that after **43** years the decoration would be rescinded; however, it was and the reason for the revocation and return of the Order are unavailable.

* * *

* Appointment of Prince Wilhelm as Regent *

During the last few years of his life, the mental and physical health of Friedrich Wilhelm IV. deteriorated. In the summer of 1857, the king suffered a stroke which seriously effected his ability to attend to the affairs of state. Within only a few months, Friedrich Wilhelm was declared insane and, by October 1858, his brother, Prince Wilhelm (entry 24, this chapter), was appointed to rule as regent.

* * *

* November 3, 1859 *

36. **Alexander, Prince of Hesse and the Rhine,** (Alexander) Ludwig Christian Georg Friedrich Emil,
    Imperial Austrian Field Marshal.
    (Awarded the Pour le Mérite Order in recognition of outstanding leadership and distinguished military planning and operations during the 1848-1849 Italian campaigns.
    Note: This appears to be the first award of the Pour le Mérite Order made by Prince Wilhelm while he was serving as Prince Regent for his incapacitated brother.)

* * *

The Death of Friedrich Wilhelm IV.

January 2, 1861

On January 2, 1861, Friedrich Wilhelm IV. died unexpectedly after a very short illness, and his brother, Prince Wilhelm, became Wilhelm I., the seventh King of Prussia.

* * *

Prince Wilhelm at the Death Bed of Friedrich Wilhelm IV.

Additional Notes:

AWARDS OF THE POUR LE MÉRITE ORDER DURING THE REIGN OF FRIEDRICH WILHELM IV. FROM 1840 THROUGH 1861.

AWARDS OF THE POUR LE MÉRITE ORDER
DURING THE REIGN OF FRIEDRICH WILHELM IV.

1840 - 1861

Table I

Rank	1840	1845	1846	1848	1849	1850	1854	1859	Total
Field Marshal	-	-	-	-	1	-	-	1	2
General of Infantry	-	-	-	-	1	-	-	-	1
General of Cavalry	-	-	1	1	-	-	-	-	2
Lt. General	-	-	-	3	2	1	-	-	6
Major General	-	-	1	4	2	1	-	-	8
Colonel	-	-	-	2	-	-	-	-	2
Lt. Colonel	-	-	-	2	-	-	-	-	2
Major	-	1	1	1	2	-	-	-	5
Captain	-	-	-	1	-	-	-	-	1
Staff Captain	-	-	-	-	-	-	-	-	-
Rittmeister	-	-	-	-	-	-	-	-	-
Staff Rittmeister	-	-	-	-	-	-	-	-	-
1st Lieutenant	-	-	-	-	-	-	-	-	-
Lieutenant	-	-	-	-	-	-	-	-	-
2nd Lieutenant	-	-	1	-	-	-	-	-	1
Cornet	-	-	-	-	-	-	-	-	-
Officer Candidate	-	-	-	-	-	-	-	-	-
Rank Unknown*	1	-	-	1	3	-	-	-	5
Miscellaneous	-	-	-	-	-	-	1	-	1
Totals	1	1	4	15	11	2	1	1	36

* Royal Princes were serving in a military capacity but records do not indicate their respective ranks.

PERCENTAGES OF TOTAL AWARDS OF THE POUR LE MÉRITE ORDER ACCORDING TO RANK

1840 - 1861

Table II

	Rank	Number Awarded	Percentage
1.	Major General	8	22.22%
2.	Lt. General	6	16.66
3.	Major	5	13.88
4.	Rank Unknown (Princes)	5	13.88
5.	Field Marshal	2	5.55
6.	General of Cavalry	2	5.55
7.	Colonel	2	5.55
8.	Lt. Colonel	2	5.55
9.	General of Infantry	1	2.77
10.	Captain	1	2.77
11.	2nd Lieutenant	1	2.77
12.	Miscellaneous	1	2.77

SIMULTANEOUS AWARD OF BOTH THE POUR LE MÉRITE ORDER AND OAKLEAVES BY FRIEDRICH WILHELM IV.

Table III

	Name	Entry	Date
1.	Wilhelm, Prince of Prussia	3	December 18, 1846

SIMULTANEOUS AWARDS OF BOTH
THE POUR LE MÉRITE ORDER AND THE 50 YEAR JUBILEE CROWN

1840 - 1861

Table IV

	Name	Entry	Date
1.	**du Pac de Badens et Sombrelle,** Marquis Gabriel	2	May 22, 1845
2.	**von Klinckowström,** Bernhard Wilhelm	35	Aug. 8, 1854

POUR LE MÉRITE ORDER REVOKED
BY ORDER OF FRIEDRICH WILHELM IV.

Table V

Name	Entry	Awarded	Revoked
1. **Armfelt,** Count Gustaf	1369	March 19, 1814	April 16, 1857*

AWARDS OF THE POUR LE MÉRITE ORDER
BY NATIONALITY

Table VI

	Nationality	Number Awarded
1.	Austrian	3
2.	Neapolitan	2
3.	French	1
4.	Hanover	1
5.	Russian	1
6.	Saxon	1
7.	Saxe-Coburg-Gotha	1

* Revoked and returned 47 years after the award was made. Reason unknown.

TOTAL AWARDS OF THE POUR LE MÉRITE ORDER TO RECIPIENTS IN PRUSSIAN UNITS MADE BY FRIEDRICH WILHELM IV.

1840 - 1861

Table VII

A		Non-Prussian	
Army of the Rhine, Operations	3	Coburg-Gotha Contingent	1

D	
1st Division	1
4th Division	2
6th Division	1

C	
X. Corps	1

G	
Garde du Corps	1
Garde Dragoon Regiment	2
1st Garde Infantry Regiment	1
2nd Garde Infantry Regiment	1

H	
11th Hussar Regiment	1

I	
9th Infantry Brigade	1
20th Infantry Brigade	1
31st Infantry Brigade	1

K	
Kaiser Alexander Grenadier Regiment	1
Kaiser Franz Grenadier Regiment	1
2nd Königs Infantry Regiment Musketeer Battalion	1

P	
Prussian Combined Line Brigade	1

Coronation of King Wilhelm I. in Königsberg on October 18, 1861.

CHAPTER VII

Wilhelm I.

1861 – 1888

n January 2, 1861, Prince Wilhelm, the Prince Regent, then 66 years old, became the seventh King of Prussia. The suddeness of the death of Friedrich Wilhelm surprised almost everyone including Wilhelm himself.

Wilhelm I. was an extremely modest man who always thought of himself, first and foremost, as a Prussian soldier. Although he was not an exceptionally brilliant man, he was indeed a brave and fearless officer. This was amply demonstrated when, during the Napoleonic wars, on March 10, 1814, he was awarded the Iron Cross 2nd Class and the Imperial Russian Order of St. George 2nd Class for his distinguished leadership and bravery during the battle at Bar sur Aube.

Wilhelm, as King of Prussia, devoted his entire life to the army and the belief that absolute power in Prussia was vested in the Royal Crown, to which the Prussian army was obliged and pledged to defend.

* * *

* **February 20, 1861** *

1. **Franz d'Assisi, Kingdom of the Two Sicilies,** Maria Leopold.

    (Awarded the Pour le Mérite Order in recognition of outstanding leadership and distinguished military planning and operations during the siege and defense of Gaeta from November 3, 1860 until February 13, 1861, against the Italian Army of Unification under the command of Italian General Enrico Caildini.)

    * * *

The first few years of the reign of Wilhelm I. were so filled with political intrigues and internal power struggles that the king came very close to abdicating the Prussian throne. The internal politics and bickering raged for months at a time. Finally, the Minister of War, Albrecht **von Roon** (see entry 174, this chapter), sent for the Prussian Ambassador to France, Otto **von Bismarck** (see entry 305, this chapter) to return to Prussia and Wilhelm I. appointed him to the high office of Prussian Prime Minister. Bismarck's first speech to the parliament, the famous "blood and iron" speech, set the course of Prussian politics for years to come.

New army reforms and reorganizations were suggested by the king, and completed and implemented as well, by the time Prussia was prepared to engage in the first war of the 27 year reign of Wilhelm I.

* * *

* The 1864 Danish-Prussian War *

Prinz Friedrich Karl von Preußen.

The first war during the reign of Wilhelm I. concluded the problems over the duchies of Schleswig and Holstein. At this time, three small German duchies, Schleswig, Holstein and Lauenburg, were being administered by the Kingdom of Denmark under the Treaty of London, signed in 1852. However, on November 15, 1863, Friedrich VII. of Denmark died and again the fate of the duchies became questionable. There was a general disagreement throughout the German states as to their status. In fact, there was even doubt as to the right of the newly crowned Danish king, Christian IX. to the succession to the throne. Some claimed the duchies were a part of Germany, and the Diet of the German Confederation issued a decree of occupation. Basically, this was in protest against Christian IX. and his administration of the duchies. In accordance with the German edict, troops from Hanover and Saxony marched into the Duchy of Holstein. The Danish troops withdrew into Schleswig. However, this action did not suit the purpose of Prussia. Wilhelm I. diplomatically proposed that Prussia and Austria alone, as the leading German powers, execute the decree. The Saxon-Hanovarian forces were replaced by Austro-Prussian troops. The Danish response was to declare war on Prussia and Austria.

The Danish-Prussian War began on February 1, 1864. The Prussian forces commanded by Field Marshal **von Wrangel** and the Imperial Austrian Field Marshal **von der Gablenz** (see entry 3, this chapter) commanding the Austrians, moved quickly. On February 2, 1864, the bombardment of the fortifications at Missude began; by February 6, 1864, the crossing of the Schlei (Sli), an inlet of the Baltic Sea on the east coast of Schleswig-Holstein, had been accomplished.

The first award of the Pour le Mérite Order of this war was made on February 27, 1864, to Prince Friedrich Karl, a nephew of Wilhelm I.

* * *

* February 27, 1864 *

2. **Friedrich Karl, Prince of Prussia,** (Friedrich Karl) Nikolaus,
   General of Cavalry, Commanding General, Combined Army Corps.
   (Awarded the Oakleaves to the Pour le Mérite Order in recognition of outstanding leadership and distinguished military planning and operations during the bombardment of Missude on February 2, 1864. For the initial award of the Pour le Mérite Order to this officer see Chapter VI, entry 9.)
   * * *

3. **von der Gablenz,** Frhr. Karl Wilhelm Ludwig,
   Imperial Austrian Field Marshal, Commander, VI. Army Corps.
   (Awarded the Pour le Mérite Order in recognition of outstanding leadership and distinguished military planning and operations during the initial assaults against the Danish fortifications.)
   * * *

* March 22, 1864 *

Wilhelm, Duke of Württemberg, (Wilhelm) Nikolaus,
Imperial Austrian Major General, Commander, King of Belgium Infantry Regiment.
(Awarded the Pour le Mérite Order in recognition of outstanding leadership and distinguished military planning and operations during the battle at Oeversee on February 6, 1864.)
* * *

The great fortress of Düppel (Dyppöl) was protected by an outer chain of ten redoubts and had been successfully invested by 16,000 Prussian troops commanded by Prince Friedrich Karl and defended by a Danish garrison of 22,000 troops. During the assault and storming of Düppel, the Prussian forces breached

The Storming of Düppel

the first parallel on March 30, 1864. On April 17, 1864, after a very heavy bombardment, the Prussians attacked the first six of a chain of protective redoubts. After brief resistance, the Prussian assault columns overwhelmed the Danish defenders. The capture of the outer defenses of the fort resulted in the capitulation of Düppel on April 18, 1864. * * *

* April 21, 1864 *

5. **von Manstein**, Gustaf Albert,
    Lt. General, Commander, 6th Infantry Division.
    (Awarded the Pour le Mérite Order in recognition of outstanding leadership and distinguished military planning and operations. The award also recognized his distinction in action during the capture of the Danish defenses at Düppel on April 18, 1864. For the initial award of the Pour le Mérite Order to this officer see entry 113, this chapter.)
    * * *

6. **von Raven**, Eduard Gustaf Ludwig,
    Major General, Commander, 10th Infantry Brigade.
    (Awarded the Pour le Mérite Order in recognition of outstanding leadership and distinguished military planning and operations during the assault and capture of the Danish defenses at Düppel on April 18, 1864. The award also recognized his distinction in action during the battle.)
    * * *

* April 22, 1864 *

7. **Vogel von Falckenstein**, Friedrich Karl Ernst Eduard,
    Lt. General, Chief of the General Staff, High Command Headquarters of the Allied Forces.
    (Awarded the Pour le Mérite Order in recognition of outstanding leadership and distinguished military planning and operations.)
    * * *

8. **Hindersin**, Gustaf Eduard,

    Lt. General, Inspector of Artillery, 2nd Artillery Inspection Unit.
    (Awarded the Pour le Mérite Order in recognition of outstanding leadership and distinction in action.)
    * * *

9. **von Blumenthal**, Karl Konstantin Albrecht,

    Colonel, Chief of the General Staff, Combined Army Corps.
    (Awarded the Pour le Mérite Order in recognition of outstanding leadership and distinguished military planning and operations. For the subsequent award of the Oakleaves to the Pour le Mérite Order given this officer see entry 71, this chapter.)
    * * *

10. **Colomier,** Louis Max Napoleon,
    Colonel, Brigadier of the 3rd Brandenburg Artillery Brigade.
    (Awarded the Pour le Mérite Order in recognition of outstanding leadership and distinction in action during the assault and capture of the Danish defenses at Düppel on April 18, 1864.)
    * * *

11. **von Mertens,** August Ferdinand,
    Colonel, Fortress Inspector, 6th Fortress Inspection Unit.
    (Awarded the Pour le Mérite Order in recognition of outstanding leadership and distinction in action during the assault and capture of the Danish defenses at Düppel on April 18, 1864.)
    * * *

* May 30, 1864 *

12. **von Bergmann,** Richard Emil,
    Lt. Colonel, 3rd Brandenburg Artillery Brigade.
    (Awarded the Pour le Mérite Order in recognition of outstanding leadership and distinction in action during the artillery bombardment of the fortifications at Düppel in April 1864.)
    * * *

* June 7, 1864 *

13. **von Canstein,** Frhr. Philipp Christian Karl Wilhelm August,
    Major General, Commander, 11th Infantry Brigade.
    (Awarded the Pour le Mérite Order in recognition of outstanding leadership and distinguished military planning and operations during the assault and capture of the Danish defensive redoubts VIII and IX at Düppel on April 18, 1864. For the subsequent award of the Oakleaves to the Pour le Mérite Order given this officer see entry 155, this chapter.)
    * * *

* A Posthumous Award of the Pour le Mérite Order *

14. **von Beeren,** Friedrich Wilhelm Heinrich Ernst,
    Major, 4th (Queens) Garde Grenadier Regiment.
    (Special Note: While leading his assault column against the Danish defensive position VI at the fort of Düppel on April 18, 1864, Major von Beeren displayed inspiring leadership and conspicuous bravery. He was killed during the attack but because of his gallantry he was awarded the Pour le Mérite Order. This was most unusual since the Order was not given posthumously. The widow of von Beeren received the Pour le Mérite Order personally from Wilhelm I. in recognition of the outstanding deed her husband performed at the cost of his life.)
    * * *

15. **von Reinhard,** Karl,
    Captain, 3rd Garde Infantry Regiment.
    (Awarded the Pour le Mérite Order in recognition of outstanding leadership and in recognition of his distinction in action during the assault and capture of the Danish position I at Düppel on April 18, 1864.)
    * * *

4th Garde Infantry Regiment

The following two officers were decorated with the Pour le Mérite Order in recognition of outstanding leadership and conspicuous bravery in action during the battle at assault and capture of the Danish defensive position I on April 18, 1864.

16. **von Korth,** Ludwig Wilhelm Martin, Colonel, Commander.
17. **von Conta,** Karl Bernard, Major.

* * *

1st Brandenburg Leib Grenadier Regiment (No. 8)

The following three officers were decorated with the Pour le Mérite Order in recognition of outstanding leadership and conspicuous bravery in action during the assault and capture of the Danish defenses I, VI and IX at Düppel on April 18, 1864.

18. **von Berger,** August Emil Alexander, Colonel, Commander.
19. **Girodz von Gaudi,** Alphons Wilhelm Georg Heinrich, Lt. Colonel.
20. **Bekuhrs,** Georg Wilhelm Ferdinand Gustaf, 2nd Lieutenant.

* * *

21. **von Devivere,** Diederich Franz Ferdinand Maria Johann,
    2nd Lieutenant, 1st Westphalian Infantry Regiment (No. 13).
    (Awarded the Pour le Mérite Order in recognition of outstanding leadership and conspicuous bravery in action during the battle at the Danish defensive position X on April 18, 1864. Lieutenant von Devivere was responsible for the capture of 50 Danish soldiers and a Danish Company Standard.)

* * *

1st Posen Infantry Regiment (No. 18)

22. **von Kettler,** Karl Friedrich, Colonel, Commander.

The following two officers of this regiment were awarded the Pour le Mérite Order in recognition of outstanding leadership and conspicuous bravery in action during the battle at Danish position VIII during the assault and capture of the Danish defenses at Düppel on April 18, 1864. The officers named below captured 4 Danish officers and 170 soldiers during this battle.

23. **von Treskow,** Heinrich Maximilian, Captain.
24. **von Gersdorff,** Wilhelm Adolf Heinrich, 1st Lieutenant.

* * *

25. **von Krohn,** Christian Karl Gerdus Alfred,
    Major, 4th Brandenburg Infantry Regiment (No. 24).
    (Awarded the Pour le Mérite Order in recognition of outstanding leadership and distinction in action during the assault and capture of the Danish defenses at Düppel on April 18, 1864.)

* * *

Brandenburg Fusilier Regiment (No. 35)

The following three officers were decorated with the Pour le Mérite Order in recognition of outstanding leadership and conspicuous bravery in action during the assault and capture of the Danish defenses at Düppel on April 18, 1864.

26. **von Puttkamer,** Frhr. Georg Karl Konstantin, Colonel, Commander.
27. **Fragstein von Niemsdorff,** Johann Karl Eduard, Major.
28. **von Speis,** Eduard Ludwig, Captain.

* * *

5th Westphalian Infantry Regiment (No. 53)

The following four officers received the Pour le Mérite Order in recognition of outstanding leadership and conspicuous bravery in action during the battle at the assault and capture of the Danish defenses at Düppel on April 18, 1864.

29. **von Buddenbrock,** Baron Karl Gustaf Leopold, Colonel, Commander.
    (**Note:** For the subsequent award of the Oakleaves to the Pour le Mérite Order given this officer see entry 193, this chapter.)

30. **von Doering,** Karl Gustaf Alfred Wilhelm, Lt. Colonel.
31. **Kerlen,** Adolf Karl Herman, 2nd Lieutenant.
32. **Loebbecke,** Gustaf Eduard Karl Friedrich, 2nd Lieutenant.

* * *

33. **von Hartmann,** Ernst Matthias Andreas,
    Lt. Colonel, Commander, 7th Brandenburg Infantry Regiment (No. 60).
    (Awarded the Pour le Mérite Order in recognition of outstanding leadership and distinction in action during the assault and capture of the Danish defenses at Düppel on April 18, 1864.
    (**Note:** For the subsequent award of the Oakleaves to the Pour le Mérite Order given this officer see entry 234, this chapter.)

* * *

34. **von Leszczynski,** Stanislaus Paul Eduard,
    Captain, 7th Brandenburg Infantry Regiment (No.60).
    (Awarded the Pour le Mérite Order in recognition of outstanding leadership and in recognition of conspicuous bravery in action during the battle at the assault and capture of the Danish defenses at Düppel on April 18, 1864.
    (**Note:** For the subsequent award of the Oakleaves to the Pour le Mérite Order given this officer see entry 204, this chapter.)

* * *

35. **Rippentrop,** Karl Berthold Siegismund,
    Captain, Commander, Garde (4 pd.) Battery, Garde Artillery Brigade.
    (Awarded the Pour le Mérite Order in recognition of outstanding leadership and distinction in action during the bombardment of the Danish defensive positions IV and V where his battery expended 596 shells at Düppel on April 18, 1864.)

* * *

36. **von Lewinski,** Eduard Julius Ludwig August,
    Captain, Garde Artillery Brigade.
    (Awarded the Pour le Mérite Order in recognition of outstanding leadership and in recognition of conspicuous bravery in action during the battle at the assault and capture of the Danish defenses at Düppel on April 18, 1864.
    (**Note:** For the subsequent award of the Oakleaves to the Pour le Mérite Order given this officer see entry 235, this chapter.)

* * *

37. **Hundt,** Eduard Julius Ernst,
    Captain, Commander, 2nd (6 pd.) Battery, 3rd Brandenburg Artillery Brigade.
    (Awarded the Pour le Mérite Order in recognition of outstanding leadership and in recognition of conspicuous bravery in action during the bombardment of Windmühlenhöhe (Windmill Heights) during the assault and capture of the Danish defenses at Düppel on April 18, 1864.)

* * *

38. **Hübler,** Julius Bruno,
    2nd Lieutenant, 4th Madgeburg Artillery Brigade.
    (Awarded the Pour le Mérite Order in recognition of outstanding leadership and in recognition of conspicuous bravery in action while leading a section of the 4th assault column against the Danish defensive position VI at Düppel on April 18, 1864.)
    * * *

39. **Daun,** Karl Friedrich Wilhelm Leopold,
    Captain, 3rd Brandenburg Engineer (Pioneer) Battalion.
    (Awarded the Pour le Mérite Order in recognition of outstanding leadership and in recognition of conspicuous bravery in action during the assault and capture of the Danish defensive position II at Düppel on April 18, 1864.)
    * * *

40. **Bendemann,** Arnold Gottfried,
    2nd Lieutenant, 7th Westphalian Engineer (Pioneer) Battalion.
    (Awarded the Pour le Mérite Order in recognition of outstanding leadership and in recognition of conspicuous bravery in action when he assumed command of the 4th assault column after the death of Major von Beeren (see entry 14, this chapter) and the serious wounding of the second in command, Captain von Gliszczynski, during the assault on the Danish defensive position VI at Düppel on April 18, 1864.)
    * * *

* June 29, 1864 *

41. **Herwarth von Bittenfeld,** Karl Eberhard,
    General of Infantry, Commanding General, Combined Army Corps.
    (Awarded the Pour le Mérite Order in recognition of outstanding leadership and distinguished military planning and operations during the initial 1864 campaign. The award also recognized his distinction in action during the battle at Düppel on April 18, 1864.)
    * * *

The Night Assault on the Island of Alsen

After the fall of the fortress of Düppel, those Danish troops not captured fled to the island of Alsen and set about building strong defensive positions in anticipation of the arrival of the Prussian forces. As the Prussians converged on the mainland, the Danish felt relatively safe on their island. However, during the night of June 29, 1864, a large force of Prussian troops crossed from the mainland in boats. Under heavy Danish artillery bombardment and rifle fire, the Prussians successfully carried the Danish entrenchments. The capture of the island of Alsen, and the surrender of the Danish forces, brought about the eventual collapse of Danish resistance. The war, for all intents and purposes, was over.

* * *

* July 3, 1864 *

42. **von Goeben,** August Karl Friedrich Christian,

Major General, Commanding Officer, 26th Infantry Brigade.

(Awarded the Pour le Mérite Order in recognition of outstanding leadership and distinguished military planning and operations during the assault and capture of the Danish defenses at Düppel on April 18, 1864, and the capture of the island of Alsen on June 29-30, 1864. For the subsequent award of the Oakleaves to the Pour le Mérite Order given this officer see 157, this chapter.)

* * *

43. **von Roeder,** Julius Heinrich August Edwin,
    Major General, Commanding Officer, 12th Infantry Brigade.
    (Awarded the Pour le Mérite Order in recognition of outstanding leadership and distinguished military planning and operations resulting in the capture of the island of Alsen on June 29-30, 1864.)

* * *

An armistice was concluded between Denmark and Prussia and her ally, Austria, on July 30, 1864. Everything in the duchies remained in a status quo until the Treaty of Vienna was signed on October 30, 1864. Under this treaty, Denmark relinquished all claims to the Duchies of Schleswig, Holstein and Lauenburg. Prussia assumed the administration of Schleswig and Lauenburg, whereas Austria was responsible for administrating the Duchy of Holstein. Although political affairs in Europe appeared on the surface to have returned to normal, this was not the case. The relationship between Wilhelm I. and Emperor Franz Joseph I. never seemed better but many undercurrents of political intrigue began to gnaw at this delicate Austro-Prussian alliance. * * *

* August 14, 1864 *

44. **von der Goltz,** Frhr. Eduard Kuno,
    Lt. Colonel, 2nd Westphalian (Prince Friedrick of the Netherlands) Infantry Regiment (No. 15).
    (Awarded the Pour le Mérite Order in recognition of outstanding leadership and in recognition of conspicuous bravery in action during the 1864 campaigns against Denmark. For the subsequent award of the Oakleaves to the Pour le Mérite Order given this officer see entry 161, this chapter.)
    * * *

4th Brandenburg Infantry Regiment

The following two Prussian officers were decorated with the Pour le Mérite Order in recognition of conspicuous bravery in action during the battle and capture of the island of Alsen on June 29-30, 1864.

45. **von Hacke,** Count Julius Emil Eugen Ludwig, Colonel, Commander.
46. **von Brockhusen,** Friedrich Wilhelm Herman Karl, 2nd Lieutenant.
    * * *

* August 18, 1864 *

47. **von Gondrecourt,** Count Leopold,
    Imperial Austrian Major General, Lord High Steward to Crown Prince Rudolph of Austria.
    (Awarded the Pour le Mérite Order in recognition of outstanding leadership and distinction in action during several engagements while serving in the Austrian advance guard. The award also recognized his distinction in action during the battle at Königsberges.)
    * * *

* January 18, 1865 *

48. **von Berg,** Count Friedrich Wilhelm Rembert,
    Imperial Russian General of Infantry, Adjutant General and Governor of Poland.
    (**Note:** General von Berg was belatedly awarded the Pour le Mérite Order in recognition of outstanding leadership and distinction in action during the battle at Brienne in 1814, **51** years earlier.
    Special Note: He also was awarded the 50 Year Jubilee Golden Crown to the Pour le Mérite Order on this date.)
    * * *

Over a period of time, Austria came to be considered the strongest and most important of the German states. Prussia, under the firm guidance of Bismarck, coveted this position for Prussia and planned to undermine Austrian influence and preeminence. Prussia wanted to become the undisputed leader of the German Confederation. At this point, Wilhelm I. felt that Prussia was strong enough, especially after the military successes over Denmark, to challange Austria and Emperor Franz Joseph. To do this, Prussia set about staging a confrontation with Austria. Over the next year the tensions intensified between the two rulers. The minor German states began to align themselves with either Prussia or Austria in what appeared to be preparations for war.

The political maneuverings continued to increase into early summer of 1866. In the meantime, Bismarck had made an alliance with Italy, which had proclaimed itself a kingdom in 1861, and had its eyes on annexing the Austrian province of Venetia. Chancellor Bismarck had also "bought off" Napoleon III. with his

promises of parts of Austrian territories to be given to France. Prussia was about to force political issue with Austria when Vienna issued the first mobilization order in the latter part of March 1866. This Austrian action caused an electrifying reaction to pass through Prussia, Wilhelm I. and Bismarck. However, due to the general inefficiency of the call-up procedures, it took the Austrian army almost eight weeks to mobilize. Wilhelm I. was convinced that Austria was preparing to invade Prussia. On June 2, 1866, before Austria could even complete her mobilization, Wilhelm issued a royal memorandum that gave General Hellmuth **von Moltke,** (see photo on left and Chapter V-2, entry 2454) his Chief of Staff, supreme powers with the General Staff. This caused the king's Adjutant General, Lt. General Leopold von Boyen, to ask, "The King in command at the age of seventy, with a decrepit Moltke at his side!... What will come out of it all?"

Wilhelm I. reacted to the Austrian mobilization by calling into active service the Prussian military forces on May 12, 1866. On May 14, 1866, Moltke reported to the king that he could begin an invasion by June 5, 1866, with a total of 270,000 troops. The king rejected such vigorous action. However, by May 12, 1866, all the German states, Austria as well as Italy, were on military alert.

* * *

* The 1866 Austro-Prussian War *

On June 14, 1866, the Federal Diet at Frankfurt a/Main, on a motion by Austria, voted for the mobilization of all Confederation troops except those of Prussia. Prussia demanded that Saxony, Hanover and Hesse-Kassel reject the Diet's decision, but those states refused. Before Wilhelm could deal with Austria, he had to secure Prussia's rear against Hanover and Hesse-Kassel, which cut off Prussia from Westphalia and Rhinish Prussia. Therefore, as a protective move, on June 16, 1866, Prussian forces invaded Hanover and Hesse-Kassel. Austria declared war on Prussia the same day. The Kingdom of Italy, allied with Prussia, declared war on Austria on June 20, 1866. The Prussian campaigns were conducted on two fronts: the western campaign against Hanover and Hesse-Kassel, and the southern campaign directed against Austria, Bavaria, Saxony and their allies. On the western front, the most signifigant action took place in Hanover at Langensalza on June 27, 1866. An advance Prussian force, commanded by General Friedrich **Vogel von Falckenstein** (see entry 7, this chapter), engaged a Hanoverian army, generaled by Crown Prince George, the Prince Regent and son of the blind George V., King of Hanover. The action took place near Erfurt when the Prussians attacked the Hanoverians. After a seven-hour engagement, the Prussians were repulsed. General von Falckenstein brought up reinforcements of 50,000 troops and the Hanoverians, exhausted from the battle and greatly outnumbered, surrendered on June 29, 1866. King George V. abdicated the Hanoverian throne, and with his son, the prince regent, fled his kingdom. The Hanoverian army was incorporated into the Prussian forces and the Hanoverians were utilized as an occupation army along the Main River.

* * *

Returning to June 16th, the Prussian Army of the Elbe entered Saxony and occupied Dresden on June 18, 1866. The following day, the Prussian forces were placed under the command of Prince Friedrich Karl.

The first major engagement of the war took place at Podol on June 26, 1866. The 8th Division, under Prince Friedrich Karl, crossed the Isar River around 8 pm and drove the Austrians out of their positions. The Austrian forces were led by General Count Eduard von Calm-Gallas. At 9:30 pm, a brigade from the Austrian 1st Corps pushed the Prussians back across the river, and by 11 pm, the Prussians had withdrawn. However, at this time General Friedrich **von Bose** (see photo at left and entry 124, this chapter), with two fresh battalions, renewed the battle and carried the main bridge and finally drove the Austrians from the town.

* * *

On June 27, 1866, around 10 am a major battle developed at Wysokow. The Prussian advance guard of the Prussian V. Corps, under the command of General Karl Friedrich **von Steinmetz** (see photo below left and Chapter VI, entry 15),

advanced against the Austrian forces, commanded by General von Ramming. By 1 pm, after a fierce Prussian Uhlan charge, the Austrian center broke and evacuated its positions. The Prussians occupied the town of Wysokow and the Austrian VI. Corps withdrew to the town of Skalitz. On the same day, the 27th of June, the Prussian I. Corps, commanded by General Eduard **von Bonin** (see entry 7, this chapter), confronted the Austrian X. Corps, led by Field Marshal **von der Gablenz** (see entry 3, this chapter). At Trautenau, the Prussians took the initiative and attacked the Austrian defense line. The Austrians counterattacked in force and successfully pushed back the Prussians.

On June 26, 1866, the bloody battle at Skalitz took place. General von Steinmetz's Prussian V. Corps clashed with the Austrian VI. and VIII. Corps under the faulty leadership of General von Ramming. It was a long hard fought engagement, but the Prussians finally captured the town of Skalitz and forced the Austrians to retreat. The Prussian victory could almost be considered the precursor up to the final decisive battle of the 1866 war.

* * *

There has been so much written in detail covering the bloody battle of Königgrätz or Sadowa, as the Austrians called it, that it seems unnecessary to dwell on it. We will only touch on the key points.

The action began early in the morning of July 3, 1866, when the Prussian 7th Division, commanded by General Eduard **von Fransecky** (see entry 119, this chapter), attacked the Austrian positions but made little impression on the Austrian line. The Prussians, outnumbered, were forced back along an seven mile front. The battle seemed to have become a bloody deadlock. Because of a broken telegraph line delaying his orders to march, Crown Prince Friedrich Wilhelm finally arrived on the field around 2 pm.

King Wilhelm I. Leading the Prussians at Königgrätz

The Crown Prince immediately launched a fierce attack on the Austrian right flank and succeeded in breaking through, capturing the hill at Chlum, which was the important key to the Austrian defense system. With the loss of the vital hill to the Prussians, Austrian Field Marshal Benedek ordered a counterattack with his cavalry, but they were unable to drive the Prussians back. Under a very heavy Prussian artillery bombardment, the Austrians, totally defeated, finally retreated and the terrible battle ended at 4:30 in the afternoon.

Needless to say, Austria was effectively out of the war. Several other minor engagements followed the Austrian disaster at Königgrätz, but all were anticlimatic.

* * *

* June 29, 1866 *

49. **Friedrich Wilhelm, Crown Prince of Prussia,** (Friedrich Wilhelm) Nikolaus, General of Infantry, Commander-in-Chief, Prussian II. Army.
    (Special Note: Wilhelm I. awarded his son, the Crown Prince, the Pour le Mérite Order on June 29, 1866. The king sent him a telegram which was intercepted by the Austrians and never delivered to Friedrich Wilhelm. When the king met his son on the battlefield of Königgrätz and saw that he had not received the Order, he took his own Pour le Mérite Order, which he was wearing, and bestowed it on the Crown Prince. For the subsequent award of the Oakleaves to the Pour le Mérite Order given Friedrich Wilhelm see entry 55, this chapter.)

* * *

Wilhelm I. Bestowing the Pour le Mérite Order
to Crown Prince Friedrich Wilhelm on the Battlefield of Königgrätz

During the evening in the victorious Prussian camp, the army commanders joined Wilhelm I. and exchanged remarks appropriate to the occasion. After the toasts were drunk, Wilhelm mounted his favorite horse and rode toward Sadowa. After spending almost 13 hours in the saddle, he dismounted at the edge of the battlefield and looked at the carnage. One of his officers heard him say, "One feels that one's youthful years are over." Remounted, he then visited a field hospital, tended by the Knights of St. John, and sought to comfort the wounded soldiers. Later that evening, at the urging of his nephew, Prince Friedrich Karl, Wilhelm went by carriage to the town of Horwitz. There at the headquarters of his nephew, Prince Friedrich Karl, the king had a cup of hot tea and a frugal supper. Wilhelm then dictated a telegram to his wife:

> *"Complete victory over the Austrian Army won today in eight hour battle fought near the fortress of Königgrätz between Elbe and Bistritz. Losses of enemy and trophies not yet counted, but significant, including 20 cannon.... I praise God for his mercy; we are all well.*
>
> *Wilhelm*
>
> *(For Publication: the Governor is to fire a victory salute!)."*

The king then retired on a bed improvised from a sofa, two chairs and a table, and slept soundly through the night.

* * *

As the result of the apocalyptic defeat at Königgrätz, which is ranked as one of the decisive battles of history, Emperor Franz Joseph I. lost most of his military resources and sought an armistice with Wilhelm I. The preliminary peace treaty was signed at Nikolsburg, ending all hostilities on July 27, 1866. The final peace treaty was negotiated and signed at Prague on August 30, 1866. Under the terms of this treaty, Austria was not required to give up any territory, other than relinquishing the Duchy of Holstein to Prussia. However, Austria was to pay an indemnity and be excluded from all German affairs north of the Main River. Following this victory, Prussia annexed Hanover, Hesse-Kassel, Nassau and the no-longer Free City of Frankfurt a/Main, on December 15, 1866.

* * *

* July 28, 1866 *

50. **Karl, Prince of Prussia,** Friedrich (Karl) Alexander,
    General of Ordnance, Chief of Artillery.
    (Awarded the Pour le Mérite Order in recognition of outstanding leadership and distinguished military planning and operations during the 1866 campaigns.)

* * *

51. **von Mutius,** Franz Wilhelm Ludwig,
    General of Cavalry, Commanding General, Prussian VI. Army Corps.
    (Awarded the Pour le Mérite Order in recognition of outstanding leadership and distinguished military planning and operations during the 1866 campaign.)

* * *

* July 31, 1866 *

52. **Albrecht, Prince of Prussia,** Friedrich Heinrich (Albrecht),
    General of Cavalry, Commanding General, Cavalry Corps of the Prussian I. Army.

(Awarded the Pour le Mérite Order in recognition of outstanding leadership and distinguished military planning and operations during the 1866 campaigns. For the subsequent award of the Oakleaves to the Pour le Mérite Order given this officer see 187, this chapter.)

* * *

Prince Adalbert of Prussia

53. **Adalbert, Prince of Prussia,** Heinrich Wilhelm (Adalbert),
    Admiral, Commander-in-Chief, Prussian Navy.
    (Awarded the Pour le Mérite Order in recognition of distinguished naval planning and operations during the 1866 campaign.
    Note: The Pour le Mérite Order was given to Prince Adalbert personally by his brother, Wilhelm I.)

* * *

54. **Anton, Prince of Hohenzollern-Sigmaringen,** (Anton) Egon Karl Josef,
    2nd Lieutenant, à la suite of the 1st Garde Infantry Regiment.
    (Awarded the Pour le Mérite Order in recognition of outstanding leadership and distinction in action at Ober-Chlum by Königgrätz on July 3, 1866. In this battle Prince Anton was killed in action. See entry 102 and the text, this chapter.)

* * *

* August 3, 1866 *

55. **Friedrich Wilhelm, Crown Prince of Prussia,** (Friedrich Wilhelm) Nikolaus,
    General of Infantry, Commander-in-Chief, Prussian II. Army.
    (Awarded the Oakleaves to the Pour le Mérite Order in recognition

of outstanding leadership and distinguished military planning and operations during the battle at Königgrätz on July 3, 1866. For the initial award of the Pour le Mérite Order to the Crown Prince see entry 49, this chapter. For the award of the Grand Cross and Star to the Pour le Mérite Order see entry 100, this chapter.)

* * *

Crown Prince Friedrich Wilhelm of Prussia

56. **August, Prince of Württemberg,** Friedrich (August) Eberhard,
General of Cavalry, Commanding General, Garde du Corps.
(Awarded the Pour le Mérite Order in recognition of outstanding leadership and distinguished military planning and operations during the 1866 campaign. The award also recognized his distinction in action during the battle at Trautenau on June 28, 1866, and at the battle at Königgrätz on July 3, 1866. For the subsequent award of the Oakleaves to the Pour le Mérite Order given to Prince August see entry 247, this chapter.)

* * *

* August 4, 1866 *

57. **Wilhelm I., King of Prussia,** Friedrich (Wilhelm) Ludwig,
Field Marshal, Commander-in-Chief, Prussian Military Forces.
(Awarded the Oakleaves to the Pour le Mérite Order in recognition of outstanding leadership and distinguished military planning and operations at the victory over the Austrians at the battle of Königgrätz on July 3, 1866.
Note: It is of interest that the badge of the Pour le Mérite Order to which the king attached his golden oakleaves was originally the Pour

le Mérite Order which had belonged to his father, Friedrich Wilhelm III. For the initial award of the Pour le Mérite Order to Wilhelm I. see Chapter VI. entry 24. For the award of the Grand Cross and Star of the Pour le Mérite Order see entry 168, this chapter.)

* * *

Wilhelm I., King of Prussia

* August 7, 1866 *

58. **von Manteuffel, Frhr. Karl Rochus Edwin,**
    Lt. General, Adjutant General, Commander-in-Chief, Army of the Main.
    (Awarded the Pour le Mérite Order in recognition of outstanding leadership and distinguished military planning and operations support during the 1866 campaigns. For the subsequent award of the Oakleaves to the Pour le Mérite Order given this officer see entry 183, this chapter.)
    * * *

* August 9, 1866 *

59. **Friedrich Franz, Grand Duke of Mecklenburg-Schwerin,** Alexander,
    General of Infantry, Commanding General, Prussian II. Reserve Army Corps.
    (Awarded the Pour le Mérite Order in recognition of outstanding leadership and distinguished military planning and operations support during the 1866 campaign. For the subsequent award of the Oakleaves to the Pour le Mérite Order given this officer see entry 178, this chapter.)
    * * *

* September 11, 1866 *

60. **von Voigts-Rhetz,** Konstans Bernhard,
    Lt. General, Chief of Staff, High Command, Prussian I. Army.
    (Awarded the Pour le Mérite Order in recognition of outstanding leadership and distinguished military planning and operations of the I. Army during the 1866 campaign. The award also recognized his distinction in action during the battle at Königgrätz on July 3, 1866. For the subsequent award of the Oakleaves to the Pour le Mérite Order given this officer see entry 184, this chapter.)
    * * *

* September 12, 1866 *

61. **von Pogrell,** Philipp Hugo,
    Rittmeister, 2nd Silesian Dragoon Regiment (No. 8).
    (Awarded the Pour le Mérite Order in recognition of outstanding leadership and distinction in action during the battle at Nachod.)
    * * *

* September 16, 1866 *

62. **von Sperling,** Ernst Karl Oskar,
    Colonel, Chief of the General Staff, Prussian VI. Army Corps.
    (Awarded the Pour le Mérite Order in recognition of outstanding leadership and distinction in action during the battle at Königgrätz on July 3, 1866. For the subsequent award of the Oakleaves to the Pour le Mérite Order given this officer see entry 208, this chapter.)
    * * *

63. **von Zastrow,** Adolf Friedrich Heinrich Karl Alexander,
Lt. General, Commander, 11th Infantry Division.
(Awarded the Pour le Mérite Order in recognition of outstanding leadership and distinguished military planning and operations during the 1866 campaign. The award also recognized his distinction in action during the battle at Königgrätz on July 3, 1866. For the subsequent award of the Oakleaves to the Pour le Mérite Order given this officer see entry 206, this chapter.)

* * *

64. **von Hanenfeldt,** Karl Konrad Louis,
Major General, Commander, 21st Infantry Brigade.
(Awarded the Pour le Mérite Order in recognition of outstanding leadership and distinguished military planning and operations during the 1866 campaign and especially during the battle at Königgrätz on July 3, 1866, where the brigade of General von Hanenfeldt captured 25 enemy cannon and 2,000 Austrian soldiers.)

* * *

65. **von Hoffmann,** Otto Gustaf Willy Leopold Karl,
Major General, Commander, 22nd Infantry Brigade.
(Awarded the Pour le Mérite Order in recognition of outstanding leadership and distinguished military planning and operations during the battle at Königgrätz on July 3, 1866, when General von Hoffman's brigade captured 14 enemy cannon and took over 2,000 Austrian soldiers.)

* * *

66. **Baumeister,** Paul Hugo Ferdinand,
Major, 1st Silesian Grenadier Regiment (No 10).
(Awarded the Pour le Mérite Order in recognition of outstanding leadership and distinction in action on July 3, 1866. During the assault on Sweti and Briza, Major Baumeister led his battalion in the attack against the Austrian positions, breaking through the enemy lines, his battalion captured 14 enemy cannon.)

* * *

67. **von Berken,** Theodor Kasimir Rudolf,
Major, 3rd Nieder-Silesian Infantry Regiment (No. 50).
(Awarded the Pour le Mérite Order in recognition of outstanding leadership and distinction in action while leading his battalion in the assault and capture of Nedelist. After sustaining many casualties from heavy enemy artillery fire, Major von Berken re-grouped his battalion and led then in the assault against Austrian positions at Briza, breaking through the enemy line, his battalion captured two enemy cannon.)

* * *

2nd Silesian Dragoon Regiment (No. 8)

The following two officers were decorated with the Pour le Mérite Order in recognition of conspicuous bravery in action during the battle at Nachod on June 27, 1866.

68. **von Wichmann,** Karl Otto Herman, Lt. Colonel, Commander.
69. **von Paczensky-Tenczyn,** Anton Max Konrad, Major.

* * *

70. **von Barby,** Adalbert Roderich Levin,
Colonel, Silesian (Prinz Friedrich von Preussen) Curassier Regiment (No. 1).

(Awarded the Pour le Mérite Order in recognition of outstanding leadership and distinction in action when he led his 1st squadron during the assault and capture of Biskupitz on July 14, 1866.)

* * *

* September 17, 1866 *

71. **von Blumenthal,** Karl Konstantin Albrecht Leonhard,
    Major General, Chief of Staff, High Command Headquarters, Prussian II. Army.
    (Awarded the Oakleaves to the Pour le Mérite Order in recognition of outstanding leadership and distinguished military planning and operations during the 1866 campaigns. For the initial award of the Pour le Mérite Order to this officer see entry 9, this chapter.)

* * *

72. **von Stülpnagel,** Louis Ferdinand Wolf Anton,
    Major General, Senior Quartermaster, serving at the time on the Staff of the Prussian I. Army.
    (Awarded the Pour le Mérite Order in recognition of outstanding leadership and distinguished military planning and operations during the 1866 campaign. For the subsequent award of the Oakleaves to the Pour le Mérite Order given this officer see entry 94, this chapter.)

* * *

73. **von Unger,** Karl Friedrich Ernst,
    Major, General Staff Officer, High Command Headquarters, Prussian I. Army.
    (Awarded the Pour le Mérite Order in recognition of outstanding leadership and distinguished military planning and operations during the 1866 campaign. The award also recognized his distinction in action during the battle at Königgrätz on July 3, 1866.)

* * *

74. **von Stosch,** Albrecht,
    Major General, Senior Quartermaster, serving at the time on the Staff of the Prussian II. Army.
    (Awarded the Pour le Mérite Order in recognition of outstanding leadership and distinguished military planning and operations in support of the Prussian II. Army during the 1866 campaign.)

* * *

75. **von der Burg,** Ernst Engelbert Oskar Viktor,
    Major, General Staff Officer, High Command Headquarters, Prussian II. Army.
    (Awarded the Pour le Mérite Order in recognition of outstanding leadership and in recognition of conspicuous bravery in action during the battle at Trautenau on June 28, 1866, and during the battle at Königgrätz on July 3, 1866. For the subsequent award of the Oakleaves to the Pour le Mérite Order given this officer see entry 218, this chapter.)

* * *

76. **von Wnuck,** Karl Heinrich,
    Major General, serving at the time at High Command Headquarters, Prussian II. Army.
    (Awarded the Pour le Mérite Order in recognition of outstanding leadership and in recognition of conspicuous bravery in action during the engagements against the Austrians on June 27, 28 and 29, 1866. Gen-

eral K. von Wnuck commanded a combined dragoon brigade at these engagements.)
* * *

77. **von Dannenberg**, Ferdinand Franz Wilhelm,
Colonel, Chief of the General Staff, Garde du Corps.
(Awarded the Pour le Mérite Order in recognition of outstanding leadership and in recognition of conspicuous bravery in action during the battle at Königgrätz on July 3, 1866.)
* * *

78. **von Obernitz**, Hugo Moritz Anton,
Colonel à la suite of the Garde Fusilier Regiment, serving at the time as commander of the 1st Garde Infantry Regiment.

(Awarded the Pour le Mérite Order in recognition of outstanding leadership and distinguished military planning and operations during the 1866 campaign. The award also recognized his distinction in action during the battle at Chlum in the vicinity of Königgrätz.)
* * *

79. **von Alvensleben**, Konstantin Reimar,
Major General, Commander, 2nd Garde Infantry Regiment.
(Awarded the Pour le Mérite Order in recognition of outstanding leadership and distinguished military planning and operations during the 1866 campaign. The award also recognized his distinction in action during the battle at Königgrätz on July 3, 1866. For the subsequent award of the Oakleaves to the Pour le Mérite Order given this officer see entry 185, this chapter.)
* * *

80. **von Kessel**, Bernhard Alexander Heinrich,
Colonel, Commander, 1st Garde Infantry Regiment.
(Awarded the Pour le Mérite Order in recognition of outstanding leadership. The award also recognized his distinction in action during several engagements of the Prussian advance guard, especially at Soor on June 28, 1866, Königinhof on June 29, 1866, and during the battle at Königgrätz on July 3, 1866.)
* * *

1st Garde Infantry Regiment

The following two officers were awarded the Pour le Mérite Order in recognition of outstanding leadership and in recognition of conspicuous bravery in action during the nearly two hour defense of the village of Ober-Chlum. Major von Kleist was responsible for the capture of one enemy cannon.

81. **von Kleist**, Christian Ewald Leopold, Major.
82. **von Schlieffen**, Count Eugen Leo Oskar, Captain.
* * *

2nd Garde Infantry Regiment

The following two officers were decorated with the Pour le Mérite Order in recognition of distinction in action during the battles at Soor on June 28, 1866, Königinhof on June 29, 1866, and during the defense of Rosberitz on July 3, 1866.

83. **von Pape,** August Wilhelm Alexander, Colonel, Commander.

(**Note:** For the subsequent award of the Oak-leaves to the Pour le Mérite Order given this officer see entry 255, this chapter.)

84. **von Erckert,** Friedrich Wilhelm Viktor, Major.
* * *

85. **von Böhn,** Philipp Oktavio,
    Major, Kaiser Franz Garde Grenadier Regiment (No. 2).
    (Awarded the Pour le Mérite Order in recognition of outstanding leadership and distinction in action while leading his battalion in an assault against Austrian defensive positions at Alt-Rognitz on June 28, 1866.)
* * *

Garde Fusilier Regiment

The following two officers were decorated with the Pour le Mérite Order in recognition of conspicuous bravery in action during the battle at Soor on June 28, 1866, and during the battle at Königgrätz on July 3, 1866.

86. **von Werder,** Bernhard Franz Wilhelm, Colonel, Commander.
87. **von Schlichting,** Ulrich Ernst Karl, Captain.
* * *

3rd Garde Infantry Regiment

The following four officers were decorated with the Pour le Mérite Order in recognition of conspicuous bravery in action as indicated with each name.

88. **Knappe von Knappstaedt,** Julius Adalbert Ulrich, Colonel, Commander.
    (During the assault at Chlum.)

89. **von Arnim,** Richard Felix, Captain.
    (Responsible for the capture of five enemy cannon.)

90. **von Lobenthal,** Karl Friedrich, Captain.
    (While leading his company during the successful assault against the Austrian defensive positions at Chlum and the capture of 9 enemy cannon.)

91. **von Löwenfeld,** Julius Josef Adalbert, 1st Lieutenant.
    (Responsible for taking 120 enemy soldiers prisoners and capturing four enemy cannon during the battle at Königgrätz on July 3, 1866.)
* * *

92. **von Witzendorff,** Karl Friedrich Wilhelm,
Colonel à la suite of the 1st Garde Dragoon Regiment, serving at the time as Chief of the General Staff, Cavalry Corps, Prussian I. Army.
(Awarded the Pour le Mérite Order in recognition of outstanding leadership and distinguished military planning and operations of the Cavalry Corps of the Prussian I. Army. The award also recognized his distinction in action during the battle at Missude during the 1864 Schleswig-Holstein War, and during the battle at Königgrätz on July 3, 1866. For the subsequent award of the Oakleaves to the Pour le Mérite Order given this officer see entry 217, this chapter.)
* * *

93. **Wilhelm, Duke of Mecklenburg-Schwerin,** Friedrich (Wilhelm) Nikolaus,
Major General, Commander, 2nd Light Cavalry Brigade, Cavalry Corps, Prussian I. Army.
(Awarded the Pour le Mérite Order in recognition of outstanding leadership and distinguished military planning and operations during the 1866 campaign. The award also recognized his distinction in action during the battle at Königgrätz on July 3, 1866.)
* * *

94. **von der Groeben,** Count Georg Reinhold,
Major General, Commander, 3rd Light Cavalry Brigade, Prussian I. Army.
(Awarded the Pour le Mérite Order in recognition of outstanding leadership and distinguished military planning and operations during the 1866 campaign. The award also recognized his distinction in action during the battle at Königgrätz on July 3, 1866.)
* * *

* September 18, 1866 *

95. **von Podbielski,** Theophil Eugen Anton,
Major General, Director, Prussian War Department.
(Awarded the Pour le Mérite Order in recognition of outstanding leadership and distinguished military planning and operations while serving as General Quartermaster during the 1864 Schleswig-Holstein War. For the subsequent award of the Oakleaves to the Pour le Mérite Order given this officer see entry 239, this chapter.)
* * *

96. **von Medem,** Frhr. Friedrich Alexander Heinrich,
Colonel, Commander, 1st Madgeburg Infantry Regiment.
(Awarded the Pour le Mérite Order in recognition of outstanding leadership and distinction in action during the battles at Muskyberge and Münchengrätz on June 28, 1866, and during the battle at Königgrätz on July 3, 1866.)
* * *

97. **von Quadt und Hüchtenbruck,** Frhr. Ludwig Eduard Ernst,
Captain, 2nd Rhine Infantry Regiment (No. 28).
(Awarded the Pour le Mérite Order in recognition of outstanding leadership and in recognition of conspicuous bravery in action during the battle at Stöffer on July 3, 1866, where he led his company and successfully captured 260 enemy soldiers, including 4 officers, and one enemy cannon.)
* * *

* September 19, 1866 *

98. **Albrecht, Prince of Prussia,** Friedrich Wilhelm Nikolaus (Albrecht),
    Major General, Commander, 1st Garde Cavalry Brigade.
    (Awarded the Pour le Mérite Order in recognition of outstanding leadership and distinguished military planning and operations during the 1866 campaign. For the subsequent award of the Oakleaves to the Pour le Mérite Order given this officer see entry 240, this chapter.)

    * * *

99. **von Stiehle,** Gustaf Wilhelm Friedrich,
    Colonel, unidentified unit, serving at the time as Wing Adjutant.
    (Awarded the Pour le Mérite Order in recognition of outstanding leadership and distinction in action during the assault and battle at Problus on July 3, 1866. For the subsequent award of the Oakleaves to the Pour le Mérite Order given this officer see entry 192, this chapter.)

    * * *

Notes:

* The Grand Cross and Star of the Pour le Mérite Order *

* September 20, 1866 *

Established by King Wilhelm I. on this date as a special class of the Pour le Mérite Order. This class consisted of a badge, worn suspended from the neck by the Pour le Mérite Order silver edged black statutary ribbon, and a rhomboid shaped star worn attached to the left side of the tunic. This special class was called:

The Grand Cross and Star of the Pour le Mérite Order

This class of the Pour le Mérite Order was awarded only to **five** recipients (see text).

The gold badge was somewhat larger than the normal sized Pour le Mérite Order having the usual cypher, crown and inscription on a blue enameled Maltese cross with gold edges. The badge had an obverse center medallion showing the profile of Friedrich the Great, in relief, facing the viewers left. The reverse of the badge was enameled blue with gold edges. The suspension was wedge shaped between the upper points of the cross. Between each arm was a golden crowned and displayed eagle.

* * *

The golden (silver gilt) star was rayed and rhomboid in shape and had a large medallion showing the same raised profile of Friedrich the Great as on the badge. The center medallion was bordered by a blue enameled band with gold edges and showing in gold letters: "POUR LE MÉRITE." At the bottom within the blue enameled border are green enameled laurel leaves outlined in gold and tied with a golden bow. The reverse had a long vertical pin and clasp for attachment.

* * *

Note: The above illustrations are from the **Handbuch der Ritter- und VerdienstOrden**, by Maximilian Gritzner.

Obverse and reverse of the badge. The badge measured approximately 70mm. Compare the eagles and the portrait medallion of Friedrich the Great to the badges at bottom of following page.

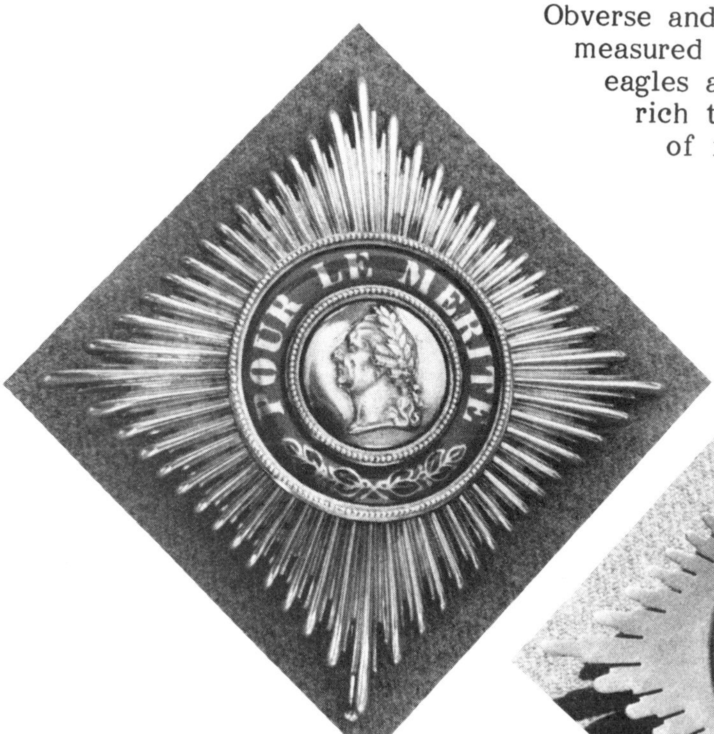

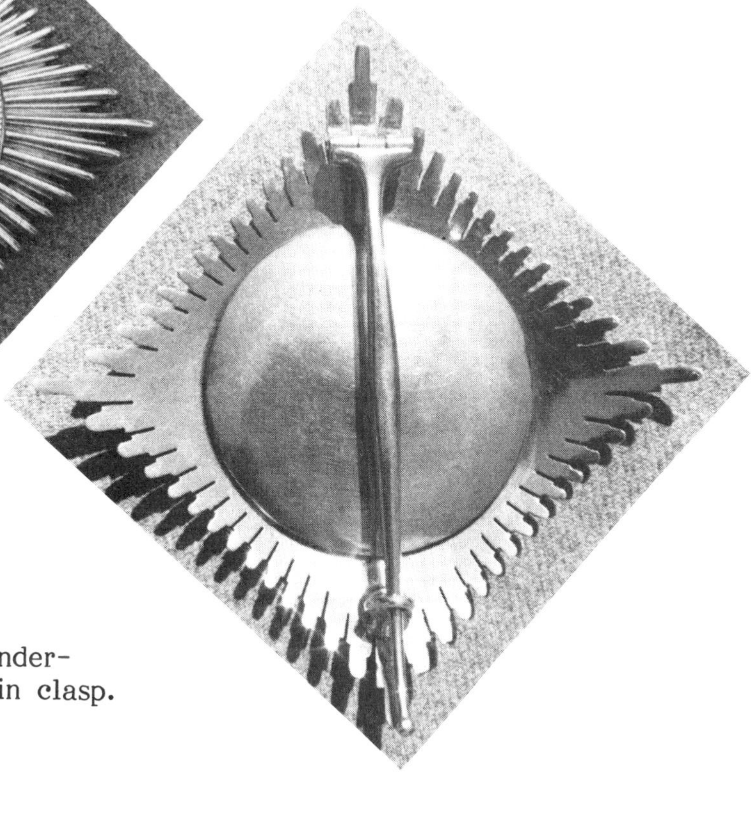

The Star measured between approximately 86 to 93mm across. This Star is marked with an "H" on the underside of the pin and below the pin clasp.

Early museum example (copy)

Current copies of the Grand Cross of the Pour le Mérite Order. Note the differences of the eagles and the portrait medallion of Friedrich the Great.

Note the plain reverse on the current replication

* First Awards of the Grand Cross and Star *
* to the Pour le Mérite Order *

* September 20, 1866 *

100. **Friedrich Wilhelm, Crown Prince of Prussia,** (Friedrich Wilhelm) Nikolaus,
General of Infantry, Commander-in-Chief, Prussian II. Army.
(Awarded the Grand Cross and Star of the Pour le Mérite Order by his father, Wilhelm I., in special recognition of outstanding leadership and distinguished military planning and successful operations during the 1866 Austro-Prussian War. The award also recognized his distinction in action during the battle at Königgrätz on July 3, 1866. For the award of the Oakleaves to the Grand Cross and Star of the Pour le Mérite Order to the Crown Prince, see entry 276, this chapter.)
* * *

101. **Friedrich Karl, Prince of Prussia,** (Friedrich Karl) Nikolaus,
General of Cavalry, Commander-in-Chief, Prussian I. Army.
(Awarded the Grand Cross and Star of the Pour le Mérite Order by his uncle, Wilhelm I., in special recognition of outstanding leadership and distinguished military planning and successful operations during the 1866 Austro-Prussian War. The award also recognized his distinction in action during the battle at Königgrätz on July 3, 1866. For the award of the Oakleaves to the Grand Cross and Star of the Pour le Mérite Order to Prince Friedrich Karl, see entry 277, this chapter.)
* * *

* Second Posthumous Award of the Pour le Mérite Order *

On September 20, 1866, Wilhelm I. personally wrote a letter to Prince Karl Anton, father of Prince Anton who was killed in action on July 3, 1866, awarding to his son the Pour le Mérite Order in recognition of conspicuous bravery in action. The young prince, a 2nd Lieutenant, was serving in the 1st Garde Infantry Regiment, and was killed during the battle at Ober-Chlum (see entry 54, this chapter). The king offered to Prince Karl Anton his sincere sympathy as the head of the House of Hohenzollern for the father's loss of an only son. Wilhelm felt this deeply as he was a father also with an only son.

102. **Karl Anton, Prince to the Hohenzollern-Sigmaringen House,** (Karl Anton) Friedrich Meinrad Joachim Zephyrin,

General of Infantry, Military Governor of the Provinces of the Rhine and Westphalia.

(Prince Karl Anton was allowed to wear his son's Pour le Mérite Order. The actual Pour le Mérite Order is presently on display at the Hohenzollern Castle in Hechingen, West Germany.)
* * *

103. **von Pape,** JohannMeinrad August Wilhelm Adolf,
Major General, Commander, 1st Infantry Brigade.
(Awarded the Pour le Mérite Order in recognition of outstanding leadership and distinguished military planning and operations during the 1866 campaign. The award also recognized his distinction in action during the battle at Trautenau on June 27, 1866, and at Chlum and the capture of Rosberitz on July 3, 1866.)

* * *

104. **von Barnekow,** Christof Gottlieb Albert,
Major General, Commander, 2nd Infantry Brigade.
(Awarded the Pour le Mérite Order in recognition of outstanding leadership and distinguished military planning and operations during the 1866 campaign. For the subsequent award of the Oakleaves to the Pour le Mérite Order given this officer see entry 203, this chapter.)

* * *

105. **von der Mülbe,** Otto Wilhelm Adolf,
Captain, 4th East Prussian Grenadier Regiment (No. 5).
(Awarded the Pour le Mérite Order in recognition of outstanding leadership and distinction in action during the battle at Trautenau on June 27, 1866.)

* * *

Konstantin von Alvensleben - Wilhelm von Tümpling - Hugo Ewald von Kirchbach
Julius von Bose - Gustaf von Alvensleben - Eduard von Fransecky

106. **Hagen**, Ernst Heinrich,
   Rittmeister, Littau (Prinz Albrecht von Preussen) Dragoon Regiment.
   (Awarded the Pour le Mérite Order in recognition of outstanding leadership and conspicuous bravery in action during the battles at Trautenau on June 27, 1866, and at Königgrätz on July 3, 1866.)
   * * *

107. **von Kameke**, Arnold Karl Georg,

Major General, Chief of the General Staff, Prussian II. Army Corps.

(Awarded the Pour le Mérite Order in recognition of outstanding leadership and distinguished military planning and operations during the 1866 campaign. For the subsequent award of the Oakleaves to the Pour le Mérite Order given this officer see entry 188, this chapter.)
* * *

108. **von Werder**, Karl Friedrich Wilhelm Leopold August,

Lt. General, Commanding Officer, 3rd Infantry Division.

(Awarded the Pour le Mérite Order in recognition of outstanding leadership and distinguished military planning and operations during the battle at Gitschin and during the battle at Königgrätz on July 3, 1866, where he commanded the right flank at Bistritz and the successful capture of the towns of Dohalitzka and Mokrowous. For the subsequent award of the Oakleaves to the Pour le Mérite Order given this officer see entry 191, this chapter.)
* * *

109. **von Keyserlingk**, Frhr. Ewald Karl Theodor,
   Captain, 1st Pomeranian (König Friedrich Wilhelm IV.) Grenadier Regiment, (No. 2).
   (Awarded the Pour le Mérite Order in recognition of outstanding leadership and conspicuous bravery in action when, seeing the battalion commander severely wounded, he took command of the battalion, rallying the troops by taking the standard and leading the troops forward

110. **von Tümpling,** Ludwig Karl Kurt Friedrich Wilhelm Georg,
Lt. General, Commanding Officer, 5th Infantry Division.
(Awarded the Pour le Mérite Order in recognition of outstanding leadership and distinguished military planning and operations during the 1866 campaign. The award also recognized his distinction in action during a battle against the Austrians when severely wounded he refused to leave the battlefield and continued to command his division until, falling unconscious, he was carried from the field.)
* * *

111. **von Schimmelmann,** Gustaf Karl Bernhard Thilo,
Major General, Commander, 9th Infantry Brigade.
(Awarded the Pour le Mérite Order in recognition of outstanding leadership and distinguished military planning and operations by directing assaults against several enemy fortified towns and forcing the Austrians to withdraw.)
* * *

112. **von Kamiensky,** Friedrich Wilhelm,
Major General, Commander, 10th Infantry Brigade.
(Awarded the Pour le Mérite Order in recognition of outstanding leadership and distinguished military planning and operations during an attack and taking over command of the 5th Infantry Division as well as commanding the 10th Infantry Brigade, after Lt. General von Tümpling was carried from the battlefield.)
* * *

113. **von Manstein,** Gustaf Albert,

Lt. General, Commander, 6th Infantry Division.

(Awarded the Oakleaves to the Pour le Mérite Order in recognition of outstanding leadership and distinguished military planning and operations during the 1866 campaigns while commanding the 6th Infantry Division. For the initial award of the Pour le Mérite Order to this officer see entry 5, this chapter.)
* * *

114. **von Debschitz,** Johann Otto Karl Kolmar,
Colonel, Commander, 2nd Brandenburg (Prinz Karl von Preussen) Grenadier Regiment (No. 12).
(Awarded the Pour le Mérite Order in recognition of outstanding leadership and conspicuous bravery in action during the battle at Gitschin.)
* * *

1st Posen Infantry Regiment (No. 18)

The following two officers were decorated with the Pour le Mérite Order in recognition of conspicuous bravery in action during the battle at Jicin on June 29, 1866.

115. **von Schkopp,** Herman Eduard, Captain.
116. **Offermann,** Franz, 1st Lieutenant.

* * *

5th Brandenburg Infantry Regiment (No. 48)

The following two officers received the Pour le Mérite Order in recognition of conspicuous bravery in action during the battle at Jicin on June 29, 1866.

117. **von Dieringshofen,** Carl Friedrich Alexander, Colonel, Commander.
  (For the subsequent award of the Oakleaves to the Pour le Mérite Order given this officer see entry 226, this chapter.)
118. **von Wulffen,** Georg Otto, Lt. Colonel.
  (For the subsequent award of the Oakleaves to the Pour le Mérite Order given this officer see entry 195, this chapter.)

* * *

119. **von Fransecky,** Eduard,

Lt. General, Commander, 7th Infantry Division.

(Awarded the Pour le Mérite Order in recognition of outstanding leadership and distinguished military planning and operations during the 1866 campaign and especially during the battles at Münchengrätz and Königgrätz and also at Pressburg. For the subsequent award of the Oakleaves to the Pour le Mérite Order given this officer see entry 207, this chapter.)

* * *

120. **von Krenski,** Paul Anton Karl,
  Major, General Staff Officer, serving at the time on the General Staff of the 7th Infantry Division.
  (Awarded the Pour le Mérite Order in recognition of outstanding leadership and of conspicuous bravery in action during the battles at Münchengrätz, Königgrätz on July 3, 1866, and at Blumenau on July 22, 1866.)

* * *

121. **von Gross (von Schwarzhoff),** Karl Julius,
  Major General, Commander, 13th Infantry Brigade.
  (Awarded the Pour le Mérite Order in recognition of outstanding leadership and distinguished military planning and operations. The award also recognized his distinction in action during the battle at Königgrätz on July 3, 1866.)

* * *

122. **von Gordon**, Hellmuth,
Major General, Commander, 14th Infantry Brigade.
(Awarded the Pour le Mérite Order in recognition of outstanding leadership and distinguished military planning and operations during the 1866 campaign. The award also recognized his distinction in action during several engagements with the enemy while his brigade was a part of the Prussian advance guard and during the battle at Königgrätz on July 3, 1866.)
* * *

123. **von Schöler**, Theodor Alexander Viktor Ernst,
Major General, Commander, 8th Infantry Division, serving at the time with the 31st Infantry Brigade.
(Awarded the Pour le Mérite Order in recognition of outstanding leadership and distinguished military planning and operations. The award also recognized his distinction in action during the battles at Hünerwasser on June 26, 1866, Münchengrätz on June 28, 1866, and Königgrätz on July 3, 1866.)
* * *

124. **von Bose**, Friedrich Julius Wilhelm,

Major General, Commander, 15th Infantry Brigade.

(Awarded the Pour le Mérite Order in recognition of outstanding leadership and his conspicuous bravery in action during the battle at Podol on June 26, 1866. The award also recognized his distinction in action during the battle at Königgrätz on July 3, 1866, and later during the battle at Pressburg on July 22, 1866.)
* * *

125. **von Zychlinski**, Franz Friedrich Heinrich Szeliga,
Colonel, Commander, 2nd Magdeburg Infantry Regiment (No. 27).
(Awarded the Pour le Mérite Order in recognition of outstanding leadership and distinction in action during the battles at Münchengrätz on June 28, 1866, Königgrätz on July 3, 1866.)
* * *

126. **von Buddenbrock**, Frhr. Robert Eduard Emil,
Captain, 2nd Magdeburg Infantry Regiment (No. 27).
(Awarded the Pour le Mérite Order in recognition of outstanding leadership and distinction in action during the battle at Königgrätz on July 3, 1866. During this battle Captain von Buddenbrock was severely wounded.)
* * *

127. **von Wedell**, Richard Georg,
Colonel, Commander, 1st Thuringen Infantry Regiment (No. 31).
(Awarded the Pour le Mérite Order in recognition of outstanding leadership and distinction in action during the battle at Königgrätz on July 3, 1866, and at Pressburg on July 22, 1866. For the subsequent award

of the Oakleaves to the Pour le Mérite Order given this officer see entry 186, this chapter.)

* * *

128. **von Avemann**, Friedrich Philipp Ludwig Karl,
Colonel, Commander, 3rd Thuringen Infantry Regiment (No. 71).
(Awarded the Pour le Mérite Order in recognition of outstanding leadership and distinction in action during the night battle at Podol on June 26, 1866, and also at Pressburg on July 22, 1866.)

* * *

129. **Hensel**, August Louis Ferdinand,
Major, 4th Thuringen Infantry Regiment (No. 72).
(Awarded the Pour le Mérite Order in recognition of outstanding leadership and distinction in action during the battle at Königgrätz on July 3, 1866, where Major Hensel was responsible for the capture of 12 Austrian officers and 900 soldiers.)

* * *

130. **von Hymmen**, Friedrich Ludwig Karl Heinrich Otto,
Major, Magdeburg Hussar Regiment (No. 10).
(Awarded the Pour le Mérite Order in recognition of outstanding leadership and his conspicuous bravery in action when during an enemy Uhlan attack at Blumenau on July 22, 1866, Major von Hymmen suffered a severe saber slash but managed to direct a counterattack against the Austrians.)

* * *

131. **von Wittich**, Friedrich Wilhelm Ludwig,

Colonel, Chief of the General Staff, Prussian V. Army Corps.

(Awarded the Pour le Mérite Order in recognition of outstanding leadership and distinguished military planning and operations during the 1866 campaign. For the subsequent award of the Oakleaves to the Pour le Mérite Order given this officer see entry 179, this chapter.)

* * *

132. **von Löwenfeld**, Julius Ludwig Wilhelm,
Major General, Commander, 9th Infantry Division.
(Awarded the Pour le Mérite Order in recognition of outstanding leadership and distinguished military planning and operations during the 1866 campaign. The award also recognized his distinction in action during the engagements against the enemy on June 28, 29, and 30, 1866.)

* * *

133. **von Ollech,** Karl Rudolf,
Major General, Commander, 17th Infantry Brigade.
(Awarded the Pour le Mérite Order in recognition of outstanding leadership and distinguished military planning and operations during the 1866 campaign. The award also recognized his distinction in action during the battle at Nachod on June 27, 1866.)
* * *

134. **von Kirchbach,** Hugo Ewald,
Lt. General, Commander, 10th Infantry Brigade.

(Awarded the Pour le Mérite Order in recognition of outstanding leadership and distinguished military planning and operations during the 1866 campaign. The award also recognized his distinction in action during the battles with the Austrians on June 27-28, 1866, and on June 29-30, 1866. For the subsequent award of the Oakleaves to the Pour le Mérite Order given this officer see entry 211, this chapter.)
* * *

2nd West Prussian (Königs) Grenadier Regiment (No. 7)

The following two officers were decorated with the Pour le Mérite Order in recognition of conspicuous bravery in action during an engagement fought against the Austrians on June 28, 1866.

135. **von Voigts-Rhetz,** Karl Wilhelm Ferdinand, Colonel, Commander.
136. **von Kaisenberg,** Leopold Karl Hugo Wilhelm Heinrich, Captain.
* * *

137. **von Below,** Ferdinand Adolf Eduard,
Colonel, Commander, Westphalian Fusilier Regiment (No. 37).
(Awarded the Pour le Mérite Order in recognition of outstanding leadership and distinction in action while serving in the Prussian advance guard during the battle at Nachod on June 27, 1866.)
* * *

138. **Walther von Monbary,** Rudolf Herman Ottomar Hugo,
Colonel, Commander, 1st Nieder-Silesian Infantry Regiment (No. 46).
(Awarded the Pour le Mérite Order in recognition of outstanding leadership and distinction in action during several engagements with the enemy. Duing the engagement at Bachod on June 27, 1866, Colonel Walther von Monbary received a serious head wound but did not relinquish his command or leave the battlefield. It was also during this engagement that his horse was shot from under him.)
* * *

139. **Hoffman,** Karl Heinrich Gustaf Arthur,
2nd Lieutenant, 2nd Nieder-Silesian Infantry Regiment (No. 47).
(Awarded the Pour le Mérite Order in recognition of outstanding lead-

ership and distinction in action during the assault on the train station at Skalitz.)

* * *

140. **von François,** Bruno Hugo Karl Friedrich,

Colonel, Commander, 3rd Posen Infantry Regiment (No. 58).

(Awarded the Pour le Mérite Order in recognition of outstanding leadership and distinction in action during the engagement against the Austrians at Nachod on June 27, 1866.)

* * *

West Prussian Uhlan Regiment (No. 1)

The following three officers were decorated with the Pour le Mérite Order in recognition of conspicuous bravery in action during the battle at Nachod on June 27, 1866, and for the capture of two enemy cannon.

141. **von Tresckow,** Julius Emil, Colonel, Commander.
142. **von Bercken,** Fedor Ernst Leopold Hans, 1st Lieutenant.
143. **von Schaubert,** Karl Friedrich Wolfgang, 2nd Lieutenant.

* * *

144. **von Prondzynski,** Konrad Ferdinand, Wilhelm,
   Lt. General, Commander, 12th Infantry Division.
   (Awarded the Pour le Mérite Order in recognition of outstanding leadership and distinguished military planning and operations during the 1866 campaign.)

* * *

Silesian Fusilier Regiment (No. 38)

The following two officers received the Pour le Mérite Order in recognition of conspicuous bravery in action during an engagement against the Austrians where they captured 100 enemy soldiers.

145. **von Dalwig,** Frhr. Louis Heinrich Elgar Josef Albert, 2nd Lieutenant.
146. **von Krane,** Adolf Anatol Wilhelm, 2nd Lieutenant.

* * *

147. **von Versen,** Felix Maximilian Christof Wilhelm Leopold Rheinhold,
   Captain, General Staff Officer, serving at the time on the General Staff of the Cavalry Division, Prussian II. Army.
   (Awarded the Pour le Mérite Order in recognition of outstanding leadership and distinction in action during several engagements against the enemy.)

* * *

West Prussian Curassier Regiment (No. 5)

The following two officers were decorated with the Pour le Mérite Order in recognition of conspicuous bravery in action during the battle at Dub on July

15, 1866. During this action these two officers by leading their squadrons captured 18 enemy cannon, 7 ammunition supply wagons, 157 horses, took 2 Austrian officers and 127 soldiers as prisoners and successfully routed the enemy.

148. **von Bredow,** Maximilian Karl Friedrich Albert, Lt. Colonel, Commander.
149. **Schach von Wittenau,** Hans Alexis Leopold, Rittmeister.

* * *

150. **von Glasenapp,** Johann Heinrich Ferdinand,
Colonel, Commander, 2nd Landwehr Hussar Regiment.
(Awarded the Pour le Mérite Order in recognition of outstanding leadership and distinction in action on July 15, 1866, when Colonel von Glasenapp, leading his Hussar Regiment advanced between Poteinitz and Dlubowitz encountered an enemy force. Leading his Hussars in a sharp engagement against the Austrians, even though severely wounded, he successfully routed them and captured 5 officers and over 200 enemy soldiers.)

* * *

151. **von Schlotheim,** Frhr. Karl Ludwig,

Colonel, Chief of Staff, Prussian Army of the Elbe.

(Awarded the Pour le Mérite Order in recognition of outstanding leadership and distinguished military planning and operations during the 1866 campaign. Colonel von Schlotheim displayed conspicuous bravery in action during the battles at Münchengrätz on June 28, 1866, and Königgrätz on July 3, 1866. For the subsequent award of the Oakleaves to the Pour le Mérite Order given this officer see entry 243, this chapter.)

* * *

152. **zu Münster-Meinhövel,** Count Hugo Eberhard Leopold Uniko,
Lt. General, Commander, 14th Infantry Division.
(Awarded the Pour le Mérite Order in recognition of outstanding leadership and distinguished military planning and operations during the 1866 campaign. The award also recognized his distinction in action during the battle at Problus on July 3, 1866.)

* * *

153. **von Schwartzkoppen,** Ferdinand Emil Karl Friedrich Wilhelm,
Major General, Commander, 27th Infantry Brigade.
(Awarded the Pour le Mérite Order in recognition of outstanding leadership and distinction in action during the battle at Problus on July 3, 1866, where his brigade drove the enemy from the field in retreat.)

* * *

154. **von Hiller,** Wilhelm August Bernhard,
Major General, Commander, 28th Infantry Brigade.
(Awarded the Pour le Mérite Order in recognition of outstanding leadership and distinguished military planning and operations during the 1866 campaign.)

* * *

155. **von Canstein,** Frhr. Philipp Christian Karl Wilhelm August,
   Lt. General, Commander, 15th Infantry Division.
   (Awarded the Oakleaves to the Pour le Mérite Order in recognition of outstanding leadership and distinguished military planning and operations during the assault and capture of Neu-Prim, Ober-Prim and Nieder-Prim on July 3, 1866. For the initial award of the Pour le Mérite Order to this officer see entry 13, this chapter.)

* * *

156. **von Kraatz-Koschlau,** Friedrich Wilhelm Alexander,
   Colonel, Chief of Staff, High Command Headquarters, Prussian Army of the Main.
   (Awarded the Pour le Mérite Order in recognition of outstanding leadership and distinguished military planning and operations along the Main River during the 1866 campaign. For the subsequent award of the Oakleaves to the Pour le Mérite Order given this officer see entry 224, this chapter.)

* * *

157. **von Goeben,** August Karl Friedrich Christian,

Lt. General, Commander, 13th Infantry Division.

(Awarded the Oakleaves to the Pour le Mérite Order in recognition of outstanding leadership and distinguished military planning and operations during the engagements at Dermbach, Kissingen, Laufach and at Aschaffenburg during the 1866 campaign. For the initial award of the Pour le Mérite Order to this officer see entry 42, this chapter.)

* * *

158. **von Kummer,** Ferdinand Rudolf,

Major General, Commander, 25th Infantry Brigade.

(Awarded the Pour le Mérite Order in recognition of outstanding leadership and distinguished military planning and operations during the engagements at Dermbach, Kissingen and especially at Aschaffenburg, Gerchsheim and Würzburg during June and July of 1866. For the subsequent award of the Oakleaves to the Pour le Mérite Order given this officer see entry 190, this chapter.)

* * *

159. **von Wrangel,** Frhr. Friedrich Wilhelm Karl Oskar,
> Major General, Commander, 26th Infantry Brigade.
> (Awarded the Pour le Mérite Order in recognition of outstanding leadership and distinguished military planning of six major operations during the 1866 campaign. For the subsequent award of the Oakleaves to the Pour le Mérite Order given this officer see entry 176. this chapter.)
> * * *

160. **des Barres,** Franz Wilhelm Herman Gustaf Adolf,
> Lt. Colonel, 2nd Silesian Grenadier Regiment (No. 11).
> (Awarded the Pour le Mérite Order in recognition of outstanding leadership and distinction in action at several engagements against the Austrians during the 1866 campaign.)
> * * *

161. **von der Goltz,** Frhr. Eduard Kuno,
> Colonel, Commander, 2nd Westphalian (Prince Friedrik of the Netherlands) Infantry Regiment (No. 15).
> (Awarded the Oakleaves to the Pour le Mérite Order in recognition of outstanding leadership and distinguished military planning and operations during the 1866 campaign. The award also recognized his distinction in action during the battle at Friedrichshall on July 10, 1866, and at Laufach on July 13, 1866. For the initial award of the Pour le Mérite Order to this officer see entry 44, this chapter.)
> * * *

162. **von Hoffmüller,** Adolf Gustaf Hugo,
> Captain, 2nd Westphalian (Prince Friedrick of the Netherlands) Infantry Regiment (No. 15).
> (Awarded the Pour le Mérite Order in recognition of outstanding leadership and distinction in action during the engagement at Gershheim on July 25, 1866.)
> * * *

163. **von Cranach,** Ludwig Otto Lukas,
> Lt. Colonel, 1st Rhine Infantry Regiment (No. 25).
> (Awarded the Pour le Mérite Order in recognition of outstanding leadership and distinction in action during the battle at Friedrichshall on July 10, 1866. For the subsequent award of the Oakleaves to the Pour le Mérite Order given this officer see entry 225, this chapter.)
> * * *

164. **von Thile,** Hugo Otto Ludwig,
> Colonel, Commander, Magdeburg Fusilier Regiment (No. 36).
> (Awarded the Pour le Mérite Order in recognition of outstanding leadership and distinction in action during the engagement at Uettingen on July 26, 1866, when Colonel von Thile personally led the assault against the Bavarian positions and successfully routed them.)
> * * *

6th Westphalian Infantry Regiment (No. 55)

The following two officers were decorated with the Pour le Mérite Order in recognition of conspicuous bravery in action during the engagement at Tauber-Bischhofsheim on July 24, 1866.

165. **Stoltz,** Johann Christian Alexander, Colonel, Commander.
166. **von Below,** Ludwig Hugo, Captain.

* * *

Wilhelm I. shown wearing the Grand Cross and Star of the Pour le Mérite Order

167. **Coester,** Rudolf Maximilian,
Captain, Battery Commander, 3rd (4 pd.) Battery, Westphalian Field Artillery Regiment (No. 7).
(Awarded the Pour le Mérite Order in recognition of outstanding leadership and distinction in action during the battles at Tauber-Bischofsheim on July 24, 1866, Gerchsheim on July 25, 1866, and especially at Würzburg where he directed the counter-bombardment and successfully destroyed four enemy batteries.)

* * *

168. **Wilhelm I., King of Prussia,** Friedrich (Wilhelm) Ludwig,
Field Marshal, Commander-in-Chief, Prussian Military Forces.
(At the request of the General Staff and his son, Crown Prince Friedrich Wilhelm, and his nephew, Prince Friedrich Karl, the Grand Cross and Star of the Pour le Mérite Order was bestowed upon the king in recognition of his distinguished leadership and the victorious end of the 1866 Austro-Prussian War. This award of the Grand Cross and Star of the Pour le Mérite Order was the **third** to be given.
Special Note: Wilhelm I.'s Grand Cross and Star of the Pour le Mérite Order is currently on display in the Hohenzollern Castle in Hechingen, West Germany.)

* * *

* December 30, 1866 *

169. **von Tiedemann,** Otto,
Major General, Commander, 19th Infantry Brigade.
(Awarded the Pour le Mérite Order in recognition of outstanding leadership and distinguished military planning and operations during the battles at Nachod on June 27, 1866, and also at Skalitz.)

* * *

With the end of the "Six Weeks" War between Prussia and Austria and the withdrawal of the political influence from north of the Main River, Chancellor Bismarck began making preparations for the next move in his plans to strengthen the position of Prussia as a major power in Europe. This brought the fateful year of 1866 to a close.

* * *

* January 15, 1867 *

170. **Chorus,** Hans Wilhelm,
2nd Lieutenant, 2nd Garde Infantry Regiment.
(Awarded the Pour le Mérite Order in recognition of outstanding leadership and conspicuous bravery in action during the battles at Soor on June 28, 1866, and at Königinhof on June 29, 1866.)

* * *

171. **Gallus,** Ewald Gotthold Hugo,
Captain, Battery Commander, 3rd (4 pd.) Battery, Pomeranian Field Artillery Regiment (No. 2).
(Awarded the Pour le Mérite Order in recognition of outstanding leadership and conspicuous bravery in action during the engagement at Jicin on June 29, 1866, and during the battle at Königgrätz on July 3, 1866.)

* * *

172.   **Bloch von Blottnitz,** Theodor Rudolf Herman,
Captain, Battery Commander, 3rd (4 pd.) Battery, Silesian Field Artillery Regiment (No. 6).
(Awarded the Pour le Mérite Order in recognition of outstanding leadership and conspicuous bravery in action During the battle at Langensalza on June 27, 1866.)   * * *

* North German Confederation of 1867 *

The first step in bringing about a strong and united Germany was the formation of the North German Confederation of 1867. Basically, the confederation was a union of all German states north of the Main River. They joined together to protect the rights of the member states in such areas as trade, defense, and to provide a united front when dealing with other foreign powers. The King of Prussia was the president of the confederation and the commander-in-chief of the combined military forces. In reality, the confederation only served to formally recognize Prussia as the leading military and economic German state in central Europe. The four German states south of the Main River, Bavaria, Württemberg, Baden and Hesse-Darmstadt, remained out of the confederation, even though they were tied to it by military and economic treaties. Bismarck knew that the only way he could overcome the reluctance of these states and bring them into the confederation was to provide a threat from outside Germany that would bring them together in a united and patriotic front.

Bismarck didn't have to look too far to find an outside enemy. Only one continental European country remained in the way of Prussia becoming the strongest nation in central Europe. This "outside enemy" was the French Empire of Napoleon III.

France made an ideal enemy, especially from the standpoint of the average German. Most Germans had never forgotten the first Napoleon for the invasions and occupation of their states. At the same time, Napoleon III. was considered the epitome of the tyrant and despot that most European countries detested. But above all, France was the traditional enemy of Germany. All Bismarck had to do was wait for the right time and reason.
* * *

* Events Leading to the Franco-Prussian War *

Bismarck's opportunity came in the fall of 1869 from a most unexpected source -- Spain. During the previous September 1868, a military revolt in Spain deposed the Queen of Spain, Isabella II. Almost immediately the Spanish government began looking for a new monarch. By mid-1869 rumor had it that the Spanish throne might be offered to a member of the House of Hohenzollern. This rumor was confirmed when in September 1869, the Spanish monarchists secretly sent representatives to meet with the head of the Roman Catholic branch of the Hohenzollern-Sigmaringen family and offered the throne of Spain to Prince Leopold.

The offer of the Spanish throne despite efforts to keep it secret, became public knowledge. The Spanish representatives officially asked King Wilhelm I. of Prussia to intercede on their behalf to persuade the reluctant Prince Leopold to accept the throne of Spain.   * * *

* December 8, 1869 *

173.   **Alexander II., Emperor of Russia.**

(**Special Note:** Records indicate that Emperor Alexander II. was given the Pour le Mérite Order in recognition of the 100th anniversary of the establishment of the Imperial Russian Order of St. George. This award of the Pour le Mérite Order was **not** given as a military bravery in action decoration but was strictly bestowed for political reasons. For the subsequent award of the Oakleaves to the Pour le Mérite Order given Alexander II., see entry 251, this chapter.) * * *

Alexander II., Emperor of Russia

When the candidature of a Hohenzollern prince for the Spanish throne became known in France on July 3, 1870, it touched off an international crisis. Just the thought of a Hohenzollern on the Spanish throne was intolerable to Napoleon III. and the French people as a whole. Bismarck knew this and he also felt sure that the French would march against Prussia before they would allow this to happen. Bismarck immediately began an intrigue in order to turn the crisis to Prussia's advantage.

The diplomatic crisis lasted until mid-July 1870, when Prince Leopold, who had actually never been too receptive to accepting the Spanish throne, publicly declined the Spanish offer. It seemed that the potential cause for war had been removed and peace would remain undisturbed. However, this was not the case. The French wanted war, or at least the opportunity to humiliate Prussia and the Hohenzollerns in particular. Napoleon III. instructed the French ambassador to the Court of Prussia, Vincent Benedetti, to get from Wilhelm I., as head of the House of Hohenzollern, a promise that the Hohenzollern prince would never again be considered for the Spanish throne. Benedetti spoke with Wilhelm I. at the city of Ems on July 13, 1870, and presented the French demand. The king told the French diplomat that he had no control over Prince Leopold and the prince could do whatever he wished. The French ambassador insisted but Wilhelm I. responded that he could not or would not give any promise that would bind his family for all time. The two men parted company somewhat cooly; a request later in the day from Benedetti for another interview was rejected by the king, who had nothing further to discuss. Wilhelm I. then sent a telegram to Bismarck informing him of the day's happenings.

This was the famous Ems Telegram, and it reached Bismarck as he was sitting down to dinner with the War Minister, **Albert von Roon** (see entry 174, this chapter), and the Chief of the General Staff, Hellmuth von Moltke. Bismarck did some minor editing and, when finished, had a telegram that, depending on the nationality of the reader, made it appear that the French ambassador had insolently accosted the Prussian King or that the king had snubbed the French diplomat. The amended telegram was then released for publication. It had the desired effect in Paris.

The French public demanded that this snub to France be avenged. Actually, Napoleon III. didn't want war with Prussia, but he was overruled by his ministers, the War Party, and even his wife, the Empress Eugénie.

On July 14, 1870, France declared war on Prussia. Napoleon had hoped that the south German states would remain neutral; however, he had not counted on the wave of nationalism and patriotism what swept throughout the German states. The Emperor of the French also did not know that the south German states were obligated, by treaty, to join forces with the North Confederation in the event of war with France, which they promptly did. The war now was to pit France against Germany.

* * *

* The 1870-1871 Franco-Prussian War *

The entire scope of the Franco-Prussian War is outside the immediate concern of this work. Many excellent books deal with this conflict, and it is suggested that the reader utilize these for further information. However, a few of the major battles will be mentioned as they are vital to the complete understanding of awards of the Pour le Mérite Order.

The efficiency of the German military plans was immediately evident. Within 12 days of the French declaration of war on Prussia, 600,000 German troops had been mobilized and organized into three separate armies and nearly 45,000 troops were already on their way to the French frontier. The French, on the other hand, had yet to complete the mobilization of 300,000 French troops, and were not in an offensive position to march to the German frontier.

The first success of the Franco-Prussian war went to the French, if it could be called a success. On August 2, 1870, a hastily formed French expeditionary force of some 25,000 troops attacked the unfortified frontier town of Saarbrücken, which was defended by a small German garrison of 1,800 men. Needless to say, the French captured the town. The news of the taking of a German city caused France to go wild. The French were sure that this was only the first of many victories to follow. As it turned out, Saarbrücken was about the only real victory France was to enjoy during this war.

On August 4, 1870, the Prussian 3rd Army, under the command of Crown Prince Friedrich Wilhelm, began crossing the French frontier and at once engaged the elements of the French I. Corps, commanded by Marshal Patrice MacMahon, near the town of Weissenburg. In a brief but furious battle, the Prussians captured the town and the French forces retreated. Marchal MacMahon concentrated his forces near the town of Wörth. However, the French commander was able to muster only a force of 37,000 before the approaching German army launched a totally unexpected attack against his positions on August 6, 1870. In a battle that lasted nearly 13 hours, the French were again forced to make a hasty retreat beyond the Vosges River with the Germans in hot pursuit. On the same day, August 6, 1870, the French suffered another defeat at the town of Spichern. The Prussian 1st Army, under the command of General Karl Friedrich **von Steinmetz,** met elements of the French "Army of the Rhine," commanded by General Charles-Auguste Frossard and Emperor Napoleon III.

These two major defeats so close to the beginning of the war caused the French army to retreat towards the fortress city of Metz, with the Prussians in close pursuit. The losses also resulted in the unexpected resignation of Napoleon III. as Supreme Commander of the French Military Forces on August 12, 1870. In his place, he appointed Marshal François Bazaine. It was hoped that the Marshal would instill a fresh spirit into the French troops. However, Bazaine continued the retreat towards Metz and by August 15, 1870, had withdrawn through Metz and onward hoping to reach the fortresses of Verdun. In the meantime, the Prussian 2nd Army, under the command of Prince Friedrich Karl, moved westward toward Verdun to cut off the French retreat. At the same time, the Prussian 1st Army continued to advance on Metz.

Initially, the Prussians thought that the French army had escaped to Verdun, but on August 16, 1870, the Prussian III. Corps, commanded by Lt. General Konstantin **von Alversleben** (see entry 185, this chapter), made contact with the French south of Vionville and Mars la Tour. Despite the fact that the entire French army was before him, General von Alvensleben immediately attacked and managed to capture Vionville and successfully cut off the French escape route. Marshal Bazaine easily could have broken through but for some reason decided that a defensive action would insure his essential communications with Metz.

The next day, Bazaine abandoned his attempt to reach Verdun, turned around and began marching back toward Metz. At this time, the King of Prussia, with Field Marshal **von Moltke,** arrived with the Prussian 2nd Army and elements of the Prussian 1st Army. Both sides started preparing for the battle that was soon to come.

The battle of Gravelotte and St. Privat began during the morning of August 18, 1870. The French army was drawn up in excellent defensive positions, while the Prussian forces thought they were facing only a rear guard and that the bulk of the French had already escaped to Verdun. Fierce fighting took place throughout the day. A crisis came for the Prussians in early evening when the Prussian Garde Corps, commanded by Prince Augustus of Württemberg, launched an attack against what was thought to be an open French flank but was in reality the French center. The Garde Corps advance was stopped under heavy fire of the French and within 20 minutes had suffered 25% casualties, and the remainder were pinned down. The timely arrival of the Saxon XII. Army Corps prevented further destruction. Instead of counterattacking, the French began withdrawing as part of a general retreat to Metz.

With the French army enclosed in Metz, only one large effective French force remained in the field. It was located at Châlon-sur-Marne under the command of Marshal MacMahon. Unfortunately, Napoleon III. stepped in and took command of the force with the intention of marching to the relief of Metz. The Prussians had anticipated this move. While part of the German armies surrounded and laid siege to Metz, the bulk of the Prussian forces moved toward Châlons to engage the French and prevent them from reaching Metz. Châlons was captured on August 25, 1870. The French army, which should have marched to defend Paris, was led northward by Napoleon to Sedan.

On August 30, 1870, the French V. Army Corps, commanded by General Pierre Louis de Failly, was surprised and defeated while in its cantonments near the city of Beaumont by the Prussian IV. and XII. Army Corps under the command of **Crown Prince Albert of Saxony** (see entry 180, this chapter). Most important was the fact that the battle, won by the Prussians, broke the French troops' will to stand and fight and hastened their panic and retreat to Sedan, which they reached on August 31, 1870. Sedan was quickly invested by the Prussian 3rd Army of Crown Prince Friedrich Wilhelm along with the forces of the Crown Prince of Saxony. On September 1, 1870, the French tried to fight their way out of Sedan but were unsuccessful. This appeared to be the final effort of the French forces. On September 2, 1870, Napoleon III. surrendered the French armies at Sedan.

The shocking news of the capitulation of Sedan and the capture of the French Emperor reached Paris on September 3, 1870. The results were quite unexpected. The scope of the French defeat could not be believed by the government or the population. It sparked an internal crisis. The French government met on September 4, 1870, to discuss which path to take in this hour of despair, but the citizens of Paris took the matter into their own hands. A large crowd invaded the Chamber of Deputies where the meeting was being held and broke up the proceedings. The people proclaimed an end to the 2nd Empire and established a Republic.

With the surrender of Sedan complete, the Prussian forces began a virtually unopposed march on Paris. By skillful deployment of the forces at his command, Field Marshal von Moltke began an investment of Paris that completely surrounded the city by September 20, 1870. The Prussians did not make an immediate assault on Paris but contented themselves with establishing a strong network of fortifications around the city, completely isolating it from the rest of France.

Meanwhile, Prince Friedrich Karl and his Prussian 2nd Army were engaged in a systematic siege of Metz. Bazaine hoped to hold out until he could be relieved by the forces of Napoleon III., but his surrender at Sedan ended this dream. The Prussians tightened their grip around the besieged city. Marshal Bazaine realized no help would be forthcoming; so on October 27, 1870, the French forces in and around Metz surrendered to the Prussians. The magnitude of the defeat was enormous and proved staggering for the new Republican government.

* * *

* October 28, 1870 *

174. **von Roon**, Albert Theodor Emil,

General of Infantry, Minister of War, Chief of the Admirality.

(Awarded the Pour le Mérite Order in recognition of outstanding leadership and distinguished military planning and operations during the 1870 campaigns. The award was given personally by Wilhelm I.)

* * *

In the meantime, other events were occuring that were to affect the history of Germany. King Wilhelm I. and the royal entourage had arrived in the area of Paris on October 5, 1870, and had set up headquarters at Versailles. During the next two months, Bismarck embarked on a campaign to bring the south German states into the North German Confederation and have the King of Prussia elevated to the Imperial throne of what would be, in fact, the German Empire. There were many obstacles standing in the path of this objective, not the least of which was Wilhelm I. who had no liking for the idea. The king, at this time, was totally involved in making the final decision on whether to bombard Paris.

* * *

* **November 1, 1870** *

175. **von Budritzki**, Rudolf Otto,

Lt. General, Commander, 2nd Garde Infantry Division.

(Awarded the Pour le Mérite Order in recognition of outstanding leadership and distinguished military planning and operations during the 1870 campaigns. The award also recognized his distinction in action during the assault and capture of the French redoubt of la Bourget, near Paris.)

* * *

* **December 5, 1870**

176. **von Wrangel**, Frhr. Friedrich Wilhelm Karl Oskar,
Lt. General, Commander, 18th Infantry Division.
(Awarded the Oakleaves to the Pour le Mérite Order in recognition of outstanding leadership and distinguished military planning and operations during the assault and capture of St. Jean de la Ruelle, a suburb of Orléans, on December 3, 1870, and the capture the following morning of over 1,000 enemy soldiers and 30 cannon. The award also recognized his distinction in action during the capture of Orléans. For the initial award of the Pour le Mérite Order to this officer see 159, this chapter.)

* * *

177. **von Tresckow**, Herman Heinrich Theodor,
Lt. General, Adjutant General, 17th Infantry Division.
(Awarded the Pour le Mérite Order in recognition of outstanding leadership and conspicuous bravery in action during the engagement at Loigny on December 2, 1870. For the subsequent award of the Oakleaves to the Pour le Mérite Order given this officer see entry 244, this chapter.)

* * *

178. **Friedrich Franz, Grand Duke of Mecklenburg-Schwerin,**

General of Infantry, Commanding an Army Group.

(Awarded the Oakleaves to the Pour le Mérite Order in recognition of outstanding leadership and distinguished military planning and operations during the battles at Artenay, Beaugency and at Orléans where units of his command captured 8 French cannon and also 7,000 enemy prisoners. For the initial award of the Pour le Mérite Order to this officer see entry 59, this chapter.)

* * *

179. **von Wittich,** Friedrich Wilhelm Ludwig,

Major General, Commander, 22nd Infantry Division.

(Awarded the Oakleaves to the Pour le Mérite Order in recognition of outstanding leadership and distinguished military planning and operations in conjunction with Grand Duke Friedrich Franz of Mecklenburg-Schwerin during the actions as shown in entry 178. For the initial award of the Pour le Mérite Order to this officer see entry 131, this chapter.)

* * *

* December 6, 1870 *

180. **Albert, Crown Prince of Saxony,** (Albert) Friedrich August Anton Ferdinand Josef Karl Maria Baptist Nepomuk Wilhelm Xaver Georg,
    Royal Saxon General of Infantry, Commander-in-Chief, Army of the Maas.
    (Awarded the Oakleaves to the Pour le Mérite Order in recognition of outstanding leadership and distinguished military planning and operations during the 1870 campaigns. For the initial award of the Pour le Mérite Order to this officer see entry 23, this chapter.
    Note: Crown Prince Albert was awarded the 50 Year Jubilee Golden Crown to the Pour le Mérite Order on July 15, 1899.)

* * *

181. **Georg, Prince of Saxony,** Friedrich August (Georg) Ludwig Wilhelm Maximilian Karl Maria Nepomuk Baptist Xaver Cyriakus Romanus,
    Royal Saxon Lt. General, Deputy Commander, Saxon XII Army Corps.

(Awarded the Pour le Mérite Order in recognition of outstanding leadership and distinguished military planning and operations in support of the Prussian armies during the 1870 campaigns. For the subsequent award of the Oakleaves to the Pour le Mérite Order given this officer see Chapter IX, entry 4.) * * *

* December 22, 1870 *

182. **von und zu der Tann-Rathsamhausen**, Frhr. Ludwig Samson Arthur,

Royal Bavarian General of Infantry, Commander-in-Chief, Royal Bavarian I. Army Corps.

(Awarded the Pour le Mérite Order in recognition of outstanding leadership and distinguished military planning and operations in support of the Prussian armies during the 1870 campaigns.) * * *

* December 24, 1870 *

183. **von Manteuffel**, Frhr. Karl Rochus Edwin,
General of Cavalry, Adjutant General and Commanding General, Prussian I. Army Corps.
(Awarded the Oakleaves to the Pour le Mérite Order in recognition of outstanding leadership and distinguished military planning and operations during the 1870 campaigns. For the initial award of the Pour le Mérite Order to this officer see entry 58, this chapter.)
* * *

* December 31, 1870 *

184. **von Voigts-Rhetz**, Konstans Bernhard,
General of Infantry, Commanding General, Prussian X. Army Corps.
(Awarded the Oakleaves to the Pour le Mérite Order in recognition of outstanding leadership and distinguished military planning and operations against the French Army of the Loire. For the initial award of the Pour le Mérite Order to this officer see entry 60, this chapter.)
* * *

185. **von Alvensleben**, Konstantin Reimar,
Lt. General, Commanding General, Prussian III. Army Corps.
(Awarded the Oakleaves to the Pour le Mérite Order in recognition of outstanding leadership and distinguished military planning and operations of the Prussian III. Army Corps against the French Army of the Loire. For the initial award of the Pour le Mérite Order to this officer see entry 79, this chapter.)
* * *

186. **von Wedell,** Richard Georg,
Major General, Commander, 38th Infantry Brigade.
(Awarded the Oakleaves to the Pour le Mérite Order in recognition of outstanding leadership and distinguished military planning and operations during the successful defense of Beaune la Rolande on November 28, 1870. For the initial award of the Pour le Mérite Order to this officer see entry 127, this chapter.)

* * *

187. **Albrecht, Prince of Prussia,** Friedrich Heinrich (Albrecht),
General of Cavalry, Commander, 4th Cavalry Division.
(Awarded the Oakleaves to the Pour le Mérite Order in recognition of outstanding leadership and distinguished military planning and operations during the 1870 campaigns. Prince Albrecht was personally awarded the Pour le Mérite Order by his brother, Wilhelm I. For the initial award of the Pour le Mérite Order to this officer see 52, this chapter.)

* * *

* January 2, 1871 *

188. **von Kameke,** Arnold Karl Georg,
Lt. General, Chief of the Combined Staffs of the Engineer and Construction Corps.
(Awarded the Oakleaves to the Pour le Mérite Order in recognition of outstanding leadership and distinguished military planning and operations during the capture of Montmédy and Thionville. For the initial award of the Pour le Mérite Order to this officer see entry 107, this chapter.)

* * *

* January 6, 1871 *

189. **von Bentheim,** Georg Ferdinand,
Lt. General, Commander, 1st Infantry Division.
(Awarded the Pour le Mérite Order in recognition of outstanding leadership and conspicuous bravery in action during the battle at Amiens on November 27, 1870.)

* * *

* January 12, 1871 *

190. **von Kummer,** Ferdinand Rudolf,

Lt. General, Commander, 15th Infantry Division.

(Awarded the Oakleaves to the Pour le Mérite Order in recognition of outstanding leadership and distinguished military planning and operations during the battles at Bapaume on January 3, 1871, and Amiens on November 27, 1870. For the initial award of the Pour le Mérite Order to this officer see entry 158, this chapter.)

* * *

* January 17, 1871 *

191. **von Werder,** Karl Friedrich Wilhelm Leopold August,
General of Infantry, Commanding General, Prussian XIV. Army Corps.
(Awarded the Oakleaves to the Pour le Mérite Order in recognition of outstanding leadership and distinguished military planning and operations during the 1870 campaigns. For the initial award of the Pour le Mérite Order to this officer see 108, this chapter.)

* * *

* January 18, 1871 *

192. **von Stiehle,** Gustaf Wilhelm Friedrich,
Major General, General à la suite to His Majesty Wilhelm I., King of Prussia, Chief of the General Staff, Prussian 2nd Army.
(Awarded the Oakleaves to the Pour le Mérite Order in recognition of outstanding leadership and distinguished military planning and operations during the 1870 campaigns. For the initial award of the Pour le Mérite Order to this officer see entry 99, this chapter.)

* * *

193. **von Buddenbrock,** Baron Karl Gustaf Leopold,

Lt. General, Commander, 6th Infantry Division.

(Awarded the Oakleaves to the Pour le Mérite Order in recognition of outstanding leadership and distinguished military planning and operations during the investment, siege and capitulation of Metz. For the initial award of the Pour le Mérite Order to this officer see 29, this chapter.)

* * *

194. **von Stülpnagel,** Louis Ferdinand Wolf Anton,
Lt. General, Commander, 5th Infantry Division.
(Awarded the Oakleaves to the Pour le Mérite Order in recognition of outstanding leadership and distinguished military planning and operations during the 1870 campaigns. The award also recognized his distinction in action during the battle at Vendôme. For the initial award of the Pour le Mérite Order to this officer see entry 72, this chapter.)

* * *

195. **von Wulffen,** Georg Otto,
Colonel, Commander, 6th Brandenburg Infantry Regiment (No. 52).
(Awarded the Oakleaves to the Pour le Mérite Order in recognition of outstanding leadership and distinguished military planning and operations during the engagements at Vendôme and at the village of Mazange. During the engagement at the village of Changé, Colonel von Wulffen displayed conspicuous bravery in action when he led the attack against French positions and successfully drove the enemy to retreat and was responsible for the capture of 800 enemy soldiers. For the initial

award of the Pour le Mérite Order to this officer see entry 118, this chapter.)
* * *

196. **von Blumenthal,** Heinrich Elie Karl,
Major General, Commander, 35th Infantry Brigade.
(Awarded the Pour le Mérite Order in recognition of outstanding leadership and conspicuous bravery in action when General von Blumenthal led his brigade in the assault and capture of the village of Cercottes.)
* * *

197. **von Voigts-Rhetz,** Julius Karl Philipp Werner,
Colonel, Chief of the General Staff, Prussian III. Army Corps.
(Awarded the Pour le Mérite Order in recognition of outstanding leadership and distinguished military planning and operations during the 1870 campaigns.)
* * *

198. **von Falkenhausen,** Frhr. Wilhelm Friedrich Eduard Heinrich Alexander,
Colonel, Commander, Holstein Infantry Regiment (No. 85).
(Awarded the Pour le Mérite Order in recognition of outstanding leadership and conspicuous bravery in action during several engagements.)
* * *

199. **von der Goltz,** Baron Moritz,
Colonel, Hanover Infantry Regiment (No. 10).
(Awarded the Pour le Mérite Order in recognition of outstanding leadership and distinction in action while personally directing artillery with exceptional accuracy during several bombardments of French defensive positions.)
* * *

200. **Sannow,** Ferdinand Heinrich Wilhelm,
Lt. Colonel, serving at the time as Commander, 3rd Westphalian Infantry Regiment (No. 16).
(Awarded the Pour le Mérite Order in recognition of outstanding leadership and distinguished military planning and operations during the defense of Beaune la Rolande on November 28, 1870.)
* * *

201. **von Caprivi,** Georg Leo,
Lt. Colonel, Chief of the General Staff, Prussian X. Army Corps.
(Awarded the Pour le Mérite Order in recognition of outstanding leadership and distinguished military planning and operations during the 1870 campaigns.)
* * *

202. **Körber,** Julius Wilhelm,
Major, Hanover Field Artillery Regiment (No. 10).
(Awarded the Pour le Mérite Order in recognition of outstanding leadership and conspicuous bravery in action during the engagements at Vendôme and at the defense of Beaune la Rolande on November 28, 1870.)
* * *

* Establishment of the German Empire *

While Bismarck was busily engaged in making concessions to the various south German states, Wilhelm I. finally gave the order for the bombardment of Paris. Once this decision had been made, negotiations over the imperial crown were resumed. After continued pressure from Bismarck and Crown Prince Friedrich Wilhelm, the king finally accepted the crown. On January 18, 1871, on the 170th anniversary of the founding of the Kingdom of Prussia, King Wilhelm I. was proclaimed Emperor of the newly constituted German Empire in the Hall of Mirrors in the Palace of Versailles. * * *

Bismarck Reading the Imperial Proclamation

* January 20, 1871 *

203. **von Barnekow**, Frhr. Christof Gottlieb Albert,
Lt. General, Commander, 16th Infantry Division.
(Awarded the Oakleaves to the Pour le Mérite Order in recognition of outstanding leadership and distinguished military planning and operations during the investment, siege and capitulation of Metz on October 27, 1870, and during the siege of the forts of Péronne. For the initial award of the Pour le Mérite Order to this officer see entry 104, this chapter.)
* * *

* The Surrender of Paris *

Eight days later, on January 28, 1871, the city of Paris, with only a few more days food supply left and with riots rampant in the city, surrendered. The provisional government of the Republic of France asked for immediate peace. Thus ended the 1870-1871 Franco-Prussian War.
* * *

The Proclamation Establishing the German Empire on January 18, 1871.

✵ February 5, 1871 ✵

204. **von Leszczynski**, Stanislaus Paul Eduard,

Grand Duchy of Baden Lt. Colonel, Chief of the General Staff, Prussian XIV. Army Corps.

(Awarded the Oakleaves to the Pour le Mérite Order in recognition of outstanding leadership and distinguished military planning and operations during the siege of Belfort between November 11, 1870, until the capitulation on January 28, 1871. For the initial award of the Pour le Mérite Order to this officer see entry 34, this chapter.) * * *

205. **von Glümer**, Heinrich Karl Ludwig Adolf,
Lt. General, Commander, Grand Duchy of Baden Field Division.
(Awarded the Pour le Mérite Order in recognition of outstanding leadership, distinguished military planning and operations during the 1870 campaigns. During the engagement at Nuits on December 18, 1870, General von Glümer displayed conspicuous bravery in action even though severely wounded, he continued to command his division and successfully routed the French from their positions.)
* * *

206. **von Zastrow**, Adolf Friedrich Heinrich Alexander,
General of Infantry, Commanding General, Prussian VII. Army Corps.
(Awarded the Oakleaves to the Pour le Mérite Order in recognition of outstanding leadership and distinguished military planning and operations during the 1870 campaigns. For the initial award of the Pour le Mérite Order to this officer see entry 63, this chapter.)
* * *

207. **von Fransecky**, Eduard Friedrich,

General of Infantry, Commander, Prussian II. Army Corps.

(Awarded the Oakleaves to the Pour le Mérite Order in recognition of outstanding leadership and distinguished military planning and operations during the 1870 campaigns. For the initial award of the Pour le Mérite Order to this officer see entry 119, this chapter.)
* * *

208. **von Sperling**, Ernst Karl Oskar,
Major General, Chief of Staff, High Command Headquarters, Prussian 1st Army.
(Awarded the Oakleaves to the Pour le Mérite Order in recognition of outstanding leadership and distinguished military planning and operations during the 1870-1871 campaigns. For the initial award of the Pour le Mérite Order to this officer see entry 62, this chapter.)

* * *

209. **von Wartensleben**, Count Wilhelm Herman Ludwig Alexander Karl,
Colonel, Senior Quartermaster of the Prussian 1st Army, Chief of Staff, High Command Headquarters, Prussian Army of the South.
(Awarded the Pour le Mérite Order in recognition of outstanding leadership and distinguished military planning and operations during the 1870-1871 Franco-Prussian War. The award also recognized his distinction in action during the battles at the Hallue on December 23-24, 1870, Péronne and at Bapaume on January 1, 1871. For the subsequent award of the Oakleaves to the Pour le Mérite Order given this officer see entry 273, this chapter.)

* * *

* February 7, 1871 *

210. **von Schmidt**, Karl Johann,
Major General, Commander, 14th Cavalry Brigade.
(Awarded the Pour le Mérite Order in recognition of outstanding leadership and distinguished military planning and operations during the 1870 campaigns.)

* * *

* February 16, 1871 *

211. **von Kirchbach**, Hugo Ewald,

General of Infantry, Commanding General of the Prussian V. Army Corps.

(Awarded the Oakleaves to the Pour le Mérite Order in recognition of outstanding leadership and distinguished military planning and operations during the 1870-1871 campaigns. The award also recognized his distinction in action during the battles at Weissenburg on August 4, 1870, Wörth on August 6, 1870, and at Mont Valérien on January 19, 1871. For the initial award of the Pour le Mérite Order to this officer see entry 134, this chapter.)

* * *

212. **von Schmidt**, Friedrich Johann Eduard Christof,
Lt. General, Commander, 10th Infantry Division.
(Awarded the Pour le Mérite Order in recognition of outstanding leadership and distinguished military planning and operations while in command of the 10th Infantry Division.)

* * *

213. **von Sandrart,** Karl Gustaf,
Major General, Commander, 9th Infantry Division.
(Awarded the Pour le Mérite Order in recognition of outstanding leadership and distinguished military planning and operations. The award also recognized his distinction in action during the battle at Mont Valérien on January 1, 1871.)

* * *

* February 17, 1871 *

214. **von Moltke,** Count Hellmuth Karl Bernhard,
General of Infantry, Chief of the General Staff, Prussian Military Forces.
(Awarded the Oakleaves to the Pour le Mérite Order in recognition of outstanding leadership and distinguished military planning and operations during the 1870-1871 Franco-Prussian War. For the initial award of the Pour le Mérite Order to this officer see Chapter V-2, entry 2454, and for the award of the Grand Cross and Star of the Pour le Mérite Order see entry 302, this chapter.)

* * *

General of Infantry Count Hellmuth von Moltke

215. **von Tresckow**, Hans Ludwig Udo,
   Lt. General, Commander, 1st Reserve Division.
   (Awarded the Pour le Mérite Order in recognition of outstanding leadership and conspicuous bravery in action during the siege and capture of Belfort. The siege lasted from November 11, 1870, until January 28, 1871.)
   * * *

216. **zu Hohenlohe-Ingelfingen**, Prince Kraft Karl August Eduard Friedrich,
   Major General, à la suite to His Majesty, Wilhelm I., King of Prussia, Commander, Garde Artillery Brigade.
   (Awarded the Pour le Mérite Order in recognition of outstanding leadership and distinction in action in several engagements during the 1870-1871 campaigns.)
   * * *

* February 24, 1871 *

217. **von Witzendorff**, Karl Friedrich Wilhelm,
   Colonel, Chief of the General Staff, Prussian VIII. Army Corps.
   (Awarded the Oakleaves to the Pour le Mérite Order in recognition of outstanding leadership and distinguished military planning and operations during the 1870-1871 campaigns. The award also recognized his distinction in action during the battles at Bapaume on January 3, 1871, and St. Quentin on January 19, 1871. For the initial award of the Pour le Mérite Order to this officer see entry 92, this chapter.)
   * * *

218. **von der Burg**, Ernst Engelbert Oskar Viktor,
   Lt. Colonel, Chief of the General Staff, Prussian I. Army Corps.
   (Awarded the Oakleaves to the Pour le Mérite Order in recognition of outstanding leadership and distinguished military planning and operations during the 1870-1871 campaigns. For the initial award of the Pour le Mérite Order to this officer see entry 75, this chapter.)
   * * *

219. **von Mermerty**, Albert Gidion Alexander Hellmuth,
   Major General, Commander, 3rd Infantry Brigade.
   (Awarded the Pour le Mérite Order in recognition of outstanding leadership and conspicuous bravery in action on January 18, 1871.)
   * * *

220. **von Boecking**, Wilhelm Theodor Karl Jobst,
   Colonel, Commander, 7th East Prussian Infantry Regiment (No. 44).
   (Awarded the Pour le Mérite Order in recognition of outstanding leadership and distinction in action during the battle at St. Quentin on January 19, 1871.)
   * * *

221. **von Strubberg**, Otto Julius Wilhelm Maximilian,
   Major General, Commander, 30th Infantry Brigade.
   (Awarded the Pour le Mérite Order in recognition of outstanding leadership and distinction in action during the battles at Amiens on November 27, 1870, on the Hallue on December 23-24, 1870, and Bapaume on January 3, 1871.)
   * * *

222. **Bumke**, Karl Friedrich Ferdinand Julius,
   Major, General Staff Officer, assigned to the Staff of the Senior Quartermaster Section, Prussian 1st Army.
   (Awarded the Pour le Mérite Order in recognition of outstanding lead-

ership and conspicuous bravery in action during the battles at the Hallue on December 23-24, 1870, and at Bapaume on January 3, 1871.)

* * *

223. **von Bock,** Louis Oskar,
Colonel, Commander, 29th Infantry Brigade.
(Awarded the Pour le Mérite Order in recognition of outstanding leadership and distinction in action during the battle at Bapaume on January 3, 1871.)

* * *

* The End of the 1870-1871 Franco-Prussian War *

The initial peace treaty was signed on February 26, 1871. Under the terms of the treaty, France was required to relinquish the Province of Alsace and most of the Province of Lorraine to Germany and pay a very large war indemnity.

* * *

* February 28, 1871 *

224. **von Kraatz-Koschlau,** Friedrich Wilhelm Alexander,
Major General, Commander, 20th Infantry Division.
(Awarded the Oakleaves to the Pour le Mérite Order in recognition of outstanding leadership and distinguished military planning and operations during the 1870-1871 campaigns. The award also recognized his distinction in action during the battle at La Mans on January 10-12, 1871. For the initial award of the Pour le Mérite Order to this officer see entry 156, this chapter.)

* * *

225. **von Cranach,** Ludwig Otto Lukas,
Colonel, Commander, 8th Westphalian Infantry Regiment (No. 57).
(Awarded the Oakleaves to the Pour le Mérite Order in recognition of outstanding leadership and distinguished military planning and operations during the engagements at Herbault, Villeporcher, St. Amand, Villechauve, Château-Renault and Tours. For the initial award of the Pour le Mérite Order to this officer see entry 163, this chapter.)

* * *

226. **von Dieringshofen,** Karl Friedrich Alexander,
Major General, Commander, 40th Infantry Brigade.
(Awarded the Oakleaves to the Pour le Mérite Order in recognition of outstanding leadership and distinguished military planning and operations during the engagement at Vendôme on the 15th and 31st of December 1870. The award also recognized his distinction in action during the battle at La Mans on January 10-12, 1871. For the initial award of the Pour le Mérite Order to this officer see 117, this chapter.)

* * *

227. **von Schwerin,** Kurt Ludwig Adalbert,
Major General, Commander, 10th Infantry Brigade.
(Awarded the Pour le Mérite Order in recognition of outstanding leadership and conspicuous bravery in action during the battles at Beaune la Rolande on November 28, 1870, Paringé and at Orléans on December 3-4, 1870, and the two engagements at La Mans on January 10-12, 1871.)

* * *

228. **von L'Estocq,** Anton Wilhelm Karl,
Colonel, Commander, Leib Grenadier (1st Brandenburg) Regiment (No. 8).
(Awarded the Pour le Mérite Order in recognition of outstanding leadership and distinction in action during the engagement at Chézy on December 4, 1870, and at several other engagements.)
* * *

229. **von Flatow,** Friedrich Gustaf,
Colonel, Commander, 3rd Brandenburg Infantry Regiment (No. 20).
(Awarded the Pour le Mérite Order in recognition of outstanding leadership and distinction in action during the engagements at Chilleurs aux bois, Baumainbert and Coulommiers during December 1870. Also on January 6, 1871, during the engagement in the vicinity of Azay.)
* * *

230. **Ludwig, Grand Duke of Hesse and by the Rhine,** Friedrich Wilhelm (Ludwig) Karl,

Lt. General, Commanding Officer of the Grand Duchy of Hesse (25th Division.

(Awarded the Pour le Mérite Order in recognition of outstanding leadership and conspicuous bravery in action during the advance of his division and the engagement at Montlivault. During this battle, Grand Duke Ludwig led his troops against the French defensive positions and successfully drove the enemy out of the village.)
* * *

231. **von Puttkamer,** Frhr. Georg Heinrich Karl,
Major General, Commander, 9th Field Artillery Brigade.
(Awarded the Pour le Mérite Order in recognition of outstanding leadership and distinction in action during the engagement at Blois on December 9, 1870, where his artillery brigade fired over 800 shells into the enemy positions, resulting in the enemy's retreat.)
* * *

232. **Lehmann,** Peter Friedrich Ludwig,
Major General, Commander, 37th Infantry Brigade.
(Awarded the Pour le Mérite Order in recognition of outstanding leadership and conspicuous bravery in action during the battle at La Mans on the January 10 and 12, 1871.)
* * *

233. **von Alvensleben,** Gustaf Herman,
Colonel, Commander, Schleswig-Holstein Uhlan Regiment (No. 15).
(Awarded the Pour le Mérite Order in recognition of outstanding leadership and distinction in action during several engagements, especially during the battles at Vancé on January 8, 1871, and at Laval also on January 8, 1871.)
* * *

* March 3, 1871 *

234. **von Hartmann,** Ernst Matthias Andreas,
Major General, Commander, 3rd Infantry Division.
(Awarded the Oakleaves to the Pour le Mérite Order in recognition of outstanding leadership and distinguished military planning and operations and conspicuous bravery in action during the engagement at Salins on January 26, 1871. For the initial award of the Pour le Mérite Order to this officer see entry 33, this chapter.)

* * *

235. **von Lewinski,** Eduard Julius Ludwig August,
Major, serving at the time on the General Staff, High Command Headquarters, Prussian Army of the South.
(Awarded the Oakleaves to the Pour le Mérite Order in recognition of outstanding leadership and distinguished military planning and operations. Major von Lewinski played a vital rôle during the successful campaigns of the Prussian Army of the South during the 1870-1871 Franco-Prussian War. For the initial award of the Pour le Mérite Order to this officer see entry 36, this chapter.)

* * *

236. **du Trossel,** Wilhelm Karl Albert,
Major General, Commander, 7th Infantry Brigade.
(Awarded the Pour le Mérite Order in recognition of outstanding leadership and distinction in action during the engagement at Pontarlier and for leading the advance guard of the 2nd Infantry Division of the Prussian II. Corps.)

* * *

237. **Schuler von Senden,** Frhr. Ernst Wilhelm Moritz Otto,
Lt. General, Commander, 14th Infantry Division.
(Awarded the Pour le Mérite Order in recognition of outstanding leadership and distinguished military planning and operations. The award also recognized his distinction in action during the battles at Noissville on September 1, 1870, St. Remy on October 2, 1870, Les Tapes-Bellevue on October 7, 1870, Pérrone on December 27 and 29, 1870, Rocroi on January 5, 1871, Bouy and Langres on January 17, 1871, Etuz on January 21, 1871, and in the vicinity of Sombacourt and Chaffois on January 29, 1871.)

* * *

238. **von Woyna,** Friedrich Wilhelm,
Major General, Commander, 28th Infantry Brigade.
(Awarded the Pour le Mérite Order in recognition of outstanding leadership and conspicuous bravery in action at Rocroi on January 5, 1871.)

* * *

* March 5, 1871 *

239. **von Podbielski,** Theophil Eugen Anton,
Lt. General, Army General Quartermaster.
(Awarded the Oakleaves to the Pour le Mérite Order in recognition of outstanding leadership and distinguished military planning and operations of the Quartermaster Corps during the 1870-1871 campaigns. For the initial award of the Pour le Mérite Order to this officer see entry 95, this chapter.)

* * *

* **March 10, 1871** *

240. **Albrecht, Prince of Prussia,** Friedrich Wilhelm Nikolaus (Albrecht),
Lt. General, Deputy Commander, 3rd Reserve Division.
(Awarded the Oakleaves to the Pour le Mérite Order in recognition of outstanding leadership and distinguished military planning and operations during the battle at St. Quentin on January 19, 1871. For the initial award of the Pour le Mérite Order to this officer see entry 98, this chapter.)
* * *

Prince Albrecht of Prussia

* **March 24, 1871** *

241. **von Mertens,** August Ferdinand,
Lt. General, serving at the time with the Siege Corps at Belfort.
(Awarded the Oakleaves to the Pour le Mérite Order in recognition of outstanding leadership and distinguished military planning and operations during the siege of Belfort. He was Chief Engineer during the siege from November 11, 1870 until January 28, 1871. For the initial award of the Pour le Mérite Order to this officer see entry 11, this chapter.)
* * *

* **June 12, 1871** *

242. **von Helden-Sarnowski,** Rudolf Franz Wilhelm,
Colonel, Commander, Garde Field Artillery Regiment.
(Awarded the Pour le Mérite Order in recognition of outstanding leadership and distinction in action while directing the artillery support

for the Prussian 2nd Division during the engagement at Le Bourget on December 21, 1870.) * * *

* June 15, 1871 *

243. **von Schlotheim**, Frhr. Karl Ludwig,

Major General, Commander, 5th Cavalry Brigade, serving at the time as Chief of Staff, High Command Headquarters, Prussian 3rd Army. (Awarded the Oakleaves to the Pour le Mérite Order in recognition of outstanding leadership and distinguished military planning and operations during the 1870-1871 campaigns. The award also recognized his distinction in action during several engagements. For the initial award of the Pour le Mérite Order to this officer see entry 151, this chapter.)
* * *

* June 16, 1871 *

244. **von Tresckow**, Herman Heinrich Theodor,

Lt. General, Adjutant General, Chief of Personnel, War Ministry and Military Cabinet.

(Awarded the Oakleaves to the Pour le Mérite Order in recognition of outstanding leadership and distinguished military planning and operations during the 1870-1871 campaigns. The Oakleaves were presented to General von Tresckow personally by Wilhelm I. during the victory parade in Paris. For the initial award of the Pour le Mérite Order to this officer see entry 177, this chapter.)
* * *

245. **von Steinmetz**, Karl Friedrich,

General Field Marshal.

(Awarded the Oakleaves to the Pour le Mérite Order in recognition of outstanding leadership and distinguished military planning and operations during the 1870-1871 Franco-Prussian War. For the initial award of the Pour le Mérite Order to this officer see Chapter VI, entry 15.)
* * *

246. **von Alvensleben,** Gustaf,
General of Infantry, Adjutant General, Commanding General, Prussian IV. Army Corps.
(Awarded the Pour le Mérite Order in recognition of outstanding leadership and distinguished military planning and operations during the 1870-1871 campaigns. The award also recognized his distinction in action during the battle at Beaumont on August 30, 1870.)
* * *

247. **August, Prince of Württemberg,** Friedrich (August) Eberhard,

General of Cavalry, Commanding General, Garde Corps.

(Awarded the Oakleaves to the Pour le Mérite Order in recognition of outstanding leadership and distinguished military planning and operations especially during the battles at Mars la Tour on August 16, 1870, St. Privat on August 18, 1870, and at the battle of Sedan on September 1, 1870. For the initial award of the Pour le Mérite Order to this officer see entry 56, this chapter.)
* * *

* November 28, 1871 *

248. **von Woyna,** Paul Peter Emil,
Major General, Commander, 39th Infantry Brigade.
(Awarded the Pour le Mérite Order in recognition of outstanding leadership and conspicuous bravery in action while personally directing his troops against the enemy during several engagements.)
* * *

249. **von der Becke,** Frhr. Friedrich Leopold Karl Alexander,
Colonel, Commander, 10th Artillery Brigade.
(Awarded the Pour le Mérite Order in recognition of outstanding leadership and conspicuous bravery in action during several engagements where he personally directed artillery fire against enemy positions.)
* * *

* December 2, 1871 *

250. **von Below,** Hans Adolf Julius,
Major General, Commander, Garde Artillery Brigade.
(Awarded the Pour le Mérite Order in recognition of outstanding leadership and distinction in action during the battle at Spichern on August 6, 1870, where General von Below received the Prussian Iron Cross 2nd Class. The award of the Pour le Mérite Order also recognized his distinction in action during the battles at Vionville on August 16, 1870, and he was also decorated with the 1st Class Iron Cross. At Orléans on December 3-4, 1870, he displayed conspicuous bravery in action during that battle.)
* * *

* December 8, 1871 *

251. **Alexander II., Emperor of Russia.**

(Awarded the Oakleaves to the Pour le Mérite Order in recognition of outstanding leadership and distinguished military planning. This award was again of a political nature rather than for military bravery. Wilhelm I. felt it necessary to show his appreciation to Alexander II. for his promise to offer military assistance to Prussia in the event that Austria chose to intervene in the 1870-1871 war on the side of France. For the initial award of the Pour le Mérite Order to Alexander II. see entry 173, this chapter.)
* * *

252. **Nikolai Nikolaieovich, Grand Duke of Russia.**

(Awarded the Pour le Mérite Order in recognition of outstanding leadership and an outstanding military career. This is another award of the Pour le Mérite Order given for political reasons. For the subsequent award of the Oakleaves to the Pour le Mérite Order to this officer, see entry 281, this chapter.)
* * *

253. **Michail Nikolaieovich, Grand Duke of Russia.**

(Awarded the Pour le Mérite Order in recognition of outstanding leadership and an outstanding military career. This is another award of the Pour le Mérite Order given for political reasons. For the subsequent award of the Oakleaves to the Pour le Mérite Order to this officer, see entry 280, this chapter.)
* * *

* March 1, 1872 *

254. **von Hartmann,** Frhr. Jakob,
Royal Bavarian General of Infantry, Commanding General, Bavarian II. Army Corps.
(Awarded the Pour le Mérite Order in recognition of outstanding leadership and distinguished military planning and operations during the 1870-1871 campaigns in conjunction with the Prussian forces.)
* * *

* March 22, 1872 *

255. **von Pape,** August Wilhelm Alexander,

Lt. General, Commander, 1st Garde Infantry Regiment.

(Awarded the Oakleaves to the Pour le Mérite Order in recognition of outstanding leadership and distinguished military planning and operations during the campaigns of the 1st Guard Infantry Regiment. The award also recognized his distinction in action during the battles at St. Privat on August 18, 1870, and at Sedan on September 1, 1870. For the initial award of the Pour le Mérite Order to this officer see entry 83, this chapter.)
* * *

256. **von Dresky,** Justus Karl Wilhelm Albert Friedrich Emil,
Colonel à la suite, Garde Field Artillery Regiment, Deputy Commander, Garde Field Artillery Brigade.
(Awarded the Pour le Mérite Order in recognition of outstanding leadership and distinction in action during several engagements and especially during the battle at Mazange on January 6, 1871.)
* * *

* May 29, 1872 *

257. **Humbert, Crown Prince of Italy,** (Humbert) Ranier Karl Emanuel Maria Ferdinand Eugene, Prince of Piedmont.

(Awarded the Pour le Mérite Order during the baptism celebration of his daughter, H.R.H Princess Margarete. Reasons for this award of the Pour le Mérite Order to Crown Prince Humbert are vague but certainly cannot be in recognition of any military achievement.)
* * *

258. **Victor Emanuel, King of Italy,** (Victor Emanuel) Maria Albert Eugene Ferdinand Thomas.

(Awarded the Pour le Mérite Order as possibly another political award.)
* * *

* January 19, 1873 *

259. **von Gottberg,** Walter Philipp Werner,
Major General, Chief of Staff, 4th Army Inspection Unit.
(Awarded the Pour le Mérite Order in recognition of outstanding leadership and distinguished military planning and operations during the 1870-1871 Franco-Prussian War.)
* * *

260. **von Geissler,** Heinrich Paul,
    Major, assigned to the Army General Staff, serving at the time as a General Staff Officer, 3rd Army Inspection Unit.
    (Awarded the Pour le Mérite Order in recognition of outstanding leadership and distinction in action during the engagements at Azay on January 7, 1871, and at Changé on January 11, 1871.)

* * *

261. **Neumeister,** Emil Georg,
    Captain à la suite, 3rd Engineer Inspection Unit, assigned and serving at the time in the War Ministry.
    (Awarded the Pour le Mérite Order in recognition of outstanding leadership and distinction in action during the battle at Metz on November 5, 1870, and several other actions.)

* * *

262. **von Maillinger,** Josef Maximilian Fridolin,
    Royal Bavarian Lt. General, Commander, 2nd Division.
    (Awarded the Pour le Mérite Order in recognition of outstanding leadership and distinguished military planning and operations. The award also recognized his distinction in action during the battles at Bagneux and Châtillon on October 13, 1870.)

* * *

263. **von Rothmaler,** Louis Karl Wilhelm Friedrich Levin,
    Major General, Commander, 11th Infantry Brigade.
    (Awarded the Pour le Mérite Order in recognition of outstanding leadership and distinction in action during the engagement at Coulommiers on December 15, 1870.)

* * *

264. **von Haesler,** Count Gottlieb Ferdinand Albert Alexis,
    Major, Senior Staff Quartermaster, Prussian Occupation Army of France.
    (Awarded the Pour le Mérite Order in recognition of outstanding leadership and conspicuous bravery in action during three engagements and especially at Vendôme on December 15, 1870.)

* * *

265. **von Scheliha,** Friedrich Ernst Ferdinand,
    Colonel, Commander, Garde Field Artillery Regiment.
    (Awarded the Pour le Mérite Order in recognition of outstanding leadership and distinction in action during the bombardments of Schlett-Stadt and near Neu-Breisach. The award also recognized his distinction in action during the siege of Belfort from November 11, 1870 until January 28, 1871.)

* * *

266. **von Massow,** Wilhelm,
    Colonel, Commander, Grenadier "Kronprinz" Regiment (1st East Prussian) (No. 1).
    (Awarded the Pour le Mérite Order in recognition of outstanding leadership and conspicuous bravery in action during the battles at Poeuilly on January 18, 1871, and at St. Quentin on January 19, 1871.)

* * *

267. **von Schachtmeyer,** Hans Rudolf Ferdinand,
    Lt. General, Commander, Prussian 8th Division.
    (Awarded the Pour le Mérite Order in recognition of outstanding leadership and distinguished military planning and operations while com-

manding the 21st Infantry Division during the battles at Weissenburg on August 4, 1870, and at Wörth on August 6, 1870. The award also recognized his distinction in action during the battle at Sedan on September 1, 1870.)

* * *

268. **von Pestel**, Eduard,
Colonel, Commander, Rhine Uhlan Regiment (No. 7).
(Awarded the Pour le Mérite Order in recognition of outstanding leadership and distinction in action during the engagement at Poeuilly on January 18, 1871.)

* * *

269. **von Lewinski**, Alfred August Louis Wilhelm,
Lt. Colonel, Chief of the General Staff, Prussian IX. Army Corps.
(Awarded the Pour le Mérite Order in recognition of outstanding leadership and conspicuous bravery in action during the battle at Villers les Plénois on October 7, 1870.)

* * *

270. **von Förster**, Otto Karl Georg,
Colonel à la suite, 2nd Thuringen Infantry Regiment (No. 32), serving at the time as Commander, 49th Infantry Brigade (1st Grand Duchy of Hesse).
(Awarded the Pour le Mérite Order in recognition of outstanding leadership and distinction in action during the engagement at Alençon on January 15, 1871.)

* * *

271. **von Wechmar**, Karl Heinrich Rudolf,
Colonel, Commander, 1st Baden Leib Grenadier Regiment (No. 109).
(Awarded the Pour le Mérite Order in recognition of outstanding leadership and distinction in action during the siege of Belfort from November 11, 1870, until January 28, 1871.)

* * *

272. **von der Esch**, Karl Wilhelm,
Colonel, Chief of the General Staff, Prussian XV. Army Corps.
(Awarded the Pour le Mérite Order in recognition of outstanding leadership and distinction in action during the battle at Sedan on September 1, 1870.)

* * *

273. **von Wartensleben**, Count Wilhelm Herman Ludwig Alexander Karl,
Colonel, Section Chief, Supreme General Staff.
(Awarded the Oakleaves to the Pour le Mérite Order in recognition of outstanding leadership and distinguished military planning and operations during the battles at Spichern, Metz, Gravelotte, on the Hallau and at Amiens. For the initial award of the Pour le Mérite Order to this officer see entry 209, this chapter.)

* * *

274. **von Brandenstein**, Karl Bernhard Herman,
Colonel, Section Chief, Supreme General Staff.
(Awarded the Pour le Mérite Order in recognition of outstanding leadership and distinction in action during several actions.)

* * *

* May 1, 1873 *

275. **Todleben**, Eduard Franz,
Imperial Russian General of Engineers and Adjutant General.

Crown Prince Friedrich Wilhelm

(Awarded the Pour le Mérite Order in recognition of outstanding leadership and distinction in action during the defense and siege of Savastopol during the Crimean War.)

* * *

* The Award of the Oakleaves to the Grand Cross and Star *
of the Pour le Mérite Order

* September 2, 1873 *

The next important event in the history of the Pour le Mérite Order occured on this date. The 1870-1871 Franco-Prussian War Victory Column was dedicated also on this date. During the dedication ceremonies, Wilhelm I. bestowed upon his son, the Crown Prince Friedrich Wilhelm, and his nephew, Prince Friedrich Karl, both now Field Marshals in the Prussian army, the Oakleaves to the Grand Cross and Star of the Pour le Mérite Order. The Oakleaves were attached to the Grand Cross badge as the suspension and attached to the upper point of the Grand Cross Star. These awards of the Oakleaves to the Pour le Mérite Order Grand Cross and Star were unique in the history of the Order since they were the **only** Oakleaves distinction **ever** given to the Grand Cross and Star of the Pour le Mérite Order.

* * *

276. **Friedrich Wilhelm, Crown Prince of the German Empire and Crown Prince of Prussia,** (Friedrich Wilhelm) Nikolaus Karl,
General Field Marshal of the Prussian Army.
(Awarded the Oakleaves to the Grand Cross and Star of the Pour le Mérite Order in recognition of his outstanding military career. For prior awards of the Pour le Mérite Order, see entries: 49, (Order badge); 55, (Oakleaves); 100, (Grand Cross and Star of the Pour le Mérite Order); all found in this chapter.)

* * *

277. **Friedrich Karl, Prince of Prussia,** (Friedrich Karl) Nikolaus,
General Field Marshal of the Prussian Army.
(Awarded the Oakleaves to the Grand Cross and Star of the Pour le Mérite Order in recognition of his outstanding military career. For prior awards of the Pour le Mérite Order, see Chapter VI, entry 9, (Order badge); this chapter, entries 2, (Oakleaves); 101, (Grand Cross and Star of the Pour le Mérite Order.)

* * *

* First Award of the Pour le Mérite Order for Science and Arts *
to a Military Officer

* May 24, 1874 *

Count Hellmuth von Moltke received the **first** award of the Pour le Mérite Order for Science and Arts to be given to a military officer. This award was given in recognition of his outstanding contributions to military tactics and operations. For prior awards of the military Pour le Mérite Order, see Chapter V-2, entry 2454, and entry 214, this chapter.

* * *

Prince Friedrich Karl

* The 1877 Russo-Turkish War *

During mid-summer of 1876, a series of uprisings occured in the Balkans against the oppressive Turkish rule. The Turkish government responded with extremely harsh and increasingly brutal methods to surpress these rebellions. The general population of Europe was aroused by this barbarous and indiscriminate slaughter of the revolutionaries. Russia was particularly incensed since she considered the Slavic populations of the Balkans under her unofficial protection. Russia felt it necessary to take action to protect the Christians of the Balkan peninsula.

In November 1876, Russia began a partial mobilization of her armed forces and engaged in secret joint military planning with the Rumanians. After these secret negotiations and plans had been completed, Russia issued a series of demands which the Turkish government ignored. Russia declared war on Turkey on April 24, 1877.

* * *

* September 25, 1877 *

278. **von Lignitz**, Friedrich Wilhelm Albert Viktor,
    Major, Prussian General Staff Officer, attached to the Imperial German Embassy and serving at the time as an official observer with the Russian forces during the Russian campaigns against the Turks.
    (Awarded the Pour le Mérite Order in recognition of outstanding leadership and distinction in action upon the recommendation of Emperor Alexander II. Major von Lignitz was also decorated with the Imperial Russian Order of St. George 4th Class and the Imperial Russian Order of St. Vladimir 4th Class with Swords.)

* * *

* Between October 23 and 25, 1877 *

279. **Elshanovski**, Kasimir Julianovich,
    Imperial Russian Colonel, Commander, 5th Kulaga (His Majesty the Emperor of Germany and King of Prussia) Infantry Regiment.
    (Awarded the Pour le Mérite Order in recognition of outstanding leadership and distinction in action during the engagement at Lovtsha. Colonel Elshanovski also received the Imperial Russian Order of St. George 4th Class.)

* * *

* November 28, 1877 *

280. **Michail Nikolaieovich, Grand Duke of Russia.**
    (Awarded the Oakleaves to the Pour le Mérite Order in recognition of outstanding leadership and distinguished military planning and operations during the 1877 campaigns against Turkey. For the initial award of the Pour le Mérite Order to this officer see entry 253, this chapter.)

* * *

281. **Nikolai Nikolaieovich, Grand Duke of Russia.**
    (Awarded the Oakleaves to the Pour le Mérite Order in recognition of outstanding leadership and distinguished military planning and operations during the 1877 campaigns against Turkey. For the initial award of the Pour le Mérite Order to this officer see entry 252, this chapter.)

* * *

282. **Alexander Alexandrovich, Heir to the Throne of Russia.**
(Awarded the Pour le Mérite Order in recognition of outstanding leadership and distinguished military planning and operations during the 1877 campaigns against Turkey.)
* * *

283. **Vladimir Alexandrovich, Grand Duke of Russia.**
(Awarded the Pour le Mérite Order in recognition of outstanding leadership and distinguished military planning and operations during the 1877 campaigns against Turkey.)
* * *

* December 18, 1877 *

284. **Karl, Prince of Rumania,** (Karl) Eitel Friedrich Zephyrin Ludwig.
(Awarded the Pour le Mérite Order in recognition of outstanding leadership and distinguished military planning and operations during the 1877 campaigns against Turkey. The award also recognized his distinction in action during the battle at Plevna.
Special Note: Prince Karl was a nephew of Wilhelm I. and eventually became Carol I., King of Rumania.)
* * *

During the bloody war, the combined Russian and Rumanian armies inflicted a major defeat on Turkey and successfully destroyed its influence in the Balkans. The driving Russian army was within sight of the Turkish capital of Constantinople and, in fact, several of the advanced units had actually entered the outskirts of the city, when Great Britain and other major European powers became concerned. They immediately stepped in to bring about a cease-fire and start negotiations for a peace settlement. The general fighting stopped on January 31, 1878.
* * *

* April 14, 1878 *

285. **Kurlov,** Grigori Nikonorovich,
Imperial Russian Major General, Commander, St. Petersburg (King Friedrich Wilhelm III.) Grenadier Regiment.
(Awarded the Pour le Mérite Order in recognition of outstanding leadership and distinguished military planning and operations during the 1877 campaigns against Turkey.)
* * *

* April 24, 1878 *

286. **Alexander II., Emperor of Russia.**
(Awarded the Grand Cross and Star of the Pour le Mérite Order in recognition of the Russian victory over Turkey during the short 1877 Russo-Turkish War. For the initial award of the Pour le Mérite Order to Emperor Alexander III., see entry 173 and 251, this chapter.
Special Note: Wilhelm I. gave the **fourth** award of the Grand Cross and Star to the Pour le Mérite Order to Alexander II. and at the same time authorized the Emperor Alexander to give **ten** Pour le Mérite Orders to deserving Russian officers for conspicuous bravery in action and outstanding leadership during the 1877 Russo-Turkish War. This was the last time authorization to award the Pour le Mérite Order by anyone other than the King of Prussia was given.)
* * *

The following ten Imperial Russian officers were awarded the Pour le Mérite Order in recognition of conspicuous bravery in action by Alexander II. as authorized by Wilhelm I.

287. **Miliutin,** Count Dmitri Alexieieovich,
Imperial Russian General of Infantry, Adjutant General and Minister of War.
(Awarded the Pour le Mérite Order by Alexander II. in recognition of outstanding leadership and distinguished military planning and operations during the 1877 campaigns. The award also recognized his distinction in action during the battle at Plevna and the capture of the Turkish army of Osman Pasha on November 28, 1877.)

* * *

288. **Nepokoitshizki,** Arthur Adamovich,
Imperial Russian General of Infantry, Adjutant General.
(Awarded the Pour le Mérite Order by Alexander II. in recognition of outstanding leadership and distinction in action during the battle at Plevna on November 28, 1877.)

* * *

289. **Sviatopolk-Mirski I.,** Prince Dmitri Ivanovich,
Imperial Russian General of Infantry, Adjutant General, Deputy to the Commander-in-Chief, Army of the Caucasus.
(Awarded the Pour le Mérite Order by Alexander II. in recognition of outstanding leadership and distinction in action during the assault at Kars during the night of November 5-6, 1877.)

* * *

290. **Loris-Melikov,** Count Michail Tarielovich,
Imperial Russian General of Cavalry, Adjutant General, Deputy to the Commander-in-Chief, Caucasus-Turkish Border Corps.
(Awarded the Pour le Mérite Order by Alexander II. in recognition of outstanding leadership and distinguished military planning and operations which resulted in the capture of the Turkish army of Muchtar Pasha at the battle of the Heights of Aladsha on October 3, 1877.)

* * *

291. **Hurko (Gurko?),** Josef Vladimirovich,
Imperial Russian General of Cavalry, Adjutant General, Imperial Russian Guard Corps.
(Awarded the Pour le Mérite Order by Alexander II. in recognition of outstanding leadership and distinguished military planning and operations during the 1877 campaigns against Turkey.)

* * *

292. **Radezki,** Fedor Fedorovich,
Imperial Russian General of Infantry, Adjutant General, Commanding General, Imperial Russian VIII. Army Corps.
(Awarded the Pour le Mérite Order by Alexander II. in recognition of outstanding leadership and distinguished military planning and operations during the defense of Shipkapasses and the capture of the entire Turkish army of Wessel Pasha on December 28, 1877.)

* * *

293. **Lasarev,** Ivan Davidovich,
Imperial Russian Lt. General, assigned to special missons by the Commander-in-Chief, Imperial Russian Army of the Causasus.
(Awarded the Pour le Mérite Order by Alexander II. in recognition of

outstanding leadership and conspicuous bravery in action during the assault at Kars during the night of November 5-6, 1877. General Lasarev personally commanded and led the attack against the Turkish southeast defensive positions and successfully caused their retreat.)
* * *

294. **Tergukassov**, Arsas Artemieovich,
Imperial Russian Lt. General, Commander, Caucasus Grenadier Regiment.
(Awarded the Pour le Mérite Order by Alexander II. in recognition of outstanding leadership and distinguished military planning and operations during the 1877 campaigns against Turkey. The award also recognized his distinction in action during the battle and capture of Bajaset in June 1877.)
* * *

295. **Imerentinski**, Prince Alexander Konstantinovich,
Imperial Russian Lt. General, Adjutant General.
(Awarded the Pour le Mérite Order by Alexander II. in recognition of outstanding leadership and distinction in action during the battle and capture of Plevna on November 28, 1877.)
* * *

296. **Skobelev II.**, Michail Dmitrieovich,
Imperial Russian Lt. General, Adjutant General, Commander, 16th Infantry Division.
(Awarded the Pour le Mérite Order by Alexander II. in recognition of outstanding leadership and distinction in action during the battle and capture of Plevna and the capture of the Turkish army of Wassel Pasha on December 28, 1877.)
* * *

* November 19, 1878 *

297. **Alexei Alexandrovich, Grand Duke of Russia.**
(Awarded the Pour le Mérite Order in recognition of outstanding leadership and distinguished military planning and operations during the building and defense of the engineering bridges at Simniza, Petroshani and Nikopol on June 14, 1877.)
* * *

298. **Sergei Alexandrovich, Grand Duke of Russia.**
(Awarded the Pour le Mérite Order in recognition of outstanding leadership and conspicuous bravery in action during an engagement against a large Turkish force while on a reconaissance patrol on October 12, 1877.)
* * *

299. **Nikolai Nikolaieovich (the Younger), Grand Duke of Russia.**
(Awarded the Pour le Mérite Order in recognition of outstanding leadership and conspicuous bravery in action during the crossing of the Danube River at Sistova on June 15, 1877.)
* * *

300. **Konstantin Konstantinovich, Grand Duke of Russia.**
(Awarded the Pour le Mérite Order in recognition of outstanding leadership and conspicuous bravery in action on the Danube River at Silistria on October 2, 1877, where he led his troops in an attack on a Turkish steamer which they successfully sank.)
* * *

301. **Nikolai Michailovich, Grand Duke of Russia.**

(Awarded the Pour le Mérite Order in recognition of outstanding leadership and distinguished military planning and operations during several engagements against Turkish forces. The award also recognized his distinction in action during the battle at the Heights of Aladsha on October 3, 1877, where the Turkish army of Muchtar Pasha was captured.)

* * *

* March 8, 1879 *

On this date Wilhelm I. made the **fifth** and **last** award of the Grand Cross and Star of the Pour le Mérite Order.

302. **von Moltke, Count Hellmuth Karl Bernhard,**

General Field Marshal, Chief of the General Staff, Prussian Military Forces.

(Awarded the Grand Cross and Star to the Pour le Mérite Order in recognition of distinguished military planning and operations and **60** years of distinguished military service. For prior awards of the Pour le Mérite Order to Count Moltke see Chapter V-2, entry 2454, (badge); entry 214, this chapter, (Oakleaves); Chapter IX, entry 1, (50 Year Jubilee Crown with Diamonds).
Special Note: General Field Marshal Count von Moltke was awarded the Pour le Mérite Order for Science and Arts on May 24, 1874, see page 312, this chapter.)

* * *

* March 22, 1879 *

303. **Shuvalov, Count Pavel Andreieovich,**
Imperial Russian Lt. General, Adjutant General, Chief of Staff, Guard Corps and all military forces in the St. Petersburg Military District.
(Awarded the Pour le Mérite Order in recognition of outstanding leadership and distinguished military planning and operations during the 1877 campaigns against Turkey. The award also recognized his distinction in action during an engagement in December 1877.)

* * *

* November 17, 1882 *

304. **Arthur, Prince of Great Britain and Ireland, Duke of Connaught,** (Arthur) William Patrick Albert.

(Awarded the Pour le Mérite Order in recognition of outstanding leadership and distinguished military planning and operations while serving as a British Major General commanding a brigade composed of three Guard battalions during the Egyptian campaigns.)

* * *

* September 1, 1884 *

305. **von Bismarck,** Prince Otto Eduard Leopold,

Chancellor of the German Empire.

(Chancellor Prince von Bismarck was awarded **both** the Pour le Mérite Order **and** the Oakleaves to the Pour le Mérite Order together on this date in recognition of outstanding leadership and his distinguished military career. It seems unusual that Prince von Bismarck was decorated with the Pour le Mérite Order so late in his career.
Special Note: Prince von Bismarck received the Pour le Mérite Order for Science and Arts on January 20, 1896, in recognition of political achievement.)

* * *

Wilhelm I. led a somewhat quiet life well into the 1880's. As the years passed he came to be revered as a monarch. This was mostly the result of his simple lifestyle and his advanced age, facts which seem to appeal greatly to the common man of the new German Empire.

* * *

* July 7, 1887 *

306. **Heinrich, Prince of Hesse and by the Rhine,** (Heinrich) Ludwig Wilhelm Adalbert Waldemar Alexander,
General of Cavalry, Commander, Grand Duchy of Hesse (25th) Division.
(A belated award of the Pour le Mérite Order in recognition of outstanding leadership and distinguished military planning and operations during the 1870-1871 Franco-Prussian War. The award also recognized his distinction in action during several engagements.
Special Note: This was the last award of the Pour le Mérite Order given by Wilhelm I.)

* * *

* The Death of Wilhelm I. *

Early in March of 1888, Wilhelm I. caught a chill that slowly grew worse and eventually confined the emperor to bed. Within days it became evident that he did not have long to live. Thirteen days short of his 91st birthday, Wilhelm I., the seventh King of Prussia and the first Emperor of the German Empire, died peacefully during the morning of March 9, 1888. With his passing, an entire era of German history came to a close.

* * *

Wilhelm I. Laying-in-state in the Berlin Catherdral

Notes:

AWARDS OF THE POUR LE MÉRITE ORDER DURING THE REIGN OF WILHELM I. FROM 1861 THROUGH 1888.

AWARDS OF THE POUR LE MÉRITE ORDER DURING THE REIGN OF WILHELM I.

1861 - 1871

Table I

Rank	1861	1864	1865	1866	1867	1869	1870	1871
Field Marshal	-	1	-	2[b]	-	-	-	-
General of Infantry	-	1	1	5	-	-	5	6
General of Cavalry	-	1	-	4	-	-	2	1
General of Artillery	-	-	-	1	-	-	-	-
General	-	-	-	-	-	-	-	-
Admiral	-	-	-	1	-	-	-	-
Lt. General	-	3	-	11	-	-	5	15
Major General	-	6	-	28	-	-	2	19
Colonel	-	9	-	27	-	-	-	14
Lt. Colonel	-	5	-	6	-	-	-	4
Major	-	4	-	11	-	-	-	3
Captain	-	8	-	14	2	-	-	-
Rittmeister	-	-	-	3	-	-	-	-
Lieutenant	-	-	-	-	-	-	-	-
1st Lieutenant	-	1	-	3	-	-	-	-
2nd Lieutenant	-	7	-	5	1	-	-	-
Rank Unknown	-	-	-	-	-	1[c]	-	3[c,d]
Miscellaneous	1[a]	-	-	-	-	-	-	-
Total	1	46	1	121	3	1	14	66

a   King of the Two Sicilies.
b   Wilhelm I. (1)
c   Alexander II. of Russia.
d   Two Russian Grand Dukes.

AWARDS OF THE POUR LE MÉRITE ORDER DURING THE REIGN OF WILHELM I.

1872 - 1888

Table II

Rank	1872	1873	1877	1878	1879	1882	1884	1887	Total
Field Marshal	-	2	-	-	1	-	-	-	7
General of Infantry	1	-	-	4	-	-	-	-	23
General of Cavalry	-	-	-	2	-	-	-	1	11
General of Artillery	-	-	-	-	-	-	-	-	1
General	-	1^g	-	-	-	-	-	-	1
Admiral	-	-	-	-	-	-	-	-	1
Lt. General	1	2	-	4	1	-	-	-	42
Major General	-	2	-	1	-	1	-	-	59
Colonel	1	8	1	-	-	-	-	-	60
Lt. Colonel	-	1	-	-	-	-	-	-	16
Major	-	2	1	-	-	-	-	-	21
Captain	-	1	-	-	-	-	-	-	25
Rittmeister	-	-	-	-	-	-	-	-	3
Lieutenant	-	-	-	-	-	-	-	-	-
1st Lieutenant	-	-	-	-	-	-	-	-	4
2nd Lieutenant	-	-	-	-	-	-	-	-	13
Rank Unknown	-	-	5^{h,i,j}	6^{k,l}	-	-	-	-	15
Miscellaneous	2^{e,f}	-	-	-	-	-	1^m	-	4
Total	5	19	7	17	2	1	1	1	306

e   King of Italy.
f   Crown Prince of Italy.
g   Russian General of Engineers.
h   Three Russian Grand Dukes.
i   Heir to the Russian Throne.
j   Prince of Rumania.
k   Alexander II. of Russia.
l   Five Russian Grand Dukes.
m   Bismarck as Chancellor.

PERCENTAGES OF TOTAL AWARDS OF THE POUR LE MÉRITE ORDER ACCORDING TO RANK

1861 - 1888

Table III

	Rank	Number Awarded	Percentage
1.	Colonel	60	20.0%
2.	Major General	59	19.0
3.	Lt. General	42	14.0
4.	Captain	25	8.0
5.	General of Infantry	23	8.0
6.	Major	21	7.0
7.	Lt. Colonel	16	5.0
8.	Rank Unknown	15	5.0
9.	2nd Lieutenant	13	4.0
10.	General of Cavalry	11	4.0
11.	Field Marshal	7	2.0
12.	1st Lieutenant	4	1.0
13.	Miscellaneous	4	1.0
14.	Rittmeister	3	1.0
15.	General of Artillery	1	0.3
16.	General	1	0.3
17.	Admiral	1	0.3

SIMULTANEOUS AWARD OF BOTH THE POUR LE MÉRITE ORDER AND OAKLEAVES

Table IV

	Name	Entry	Date
1.	**von Bismarck**, Prince Otto	305	September 1, 1884

SIMULTANEOUS AWARD OF BOTH THE POUR LE MÉRITE ORDER AND THE 50 YEAR JUBILEE CROWN

Table V

	Name	Entry	Date
1.	**von Berg**, Count Friedrich Wilhelm Rembert (Russian)	48	January 18, 1865

PERCENTAGES OF TOTAL AWARDS OF THE POUR LE MÉRITE ORDER BY NATIONALITY

1861 - 1888

Table VI

	Nationality	Number Awarded	Percentage
1.	Prussia	259	84.64%
2.	Russia	29	9.47
3.	Austria	3	0.98
4.	Baden	3	0.98
5.	Bavaria	3	0.98
6.	Hesse	2	0.65
7.	Italy	2	0.65
8.	Saxony	2	0.65
9.	England	1	0.33
10.	Rumania	1	0.33
11.	Sicily	1	0.33

AWARDS OF THE GRAND CROSS AND STAR OF THE POUR LE MÉRITE ORDER

Table VII

	Name	Entry	Date
1.	**Friedrich Wilhelm,** Crown Prince, of Prussia	100 276*	September 20, 1866 September 1, 1873
2.	**Friedrich Karl,** Prince of Prussia	101 277*	September 20, 1866 September 1, 1873
3.	**Wilhelm I.,** King of Prussia	168	November 11, 1866
4.	**Alexander II.,** Emperor of Russia	286	April 24, 1878
5.	**von Moltke,** Field Marshal Hellmuth	302	March 8, 1879

* Awarded the Oakleaves to the Grand Cross and Star of the Pour le Mérite Order.

TOTAL AWARDS OF THE POUR LE MÉRITE ORDER TO RECIPIENTS IN PRUSSIAN UNITS BY WILHELM I.

1861 - 1888

Table VIII

A

I. Army	8
II. Army	8
III. Army	1
I. Army Corps	2
II. Army Corps	2
III. Army Corps	2
IV. Army Corps	1
V. Army Corps	2
VI. Army Corps	2
VII. Army Corps	1
VIII. Army Corps	1
IX. Army Corps	1
X. Army Corps	2
XIV. Army Corps	2
XV. Army Corps	1
3rd Army Inspection Unit	1
4th Army Inspection Unit	1
2nd Artillery Inspection Unit	1

B

3rd Brandenburg Artillery Regiment	3
3rd Brandenburg Engineer Regiment	1
Brandenburg Fusilier Regiment	3
2nd Brandenburg Grenadier Regt.	1
3rd Brandenburg Infantry Regiment	1
4th Brandenburg Infantry Regiment	3
5th Brandenburg Infantry Regiment	2
6th Brandenburg Infantry Regiment	1
7th Brandenburg Infantry Regiment	2
1st Brandenburg Leib Grenadier Rgt.	4

C

Cavalry Corps, I Army	1
Cavalry Division, II. Army	1
4th Cavalry Division	1
Combined Army Corps	3

1st East Prussian Grenadier Regiment	1
4th East Prussian Grenadier Regiment	1
7th East Prussian Infantry Regiment	1
Elbe, Army of the	1
3rd Engineer Inspection Unit	1

F

9th Field Artillery Brigade	1
10th Field Artillery Brigade	1
6th Fortress Inspection Unit	1

G

Garde du Corps	3
Garde Artillery Brigade	3
Garde Field Artillery Regiment	4
1st Garde Cavalry Brigade	1
Garde Fusilier Regiment	2
Garde Grenadier Regiment	1
4th Garde Grenadier Regiment	1
1st Garde Infantry Brigade	1
2nd Garde Infantry Brigade	1
2nd Garde Infantry Division	1
1st Garde Infantry Regiment	5
2nd Garde Infantry Regiment	3
3rd Garde Infantry Regiment	5
4th Garde Infantry Regiment	2

H

Hanover Field Artillery Regiment	2
Holstein Infantry Regiment	1

I

1st Infantry Brigade	1
2nd Infantry Brigade	1
3rd Infantry Brigade	1
7th Infantry Brigade	1
9th Infantry Brigade	1
10th Infantry Brigade	3
11th Infantry Brigade	2
12th Infantry Brigade	1
13th Infantry Brigade	1
14th Infantry Brigade	1
15th Infantry Brigade	1

17th Infantry Brigade	1
19th Infantry Brigade	1
21st Infantry Brigade	1
22nd Infantry Brigade	1
25th Infantry Brigade	1
26th Infantry Brigade	2
27th Infantry Brigade	1
28th Infantry Brigade	1
29th Infantry Brigade	1
30th Infantry Brigade	1
31st Infantry Brigade	1
35th Infantry Brigade	1
37th Infantry Brigade	1
38th Infantry Brigade	1
39th Infantry Brigade	1
40th Infantry Brigade	1
1st Infantry Division	1
3rd Infantry Division	2
5th Infantry Division	2
6th Infantry Division	3
7th Infantry Division	2
9th Infantry Division	2
10th Infantry Division	2
11th Infantry Division	1
12th Infantry Division	1
13th Infantry Division	1
14th Infantry Division	2
15th Infantry Division	2
16th Infantry Division	1
17th Infantry Division	1
18th Infantry Division	1
20th Infantry Division	1
22nd Infantry Division	1

L
2nd Landwehr Hussar Regiment	1
2nd Light Cavalry Brigade	1
3rd Light Cavalry Brigade	1
Litthau Dragoon Regiment	1

M
Maas, Army of the	1
Magdeburg Fusilier Regiment	1
Magdeburg Hussar Regiment	1
1st Magdeburg Infantry Regiment	1
2nd Magdeburg Infantry Regiment	2
4th Magdeburg Artillery Brigade	1
Main, Army of the	2

N
1st Nieder-Silesian Infantry Regiment	1
2nd Nieder-Silesian Infantry Regiment	1
3rd Nieder-Silesian Infantry Regiment	1

P
Pomeranian Field Artillery Regiment	1
1st Pomeranian Grenadier Regiment	1
1st Posen Infantry Regiment	5
3rd Posen Infantry Regiment	1

R
II. Reserve Army Corps	1
1st Reserve Division	1
3rd Reserve Division	1
1st Rhine Infantry Regiment	1
2nd Rhine Infantry Regiment	1
Rhine Uhlan Regiment	1
Royal Prussian Navy	1

S
Schleswig-Holstein Uhlan Regiment	1
Silesian Curassier Regiment	1
2nd Silesian Dragoon Regiment	3
Silesian Field Artillery Regiment	1
Silesian Fusilier Regiment	2
1st Silesian Grenadier Regiment	1
2nd Silesian Grenadier Regiment	1
South, Army of the	1

T
1st Thuringen Infantry Regiment	1
2nd Thuringen Infantry Regiment	1
3rd Thuringen Infantry Regiment	1
4th Thuringen Infantry Regiment	1

U
Unit Unknown	1

W
West Prussian Curassier Regiment	2
West Prussian Uhlan Regiment	3
2nd West Prussian Grenadier Regiment	2
Westphalian Field Artillery Regiment	1
Westphalian Fusilier Regiment	1
7th Westphalian Engineer Battalion	1
1st Westphalian Infantry Regiment	1
2nd Westphalian Infantry Regiment	3
3rd Westphalian Infantry Regiment	1
5th Westphalian Infantry Regiment	4

6th Westphalian Infantry Regiment	2	**Miscellaneous Unit**	
8th Westphalian Infantry Regiment	1	8th Division	1

TOTAL AWARDS OF THE POUR LE MÉRITE ORDER TO RECIPIENTS IN NON-PRUSSIAN UNITS BY WILHELM I.

1861 - 1888

Table IX

AUSTRIA		**SAXONY**	
VI. Austrian Army Corps	1	XII. Saxon Army Corps	1
King of Belgium Infantry Regiment	1		
		RUSSIA	
BADEN		VIII. Russian Army Corps	1
Baden Field Division	1	Caucasus Grenadier Division	1
1st Baden Leib Grenadier Regiment	1	Caucasus-Turkish Border Corps	1
		Guard Corps	2
BAVARIA		16th Infantry Division	1
I. Bavarian Army Corps	1	5th Kaluga Infantry Regiment	1
II. Bavarian Army Corps	1	St. Petersburg Grenadier Regiment	1
2nd Bavarian Division	1	* * *	
HESSE			
25th Hesse Division	2		

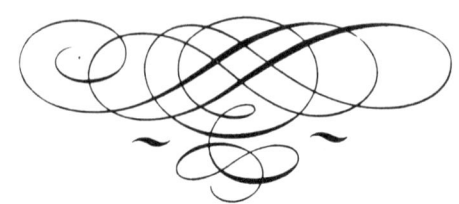

Additional Notes:

CHAPTER VIII

Friedrich III.

1888

ith the death of Wilhelm I. on March 9, 1888, the Crown of Prussia and the German Empire went to his only son, Crown Prince Friedrich Wilhelm, who became Friedrich III. and the eighth King of Prussia.

Friedrich III. was 57 years old when ascending the Prussian and German Empire throne. His upbringing was in the best tradition of a Prince of the House of Hohenzollern. At the age of ten he was commissioned a Second Lieutenant in the 1st Garde Regiment and was trained from that moment on to be a professional soldier. He was to be a proficient soldier; however, the military was not the profession he would have entered had he been given the opportunity to choose.

Friedrich III. was, basically, a peace loving man. He combined all the best characteristics of his parents. He was goon natured, and had his father's excellent presence and his mother's enlightened outlook at life. He was a handsome man and stood a good head taller than his father. He was well built with head of golden blond hair and deep blue eyes.

At the insistence of his mother, Queen Augusta, Friedrich was the first prince of the Hohenzollern dynasty to receive a university education. While at the University of Bonn he studied literature, history, law and English. The atmosphere seemed to agree with Friedrich, and his exposure to a somewhat more democratic life outside the royal court began to awaken a sense of liberalism that was to be with him the rest of his life. However, he had obvious weaknesses which were also to plague him. Friedrich was a chronic worrier and subject to periods of intense depression. He was easily discouraged, lacked a strong drive and had little stamina. His respect for authority, fowever, was a deep part of his personality.

During the summer of 1855, on a trip to England to visit Queen Victoria and Prince Albert, Friedrich met and fell in love with their eldest daughter, Victoria, the Princess Royal. Only six days after they met, Friedrich asked for her hand in marriage. Queen Victoria and Prince Albert approved and gave their consent. The marriage of the Crown Prince of Prussia and the Princess Royal of England took place on January 25, 1858.

As the years passed Friedrich III. continued to pursue his military career. During the wars of the 1860's and especially during the 1870-1871 Franco-Prussian War, he displayed an excellent military promise of outstanding leadership. However, he was denied any real opportunity to take an active part in the Prussian government and finally withdrew from the effort in frustration.

In late winter of 1886, Friedrich developed a persistent hoarseness that eventually became so bad that throat specialists were called in. They discovered a small growth on his vocal cords. Treatment began immediately and more specialists were summoned. There was no response to the harsh treatments the Crown Prince was subjected to. In early November 1887, it was determined that Friedrich had cancer of the larynx and it became only a matter of time before death would take him.

Friedrich received the sad news of his father's death while staying in San Remo in Italy. He and his wife were vacationing there to escape the hard, cold German winter. By this time the Crown Prince could not even speak.

The new German Emperor and King of Prussia, Friedrich III., returned to Berlin on March 11, 1888, but was so ill he was immediately confined to bed. During the following three months his condition continued to deteriorate.

Death finally claimed Friedrich III. on June 15, 1888. He had reigned as Emperor of Germany and King of Prussia only 99 days. One wonders what changes in history would have taken place had Friedrich III. lived. He was succeeded by his son Crown Prince Wilhelm who was to become the last Emperor of Germany and King of Prussia.

Available records do not indicate that Friedrich III. made any awards of the Pour le Mérite Order.

* * *

Additional Notes:

APPENDIX I

A translation of the famous "To My People" appeal made by Friedrich Wilhelm III. on March 20, 1813, which appeared in the Silesian Newspaper number 34, is as follows:

His Majesty the King has with His Majesty the Emperor of All Russia concluded an offensive and defensive alliance.

To My People

With the commencement of the war it is required that my people, as for all true Germans, be held accountable for its success. Previously it has been clear that the eyes of Europe have been blind.

We are under French domination. Because of the war, a profound blow has been struck us and we have not been granted the blessings of peace. The skill of the state, the strength of the land, will be highly tested while the strongholds of the enemy remain. The freedom of individual action and thereby the source of wealth and livelihood will stop. The land is being plundered and impoverished. I hope to lighten the severe obligations binding my people and to finally convince the French Emperor that it is to his own advantage to leave alone the independence of Prussia. Though it is my intention to do this peacefully and thereby thwart the treachery of the Emperors treaties, we are obliged not to be slow in preparing for war. The moment has come in which all deception must cease.

Brandenburgers, Prussians, Silesians, Pomeranians and Litthauers! The beginning of the war was not honorable and for seven years we have suffered and I have shared the same sad lot as you to that end. Call to mind another time, of the Great Elector, the great Friedrich. Continue to remember their greatness and what was gained by our forefathers through bloody fighting: freedom of conscience, honor, independence, trade, arts and sciences. Remember the great example of a strong united Russia, remember the Spanish, remember the Portugese. I myself remember these people for their greatness. For they have faced a strong enemy and drawn out the battle to win the victory. Call to mind the heroism of the Swiss and Dutch.

Great sacrifices shall come to be made by all, because the undertaking is great and the number of our enemy is not small. We have learned so many lessons, that for the fatherland, for your king and from foreign occupation, your sons, and your last strength should be dedicated that we shall be free of foreigners. Trusting in God and the strength and courage of our allies, we will be victorious. But we, as Prussians and Germans, must cease our quarreling if our sacrifices are to insure the success of our just cause and bring us victory.

I am determined that the battle we are to undergo for our independence and our prosperity shall be the last. There is no other way out but an honorable peace or a glorious destruction. I am confident and will proceed with honor and dignity, for as long as I live I will not dishonor Prussia and the German people. This alone we must have confidence in. God and our strong will in our righteous cause will award us victory bringing a glorious peace and auspicious future.

Breslau, 17 March 1813. /s/ *Friedrich Wilhelm.*

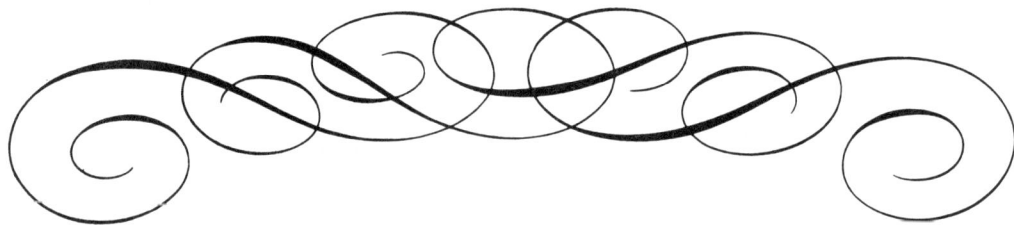

APPENDIX II

A translation of special supplement in the Linz Newspaper edition number 73, dated 1813, which first appeared in the Prague Newspaper edition number 107, dated 1813, where Army Commander, General Blücher announced the Prussian victory at Katzbach.

The Royal Prussian General von Blücher has announced from his headquarters at Löwenberg on 1 September the following daily order:

Silesia has been freed of the enemy. Your bravery, soldiers of the Russian and Prussian armies under my command, your efforts and persistence, your endurance at striking at the enemy, have driven him back, and we thank the Hand of Providence.

At the battle of Katzbach, the enemy supply line was broken and by your display of courage, endeavor, and lightening speed broke the enemy. You showered them with musket fire and without breaking stride your bayonet routed them down the Niesse and Katzbach.

Since the rains have come and the river has risen, in the mud you have brought your revenge.

You have endured the lack of food, the endless road, the wagons that impede you, cold, wet, self denied, you have battled and succeeded. You have not complained at this strained and torturous cause against the enemy. I have come to give thanks to you for the high and outstanding qualities. Only soldiers united in a common cause can succeed as you have.

In your hands are 103 cannon, 250 ammunition wagons, an enemy military field hospital, a mobile forge, and a large number of flour wagons, as well as, 1 Division General, 2 Brigade Generals, a large number of Colonels, Staff and other officers, 18,000 prisoners, 2 Eagles and other trophies. The remainder of the enemy faced you at the battle at Katzbach and in the face of your attack and the sight of your bayonets, he became fearful and could suffer no more.

The streets and fields between the Katzbach and the Bober have conveyed this sign to the fearful and fleeing enemy.

Let us give thanks to the Lord of the Heavenly Hosts, who has aided us against the enemy, sing a hymn of praise and proclaim our service to God for having given us this glorious victory. Three bonfires will dedicate the hour you devote to prayers. At that time, remember a new enemy will soon be upon us.

Headquarters, Löwenburg, 1 September, 1813.
v. Blücher

APPENDIX III

RECIPIENTS OF THE OAKLEAVES
TO THE POUR LE MÉRITE ORDER
BETWEEN 1813 AND 1888

	Name	Chapter	Entry	Date
	1813			
1.	von Yorck, Johann David Ludwig	V-2	790	Jun. 10, 1813
2.	von Zeiten, Wieprecht Hans Karl	V-2	849	Sep. 5, 1813
3.	von Bülow, Friedrich Wilhelm	V-2	851	Sep. 6, 1813
4.	von Oppen, Adolf Friedrich	V-2	852	Sep. 6, 1813
5.	von dem Knesebeck, Karl Friedrich	V-2	988	Oct. 19, 1813
6.	von Thüman, Heinrich August	V-2	989	Oct. 21, 1813
7.	von Borstell, Karl Leopold Ludwig	V-2	991	Oct. 21, 1813
8.	von Klüx, Friedrich Karl Leopold	V-2	1225	Dec. 8, 1813
9.	von Grolman, Karl Wilhelm Georg	V-2	1226	Dec. 8, 1813
10.	von Horn, Heinrich Wilhelm	V-2	1227	Dec. 8, 1813
11.	von Wohlen-Jürgass, Alexander Georg	V-2	1228	Dec. 8, 1813
12.	von Borcke, Karl August Ferdinand	V-2	1229	Dec. 8, 1813
	1814			
13.	von Kleist, Friedrich Emilius	V-2	1370	Mar. 31, 1814
14.	Niedhardt von Gneisenau, Wilhelm	V-2	1372	Mar. 31, 1814
15.	von Hake, Karl Georg Albrecht	V-2	1379	Apr. 3. 1814
16.	von der Goltz, Count Karl Friedrich	V-2	1514	Apr. 13, 1814
17.	von Clausewitz, Vollmar Karl Friedrich	V-2	1664	May 31, 1814
18.	von Schmidt, Johann Heinrich Otto	V-2	1646	May 31, 1814
19.	Hiller von Gaertringen, Frhr. Johann	V-2	1647	May 31, 1814
20.	von Loebell, Friedrich Ernst	V-2	1650	May 31, 1814
21.	von Rauch, Johann Gustaf Georg	V-2	1656	Jun. 3 1814
22.	von Röder, Friedrich E.	V-2	1689	Sep. 7, 1814
	1815			
23.	von Below, Theodor Werner Christian	V-2	2293	Jan. 1, 1815
24.	von Thile II., Heinrich Adolf Eduard	V-2	2306	Jun. 24, 1815
25.	von Holtzendorff, Karl Friedrich	V-2	2317	Oct. 2, 1815
26.	von Steinmetz, Karl Friedrich	V-2	2319	Oct. 2, 1815
27.	von Lützow, Frhr. Ludwig Adolf Wilhelm	V-2	2321	Oct. 2, 1815
28.	Stach von Goltzheim, Engel Ludwig	V-2	2327	Oct. 2, 1815
29.	von Rohr, Karl Heinrich Christian	V-2	2328	Oct. 2, 1815
30.	von der Osten, Otto Albrecht Philipp	V-2	2331	Oct. 2, 1815
31.	von Tippelskirch, Ernst Ludwig	V-2	2335	Oct. 2, 1815
32.	von Krafft, Karl Thilo Ludwig	V-2	2334	Oct. 2, 1815

33.	**von Kemphen,** Johann Karl Jakob	V-2	2336	Oct. 2, 1815
34.	**von Brandenstein,** Friedrich August Karl	V-2	2337	Oct. 2, 1815
35.	**von Losthin,** Michael Heinrich	V-2	2341	Oct. 2, 1815
36.	**von Sydow,** Johann Joachim Friedrich	V-2	2342	Oct. 2, 1815
37.	**von Hedemann,** August Georg Friedrich	V-2	2345	Oct. 2, 1815
38.	**Beier,** Johann Peter Paul	V-2	2346	Oct. 2, 1815
39.	**Krausenek,** Johann Wilhelm	V-2	2364	Oct. 2, 1815
40.	**von Funck,** Friedrich Wilhelm	V-2	2367	Nov. 3, 1815

1816

41.	**von Zepelin,** Konstantin Gottlieb	V-2	2372	Jan. 14, 1816
42.	**von Clausewitz,** Wilhelm	V-2	2376	Jun. 18, 1816

1831

43.	**von Canitz und Dallwitz,** Frhr. Karl	V-2	2442	Oct. 11, 1831
44.	**von Pfuel,** Ernst Adolf Heinrich	V-2	2444	Dec. 31, 1831

1848

45.	**von Wrangel,** Friedrich Heinrich	VI	8	Sep. 13, 1848

1849

46.	**von der Groeben,** Count Karl	VI	25	Jul. 27 1849

1864

47.	**Friedrich Karl,** Prince of Prussia	VII	2	Feb. 27, 1864

1866

48.	**Friedrich Wilhelm,** Crown Prince of Prussia	VII	55	Aug. 3, 1866
49.	**Wilhelm I.,** King of Prussia	VII	57	Aug. 4, 1866
50.	**von Blumenthal.** Karl Konstantin	VII	71	Sep. 17, 1866
51.	**von Manstein,** Gustaf Albert	VII	113	Sep. 20, 1866
52.	**von Canstein,** Frhr. Philipp Christian	VII	155	Sep. 20, 1866
53.	**von Groeben,** August Karl Friedrich	VII	157	Sep. 20, 1866
54.	**von der Goltz,** Frhr. Eduard Kuno	VII	161	Sep. 20, 1866

1870

55.	**von Wrangel,** Frhr. Friedrich Wilhelm	VII	176	Dec. 5, 1870
56.	**Friedrich Franz,** Mecklenburg-Schwerin	VII	178	Dec. 5, 1870
57.	**von Wittich,** Friedrich Wilhelm Ludwig	VII	179	Dec. 5, 1870
58.	**Albert,** Crown Prince of Saxony	VII	180	Dec. 6, 1870
59.	**von Manteuffel,** Frhr. Karl Rochus Edwin	VII	183	Dec. 24, 1870
60.	**von Voigts-Rhetz,** Konstans Bernhard	VII	184	Dec. 31, 1870
61.	**von Alvensleben,** Konstantin Reimar	VII	185	Dec. 31, 1870
62.	**von Wedell,** Richard Georg	VII	186	Dec. 31, 1870

1871

63.	**von Kameke,** Arnold Karl Georg	VII	188	Jan. 2, 1871
64.	**von Kummer,** Ferdinand Rudolf	VII	190	Jan. 12, 1871
65.	**von Werder,** Karl Friedrich Wilhelm	VII	191	Jan. 17, 1871
66.	**von Stiehle,** Gustaf Wilhelm Friedrich	VII	182	Jan. 18, 1871
67.	**von Buddenbrock,** Baron Karl Gustaf	VII	193	Jan. 18, 1871

68.	von **Stülpnagel**, Louis Ferdinand Wolf	VII	194	Jan. 18, 1871
69.	von **Wulffen**, Georg Otto	VII	195	Jan. 18, 1871
70.	von **Barnekow**, Frhr. Christof Gottlieb	VII	203	Jan. 20, 1871
71.	von **Leszcynski**, Stanislaus Paul Eduard	VII	204	Feb. 5, 1871
72.	von **Zastrow**, Adolf Friedrich Heinrich	VII	206	Feb. 5, 1871
73.	von **Fransecky**, Eduard Friedrich	VII	207	Feb. 5, 1871
74.	von **Sperling**, Ernst Karl Oskar	VII	208	Feb. 5, 1871
75.	von **Kirchbach**, Hugo Ewald	VII	211	Feb. 16, 1871
76.	von **Moltke**, Count Hellmuth Karl	VII	214	Feb. 17, 1871
77.	von **Witzendorff**, Karl Friedrich Wilhelm	VII	217	Feb. 24, 1871
78.	von **der Burg**, Ernst Engelbert Oskar	VII	218	Feb. 24, 1871
79.	von **Kraatz-Koschlau**, Friedrich Wilhelm	VII	224	Feb. 28, 1871
80.	von **Cranach**, Ludwig Otto Lukas	VII	225	Feb. 28, 1871
81.	von **Dieringshofen**, Carl Friedrich	VII	226	Feb. 28, 1871
82.	von **Hartmann**, Ernst Matthias Andreas	VII	234	Mar. 3, 1871
83.	von **Lewinski**, Eduard Julius Ludwig	VII	235	Mar. 3, 1871
84.	von **Podbielski**, Theophil Eugen Anton	VII	239	Mar. 5, 1871
85.	**Albrecht**, Prince of Prussia	VII	240	Mar. 10, 1871
86.	von **Mertens**, August Ferdinand	VII	241	Mar. 24, 1871
87.	von **Schlotheim**, Frhr. Karl Ludwig	VII	243	Jun. 15, 1871
88.	von **Treskow**, Herman Heinrich Theodor	VII	244	Jun. 16, 1871
89.	von **Steinmetz**, Karl Friedrich	VII	245	Jun. 16, 1871
90.	**August**, Prince of Württemberg	VII	247	Jun. 16, 1871
91.	**Alexander II.**, Emperor of Russia	VII	251	Dec. 8, 1871
	1872			
92.	von **Pape**, August Wilhelm Alexander	VII	255	Mar. 22, 1872
	1873			
93.	von **Wartensleben**, Count Wilhelm Herman	VII	273	Jan. 19, 1873
	1877			
94.	**Michail Nikolaieovich**, Grand Duke of Russia	VII	280	Nov. 28, 1877
95.	**Nikolai Nikolaieovich**, Grand Duke of Russia	VII	281	Dec. 16, 1877

APPENDIX IV

RECIPIENTS OF THE 50 YEAR GOLDEN CROWN TO THE POUR LE MÉRITE ORDER UNTIL 1888

The volume, chapter and entry number indicate when the recipient was awarded the Pour le Mérite Order. The date shows when the recipient received the 50 Year Jubilee Golden Crown to the Pour le Mérite Order.

	Name	Vol	Chap	Entry	Crown Date
	1844				
1.	von Zieten, Weiprecht Hans Karl	I	IV	242	Jul. 18, 1844
2.	von Schöler, Moritz Ludwig Wilhelm	I	IV	276	Jul. 18, 1844
3.	von Pückler, Count Maximilian Erdmann	I	IV	283	Jul. 18, 1844
4.	Henckel von Donnersmark, Count Karl	I	IV	291	Jul. 18, 1844
5.	von der Malsburg, Frhr. Christian K.	I	IV	299	Jul. 18, 1844
6.	Schmied, Friedrich	I	IV	310	Jul. 18, 1844
7.	von Corvin-Wiersbitzki, August F.	I	IV	315	Jul. 18, 1844
8.	von Beckendorff, Hans Friedrich	I	IV	329	Jul. 18, 1844
9.	von Klüx, Franz Karl Friedreich Ernst	I	IV	335	Jul. 18, 1844
10.	von Waldow, Achatius Wilhelm August	I	IV	363	Jul. 18, 1844
11.	Heidenreich, Heinrich Leopold	I	IV	434	Jul. 18, 1844
12.	von Lindenau, Adam Friedrich August	I	IV	474	Jul. 18, 1844
13.	von Normann, Ernst Ludwig	I	IV	499	Jul. 18, 1844
14.	von Graevenitz, Heinrich Ernst Hans	I	IV	555	Jul. 18, 1844
15.	von Bandemer, Ernst Friedrich Wilhelm	I	IV	611	Jul. 18, 1844
16.	von Jaski (Köhn), Karl Friedrich	I	IV	629	Jul. 18, 1844
17.	Jochens, Gottfried Wilhelm	I	IV	672	Jul. 18, 1844
18.	von Berg, Karl Friedrich Wilhelm	I	IV	720	Jul. 18, 1844
19.	von Reisewitz, Frhr. Gottlob Johann	I	IV	724	Jul. 18, 1844
20.	Gans Edler Herr zu Puttlitz, Kaspar	I	IV	737	Jul. 18, 1844
21.	von Lindern, Jodokus	I	IV	738	Jul. 18, 1844
22.	von Schallern, Hans Christof	I	IV	740	Jul. 18, 1844
23.	Edler von Paschwitz, Johann Gottlieb	I	IV	746	Jul. 18, 1844
24.	von Akiewitz, Franz Xaver	I	IV	763	Jul. 18, 1844
25.	von der Schulenburg-Blumberg, Count C.	I	IV	793	Jul. 18, 1844
26.	von Kottulinsky, Ernst Daniel Gottlob	I	IV	809	Jul. 18, 1844
27.	Fausser, Johann Heinrich	I	IV	814	Jul. 18, 1844
28.	Igelström,* Count Alexander	I	IV	826	Jul. 18, 1844
29.	Tolstoi,* Count Peter Alexandrovich	I	IV	830	Jul. 18, 1844
30.	von Wallmoden, Count Ludwig Georg	I	IV	839	Jul. 18, 1844

31.	von Belling, Karl Friedrich Bernhard	I	IV	840	Jul. 18, 1844
32.	von Koschembar, Ernst Friedrich	I	IV	848	Jul. 18, 1844
33.	von Romberg, Konrad Philipp	I	IV	860	Jul. 18, 1844
34.	von Chartron, Ferdinand Heinrich	I	IV	867	Jul. 18, 1844
35.	von Manteuffel, Friedrich August	I	IV	868	Jul. 18, 1844
36.	von Haas, Peter Franz	I	IV	872	Jul. 18, 1844
37.	von Ledebur, Heinrich Friedrich	I	IV	886	Jul. 18, 1844
38.	von Sohr, Friedrich Georg Ludwig	I	IV	967	Jul. 18, 1844
39.	Gortschakov,* Prince Andrei Ivanovich	I	IV	987	Jul. 18, 1844

1845

40.	von Steinmetz, Moritz Christof	I	IV	941	Jan. 16, 1845
41.	von der Schulenburg, Friedrich F.	I	IV	985	Apr. 12, 1845
42.	von Kathen, Johann Gottlieb Christian	I	IV	658	Jun. 26, 1845

1847

43.	von Schlotheim, Friedrich Wilhelm	I	IV	266	Mar. 6, 1847

1857

44.	von Massow, Heinrich Erdmann Gotthard	I	V-1	64	Jan. 13, 1857
45.	von Stutterheim, Friedrich Wilhelm	I	V-1	81	Jan. 13, 1857
46.	von Rotberg, Wilhelm Emilius Heinrich	I	V-1	133	Jan. 13, 1857
47.	von Wedell, Heinrich Kaspar	I	V-1	157	Jan. 13, 1857
48.	von Rexin, Ludwig Bogislaf Nikolaus	I	V-1	182	Jan. 13, 1857
49.	von Tiedewitz, Friedrich Wilhelm	I	V-1	241	Jan. 13, 1857
50.	von Obernitz, Moritz Karl Heinrich	I	V-1	256	Jan. 13, 1857
51.	von Wedell, Karl Friedrich Heinrich	I	V-1	295	Jan. 13, 1857
52.	von Ostau, Friedrich Egidius	I	V-1	333	Jan. 13, 1857
53.	von Wrangel, Friedrich Heinrich	I	V-1	334	Jan. 13, 1857
54.	zu Dohna-Wartenberg-Schlobitten, Count	I	V-1	335	Jan. 13, 1857
55.	Gebhardt, Wilhelm Karl	I	V-1	344	Jan. 13, 1857
56.	von Cosel, Karl Wilhelm Gustaf	I	V-1	354	Jan. 13, 1857
57.	von Sandrert, Karl Wilhelm Emanuel	I	V-1	355	Jan. 13, 1857
58.	von Siegroth, Adolf Rudolf	I	V-1	359	Jan. 13, 1857
59.	von Petersdorff, Johann Karl	I	V-1	396	Jan. 13, 1857
60.	von Bülow, Friedrich Wilhelm Arweg	I	V-1	398	Jan. 13, 1857
61.	von Brandenstein, Friedrich August	I	V-1	399	Jan. 13, 1857
62.	von Flemming, Julius Friedrich Gottlob	I	V-1	444	Jan. 13, 1857
63.	von der Wolffsburg, Josef Sylvius	I	V-1	509	Jan. 13, 1957
64.	von Prittwitz, Moritz Heinrich	I	V-1	511	Jan. 13, 1857
65.	von Wedell, Count Ernst Ludwig August	I	V-1	512	Jan. 13, 1857
66.	von Lundt, Friedrich Wilhelm	I	V-1	520	Jan. 13, 1857
67.	von Hirschfeld, Karl Alexander Adolf	I	V-1	527	Jan. 13, 1857
68.	de Constant Rebecque de Villars, August	I	V-1	531	Jan. 13, 1857
69.	von Eberhardt, Friedrich Wilhelm Magnus	I	V-1	597	Jan. 13, 1857
70.	von Hedemann, August Georg Friedrich	I	V-1	607	Jan. 13, 1857
71.	von der Groeber, Count Karl	I	V-1	608	Jan. 13, 1857
72.	du Rosey, Adolf Ernst	I	V-1	621	Jan. 13, 1857
73.	Reuter, Johann Wilhelm Ferdinand	I	V-1	630	Jan. 13, 1857
74.	zu Eulenburg, Count Albrecht Ludwig	I	V-1	641	Jan. 13, 1857
75.	von Steinwehr, Christian Ferdinand	I	V-1	644	Jan. 13, 1857
76.	von Bremen,* Karl Ivanovich	I	V-1	593	Dec. 12, 1857

1858

77.	Sabir,* Josef Josefovich	I	V-1	73	May 18, 1858
78.	von Tornow (Turnau), Ferdinand	I	V-1	132	May 18, 1858
79.	Scieptschenko(v),* Peter Ivanovich	I	V-1	152	May 18, 1858
80.	Jermolov,* Alexei Petrovich	I	V-1	167	May 18, 1858
81.	Sakrevski,* Arseni Andreieovich	I	V-1	208	May 18, 1858
82.	Tshetvertinski,* Prince Boris Anton	I	V-1	276	May 18, 1858
83.	von Bennigsen,* Frhr. Adam Johann	I	V-1	278	May 18, 1858
84.	Friderici,* Herman Karlovich	I	V-1	281	May 18, 1858
85.	Nauendorff,* Gustaf Viliamovich	I	V-1	436	May 18, 1858
86.	Begitshev,* Dmitri Nikititsh	I	V-1	467	May 18, 1858
87.	Pegrebov,* Alexander Andreieovich	I	V-1	468	May 18, 1858
88.	Olenin,* Vladimir Ivanovich	I	V-1	476	May 18, 1858
89.	Rshenskoi,* Konstantin Vladimirovich	I	V-1	477	May 18, 1858
90.	Radulovich,* Dmitri Gavrilovich	I	V-1	478	May 18, 1858
91.	Tenner,* Karl Ivanovich	I	V-1	498	May 18, 1858
92.	Desbout,* Jossif Lvovich	I	V-1	501	May 18, 1858
93.	Dozenkov,* Ivan Vassilieovich	I	V-1	549	May 18, 1858
94.	Shivkovovich,* Iliä Petrovich	I	V-1	563	May 18, 1858
95.	Gorgoli,* Ivan Savvich	I	V-1	573	May 18, 1858
96.	Burnashev,* Peter Alexieieovich	I	V-1	577	May 18, 1858
97.	Gunderstrup,* Karl Ivanovich	I	V-1	581	May 18, 1858
98.	Loshkarev,* Alexei Sergeieovich	I	V-1	582	May 18, 1858
99.	Rashevski,* Alexander Jakovleovich	I	V-1	583	May 18, 1858
100.	Chovrin,* Alexander Lvovich	I	V-1	588	May 18, 1858
101.	Lupadin,* Nikolai Antonovich	I	V-1	589	May 18, 1858
102.	Schele II,* Kyrill Chrestianovich	II	V-2	2424	May 18, 1858

1862

103.	von Wnuck, Karl Wilhelm	I	V-1	656	Jan. 9, 1862
104.	von Uttenhoven, Philipp Friedrich	I	V-1	657	Jan. 9, 1862
105.	von Schack, Hans Wilhelm	I	V-1	693	Jan. 9, 1862
106.	Hintzmann, Karl Ludwig Wilhelm	I	V-1	698	Jan. 9, 1862
107.	von Massow, Karl Ludwig Ferdinand	I	V-1	722	Jan. 9, 1862
108.	von Uthmann, Rudolf Gottlieb	I	V-1	724	Jan. 9, 1862
109.	von Strantz, Karl Adolf Ferdinand	II	V-2	730	Jan. 9, 1862
110.	von Rudorff, Wilhelm Heinrich	II	V-2	732	Jan. 9, 1862
111.	von Szerdahelyi, Karl Adolf Eduard	II	V-2	735	Jan. 9, 1862
112.	Westphal, Heinrich Ernst Adolf	II	V-2	736	Jan. 9, 1862
113.	Dallmer, Karl Friedrich Franz	II	V-2	787	Jan. 9, 1862
114.	Heuduch, Heinrich Gottlieb Konrad	II	V-2	788	Jan. 9, 1862
115.	von Hobe, August Johann Ludwig Elias	II	V-2	789	Jan. 9, 1862
116.	von Lupinski, Vinzentius Ferrerius	II	V-2	810	Jan. 9, 1862
117.	von Stülpnagel, George Karl Leonhard	II	V-2	828	Jan. 9, 1862
118.	von Dunker, Friedrich Wilhelm	II	V-2	829	Jan. 9, 1862
119.	von Kalckreuth, August Friedrich	II	V-2	2381	Jan. 9, 1862

1863

120.	Stsherbinin,* Alexander Andreieovich	II	V-2	756	Jan. 22, 1863
121.	Obrutshev,* Vladimir Afanasseovich	II	V-2	759	Jan. 22, 1863
122.	Engelhart,* Anton Jevstafieovich	II	V-2	772	Jan. 22, 1863
123.	Raben,* Karl Ivanovich	II	V-2	779	Jan. 22, 1863
124.	Shabelski,* Ivan Petrovich	II	V-2	808	Jan. 22, 1863
125.	Nasimov,* Jevgeni Petrovich	II	V-2	879	Jan. 22, 1863

126.	Kisselev,* Pavel Dmitrieovich	II	V-2	936	Jan. 22, 1863
127.	von der Osten-Sacken,* Baron Dmitri	II	V-2	937	Jan. 22, 1863
128.	von Grotenhelm,* Maxim Maximovich	II	V-2	1004	Jan. 22, 1863
129.	Mikulin,* Sergei Ivanovich	II	V-2	1059	Jan. 22, 1863
130.	Frolov,* Peter Nikolaieovich	II	V-2	1088	Jan. 22, 1863
131.	Vielhorski,* Count Matbei Jureovich	II	V-2	1129	Jan. 22, 1863
132.	Messing,* Alexander Ivanovich	II	V-2	1151	Jan. 22, 1863
133.	Schubert,* Fedor Fedorovich	II	V-2	1196	Jan. 22, 1863
134.	Kronstein,* Gustaf Vassilieovich	II	V-2	1215	Jan. 22, 1863
135.	Le Coq, Karl August (Saxon)	II	V-2	1234	Jan. 22, 1863
136.	Pantshulidsev,* Alexander Alexeieovich	II	V-2	1243	Jan. 22, 1863
137.	von dem Bussche-Ippenburg,* Frhr. Karl	II	V-2	1270	Jan. 22, 1863
138.	Helfreich,* Igor Ivanovich	II	V-2	1290	Jan. 22, 1863
139.	Vilhelmov,* Pavel Fedorovich	II	V-2	1310	Jan. 22, 1863
140.	Menshikov,* Prince Alexander	II	V-2	1509	Jan. 22, 1863
141.	Glinka,* Grigori Nikolaieovich	II	V-2	1681	Jan. 22, 1863
142.	von Knorring,* Pontus Voldemar	II	V-2	2100	Mar. 22, 1863
143.	Bibikov,* Ilia Gavrileovich	II	V-2	908	Nov. 16, 1863

1864

144.	Panutin,* Fedor Sergieieovich	II	V-2	1817	Mar. 3, 1864
145.	Schmaltz, Johann Heinrich (Bavarian)	II	V-2	1526	Jun. 18, 1864
146.	Küpfer,* Heinrich Karl Wilhelm	II	V-2	1569	Jun. 18, 1864
147.	Hess, Heinrich (Austrian)	II	V-2	1595	Jun. 18, 1864
148.	Vratislav, Count Eugen (Austrian)	II	V-2	1596	Jun. 18, 1864
149.	Wood, Charles (British)	II	V-2	1662	Jun. 18, 1864
150.	de Maistre,* Count Rudolf Ossipovich	II	V-2	1910	Jun. 18, 1864
151.	von Fabecky,* Ferdinand Friedrich	II	V-2	2034	Jun. 18, 1864
152.	Fanshave,* Grigori Andreieovich	II	V-2	2085	Jun. 18, 1865
153.	Ulfsparre, Erik Georg (Swedish)	II	V-2	2143	Jun. 18, 1864
154.	von Pfuel, Ernst Adolf Heinrich	II	V-2	2292	Jun. 18, 1864
155.	Wachten,* Hans Otto	II	V-2	780	Oct. 25, 1864
156.	Sternhelm,* Alexander Vassilieovich	II	V-2	1003	Oct. 25, 1864
157.	von Korff,* Baron Nikolai Ivanovich	II	V-2	1389	Oct. 25, 1864
158.	Vikinski,* Ivan Michailovich	II	V-2	1466	Oct. 25, 1864
159.	Antonivski,* Anton Ivanovich	II	V-2	1498	Oct. 25, 1864
160.	Lechner,* Andrei Andreieovich	II	V-2	1515	Oct. 25, 1864
161.	Stroganov,* Baron Alexander	II	V-2	1556	Oct. 25, 1864
162.	Jushkov,* Vladimir Ivanovich	II	V-2	1564	Oct. 25, 1864
163.	von Salza,* Baron Roman Alexandrovich	II	V-2	1584	Oct. 25, 1864
164.	von Berg,* Karl Borissovich	II	V-2	1587	Oct. 25, 1864
165.	Dieiev,* Ivan Michailovich	II	V-2	1613	Oct. 25, 1864
166.	von Sievers,* Ivan Lavrentieovich	II	V-2	1665	Oct. 25, 1864
167.	Tshertov,* Pavel Apollonovich	II	V-2	1711	Oct. 25, 1864
168.	Melnikov,* Michail Ivanovich	II	V-2	1727	Oct. 25, 1864
169.	Sumarokov,* Sergei Pavlovich	II	V-2	1772	Oct. 25, 1864
170.	Bibikov,* Larion Michailovich	II	V-2	1774	Oct. 25, 1864
171.	Shipov,* Sergei Pavlovich	II	V-2	1802	Oct. 25, 1864
172.	Annenkov,* Nikolai Petrovich	II	V-2	1810	Oct. 25, 1864
173.	Bushen,* Christian Nikolaieovich	II	V-2	1903	Oct. 25, 1864
174.	Sacharshevski,* Jakob Vassilieovich	II	V-2	1931	Oct. 25, 1864
175.	Tishin,* Vassili Grigorieovich	II	V-2	1938	Oct. 25, 1864
176.	Deroshinski,* Vladimir Kosmish	II	V-2	2028	Oct. 25, 1864
177.	von Patkul,* Friedrich	II	V-2	2076	Oct. 25, 1864
178.	Timiriasev,* Ivan Semenovich	II	V-2	2084	Oct. 25, 1864

179.	**Stahn**,* Andrei Antonovich	II	V-2	2129	Oct. 25, 1864
180.	**Burmeister**,* Fedor Fedorovich	II	V-2	2289	Oct. 25, 1864

1865

181.	**von Berg**, Count Friedrich Wilhelm	II	VII	48	Jan. 18, 1865
182.	**von Kliest**,* Ewald Johann	II	V-2	1157	Nov. 16, 1865
183.	**Chvostovski**,* Nikolai Alexandrovich	II	V-2	1467	Nov. 16, 1865
184.	**Jermakov**,* Alexander Dmitrieovich	II	V-2	1780	Nov. 16, 1865
185.	**Klein**, Fedor Borissovich	II	V-2	1885	Nov. 16, 1865
186.	**Urussov**,* Prince Sergei Dmitrieovich	II	V-2	1906	Nov. 16, 1865
187.	**O'Rurk III.**,* Count Korneli	II	V-2	1996	Nov. 16, 1865
188.	**von Kahlen II.**,* Paul Bogdanovich	II	V-2	2103	Nov. 16, 1865
189.	**Pusin**,* Karl Karlovich	II	V-2	2137	Nov. 16, 1865

1866

190.	**Schulz**, Heinrich Christian (Hessian)	II	V-2	2362	Mar. 20, 1866

1867

191.	**Vonliarliarski**,* Ivan Andreieovich	II	V-2	1449	Mar. 9, 1867
192.	**Kobiakov**,* Ivan Nikolaieovich	II	V-2	1570	Mar. 9, 1867
193.	**Bibikov**,* Vassili Alexandrovich	II	V-2	1574	Mar. 9, 1867
194.	**Dsitshkanez**,* Adam Jakovleovich	II	V-2	1693	Mar. 9, 1867
195.	**Barishnikov**,* Peter Petrovich	II	V-2	1783	Mar. 9, 1867
196.	**Stremouchov**,* Alexander Sergieieovich	II	V-2	1799	Mar. 9, 1867
197.	**von Arpshofen**,* Baron Karl Karlovich	II	V-2	1813	Mar. 9, 1867
198.	**Muromzov**,* Alexander Matvieieovich	II	V-2	1864	Mar. 9, 1867
199.	**Velenin**,* Peter Alexandrovich	II	V-2	1905	Mar. 9, 1867
200.	**Shishkin**,* Pavel Sergieieovich	II	V-2	1909	Mar. 9, 1867
201.	**Reich**,* Ivan Ivanovich	II	V-2	1959	Mar. 9, 1867
202.	**Shishkov (Shishkin)**,* Peter Ivanovich	II	V-2	2130	Mar. 9, 1867
203.	**von der Hoven**,* Igor Christoforovich	II	V-2	2265	Mar. 9, 1867

1870

204.	**zu Ysenburg-Philippseich**, (Bavarian)	II	V-2	2398	Jan. 27, 1870
205.	**Gortshakov**,* Prince Sergei Dmitrieovich	II	V-2	1303	Mar. 24, 1870
206.	**Lermantov**,* Vladimir Nikolaieovich	II	V-2	1977	May 4, 1870

1871

207.	**Nekludov**,* Sergei Petrovich	II	V-2	1518	Apr. 18, 1871

1872

208.	**Bellegarde**, Count August (Austrian)	II	V-2	2402	Dec. 14, 1872

1879

209.	**von Reitzenstein**, Frhr. Karl	II	V-2	2439	Jan. 18, 1878

1881

210.	**von Seydlitz und Kurzbach**, Karl	II	V-2	2443	Sep. 24, 1881

* Indicates Russian recipient.

NAME DIRECTORY

Volume II

1813 – 1888

The numbers following each name indicate:

Volume / Entry number / Chapter / Page number

Special Note: In order to maintain a continuity and provide for the reader an important cross-reference between Volumes II and III, the Name Directory includes the names of the recipients of the Pour le Mérite Order from both volumes. This will provide a more complete access to the recipients during the years 1813 and 1918.

The recipients of the Oakleaves and the Grand Cross and Star
to the Pour le Mérite Order
are each shown as a separate entry.

A

Abakumov,* II/2062/V-2/149
Achlestishev, Michail, II/891/V-2/38
Adabashev,* II/1775/VII/256
Adalbert, Prince of Prussia, II/53/VII/256
Adam, Hans, III/345/IX/520
von Aderkas,* II/765/V-2/18
Adlercreutz, Friedrich, (Frhr.), II/969/V-2/44
Adlercreutz, Gustaf, II/2142/V-2/154
von Aexkull-Gyllenbandt, Roman, II/1032/V-2/59
Afanassiev,* II/1486/V-2/105
af Wirsén, Karl J., II/963/V-2/44
Agte (Achte), Igor A. II/896/V-2/39
Aksakov,* II/1072/V-2/61
Akutin, Alexander N. II/1674/V-2/122
Aladin, Fedor A. II/2200/V-2/159
Albert, Christof J.F., II/2403/V-2/190
Albert, Crown Prince of Saxony, F., II/180/VII/290
Albert, Prince of Saxony, F., II/23/VI/229
von Alberti, Armand, III/813/IX/635
Albrecht, Alexander Ivanovich, II/1149/V-2/67
Albrecht, Archduke of Austria, F., II/22/VI/229
Albrecht, Duke of Württemberg, III/83/IX/435
Albrecht, Duke of Württemberg, III/431/IX/543
Albrecht II., Karl Ivanovich, II/1543/V-2/110
Albrecht, Peter Ivanovich, II/2238/V-2/161
Albrecht, Prince of Prussia, F.H., II/52/VII/255
Albrecht, Prince of Prussia, F.H., II/187/VII/292
Albrecht, Prince of Prussia, F.W., II/98/VII/264
Albrecht, Prince of Prussia, F.W., II/240/VII/304
Albrecht, Victor, III/474/IX/555
Alexander Alexandrovich, (Heir), II/282/VII/315
Alexander II., Emperor of Russia, II/173/VII/285
Alexander II., Emperor of Russia, II/251/VII/307
Alexander II., Emperor of Russia, II/286/VII/315
Alexander, Prince of Hesse, II/36/VI/232
Alexandrovich, Dmitri Ivanovich, II/2946/V-2/148
Alexei Alexandrovich, Grand Duke, II/297/VII/317
Alexieiev, Alexie Petrovich, II/2954/V-2/148
Alexieiev, Ivan Alexieieovich, II/1639/V-2/118
Alferiev, Pavel Vassilieovich, II/2245/V-2/162
Almifov,* II/2150/V-2/155
Allissov,* II/1451/V-2/104
Allmenröder, Karl, III/258/IX/494
Almásy von Zsádany und Török-Sz. II/2303/V-2/168
von Althaus, Ernst (Frhr.), III/130/IX/456
von Alvensleben, Gustaf Herman, II/233/VII/302
von Alvensleben, Gustaf Herman, II/246/VII/306
von Alvensleben, Johann Friedrich, II/1371/V-2/99
von Alvensleben, Konstantin Reimar, II/79/VII/262
von Alvensleben, Konstantin Reimar, II/185/VII/291
Ampach, Pavel Adamovich, II/1444/V-2/103
Andreievski, Konstantin S. II/1002/V-2/57
Andreievski, Konstantin S. II/1829/V-2/134
Andrusski, Nikolai I., II/2956/V-2/148
Annenkov, Nikolai P., II/1810/V-2/134
Antonovski, Anton I., II/1498/V-2/106
Appel, Christian, II/1600/V-2/114
Apraxin, Alexander P., II/2044/V-2/148
Apraxin, Vassili I., II/1616/V-2/116
Apraxin, Vladimir S., II/1522/V-2/108
Apushkin, (Apuchtin),* II/1861/V-2/136
Apushkin, Alexander N., II/1999/V-2/144
Arbussov, Alexei F., II/1836/V-2/135
Arens, Walther, III/759/IX/623
Arfedson, Elias, II/966/V-2/44
Armfelt, Gustaf G. II/1369/V-2/98
von Arnauld de la Perière, August, II/2324/V-2/179, Lothar, 180/IX/470
von Arnim, Achim, III/489/IX/559
von Arnim, Richard Felix, II/89/VII/263
Arnoldi, Ivan Karlovich, II/1018/V-2/58
von Arpshofen, Karl K., II/1813/V-2/143
Arseniev, Nikolai V., II/2007/V-2/145
Artemiev,* II/1076/V-2/61
Arthur, Prince of Great Britain, II/304/VII/318
Artiuchov, Jefim T., II/1083/V-2/62
Arz von Straussenburg, A. III/92/IX/437
Arz von Straussenburg, A. III/184/IX/501
Arzishevski, Anton K. II/1317/V-2/82
Asantshevski, Fedor S. II/1251/V-2/77
Ashakov, Alexei, II/1997/V-2/144
Asovski,* II/2276/V-2/163
Astachov, Michail N. II/1140/V-2/66
Astafiev, Lev A. II/782/V-2/20
Aster, Ernst Ludwig, II/1030/V-2/59
Atreshkov, Lev I., II/1222/V-2/74
Audé de Sion, Karl, II/1588/V-2/113
August, Prince of Württembg, II/56/VII/257
August, Prince of Württembg, II/247/VII/306
von Avemann, Friedrich P. II/128/VII/276

B

Baader,* III/754/IX/621
Babst, Kondrati K., II/1914/V-2/139
Bachmann, Jakob I. II/1704/V-2/125
von Bacmeister, Ernst, III/314/IX/509
Bagaievskov, Stepan, II/2156/V-2/156
Bagdanovski, Andrei V., II/1358/V-2/96
Bakaiev II., Michail I., II/1434/V-2/103
Bakunin, Vassili M. II/2008/V-2/145
Balbekov, Alexei A. II/1328/V-2/85
Balck, William, III/437/IX/545
von Balcke, Hermann, III/274/IX/498
Balkashin, Michail N. II/1334/V-2/85
Balkashin, Nikanor N. II/1835/V-2/135
Bangert, Viktor, III/356/IX/524

Baranov, Jevstafi J. II/1961/V-2/142
Baranovski, Josef, II/2020/V-2/145
Barateiev II., Prince Peter, II/1386/V-2/102
von Barby, Adalbert R. II/70/VII/260
von Bardeleben, Wilhelm F. II/2361/V-2/183
Bardolff,* III/272/IX/498
Barishnikov, Pavel P. II/1828/V-2/134
Barishnikov, Peter P. II/1783/V-2/132
von Barnekow, Christof G. II/104/VII/271
von Barnekow, Christof G. II/203/VII/295
Barokov, Lev L. II/2248/V-2/162
Barozzie, Jakob I. II/1283 /V-2/79
Bartenbach, Karl, II/327/VII/463
Barth,* III/641/IX/595
Bartholomai, Fedor I. II/1550/V-2/110
Bashmakov, Dmitri J. II/1519/V-2/108
Bashmakov, Flegon M. II/1102/V-2/64
Batashev, Alexei A. II/1016/V-2/58
Baturin, Sergei G. 1425/V-2/103
Bauer, Max, III/202/IX/477
Bauer, Max, III/459/IX/551
Baumeister, Paul Hugo, II/66/VII/260
Bäumer, Paul, III/793/IX/630
Baumgarten, Johann J. II/1070/V-2/61
von Beaulieu-Marconnay, Lothar, III/775/IX/626
Beck Ivan Ivanovich, II/1080/V-2/62
von der Becke, Friedrich, II/249/VII/306
Becker, Friedrich, III/689/IX/605
Becker, Johann, II/1728/V-2/127
Beckmann, Fedor P. III/878/V-2/36
Bedriaga, Ivan Ivanovich, II/1688/V-2/123
von Beeren, Friedrich W. II/12/VII/245
von Beerfeld, Kurt, III/496/IX/560
Behncke, Paul, III/332/IX/515
von Behr, Franz, III/315/IX/509
Behrends (Behrens), Vassili, II/769/V-2/19
Behrendt, Stanislaus, III/712/IX/611
Beier, Johann Peter, II/2346/V-2/183
Bekuhrs, Georg Wilhelm, II/20/VII/246
Bellegarde, August, II/2402/V-2/189
von Belli,* II/1975/V-2/142
Bellinghausen, Fedor C. II/1487/V-2/105
Bellinghausen, Fedor I. II/1105/V-2/64
von Below, Eduard, III/286/IX/502
von Below, Ernst, III/357/IX/524
von Below, Ernst, III/743/IX/619
von Below, Ferdinand, II/137/VII/277
von Below, Fritz, III/34/IX/415
von Below, Fritz, III/138/IX/459
von Below, Hans, III/358/IX/524
von Below, Ludwig Hugo, II/166/VII/281
von Below, Otto, III/35/IX/415
von Below, Otto, III/231/IX/487

von Below, Theodor W. II/2293/V-2/165
Bendemann, Arnold G. II/40/VII/248
Benderski, Konstantin A. II/1199/V-2/72
von Benning, Karl August, II/2354/V-2/183
von Bentheim, Georg F. II/189/VII/292
von Bercken, Fedor E. II/142/VII/278
von Berendt, Richard, III/212/IX/481
von Berendt, Richard, III/367/IX/526
von Berenhorst, Johann G. II/2375/V-2/186
von Berg, Friedrich W. II/48/VII/250
von Berg, Karl B. II/1587/V-2/113
Bergencreutz, Lars A. II/1337/V-2/89
Bergenstrale, Peter I. II/2037/V-2/147
Berger,* III/490/IX/559
Berger, August Emil, II/18/VII/246
Bergmann, Alexander P. II/996/V-2/56
Bergmann, Jermolai A. II/1479/V-2/105
von Bergmann, Richard E. II/12/VII/245
Bergmann, Walter, III/546/IX/571
Berka, Waldemar, III/592/IX/582
von Berken, Theodor K. II/67/VII/260
Bernert, Otto (Fritz), III/222/IX/486
von Bernhardi, Friedrich, III/141/IX/460
von Bernhardi, Friedrich, III/552/IX/573
Bernikov, Pavel S. II/1356/V-2/96
von Bernuth, Felix, III/726/IX/615
Berr, Hans, III/192/IX/474
von Berrer, Albert, III/292/IX/503
Bersilov, Arseni J. II/1844/V-2/135
Berthold, Rudolf, III/181/IX/470
Beseler, Hans, III/374/IX/528
von Beseler, Hans, III/24/IX/409
von Beseler, Hans, III/79/IX/433
Besgin, Konstantin M. II/2209/V-2/159
Besobrasov, Grigori M. II/2407/V-2/190
Besebrasov, Peter M. II/1815/V-2/134
Besserer von Thalsingen, A. II/1531/V-2/109
Bestushev, Grigori V. II/843/V-2/29
Bestushev-Riumin, Michail, II/1166/V-2/68
von Beust, Franz J. II/1382/V-2/101
Biakov, Ivan Ivanovich, II/911/V-2/40
Bibikov, Dmitri I. II/1311/V-2/81
Bibikov, Ilia G. II/908/V-2/39
Bibikov, Ivan P. II/1684/V-2/123
Bibikov, Larion M. II/1774/V-2/132
Bibikov, Vassili A. II/1574/V-2/112
Bichalov, Ivan, II/1147/V-2/66
Bichalov, Jossif I. II/1634/V-2/117
Bichalov, Jossif M. II/2114/V-2/152
Bichalov, Konon V. II/1146/V-2/66
Bichalov, Vassili, II/1231/V-2/75
Biegidov, David G. II/1135/V-2/66
Bielaievski,* II/1192/V-2/72

Bielogradski, Grigori G. II/1296/V-2/80
Bielogradski, Jemelian O. II/1446/V-2/104
Bikov III., Peter M. II/1413/V-2/103
von Bila, Ernst, III/455/IX/550
Biros von Kurland, Prince Gustaf, II/1590/V-2/113
Bischoff, Josef, III/598/IX/584
von Bismarck, Prince Otto E. II/305/VII/319
Bistrom, Alexander I. II/1949/V-2/141
Bistrom, Anton A. II/1097/V-2/63
von Bistrom, Filipp A. II/1549/V-2/110
von Bistrom, Filipp A. II/2112/V-2/152
von Björnstjerna, Magnus F. II/964/V-2/44
Blanov, Gavrilo V. II/1167/V-2/68
Blashievski, Valenti V. II/1895/V-2/138
Bloch von Blottnitz, Theodor, II/172/VII/284
von Blomburg, Werner, III/571/IX/578
Blum, Paul Petrovich, II/1801/V-2/133
Blume, Walter, III/706/IX/610
von Blumenthal, Heinrich E. II/196/VII/294
von Blumenthal, Karl K. II/9/VII/244
von Blumemthal, Karl K. II/71/VII/261
von Blumenthal, Karl K. III/5/IX/391
von Bock, Fedor, III/462/IX/553
von Bock, Franz-Karl, III/739/IX/617
von Bock, Louis O. II/223/VII/301
von Bock, Timofei I. II/977/V-2/45
von Böckmann, Alfred, III/179/IX/469
von Böchmann, Alfred, III/253/IX/493
von Bode, Lev Karlovich, II/798/V-2/24
von Boecking, Wilhelm T. II/220/VII/300
Boedicker, Ludwig, II/2348/V-2/183
von Boehler, Johann C. II/2325/V-2/179
von Boehn, Max, III/145/IX/461
von Boehn, Max, III/251/IX/492
Boelcke, Oswald, III/110/IX/444
von Boenigk, Oskar, III/769/IX/625
von Boetticher, August F. II/928/V-2/40
von Boetticher, Gustaf I. II/950/V-2/43
von Boetticher, Moritz I. II/811/V-2/25
Bogatirev, Vassili I. II/2157/V-2/156
Bogdanov,* II/943/V-2/42
Bogdanov, Alexander I. II/1572/V-2/112
Bogdanov, Alexander N. II/1020/V-2/58
Bogdanovich, Ivan F. II/916/V-2/40
Bogdanovich, Vassili I. II/1714/V-2/126
von Bogendörfer, Friedrich, III/625/IX/591
Bogulterov,* II/2155/V-2/156
Boguslavski, Ivan Pavlovich, II/1758/V-2/130
Bohm, Helmuth, III/537/IX/570
von Böhm, Maximilian, II/1010/V-2/57
von Böhm-Ermolli, Eduard, III/176/IX/469
von Böhm-Ermolli, Eduard, III/273/IX/498
Böhme, Erich, III/543/IX/571
Böhme, Erwin, III/371/IX/526
von Böhn, Philipp O. II/95/VII/263
Bolatuk, Prince Kai, II/971/V-2/45
Bolle, Karl, III/664/IX/600
Bologovski, Dmitri N. II/1690/V-2/123
Bongartz, Heinrich, III/410/IX/537
von Bonin, Eduard Ludwig, II/7/VI/226
von Borcke, Karl August, II/1229/V-2/75
von Borcke, Kurt Friedrich, II/733/V-2/4
Borgraf, Ivan F. II/1756/V-2/30
Boris, Crown Prince, Bulgaria, III/187/IX/472
Borissov, Christofor S. II/886/V-2/38
Borissov, Nikolai I. II/1051/V-2/60
von dem Borne, Kurt, III/475/IX/555
von dem Borne, Kurt, III/810/IX/634
Bornovolokov, Alexander P. II/1431/V-2/103
Boroević von Bojna, Svetozar, III/338/IX/518
von Borries, Karl, III/582/IX/580
von Borries, Rudolf, III/280/IX/500
von Borstell, Karl L. II/991/V-2/54
von Borstell, Ludwig F. II/2343/V-2/182
von Bose, Ernst Ludwig, II/1873/V-2/137
von Bose, Friedrich J. II/124/VII/275
von Both, Kuno-Hans, III/484/IX/557
von Bothmer, Felix, III/66/IX/428
von Bothmer, Felix, III/265/IX/496
von Boyen, Ludwig L. II/1654/V-2/76
Brahe, Magnus, II/1240/V-2/76
Brams, Alexander I. II/1212/V-2/74
Brandenburg, Ernst, III/256/IX/493
von Brandenstein, Otto, III/550/IX/572
von Brandenstein, Friedrich, II/2337/V-2/181
von Brandenstein, Hermann, III/293/IX/504
von Brandenstein, Joachim, II/2391/V-2/188
von Brandenstein, Karl B. II/274/VII/310
von Brandenstein, Kurt, III/701/IX/609
von Brandis, Cordt, III/116/IX/449
von Brandis, Cordt, III/496/IX/561
von Brandt, August H. II/21/VI/228
Brandt, Johann (Ivan), II/1347/V-2/93
Brandt, Johann (Ivan), II/2165/V-2/156
Branicki, Stanislav S. II/1005/V-2/57
Braun,* II/2154/V-2/156
Braun, Johann Karl, II/2340/V-2/182
von Brederlow, Tido, III/727/IX/615
von Bredow, Anatol, II/69/IX/429
von Bredow, Maximilian, II/148/VII/279
von Bremen,* II/865/V-2/36
Brenner, Ivan Ivanovich, II/1951/V-2/142
Breshinski, Michail P. II/1713/V-2/126
Breshinski, Semen P. II/1156/V-2/67
Breshinski, Semen P. II/1901/V-2/138
Bresin, Alexei D. II/2177/V-2/157
Bresovski, Anton V. II/1852/V-2/135
Bresovski, Appollon V. II/1668/V-2/122

Bressler, Ludwig, III/728/IX/615
von Brewern, Christofor L. II/2180/V-2/157
Brieskorn, Bogdan J. II/777/V-2/19
Brilkin, Dmitri M. II/2947/V-2/148
von der Brincken, Karl V. II/993/V-2/41
von Brincken, Christofor A. II/1808/V-2/134
Brinkmann, Friedrich, III/436/IX/545
Brinkord, Heinrich, III/755/IX/622
Briskin, Ferdinand, III/525/IX/567
von Brockhausen, Friedrich, II/46/VII/250
Broglio de Revel I., Alfons, II/1406/V-2/102
Bronevski, Nikolai B. II/2174/V-2/157
Bronsart von Schellendorff, B. III/165/IX/465
Bronsart von Schellendorff, H. III/760/IX/623
Bronsart von Schellendorff, W. III/567/IX/577
Brosin II., Jakob N. II/1659/V-2/121
Brosin, Pavel Ivanovich, II/754/V-2/17
Brozowsky, Wilhelm F. II/1691/V-2/124
Bruchmüller, Georg, III/232/IX/488
Bruchmüller, Georg, III/449/IX/549
Bruckendahl (Brückental),* II/1091/V-2/62
Bruckendahl, Karl V. II/854/V-2/34
Brückner, Erich, III/681/IX/603
Brummel,* II/1630/V-2/117
Brümmer I.,* II/958/V-2/43
Brunner,* II/2300/V-2/168
Bruns, Friedrich, III/799/IX/632
Brunsich Edler von Brun, G. II/32/VI/230
Bruslianski, Ivan I. II/1490/V-2/105
Bublik, Jakob P. II/1833/V-2/135
Büchner, Franz, III/767/IX/624
Buckler, Julius, III/383/IX/530
von Budberg, Peter L. II/1666/V-2/122
von Budberg, Fedor V. II/1929/V-2/140
Buddecke, Hans J. III/199/IX/452
von Buddenbrock, Karl G. II/29/VII/247
von Buddenbrock, Karl G. II/193/VII/293
von Buddenbrock, Robert E. II/126/VII/275
von Budritzki, Rudolf O. II/175/VII/289
Bulashov,* II/1484/V-2/105
Bulgakov, Fedor V. II/2285/V-2/164
Bulgarin, Peter D. II/1169/V-2/68
Bulgarski, Peter V. II/1703/V-2/125
Bullach,* II/813/V-2/25
von Bülow, Friedrich W. II/851/V-2/34
von Bülow, Hans Adolf, II/250/VII/306
von Bülow, Karl, III/47/IX/420
von Bülow-(Bothkamp), Walther, III/321/IX/511
Bumke, Karl Friedrich, II/222/VII/300
von Bünau, Heinrich, III/690/IX/606
von der Burg, Ernst E. II/75/VII/261
von der Burg, Ernst E. II/218/VII/300
von Burkardt, Hermann, III/239/IX/489
Bürkner, Robert, III/556/IX/574

Burmeister, Adolf C. II/1676/V-2/122
Burmeister, Fedor F. II/2289/V-2/164
Burmeister, Jevdokim R. II/1677/V-2/122
Burssak II., Afanassi F. II/1582/V-2/113
Busch, Ernst, III/713/IX/611
Bushen, Christian N. II/1903/V-2/138
Bushuiev,* II/1973/V-2/142
von dem Bussche-Haddenhausen, III/692/IX/607
von dem Bussche-Ippenburg, II/1270/V-2/78
von Busse, Johannes, III/524/IX/566
Bussov, Semen J. II/1710/V-2/125
Butkovski, Nikolai J. II/1361/V-2/96
Buturlin, Dmitri P. II/1249/V-2/77
von Buxhöwden, Peter F. II/2425/V-2/193

C

Call, Karl, II/995/V-2/55
von Canitz u Dallwitz, Karl W. II/2442/V-2/195
von Canstein, Philipp C. II/13/VII/245
von Canstein, Philipp C. II/155/VII/280
Capelle, Eduard, III/415/IX/538
von Caprivi, Georg Leo, II/201/VII/294
Caracciola-Delbrueck,* III/655/IX/598
von Cardell, Karl F. II/1237/V-2/76
Carlheim-Gyllensköld, Karl, II/1335/V-2/89
von Carlowitz, Adolph, III/275/IX/498
von Carlowitz, Adolph, III/562/IX/575
Caspari, Walter, III/499/IX/561
Chales de Beaulieu, Martin, III/304/IX/507
Chanikov, Nikolai P. II/1262/V-2/78
Charles, James N. II/979/V-2/45
Chartshenko-Denissenko, A. II/1477/V-2/105
Chérisey, Charles Louis, II/2386/V-2/187
Chilkov, Prince Stepan, II/1534/V-2/109
Chitrovo, Vassili J. II/1442/V-2/103
Chmielievski, Anton O. II/2204/V-2/159
Cholodovski, Igor, V. II/856/V-2/34
Choliakov, Alexei A. II/1189/V-2/71
Chomaikov,* II/1440/V-2/103
Chomutov, Grigori S. II/1302/V-2/80
Chorus, Hans Wilhelm, II/170/VII/283
Chrapatshov, Vassili S. II/2287/V-2/164
Chrapovizki, Grigori S. II/1205/V-2/73
Chrapovizki, Ivan I. II/2094/V-2/151
Chrapovizki, Jason S. II/1279/V-2/79
Chrapovizki, Matvei J. II/1797/V-2/133
Chriestshatizki, Pavel, II/1282/V-2/79
Christiansen, Friedrich, III/392/IX/532
Churstshov, Sergei P. II/2059/V-2/148
Chvostovski, Nikolai A. II/1467/V-2/105
von Claer, Eberhard, III/64/IX/427
Clam-Martinez, Karl J. II/1632/V-2/117
von Clausewitz, Vollmar K. II/1644/V-2/119
von Clausewitz, Wilhelm, II/2376/V-2/186

Clausius, Max, III/748/IX/620
von Cler, Ignaz Heinrich, II/2441/V-2/195
Coester, Rudolf M. II/167/VII/283
von Collani, Erwin, III/544/IX/571
Colomier, Louis Max, II/10/VII/245
Commichau, Oskar, III/498/IX/561
Conrad von Hötzendorf, Franz, III/50/IX/422
Conrad von Hötzendorf, Franz, III/214/IX/482
von Conta, Karl Bernhard, II/17/VII/246
von Conta, Richard, III/182/IX/470
von Conta, Richard, III/450/IX/549
Cooke, Henry Frederic, II/978/V-2/45
von Cranach, Elimar, III/514/IX/565
von Cranach, Ludwig Otto, II/163/VII/281
von Cranach, Ludwig Otto, II/225/VII/301
von Crayen, Karl August, II/734/V-2/10

D

von Dahlen, Nikolai I. II/2369/V-2/185
d'Ainesy, Leopold, II/1636/V-2/118
Dallmer, Karl Friedrich, II/787/V-2/20
Dallmer, Viktor, III/225/IX/486
Dallmer, Viktor, III/578/IX/579
d'Alton-Rauch,* III/643/IX/595
von Dalwig, Louis H. II/145/VII/278
Dambrovski, Ivan I. II/1726/V-2/127
Damitsh, Feodissi I. II/1481/V-2/105
Dammann, Gustav, III/800/IX/632
Danilov, Dmitri P. II/1469/V-2/104
Danilov, Pavel V. II/1130/V-2/65
von Dannenberg, Ferdinand, II/77/VII/262
Dannenberg, Ivan Petrovich, II/1925/V-2/140
Dannenberg, Samuil (Peter), II/2228/V-2/160
Dänner, Rudolf, III/771/IX/625
d'Artis de Bequignolles, E. II/14/VI/227
von Dassel, Johannes, III/761/IX/623
Daun, Karl Friedrich, II/39/VII/248
Davidov I.,* II/1114/V-2/64
Davidov, Dmitri V. II/1436/V-2/103
Davidov II., Jevdokim V. II/1122/V-2/65
Davidov, Jevdokim V. II/2092/V-2/150
Davidov, Nikolai D. II/1870/V-2/136
Davidov, Peter Ivanovich, II/2032/V-2/46
Dawson, George L. II/982/V-2/46
de Balmaine, Alexander, II/2040/V-2/147
de Boissesson, Josef P. II/1536/V-2/109
von Debschitz, Johann, II/114/VII/273
de Chamborant, Viktor, II/1223/V-2/75
Dechterev, Jevgraf S. II/2013/V-2/145
Dedeniev (Dederiev), A. II/760/V-2/18
Degelow, Carl, III/821/IX/636
de Gervais, Alexander K. II/1671/V-2/122
de Grossard, Jean Baptiste, II/1508/V-2/106
von Deimling, Berthold, III/147/IX/461

de la Rochejaquelein, A. II/2389/V-2/188
van Delen, Leonhard A. II/1653/V-2/120
von Delius, Walter, III/418/IX/539
von Dellinghausen, Ivan F. II/1877/V-2/137
d'Elsa, Karl Ludwig, III/155/IX/463
de Mendoza-Butello, Ossip, II/862/V-2/36
Demiankov, Parfeni S. II/1398/V-2/102
Demtshenkov, Semen S. II/1034/V-2/59
Denissievski, Andronik A. II/1892/V-2/138
Dennissov, Peter A. II/2027/V-2/146
de Polignac, Heraklius A. II/1669/V-2/122
de Rainville, Franz, III/805/IX/633
Dernen, Friedrich W. III/665/IX/600
de Rochechouart, Louis, II/893/V-2/38
de Rochechouart, Ludwig, II/1007/V-2/57
Deroshinski, Leopold, II/2193/V-2/158
Deroshinski, Vladimir, II/2028/V-2/146
von Derschau, Karl F. II/2102/V-2/151
de St. Priest, Louis F. II/1163/V-2/68
de Sauveplan, Karl A. II/1708/V-2/125
des Barres, Franz W. II/160/VII/281
Deskur (Descours), Ivan, II/1345/V-2/92
Deskur (Descours), Ivan, II/2163/V-2/156
de Surmain, Charles Jean, II/1238/V-2/76
von Detten, Arnold, III/660/IX/599
von Devivere, Diederich F. II/21/VII/246
von Dewitz, Kurt, III/515/IX/565
de Zerbi, Sir Johann, 1605/V-2/115
Diakov, Alexei N. II/1521/V-2/108
Diakov, Peter N. II/2081/V-2/150
Dickinson, Richard, II/2371/V-2/185
Dieiev, Alexander M. II/1612/V-2/115
Dieiev, Ivan M. II/1613/V-2/115
Diemal Pasha, III/303/IX/506
von Diepenbroick-Grüter, O. III/583/IX/581
von Dieringshofen, Carl, II/117/VII/274
von Dieringshofen, Karl, II/226/VII/301
Diessenbach, Karl, III/226/IX/487
von Diest, Heinrich F. II/804/V-2/24
Dieterichs (Dieteriks),* II/1880/V-2/137
Dieterichs III., Christian, II/956/V-2/43
Dieterichs, Andrei I. II/1100/V-2/63
Dieterichs (Diedrich), Andrei, II/1164/V-2/68
von Ditfurth, Wilhelm, III/500/IX/561
von Ditfurth, Wilhelm H. II/2339/V-2/181
Dittmar, Peter (Igor), II/1849/V-2/135
Dluski, Jevgeni M. II/1619/V-2/116
Dmitriev, Ivan D. II/1368/V-2/98
Dmitriev-Mamonov, A.I. II/1439/V-2/103
Dobrishin, Nikolai I. II/2263/V-2/162
Dobrovolski, Lavrenti L. II/1092/V-2/62
Dobrovolski, Semen I. II/748/V-2/17
von Doering, Karl Gustaf, II/30/VII/247
von Doernberg, Wilhelm K. II/739/V-2/14

zu Dohna (Schlodien), Nikolaus, III/114/IX/439
Dolgoruki, Prince Nikolai, II/1916/V-2/139
Dolinski, Lev, II/1628/V-2/117
Doliva-Dobrovolski, Frol, II/962/V-2/44
Dolomanov, Nikolai K. II/867/V-2/36
d'Olonne, Ossip F. II/917/V-2/40
Dombrovski, Pavel F. II/2196/V-2/158
Dombrovski, Roman A. II/1847/V-2/135
von Dommes, Wilhelm, III/591/IX/582
Dorndorf, Georg, III/463/IX/553
Dossenbach, Albert, III/191/IX/474
von Dostler, Eduard, III/283/IX/501
Drause, Ossip Ivanovich, II/1874/V-2/137
Drechsel, Hermann, III/467/IX/553
von Dresky, Justus Karl, II/256/VII/308
von Dresler u Scharfenstein, H. III/346/IX/521
Dresler von Scharffenstein, W. II/822/V-2/27
Drevich,* II/921/V-2/40
Driese, Carl, III/670/IX/601
von Drigalski, Hans III/456/IX/550
Drobishevski, Karp, II/1957/V-2/142
Drosdovski, Faddei A. II/955/V-2/43
von Drost zu Vischering, Josef, II/2258/V-2/162
Drulski-Sakolinski,* Prince, II/767/V-2/18
Dsevonski, Ivan, II/1123/V-2/65
Dsheshelei, Grigori A. II/2252/V-2/162
Dsheshelinski,* II/1109/V-2/64
Dsitshkanez, Adam J. II/1693/V-2/124
Dubelt, Leonti V. II/2315/V-2/177
Dubelt, Peter V. II/1680/V-2/122
Dubois Descours, de la Maisonfort, II/1516/V-2/108
Du Boy (Deboar), Ossip, II/1309/V-2/81
Dubrovin, Peter S. II/2176/V-2/157
von Dücker, Wilhelm, III/666/IX/600
Dunaiev, Alexander I. II/1998/V-2/144
von Dunker, Friedrich W. II/829/V-2/28
du Pac de Badens et Sombrelle, G. II/2/VI/225
von Düring, Ernst Johann, II/980/V-2/45
Durnovo, Ivan N. II/1185/V-2/71
Durnovo, Nikolai D. II/1000/V-2/57
Durov, Fedor Fedorovich, II/1187/V-2/71
Dushek (Dussek),* II/2025/V-2/146
du Trossel, Wilhelm K. II/236/VII/303
Dutshinski, Ossip I. II/2414/V-2/191
Duvanov, Akim V. II/2045/V-2/148

E

von Eben, Johannes, III/117/IX/469
von Eben, Johannes, III/310/IX/508
von Eberhardt, Magnus, III/243/IX/490
von Eberhardt, Magnus, III/531/IX/568
Edelbüttel, Gottfried, III/325/IX/512
von Edelsheim, Franz, III/714/IX/611
Edenhjelm, Gillis, 1241/V-2/76

Edler von Graeve, Wilhelm, III/815/IX/635
von Egidy, Ralph, III/786/IX/629
von Ehrenthal, Oskar, III/259/IX/495
von Eichmann, Hermann, III/77/IX/433
von Eichmann, Hermann, III/96/IX/439
von Einem (Rothmaler), Karl, III/41/IX/418
von Einem (Rothmaler), Karl, III/184/IX/471
von Eisenhart, Johann E. II/726/V-2/2
Eismont, Alexei M. II/1153/V-2/67
Eismont, Kosma M. II/1736/V-2/128
Eital Friedrich, Prince of Prussia, III/45/IX/419
Eitel Friedrich, Prince of Prussia, III/57/IX/424
Elshanovski, Kasimir J. II/279/VII/314
Elstermann von Elster, Hugo, III/309/IX/508
Emme, Alexander Ivanovich, II/1918/V-2/139
Emme, Alexei F. II/949/V-2/43
von Emmich, Otto, III/18/IX/404
von Emmich, Otto, III/55/IX/423
von Ende, Siegfried, III/329/IX/514
von Endres, Nikolaus, III/491/IX/559
von Endres, Nikolaus, III/635/IX/593
von Engelbrechten, George, III/618/IX/588
von Engelhart, Adam G. II/1994/V-2/144
Engelhart, Andrei V. II/1267/V-2/78
Engelhart, Anton J. II/772/V-2/19
von Engelhart, Karl L. II/2332/V-2/180
von Engelström, Gustaf S. II/1239/V-2/76
Enver Pasha, III/86/IX/435
Enver Pasha, III/108/IX/444
von Epp, Franz, III/563/IX/576
von Erckert, Friedrich W. II/84/VII/263
Ernst II., Duke, Saxe-Altenburg, III/58/IX/424
Ernst, Duke Saxe-Coburg-Gotha, II/31/VI/230
von der Esch, Hans, III/740/IX/618
von der Esch, Karl W. II/272/VII/310
von Eschwege, Ludwig, II/2360/V-2/183
von Esebeck, Friedrich, III/468/IX/554
von Essen, Alexander F. II/1350/V-2/94
von Essen, Karl K. II/855/V-2/34
von Essen, Karl K. II/2415/V-2/191
von Estorff, Ludwig, III/305/IX/507
von Etzel, Günter, III/627/IX/592
von Etzel, Günter, III/770/IX/625
Eugen, Archduke of Austria, III/252/IX/492
Eugen, Archduke of Austria, III/340/IX/518
zu Eulenburg, Siegfried, III/294/IX/504
zu Eulenburg, Siegfried, III/684/IX/604

F

von Fabeck, Max, III/84/IX/435
von Fabecky, Ferdinand F. II/2034/V-2/147
Fahlenberg,* II/2236/V-2/161
von Fahnenberg, Anton, II/2302/V-2/168
Falk, Fedor Bogdanovich, II/2295/V-2/166

von Falkenhausen, Alexander, III/545/IX/571
von Falkenhausen, Ludwig, III/85/IX/435
von Falkenhausen, Ludwig, III/120/IX/453
von Falkenhausen, Wilhelm, II/198/VII/294
von Falkenhayn, Erich, III/36/IX/415
von Falkenhayn, Erich, III/61/IX/425
von Falkenhayn, Eugen, III/89/IX/436
von Falkenhayn, Eugen, III/101/IX/441
Fallon, Ludwig August, II/1592/V-2/114
Fanshave, Friedrich A. II/1577/V-2/113
Fanshave, Grigori A. II/2085/V-2/150
Fanshave, Vassili A. II/952/V-2/43
von Fasbender, Karl, III/163/IX/465
Faupel, Wilhelm, III/576/IX/579
Faupel, Wilhelm, 636/IX/593
Fedorov,* II/1876/V-2/142
Fedosseiev, Michail D. II/1493/V-2/106
Felgentreu, Adolf Erikus, II/819/V-2/27
Ferdinand I., Czar of Bulgaria, III/161/IX/464
Figner, Alexander S. II/1360/V-2/96
Filangieri, Prince of Satriano, II/33/VI/230
von Filies, Johann K. II/2355/V-2/183
Filipov I., Nikolai F. II/906/V-2/39
Filipov, Alexei A. II/1378/V-2/100
Filipov, Alexei A. 2153/V-2/155
Finck von Finckenstein, Bernhard, III/476/IX/555
Firssov, Peter S. II/2395/V-2/189
Fischer,* II/2188/V-2/158
Fischer, Kurt, III/341/IX/518
von Fischer, Udo, III/599/IX/584
von Flatow, Friedrich G. II/229/VII/302
Fleck, Paul, III/42/IX/418
Fokin,* II/2184/V-2/157
Fomin,* II/1136/V-2/66
Forcade de Biaix, Wilhelm, II/1635/V-2/77
Forsell, Karl Gustaf, II/967/V-2/44
von Förster, Arthur S. III/9/IX/396
von Förster, Otto Karl, II/270/VII/310
Forstmann, Walter, III/139/IX/459
von Forstner, Ernst, III/331/IX/515
von Forstner, Ernst, III/590/IX/582
Fragstein von Niemsdorff, Johann, II/27/VII/246
Frahnert,* III/342/IX/519
von François, Bruno Hugo, II/140/VII/278
von François, Hermann, III/51/IX/402
von François, Hermann, III/271/IX/498
Franke, Adolf, III/752/IX/621
Franke, Erich Viktor, III/17/IX/402
von Frankenberg, Hans, III/608/IX/586
Frankl, Wilhelm, III/140/IX/459
von Fransecky, Eduard F. II/119/VII/274
von Fransecky, Eduard F. II/207/VII/297
Frantz, Rudolf, III/262/IX/495
Franz Joseph I., Emperor of Austria, III/20/IX/406

Franz d'Assisi, Two Sicilies, II/1/VII/241
Franz, Prince of Bavaria, III/555/IX/574
Frederiks, Peter A. II/1682/V-2/123
Freigang, Johann (Ivan), II/2417/V-2/192
Freigang, Peter Ivanovich, II/1033/V-2/59
Freigang, Peter Ivanovich, II/2235/V-2/161
Freyer, Erich, III/492/IX/559
von Freyhold, Karl, III/585/IX/581
Freymann, Rudolf (Roman), III/1305/V-2/81
Freytag von Loringhoven, R. II/2222/V-2/160
Fricke, Hermann, III/408/IX/536
von Fricks, Gustaf F. II/2132/V-2/153
Friedberg, Ivan Petrovich, II/1042/V-2/59
von Friedeburg, Friedrich, III/697/IX/608
Friederici, Karl, III/600/IX/584
Friedrich August III., Saxony, III/206/IX/479
Friedrich Franz, M-Schwerin, II/59/VII/259
Friedrich Franz, M-Schwerin, II/178/VII/290
Friedrich Karl, Prince of Prussia, II/9/VI/227
Friedrich Karl, Prince of Prussia, II/2/VII/243
Friedrich Karl, Prince of Prussia, II/101/VII/270
Friedrich Karl, Prince of Prussia, II/277/VII/312
Friedrich Wilhelm, Crown Prince, II/49/VII/254
Friedrich Wilhelm, Crown Prince, II/55/VII/256
Friedrich Wilhelm, Crown Prince, II/100/VII/270
Friedrich Wilhelm, Crown Prince, II/276/VII/312
Friedrich, Archduke of Austria, III/49/IX/422
Friedrich, Archduke of Austria, III/207/IX/479
Friedrich, F. Archduke of Austria, II/1/VI/221
Friedrich, Prince of Schleswig etc. II/19/VI/228
Fritsch, Albert H. III/678/IX/603
Fritsch, Lothar, III/540/IX/570
von Froelich, Ernst A. II/2323/V-2/179
Frolov, Peter N. II/1088/V-2/62
Frolov-Bargrieiev, Viktor, II/1427/V-2/103
Frotscher, Georg, III/538/IX/570
Fuchs, Georg, III/287/IX/502
Fuhrmann, Alexander F. II/1576/V-2/112
von Funck, Friedrich W. II/2367/V-2/185

G

von Gabain, Arthur, III/347/IX/521
von Gabain, Arthur, III/495/IX/560
Gabcke,* III/674/IX/602
von der Gablenz, Karl W. II/3/VII/243
Gaede, Hans, III/88/IX/436
Gaertner, Erich, III/814/IX/635
Gagarin,* Prince, II/2409/V-2/191
Gagin, Pavel N. II/2105/V-2/151
Gaievski, Fedor S. II/1734/V-2/128
Galagan, Andrei P. II/1754/V-2/130
Galionka, Afanassi J. II/1161/V-2/68
Gallus, Ewald Gotthold, II/171/VII/283
von Gallwitz, Max, III/72/IX/430

von Gallwitz, Max, III/97/IX/439
Ganskau, Jakob F. II/1089/V-2/62
Garichvostov, Alexander S. II/1898/V-2/138
von Garnier, Otto, III/183/IX/471
Gatovski, Semen O. II/1207/V-2/73
Gavrilenko, Ivan Ivanovich, II/1575/V-2/112
von Gayl, George, III/547/IX/572
von Gazen (Gaza), Wilhelm, III/359/IX/524
von Gabsattel, Ludwig, III/174/IX/468
Gedeonov, Alexander M. II/1264/V-2/78
von Geismar, Friedrich K. II/938/V-2/41
von Geissler, Heinrich P. II/260/VII/309
Gelber, Georg, II/1606/V-2/115
Gentsy de Gents, Josef, II/2388/V-2/188
von Georg, Carl-Siegfried, III/528/IX/567
Georg, Prince of Saxony, III/4/IX/391
Georg, Prince of Saxony, II/181/VII/290
von Gorgii, August E. II/1013/V-2/57
Geppert, Georg, II/1594/V-2/114
Gerassimov, Alexander S. II/1900/V-2/138
Gerassimov, Alexander S. II/1952/V-2/142
Gerbel II., Gustaf V. II/954/V-2/43
von Gerbel III., Karl G. II/1504/V-2/106
von Gerbel III., Karl G. II/1665/V-2/121
von Gerbel, Vassili V. II/2109/V-2/151
Germar, Ullrich, III/516/IX/565
Gerngross, Renatus, II/743/V-2/16
von Gerok, Friedrich, III/67/IX/428
von Gersdorff, Wilhelm A. II/24/VII/246
von Gerstenzweig, Danilo A. II/1548/V-2/110
von Gerstenzweig, Danilo A. II/2111/V-2/151
Gerth, Daniel, III/708/IX/610
Giese, Johann, II/737/V-2/10
Gilein von Gembitz, Karl O. II/2449/V-2/197
Girodz von Gaudi, Alphons, II/19/VII/246
von Glasenapp II., Wilhelm, II/1541/V-2/110
von Glassenapp, Johann H. II/150/VII/279
Glasko,* II/797/V-2/24
Gleitzmann, Fedor A. 1482/V-2/105
Gliebov,* II/877/V-2/36
Glinka, Fedor N. II/930/V-2/41
Glinka, Grigori N. II/1681/V-2/122
Gluchov, Feofilakt A. II/2368/V-2/185
von Glümer, Heinrich K. II/205/VII/297
von Gluszewski-Kwilecki, Wilhelm, III/360/IX/524
Glutshkovius, Michail, II/836/V-2/29
von Goeben, August Karl, II/42/VII/249
von Goeben, August Karl, II/157/VII/280
von Goerne, Wilhelm, III/244/IX/491
von Goerne, Wilhelm, III/658/IX/598
Goesch, Martin, III/501/IX/562
Goeschl, Ignaz, II/1525/V-2/109
Goiarrin, Michail G. II/2074/V-2/149
Golizin I., Prince Andrei, II/1716/V-2/126

Golizin II., Prince Michail, II/1717/V-2/126
Golizin, Prince Alexander S. II/1366/V-2/98
Golizin, Prince Ivan A. II/2088/V-2/150
Golizin, Prince Pavel A. II/2042/V-2/148
Golizin, Prince Vassili S. II/2135/V-2/153
Golizin, Prince Vladimir, II/1773/V-2/31
Golofeiev, Appolon V. II/814/V-2/25
Goloshtshapov, Alexei, II/1476/V-2/105
Golovin, Yevgini A. 1041/V-2/59
von der Goltz, Eduard Kuno, II/44/VII/250
von der Goltz, Eduard Kuno, II/161/VII/281
von der Goltz, Karl F. II/1514/V-2/107
von der Goltz, Moritz, II/199/VII/294
von der Goltz, Rüdiger, III/551/IX/572
von Gondrecourt, Leopold, II/47/VII/250
von Gontard, Friedrich, III/477/IX/556
von Gontard, Friedrich, III/637/IX/594
Gontermann, Heinrich, III/241/IX/490
Gontsharov,* II/1785/V-2/132
Gordieiev, Jakob F. II/1699/V-2/124
von Gordon, Hellmuth, II/122/VII/275
Göring, Hermann, III/570/IX/577
Gorlenkov, Andrei Ivanovich, II/738/V-2/14
Gorski, Karl Petrovich, II/2239/V-2/161
Gortalov, Ivan Kusmitsh, II/2452/V-2/198
Gortshakov I., Prince Peter, II/742/V-2/16
Gortshakov, Prince Michail, II/1095/V-2/62
Gortshakov, Prince Sergei, II/1303/V-2/81
von Gossler, Konrad, III/134/IX/458
von Gottberg, Walter P. II/259/VII/308
von Götz, Georg, III/750/IX/620
von Götzen, August, III/162/IX/464
von Graessendorff, Wolf, III/362/IX/525
Gratshov, Peter A. II/2057/V-2/148
Grave, Pavel Semenovich, 2029/V-2/146
von Greiff, Kurt, III/580/IX/580
von Greim, Robert, III/725/IX/614
Grekov VIII., Alexei D. II/2428/V-2/193
Grekov XVIII., Alexei J. II/1255/V-2/77
Grekov, Sergei N. II/2217/V-2/159
Griebsch, Wilhelm, III/705/IX/609
Grigoriev, Peter F. II/1751/V-2/129
Grigoriev, Peter V. II/907/V-2/39
Grigorov, Fedor Ivanovich, II/2197/V-2/158
Grimmer von Adelsbach,* II/1604/V-2/114
Grinkevich,* II/1257/V-2/78
von Groddeck, Wilhelm, III/478/IX/556
von Grodzki, Hieronymus, II/2383/V-2/187
von der Groeben, Albrecht, II/6/VI/226
von der Groeben, Georg, II/94/VII/264
von der Groeben, Karl, II/25/VI/229
Groener, Wilhelm, II/94/IX/438
von Grolman, Karl Wilhelm, II/1226/V-2/75
Gromov,* II/2071/V-2/149

von Gronau, Hans, III/175/IX/468
von Gronau, Hans, III/640/IX/594
von Grone, Jürgen, III/744/IX/619
Groppe, Theodor, III/801/IX/632
von Gross (Schwarzhoff), Karl, II/121/VII/274
Gross, Gottlieb, Wilhelm, II/34/VI/230
von Grotenhelm, Maxim M. II/1004/V-2/57
von Grothe, Hans, III/792/IX/630
von Grothuss,* II/2299/V-2/168
von Grothuss, Dmitri U. II/1047/V-2/60
Grudsinski, Sachar Ivanovich, II/1991/V-2/143
Grünert, Paul, III/533/IX/569
Grusinov,* II/1497/V-2/106
Gruson, Ernst, III/614/IX/587
Gubin,* II/1071/V-2/61
Gudovich, Nikolai N. II/1395/V-2/102
Gudoxius, Erich, III/628/IX/592
Guérois, Alexander K. II/1134/V-2/66
von Gündell, Erich, III/148/IX/462
Günzell II., Alexander K. II/912/V-2/40
von Guretzky-Cornitz, Hans, III/115/IX/448
Guriev, Nikolai D. II/794/V-2/24
Gurov, Ivan Antonovich, II/1611/V-2/115
Gutjahr, Karl Petrovich, II/771/V-2/19
Güzel I.,* II/2416/V-2/192

H

von Haack, Friedrich, III/629/IX/592
Habbe, Michail A. II/1304/V-2/81
von Hacke, Julius Emil, II/45/VII/250
von Hadelin, Heinrich, III/290/IX/503
Haenicke, Siegfried, III/586/IX/581
von Haeseler, Gottlieb, III/44/IX/419
von Haeseler, Gottlieb, II/264/VII/309
Hagedorn, Wilhelm, III/276/IX/499
Hagen, Ernst Heinrich, II/106/VII/272
von Hagen, Karl, III/470/IX/554
Hahnke, Oskar, III/721/IX/613
von Hake, Karl Georg, II/1379/V-2/101
Halkett, Hugh, II/18/VI/228
Hammacher, Ernst, III/785/IX/628
Hammer, Rudolph, III/361/IX/525
von Hammerstein-Equord, W. II/2145/V-2/155
von Hammerstein-Gesmold, F. III/787/IX/629
von Hammerstein-Gesmold, H. III/802/IX/632
von Hanenfeldt, Karl K. II/64/VII/260
Hanson, Karl, III/817/IX/636
von Harder, Georg, III/656/IX/598
Harder, Karl Vassilieovich, II/2405/V-2/190
Harding, Sir Henry, II/2370/V-2/185
Harris, Thomas Noel, II/1591/V-2/113
Harting, Martin N. II/803/V-2/24
von Hartmann, Ernst Matthias, II/33/VII/246
von Hartmann, Ernst Matthias, II/234/VII/303

von Hartmann, Jakob, II/254/VII/307
Hartwig, Kurt, III/711/IX/611
Hasse, Otto, III/395/IX/535
Hasse, Otto, III/549/IX/572
von Hassy, Wilhelm, III/574/IX/578
Haupt, Hans-Joachim, III/117/IX/449
Haupt, Wilhelm, III/652/IX/597
Hauss, Ludwig, III/687/IX/605
Haverlandt I., Fedor, II/2447/V-2/197
von Haxthausen, Walter, III/584/IX/581
Head, Sir Francis Bond, II/2451/V-2/198
Hebener, Pavel N. II/1707/V-2/125
Heckel, Johann G. II/1331/V-2/85
von Hedemann, August G. II/2345/V-2/182
von Heeringen, Josias, III/90/IX/437
von Heeringen, Josias, III/154/IX/462
von Heimburg, Heino, III/285/IX/501
Heinecke, Oskar, III/434/IX/544
Heinrich, Prince of Hesse, II/306/VII/319
Heinrich, Prince of Prussia, III/133/IX/457
Heinrigs, Franz, III/348/IX/521
von Held, Siegfried, III/809/IX/634
von Helden-Sarnowski, Rudolf, II/242/VII/304
Helfreich, Igor Ivanovich, II/1290/V-2/80
Hell, Emil, III/167/IX/466
Hell, Emil, III/209/IX/480
von Helldorff, Heinrich, II/1967/V-2/142
Helmersen, Anton A. II/1131/V-2/65
Helwig, Alexander J. II/1778/V-2/132
von Hemmer, Hans, III/263/IX/496
Henckel von Donnersmarck, W. II/1242/V-2/77
Hensel, August Louis, II/129/VII/276
Hentsch, Richard, III/311/IX/508
(von) Herbert, Ernst, II/2262/V-2/162
Hermann, Alexander I. II/2396/V-2/189
Herold, Ferdinand, III/316/IX/510
Herrgott, Adolf, III/630/IX/592
Hersing, Otto, III/62/IX/426
von Hertsberg, Friedrich, III/797/IX/631
Hervey, Sir Felton Elwill, II/2393/V-2/188
Herwarth von Bittenfeld, K. II/41/VII/248
Hess, Heinrich, II/1595/V-2/114
Hesse, Hans, III/195/IX/475
von Hessenstein, Karl, II/1571/V-2/112
Heuck, Albert, III/776/IX/626
Heuduck, Heinrich, II/788/V-2/22
Heydenreich, Adolf H. II/2392/V-2/188
Heye, Wilhelm, III/142/IX/460
Heye, Wilhelm, III/469/IX/554
Heym, Hubert, III/479/IX/556
von Heynitz, Hans, III/379/IX/529
Hieronymus, Robert, III/593/IX/583
Hiller von Gaertringen, A. II/1647/V-2/119
von Hiller, Wilhelm A. II/154/VII/279

von Hindenburg, Paul, III/21/IX/407
von Hindenburg, Paul, III/38/IX/416
Hindersin, Gustaf Eduard, II/8/VII/244
Hingliat, Ivan M. II/2203/V-2/159
von Hipper, Franz, III/123/IX/454
Hippius, Karl Fedorovich, II/1622/V-2/116
Hippius, Karl Fedorovich, II/2208/V-2/159
Hirsch, Ivan, II/746/V-2/17
Hjerta, Gustaf Adolf, II/1338/V-2/89
von Hobe, August Johann, II/789/V-2/22
von Hobe, Kord Friedrich, II/1643/V-2/118
von Hoeck (Huek),* II/750/V-2/17
Hoefer, Karl, III/131/IX/457
Hoefer, Karl, III/487/IX/558
von Hoeppner, Ernst, III/217/IX/484
von Hofacker, Eberhard, III/227/IX/487
von Hofacker, Eberhard, III/368/IX/526
Hoffmann, Karl Heinrich, II/139/VII/277
Hoffmann, Max, III/178/IX/469
Hoffmann, Max, III/266/IX/497
von Hoffmann, Otto Gustaf, II/65/VII/260
von Hoffmüller, Adolf G. II/162/VII/281
von Hofmann, Georg Wilhelm, II/774/V-2/19
von Hofmann, Heinrich, III/351/IX/522
von Hofmann, Heinrich, III/695/IX/607
Hofmann, Max, III/91/IX/437
Hofmann, Max, III/613/IX/587
von Hohendorff, Otto Wilhelm, II/817/V-2/26
zu Hohenlohe-Ingelfingen, K. II/216/VII/300
von Hohenzollern-Hechingen, F. II/975/V-2/45
von Hohenzollern-Hechingen, F. II/1383/V-2/101
von Hohenzollern-Hechingen, Johann, II/1529/V-2/109
von Hohenzollern-Sigmaringen, A. II/54/VII/256
von Hohenzollern-Sigmaringen, K. II/102/VII/270
Hohnhorst, Ernst, III/541/IX/570
von Holleben, Ludwig F. II/2338/V-2/181
von Holtzendorff, Henning, III/215/IX/483
von Holtzendorff, Henning, III/426/IX/541
von Holtzendorff, Karl F. II/2317/V-2/178
Homburg, Erich, III/745/IX/619
Höndorf, Walter, III/129/IX/456
Höring, Wenzel, II/1593/V-2/114
Horn, Hans-Georg, III/409/IX/536
von Horn, Heinrich W. II/1227/V-2/75
von Horn, Rudolf, III/698/IX/608
von der Hoven, Igor C. II/2265/V-2/162
von der Hoven, Igor F. II/1367/V-2/98
Howaldt, Hans, III/407/IX/536
von Hoym,* Baron, II/2215/V-2/159
Hrabovsky von Hrabova, Johann, II/2400/V-2/189
Huberti, Vassili J. II/2270/V-2/163
Hübler, Julius Bruno, II/38/VII/248
von Hugel, Otto, III/149/IX/462
von Huhn, Otto (Wilhelm), II/1948/V-2/141

von Huhn, Otto F. II/1776/V-2/132
von Hülsen, Walter, III/480/IX/556
Humbert, Crown Prince, Italy, II/257/VII/308
Humser, Wilhelm, III/557/IX/574
Hundius, Paul, III/653/IX/597
Hundrich, Wilhelm, III/526/IX/567
Hundt, Eduard, Julius, II/37/VII/247
Hurko (Gurko), Josef V. II/291/VII/316
Hurko (Gurko), Ossip A. II/1285/V-2/79
von Huth, Friedrich Franz, III/424/IX/541
von Hutier, Oskar, III/306/IX/507
von Hutier, Oskar, III/440/IX/547
Hütterod, Wilhelm, II/2350/V-2/183
von Hymmen, Friedrich L. II/130/VII/276

I

Igelstroem, Gustaf G. II/2246/V-2/162
Ignatiev, Dmitri L. II/791/V-2/24
Ikonnikov, Ivan J. II/1292/V-2/80
Iljin,* II/2226/V-2/160
Iljinski, Alexander I. II/766/V-2/18
Ilovaiski XII., Ivan D. II/1871/V-2/137
Ilovaiski XVII., Fedor S. II/1566/V-2/112
Ilse, Emil, III/151/IX/462
Iltis, S.M.S. (Gunboat), III/12/IX/396
von Imeretien, Konstantin, II/1008/V-2/57
Imeretinski, Prince Alexander, II/295/VII/317
Immelmann, Max, III/111/IX/445
Isbash, Nikita N. II/2002/V-2/144
Isdemirov,* II/2183/V-2/157
Iskrizki, Peter M. II/2192 /V-2/158
Ismailov, Lavr T. II/1982/V-2/143
Issiumov, Nikolai G. II/1921/V-2/140
Itshkov, Nikolai N. II/1184/V-2/70
Ivanov III., Igor S. II/1984/V-2/143
Ivanov III., Igor S. II/2219/V-2/160
Ivanov, Stepan E. II/776/V-2/19
Ivanov, Stepan E. II/1492/V-2/106
Ivanov, Stepan J. II/2233/V-2/161
Ivashkevich, Ustin T. II/1248/V-2/77
Ivashkin,* II/2267/V-2/163

J

Jachontov, Alexander A. II/2413/V-2/191
von Jacobi, Albano, III/220/IX/485
Jacobs, Josef, III/623/IX/590
Jagnizki, Ivan T. II/2009/V-2/145
Jagodovski, Matwei I. II/1339/V-2/92
von Jagow, Christian F. II/2318/V-2/178
Jakimach, Moissei A. II/2170/V-2/156
Jakobson, Adelbart D. II/2015/V-2/145
Jakovlev, Alexander I. II/1087/V-2/62
Jakovlev, Stepan M. II/1125/V-2/65

Jakovlev, Stepan M. II/1193/V-2/72
James, George, II/981/V-2/46
Jaminski, Nikonor V. II/1511/V-2/107
Jaminski, Nikonor V. II/1657/V-2/120
Jannau II., Grigori Ivanovich, II/1456/V-2/104
Jaroslavzev, Ivan A. II/2075/V-2/149
Jefimovich, Grigori Ivanovich, II/1812/V-2/134
Jekov,* III/112/IX/445
Jelagin, Nikolai A. II/2218/V-2/159
Jemelianov, Nikolai F. II/1329/V-2/85
Jemilovski,* II/1971/V-2/142
Jereovski,* II/873/V-2/36
Jergeniev II., Peter M. II/1457/V-2/104
Jermakov, Alexander D. II/1780/V-2/132
Jermolaiev,* II/2178/V-2/157
Jermolov, Michail A. II/1430/V-2/103
Jermolov, Peter N. II/1409/V-2/103
Jeropkin,* II/1558/V-2/111
Jeropkin, Fedor Alexandrovich, II/2152/V-2/155
Jershov, Ivan Sacharieovich, II/1460/V-2/104
Jershov, Ivan Sacharieovich, II/2031/V-2/146
Jeschin, Vassili V. II/1118/V-2/65
Jesimovich, Andrei A. II/2049/V-2/148
Jessakov, Dmitri Semenovich, II/2086/V-2/150
Jessaulov,* II/1218/V-2/74
Johow, Georg, III/168/IX/466
Josenhanss, Edgar, III/777/IX/627
Joseph, Archduke of Austria, III/216/IX/484
Joseph, Archduke of Austria, III/452/IX/549
Julius,* II/1258/V-2/78
Julius, Karl Johann, II/824/V-2/27
Juncker, Karl Filippovich, II/935/V-2/41
Jünger, Ernst, III/696/IX/607
Jurgenev,* II/1038/V-2/59
Jushkov, Vladimir Ivanovich, II/1564/V-2/111

K
Kabisch, Ernst, III/729/IX/615
Kachovski, Michail Ivanovich, II/799/V-2/24
Kaether, Ernst, III/816/IX/635
von Kageneck, Karl, II/1373/V-2/99
von Kahlden, Hans-Heinrich, III/803/IX/633
von Kahlen I., Alexander B. II/2106/V-2/151
von Kahlen II., Paul B. II/2103/V-2/151
von Kaisenberg, Leopold, II/136/VII/277
Kalatshevski, Nikolai, II/1928/V-2/140
Kalau von Hofe, Konrad, III/132/IX/457
von Kalckreuth, August F. II/2381/V-2/187
Kalinin, Alexander Ivanovich, II/1168/V-2/68
Kalinovski, Vassili J. II/2198/V-2/158
Kalm, Fedor Grigorieovich, II/1172/V-2/69
von Kameke, Arnold Karl, II/107/VII/272
von Kameke, Arnold Karl, II/188/VII/292
Kamenov, Alexander M. II/1579/V-2/113

Kamenski,* II/1284/V-2/79
von Kamiensky, Friedrich W. II/112/VII/273
Kampan, Franz Ivanovich, II/1784/V-2/132
Kanattshikov,* II/1133/V-2/65
Kandiba II., David, II/957/V-2/43
Kantshialov, Alexander, II/1108/V-2/64
Kapustin, Ivan Fedorovich, II/1086/V-2/62
Kapzevich, Ivan M. II/2288/V-2/164
Karaczay von Walie-Szaka, F. II/1159/V-2/114
Karaoulov I., Dmitri, II/2138/V-2/153
Karaoulov, Alexander D. II/1792/V-2/132
Karaoulov, Nikolai D. II/1791/V-2/132
Karatshinski, Ivan, II/1385/V-2/102
Karatshinski, Ivan, II/2278/V-2/163
Karishev,* II/1341/V-2/92
Karl I., Emperor of Austria, III/193/IX/475
Karl, Archduke of Austria, III/121/IX/453
Karl, Prince of Prussia, F. II/50/VII/255
Karl, Prince of Rumania, E. II/284/VII/315
Karpov V., Akim A. II/2063/V-2/149
Karpov, Alexei Karpovich, II/1512/V-2/107
Karpov, Ivan Michailovich, II/895/V-2/38
Karshin, Christofor P. II/1276/V-2/79
Kartaminshev, Ivan N. II/1782/V-2/132
Kartshevski, Ivan S. II/2189/V-2/158
Karzov I., Ivan Petrovich, II/1432/V-2/103
Karzov, Pavel Stepanovich, II/1390/V-2/102
Kasadaven, Nikolai, II/1026/V-2/59
Kasha, Kosma Ivanovich, II/1729/V-2/127
Kashinzov II., Porfiri S. II/1414/V-2/103
Kashinzov, Alexander, II/1862/V-2/136
Kashirinov, Nikanor F. II/1085/V-2/62
Kashperov, Nikita P. II/2120/V-2/152
Kasin I., Peter Andreieovich, II/1552/V-2/110
Kasin II., Ivan Petrovich, II/1025/V-2/59
Kastriot-Drekalovich-etc., II/1116/V-2/64
Kastrov II., Prince Alexei, II/2077/V-2/149
Katashev,* II/1902/V-2/138
von Kathen, Hugo, III/150/IX/462
von Kathen, Hugo, III/298/IX/504
Katshoni, Lukurg L. II/1388/V-2/102
Kaufmann, Peter F. II/2212/V-2/159
Kaulbach, Georg, III/568/IX/577
Kaupert, Wilhelm, III/780/IX/627
Kaver, Jevstafe V. II/826/V-2/27
von Keiser, Karl, III/363/IX/525
von Keiser, Richard, III/502/IX/562
Keldermann,* II/1963/V-2/142
Keldermann, Konstantin, II/1084/V-2/62
Keldijarev, Michail G. II/1175/V-2/69
Keller, Alfred, III/382/IX/530
von Keller, Theodor L. II/792/V-2/24
von Keller, Heinrich Eugen, II/2344/V-2/182
Keller, Viktor, III/454/IX/550

Kellner, Alexander K. II/2067/V-2/149
von Kemphen, Johann Karl, II/2336/V-2/181
Kerlin, Adolf Karl, II/31/VII/247
Kern, Jermolai F. II/1064/V-2/61
von Kessel, Bernhard A. II/80/VII/262
von Kettler, Karl Friedrich, II/22/VII/246
Kewisch,* III/631/IX/592
von Keyserlingk, Ewald Karl, II/109/VII/272
von Keyserlink, Otto Karl, II/1883/V-2/137
von Kiefhaber, Christoph, III/365/IX/525
Kienitz, Paul, III/621/IX/589
von Kietzell, Karl, III/609/IX/586
Kindiakov, Semen Ivanovich, II/2280/V-2/163
Kiov, Ivan Ivanovich, II/2281/V-2/163
Kirchbach, Günter, III/295/IX/504
von Kirchbach, Hans, III/136/IX/458
von Kirchbach, Hugo Ewald, II/134/VII/277
von Kirchbach, Hugo Ewald, II/211/VII/298
Kirchfeldt, Friedrich W. II/26/VI/229
Kirchheim, Heinrich, III/741/IX/618
Kireiev V., Michail Igorovich, II/2431/V-2/194
Kireievski, Fedor (Theodor), II/2128/V-2/152
Kirpitshev, Matvei K. II/2312/V-2/177
Kirschstein, Hans, III/597/IX/583
Kishinski, Dmitri Igorovich, II/1798/V-2/133
Kishkin, Vassili Michailovich, II/1851/V-2/135
Kisselev, Pavel Dmitriovich, II/936/V-2/41
Kissenberth, Otto, III/605/IX/585
Kisslovski, Dmitri A. II/1057/V-2/60
Kladishtshev, Peter A. II/1899/V-2/138
Klebek, Igor Jermolaieovich, II/1363/V-2/98
Klein, Fedor Borissovich, II/1885/V-2/137
Klein, Hans, III/384/IX/530
Kleine, Rudolf, III/313/IX/509
von Kleist, Alfred, III/722/IX/614
von Kleist, Christian Ewald, II/81/VII/262
von Kleist, Ewald Johann, II/1157/V-2/68
von Kleist, Friedrich Emilius, II/1370/V-2/99
von Kleist, Peter, II/2134/V-2/153
Klette, Paul, III/503/IX/562
Klevesahl, Nikolai Jesimovich, II/2384/V-2/187
von Klewitz, Willi, III/281/IX/501
von Klewitz, Willi, III/659/IX/599
Klimovski, Lev Vassilieovich, II/1153/V-2/109
Klinckowström, Bernhard Wilhelm, II/35/VI/231
Klinckowström, Karl Friedrich, II/1658/V-2/121
Klingenberg, Jevstafi C. II/1188/V-2/71
Kloebe, Hans, III/419/IX/539
Klotzsch, Karl, II/2304/V-2/168
von Klüber, Robert, III/257/IX/494
von Kluck, Alexander, III/46/IX/419
von Klugen III., Gustaf, II/2446/V-2/197
von Klüser,* III/505/IX/562
von Klüx, Friedrich Karl, II/1225/V-2/75

Knappe von Knappstaedt, J. II/88/VII/263
von dem Knesebeck, Karl F. II/988/V-2/54
Kniasev, Peter Fedorovich, II/2061/V-2/149
Kniashnin, Boris J. II/1037/V-2/59
Knishnikov, Vassili D. II/2173/V-2/157
Knobel, Vassili F. II/1698/V-2/124
von Knobloch, Karl S. II/725/V-2/2
von Knoch, Maximilian, III/644/IX/595
von Knorring, Pontus V. II/2100/V-2/151
von Knorring, Vladimir K. II/1298/V-2/80
von Knuessl, Paul, III/59/IX/425
von Knuessl, Paul, III/210/IX/480
Kobiakov, Ivan N. II/1570/V-2/112
Koch, Otto, III/504/IX/562
Kochius,* II/1157/V-2/111
Koehl, Hermann, III/559/IX/574
Koenemann, Armin, III/375/IX/528
Köhn (von Jaski), Andreas, II/1645/V-2/119
Koilenski,* II/1746/V-2/129
Koilenski, Fedor (Ivan), II/825/V-2/27
Koletshizki, Ivan N. II/1376/V-2/100
Koletshizki, Ivan N. II/2149/V-2/155
Koliubakin, Vassili I. II/2264/V-2/162
Kologrivov, Stepan I. II/1868/V-2/136
Kolotinski, Konstantin M. II/1364/V-2/98
Kolsakov, Pavel A. II/2082/V-2/150
Komstadius, August F. II/1293/V-2/80
von König, Götz, III/70/IX/429
Konivalski, Ivan M. II/2018/V-2/145
Könnecke, Otto, III/702/IX/609
Konovkin, Gavril Ilitsh, II/1969/V-2/142
Konstantin, Grand Duke, Russia, II/30/VI/230
Konstantin, K. "   "   "   II/300/VII/317
Kophamel, Waldemar, III/411/IX/537
Korber, Julius Wilhelm, II/202/VII/294
Korf (Korsh), Nikolai, II/2201/V-2/158
von Korff I., Ossip I. II/1266/V-2/78
von Korff, Nikolai I. II/1389/V-2/102
Korobin III., Porfiri P. II/1400/V-2/102
Korovin, Ivan Stepanovich, II/2194/V-2/158
Korovkin, Arseni J. II/1433/V-2/103
Korshavin, Vassili Ivanovich, II/1203/V-2/73
Korssak, Roman Ossipovich, II/1983/V-2/143
Korssakov I., Pavel N. II/1426/V-2/103
Korssakov, Michail A. II/1803/V-2/134
Korssakov, Semen N. II/1320/V-2/82
von Korth, Ludwig Wilhelm, II/16/VII/245
Kosch, Robert, III/37/IX/416
Kosch, Robert, III/104/IX/442
von Koschembahr, Lev I. II/1447/V-2/104
Koshkin, Vassili Ivanovich, II/2078/V-2/149
Koshkin, Vassili Ivanovich, II/2227/V-2/160
von Kosküll, Josef Wilhelm, II/1932/V-2/140
von Kosküll, Peter Ivanovich, II/2099/V-2/151

Koslainov, Vladimir Petrovich, II/2313/V-2/177
Koslov, Nikolai Fedorovich, II/1277/V-2/78
Koslovski, Prince Vladimir, II/1422/V-2/103
Kostin IV., Grigori A. II/1274/V-2/79
Kostin, Nikolai G. II/1441/V-2/103
Kostirev, Nikolai Ivanovich, II/1475/V-2/105
Kostomarov, Sergei A. II/1404/V-2/102
Kotshetov, Fedor Nikititsh, II/1043/V-2/60
Kotshubei I., Arkadi V. II/800/V-2/24
Kotshuubei, Vassili V. II/934/V-2/41
Kovalevski,* II/1066/V-2/61
Kovankov. Michail Michailovich, II/1219/V-2/74
Koverniev,* II/868/V-2/36
Kövess von Kövessháza, Hermann, III/106/IX/443
Kövess von Kövessháza, Hermann, III/453/IX/549
Kovrigin, Michail A. II/1355/V-2/96
von Kraatz-Koschlau, Friedrich, II/156/VII/280
von Kraatz-Koschlau, Friedrich, II/224/VII/301
Kraehe, Konrad, III/317/IX/510
Kraehe, Konrad, III/650/IX/596
Krafft von Dellmensingen, Konrad, III/159/IX/464
Krafft von Dellmensingen, Konrad, III/200/IX/476
von Krafft, Karl Thilo, II/2334/V-2/181
Kramer, Lev Fedorovich, II/876/V-2/36
von Krane, Adolf Anatol, II/146/VII/278
von Kranold, Georg, III/675/IX/602
Krasinski, Leonid Yureovich, II/1491/V-2/106
Krasnakov, Gennadi Ivanovich, II/1809/V-2/134
Krasnokutski, Alexander G. II/1269/V-2/78
Krasnokutski, Ivan Nikolaiovich, II/863/V-2/36
Krasnokutski, Semen G. II/1807/V-2/134
Krassovski, Ivan Ivanovich, II/2014/V-2/145
Krassovski, Jakob Petrovich, II/1022/V-2/58
Kratz, Fedor Ivanovich, II/1289/V-2/80
Krause, Paul, III/464/IX/553
Krausenek, Johann Wilhelm, II/2364/V-2/183
Krauss, Alfred, III/353/IX/522
Krebs, Erich, III/396/IX/535
Krekshin, Dmitri Ivanovich, II/1435/V-2/103
Krekshin, Nikolai, II/1321/V-2/82
Kremkow, Fritz Theodor, III/8/IX/395
von Krenski, Paul Anton, II/120/VII/274
Kress von Kressenstein, F. III/302/IX/506
von Kretschmann, Ernst, III/577/IX/579
Kreuger, Johann Heinrich, II/1233/V-2/76
Kreuter, Eduard, III/747/IX/620
von Kriegsheim, Friedrich, III/457/IX/550
Krilov, Alexander A. II/1936/V-2/141
Krilov, Dmitri S. II/1428/V-2/103
Krishanovski, Andrei Ivanovich, II/1208/V-2/73
Krishanovski, Maxim K. II/761/V-2/18
Krishtofovich, Evgeni J. II/1988/V-2/143
Krishtofovich, Igor Konstantinovich, II/898/V-2/39
Kritshinski, Semen Jossifovich, II/2118/V-2/152

Krivonossov,* II/882/V-2/36
Krivski, Alexander J. II/1891/V-2/138
Krivzov, Alexander I. II/2083/V-2/150
Krivzov, Nikolai I. II/1424/V-2/103
Krizin, Jefim N. II/1922/V-2/140
von Krohn, Christian K. II/25/VII/246
Krohnstein, Gustaf V. II/1215/V-2/74
Kroll, Heinrich, III/460/IX/551
von Krüdener, Peter A. II/1733/V-2/128
Krug von Nidda, Hans, III/719/IX/613
Kruglikov, Ivan Gavrilovich, II/1546/V-2/110
von Krummes, Theodor E. II/1894/V-2/138
Krupenin, Vladimir P. II/1412/V-2/103
Krus, Alexander A. II/918/V-2/40
Kubitovich, Danilo A. II/1947/V-2/141
von Kuczkowski, Voleslaus, III/364/IX/525
von Kuhl, Hermann, III/152/IX/462
von Kuhl, Hermann, III/204/IX/478
Kühme, Kurt, III/671/IX/601
Kuhn, Josef Ignatieovich, II/2243/V-2/161
Kühne, Viktor, III/197/IX/476
Kuliabka, Ivan, II/1340/V-2/92
von Kummer, Ferdinand, II/158/VII/280
von Kummer, Friedrich, II/190/VII/282
Kundt, Friedrich, III/738/IX/617
Kunizki,* II/1562/V-2/111
Kupfer, Alexander I. II/2244/V-2/162
Küpfer, Heinrich Karl, II/1569/V-2/112
Kurdiumov, Igor S. II/1455/V-2/104
Kurlov, Grigori N. II/285/VII/315
Kurnossov, Nikolai A. II/1050/V-2/60
Kurshenski, Vladimir G. II/1830/V-2/135
von Kurssel, Fedor Fedorovich, II/781/V-2/19
Kushin, Vassili V. II/1450/V-2/104
Kusmin, Alexander Ivanovich, II/953/V-2/43
Kusmin, Nikita Petrovich, II/1465/V-2/104
Kusmin, Stepan Ivanovich, II/1209/V-2/73
Kusnezov, Michail M. II/1268/V-2/78
von Küster, Karl Gustaf, II/2440/V-2/195
Kuteinikov IV., Fedor, II/1702/V-2/125
Kuteinikov VI.,* II/984/V-2/47
Kutsherov,* II/1139/V-2/66
Kvitnizki, Xenofint F. II/1535/V-2/109

L

L'Coq, Karl August, II/1234/V-2/76
von L'Estocq, Anton Wilhelm, II/228/VII/302
von La Chevallerie, Siegfried, III/417/IX/539
von La Chevallerie, Siegfried, III/735/IX/626
Labutin,* II/1453/V-2/104
Lachmann,* II/2259/V-2/162
Lada, Hippolit M. II/1617/V-2/116
Ladigin, Nikolai Ivanovich, II/1503/V-2/106
Ladomirski, Vassili N. II/1819/V-2/134

von Leffert, Maximilian, III/156/IX/463
von Lamsdorff, Jakob M. II/1006/V-2/57
Lancelle, Otto, III/730/IX/615
Lange, Rudolf, III/624/IX/590
Langer, Felix, III/318/IX/510
Langer, Felix, III/811/IX/634
von Langsdorff, Julius, III/517/IX/565
Lans, Wilhelm Andreas, III/6/IX/393
Lappa, Peter Pavlovich, II/1459/V-2/104
Lappa, Wilhelm Michailovich, II/1513/V-2/107
Laptiev, Nikolai (Ivanovich), II/2269/V-2/163
von Larisch, Alfred, III/657/IX/598
Lasarev, Ivan Davidovich, II/293/VII/316
Latshinov, Alexander Petrovich, II/1520/V-2/108
Latshinov, Peter Petrovich, II/1771/V-2/131
Latshinov, Peter Petrovich, II/1058/V-2/148
Laumann, Artur, III/768/IX/625
Laveika, Alexander J. II/1474/V-2/104
Le Blanc, Albert, II/946/V-2/42
Lechner, Andrei Andreieovich, II/1515/V-2/107
von Ledebur, Leopold, III/776/IX/600
Leffers, Gustav, III/190/IX/473
Lehmann, Peter Friedrich, II/232/VII/302
von Leistner, Franz, II/236/V-2/185
von Lemke, Friedrich Wilhelm, II/2305/V-2/175
von Lens, Herman, III/485/IX/558
Leonhardy, Leo, III/710/IX/610
Leontovich, Ossip V. II/1743/V-2/129
Leopold, Prince of Bavaria, III/75/IX/431
Leopold, Prince of Bavaria, III/264/IX/496
Lepechin,* II/1485/V-2/105
Lequis, Arnold, III/323/IX/511
Lequis, Arnold, III/387/IX/531
Lermantov, Vladimir N. II/1977/V-2/142
Lessovski, Stepan Ivanovich, II/111-/V-2/64
von Leszczynski, Stanislaus, II/34/VII/247
von Leszczynski, Stanislaus, II/204/VII/297
von Lettow-Vorbeck, Paul, III/189/IX/473
von Lettow-Vorbeck, Paul, III/322/IX/511
Levandovski, Justin V. II/2273/V-2/163
von Levetzow, Magnus, III/334/IX/516
Levin, Dmitri Andreiovich, II/1044/V-2/60
Levoshka, Artemi Danilovich, II/2069/V-2/149
Levshin, Vladimir Vassilieovich, II/884/V-2/38
Levtshenko, Fedor G. II/1443/V-2/103
von Lewinski, Alfred August, II/269/VII/310
von Lewinski, Eduard Julius, II/36/VII/247
von Lewinski, Eduard Julius, II/235/VII/303
von Lewinski, Karl, III/234/IX/488
Liatkovski, Alexander J. II/2205/V-2/159
Liatuchin, Nikolai Petrovich, II/1827/V-2/134
Licharev, Afanassi, II/1462/V-2/104
von Liebert, Eduard, III/255/IX/493
Liebstein, Andrei Ivanovich, II/775/V-2/19

Liechtenstein, Prince Wenzel, II/1011/V-2/57
von der Lieth-Thomsen, H. III/218/IX/485
von Lignitz, Friedrich, II/278/VII/314
Liman von Sanders, Otto, III/107/IX/443
Lincke, Wilhelm, III/240/IX/490
von der Linde, Otto, III/23/IX/408
von Lindequist, Arthur, III/397/IX/535
von Lindequist, Arthur, III/812/IX/634
Lingren, Jevstafi M. II/1445/V-2/104
von Linsingen, Alexander, III/52/IX/423
von Linsingen, Alexander, III/65/IX/428
Lisagub, Alexander Ivanovich, II/1620/V-2/116
Lishin, Nikolai Fedorovich, II/1896/V-2/143
Lishin, Nikolai Fedorovich, II/2231/V-2/161
Lissanevich, Ivan G. II/1923/V-2/140
Lissanovski,* II/1761/V-2/130
Listovski,* II/1202/V-2/73
Litov, Andrei Jefremovich, II/837/V-2/29
Litvinov, Ivan Vassilieovich, II/1831/V-2/135
Litzmann, Karl, III/28/IX/412
Litzmann, Karl, III/78/IX/433
Liubushin,* II/922/V-2/40
Lobanov-Rostovski, Prince B. II/1915/V-2/139
von Lobbecke, Gerhard, III/685/IX/604
von Lobenthal Karl F. II/90/VII/263
Lobo da Silbeira, Count of Oriola, II/5/VI/226
von Lochow, Ewald, III/102/IX/441
Loeb, Robert, III/587/IX/581
Loebbecke, Gustaf Eduard, II/32/VII/247
Loebell, Friedrich Ernst, II/1650/V-2/119
Loeben, Eckhart, III/703/IX/609
Loerzer, Bruno, III/429/IX/542
von Loewenstein-Wertheim-R. II/1528/V-2/109
von Lowenstern, Karl K. II/2004/V-2/144
von Lowenstern, Ivan Peter, II/2297/V-2/167
von Lowenstern, Woldemar, II/890/V-2/38
Loewenthal, Fedor K. II/1621/V-2/116
Lohmann (Loman), Roman, II/1725/V-2/127
Lohs, Johannes, III/529/IX/568
Lopuchin, Alexander P. II/1165/V-2/68
Lopuchin, Prince Pavel, II/2038/V-2/147
Loris-Melikov, Michail T. II/290/VII/316
Loshkarev, Alexander S. II/2242/V-2/161
von Lossberg, Friedrich K. III/169/IX/466
von Lossberg, Friedrich K. III/224/IX/486
von Lossberg, Friedrich W. II/2353/V-2/183
Lossenkov, Vassili Ivanovich, II/869/V-2/36
Lossovski, Ivan V. II/2434/V-2/194
Losthin, Michail Heinrich, II/2341/V-2/182
Lour, Ivan Ivanovich, II/1494/V-2/106
Lovieko, Ivan, II/2127/V-2/152
Lowe, Sir Hudson, II/1384/V-2/101
Löwenfeld, Julius Josef, II/91/VII/263
Löwenfeld, Julius Ludwig, II/132/VII/276

Löwenhardt, Erich, III/565/IX/576
Löwenhof, Timofei Antonovich, II/1048/V-2/60
Löwenhof, Timofei Antonovich, II/1944/V-2/141
von Luchow, Ewald, III/32/IX/414
von Luck, Friedrich, III/668/IX/600
Ludendorff, Erich, III/19/IX/405
Ludendorff, Erich, III/39/IX/416
von Lüdinghausen, Peter J. II/778/V-2/19
von Lüdinghausen, Peter J. II/1978/V-2/143
Ludwig III., King of Bavaria, III/194/IX/475
Ludwig, Auchduke of Hesse, II/230/VII/302
Ludwig, Max, III/610/IX/586
Lukitsh, Panteleimon S. II/2050/V-2/148
Lukomski, Dmitri Nikolaiovich, II/1120/V-2/65
Lukovkin, Amvrosi Gavrilovich, II/2011/V-2/145
von Lupin, Kurt, III/447/IX/548
von Lupinski, Vinzentius F. II/810/V-2/25
Lüters, Rudolf, III/704/IX/609
von Lüttwitz, Arthur, III/349/IX/521
von Lüttwitz, Walther, III/146/IX/461
von Lüttwitz, Walther, III/445/IX/548
von Lützow, Ludwig Adolf, II/2321/V-2/178
von Lützow, Friedrich, II/1028/V-2/59
Lvov, Alexander Nikolaiovich, II/1618/V-2/116
Lvov, Dmitri Michailovich, II/2089/V-2/150
von Lyncker, Moritz, III/337/IX/518

M
von Mach II., Leopold, II/783/V-2/20
von Mach II., Leopold, II/816/V-2/25
von Mach, August Friedrich, II/1374/V-2/99
von Mackensen, August, III/27/IX/412
von Mackensen, August, III/60/IX/425
Madatov, Prince Valerian, II/961/V-2/43
Maercker, Georg, III/312/IX/509
Maercker, Georg, III/536/IX/569
Magdenko I., Ivan Semenovich, II/1794/V-2/133
Magdenko II., Michail S. II/1197/V-2/72
von Magnus, Franz, III/682/IX/604
Maievski, Sergei Ivanovich, II/2017/V-2/145
von Maillinger, Josef M. II/262/VII/309
Maiorov, Alexei Ivanovich, II/1532/V-2/109
Maistre (de), Rudolf O. II/1910/V-2/139
Makalinski, Ivan, II/914/V-2/40
Makazarov, Ivan Vassilieovich, II/1176/V-2/69
Makuchin,* II/1348/V-2/93
Makuchin,* II/2166/V-2/156
Maleiev, Alexander Semenovich, II/1103/V-2/64
Malevanov,* II/1068/V-2/61
Malinovski, Silvester S. II/1715/V-2/126
Mandrika, Nikolai J. II/1920/V-2/140
Manfredi, Ossip Ivanovich, II/1315/V-2/82
Manonov, Ivan Averianovich, II/1960/V-2/142
Mansei, Nikolai Loginovich, II/2146/V-2/155

von Manstein, Gustaf Albert, II/5/VII/244
von Manstein, Gustaf Albert, II/113/VII/273
von Manteuffel,* II/2211/V-2/159
von Manteuffel, August K. II/731/V-2/4
von Manteuffel, Karl R. II/58/VII/259
von Manteuffel, Karl R. II/183/VII/291
Manuilov, Matvei I. II/1718/V-2/126
Maratshinski, Ivan A. II/2024/V-2/145
von der Marck, Josef, II/1527/V-2/109
Marianovich, Markiss P. II/2051/V-2/148
Markevich, Filipp P. II/1626/V-2/117
Markevitsh (Markovitsh), A. II/1739/V-2/128
Markmann, Hans, III/428/IX/542
Markov III., Alexander I. II/745/V-2/17
Marquard, Gottfried, III/172/IX/467
von Marschall, August L.2 II/352/V-2/183
Marschall, Wolf, III/166/IX/465
Marschall, Wolf, III/554/IX/574
von Marschall, Wenzel P. II/1322/V-2/82
Marschall, Wilhelm, III/607/IX/586
Martianov, Danilo J. II/2119/V-2/152
Martinov, Pavel Petrovich, II/1820/V-2/134
von der Marwitz, Friedrich, II/2373/V-2/186
von der Marwitz, Georg, III/40/IX/417
von der Marwitz, Georg, III/56/IX/423
Masaraki, Semen S. II/1019/V-2/58
Maske (Masska), Ivan J. II/1893/V-2/138
Massalov, Ivan G. II/1822/V-2/134
Masslenizki, Fedor T. II/1822/V-2/134
Masslov,* II/1093/V-2/63
Masslov, Alexander P. II/1845/V-2/135
von Massow, Wilhelm, II/266/VII/309
Matov,* II/887/V-2/38
Matshulski, Fedor S. II/2023/V-2/145
Matthiass, Robert, III/632/IX/593
Matthiass, Willi, III/354/IX/523
Mattshinski, Adam O. II/2399/V-2/189
von Maur, Heinrich, III/245/IX/491
Maznev, Michail N. II/2290/V-2/164
Meckel, Wilhelm, III/291/IX/503
Mecklenburg von Kleeberg, J. II/1603/V-2/114
von Mecklenburg-Strelitz, K. II/986/V-2/49
von Medem, Friedrich A. II/96/VII/264
von Medem, Vassili A. II/903/V-2/39
von Medem, Vassili I. II/2090/V-2/150
Medinzov, Jakob A. II/1177/V-2/69
Medviedev, Alexei D. II/1496/V-2/106
Medviedev, Peter I. II/749/V-2/17
Medviedev, Peter I. II/762/V-2/18
Meier II., Karl C. II/1539/V-2/110
Meister, Karl Theodor, III/16/IX/402
Meknob,* II/1473/V-2/104
Melikov, Pavel M. II/2101/V-2/151
Mellard, Karl K. II/1480/V-2/105

Mellenthin, Hans, III/432/IX/543
Melnikov IV.,* II/1651/V-2/120
Melnikov V., Nikolai G. II/1652/V-2/120
Melnikov,* II/845/V-2/29
Melnikov, Michail, II/1732/V-2/128
Melnikov, Michail I. II/1727/V-2/127
Menckhoff, Karl, III/527/IX/567
von Mensdorff, Emanuel, II/987/V-2/49
Menshikov, Prince A. II/1509/V-2/107
Menshikov, Prince Nikolai, II/846/V-2/29
Menshinski, Jossif S. II/2165/V-2/156
Merkel, Carl, III/534/IX/569
von Merlin, Karl D. II/1882/V-2/137
von Mermerty, Albert G. II/219/VII/300
von Mertens, August F. II/11/VII/245
von Mertens, August F. II/241/VII/304
von Mertens, Max, III/688/IX/605
Mertz von Quirnheim, H. III/458/IX/550
Messing, Alexander I. II/1151/V-2/67
von Metzsch, Horst, III/720/IX/613
von Meyendorf, Georg Otto, II/2450/V-2/197
Meyer,* III/818/IX/636
Meyer, Dmitri Petrovich, II/1585/V-2/113
von Meyerdorff, Igor K. II/915/V-2/40
Meyerlinck, Wichard Georg, II/2087/V-2/150
Miagkov,* II/816/V-2/34
Miagkov, Vassili N. II/1154/V-2/67
Miakinin, Nikolai D. II/2139/V-2/153
von Miaskowski, Friedrich, III/506/IX/563
von Michaelis, Christof J. II/785/V-2/20
Michail, Grand Duke, Russia, N. II/253/VII/307
Michail, Grand Duke, Russia, N. II/280/VII/314
Michailovski, Nikolai, II/2214/V-2/159
Michailovski-Danilevski, Alex. II/998/V-2/56
Michaud, Ludwig Franzovich, II/838/V-2/29
Michelsen, Andreas, III/564/IX/576
Mikulin, Sergei Ivanovich, II/1059/V-2/60
Mikulin, Vassili J. II/2301/V-2/168
Mileant, Igor Dmitrieieovich, II/2406/V-2/190
Mileoka, Ivan Ossipovich, II/1787/V-2/132
Milisch, Leopold, III/762/IX/623
Miliutin, Dmitri Alexeiovich, II/287/VII/316
Milochov, Alexei Alexeiovich, II/815/V-2/25
Miloradovich, Alexei G. II/931/V-2/41
Miloradovich, Andrei N. II/1031/V-2/59
Mirkovich, Ivan Petrovich, II/880/V-2/36
Mironov, Ivan Semenovich, II/1687/V-2/123
Moeller, Richard, III/246/IX/491
von Möhl, Arnold, III/731/IX/615
Moisseviev, Alexander L. II/894/V-2/38
Moliere, Louis Auguste, II/2438/V-2/195
von Möllendorf, Johann Karl, II/11/VI/227
Molokov, Kornili I. II/2410/V-2/192
Molostvov, Panfemir C. II/1438/V-2/103
Molostvov, Porfiri C. II/1162/V-2/68
Molostvov, Vladimir P. II/1942/V-2/141
von Moltke, Hellmuth K. II/214/VII/299
von Moltke, Hellmuth K. II/302/VII/318
von Moltke, Hellmuth K. III/1/IX/388
von Moltke, Hellmuth K. II/2454/V-2/198
von Moltke, Helmuth, III/74/IX/431
von Moltke, Paul A. II/2397/V-2/189
Moltshanov (Multshanov),* II/1640/V-2/118
Moltshanov,* II/1143/V-2/66
Möner, Axel Otto, II/1336/V-2/89
Moraht, Robert, III/352/IX/522
Mordvinov II., Ivan N. II/1410/V-2/103
Mordvinov, Vladimir M. II/2404/V-2/190
von Morgen, Kurt, III/29/IX/412
von Morgen, Kurt, III/201/IX/476
Morkovnikov, Kosma I. II/2255/V-2/162
Morosov, Ivan Semenovich, II/929/V-2/41
von Morsbach, Engelbert, III/611/IX/587
Morshin, Michail M. II/1722/V-2/126
Mortshalov, Ivan P. II/1463/V-2/104
von Moser, Otto, III/228/IX/487
Moshenski, Denis D. II/1045/V-2/60
Moshenski, Filipp D. II/1777/V-2/132
Muchanov,* II/1278/V-2/79
von Mudro, Bruno, III/21/IX/414
von Mudro, Bruno, III/185/IX/471
von Müffling, Friedrich K. II/1655/V-2/120
von Müffling, Wilhelm, II/1381/V-2/101
von Mühlbach, Traugott, W. II/2453/V-2/198
von zur Mühlen, Vassili W. II/805/V-2/24
Mühry, Georg, III/763/IX/624
von der Mülbe, Otto W. II/105/VII/271
Müller,* II/1956/V-2/142
Müller, Fedor Fedorovich, II/2429/V-2/193
Müller, Ferdinand, III/645/IX/596
von Müller, Georg, III/446/IX/548
Müller, Karl Ivanovich, II/2412/V-2/191
von Müller, Karl, III/439/IX/546
von Müller, Max, III/301/IX/506
Müller, Otto, III/691/IX/606
Müller, Rudolf, III/646/IX/596
Müller-Kahle, Albert, III/746/IX/619
von Mulzer, Max, III/127/IX/455
von Münch, Friedrich W. II/2357/V-2/183
zu Münster-Meinhövel, Hugo, II/152/VII/279
Murat Bieiev, Saltan D. II/1510/V-2/107
Muraviev, Alexander S. II/1351/V-2/94
Muraviev, Artamon S. II/1352/V-2/94
Muromzov, Alexander M. II/1864/V-2/136
Muromzov, Matvei M. II/1417/V-2/103
Mussin-Pushkin, Michail, II/1814/V-2/134
Mussin-Pushkin, Ivan A. II/830/V-2/28
Mustafin, Prince Alexander, II/859/V-2/34

von Mutius, Albert, III/683/IX/604
von Mutius, Franz Wilhelm, II/51/VII/255

N

Nabel, Andrei Andreiovich, II/1912/V-2/139
Nagatkin* II/1752/V-2/129
Nagin,* II/864/V-2/36
Nahbel, Carl, III/707/IX/610
Nakovalnin, Nikolai F. II/1316/V-2/82
Narbut, Heinrich Karlovich, II/1074/V-2/61
Narishkin, Dmitri V. II/2006/V-2/145
Narvoish, Franz G. II/1697/V-2/124
Nasimov, Yevgeni P. II/879/V-2/36
Natara (I.), Stepan S. II/2279/V-2/163
Natara II., Stepan J. II/2232/V-2/161
Natara III. Dmitri J. II/2234/V-2/161
Naumov, Sergei Alex. II/1507/V-2/106
Neckel, Ullrich, III/820/IX/636
von Niedhardt II., Alex. W. II/733/V-2/19
Niedhardt von Gneisenau, W. II/1372/V-2/99
Neielov II., Ivan Ivanovich, II/2124/V-2/152
Neielov, Peter, Alex. II/2039/V-2/147
Nekludov, Sergei Petrovich, II/1518/V-2/108
Nelidov,* II/1759/V-2/130
Nepenin, Andrei G. II/1170/V-2/68
Nepieizin, Sergei V. II/1160/V-2/68
Nepokoitshizki, Arthur V. II/288/VII/316
Nerger, Karl August, III/430/IX/543
Nesterovski, Avim V. II/1200/V-2/73
Netshaiev, Nikolai A. II/2026/V-2/146
Neumann, Alexander I. II/1979/V-2/143
Neumeister, Emil Georg, II/261/VII/309
Nielebock, Friedrich, III/569/IX/577
Nikiforov, Michail K. II/1470/V-2/104
Nikitin, Michail Fedorovich, II/1327/V-2/85
Nikolai, Grand Duke, Russia, M. II/301/VII/318
Nikolai, Grand Duke, Russia, N. II/299/VII/317
Nikolai, Grand Duke, Russia, N. II/252/VII/307
Nikolai, Grand Duke, Russia, N. II/281/VII/314
Nikolaiev, Ivan Yurieovich, II/1313/V-2/81
Nikolev, Vladimir Ivanovich, II/1853/V-2/135
Nikonov, Kyrill Nikititsh, II/1260/V-2/78
Nilus, Bogdan Bogdanovich, II/905/V-2/39
Noailles, Alexis, II/850/V-2/33
Nogi, Kiten, III/14/IX/399
Nolde, Karl, II/1104/V-2/64
Noldken, Igor Fedorovich, II/747/V-2/17
Nordstein, Sergei N. II/1993/V-2/144
Norov, Vassili S. II/2411/V-2/191
von Nostitz, August L. II/2436/V-2/195
Novak, Peter Ivanovich, II/892/V-2/38
Novikov,* II/1063/V-2/61
Novikov, Nikita I. II/1793/V-2/132
Novizki,* II/1489/V-2/105
Novopoliez, Andrei A. II/2206/V-2/159
Novossilzov, Ivan P. II/801/V-2/24
Novossilzov, Vladimir G. II/2298/V-2/167

O

von Obernitz, Hugo M. II/78/VII/262
Oblenski, Alexander P. II/1065/V-2/61
Oblenski, Prince Nikolai, II/1210/V-2/74
Oblenski, Prince Vassili, II/1191/V-2/72
Obrutshev, Vladimir A. II/759/V-2/17
Obrutshev, Vladimir A. II/1795/V-2/133
Obuchovski, Peter S. II/1078/V-2/61
von Oesterreich, Kurt, III/573/IX/578
von Oetinger und Edler, H. III/448/IX/549
Offermann, Franz, II/116/VII/274
Ofrossimov, Konstantin, II/2421/V-2/192
Ogoreliz, Stepan, II/1869/V-2/136
Okuniev, Gavril S. II/1806/V-2/134
Okuniev, Nikolai A. II/944/V-2/42
Oldenborgen, Ivan F. II/1245/V-2/77
von Oldershausen, Erich, III/398/IX/535
von Oldershausen, Erich, III/451/IX/549
von Oldershausen, Martin, III/247/IX/491
von Ollech, Karl Rudolf, II/133/VII/277
Olshevski II., Franz D. II/770/V-2/19
Olshevski, Anton D. II/874/V-2/36
Olshenski, Matvei A. II/1082/V-2/62
Olshevski, Ossip D. II/2055/V-2/148
Olsuviev, Alexander D. II/2043/V-2/148
von Oppen, Adolf F. II/852/V-2/34
von Oppen, Gustav, III/788/IX/629
von Oppenkowsky, S. II/2329/V-2/180
Oranski, Ivan A. II/1889/V-2/138
O'Rurk III. Korneli J. II/1996/V-2/144
O'Rurk IV., Vladimir I. II/1995/V-2/144
Orlov, Alexander V. II/1581/V-2/113
Orlov, Alexei F. II/942/V-2/41
Orlov, Alexei F. II/976/V-2/45
Oserski,* II/1488/V-2/105
Oserski, Ivan, II/764/V-2/18
Osharovski, Ignati O. II/2005/V-2/144
Osiander, Wilhelm, III/804/IX/633
Osmolovski,* II/2221/V-2/160
Ossipov, Nikolai J. II/1039/V-2/59
Ossipovich, Saveli A. II/2210/V-2/159
von der Osten, Otto A. II/2331/V-2/180
von der Osten-Sacken, D. II/973/V-2/41
Osterkamp, Theo, III/677/IX/602
Ostragradski, Matvei I. II/875/V-2/36
Ostreshkovski, Franz, K. II/2283/V-2/163
von Othegraven, Thomas, II/1649/V-2/119
Otto, Martin, III/647/IX/596
Ovander, Vassili J. II/2126/V-2/152
von Oven, Adolf, III/699/IX/608

von Oven, Ernst, III/764/IX/624
von Oven, Georg, III/261/IX/495

P

Paar, Johann Baptist, II/1009/V-2/57
Pachert, Ivan Ivanovich, II/809/V-2/25
von Paczensky-Tenczyn, Anton, II/69/VII/260
von Paczynski-Tenczin, Leo, III/372/IX/527
von der Pahlen, Ivan P. II/1934/V-2/141
von Paikul (Paykull), Anton F. II/902/V-2/39
Paissel, Peter P. II/1306/V-2/81
Palizin, Michail J. II/1856/V-2/136
Palizin, Vladimir, II/2080/V-2/150
Panin, Alexander N. II/2309/V-2/177
Pankratiev, Nikolai, II/1692/V-2/124
von Pannewitz, Günther, III/164/IX/465
Pantenius, Fedor I. II/1354/V-2/96
Pantshulidsev, Alexander A. II/1243/V-2/77
Panutin, Fedor S. II/1817/V-2/134
von Pape, August Wilhelm, II/83/VII/263
von Pape, August Wilhelm, II/255/VII/308
von Pape, Johann Meinard, II/103/VII/271
von Pappenheim, Karl T. II/1663/V-2/121
Parenssov, Dmitri T. II/741/V-2/16
Parfazki, Apollon A. II/2052/V-2/148
Parschau, Otto, III/128/IX/456
Pashkov, Andrei I. II/889/V-2/38
Paskevich, Ossip F. II/932/V-2/41
Pastshenko, Lev K. II/832/V-2/28
von Patkul, Friedrich, II/2076 /V-2/149
Patkul, Vladimir G. II/1405/V-2/102
Paton de Merieran,* II/1769/V-2/131
Pauli (Paoli), Peter I. II/1625/V-2/116
Pauli (Paoli), Peter I. II/1738/V-2/128
Paulus, Karl, III/742/IX/618
Pavlenko, Dorofei J. II/1076/V-2/125
Pavlenkov, Jemelian O. II/1035/V-2/59
Pavloski II., Ferdinand A. II/927/V-2/40
Pavlov,* II/940/V-2/41
Pavlov, Dmitri Pavlovich, II/2022/V-2/145
Pavlov, Grigori, II/1941/V-2/141
Pavlov, Pavel A. II/2068/V-2/149
von Paweltz, Richard, III/399/IX/535
von Pechmann, Paul, III/278/IX/499
Peiker, Matvei M. II/1675/V-2/122
Penskoi IV., Ivan I. II/1420/V-2/103
Perepietshin,* II/1211/V-2/74
Perovski, Lev Alexieovich, II/999/V-2/57
Perski, Michail S. II/1672/V-2/122
Peshtshanski, Grigori, II/2186/V-2/158
von Pestel, Eduard, II/268/VII/310
Pestel, Pavel Ivanovich, II/1937/V-2/141
von Petersdorff, Axel, III/518/IX/565
Peterson, Ivan Fedorovich, II/812/V-2/25
Peterson, Jakob I. II/1766/V-2/130
Petri, Hans, III/778/IX/627
Petrov, Ivan A. II/860/V-2/34
Petrov, Ivan M. II/901/V-2/39
Petrovich, Andrei P. II/2035/V-2/147
Petrovski, Andrei A. II/2060/V-2/148
Petrovski-Muravski,* II/1213/V-2/74
Petrovski-Muravski,* II/2275/V-2/163
Petrovski-Muravski, N. II/1965/V-2/142
Petrulin, Jakob V. II/793/V-2/24
Petrulin, Jakob V. II/1933/V-2/140
Petrulin, Yuri V. II/1939/V-2/141
Peyron, Gustaf A. II/965/V-2/44
Pfaehler, Wilhelm, III/732/IX/616
Pfafferot, Clemens, III/782/IX/628
Pflugradt, Benno, III/794/IX/630
von Pfuel, Ernst A. II/2292/V-2/164
von Pfuel, Ernst A. II/2444/V-2/196
von Pfuel, August F. II/27/VI/229
Piatkin, Vassili G. II/1863/V-2/136
Pichatshev, Matvei I. II/1021/V-2/58
Pichelstein, Johann S. II/1987/V-2/143
Pietin, Ivan A. II/1418/V-2/103
Pikardi, Arthur, III/615/IX/587
Pilchovski, Ivan C. II/1943/V-2/141
Piliugin, Vassili A. II/2070/V-2/149
Pimanov, Ivan A. II/2079/V-2/149
von Pirch I., Karl K. II/1396/V-2/102
von Pirch, Georg D. II/1324/V-2/82
von Pirch, Otto K. II/2320/V-2/178
von Pirscher, Friedrich, III/539/IX/570
Pishnizki,* II/1058/V-2/60
Pissarev, Alexander A. II/1040/V-2/59
von der Planitz (Edler) H. III/248/IX/441
von Platen, Axel, III/507/IX/563
Plath, Otto, III/616/IX/599
Platov, Ivan M. II/2314/IX/177
von Plehwe, Karl III/508/IX/563
Pleski, Wilhelm A. II/1454/V-2/104
von Plessen, Hans, III/444/IX/548
von Plattenberg, Karl, III/53/IX/423
Plochovo, Sergei N. II/1273/V-2/79
von Plüskow, Otto, III/238/IX/489
Pochvisniev, Ivan I. II/1127/V-2/65
von Podbielski, Theophil II/95/VII/264
von Podbielski, Theophil II/239/VII/303
Pogorski-Linkevich, N. II/2422/V-2/192
von Pogrell, Philipp, II/61/VII/259
Pohl, Ivan L. II/1121/V-2/65
Pohlmann, Georg, III/715/IX/612
Pokrovski, Jevstafi C. II/1375/V-2/100
Pokrovski, Jevstafi C. II/2148/V-2/155
Polossov, Danilo P. II/1152/V-2/67
Poltarazki, Alexander, II/2012/V-2/145

Pomeranski, Narkiss, II/1968/V-2/142
Ponerovski, Vassili J. II/1069/V-2/61
Poniński, August, II/1629/V-2/117
Popelka, Rudolph, III/737/IX/617
Popov XIII.,* II/2001/V-2/144
Popov,* II/821/V-2/27
Popov,* II/993/V-2/54
Popov, Alexander J. II/2115/V-2/152
Porochovnikov, Nikolai P. II/1679/V-2/122
Posdieiev, Ivan V. II/1860/V-2/136
Possiet, Alexander P. II/2160/V-2/156
Possudovski,* II/2168/V-2/156
Postelnikov, Nikolai J. II/758/V-2/17
Postels, Siegismund F. II/768/V-2/19
Potapov, Peter Igorovich, II/1096/V-2/62
Potemkin I., Alexander D. II/1505/V-2/106
Potemkin, Alexander M. II/1800/V-2/133
Potemkin, Jakob A. II/1796/V-2/133
Potocki, Jaroslav S. II/1614/V-2/116
Potocki, Stanislaus S. II/1126/V-2/65
von Pott, Georg Heinrich, II/1878/V-2/137
Potulov V., Peter, II/1397/V-2/102
Potulov, Ivan T. II/1346/V-2/92
Potulov, Ivan T. II/2164/V-2/156
Potvig,* II/919/V-2/40
von Prager, Karl, III/400/IX/535
Priess, Nikolai I. II/1377/V-2/100
Priess, Nikolai I. II/2151/V-2/155
Preuschen-(von u zu Liebenstein), III/588/IX/581
Preusker, Hans, III/267/IX/497
Preusker, Hans, III/616/IX/587
Priashevski, Nikolai I. II/1768/V-2/131
Priashevski, Nikolai I. II/2230/V-2/160
Prigara, Pavel O. II/1186/V-2/71
Prinz von Buchau, Kurt, III/548/IX/572
von Prittwitz, Karl L. II/28/VI/229
von Prittwitz, Paul K. II/1300/V-2/80
Pritzelwitz, Kurt, III/109/IX/444
von Probst, Friedrich W. II/818/V-2/27
Prokofiev, Tichon F. II/1789/V-2/132
von Prondzynski, Konrad F. II/144/VII/278
Prosorkevich, Lavrenti J. II/1452/V-2/104
Prosvirkin,* II/842/V-2/29
Protassov, Grigori G. II/1060/V-2/60
Protopopov, Ivan A. II/1578/V-2/113
Protopopov, Peter S. II/1046/V-2/60
Protopopov, Stepan D. II/820/V-2/27
Prozikov, Andrei F. II/1275/V-2/79
Prudnikov, Alexander F. II/2256/V-2/162
Pshenitshonoi, Alexei A. II/1137/V-2/66
Puetling, Andrei A. II/1720/V-2/126
Pushkarev, Fedor N. II/1353/V-2/95
Pusin,* II/1344/V-2/92
Pusin, Karl Karlovich, II/2137/V-2/153

Pusirevski,* II/1890/V-2/138
Pustshin, Nikolai N. II/2365/V-2/185
Pustshin, Pavel S. II/1805/V-2/134
Pütter, Fritz, III/566/IX/576
von Puttkamer, Georg H. II/231/VII/302
von Puttkamer, Georg K. II/26/VII/246
von Puttkammer, Wilhelm, III/772/IX/625

Q

von Quadt u Huchtenbruck, L. II/97/VII/264
von Quast, Ferdinand, III/137/IX/459
von Quast, Ferdinand, III/486/IX/558
von Quednow, Kurt M. III/672/IX/601
von Quitzow, Siegfried G. II/740/V-2/16

R

Raben, Karl Ivanovich, II/779/V-2/19
Rachmanov, Alexander I. II/839/V-2/29
Rackow, Kurt, III/125/IX/454
Radezki, Fedor F. II/292/VII/316
Raditsh, Jakob, N. II/1867/V-2/136
Radziwill, Prince Friedrich, II/12/VI/227
Raievski, Alexander N. II/939/V-2/41
Raiski,* II/924/V-2/40
Raiski, Ivan S. II/1297/V-2/80
Rall III., Fedor F. II/1419/V-2/103
Rall IV., Vassili F. II/1857/V-2/136
von Ramburg,* II/1001/V-2/57
Ramm, Karl K. II/2097/V-2/151
Raslov,* II/1235/V-2/76
Rassochin,* II/1483/V-2/105
Rastkovski, Justin S. II/1332/V-2/85
Rateiev, Prince Yuri, II/1204/V-2/73
von Rauch, Johann G. II/1656/V-2/120
von Rauchenberger, Otto, III/307/IX/507
von Rauchenberger, Otto, III/753/IX/621
von Raven, Eduard Gustaf, II/6/VII/244
von Ravenstein,* III/594/IX/583
Read V., Andrei A. II/1624/V-2/116
Read, Evgeni A. II/2435/V-2/194
Read, Jakob A. II/1387/V-2/102
Read, Nikolai A. II/1917/V-2/139
Rebrikov III.,* II/1926/V-2/140
Redrikov,* II/2030/V-2/146
von Rehbinder, Boris B. II/2073/V-2/149
Reibnitz, Karl Pavlovich, II/1054/V-2/60
Reich, Ivan Ivanovich, II/1959/V-2/142
Reichard (Reichert),* II/2418/V-2/192
Reichel, Avram A. II/1723/V-2/126
Reichenbach,* III/509/IX/563
von Reinhard, Karl, II/15/VII/245
Reinhard, Wilhelm, III/296/IX/504
Reinhard, Wilhelm, III/709/IX/610
Reinhardt, Walter, III/221/IX/485

Reinhardt, Walter, III/572/IX/578
Reinicke, Hermann, III/388/IX/531
von Reitenstein,* III/819/IX/636
Reitz, Leonti L. II/827/V-2/27
von Reitzenstein, Karl H. II/2439/V-2/195
von Rennenkampff, Gustaf, II/1359/V-2/96
von Rennenkampff, Karl P. II/1132/V-2/65
von Rennenkampff, Karl P. II/1748/V-2/129
von Rennenkampff, Paul J. II/1586/V-2/113
Renner, Theodor, III/676/IX/602
Renni, Robert (Igorovich), II/752/V-2/17
Repninski, Nikolai J. II/1832/V-2/135
Retkin (Redkin), Nikolai N. II/2426/V-2/193
Retsey de Retse, Adam, II/994/V-2/54
von Rettberg, Karl, III/366/IX/526
von Reutern, Christofor R. II/1112/V-2/64
von Reutern Erhard R. II/1865/V-2/136
Reuterskjöld, Leonhard A. II/968/V-2/44
Ribbontrop, Wilhelm, III/693/IX/607
Richter, Karl Ivanovich, II/2237/V-2/161
von Richthofen, Lothar, III/242/IX/490
von Richthofen, Manfred, III/211/IX/481
von Richthofen, Manfred III/416/IX/538
Riemann, Julius, III/43/IX/418
Rieper, Peter, III/617/IX/588
von Reisenthal, Hans E. III/519/IX/566
Rikov, Vassili D. II/1295/V-2/80
Rindin, Feladelf K. II/2274/V-2/163
Rippentrop, Karl B. II/35/VII/247
Risvanovich I., Chalil I. II/1501/V-2/106
Ritshkov, Nikolai V. II/1685/V-2/123
von Röder, Friedrich E. II/1689/V-2/123
Rodig, Siegfried, III/510/IX/563
Rodsianko, Michail P. II/2311/V-2/177
von Roeder, Dietrich, III/493/IX/560
von Roeder, Julius H. II/43/VII/249
Rogatshev, Semen, I. II/848/V-2/32
Rogovski, Alexander V. II/2175/V-2/157
Rohr, Karl Heinrich, II/2328/V-2/179
Röhren, Ivan Bogdanovich, II/1077/V-2/61
Röhren, Ivan Bogdanovich, II/1183/V-2/70
Rokotov, Nikolai M. II/1247/V-2/77
Rokshanin, Semen O. II/2053/V-2/148
Romanov, Peter Danilovich, II/1609/V-2/115
Romanovski II., Matvei M. II/1502/V-2/106
Romanovski, Ivan K. II/2019/V-2/145
Rommel, Erwin, III/390/IX/532
von Rommel, Theodor K. II/16/VI/228
von Rönne, Gustaf, II/806/V-2/24
von Rönne, Otto F. II/2036/V-2/147
von Rönne, Vassili I. II/2385/V-2/187
von Roon, Albert T. II/174/VII/288
Roosen, Berend, III/481/IX/556
Rördanz, Karl Heinrich, II/728/V-2/2

Rosalion-Soshalski, Fedor, II/1749/V-2/129
Rose, Hans, III/393/IX/533
von Rosen, Andrei F. II/807/V-2/24
von Rosen, Andrei F. II/2241/V-2/171
von Rosen, Otto F. II/2225/V-2/160
von Rosen, Peter (Fedor), II/2136/V-2/153
von Rosen, Axel, II/1380/V-2/101
Rosen, Vladimir I. II/1099/V-2/63
von Rosenberg, Hugo, III/381/IX/529
Rosenstein, Fedor I. II/2240/V-2/161
von Rosenthal, Gustaf, II/2010/V-2/145
Rostopshin, Sergei F. II/1349/V-2/94
Roszner von Roszenegg, J. II/1365/V-2/98
von Rotberg, Albert, III/601/IX/584
von Röth, Fritz, III/686/IX/604
Roth, Ludwig C. II/1953/V-2/142
Röthenbucher, Moritz, III/648/IX/596
Rothenburg,* III/602/IX/585
Von Rothmaler, Louis K. II/263/VII/309
Rshenski, Konstantin A. II/2419/V-2/192
Rshevski, Pavel A. II/1881/V-2/137
Rubzov, Peter Igorovich, II/1461/V-2/104
Rudakov, Ivan Pavlovich, II/2172/V-2/157
Rudnizki, Konstantin I. II/1786/V-2/132
Rudolph, Hermann, III/765/IX/624
von Rudorff, Wilhelm H. II/732/V-2/4
Rühl, Andrei Fedorovich, II/841/V-2/29
Ruhnau, Otto, III/520/IX/566
Rumey, Fritz, III/619/IX/588
von Rummel, Friedrich A. II/835/V-2/28
Rümmelein, Fritz, III/779/IX/627
Runge, Siegfried, III/673/IX/602
Rupprecht, Crown Prince, III/80/IX/434
Rupprecht, Crown Prince, III/203/IX/478
Rusche, Rudolph, III/798/IX/631
Russanov, Dmitri M. II/1742/V-2/127

S

Saba, Ivan Petrovich, II/900/V-2/39
Sabanieiev, Peter V. II/1 291/V-2/80
Sablin, Michail J. II/913/V-2/40
Sablin, Pavel I. II/1764/V-2/130
Sablozki, Ivan D. II/1500/V-2/106
Saporinski II., Semen N. II/1538/V-2/110
Saborinski II., Alex N. II/1537/V-2/109
Sabudski, Ivan G. II/1474/V-2/104
Sacharshevski, Jakob, V. II/1931/V-2/140
Sachsenberg, Gotthard, III/639/IX/594
Sadluzki, Anton, II/1760/V-2/130
Sadonski, Voin D. II/2072/V-2/149
Safianov, Peter, II/2272/V-2/163
von Sahlhausen, Moritz, II/2401/V-2/189
von Saldern, Sieghard, III/560/IX/575
Salov, Fedor A. II/2096/V-2/151

von Salza, Karl A. II/2110/V-2/151
von Salza, Roman A. II/1584/V-2/113
Salzwedel, Reinhold, III/288/IX/502
Samarin,* II/847/V-2/33
Samburski, Akim P. II/1850/V-2/135
Samkovski, Alexei D. II/2229/V-2/160
Samoilovich, Ivan V. II/1081/V-2/62
Samsanov, Sergei V. II/1826/V-2/134
Samsonov, Sergei V. II/2179/V-2/157
Samuizki, Nikolai I. II/1415/V-2/103
von Sanden-Peskovich, K. II/2291/V-2/164
Sander, Philipp, III/542/IX/571
von Sandrart, Karl G. II/213/VII/299
Sannow, Ferdinand H. II/200/VII/294
Sasonov, Nikolai V. II/755/V-2/17
Sass, Peter A. II/1565/V-2/112
Sass, Peter A. II/1637/V-2/118
Sass, Peter A. II/1940/V-2/141
Sassajädko I., Danilo D. II/831/V-2/28
Sassajädko II., Alexander D. II/833/V-2/28
von Sauberzweig, Traugott, III/308/IX/507
von Sauberzweig, Traugott, III/442/IX/547
von Saucken, Ernst F. II/823/V-2/27
Savieskin, Michail V. II/959/V-2/43
Savieskin, Michail V. II/1023/V-2/58
Savinitsh,* II/1073/V-2/61
Savostianov, Platon (P), II/1972/V-2/142
von Sayn-Wittgenstein, L. II/1875/V-2/137
Schach von Wittenau, Hans II/149/VII/279
Schachtmeyer, Hans R. II/267/VII/309
von Schack, Magnus F. II/729/V-2/2
Schaefer, Karl Emil, III/230/IX/487
von Schanzenbach, Xaver, II/2432/V-2/194
Scharenberg, Wilhelm F. II/1779/V-2/132
von Scharpffenstein, Karl, II/1633/V-2/117
Schaubert, Friedrich W. II/143/VII/278
Schaumburg, Ernst, III/511/IX/564
von Scheel, Peter R. II/2390/V-2/188
Scheer, Reinhard, III/122/IX/453
Scheer, Reinhard, III/427/IX/542
Scheffer, Johann E. II/2347/V-2/183
von Scheffer-Boyadel, R. III/30/IX/413
Scheffler, Gustaf, I. II/1972/V-2/137
von Scheither, Georg, II/2144/V-2/155
Schele, Friedrich Rabot, III/2/IX/390
Scheliha, Friedrich E. II/265/VII/309
Schelle, Felix, III/603/IX/585
von Schenck, Dedo, III/173/IX/468
Scheping, Dmitri A. II/925/V-2/40
Schering, Werner, III/679/IX/603
Scheüch, Heinrich, III/471/IX/554
Scheunemann, Peter, III/465/IX/553
Schiermann, Fedor K. II/1864/V-2/135
Schiermann, Karl K. II/1848/V-2/135

von Schilling, Jakob V. II/2033/V-2/147
von Schimmelmann, E. III/622/IX/589
von Schimmelmann, G. K. II/111 /VII/273
von Schkopp, Herman E. II/115/VII/274
von Schlechtendal, Max F. III/268/IX/497
von Schleich, Eduard, III/385/IX/530
Schlein, Fedor M. II/2107/V-2/151
von Schleinitz, Walter, III/330/IX/515
von Schlichting, Ulrich E. II/87/VII/263
von Schlieffen, Eugen L. II/82/VII/262
Schlippenbach, Anton, A. II/1448/V-2/104
von Schlippenbach, Nikolai, II/1253/V-2/77
Schlodhauer, Jakob F. II/1307/V-2/81
von Schlotheim, Karl L. II/151/VII/279
von Schlotheim, Karl L. II/243/VII/305
Schlüter, Ivan I. II/763/V-2/18
Schmaltz, Johann H. II/1526/V-2/109
Schmedes, Heinrich, III/718/IX/612
von Schmettow, Eberhard, III/196/IX/475
von Schmettow, Eberhard, III/638/IX/594
von Schmettow, Egon, III/343/IX/519
Schmid, Hans, III/269/IX/497
Schmidt von Knobelsdorf, K. III/99/IX/440
Schmidt von Knobelsdorf, K. III/144/IX/460
Schmidt, Alexander C. II/2122/V-2/152
Schmidt, Erhard, III/333/IX/515
von Schmidt, Friedrich J. II/212/VII/298
Schmidt, Heinrich T. II/2349/V-2/183
von Schmidt, Johann H. II/1646/V-2/119
von Schmidt, Karl J. II/210/VII/298
von Schmidtler, Johann, III/773/IX/626
Schneider von Arno, K. II/1330/V-2/85
Schnieber, Walther, III/328/IX/513
Schniewindt, Rudolf, III/633/IX/593
Schniewindt, Wilhelm, III/561/IX/575
von Schnizer, Emil, III/662/IX/599
Schoedde, Ernst F. II/2359/V-2/183
von Schoeler, R. III/604/IX/585
Schoen, Albert, III/766/IX/624
Schoerner, Ferdinand, III/386/IX/530
von Schöler, Theodor A. II/123/VII/275
von Scholtz,* III/93/IX/438
von Scholtz,* III/254/IX/493
Scholtz, Erich, III/401/IX/535
von Schon, Johann K. II/1641/V-2/118
von Schon, Johann K. II/2333/V-2/180
von Schönfeldt, Ernst, III/806/IX/633
Schott, Christofor K. II/1879/V-2/137
Schröder, Karl G. II/1318/V-2/82
von Schroeder, Ludwig, III/100/IX/440
von Schroeder, Ludwig, III/406/IX/536
Schubert, Fedor F. II/1196/V-2/72
Schubert, Grigori I. II/1841/V-2/135
von Schubert, Richard, III/153/IX/462

von der Schulenburg, F. III/223/IX/486
von der Schulenburg, F. III/441/IX/547
von der Schulenburg, Karl, II/1598/V-2/114
von der Schulenburg-Wolfburg, K. III/319/IX/510
Schulgan,* II/866/V-2/36
Schulinius, Karl L. II/2161/V-2/156
Schulmann, Fedor M. II/947/V-2/42
Schultz, Jakob, II/2261/V-2/162
Schultz, Otto, III/438/IX/545
von Schulz, Igor V. II/840/V-2/29
Schulz, Heinrich C. II/2362/V-2/183
Schulz, Walter, III/716/IX/612
von Schüssler, Georg, III/521/IX/566
von Schutter, Arnold, II/2330/V-2/180
Schütz, Ernst, III/249/IX/492
Schütz, Karl A. II/1648/V-2/119
Schwab, Adolf, III/807/IX/633
von Schwartzkoppen, F. II/153/VII/279
Schwarz, Fedor J. II/897/V-2/39
von Schwerin, Detlof, III/581/IX/580
von Schwerin, Kurt L. II/227/VII/301
Schwerk, Oskar, III/170/IX/466
Schwerk, Oskar, III/236/IX/489
Schweiger, Walther, III/277/IX/499
von Seddler, Ludwig I. II/2316/V-2/178
von Seeckt, Hans, III/54/IX/423
von Seeckt, Hans, III/105/IX/442
von Seelhorst, Just F. III/373/IX/527
Sehmsdorf, Hans, III/751/IX/621
Seidel, Karl, III/733/IX/616
Seiler, Richard, III/425/IX/541
Sekretov, Peter T. II/983/V-2/46
von Selasinsky, Karl F. II/2322/V-2/179
Selesniev,* II/2117/V-2/152
Selezki, Dmitri P. II/1553/V-2/110
Seliavin, Nikolai I. II/753/V-2/17
Selieniezki, Michail P. II/1737/V-2/128
Selivanov I.,* II/2408/V-2/190
Selivanov II., Andrei A. II/827/V-2/36
Selivanov III., Alexei A. II/1144/V-2/66
Selivanov,* II/2116/V-2/152
Selivanov, Andrei A. II/1701/V-2/125
Selivanov, Grigori A. II/2271/V-2/163
von Selle, Fritz, III/412/IX/538
Semenov,* II/2427/V-2/193
Semenov, Danilo, II/1884/V-2/137
Semenstshenkov, Stepan, II/1141/V-2/66
Sergei A. Grand Duke, II/298/VII/317
Sergieiev, Grigori A. II/1138/V-2/66
Seslavin III., Fedor N. II/858/V-2/34
Seslavin (III.), Fedor N. II/960/V-2/43
von Seydlitz u Kurzbach, Karl, II/2443/V-2/196
Shabelski, Ivan Petrovich, II/808/V-2/25
Schuler von Senden, Ernst W. II/237/VII/303

Shachmatov, Nikolai A. II/1950/V-2/142
Shachovskoi, Nikolai, II/1254/V-2/77
Shafranski, Ludwig M. II/2250/V-2/162
Shaglevski, David, II/2195/V-2/158
Shamshev,* II/1148/V-2/66
Shamshev, Jakob I. II/1824/V-2/134
Shamshev IV., Yuri I. II/1280/V-2/79
Shatalov, Timofei A. II/883/V-2/38
Shatalov, Ivan V. II/2131/V-2/153
Shele II., Kyrill C. II/2424/V-2/193
Shelechov, Dmitri N. II/1866/V-2/136
Shelvinski, Jakob S. II/1049/V-2/60
Shemonin, Nikolai, II/1735/V-2/128
Shemshushnikov, Apollon, II/2121/V-2/152
Shemshushnikov, Michail, II/1985/V-2/143
Shenne, Karl, II/1755/V-2/130
Shenshin, Vassili N. II/1061/V-2/61
Shenshin, Vassili N. II/1182/V-2/70
Shenshin, Vladimir N. II/1627/V-2/117
Shetochin, Kapitan B. II/1342/V-2/92
Sheviakov,* II/1705/V-2/125
Shibaiev,* II/1962/V-2/142
Shimanov,* II/1232/V-2/76
Shimanovski, Maxim, II/1312/V-2/81
Shipov, Peter I. II/1790/V-2/132
Shipov, Sergei P. II/1802/V-2/133
Shirov, Ivan I. II/923/V-2/40
Shishkin, Pavel S. II/1909/V-2/139
Shishkov, Peter I. II/2130/V-2/153
Shishmarev, Michail V. II/2249/V-2/162
Shitov, Alexei I. II/1015/V-2/58
Shkurin, Paul S. II/2308/V-2/177
Shliachtin, Nikolai N. II/1958/V-2/142
Shmarov, Timofei A. II/1747/V-2/129
Shmurin, Vassili M. II/1580/V-2/113
Shochov, Peter A. II/1178/V-2/69
Sholobov,* II/1416/V-2/103
Shoshin, Peter A. II/2048/V-2/148
Shtsherbov, Vassili P. II/1730/V-2/127
Shubin, Alexander F. II/1256/V-2/78
Shubinski, Nikolai P. II/1067/V-2/61
Shuchov, Andrei P. II/1357/V-2/96
Shukovski, Galaktion S. II/1745/V-2/129
Shukovski, Michail S. II/1935/V-2/141
Shulgin, Dmitri I. II/1854/V-2/135
Shulgin, Peter (A), II/1945/V-2/141
Shumkov, Ivan F. II/1145/V-2/66
Shumovski,* II/1721/V-2/126
Shuravlov, Alexander A. II/1155/V-2/67
Shusherin, Sachar S. II/1098/V-2/63
Shusherin, Sachar S. II/1198/V-2/72
Shusherin, Sachar S. II/1740/V-2/128
Shuvalov, Pavel A. II/303/VII/318
Shvedkin, Alexei F. II/1568/V-2/112

Sibin, Sergei V. II/1323/V-2/82
Sick, Georg, III/250/IX/492
Sieger, Ludwig, III/532/IX/568
Sieger, Ludwig, III/795/IX/631
von Siegroth,* II/1055/V-2/60
Siess, Gustav, III/530/IX/568
von Sievers, Ivan L. II/1665/V-2/121
von Sievers, Karl I. II/1287/V-2/80
Sikorski,* II/2282/V-2/163
Simonyi von Vitetzvár, Josef, II/2374/V-2/186
Sinelnikov, Alexander N. II/1506/V-2/106
Sipiagin, Nikolai M. II/941/V-2/41
Sivai, Alexander I. II/1946/V-2/141
Sixt von Armin, Friedrich, III/135/IX/458
Sixt von Armin, Friedrich, III/626/IX/591
Skardovi-Rington, Fedor L. II/2169/V-2/156
Skobelev II., Michail D. II/298/VII/317
Skobelev, Ivan Nikititsh, II/1767/V-2/131
Skobelzin, Nikolai D. II/1544/V-2/110
Skobelzin, Nikolai D. II/1563/V-2/111
Sliepzov,* II/2181/V-2/157
Sliuniaiev, Grigori D. II/2268/V-2/163
von Smitten, Gustaf G. II/1583/V-2/113
von Smitten, Igor F. II/1589/V-2/113
Smoliak, Ossip I. II/1265/V-2/78
Smolianinov, Alexander O. II/1908/V-2/139
Smolkov, Peter G. II/1079/V-2/62
Sololevski, Stepan G. II/2207/V-2/159
Sochazki, Michail N. II/1478/V-2/105
von Soden, Anton Georg, III/7/IX/395
von Soden, Franz, III/270/IX/498
Sokolovski, Xavier P. II/2253/V-2/162
Soldaen, Christofor F. II/2095/V-2/151
Soldan, George, III/522/IX/566
Solezki, Alexei P. II/2251/V-2/162
Sologub, Ignati M. II/2104/V-2/151
Solotarev, Afannasi I. II/1281/V-2/79
Solotosevski, Peter P. II/1559/V-2/111
Solovov, Martemian A. II/1214/V-2/74
von Somnitz, Christof G. II/985/V-2/47
Sonn, Grigori K. II/1781/V-2/132
von Sonneberg, Albrecht, II/2356/V-2/183
Sontag, Igor V. II/844/V-2/29
Sorokin, Peter J. II/870/V-2/36
Sosnin,* II/948/V-2/43
Sosnin,* II/974/V-2/45
Sottorf, Hans, III/789/IX/629
Souchon, Wilhelm, III/188/IX/472
von Speis, Eduard L. II/28/VII/246
von Sperling, Ernst K. II/62/VII/259
von Sperling, Ernst K. II/208/VII/298
Spiridov, Alexei M. II/1825/V-2/134
Spiridov, Ivan M. II/1159/V-2/68
Sproesser, Theodor, III/391/IX/532

von Staabs, Hermann, III/198/IX/476
von Staabs, Hermann, III/553/IX/573
Stach von Goltzheim, Engel, II/2327/V-2/179
Stachovski, Martin M. II/2199/V-2/158
Stachow, Markus, III/376/IX/528
von Stackelberg, Fedor, II/1695/V-2/124
von Stackelberg, Vladimir, II/1753/V-2/129
Staden, Gustaf G. II/744/V-2/16
von Stael, Alexander F. II/2093/V-2/151
Stahn, Andrei A. II/2129/V-2/153
Stalipin, Dmitri A. II/1547/V-2/110
Stankovich, Michail M. II/1111/V-2/64
Stapanov, Matvei, II/1964/V-2/142
Stapff, Max, III/402/IX/535
Starkov, Jakob, M. II/1981/V-2/143
Stashevski, Matvei I. II/1981/V-2/143
Stavrakov, Sachar C. II/1221/V-2/74
Stegmann, Anton O. II/1220/V-2/74
Stegmann, Christofor O. II/1673/V-2/122
von Stein, H. (Frhr.) III/289/IX/503
von Stein, H. (Frhr.) III/369/IX/526
von Stein, Hermann, III/157/IX/463
von Stein, Hermann, III/473/IX/555
von Stein, Karl M. II/2351/V-2/183
Steinbauer, Wolfgang, III/433/IX/544
Steinbrinck, Otto, III/118/IX/451
von Steinmetz, Karl F. II/2319/V-2/178
von Steinmetz, Karl F. II/15/VI/227
von Steinmetz, Karl F. II/245/VII/305
Steinwachs, Adolf, III/235/IX/488
Stepanov,* II/1897/V-2/138
Stepanov,* II/2284/V-2/164
von Stephani, Karl, II/2113/V-2/152
Steppuhn, Albrecht, III/589/IX/582
von Sternheim, Alexander, II/1003/V-2/57
von Stetten, Otto, III/171/IX/467
Stetter, Ivan, II/2003/V-2/144
Steuben, Kuno, III/98/IX/440
Steven, Alexander C. II/1670/V-2/122
von Stiehle, Gustaf W. II/99/VII/265
von Stiehle, Gustaf W. II/192/VII/293
Stiemer, Christian W. II/2379 /V-2/187
Stobbe, Adolf, III/808/IX/634
von Stockhausen, August W. II/13/VI/227
von Stoeklern zu Grünholzek, J. III/595/IX/583
von Stoessel, Anatoli M. III/13/IX/398
Stoffleth, Gustav, III/420/IX/539
Stolipin, Dmitri A. II/2108/V-2/151
Stoltz, Johann C. II/165/VII/281
von Stolzmann, Paulus, III/68/IX/428
von Stosch, Albrecht, II/74/VII/261
von Stosch, Albrecht, III/756/IX/622
Strack, Heinrich, III/783/IX/629
Strahlborn, Vladimir K. II/1252/V-2/77

Strahlmann, Peter K. II/1124 /V-2/65
von Strandmann, Fedor A. II/1839/V-2/135
von Strandmann, Karl G. II/1542/V-2/110
von Strandmann, Karl O. II/1429/V-2/103
von Strantz, Karl A. II/730/V-2/4
von Strantz, Karl F. II/1686/V-2/123
von Stranz, Hermann, III/82/IX/435
Strasser, Peter, III/299/IX/505
Stremouchov, Alexander, II/1799/V-2/133
Striabin, Fedor J. II/1495/V-2/106
Stroganov, Alexander G. II/1556/V-2/111
von Strubberg, Otto J. II/221/VII/300
van der Struf, Ivan, II/2171/V-2/157
Stshelkan, Afanassi J. II/784/V-2/20
Stsherbatov, Prince N. II/1190/V-2/71
Stsherbatshev, Alexander, II/1840/V-2/134
Stsherbinin, Alexander, II/756/V-2/17
Stshulepnikov, Michailo, II/1314/V-2/81
Studsinski, Lev S. II/1631/V-2/117
von Stülpnagel, Edwin, III/634/IX/593
von Stülpnagel, George K. II/828/V-2/28
von Stülpnagel, Louis F. II/72/VII/261
von Stülpnagel, Louis F. II/194/VII/293
von Stumpff, Karl, III/523/IX/566
von Stürler, Nikolai K. II/1811/V-2/134
von Stutterheim, August L. II/2326/V-2/179
von Stutterheim, Karl A. II/1642/V-2/118
von Stutterheim, Wolff, III/669/IX/601
Suchosanet I., Ivan O. II/1294/V-2/80
Suchosanet II., Peter O. II/1014/V-2/58
Suchosanet III., Nikolai O. II/1555/V-2/111
Suchovo-Kobulin, Vassili A. II/1554/V-2/111
van Suchtelen, Konstantin P. II/1421/V-2/103
von Suchtelen, Paul P. II/1886/V-2/137
Sück, Jakob, II/945/V-2/42
Suiev, Sergei C. II/1029/V-2/59
Sukovkin, Peter L. II/2307/V-2/177
Sulima, Ossip I. II/2223/V-2/160
Sumarokov, Sergei P. II/1772/V-2/131
Sushkov, Vassili V. II/1788/V-2/132
Suthof I., Nikolai I. II/1090/V-2/62
Suvorov II., Peter, II/1107/V-2/64
Suvorov II., Peter, II/1201/V-2/73
Svarkovski, Nikolai A. II/1990/V-2/143
Sviagin, Nikolai M. II/1966/V-2/142
Sviatopolk-Mirski I., Prince D. II/289/VII/316
Svida, Michail S. II/2216/V-2/159
Svieriev,* II/881/V-2/36
Svietshin, Peter A. II/2410/V-2/191
von Sydow, Hans, III/413/IX/538
von Sydow, Johann J. II/2342/V-2/182
Széchényi, Stefan, II/1601/V-2/114
von Szerdahelyi, Karl A. II/735/V-2/10

T

von und zu der Tann-Raths. II/182/VII/291
Tannauer,* II/1970/V-2/142
Tappen, Gerhard, III/95/IX/438
Tappen, Gerhard, III/113/IX/445
Tarashkevich, Ossip F. II/1709/V-2/125
Tarassov, Ivan I. II/2310/V-2/177
Tarassov, Peter I. II/1244/V-2/77
Tarbeiev, Pavel P. II/1887/V-2/137
Tarnovski, Peter I. II/1036/V-2/59
Tarshevski, Afanassi P. II/1052/V-2/60
von Taube, Anton, II/1919/V-2/139
Taube, Karl Karlovich, II/1094/V-2/62
von Taysen, Friedrich, III/414/IX/538
Tazin IV., Peter F. II/1106/V-2/64
Tazin IV., Peter F. II/1271/V-2/78
Teetzmann, Theodor, III/324/IX/512
Teglev, Nikolai J. II/1319/V-2/82
Teichmann Rudolf, III/558/IX/574
Teliegin, Igor I. II/1171/V-2/69
Temirov (Timirov),* II/2158/V-2/156
Temirov, Pavel L. II/1128/V-2/65
Teplov,* II/899/V-2/39
Teplov,* II/2181/V-2/157
Teplov, Michail A. II/951/V-2/43
Tergukassov, Arsas A. II/294/VII/317
Termin, Leonti A. II/1770/V-2/131
Terne, Fedor F. II/1173/V-2/69
Terne, Fedor F. II/2187/V-2/158
Terpielivski, Ivan F. II/1763/V-2/130
Terpielivski, Jevgeni O. II/1700/V-2/125
Teschner, Otto, III/421/IX/539
Teslev, Alexander P. II/802/V-2/24
von Thadden, Wilhelm, III/320/IX/510
von Thaer Albrecht, III/282/IX/501
Thal (Thalen),* II/1876/V-2/137
von Thile II., Heinrich, II/2306/V-2/175
von Thile, Hugo O. II/164/VII/281
Thom, Karl, III/791/IX/629
von Thümen, Heinrich, II/989/V-2/54
von Thun, Wilhelm U. II/2437/V-2/195
von Thurn und Taxis, A. II/1530/V-2/109
von Thurn und Taxis, K. II/2147/V-2/155
Thuy, Emil, III/606/IX/585
Tichanov, Fedor A. II/1842/V-2/135
Tichmenev, Vassili I. II/2423/V-2/192
Tichozki, Alexei M. II/2191/V-2/158
Tiede, Paul, III/494/IX/560
Tiede, Paul, III/758/IX/622
von Tiedemann, Otto, II/169/VII/283
von Tiele, Karl F. II/786/V-2/20
von Tiesenhausen, Bogdan, II/2162/V-2/156
von Tiesenhausen, Gottard, II/871/V-2/36
Timiriasev, Ivan S. II/2084/V-2/150

Timofeiev, Pavel P. II/1741/V-2/128
Timrodt, Alexander I. II/2296/V-2/166
Timrodt, Fedor K. II/1150/V-2/67
von Tippelskirch, August, III/749/IX/620
von Tippelskirch, Ernst L. II/2335/V-2/181
Tirkov, Alexei D. II/1308/V-2/81
von Tirpitz, Alfred, III/76/IX/432
Tishevski, Yeugeni I. II/1288/V-2/80
Tishin, Vassili G. II/1062/V-2/61
Tishin, Vassili G. II/1938/V-2/141
Tishkievich, Anton D. II/2098/V-2/15
Titov I., Vladimir M. II/1392/V-2/102
Titov II., Nikolai M. II/1393/V-2/102
Titov IV. Ivan A. II/1401/V-2/102
Titov, Alexei I. II/1837/V-2/135
Tiumenev, Prince S. II/2065/V-2/149
Tiunin, Pavel Semenovich, 1180/V-2/69
Tiutshev I., Afanassi P. II/1402/V-2/102
Tiutshev II., Alexei P. II/1403/V-2/102
Todleben, Eduard Franz, II/275/VII/310
Todorov,* III/326/IX/512
Togaitshinov, Michail I. II/1343/V-2/92
Tokarev, Konstantin A. II/2387/V-2/188
Tolmatshev, Afanassi J. II/1834/V-2/135
Tolmatshov, Jevdokin, P. II/1174/V-2/69
Tolsdorff, Ivan A. II/1696/V-2/124
Tolstoi,* II/1907/V-2/139
Tolstoi,* II/1362/V-2/96
Tolstoi, Alexander, II/2140/V-2/153
Tolstoi, Alexander D. II/1804/V-2/134
Tomilovski, Andrei S. II/2041/V-2/147
Tompson, Ludwig, II/2294/V-2/166
von Tornow, Otto W. II/2380/V-2/187
Totshinski, Ignati P. II/1053/V-2/60
Totshinski, Ignati P. II/2448/V-2/197
Trautmann,* II/920/V-2/40
Travin, Pavel A. II/1115/V-2/64
Trebing, Emil, III/488/IX/558
Tregubov, Andrei V. II/1980/V-2/143
Tregubov, Ossip G. II/2159/V-2/156
Trenk, Walter, III/620/IX/589
von Tresckow, Hans L. II/215/VII/300
von Tresckow, Herman H. II/177/VII/289
von Tresckow, Herman H. II/244/VII/305
von Tresckow, Julius E. II/141/VII/278
Treskin, Igor I. II/1301/V-2/80
Treskin, Michail L. II/973/V-2/45
von Treskow, Heinrich M. II/23/VII/246
Tretiakov, Jakob M. II/1471/V-2/104
Treuberg, Friedrich, II/1524/V-2/109
Treulebem, Nikolai J. II/909/V-2/39
Treusch von Buttlar-Brandenfels, H. III/484/IX/557
Triapizin, Vassili I. II/853/V-2/34
Trinchiere, Joseph (V), II/1206/V-2/73

Trishanti, Alexander L. II/2123/V-2/152
Trizinski Nikolai, II/2433/V-2/194
von Troilo, Hans, III/612/IX/587
von Trotha, Adolf, III/124/IX/454
Trotha, Adrian D. III/15/IX/402
Trousson, Peter C. II/1573/V-2/112
Trubezkoi I., Prince S. II/1818/V-2/134
Trubezkoi II., Prince A. II/904/V-2/39
Trubezkoi, Peter P. II/2394/V-2/188
Trubezkoi, Prince Y. II/1750/V-2/129
Trubtsheninov, Igor M. II/757/V-2/17
Truchsess zu Waldburg etc. H. II/885/V-2/38
von Tschischwitz, Erich, III/350/IX/521
von Tschischwitz, Erich, III/443/IX/548
Tshagin, Nikolai G. II/1411/V-2/103
Tshagin, Peter N. II/795/V-2/24
Tshagin, Vladimir N. II/1911/V-2/139
Tshaplin, Michail, II/2257/V-2/162
Tshavtshavadse, A. II/1286/V-2/80
Tshekalov, Michail P. II/1843/V-2/135
Tshemessov, Ivan J. II/1823/V-2/134
Tsheodaiev, Michail I. II/1056/V-2/60
Tsheodaiev, Michail J. II/1407/V-2/103
Tsherkassov, Pavel P. II/1678/V-2/122
Tshernaiev, Peter N. II/1765/V-2/130
Tshernievich, Prince P. II/1608/V-2/115
Tshernosubov,* II/2064/V-2/149
Tshernosubov, G. II/1142/V-2/66
Tshernosubov V., Peter, II/1638/V-2/118
Tshertorishski, Vassali, II/1859/V-2/136
Tshertov, Pavel A. II/1711/V-2/126
Tshetshenski, Alexander, II/2021/V-2/145
Tshcvakinski, Michail I. II/2445/V-2/197
Tahichatshev, Matvei N. II/2838/V-2/135
Tshoglokov, Andreian N. II/2125/V-2/152
Tshudovski, Kasimir I. II/1551/V-2/110
Tshumakov, Peter P. II/1472/V-2/104
Tshurakovski, Michail D. II/1712/V-2/126
Tshurilov, Ivan I. II/1075/V-2/61
von Tucholka, Leo J. II/1391/V-2/102
Tuleninov, Platon G, II/2224/V-2/160
Tulubiev, Alexander D. II/1683/V-2/123
Tulubiev, Arseni S. II/2254/V-2/162
Tulubiev, Dorimedont T. II/1913/V-2/139
von Tümpling, Ludwig K. II/110/VII/273
Turgeniev, Lev A. II/2185/V-2/158
Turtshaninov, Andrei P. II/910/V-2/40
Turtshaninov, Andrei P. II/972/V-2/45
von Tutschek, Adolf, III/279/IX/500
von Tutschek, Ludwig, III/389/IX/531

U

Udet, Ernst, III/483/IX/557
von Uechtritz und Steinkirch, III/757/IX/622

von Uexkull-Gyllenbandt, P. II/1195/V-2/72
Ugriumov, Pavel A. II/1667/V-2/122
Ugriumov, Pavel A. II/1179/V-2/69
Ukinsiev, Fedor V. II/1437/V-2/103
Ulfasparre, Erik G. II/2143/V-2/154
von Under, Karl F. II/73/VII/261
von Ungern-Sternberg, G. II/992/V-2/54
Unknown, British Officer, II/1660/V-2/121
Unknown, British Officer, II/1661/V-2/121
Unknown, Russian Officer, II/1236/V-2/76
von Unruh, Walter, III/512/IX/564
Urussov, Prince Sergei, II/1906/V-2/139
von Usedom, Ernst A. III/11/IX/396
von Usedom, Ernst A. III/87/IX/436
Ushakov I., Michail A. II/1399/V-2/102
Ushakov, Nikolai P. II/1423/V-2/103
Ushakov, Peter S. II/1216/V-2/74
Ushakov, Peter S. II/1855/V-2/136
Uvarov, Fedor A. II/2091/V-2/150
Uvarov, Fedor F. II/1468/V-2/104
Uvarov, Fedor S. II/2066/V-2/149

V

Vadkovski I., Ivan F. II/1816/V-2/134
Vadkovski II., Pavel F. II/1408/V-2/103
von Vaernewyck, Hans P. III/694/IX/607
Valchovski, Dmitri N. II/1217/V-2/74
Valentiner, Max, III/205/IX/478
von Valentini, Georg W. II/1230/V-2/75
Valory, Franz Florentin, II/1523/V-2/108
Varlovski, Adam S. II/2286/V-2/164
Varnhagen von Ense, Karl, II/2260/V-2/162
Vassiliev,* II/1974/V-2/142
Vassiliev¥ Michail V. II/2247/V-2/162
Vassiltshikov, Nikolai V. II/1694/V-2/124
Vastianov (Vassianov),* II/1560/V-2/111
Velenin, Peter A. II/1905/V-2/138
Velenti, Ivan Lukitsh, II/2190/V-2/158
Veliaminov, Nikolai S. II/834/V-2/28
Veliaminov, Nikolai S. II/1858/V-2/136
Veltjens, Josef, III/651/IX/597
Verbovski, Platon V. II/2277/V-2/163
Verchovski, Peter I. II/1027/V-2/59
von Versen, Felix M. II/147/VII/278
Vesselovski, Stepan S. II/113/V-2/64
Vett, Detlev, III/717/IX/612
Vichodsevski, Peter P. II/1181/V-2/70
Victor Emanuel, King of Italy, II/258/VII/308
Veibeg, Max, III/423/IX/541
Vielhorski, Matvei J. II/1129/V-2/65
von Vietinghoff,* II/1119/V-2/65
von Vietinghoff,* II/1499/V-2/106
von Vietinghoff, Andrei I. II/1325/V-2/84
von Vietinghoff, Anton M. II/1246/V-2/77
von Vietinghoff, Karl F. II/1597/V-2/114
Vikinski, Ivan M. II/1466/V-2/104
Viktorov, Vladimir M. II/1017/V-2/58
Vilhelmov, Pavel F. II/1310/V-2/81
Viltshinski, Ivan F. II/1924/V-2/140
Viniarski, Adam A. II/1194/V-2/72
Virubov, Andrei P. II/2220/V-2/160
Vishizki, Michail F. II/1561/V-2/111
Vishizki, Michail F. II/1610/V-2/115
Vishniakovski, S. II/2266/V-2/162
Vissitski, Jevgraf, S. II/1458/V-2/104
Vissozki, Josef F. II/1259/V-2/78
Vitkovski, Adam L. II/1567/V-2/112
Vitkovski, Adam L. II/2133/V-2/153
Vladimir A. Grand Duke, II/283/VII/315
Vlassov, Michail, II/1927/V-2/140
Vnukov, Vassili M. II/857/V-2/34
Vogel von Falckenstein, F. II/7/VII/244
Voievodski, Lev G. II/1992/V-2/144
Voievodski, Pavel J. II/1989/V-2/143
Voigt (Focht), Peter A. II/1623/V-2/116
Voigt (Focht), Peter A. II/1744/V-2/129
von Voigts-Rhetz, Julius K. II/197/VII/294
von Voigts-Rhetz, Karl W. II/135/VII/277
von Voigts-Rhetz, Konstans, II/60/VII/259
von Voigts-Rhetz, Konstans, II/184/VII/291
Voinov,* II/970/V-2/44
Volevatsh, Jakob I. II/1101/V-2/63
Volevatsh, Jakob I. II/1742/V-2/128
Volkonski, Prince Sergei, II/888/V-2/38
Volkonski, Prince Sergei, II/1731/V-2/128
Volkov, Mikolai A. II/1718/V-2/126
Volkov, Vassili S. II/2213/V-2/159
von Vollard-Bockelberg, A. III/344/IX/519
Volodimirov, Semen I. II/2202/V-2/159
Volshenski, Peter L. II/1224/V-2/75
Vonliarliarski, Ivan A. II/1449/V-2/104
Voroniez, Ivan A. II/1954/V-2/142
Voropanov, Nikolai F. II/1821/V-2/134
von Voss,* III/403/IX/535
Voss, Werner, III/219/IX/485
Vranizki,* II/751/V-2/17
Vratislav, Eugen, II/1596/V-2/114
Vuitsh II., Ivan A. II/1540/V-2/110
Vulffert, Ivan G. II/1896/V-2/138
Vunkov, Vassili M. II/1024/V-2/58

W

Wachamuth, Alexander, II/1930/V-2/140
Wachtem, Hans Otto, II/780/V-2/19
von Wahlen-Jürgass, A. II/1228/V-2/75
Waldemar, Prince of Prussia, II/4/VI/226
von Waldersee, Alfred L. III/10/IX/396
von Waldersee, Friedrich G. II/10/VI/227

Waldorf, Emil, III/790/IX/629
von Waldstätten, Alfred, III/339/IX/518
Walther von Monbary, Rudolf, II/138/VII/277
Walther, Hans, III/208/IX/479
Walz, Franz, III/642/IX/595
von Wangenheim, Kurt, III/300/IX/506
Wardenburg, Wilhelm G, II/2358/V-2/183
von Wartensleben, K. II/1602/V-2/114
von Wartensleben, W. II/209/VII/298
von Wartensleben, W. II/272/VII/310
Wassner, Erwin, III/435/IX/544
von Watter, Oskar, III/404/IX/535
von Watter, Oskar, III/796/IX/631
von Watter, Theodor, III/158/IX/463
Weber, Theodor, III/723/IX/614
von Wechmar, Karl H. II/271/VII/310
Weddigen, Otto, III/25/IX/410
von Wedekind, Fritz, III/649/IX/596
von Wedel, Hasso, III/297/IX/504
von Wedel, Hasso, III/370/IX/526
von Wedell, August H. II/20/VI/228
von Wedell, August L. II/1517/V-2/108
von Wedell, Richard G. II/127/VII/275
von Wedell, Richard G. II/187/VII/292
von Weks, Franz, II/2141/V-2/154
Wellmann, Richard, II/405/V-2/485
Wellmann, Richard, III/774/IX/626
Wenckstern, Karl, III/663/IX/599
von Wenninger, Karl, III/233/IX/488
Wenninger, Ralph, III/461/IX/551
von Werder, Bernhard F. II/86/VII/263
von Werder, Hans, III/535/IX/569
von Werder, Karl F. III/108/VII/272
von Werder, Karl F. II/191/VII/293
Werner, Wilhelm, III/654/IX/597
von Wernhardt, Paul, II/1333/V-2/85
von Westhoven, Eduard, III/466/IX/553
Westphal, Heinrich E. II/736/V-2/10
Wetzell, Georg, III/199/IX/476
Wetzell, Georg, III/336/IX/517
von Weyrauch, Alexander J. II/1299/V-2/80
von Wichmann, Karl O. II/68/VII/260
Wichura, Georg, III/229/IX/487
Wichura, Georg, III/579/IX/579
Wiedburg, Friedrich K. II/2363/V-2/183
Wiesner, Friedrich A. II/17/VI/228
Wilck, Hermann, III/734/IX/616
Wild von Hohenborn, A. III/73/IX/431
Wild von Hohenborn, A. III/736/IX/617
Wilhelm I., King of Prussia, II/57/VII/257
Wilhelm I., King of Prussia, II/168/VII/283
Wilhelm II., German Emperor, III/33/IX/415
Wilhelm II., German Emperor, III/48/IX/421
Wilhelm II., King, Württemberg, III/213/IX/481
Wilhelm, Crown Prince, III/81/IX/434
Wilhelm, " III/160/IX/414
Wilhelm, Duke, M-Schwerin, II/93/VII/264
Wilhelm, Duke of Württemberg, II/4/VII/243
Wilhelm, Prince of Baden, III/3/IX/390
Wilhelm, Prince of Prussia, II/3/VI/225
Wilhelm, Prince of Prussia, II/24/VI/229
von Willisen, Ludwig W. III/335/IX/517
von Willisen, Friedrich A. II/29/VI/230
Willweber, Karl, III/680/IX/603
von Winckler, Arnold, III/103/IX/442
von Winckler, Arnold, III/260/IX/495
Windish, Rudolf, III/575/IX/578
Winspeare, Robert A. II/2000/V-2/144
Wintgens, Kurt, III/126/IX/455
Wirjubov, Andrei, II/926/V-2/40
von Wisin, Ivan A. II/132/V-2/84
von Wisin, Michail A. II/1158/V-2/68
von Witte I., Ivan O. II/1394/V-2/102
von Witte (I.), Ivan O. II/2430/V-2/193
Wittekind, Eduard, III/380/IX/529
von Wittich, Friedrich W. II/131/VII/276
von Wittich, Friedrich W. II/179/VII/290
von Witzendorff, Karl F. II/92/VII/264
von Witzendorff, Karl F. II/217/VII/300
Witzleben, Friedrich H. II/727/V-2/2
von Witzleben, Friedrich K. III/596/IX/583
von Wnuck, Karl H. II/76/VII/261
von Wolff, Alexander (E), II/1615/V-2/116
von Wolff, Horst, III/377/IX/528
Wolff, Kurt, III/237/IX/489
Woltersdorf, Siegfried, III/781/IX/628
von Wolzogen, Justus P. II/997/V-2/56
Wood, Charles, II/1662/V-2/121
Wossidlo, Georg C. II/2377/V-2/187
Woyna, Felix, II/1012/V-2/57
von Woyna, Friedrich W. II/238/VII/303
von Woyna, Paul Peter, II/248/VII/306
von Woyrsch, Remus, III/25/IX/410
von Woyrsch, Remus, III/71/IX/429
von Wrangel, Friedrich W. II/159/VII/281
von Wrangel, Friedrich W. II/176/VII/289
von Wrangel, Friedrich H. II/8/VI/226
von Wrangel, Ludwig A. II/1955/V-2/142
von Wrisberg, Ernst, III/472/IX/555
Wulff, Fritz, III/724/IX/614
von Wulffen, August F. II/2283/V-2/187
von Wulffen, Georg O. II/118/VII/274
von Wulffen, Georg O. II/195/VII/293
von Wulffen, Gustaf A. III/513/IX/564
Wülfing, Herman, III/784/IX/628
Wünsche, Otto, III/394/IX/533
Wurst, Alexander F. II/1762/V-2/130
Württemberg, Prince A. II/2378/V-2/187

Westoff, Kurt, III/355/IX/523

X
von Xylander, Oskar, III/143/IX/460

Y
Yorck von Wartenburg, Ernst, III/700/IX/608
von Yorck, Johann David, II/790/V-2/23
Ypsilanti, Prince Alexander, II/1117/V-2/64
zu Ysenburg-Philippseich, G. II/2398/V-2/189
Yushkov, Ossip Ivanovich, II/1545/V-2/110

Z
von Zastrow, Adolf F. II/63/VII/260
von Zastrow, Adolf F. II/206/VII/54
von Zepelin, Konstantin, II/2372/V-2/186
Zickel (Zickeln),* II/1263/V-2/78
von Zieten, Wieprecht H. II/849/V-2/33
Ziethen, Alfred, III/63/IX/426
Zireniev,* III/1904/V-2/138
Zunehmer, Max, III/378/IX/528
Zvietkov, Vassili N. II/2016/V-2/145
von Zwehl, Hans, III/22/IX/407
von Zwehl, Hans, III/186/IX/471
Zweibrücken, Christian, II/1607/V-2/115
von Zychlinski, Franz F. II/125/VII/275

* Indicates the first name of the recipient is either unknown or obscure.

Additional Notes:

SELECTED BIBLIOGRAPHY
Volume II
(Including Bibliography of Volume III)

Abbot, John S.C., **Austria, Its Rise and Present Power.** New York: P.F. Collier, 1877.

Alexander, Roy, **The Cruise of the Raider "Wolf",** New York: Garden City Publishing Co. Inc., 1941.

Anderson, J.H., **The Austro-Prussian War in Bohemia, 1866,** London: Hoag Rees, Ltd., 1908.

Angolia, John R. & Hackney, Jr. Clint R, **The Pour le Merite and Germany's First Aces,** Texas: Hackney Publishing Co., 1984.

Aronson, Theo, **The Golden Bees, The Story of the Bonapartes,** Connecticut: NY Graphic Soc., 1964.

Aronson, Theo, **Royal Vendetta: The Crown of Spain 1829-1965,** New York: Bobs-Merrill Co. Inc., 1966.

Aronson, Theo, **The Kaisers,** Indianapolis - New York: Bobs-Merrill Co. Inc. 1971.

Asprey, Robert B., **The First Battle of the Marne,** Philadelphia & New York: J.B. Lippencott Co., 1962.

Bennett, Geoffrey, **Naval Battles of the First World War,** New York: C. Scribner's, 1968.

Blond, Georges, **Verdun,** New York: The Macmillan Co., 1961.

Bodin, Lynn E., **The Boxer Rebellion,** London: Osprey Publishing Ltd. 1979.

Botting, Douglas, **The U-Boats,** Virginia: Time-Life Books Inc., 1979.

Bourne, Kenneth, **The Foreign Policy of Victorian England 1830-1902,** Oxford: Clarendon Press, 1970.

Bowen, Ezra, **Knights of the Air,** Virginia: Time-Life Books Inc., 1980.

Brockett, L.P., **The Year of Battles: or the Franco-Prussian War of 1870-71,** New York, J.W. Goodspeed & Co., 1871.

Chalfont, Lord, Ed., **Waterloo, Battle of Three Armies,** New York: Alfred A. Knopf, Inc., 1979.

Chandler, David G., **The Campaigns of Napoleon,** New York: The Macmillan Co., 1966.

Chandler, David G., **Dictionary of the Napoleonic Wars,** New York: The Macmillan Co., 1979.

Chandler, David G., **Waterloo - The Hundred Days,** New York: The Macmillan Co., 1980.

Congdon, Don, Ed., **Combat: World War I,** New York: The Dial Press, 1964.

Connelly, Owen, **Napoleon's Satellite Kingdoms,** New York, The Free Press, 1969.

Constant, Stephen, **Foxy Ferdinand, Tsar of Bulgaria,** New York: Franklin Watts, Inc., 1979.

Cowles, Virginia, **The Kaiser,** New York: Harper & Row, Publishers, 1963.

Craig, Gordon A., **The Battle of Koniggratz,** Philadelphia & New York: Lippencott Co., 1964.

Crankshaw, Edward, **Bismarck,** New York: The Viking Press, 1981.

Delderfield, R.F., **Imperial Sunset, The Fall of Napoleon, 1813–14,** New York: Stein & Day, 1980.

Dobbettin, Walther, **Die Soldaten Lettow-Vorbecks,** Halberstadt: Louis Koch, 1932.

Durant, Will; Durant Ariel, **The Story of Civilization, Volume XI, The Age of Napoleon,** New York, Simon & Schuster, 1975.

Edkins, David, **The Preussen Orden Pour le Merite,** Falls Church, Virginia: 1981.

Engelmann, Joachin von, **Feldmarshall Blücher,** Friedburg: Podzun-Pallas-Verlag GMBH., 1984.

Esposito, BG Vincent J., Elting, Col. John R., **A Military History and Atlas of the Napoleonic Wars,** New York: F.A. Praeger, Inc., 1964.

Falls, Cyril, **A Hundred Years of War,** London: Gerald Duckworth & Co., 1953.

Farrar-Hockley, Anthony, **Death of an Army,** New York: Wm. Morrow & Co., Inc., 1968.

Fay, Sidney B., **The History of Nations, "Germany." Volume XVIII,** New York: P.F. Collier & Co., 1928.

Fuller, MG J.F.C., **A Military History of the Western World, Volume II,** New York: Funk & Wagnalls Co., 1955.

Geeb, Hans Karl von, Kirchner, Heinz & Thiemann, Hermann-Wilhelm, **Deutsche Order und Ehrenzeichen,** Cologne-Berlin-Bonn-Munich: Carl Heymanns Verlag KG, 1970.

Gardner, Brian, **On to Kilimanjaro,** Philadelphia, PA: Macrae Smith Co., 1963.

Gilbert, Martin, **Atlas of World War I,** London: Dorset Press, 1984.

Goodspeed, D.J., **The German Wars 1914–1945,** Boston, MS: Houghton Mifflin Co., 1977.

Graudenz, Karl-Heinz, **Die Deutschen Kolonien,** Munich: Sudwest Verlag GMBH, 1982.

Graudenz, Karl-Heinz, **Deutsche Kolonial-Geschichte,** Munich, Sudwest Verlag GMBH & Co., 1984.

Gray, Edwyn A., **The Killing Time, The U-Boat War 1914–18,** New York: Chas. Schribner's Sons, 1972.

Gritzner, Maximilian, **Handbuch der Ritter- Und Verdienstorden,** Graz: Akademische Druck-U. Verlaganstalt, 1962, (Reprint).

Hamelman, William E, **Of Red Eagles and Royal Crowns,** Dallas, TX: Matthaus Pub., 1978.

Hamelman, William E.; Martin Dennis, **The History of the Prussian Pour le Merite Order 1740–1812,** Volume I, Hamburg: Ernst Blass, Verlag Sammlerfreund, 1982.

Harbottle, Thomas, **Dictionary of Battles,** New York: Stein & Day, 1971.

Harvey, W.J.; Reppien, C., **Denmark and the Danes,** New York: Kennikat Press, 1915.

Haupt, Werner, **Deutschlands Schutzgebiete in Übersee 1884–1918,** Friedberg: Podzun-Pallas-Verlag GMBH., 1984.

Hawtrey, H.C.; Flattery, Amanda M., **A Short History of Germany,** Detroit, MI: Longmans, Green & Co., 1903.

Herold, J. Christopher, **The Battle of Waterloo,** New York: American Heritage Pub. Co., 1967.

Holborn, Hajo, **A History of Modern Germany 1840–1945,** New York: Knopf Inc., 1975.

Howard, Michael, **The Franco-Prussian War,** New York: The Macmillan Co., 1962.

Howarth, David, **Waterloo, Day of Battle,** New York: Atheneum, 1968.

Hoeling, A.A., **The Great War at Sea,** New York: Thomas Y. Crowell Co., 1965.

Horold, J. Christopher, **The Age of Napoleon,** New York: American Heritage Pub. Co., 1963.

Hoyt, Edwin P., **Raider Wolf, The Voyage of Captain Nerger, 1916-1918,** New York: Pinnacle Books, 1977.

Hoyt, Edwin P., **Guerilla, Colonel von Lettow-Vorbeck and German's East Africa Empire,** New York: The Macmillan Pub. Co. Inc., 1981.

Hythe, Viscount, Ed., **The Naval Annual, 1913,** New York: Arco Publishing Co. Inc., 1970, (Reprint).

Imrie, Alex, **Pictorial History of the German Army Air Service 1914-1918,** Chicago, IL: Henry Regnery Co., 1973..

Jansson, Per-Eric, **Leipzig,** London: Almark Publishing Co. Ltd., 1975.

Jones, Dorsey D., **Russia: A Concise History,** Harrisburg, PA: The Stakepole Co., 1955.

Jones, W. Glyn, **Denmark,** Washington, New York: Praeger Publishers, 1970.

Kannik, Preben, **Military Uniforms In Color,** New York: The Macmillan Co., 1971.

Klietmann, Dr. K-G., **Pour le Merite und Tapferkeitsmedaille,** Berlin: Verlag "Die Ordenssammlung", 1966.

Koeppen, Georg, **Der Deutsche-Franzoesische Krieg 1870 und 1871,** Milwaukee WI: Geo. Brumber, 1890.

Kroschel, Guenter; Evers, August-Ludwig, **Die Deutsche Flotte 1848-1945,** Wilhemshaven: Verlag Lohse Eissing, 1962.

Kugler, Dr. Bernhard, **Deutschlands Groesster Held,** Dresden, Vaterlaendischer Buchverlag, 1893.

Kurtz, Herold, **The Second Reich, Kaiser Wilhelm II. and His Germany,** New York: American Heritage Press, 1970.

Lawford, James, **Napoleon, The Last Campaigns 1813-15,** New York: Crown Publishers Inc., 1979.

Lehmann, Gustaf, **Die Ritter des Ordens Pour le Merite, Erster Band, 1740-1811,** Berlin: Ernst Siegfried Mittler und Sohn, 1913.

Lehmann, Gustaf, **Die Ritter des Ordens Pour le Merite, Zweiter Band, 1812-1913,** Berlin: Ernst Siegfried Mittler und Sohn, 1913.

Lindner, Th., **Der Krieg gegen Frankreich 1870-71,** Berlin: A. Asher & Co., 1895.

MacCloskey, BG Nonro, **Reillys Battery: A Story of the Boxer Rebellion,** New York: Richards Rosen Press, Inc. 1969.

MacDonald, Lyn, **Somme,** London: Michael Joseph, 1983.

Martin, W.A., **The Siege of Peking,** Shannon, Ireland: Irish University Press, 1972, (Reprint).

Maurois, Andre, **Napoleon and His World,** New York: The Viking Press, 1963.

May, Robin, Embleton, G.A., **The Franco-Prussian War,** London: Almark Publishing Co., 1975.

Menzel, Wolfgang, **Nations of the World - Germany,** Volume III, New York: P.F. Collier & Sons, 1902.

Middlebrook, Martin, **The First Day on the Somme 1 July 1916,** New York: W.W. Norton & Co. Inc., 1972.

Miliukov, Paul; Seignobos, Charles; Eisenman, L., **History of Russia: Reforms, Re-**

actions, Revolutions 1855-1932, Volume III, New York: Funk & Wagnalls, 1969.

Miller, Charles, **Battle for the Bundu,** New York: The Macmillan Publishing Co. Inc., 1974.

Moeller, Hanns, **Geschichte der Ritter des Ordens Pour le Merite in Weltkrieg, Erster Band A-L,** Berlin, Verlag Bernard & Graese, 1935.

Moeller, Hanns, **Geschichte der Ritter des Ordens Pour le Merite in Weltkrieg, Zweiter Band M-Z,** Berlin: Verlag Bernard & Graese, 1935.

Mollo, Boris, **Uniforms of the Imperial Russian Army,** Poole, Dorest: Blandford Press Ltd., 1979.

Moltke, FM Count Helmuth von, **The Franco-German War of 1870-71,** New York: Harper & Brothers, 1892.

Mühlbach, Louise, **Napoleon and Bluecher,** New York: P.F. Collier & Son, 1911.

Narbeth, Colin, **Admiral Seymour's Expedition & Taku Forts 1900,** Chippenham, Wiltshire: Picton Publishing, 1980.

Nash, David, **The Prussian Army 1808-1815,** London: Almark Publishing Co., 1972.

Nash, D.B., **Imperial German Army Handbook 1914-1918,** London: Ian Allan Ltd., 1980.

Nelson, Walter Henry, **The Soldier Kings, The House of Hohenzollern,** New York: G.P. Putnam's Sons, 1970.

Nicolson, Harold, **The Congress of Vienna - A Study in Allied Unity: 1812-1822,** New York: Harcourt Brace Jovanovich, 1946.

Nimmergut, Jörg, **Der Orden Pour le Merite für Wissenschaft und Kunste, Band I,** Gunzenhausen, Siebentritt, 1979.

Orlandi, Enzo, Ed., **The Life and Times of Napoleon,** Philadelphia, PA: The Curtis Publishing Co., 1966.

Over, Keith, **Flags and Standards of the Napoleonic Wars,** London: Bivouac Books Ltd., 1976.

Palmer, Alan, **Bismarck,** New York: Charles Scribner's Sons, 1976.

Petain, Henri Philippe, **Verdun,** New York: The Dial Press, 1930.

Petre, F. Loraine, **Napoleon's Last Campaign in Germany - 1813,** New York: Hippocrene Books, Inc., 1974.

Petre, F. Loraine, **Napoleon at Bay 1814,** New York: Hippocrene Books, Inc., 1977.

Pflugk-Harttung, Dr. J. von, **Krieg und Sieg 1870-71,** Berlin: Schall & Grund. (No Year).

Pivak, Otto von, **Armies of the Napoleonic Era,** New York: Taplinger Publishing Co., 1979.

Preston, Antony, **U-Boats,** London: Excalibur Books, 1978.

Purves, Alec A., **The Medals, Decorations & Orders of the Great War 1914-1918,** London: J.B. Hayward and Son, 1975.

Reimer, Dr. Erwin Heinrich, **Des Deutschen Volkes Freiheitskampf 1806-1815,** Hamburg: Hansa-Verlag, 1906.

Robertson, Bruce, Ed., **Air Aces of the 1914-1918 War,** Fallbrook, CA: Aero Publishers Inc., 1964.

Robertson, Bruce, Ed., **von Richthofen and the Flying Circus,** Fallbrook, CA: Aero Publishers, Inc., 1964.

Sauer, Werner, Ed., **Orden & Militaria Journal,** No. 33, No. 34, 5 Jahrgang, 1980.

Scheibert, J., **Der Krieg von 1870-71,** Berlin: Vaterländischer Verlag, 1906.

Schreckenbach, Paul, **Der Weltbrand,** Volumes I, II, III, Leipzig: J.J. Weber, 1919.

Sigel, Gustav A., **Deutschlands Heer und Flotta,** Akron, OH: The Warner Co., 1900.

Snyder, Louis L., **Historic Documents of World War I,** Princeton, NJ: D. Van Nostrand Co. Inc., 1958.

Tan, Chester C., **The Boxer Catastrophe,** New York: W.W. Norton & Co. Inc., 1967.

Taylor, J.C., **German Warships of World War I,** Garden City, New York: Doubleday & Co. Inc., 1970.

Thomas, Lowell, **Raiders of the Deep,** Garden City, New York: Doubleday, Doran & Co. Inc., 1928.

Vat, Dan van der, **Gentlemen of War,** New York: Wm. Morrow & Co. Inc., 1984.

Warner, Philip, Ed., **Blücher's Army 1813–1815,** Reading, Berkshire: Osprey Publishing Ltd., 1973.

Westwood, J.N., **The Illustrated History of the Russo–Japanese War,** Chicago, IL: H. Regnery Co., 1963.

Wilson, Lawrence, **The Incredible Kaiser,** New York: A.S. Barnes & Co. Inc., 1963.

Windrow, Martin, Ed., **The Army of the German Empire 1870–1888,** London: Osprey Publishing Ltd., 1973.

Windrow, Martin, Ed., **The Boxer Rebellion,** London: Osprey Publishing Ltd., 1979.

Wise, Terence, **Flags of the Napoleonic Wars (2),** London: Osprey Publishing Ltd., 1978.

Wise, Terence, **Flags of the Napoleonic Wars (3),** London: Osprey Publishing Ltd., 1981.

Wolff, Leon, **In Flanders Fields, The 1917 Campaign,** New York: The Viking Press, 1958.

Zimmermann, Dr. G.A., **Kriegs-Erinnerungen,** Milwaukee, WI: Geo. Brumder, 1895.

* * *

German General Staff, **Die Kaempfe der Deutschen Truppen in Suedwestafrika,** Berlin: Ernst Siegfried Mittler & Sohn, 1908.

Her Majesty's Stationary Office, **German Army Handbook April 1918,** New York: Hippocrene Books Inc., 1977, (Reprint).

His Majesty's Stationary Office, **British Vessels Lost at Sea 1914–1918,** London: 1977, (Reprint).

Multiple Authors, **Krieg und Sieg 1870–71,** Berlin, Schall & Grund, (No Date).

Multiple Authors, **Unser Kaiser, Fuenfundzwanzig Jahre der Regierung Kaiser Wilhelm II 1888–1913,** Berlin: Deutsches Verlagshaus Bong & Co., 1913.

Multiple Authors, **Das Bayernbuch vom Weltkrieg 1914–1918, I. Band,** Stuttgart: Chr. Belser A.G., 1930.

Multiple Authors, **Der Erste Weltkrieg,** Wiesbaden: R. Loewit, 1965.

Multiple Authors, **Das Kaiserreich,** Weisbaden: R. Loewit, 1966.

Multiple Authors, **Die Groesse Zeit,** Vienna, Berlin: Ullstein & Co., 1915.

* * *